SECOND
EDITION

The
United
States

brief edition

WINTHROP D. JORDAN

LEON F. LITWACK

RICHARD HOFSTADTER

WILLIAM MILLER

DANIEL AARON

Prentice-Hall, Inc., Englewood Cliffs, New Jersey 07632

Library of Congress Cataloging in Publication Data

Main entry under title:

The United States.

Includes bibliographies and index.
1. United States—History. I. Jordan, Winthrop D.
E178.1.U55321985   973   84-23743
ISBN 0-13-937103-6

Editorial supervision and interior design: Serena Hoffman
Cover design: Diane Saxe
Cover illustration: Maude Mahlman, University of Mississippi
Manufacturing buyer: Barbara Kelly Kittle

PRINTED IN THE UNITED STATES OF AMERICA

10 9 8 7 6 5 4 3 2 1

ISBN 01-13-937103-6 01

PRENTICE-HALL INTERNATIONAL, INC., *London*
PRENTICE-HALL OF AUSTRALIA PTY. LIMITED, *Sydney*
EDITORA PRENTICE-HALL DO BRASIL, LTDA., *Rio de Janeiro*
PRENTICE-HALL CANADA INC., *Toronto*
PRENTICE-HALL HISPANOMERICANA, S. A., *Mexico*
PRENTICE-HALL OF INDIA PRIVATE LIMITED, *New Delhi*
PRENTICE-HALL OF JAPAN, INC., *Tokyo*
PRENTICE-HALL OF SOUTHEAST ASIA PTE. LTD., *Singapore*
WHITEHALL BOOKS LIMITED, *Wellington, New Zealand*

Contents

Preface

To that persistent question "Why study the past, when we live in the present?" the best answer we can give you is so simple that it may be difficult to understand. Perhaps an analogy will make the point. Each of us lives in the present, but our immediate experiences, thoughts, and perceptions are shaped by our previous ones. We are, in a very real sense, what we have been. And an important aspect of our present is our consciousness of that past. We cannot tell where we are (much less where we are going) without knowing where we have been.

In the United States, the situation is an involved one because of the country's size and complexity. When we speak of our "national experience," we are using shorthand for a collection of many experiences of various groups—economic, religious, ethnic, or whatever. Indeed, the national experience is not merely the experience of the United States as such, but of millions of individuals who have lived, at least in part, in a specifically defined geographical space. Not only is the history of our country complex, but it abounds in ambiguities, paradoxes, and contradictions— like the experience of any people—and more often than not it defies measurement and exactitude. These are the very qualities, we think, that make the study of history so challenging and fascinating.

Since no two historians view the past in exactly the same manner, a few words should be said about the new writing and new contents of this book. It is a briefer version of our The United States, fifth edition, which is itself a much modified text originally authored by Richard Hofstadter, William Miller, and Daniel Aaron. We have thoroughly rewritten that work, updating it and placing greater emphasis on social history—the history of the various groups of people in America from the time when no *human beings lived on this continent. We have constantly borne in mind both the most recent research in American history and the interests and concerns of students in the mid-1980s. Both of us teach survey courses in the history of the United States, and we learn by doing so.*

A note about our cooperation. The chapters prior to Reconstruction have been Winthrop Jordan's responsibility; the chapters from Reconstruction to the present are Leon Litwack's. From the outset, we agreed to aim for a volume that is readable, challenging, and judicious without being insipid in its interpretations. Our objective is not merely to present some formal knowledge about American history, but to convey the complexity and diversity of the American experience with a deeper, more subtle sense of what it means to live in this often ambiguous nation. We challenge our readers to accept the rewards of such learning.

WINTHROP D. JORDAN
University of Mississippi

LEON F. LITWACK
University of California, Berkeley

1

Migrants to America

The first Americans were immigrants. They came on foot in small groups many thousands of years ago across a bridge of dry land between Asia and Alaska—a pathway that is now under water. Gradually they moved into North, Central, and South America, and as they did so they developed a wide variety of societies. These "Indians" were the first Americans.

Much later, 500 years ago, people came by sea from western Europe and from West Africa. The Europeans thought they had found a new world. The land was indeed new to them, and they began describing their homeland as the Old World, in order to distinguish it from the new one. The

nations of western Europe, especially England, France, Spain, Portugal, and the Netherlands, set about settling this land, often with disastrous consequences for the earliest inhabitants. The Indians died very rapidly, largely from new diseases imported from Africa and Europe. Measles and smallpox, which are nearly extinct today, killed millions of Indians, who had had no previous contact with the microbes that cause them.

Christopher Columbus, an Italian ship captain working for the rulers of Spain, "discovered" this ancient land. He died thinking he had reached Asia, not America.

THE FIRST AMERICANS

The eastern-woodland Indians in the region stretching from what is now Georgia to Maine had many common characteristics, though with variations. Anthropologists usually divide them into three large groups, principally on the basis of language. The Algonkian tribes who lived along the coast from Canada to North Carolina became, for

the early English migrants, the "typical" Indians. Further south and west were several large groups who spoke Muskogean languages. A third language, Iroquoian, prevailed in the area around the eastern Great Lakes. The Iroquoian peoples were probably relative newcomers, having come from the Mississippi Valley into what is now upstate New York and neighboring parts of Canada.

Indian Economic Life

All these peoples had common cultural characteristics, but climate and the available supplies of food and housing made for important differences. Although they had several technological skills Europeans lacked, their lack of other skills put them at a severe disadvantage when they were confronted by the migrants from northern Europe. The Iroquois and Algonkian had developed a highly efficient means of transportation at a time when "roads" in most parts of the world were inferior to the highways of ancient Rome. The Indian elm and birch-bark canoes were brittle, but they had the great advantage of light weight for carrying between lakes and streams. Hollowed-out logs were also used, but more often on the ocean. Many of the coastal Indians fished with great efficiency in shallow waters, using nets and weirs. They were not, however, fishers of the deep sea, for they had not developed sails.

All the eastern-woodland Indians grew corn (maize) and various kinds of squash, pumpkins, and beans. And of course they hunted deer, which provided clothing as well as food, and they trapped and hunted a variety of smaller animals unknown in the Old World, such as beaver, opossum, and raccoon. Hunting was done with bows and arrows, which in skillful hands were as accurate as European muskets and much more rapid firing. They also used tomahawks in warfare, and the Muskogean carried, in addition, spears and shields woven from bark and vines. Their housing usually consisted of bent poles covered with thatch or hides. The word *wigwam* is the Algonkian term for *house*. Metalworking was unknown, so stones and shells served as weapons and tools. However, these Indians lacked three technological advantages widely used by Europeans: the wheel, the plow, and draft animals such as oxen and horses.

Nature and Society

Eastern-woodland Indians lived closer to nature than Europeans did, though of course Europeans then lived much closer to nature than we do now. They still kept time by the sun or moon or walking distances, in an age when Europeans were increasingly using clocks and calendars. The Indians had a close psychological rapport with animals and even with trees and mountains; many tribes believed that animals had souls. Their religious faiths reflected their strong ties with natural surroundings. Most—perhaps all—believed in a high god, a single deity who was superior to other deities, who were often identified with specific animals, vegetation, or places. This closeness with nature also reflected the way that they thought about their societies. Many tribes considered themselves to be divided into *clans*, groups of people thought to be related to one another, and these clans were often identified by such names as wolf, bear, deer and beaver.

The Indians were strongly attached to their land, which they felt was theirs by reason of tradition and use, not because they "owned" it. The land almost seemed to own them. This way of thinking about territory was very different from the one that prevailed in Europe, where various groups of people staked out their own turf by means of national boundaries and carved up those spaces among individuals who "owned" land as "real estate." The gap between these two concepts of land was to prove an enduring source of conflict between Indians and Europeans in America.

The social and political organizations of the tribes varied considerably, but it is

A drawing of early Indian settlers in Virginia. (Theodore de Bry, engraving after the watercolor by John White, 1590; New York Public Library)

impossible today to describe them accurately, largely because early Europeans tended to talk about Indian tribes in terms of their own societies. European observers expected to find kings, nobles, and commoners, and they became confused when they discovered that such groups did not fit the societies they were describing. There was similar confusion about the different Indian groups, which the English variously called *nations*, *tribes*, or simply *sorts*. It is clear, however, that there were at least a hundred Algonkian tribes; sometimes groups of them were shaped into confederacies by forceful leaders.

The famous League of the Iroquois in upstate New York came about because five tribes fashioned a sophisticated, powerful, and remarkably enduring political alliance. Each tribe sent a specific number of representatives to a central council for decisions about war and diplomacy. The Iroquois fascinate historians and anthropologists because of the unusual strength of this confederation and also because of other distinguishing aspects of their society: their *longhouses*, huge wigwams occupied by four to six families; their reputation as fierce warriors; their reliance on communal interpretation of individual dreams; and the powerful influence of Iroquois women, who farmed while their men hunted and warred and who chose which men would lead them in both war and peace. Among all eastern Indians, political leadership depended on maturity, wisdom, and forcefulness much more than on heredity or wealth.

The woodland Indians were no more peaceful than Europeans. They fought frequently against each other, more for sport and manhood than for territory. By European standards, casualties were low. Silence and surprise were the usual methods of attack. Many tribes practiced ritual torture of captives and/or formal tribal adoption.

Their style of peace resembled their style of war; Europeans were struck by their quiet dignity in diplomatic negotiations. Carefully weighing their words, they spoke with brief eloquence, confident that those few words would seal whatever agreement was being made.

THE OLD WORLD MEETS THE NEW

People from the Old World discovered Indian America at least twice, but the first discovery had little effect. The impact of the second discovery was momentous in Europe as well as in America. In each instance, "America" was not discovered as a whole. Rather, European navigators stumbled onto particular landfalls, unaware in the slightest that they had found two "new" continents.

The Norsemen

The Norse (Norwegian) contacts with America took place about a thousand years ago. Norwegians had long been settled in Iceland; from there they pushed westward. About 980 they established tiny settlements near the southern tip of Greenland. Some four thousand Norse people were living there, but for unknown reasons they lost contact with Europe in the second half of the fifteenth century and died out for lack of food and supplies.

That thrust westward had gone further. In 986 Biarni Heriulfson set sail from Iceland and ended up cruising along a shore he was sure could not be Greenland because it was "a flat and wooded country" and had no mountains of ice. He was, in fact, running along the coasts of Baffin Island and Labrador, but he did not land.

Although Biarni was the first European we know of who saw American shores, Leif

Ericson was the first to set foot on American soil. He landed on Baffin Island and then made his way south down the coast of Labrador and Newfoundland. At last the voyagers came ashore at a place they called Vinland "in accordance with all the good things they found in it."

This original European discovery of America remained unknown, except in some obscure old Norse stories, until the nineteenth century. Some people have made claims for earlier contact with Indian America—by ancient Phoenicians from the Mediterranean, by black Africans, and even by Pacific islanders. None of these claims is totally improbable, but all are very far from firmly established. Much more to the point, if such contacts did occur, they had no widespread effect. The voyages of Christopher Columbus did.

European Expansion

There is no easy explanation for the sudden expansiveness of western Europeans in the fifteenth century. Contributing to their thrust overseas were various factors, which we might label economic, political, technological, and demographic.

For centuries Europeans had traded with the peoples of southeastern Asia for certain highly valued commodities that could not be found or grown in Europe, among them jewels, silk, and especially spices. (Spices improved the taste of food and, in an age without refrigeration, preserved meat and disguised its taste when rotten.) That trade was carried on over thousands of miles across the Indian Ocean, through the Middle East, over the Mediterranean Sea to the ports of southern Europe, and then overland to the north and west. At the western ports of entry, the trade was controlled by the merchants of Venice and other city-states in what is now Italy. As

time went on, merchants in the western parts of Europe grew more and more discontented with the problems of this trade: high prices, piracy, too many middlemen, and lack of reliability. At the same time, new financial practices developed in Italy were beginning to spread north and west: double-entry bookkeeping of financial records, pooling of capital among several individuals or families, rudimentary banks, and the use of Arabic numerals rather than Roman numerals in account books.

Politically, the monarchs of western Europe were becoming more successful in their struggles with powerful feudal warlords. Geographical areas that are now single countries, such as France, Portugal, and Spain, were then collections of separate provinces and dukedoms. During the fifteenth century, monarchs consolidated their authority over larger territories, and it was these powerful new monarchies that became the modern countries of western Europe. Many historians summarize these developments as *the rise of nation-states.*

A third development in European society was just as complicated but much less dramatic. Trade with the Far East had resulted in knowledge of both gunpowder and the compass. Although neither of these Chinese inventions had an immediate impact on European methods of warfare and navigation, in the long run they helped give Europeans a sense of mastery over other peoples and the sea. Also important to overseas expansion were hundreds of small improvements in ship design. Taken together, these improvements enabled Europeans to build vessels that could handle ocean waves without capsizing, be steered by workable rudders, and be propelled entirely by sails—there was no need for oars.

The demographic change that helped set off European expansion was the result of a disaster. In the fourteenth century, Europe was struck by bubonic plague, a deadly infection carried by infected lice on rats. The Black Death swept away about a third of western Europe's population. Even though it damaged the economy, the tragedy raised the economic and social status of the serfs (agricultural laborers) who survived, because it meant that their labor came into greater demand. The notion that people were bound to the land began to break down. As people grew less attached to custom and more to individual initiative, they grew restless and no longer assumed they had to stay where they had been born.

Exploration

Early in the fourteenth century, Italian, Spanish, and French mariners began to explore the west coast of Africa in search of a way around that continent. They came upon and occupied the Canary Islands, then the Madeiras, and ultimately the still more westerly Azores. But it remained for the Portuguese, after 1420, to begin the systematic collection of geographic information that calmed ancient fears of the "green sea of gloom," as the Arabs called the Atlantic. The Portuguese transformed that waterway into a path of adventure and commerce in enslaved blacks.

In 1488 Bartholomeu Dias rounded Cabo Tormentoso (Cape of Storms) at Africa's southernmost tip and opened the first all-water route from Europe to the Indies. The king of Portugal was so impressed by this feat that he renamed the treacherous neck of land Cape of Good Hope.

Nine years after Dias's voyage, four Portuguese ships under Vasco da Gama sailed for India from Lisbon and returned in 1499 with spices and jewels. Gama's voyage marked the end of Middle Eastern supremacy in the Oriental trade and the eclipse of the Italian merchants. The Portuguese, moreover, soon drove Muslim merchants from the Indian Ocean itself, reduced their strongholds at the sources of supply, and established an Oriental empire of their own that lasted, at least in fragments, almost to our day.

THE SPANISH EMPIRE IN THE NEW WORLD

Compared with the Portuguese, the Spanish were latecomers to overseas expansion. Columbus himself had sailed as a youth in the service of the Portuguese in ships similar to the little Niña, Pinta, and Santa Maria, but when he asked for royal support for his voyage westward he was turned down flat. Columbus left Portugal to try his luck with King Ferdinand and Queen Isabella of Spain. But the Spanish monarchs had no time for his "impossible and vain" scheme. So for five years, Columbus appealed in turn to England, France, and again to Portugal.

In 1492, the situation in Spain changed. The Spanish finally expelled Islamic people from their last foothold in Spain. The hope of converting the "princes and people" of the Indies to the holy faith and taking their fabled treasure prompted Ferdinand and Isabella to give in. They gave their backing to the explorer's search for the Orient and agreed further, as Columbus noted for himself, "that henceforth I might call myself by a noble title and be Admiral-in-Chief of the Ocean Sea and Viceroy and Perpetual Governor of all the islands and mainlands that I should discover."

We know now what Columbus found. After a few months of exploring the Caribbean, he left some of his men behind on the island of Hispaniola and set out for Spain with a few gold nuggets and several

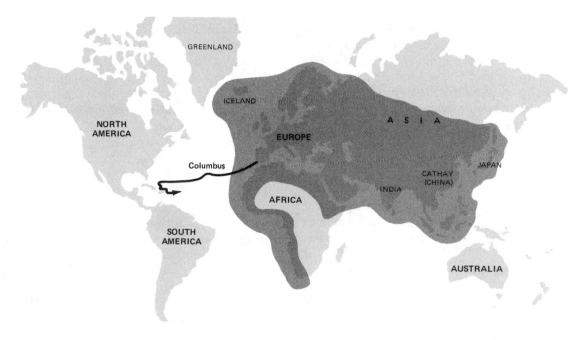

The World Known to Europeans in 1492

"Indians" to prove the success of his voyage. None of the Indians survived.

Columbus made three more voyages. His search on these visits was for a passage through the land barrier just beyond which, he remained certain, must lie Japan. Naturally, he found no passage. Not until Ferdinand Magellan's men circumnavigated the globe in the service of Spain (1519–22) did the truth become known about how enormously long was the westward passage to the East.

Upon learning of Columbus's stunning discoveries in 1493, the pope proceeded to divide the newly discovered world between the Spanish and the Portuguese. The next year, in the Treaty of Tordesillas, Spain and Portugal agreed on the specific boundary separating their portions of the globe. Portugal, in effect, received the Orient; Spain, the New World except for the region that became Brazil.

Spain soon encouraged other mariners to occupy her claim, to search out its limits, convert its inhabitants, and uncover its wealth. One of the first to sail under her flag was a Florentine, Amerigo Vespucci, who in 1497 began a series of voyages on which he explored the American coastline southeast from Mexico all the way to Brazil. Ten years later, a German geographer first called the New World *America* in honor of Vespucci.

Long before other Atlantic nations challenged it, Spain had established a vast empire in the New World. Small numbers of Spaniards occupied the largest Caribbean islands: Cuba, Hispaniola, Puerto Rico, and Jamaica. Led by Hernando Cortés, Spanish *conquistadores* went on to conquer the high

Indian civilizations in Mexico. Francisco Pizarro began the Spanish occupation of Peru in 1528. In both regions the Spanish found fabulous sources of gold and silver. Other Spanish explorers wandered through Florida, the lower Mississippi Valley, and the American Southwest, but they were discouraged by the apparent absence of precious metals in those regions.

The Indians of the Caribbean Islands—the Arawaks and Caribs—were relatively primitive in technology and political organization, although they had mastered the art of interisland boating. The first European drawings of these Indians showed them eating human flesh. They may or may not have been cannibals; what is certain is that the Arawaks told the Spanish that the Caribs, their enemies, were. On the mainland of Mexico and Peru, the Spanish found densely populated, advanced civilizations, genuine empires with powerful kings, highway systems, enormous temples, and stunning works of art in silver and gold.

Until recently, the success of the small numbers of Spanish explorers has been explained largely in terms of their superior boldness and technology. The Spanish conquerors were indeed brutal, but the Aztecs in Mexico were themselves conquerors of earlier peoples and practiced ritual human sacrifice and perhaps cannibalism as well. The Spanish advantage was mainly psychological. Many more Indians were overawed by Spanish firearms than were killed by them. The Indians were also amazed by the sight of men on horseback, who they thought were single animals.

In recent years, however, it has become clear that the Spanish had one enormous advantage of which neither they nor the Indians were aware. Over hundreds of centuries, most of the peoples of the Old World had developed partial immunity to certain diseases unknown in the New World. Within fifty years of first contact with the Spanish, the Indians of Hispaniola nearly died out. In Mexico the Indian population appears to have dropped to something like 10 percent of its previous level. Measles and especially smallpox were probably the two chief killers. Whatever the diseases, it is clear that no society can survive when it loses 90 percent of its people in two or three generations. Unwittingly the Indians had their revenge, for Columbus's sailors introduced syphilis into Europe. But that disease did not kill masses of people in a short period of time.

The political and social consequences of these diseases were profound. Many Indian societies were virtually destroyed. Depopulation among the Indians was largely responsible for the demand for slaves from the Old World to work the fields and mines of the New. Starting about 1522, the Spanish began importing slaves from Africa. Though they too died in large numbers, the Africans had had sufficient contact with Europeans across the Sahara Desert to acquire partial immunities themselves, so they did not suffer the drastic mortality rates of the Indians. But they too had a measure of revenge, for many European slave traders died from tropical diseases. The dimensions of this human tragedy, then, were enormous and bitterly ironic.

THE FRENCH

Except in Brazil, the Spanish claimed a monopoly on the entire New World, one that was endorsed by the pope. Yet other Christian nations refused to recognize Spain's exclusive jurisdiction. The French were the first to challenge it. The French king sent Jacques Cartier on a mission in search of what had become known as the Northwest Passage—not because it was expected to run northwest, but because it was supposed to be in the north and to run directly west to the Indies. Cartier hit upon the mouth of the St. Lawrence River, and he was able to sail so far up that stream that he was convinced he had found the route to the Orient. But then, at the site of modern Montreal, he came up against rapids that prevented further progress to the west. Despite his disappointment, he was impressed by "the immense numbers of people in Hochelga" and by "their kindness and peacefulness."

The Spanish showed little interest in the northern voyages, but they were deeply concerned by a French settlement in Florida that was uncomfortably close to the shipping lanes of their treasure ships from Peru and Mexico. They wiped it out and confidently built Fort Augustine on the northeast coast of that region.

It was the French and not the Spanish who gained control in North America. In the early seventeenth century, under the leadership of Samuel de Champlain, French explorers established outposts at Quebec, Montreal, and various other points along the St. Lawrence River, the great gateway to the interior of the continent. Then they pressed on through the regions of the Great Lakes and the Ohio and Mississippi valleys. The French also established settlements at New Orleans and Biloxi on the Gulf of Mexico, and at St. Domingue, the western end of the island of Hispaniola.

Most French settlements in the Midwest were not really towns; they were forts and trading stations, aimed primarily at serving the fur trade. Many French fur traders married Indian women and adopted Indian ways. French farmers were widely scattered and remained sufficiently few in number to take very little land from the Indians. Thus the French avoided conflict with the native inhabitants, unlike the Spanish and English.

RELIGIOUS CHANGE IN EUROPE

A century after the Portuguese and Spanish began their conquest of distant regions, a religious revolution swept through Germany and the rest of northwestern Europe. The Protestant Reformation broke into the open in Germany in 1517 when Martin Luther challenged the Church by denouncing the "indiscriminate" sale of "pardons" for sins. Luther asserted that people could not save themselves by accomplishing outward charities, or "good works," but only "by faith alone." He went on to claim that Christians must acquire faith not through priestly intermediaries but directly from the Bible, the Word of God. Luther's assault on the Church's hierarchy began an age of religious warfare that wracked northwestern Europe for more than a century.

Calvinism

Intellectual leadership of the Protestant revolution soon passed to John Calvin, a French refugee who established a theocratic city-state in Geneva, Switzerland. Calvin stressed man's helplessness in the face of an omnipotent God. He insisted that from the beginning of all time, God had decided the eternal fate of every individual, whether he or she was to be saved or damned. There was nothing anyone could do, Calvin insisted, to change God's decision. At the same time, he said, God required rigidly good behavior on the part of all His subjects.

John Calvin. (New York Public Library)

Calvin also sought to eliminate from Protestant services the forms and ceremonials of Roman Catholic ritual. The community must be dedicated to God's purposes, the Christian purified of sin. Above all, every dweller in Calvin's righteous community must constantly examine the condition of his own soul. Although people could not earn their way to Heaven by work or win God's favor by performing good deeds, diligent labor and devotion to one's job or "calling," Calvin taught, were often signs of redemption.

The inherent ambiguity in these injunctions was compelling to many people in the sixteenth century. One could not earn eternal salvation, because "God did all." On the other hand, the person who labored and lived in godly fashion seemed to be the more likely candidate for God's arbitrary (but always just) decision on whether he or she was damned or saved in later life—which was the life that mattered. Furthermore, it seemed to Calvinists that God would favor entire communities that were committed to His ends.

English Reformation and Nationalism

These doctrines began to seep into England in the middle of the sixteenth century. The English nation first broke with the Roman Catholic Church because a willful Henry VIII became entangled in marital difficulties, which embroiled him with the Pope, and in dynastic entanglements with Spain, whose monarch was rapidly becoming the international champion of Catholicism. Two short reigns followed Henry's death— one Protestant, the next Catholic. Then Queen Elizabeth, monarch from 1558 to 1603, tried to compromise at home between a nationalized Church of England, still partially Catholic in doctrine, and the growing number of English Calvinists, called Puritans, who wanted further reform and purification of the national church. At the same time, she became the international champion of Protestantism against the counter-crusade being mounted by Spain. The eventual battle came in 1588, when English vessels defeated a massive Spanish invasion attempt, the famous Armada.

The war with Spain dragged on until 1604, but the defeat of the Armada established the little English nation as a world power and leader of the Protestant cause. As such, she began to think more seriously about challenging her international rivals in the New World.

England and the New World

While English sea dogs could harry the Spanish at sea, they had no hope of dislodging well-established Spanish settlements in America. England's only legitimate claim to land in America came from John and Sebastian Cabot's two voyages to the northeastern coast, years before, in the 1490s. The French had claimed and then thinly settled a large area in what is now called Canada. Thus, for the English the only remaining territory that seemed unclaimed and unoccupied was the ill-defined Atlantic seaboard southward from the French and north of the Spanish in Florida.

English interest in New World colonization was not merely a matter of challenging international rivals. Just prior to Elizabeth's reign, English merchants began to organize commercial joint-stock companies for trading overseas to Russia, Africa, and the Near East. No one knew it at the time, but England was just on the verge of taking off as a major economic power among European nations. In the 1570s, a number of merchants combined with gentlemen adventurers to send expeditions to the New World. They were to set up trading forts, find gold, and discover the elusive Northwest Passage to the Orient.

Most persistent of all was Sir Walter Raleigh, who organized numerous expeditions. On his third (but not final) attempt, Raleigh sent 120 persons under the leadership of John White to Roanoke Island in the region he had tactfully named Virginia, after his unmarried queen. The Armada prevented supplies from reaching them for three years, and when the relief expedition finally arrived they found virtually no trace of the settlers. Their fate remains unknown to this day.

Ideology of English Expansion

Because of bad luck, overly romantic expectations, insufficient financial resources, and the ongoing war with Spain, English colonizing efforts seemed to be going nowhere during the last quarter of the sixteenth century. Yet there was a significant change at home in England, which may in the long run have been as important as all these failures. Richard Hakluyt was an Elizabethan preacher and adventurer who never ventured overseas himself, but his writings did much to turn English attention in that direction. In 1584 Hakluyt set forth the case for English settlement in the New World in his *Discourse Concerning Western Planting*. Then in the 1590s he captivated a wide reading public with his highly nationalistic *The Principal Navigations, Voyages, Traffiques, and Discoveries of the English Nation*. Here were words to stir the hearts and ambitions of Hakluyt's island countrymen. He set forth the case for "western planting": "This enterprise may stay the Spanish king from flowing over all . . . of America, if we seat and plant there in time." "We shall," Hakluyt cried, "by planting there enlarge the glory of the gospel, and from England plant sincere religion." He meant, of course, Protestantism. As for the possibilities of trade, "the subjects of this realm for many years shall change many cheap commodities of those parts for things of high value there not esteemed." Hakluyt predicted that his countrymen "shall have by that means ships . . . of great strength for the defence of this realm." And for the further benefit of the nation, the soldiers at "the end of the wars, . . . the wandering beggars of England, that grow up idly, and hurtful and burdensome to this realm, may there be unladen, better bred up, and may people waste countries . . . to their own more happy state."

Few individuals have so completely stated the mood and intentions of an expansive people.

SUGGESTED READINGS

H. Driver, *Indians of North America* (1970). J. Axtell, ed., *The Indian Peoples of Eastern America* (1981). J.H. Parry, *The Age of Reconnaisance* (1963). C. Gibson, *Spain in America* (1966). C. Bridenbaugh, *Vexed and Troubled Englishmen, 1590-1642* (1968). C. Cipolla, *European Culture and Overseas Expansion* (1970).

SUMMARY

European voyages of exploration and discovery had by the late fifteenth century reached the Americas, which until then had known only Asian immigrants. This new expansionism was motivated by desire for the trade and wealth on which the new economic system of commercial capitalism was based, as well as by political rivalry. The latter, in turn, was based on the religious conflicts that had grown out of the Protestant Reformation.

The most important immediate effect of this "invasion" of the New World by Europeans was the destruction of the native populations, who died by the thousands of diseases to which they had no resistance. These Indians, as the Europeans called them, were extremely varied in language, culture, and appearance. Their societies and political organizations ranged from the sophisticated empires of the Aztecs and Incas to the simple family or tribal groupings of nomadic hunters.

The woodland Indians of the Atlantic seacoast lived primarily by hunting, fishing, trapping, and simple agriculture. Political organization was based on tribes or nations, and sometimes on confederations or alliances of a number of tribes. These societies were remarkably "classless." There were leaders, but leadership was based on age and merit, not birth.

Although we say Christopher Columbus discovered America, it had actually been known to Europeans much earlier, though no one then, including Columbus, had any idea of its size. The tenth-century Norwegians who found and settled Iceland and Greenland also made their way to Labrador and Newfoundland. But it was not until late in the fifteenth century that economic, political, and technological development made long sea voyages and large-scale colonization possible.

The Portuguese were the first to venture out. They reached the Far East by sailing south along the coast of Africa and then northeast to India and beyond. By chance they stumbled onto the eastern bulge of South America, which was soon named Brazil. When Columbus tried to go west, he landed among the islands of the Caribbean Sea (the West Indies), though he thought he was near Japan.

Eventually five nations of western Europe established empires in the New World. Many of their claims overlapped. The Spanish claimed by far the largest part, including much of South America, all of Central

America, what is now the southwestern part of the United States, and Florida. The Portuguese took Brazil, and the Dutch various small colonies including New Netherlands, now New York. French fur traders and farmers established good relations with the Indians in New France—Canada, the Great Lakes region, and the Mississippi Valley as far south as the Gulf of Mexico. English claims were established only along the North Atlantic coastline southward from Maine to Georgia.

Martin Luther's challenge in 1517 of the supreme authority of the Catholic Church started centuries of religious conflict in Europe. Spain, Portugal, and France became loyal supporters of the pope; England, Scotland, the Netherlands, and Scandinavia were split among various Protestant denominations. The defeat of the Spanish Armada in 1588 made England a major maritime power; its merchants were by this time eager to share in the rewards of overseas trade. But the first attempts to establish English settlements in North America all failed. It would take much trial and error before the English would find the right formula for an overseas empire in North America.

2
An Overseas Empire

Between 1600 and 1700, England acquired a permanent empire in the New World. The colonies that grew up on the coast of North America became linked with one another and with England in a mercantile system of empire. Theirs was an economy based on the exchange and sale of goods in a pattern designed to build the prosperity and power of England as the center. Making and running an overseas empire was a new venture for England; making a new life was a new venture for the colonists. It was inevitable that there would be problems, particularly because England sent colonists rather than conquerors to North America. The colonies themselves differed from one another because they were established for different reasons.

By the end of the century, government officials in England began to realize that they had the makings of an overseas empire. In actuality, that empire consisted of nearly twenty different settlements stretching from the Caribbean to New England. They knew what they wanted the colonies to become, but enforcing their wishes was difficult at a time when it took three months to get an answer in London to the simplest question about what was going on in America. But none of this was apparent in 1603–4, when events in England made permanent settlement on the Atlantic coast a possibility.

CHANGES IN ENGLAND

Several factors combined to make many English people suddenly decide to emigrate to the forbidding wilderness across the Atlantic. The war between Spain and England came to an end in 1604, and peace encouraged merchants to invest their capital in overseas enterprises. James I, who had succeeded Elizabeth, proved hostile to the Puritans. They then decided they could establish truly godly communities more easily in America than in England. Many of his subjects thought James was undermining the traditional English freedoms of representative government, free speech, taxation by consent, and trial by due process. In addition, economic dislocations convinced many observers that England was overpopulated: there seemed to be too many "beggars" roaming the countryside and flooding into London. Finally, a sense of exhilaration and expansive power was sweeping the nation after its victories over Catholic Spain.

James I died in 1625, but his son Charles I took a hard line on taxation and the privileges of Parliament. After a major constitutional crisis in the late 1620s, Charles I tried for more than a decade to rule without Parliament. When forced by financial necessity to call Parliament together in 1639, he became involved in a civil war that resulted in his execution in 1649. This was followed by the Puritan dictatorship of Oliver Cromwell and his "saints." After Cromwell's death, the monarchy was "restored" in 1660.

The Restoration of Charles II marked a turning point in English history that had a great effect on the colonies, just as the outbreak of the civil war had in 1640. After twenty years of civil turmoil, the English government was able to encourage the establishment of more colonies and to set up a system for supervising them. Yet the religious issue in England was only partially settled. Most of the people still belonged to the Church of England, but a large minority of Dissenters still held to Puritan principles in the face of some persecution. The constitutional issue remained less clear. It was not until another revolution in 1689 that the primacy of Parliament over the Crown was firmly established.

VIRGINIA

When James I assumed the throne in 1603, he was quite willing to issue land grants in America. James gave his backing to the Virginia Company, which had two branches, one in London and the other in the little port city of Plymouth. He awarded Sir Ferdinando Gorges's Plymouth branch an enormous territory on the northern portion of the Atlantic coast, and in the spring of 1607 Sir Ferdinando sent an expedition to Sagadahoc on the Kennebec River in Maine. The settlement lasted barely one winter. After an "extreme, unseasonable, and frosty" season, the men simply quit. It was the Jamestown settlement that finally succeeded.

The Jamestown Settlement

In 1607 three tiny English ships sailed up a broad river in Virginia. There were 160 men aboard. These settlers tactfully named the river the James and chose an island they called Jamestown, a site well situated for defense—and also, as it turned out, for the spread of disease. Here, after the most terrible experiences, England won its first foothold in America. (One can visit a reconstruction of this little colony today.)

This first permanent English settlement in the New World came very close to failure; only an accident of timing saved it from going the way of Roanoke. At first it was an all-male enterprise, but gradually a few women braved the hardships of the Atlantic voyage and the crude life in the struggling colony. In order to survive, an overseas colony needed a reliable source of income, and this first successful English settlement found one in a new crop, tobacco. These early English settlers also had to deal with the fact that the land was already occupied. In those early years, the Indian residents of the area could easily have wiped out the tiny settlement, and they came quite close to doing so.

During the bleak winter of 1608–9, the "starving time," the colony was held together by the efforts of Captain John Smith, an energetic and iron-willed war veteran. Smith was aided by Powhatan, an Indian chief who had forged a powerful confederacy of tribes in the area. Powhatan at first regarded the English as pawns in his power game and befriended them with food.

The English undertaking in Virginia had three principal objectives: to find a northwest water passage to the wealth of Asia, to exploit the gold and silver of America, and to find suitable lands for producing crops such as silk, grapes, dyes, and oranges. All three efforts failed. The James River did not go very far west. Smith's explorations aroused the hostility of Powhatan's people, who soon realized that the English had come not merely to trade metal for corn, but to take Indian land.

When Smith was injured in 1609 and left Virginia for good, the settlement remained, as he accurately described it, "a miserie, a ruine, a death, a Hell." The colony had been financed by the Virginia Company, a group of wealthy English capitalists who hoped to profit from the settlement. They were more than disappointed.

The Virginia Company struggled to support its overseas enterprise but met with little success. In 1624, when James I canceled Virginia's charter and made it a royal province, the colony had only 1200 people. About 6000 had set out for Jamestown, but 4000 had died on the ocean voyage or in the New World, and hundreds of others had given up and gone home.

By then, however, conditions had begun to improve. Some of the earliest settlers in Virginia had been mere servants, men who signed contracts called *indentures*, by which they agreed to work for a certain number of years in return for their passage to the New World. Once in Virginia, these servants proved very hard to control, despite the use of brutal punishments. The promoters recognized the shortcomings of this system in 1619. They gave each of the old settlers 100 acres and began a *head-right* system, under which each new settler received 50 acres of land for himself and an additional 50 acres for every servant he brought to the colony. In the same year, the company sought to make the colony more attractive and orderly by creating a House of Burgesses, the first legislature of elected representatives in America.

As important as these formal changes was the discovery, several years earlier, that tobacco could be grown successfully in Virginia. A market for tobacco had been growing in Europe since the middle of the sixteenth century.

The explosion of tobacco production that followed had important social and political effects. Tobacco rapidly wore out the soil: four years on the same ground was the normal limit. In their search for more and more land, Virginia planters gradually pushed small farmers from the rich coastal plain onto marginal lands and into upland areas farther west, far from easy water transport. This trend was accompanied by a concentration of economic and political power in the hands of a relatively small group, whose members, no matter how humble their origins, came rapidly to regard themselves as a ruling class, an aristocracy.

Yet the most lasting impact of the tobacco economy worked in another direction—toward a lack of freedom. Tobacco production required a stable labor force, but indentured servants left after a few years. Slaves did not, nor did their descendants.

English and Indians

The one-crop system became the source for some of the grievances that led in 1676 to Bacon's Rebellion. In 1622, several years after tobacco culture had begun to push settlers into Indian territory, Powhatan's successor led an attack on the English settlements in which nearly a third of the colonists were killed. The English response was bitter and violent. All Indians, whether friendly or not, were now seen as enemies. Instructions from London directed settlers "to root out [the Indians] from being any longer a people."

There was another conflict in the 1640s. When the fighting was over, in 1646, leaders on both sides agreed to occupy separate territories. The Indians and the English lived in relative peace for the next thirty years, until a new wave of settlers began spreading onto the Indian lands. In the 1670s these settlers complained of Indian raids on their hogs and demanded official permission to push the Indians out of the lands near white settlements. Virginia's governor, William Berkeley, was reluctant to upset relations with the Indians, so the frontiersmen took matters into their own hands. They attacked a group of about 400 Susquehannocks living in an abandoned fort. Weakened by European diseases and warfare, they and several other local tribes were extremely vulnerable. In the war of extermination that followed, revenge was taken on both sides. When Governor Berkeley failed to provide a force that could remove or destroy the Indians, Nathaniel Bacon had his chance.

An aristocrat with a shady past, Bacon was in his twenties when he arrived in Virginia and set himself up on more than 1000 acres in the interior. The elderly governor was his cousin by marriage, and within a year of his arrival Bacon was given a seat on the governor's council. Bacon, however, remained an outsider. The Virginia country, he said, wanted dead Indians, not friendly ones, and he demanded that Berkeley grant him a military commission to do the job. When Berkeley refused, Bacon set himself up as the leader of an anti-Berkeley party. He gathered a force of volunteers and led them in successful raids against the Indians and then against Jamestown itself. They burned the capital. News reached England in September 1676, and the king shipped out 1100 soldiers to restore order. But by that time Nathaniel Bacon had died of "swamp fever," and his followers had scattered into the woods. Probably fewer than 100 Englishmen died in the rebellion; 23 more were hanged as rebels.

The surviving Indians declared themselves subject to English law and fought other tribes from the interior for the English. But they were not considered equals. They were always the first to be abandoned by the colonial government in conflicts over land. The results of Bacon's Rebellion made it clear that even when the white population divided in civil war over the issue of Indian relations, it was the Indians who lost.

PURITAN NEW ENGLAND

The Puritans who migrated to New England were very different from the settlers of Virginia and subsequent tobacco-growing colonies. They were committed to dynamic religious beliefs that had profound and lasting effects on the settlement of the region and later on much of English America as well. They were not seeking religious liberty. Rather, they intended to set up their own Puritan churches, and they expected all settlers to follow Puritan principles and leadership. In order to do this, Puritan leaders tried to keep tight control over the pattern of settlement; they wanted compact village communities rather than scattered farms. And the Puritans migrated as families rather than as individuals. Thus, from the beginning there were more women and children in New England than in the other English colonies.

Puritan Ideology

Much nonsense has been written about the Puritans. They did not all wear tall black hats and drab clothing. They drank liquor, but not to excess. "Wine is from God," one of them wrote, "but drunkenness is from the devil." Far from denouncing sex, they enjoyed it, but they firmly believed that it ought to take place only between a married man and woman. Not only that, they insisted that a husband and wife *ought* to love each other both physically and spiritually. On this score they had only one reservation—that married love should not distract the partners from the higher love of God.

These English Calvinists kept God at the center of their attention. As Calvin himself had taught, they were certain that from the beginning of creation God had either saved or damned every single person for eternity. Yet this conviction did not make Puritans give up trying to lead good and moral lives. Both God and His Word, the Bible, required good behavior on the part of the individual and the community as a whole. Puritans knew that God would see fit to punish violations of His laws both in this world and in the next; surely He would punish an individual sinner. It was also entirely within His power to show His displeasure with entire communities by means of storms, disease, and other natural disasters. What could a person do in order to be saved? Strictly speaking, the answer was nothing, because the decision was in the hands of God. At the same time, Puritans believed they should watch for signs of God's pleasure toward them. They should prepare their hearts to receive salvation. Through faith in Christ, people should try to gain assurance that they were saved.

The problem was that a person could never be absolutely certain about God's decision. In daily life, therefore, Puritans were constantly examining themselves for signs of their eternal life. Puritans also watched their neighbors. They believed they had excellent reasons for doing so, since God, speaking through the Bible, required good behavior of everyone. So the Puritans looked for sinful words and deeds in their communities. They expected to find them, and of course they did, for they regarded all people as sinful by nature. They kept a watchful eye out for such sins as swearing, drunkenness, unlawful sex, theft, assault, murder, and idleness.

Puritans included idleness in the catalogue of sins because they believed that God required everyone to be busy at his or her work. God "called" men and women to their jobs—minister, farmer, mother, servant, seamstress, or carpenter. Whatever the calling, God required that men and women work long and hard at it. Thus the humblest farmer and the greatest merchant had to meet the same requirements for the performance of their appointed duties.

As we look back now, we can easily see that these requirements produced men and women of great faith and little tolerance. In the early years of New England settlement, this world view resulted in impatience toward anyone who stood in the Puritans' way, whether it was an English king and his bishops, the Atlantic Ocean, or the Indians who already lived on land the Puritans decided ought to be their own.

Pilgrims in Plymouth

The first Puritans who migrated to New England were a small and somewhat peculiar group. Though today we know them as Pilgrims, at the time they were called Separatists because they wished to break completely from the Church of England. The Separatists regarded the English church as hopelessly corrupt. King James and the church authorities responded by harassing their ministers and little congregations. In 1614 one of these Separatist congregations fled to Holland, where the authorities were more tolerant. After several years there, however, some of them grew worried about the condition of their children. They decided to attempt to go to America.

Thirty-five Pilgrims set out aboard the *Mayflower* in the autumn of 1620. Also in the ship's company were some sixty "strangers"—artisans, soldiers, and indentured servants. Finding themselves off Cape Cod, they decided not to seek Virginia, where they had been given a land grant. Rather, they would find a suitable harbor in the region where God had sent them. A month later their search was rewarded by discovery of the place they called Plymouth, on the inner shore of Massachusetts Bay.

The Pilgrims knew very little about fishing and hunting and not much more about farming in the extreme New England climate. The tiny settlement barely survived the "starving time" of that first winter, when half the group died. Yet eventually it grew, by means of luck, fortitude, and faith. Only a few years before, a plague carried by European fishermen had wiped out many Indians in southeastern New England. Those the English met were wary but not unfriendly.

Six years after they landed, the Pilgrims were able to buy out their financial backers with shipments of lumber and furs. That purchase virtually cut their connection with England. After ten years on their own, during which new towns scattered southward and onto Cape Cod, the Pilgrims adopted a system of elective, representative government. Each town sent representatives to the central government at Plymouth. Still, only those orthodox in religion and owning property were given the vote.

Until 1691, when their little towns were absorbed into Massachusetts Bay Colony, the Pilgrims led an independent existence, sustained by fish, fur, lumber, and religious faith. They were, as one of their friends in England wrote, "the instruments to break the ice for others."

The Commonwealth of Massachusetts Bay

Unlike the Separatist Pilgrims, most English Puritans intended to remain within the Church of England. By the late 1620s, however, many had grown discouraged about the future of their movement. The new king, Charles I, tried to suppress their preachers. This made some Puritans think of emigrating to America in order to establish a holy commonwealth of their own. In 1629 a wealthy Puritan lawyer, John Winthrop, led a successful effort to establish a

Governor John Winthrop. (New York Public Library)

company with rights of settlement in New England. Winthrop became the first governor of Massachusetts.

The Great Migration began in 1630. By the end of that year, a thousand selected settlers had landed in Massachusetts. Moving outward from Boston, the Puritans laid out other little towns. Migrants kept coming, and by the end of the decade, about 15,000 persons had crossed the Atlantic. This large migration sustained the prosperity of the colony; there was no "starving time" in Massachusetts. Few of the Puritan settlers were very wealthy, but many of them were able to pay for their own passage, with enough savings left over to support themselves for the first few months. The earlier settlers prospered by selling food and other articles to the newcomers. The arrangement worked very well as long as immigration lasted. But about 1640 the Great Migration came to a halt—civil war had broken out in England. Massachusetts faced its first economic depression. Yet the colony escaped disaster because, as Winthrop wrote, "the Lord was pleased to open up a trade with the West Indies." After only a dozen years of settlement, Massachusetts found its economic prosperity resting not on any single crop, but on overseas trade with other colonies and with England.

The search for a suitable form of government proved more difficult. The colony had control over its own charter and thus was able to act like an independent republic while acknowledging allegiance to the king. But it was not at all clear which settlers should control that government. Winthrop and other Puritan leaders, convinced that most settlers were not truly godly persons, struggled to keep control of the colony in the hands of the Puritan elite. They never thought that Puritan ministers should rule the holy commonwealth, though they often turned to them for advice and support. They simply assumed that any truly godly community should be governed by thoroughly orthodox Puritan men.

Thus Massachusetts Bay, not formally a theocracy since the clergy did not hold public office, was run by a Calvinist oligarchy of "visible saints." Authority rested with a legislature, called the General Court, which was made up of company officials, shareholders called freemen, and assistants elected by the freemen. All had to be members of a Puritan church.

At the outset the freemen, who alone had the franchise, constituted a small minority of the adult population. As the colony thrived and disfranchised men demanded a voice in the government, certain liberalizing steps were taken, chief among them the extension of the rank of freeman to all church members. To become a church member, a man still had to undergo intense scrutiny of his life and character by the Puritan divines. But thereafter, the franchise and even officeholding rights might be extended to him. In 1644 the towns beyond Boston gained the right to send representatives to a Chamber of Deputies, which became the lower house of the General Court; the upper house of Assistants still retained more power.

Dissidents in Rhode Island

The first American colonies to be established as offshoots of earlier ones were in New England. In many respects the most interesting was founded by Roger Williams, a talented Puritan minister who arrived in Massachusetts in 1631. Williams quickly got into hot water by embarrassingly asserting that the Bay Colony had no just claims to Indian lands. He also was so concerned with the purity of the churches that he took the radical position that civil authorities had no right to interfere with religious matters. Threatened with banishment to England, he fled to the region of Narragansett Bay, where he lived with the Indians. The following spring, having been joined by some of his sympathizers, he established his own community there, which he called Providence, the foundation of later Rhode Island.

In 1638 Massachusetts banished another troublemaker, the sharp-witted Anne Hutchinson, who had moved from practical discussions of midwifery in Boston to more touchy analyses of sermons she heard on Sundays. At her trial she finally challenged the core of Puritan theology by asserting that she had heard from God "by an immediate voice." Such a claim was clearly a threat to the primacy of the Bible and the powers of the clergy. Banished from Massachusetts, she moved with her family and some supporters to Rhode Island and later migrated westward, where she was killed by Indians—a brutal end that several Massachusetts leaders saw as a special instance of God's providence.

Roger Williams's settlement also drew voluntary exiles from Massachusetts who founded towns nearby. To insure the land titles of these loosely federated settlements, Williams obtained a charter from Parliament in 1644. For many years Rhode Island was the only colony in which all Christian sects enjoyed "liberty in religious concernments," as the charter put it, including the liberty to vote, whether one was a church member or not.

Connecticut, New Hampshire, and Maine

In the meantime, orthodox Puritan settlers were venturing far from the cluster of towns around Boston. Some moved northward onto land between the Merrimack and Kennebec rivers claimed by Massachusetts and also by several wealthy individuals in England. After considerable confusion about boundaries and land titles, New Hampshire emerged as a separate Puritan colony with a governor appointed by the king. The coastal land to the northeast, known as the district of Maine, remained part of Massachusetts.

Other Puritans left Massachusetts in favor of the fertile lands of the lower Connecticut valley. The Reverend Thomas Hooker led the first sizable migration and established the town of Hartford in 1636. More settlers from Massachusetts arrived and set up towns of their own. Puritans from England migrated to the Connecticut coast, where they founded New Haven. Eventually these towns banded together, applied for a charter much like those of Massachusetts and Rhode Island, and emerged in 1662 as the colony of Connecticut.

Thus five separate colonies had been established in New England. Of the five, Massachusetts was by far the most populous. All were thoroughly Puritan in their origins, and only Rhode Island was wayward and unorthodox. Yet Rhode Island was Puritan too. Religious tolerance in that colony demonstrated that orthodox Puritanism contained the seeds of disagreement and of change.

Puritans and Indians

The Puritans in Massachusetts, like the Pilgrims in Plymouth, had at first encountered small and sparsely settled Indian tribes who usually were peaceful and even generous to them. The colonists were not as generous in return. Although the Puritans talked about an obligation to convert the Indians to Christianity, they did little about it. The first missionary activity did not take place until thirteen years after the Puritans' arrival, and even then only a few ministers took any interest. Puritan governments forbade the sale of firearms to Indians and barred them from entering English settlements.

The Indians were puzzled and angered by the English encroachment on their lands. For their part, the Puritans wished the Indians would become civilized or simply go away. Intent on establishing their holy commonwealths, the English settlers regarded the Indians with a combination of hostility, contempt, and indifference. When smallpox killed several thousand Indians in eastern Massachusetts, for example, Governor John Winthrop explained the tragedy by saying, "The Lord hathe cleared our title to what we possess."

Given these attitudes, conflict was unavoidable. Usually the Puritans took advantage of old hostilities between Indian tribes. In 1637 the Pequots chose to resist the English by force. In May of that year, the English and their allies, the Narragansetts, set fire to the last Pequot stronghold, a fort on the Mystic River. They slaughtered or captured nearly the entire nation. The Narragansetts, shocked at this savagery, thought that the warfare of their English allies "is too furious and slays too many men."

A generation later, one tribe, the Wampanoags, organized a last-ditch offensive to oust the white invaders. The alliance was led by Metacom (or King Philip, as the Puritans called him), who won support from tribes whose lands and livelihood had been taken by the whites. These Indians had become dependent on European trade goods but could no longer supply beaver furs in exchange, since the animals had been hunted out of their eastern territories. Successful guerrilla raids on outlying Puritan villages attracted more and more tribes (including the Narragansetts) to the Wampanoags' cause.

During the winter of 1675–76, the Indians devastated the New England frontier. By March they were attacking towns twenty miles west of Boston. In response, the Puritans followed the usual policy of extermination, massacring both friendly and hostile tribes. Food shortages and disease finally halted Metacom's forces. Of some ninety Puritan villages, fifty-two had been attacked and twelve destroyed, and the white frontier had been moved back. A higher proportion of the white New England population had died than in any American war before or since.

New England's Economy: Trade

Except for the Connecticut and Merrimack valleys, New England was much more hilly and far less fertile than the Chesapeake region. Small farms rather than large plantations were the rule. Farming families settled in villages where the houses clustered around the church and the village green instead of being scattered over the countryside.

When a group wished to establish a new town, it obtained permission from the colonial legislature to settle a block of land of approximately six square miles, usually adjoining an older town. All freemen were eligible to draw for the town lots and to use the woods and meadows. The richer settlers sometimes got additional lots, but even they never received more than two or three times as much land as the poorest. The system had certain disadvantages. By keeping control of the undivided land, the original owners could discriminate against newcomers, who often formed a deprived majority, along with landless and voteless tenants and laborers. Disputes between the old settlers and the new frequently ended with the newcomers moving west or north to areas beyond the town's control. Eventually the system of planned expansion broke down. During most of the seventeenth century, however, the system worked, and Puritan culture was carried to new frontiers.

Most settlers in this period lived by farming and home industry; there was relatively little hired help or indentured labor. But as early as 1644, iron was being smelted commercially in Massachusetts, rum was being made from West Indian molasses, and cider pressed from local fruits had become available for sale locally and overseas. New England craftsmen also made many of the commodities needed in the colony, such as furniture, pottery, hardware, and tools. The Puritans, who did not have an export staple such as tobacco, could not easily pay to import such articles from abroad.

Some New Englanders turned to the sea for a living. Fishing off the banks of Newfoundland became so important in Massachusetts that the cod became the symbol of the colony. Enough fish were caught for export to the West Indies and elsewhere, along with foodstuffs, horses, lumber, rum, and even captive Indians to be sold as slaves.

Commerce, like fishing, greatly stimulated shipbuilding, and Yankee ships were so seaworthy and so cheap that they were soon being built for foreign as well as domestic sale.

THE DUTCH BEACHHEAD

In the first half of the seventeenth century, the Netherlands was a major commercial and naval power. During the same years that the English were establishing themselves in the Chesapeake and New England, the Dutch suddenly grabbed the strategically most valuable portion of the seaboard. In 1620, at the foot of a little island at the

mouth of the Hudson River, the Dutch set up a fort that they called New Amsterdam. They then established Fort Orange (later renamed Albany) at the critical junction of the Mohawk and Hudson rivers. From there they rapidly extended their influence westward to the most powerful and politically sophisticated group of Indians in northeastern America, the Iroquois Confederacy. By the 1630s, the Dutch were engaged in a lucrative fur trade with the Iroquois and had probed east to the Connecticut River and south to the Delaware. Though the English were not yet fully aware of the fact, the three major water-level routes into the interior—the St. Lawrence, the Mississippi, and the Hudson—were in the hands of foreign powers.

England and the Netherlands—two Protestant, commercial powers fighting for national supremacy—battled at sea in a series of three wars in the mid seventeenth century. The English won. New Netherland, as the Dutch colony in North America was called, changed hands several times, but it ended up as New York. Owing to half a century of Dutch settlement and governance prior to 1664, however, the region remained for many years a culturally distinct province among the English colonies, characterized by ethnic tensions that Virginia and New England escaped.

THE PROPRIETARY COLONIES

Most of the early English colonies, except Rhode Island and Connecticut, were founded by joint-stock trading companies. By the 1630s, however, the English Crown had begun to take a more direct interest in controlling land grants. King Charles I granted a portion of the American coast to a single individual and his heirs. Then, after the Restoration of 1660, his son Charles II gave out enormous tracts of land to various wealthy individuals. Recipients of these grants were called *proprietors* because they owned the land. Yet in the long run the proprietary colonies developed along much the same lines as the earlier settlements, largely because the proprietors found that the settlers insisted on having representative legislatures of their own.

Maryland

George Calvert was a major figure in the English court. He wanted to found a colony in America as a refuge for English Catholics, who remained a small and unhappy minority in England. Charles I was well aware that the settlements around Jamestown did not occupy all of what was called Virginia. So he was happy to respond to Calvert's request for a land grant. The king simply gave Calvert the area of Virginia that surrounded the northern part of Chesapeake Bay.

The gift was personal. Calvert and his heirs were to be the proprietors of an entire colony. The royal charter provided that the Calvert family would own the land and collect rents from people who settled on it. The charter gave Calvert broad powers of government in the colony, but it also provided for a representative assembly.

Calvert died while the charter was still being processed by royal bureaucrats. His son Lord Baltimore organized the expedition that set out for the Chesapeake in 1634 and first settled on an island in the upper part of the bay. There was no starving time in Maryland; the settlers had learned from the sad experiences at Jamestown. They brought plenty of provisions, and they were able to trade for supplies with other colonies. They soon discovered that tobacco grew as well in Maryland as in Virginia. Economically, the two colonies became almost twins.

The Calvert-Baltimore family realized from the start that Protestant settlers might outnumber Catholics in Maryland, even though the early leaders of the settlement were Catholic. The Baltimores had no desire to persecute Protestants, and as things turned out, they had little opportunity. When Protestants settled in large numbers in Maryland, Lord Baltimore began to fear that Catholics in the colony might themselves become victims of religious persecution. In 1649 he requested the Maryland assembly to pass his Toleration Act, and the assembly did so. This landmark act provided for freedom of worship for all Christians except those few who did not believe in the Holy Trinity. The important principle of religious toleration was firmly established thereby, largely out of necessity.

Carolina

Carolina, which extended from the southern boundary of Virginia to the borders of Spanish Florida and as far westward as the continent itself, was the first colony established after the Restoration of Charles II. This enormous territory was granted by Charles II in 1663 to eight friends at court. The first permanent settlement began in 1670.

The new colony grew slowly, but without starvation. The capital of Charlestown became a thriving commercial center. The colonists traded actively with the Indians for deer hides. They also experimented with a variety of crops, but the weather proved too warm for tobacco and too cold for tropical fruits. Finally they found a crop that could be profitably exported—rice. It came to be the staple crop of Carolina and the source of great wealth for successful planters. Some African slaves had been brought in at the very beginning, and it was they who probably introduced the cultivation of rice—a crop not grown in England but well known in parts of West Africa. Rice came to dominate the low-country land, and more and more African slaves were dragged in to cultivate it.

In 1721 the king made South Carolina a royal colony; henceforth the governor was appointed by the crown. A few years later North Carolina was also made a royal colony. Both kept their representative assemblies, for by this time assemblies were regarded as normal and essential parts of colonial governments.

New York and New Jersey

King Charles II had been generous to the Carolina proprietors, and he was even more so to his younger brother James, the Duke of York. He turned over to James all the territory captured from the Dutch. Partly because the Dutch settlers were foreigners, no provision was made for a representative assembly. James simply sent over a royal governor to rule the colony, which was renamed New York. James also granted the southern portion of this vaguely defined territory to two of his friends. This area eventually became the colony of New Jersey.

Pennsylvania and Delaware

Only one section of the Atlantic seaboard remained to be given away, and Charles II gave it to a most unlikely person. William Penn was the son of an admiral and was raised as a conventional gentleman. In 1681 Charles gave him a huge tract of land north and west of the Delaware River and its bay. The king owed Admiral Penn both gratitude and money, and he decided to repay the son. But rather than naming his colony after a member of the royal family, William Penn chose to call it Penn's Woods, or Pennsylvania.

Tilling the soil on a farm in Pennsylvania. (New York Public Library)

The younger Penn had become a Quaker. By doing so he shocked and angered his father and many of his friends. He remained a gentleman, but his Quaker ideas were regarded by many people as radical, foolish, and dangerous. The Quakers (who called themselves Friends) had emerged from the turmoil of the English civil war as a religiously and socially radical group of Protestant Christians. They pressed certain Christian beliefs to extremes. All Christians, for example, believed in good will toward men; Quakers acted upon this principle. They believed that love of God could best be shown by love for every man and woman, and they believed that everyone could be saved. Quakers insisted that there was an Inner Light in every person that enabled him or her to learn God's will. Accordingly, Quakers had no ministers, for they felt that every person was both a minister and a child of God. Quakers insisted on a life of simplicity, and for this reason dressed plainly.

In addition, Quakers were firm pacifists. To most Christians, Quakerism was Christianity gone mad. When Quakers tried to gain converts, not only in England but elsewhere, they met resistance. In Massachusetts, the Puritan authorities hanged two Quakers who returned after being banished.

In England, many Quakers were jailed for holding religious meetings. As time went on, however, the group became somewhat more conventional and conservative. People began to realize that Quakers were not trying to undermine all good government. It was in this changing atmosphere that William Penn received the charter for his colony in 1681.

Penn provided a liberal plan of government for his colony. He kept his own authority at a minimum, and gave the right to vote to all adult male landowners and taxpayers. All Christians of whatever sort were to have complete freedom of worship.

The colony proved to be a great success. Its liberal government and its policy of religious freedom attracted large numbers of settlers. At first, most of the colonists were English and Welsh Quakers, and they continued to dominate the government of the colony. But Penn's policies attracted many other groups. When he sent agents to western Germany to advertise the virtues of his colony, large numbers of German Protestants emigrated, drawn by promises of religious freedom and cheap land. The immediate success of Pennsylvania showed how much the colonists had learned since Jamestown and Plymouth. Penn carefully selected the site for Philadelphia before the first settlers arrived. His province turned out to be highly fertile. As in New England, a flourishing trade quickly sprang up with the West Indies, where Pennsylvania pork, beef, wheat, and flour were in great demand.

A unique feature of this colony was the Quaker policy of nonviolence and peaceful coexistence with the Indians. Penn was one of the few Englishmen to learn an Indian language. He recognized Indian ownership of the land and allowed colonists to settle only on tracts he had purchased from tribal chiefs.

William Penn's colony became the most populous and the richest in North America. But he did not share in its good fortune. After returning to England in 1701 in order to prevent the Crown from taking his charter, Penn had financial difficulties, spent a short time in debtor's prison, and died in 1718. More than any other proprietor, Penn had sought to establish a good society, what he called a "Holy Experiment." As things turned out, the experiment worked very well.

BUILDING AN EMPIRE

The permanent settlement of the mainland colonies and their economic growth, political maturity, and territorial expansion all took place within the framework of an emerging imperial system.

Mercantilism

The English had a theory of empire long before they had an empire. That theory, known as mercantilism, was simple, and was used by other Europeans. People saw two main sources of national strength: wealth and military power. National leaders were well aware that it was best to sell more things abroad than were bought from other countries.

Mercantilists were also very much concerned about military strength, which for the English meant naval power. The ships of His Majesty's navy had to be built and supplied and manned. The vessels could be built in England, but trees for masts and spars had to be imported, so the largest pines in northern New England were reserved for the use of His Majesty's navy.

The two aspects of mercantilism usually worked well together. In the seventeenth century and even later, these principles were in the best interests of the colonies. The colonies did not have enough people to engage in large-scale manufacturing. The colonists produced raw materials that sold well in England, and English manufacturers could supply them with a broad range of finished goods. Yet the fit between mercantilist principles and the interests of the colonies was not a perfect one. Left to themselves, the colonists might prefer to buy cloth from French or Dutch rather than English manufacturers. They might prefer to sell masts, pitch, and tar to outfitters of Dutch ships rather than English ones. In order to work well, the mercantilist system required supervision by the home government.

The royal government never doubted that it had the right to undertake such supervision. Nor did the colonists—although they sometimes found it convenient to evade regulations that hurt their interests. Obviously the colonists had no desire to weaken England's naval power or to lessen its wealth.

Although the need for supervision was clear, setting up an effective system was not easy. The colonies were 3000 miles and many weeks away from London. English bureaucrats had no experience or training in administering overseas lands. They did have experience in regulating economic activity at home, and they had little doubt that they could do the same abroad. But if they knew what sort of activity *ought* to be going on in the colonies, they often found it difficult to discover what actually *was* going on. And sometimes the colonists were less than helpful in letting them know.

The mercantilist system worked best when the colonies produced agricultural staples, such as the tobacco of Virginia and Maryland, the rice of South Carolina, and the sugar of the West Indies. Planters found

a protected market for their products in the mother country, and were granted credit for the manufactures they bought. British exporters, assured of payment in marketable crops each year, encouraged the colonial planters to live well—indeed, well beyond their means. The system had fewer attractions for merchants of the Middle Colonies and fewest of all for those of New England, who had no staple crops that were marketable in England. The northern colonies developed an extensive trade with the West Indies and looked about for other means of profiting from overseas trade. Meanwhile, England was still battling the Dutch for maritime supremacy. In addition to three naval wars and the English capture of New Netherland, the struggle resulted in several important acts of Parliament aimed at regulating the trade of the American colonies as well as weakening the Dutch merchant marine. These were the Navigation Acts.

The Navigation Acts: Regulation and Enforcement

The Navigation Acts of 1660 and 1663 set up certain basic regulations that were later enlarged and tinkered with, but never abandoned. First, they banned all trade with the colonies except in colonial or English-built ships. These vessels had to be manned by crews that were at least three-quarters English or colonial. Second, the acts required that certain colonial products be exported only to England or another colony. The list included such important items as sugar and tobacco. Third, most European goods imported by the colonies had to be shipped by way of England. The system was tightened up and extended over a period of many years.

The colonists observed most of these laws. After all, the regulations were intended to benefit English subjects everywhere. But when people in the American colonies found it profitable to avoid sticking to the letter of the law, they did not. In short, they smuggled.

From London's point of view, all these laws had to be enforced. Within the English government, a small group of bureaucrats were responsible for colonial affairs. They were commonly known as the Lords of Trade, but their powers were not clear. In 1664 the Lords of Trade sent a royal commission to the colonies to find out what was going on and to remind the colonists about their obligations under the new Navigation Acts. The commissioners decided to investigate New England. Both Virginia and Maryland were exporting large quantities of tobacco, on which the Crown was collecting handsome taxes, but New England did not seem to fit into the system nearly as well. These colonies were exporting masts and spars, but otherwise were not contributing to the wealth and power of the mother country.

When the commissioners arrived in Boston, the leaders of Massachusetts did their best to ignore them and then questioned their authority to make inquiries. Used to having their own way for thirty-five years, they did not take kindly to the agents of a monarch who was persecuting Puritans in England.

The frustrated commissioners returned to London, where they recommended that Massachusetts be made to observe the Navigation Acts and that its charter be recalled and canceled. Nothing came immediately from the report. During the next twenty years it was followed (as such reports often are) by more commissions and more reports. Massachusetts went on as it had before.

Over the years royal officials repeated the same recommendation: the Massachu-

setts charter ought to be revoked. Charles II was finally convinced. An English court declared the charter null and void in 1684. The most populous English colony in America no longer had any legal basis.

The Glorious Revolution

A series of dramatic events followed, but they were not caused by the loss of the Massachusetts charter. A great and general crisis shook the English-speaking world. When Charles II died in 1685 he was succeeded by his brother, the Duke of York, who became James II. He had become a Roman Catholic. At the time he had no children and therefore no Roman Catholic heir, but he was still young and might yet produce one. His Protestant subjects were appalled by this possibility. In addition, James was determined to rule with an iron hand. A stubborn and tactless man, he had little idea how much his subjects valued their Protestantism and the privileges of their Parliament.

The king took drastic action to settle the Massachusetts problem. He created a single vast colony called the Dominion of New England, a new administrative unit that included all the New England colonies, and New York and New Jersey as well. There were to be no representative assemblies in any part of the dominion. This sweeping reorganization sent a shudder through the colonies. What would government be like without the protections provided by elected legislatures?

The man James II appointed as governor of the Dominion of New England did nothing to calm these fears. Within a few weeks of arriving in Boston, Edmund Andros managed to make thousands of enemies. Andros levied taxes on his own authority. Puritan leaders pointed out that such taxes violated their rights as freeborn

Englishmen; Andros replied that such rights did not necessarily exist in the Dominion of New England. He announced that the town governments established under the old Massachusetts charter were illegal. The Massachusetts colonists were outraged.

Andros's rule was matched in severity by that of James in England, and when the king was overthrown in the Glorious Revolution of 1688 by great Whig merchants and others, the colonists in Massachusetts took it upon themselves to throw out Andros as well. When William of Orange became King William III of England by parliamentary invitation in 1688, America looked forward to a more tolerant regime. In 1691 Massachusetts was granted a new and more liberal charter. But in the critical matter of trade regulation, as Dutch William undertook to mobilize England's resources for his traditional wars with France, merchants in the northern colonies were to be disappointed.

Administration of the Colonies

As the Crown's chief representative in a colony, the royal governor possessed broad powers. He could summon and dissolve the assembly, veto its legislation, and appoint minor officials. The upper house, or council, served as his advisory board and had executive, legislative, and judicial functions. Except in Massachusetts, this house was chosen from among leading colonials by the Board of Trade in England. But since the governor's recommendations influenced the board's choices, his friendship counted for much among wealthy and aspiring Americans. With all his dignity and authority, however, the governor often found himself caught in the crossfire between colony and Crown. As the symbol and spokesman of the Crown, he was expected to follow the rigid policies of British bureaucrats made thousands of miles from the scene. At the same time, he had to respect the needs of his colony and its leaders, among whom he had to live. The job called for remarkable tact, but even the best of governors gradually lost power to the colonial assemblies.

William III brought with him to England his rivalry with the Catholic French. As early as 1689, this rivalry led to war. It was the opening conflict in the world wars of the eighteenth century fought over North America and other regions. To bolster his position in the New World, William III established a new committee for governing the colonies in 1696, called the Board of Trade, and strengthened the administration of the Navigation Acts.

Yet the colonies prospered, and the richness of America's natural resources contributed heavily to their success. Smuggling and other kinds of evasion continued to go largely unpunished. American as well as English merchants benefited from the exclusion of other nations from their trade and from protection against enemies at sea. With all these benefits, the colonists took pride in their role as overseas subjects. They were not yet conscious that they were creating a distinctively American way of life.

SUGGESTED READINGS

A.T. Vaughn, *American Genesis: Captain John Smith and the Founding of Virginia* (1975). E.S. Morgan, *The Puritan Dilemma: The Story of John Winthrop* (1958). R. Middlekauff, *The Mathers* (1971). W.F. Craven, *The Southern Colonies in the Seventeenth Century* (1949). E.B. Bronner, *William Penn's "Holy Experiment"* (1962). C.M. Andrews, *The Colonial Period of American History*, vol. IV (1938). R.R. Johnson, *Adjustment to Empire: The New England Colonies, 1675-1715* (1981).

SUMMARY

The pattern of English colonization and the push to establish permanent settlements in North America were the result of several conditions in England and Europe at the turn of the seventeenth century: religious and political discontent, economic changes that uprooted people, and a sense of power and opportunity in England after the victory over Spain.

The first permanent English settlement in North America was at Jamestown in Virginia. It survived early hardships and began to prosper with the discovery of a valuable export crop—tobacco. Another factor in the growth of Virginia and the other agricultural southern colonies was the discovery of a new system of cheap labor: black slaves imported from Africa.

The Jamestown settlement was followed by the Puritan migration to New England, which grew into the Commonwealth of Massachusetts Bay and set yet another colonial economic pattern: shipping and trade. By the middle of the seventeenth century, New England included Connecticut, Rhode Island, and New Hampshire, as well as Massachusetts and Plymouth.

What were to become the Middle Colonies—New York, New Jersey, Pennsylvania, and Delaware—began with the Dutch settlement of New York. Except for New York, all the Middle Colonies, as well as
Carolina, began as proprietary colonies—huge grants of land to wealthy individuals—rather than smaller grants to joint-stock companies.

Although the colonies were settled by different types of people and for different reasons, they soon began to develop a new way of life. One factor in this development was the colonists' attachment to representative assemblies and representative government.

The close supervision by governors and agents sent from London was not always welcome in America. Nor were the Navigation Acts, a series of laws passed by Parliament to regulate trade and to strengthen the navy. The Navigation Acts were passed with the intention of benefitting the empire as a whole, but some of the requirements were unpopular in the colonies.

Discontent on these matters came to a head when James II, in an effort to tighten control, lumped New York, New Jersey, and the New England colonies into the Dominion of New England and appointed a royal governor to rule it without any colonial assembly. The Glorious Revolution of 1688 in England toppled this short-lived attempt at arbitrary government in the colonies, but Americans were left with an abiding horror of what they called "tyranny."

3

Colonial Society

During the first two-thirds of the eighteenth century, the Anglo-American colonies grew rapidly in population. This growth meant geographical expansion, but it also gave rise to certain population patterns that had important social and economic consequences. Many new settlers in the English colonies were not English at all, and outside of New England ethnic diversity became the rule rather than the exception.

As the colonies grew, distinct social patterns emerged in various regions. Along the southern part of the Atlantic coast, slavery transformed the English settlements; after 1720 it begins to make sense to speak of southern and northern colonies. We can

also begin to talk about a frontier culture in all the colonies to the west. And in the east, the rapid growth of towns marked the emergence of an urban way of life.

Yet the single most common experience of the colonists was life on a family farm. This dominance of rural over urban life was of course exactly opposite the situation in the United States today; it did a good deal to shape the structure and practices of colonial politics. Yet political life in the colonies was shaped by other factors as well. Among them were the continuing tie with the mother country, the nature of the colonial economy, and the idea that government should remain in the hands of the rich, the well born, and the able.

PATTERNS OF POPULATION

In many ways the population of the English colonies in America was unique. The number of people grew faster, probably, than anywhere else in the world. This rapid growth had a deep impact on the colonial economy and the nature of colonial society. In addition, the English colonies attracted a great many non-English peoples. By the time of

the American Revolution, colonists of English descent made up only slightly more than half the entire population.

The Population Explosion

At the end of the Great Migration in 1640, the non-Indian population of the colonies was about 27,000. This figure includes all the English colonies along the Atlantic seaboard, as well as New Netherland, but not the English colonies in the West Indies. It does not include Indians because no one knows how many Indians there were. Today, 27,000 people would make a very small town; modern football stadiums hold about three times that number.

By 1700 the non-Indian population in these colonies was nearly ten times as large, about 250,000. This rapid growth continued during the eighteenth century. No other European settlements in the New World grew as fast. Though this increase was remarkable, we still need to bear in mind that 250,000 is about the population of a medium-sized city in the United States today.

There were several reasons for the rapid increase. One, of course, was the founding of new colonies: each new colony offered more land, and more land attracted more settlers. Another was the continued migration from England to the older colonies. In addition, the birth rate in the colonies was considerably higher than that in England. Probably this was largely because of the relative ease of obtaining land, which enabled couples to marry younger than in Europe and therefore to have more children.

Rapid population growth also reflected a relatively low death rate. After the early years of settlement, the death rate in the American colonies was far lower than in England, where large cities killed off people much faster than they produced them. Crowding encouraged the spread of disease, especially because the drinking water in almost all cities was badly polluted by garbage and sewage. In 1700 London was the largest city in the world. By comparison, Boston, New York, and Philadelphia were tiny towns. And because they were so much smaller, they had far fewer urban problems.

The population explosion in the American colonies had several important effects. It stimulated economic growth and helped raise the standard of living since natural resources were so plentiful. A small settlement could not afford to undertake activities other than growing food and making clothes and shelter. A larger one could support a greater variety of jobs.

The high birth rate also shaped early American society by making it very youthful. Today, half the people of the United States are under the age of thirty. In the seventeenth and eighteenth centuries, half the people were under the age of sixteen. This youthfulness had several important effects. Obviously, only a relatively small number of men could take part in politics and government. It also meant that the military power of the colonies was relatively small. The colonists did their best to meet the situation by setting the age for service in the colonial militias between sixteen and sixty.

The youthfulness of the colonial population had an even more important result: the absence of a large group of people who were too old to work. Some people lived to be seventy or eighty, but not many. Elderly people assumed they should work until they died or became too feeble. The age of sixty-five had no particular meaning, and no one thought about retirement. Most people did a full day's work from about age twelve on, unless they were disabled. In sharp contrast, the United States today has a very large group of old people who either do not or cannot work. They are supported partly by savings from their working years and by the social-security and welfare systems. But as a group they are not self-supporting; they are supported by younger people who can and do work.

Non-English Immigrants

By sheer coincidence, social conditions in western Germany and northern Ireland created a large pool of discontented persons willing, if not eager, to migrate overseas. The people from western Germany and the Scotch-Irish, as those from the province of Ulster in northern Ireland were called, made up by far the largest groups of eighteenth-century white newcomers. But easily the largest group of immigrants came from West and West Central Africa—all of them against their will.

Forced Immigrants from Africa

The first few Africans brought to the English colonies were sold by a Dutch shipmaster at Virginia in 1619. Whether most of these early arrivals were treated as slaves-for-life or servants-for-term is uncertain, but they were never regarded as merely another sort of settler. After 1640 in Virginia and Maryland, some but not all Africans and their offspring were being enslaved for life. By 1660 a pattern had clearly emerged: Negroes (a term borrowed from the Portuguese-Spanish word for black) customarily were lifetime, hereditary slaves.

About the same year, the legislatures of Virginia and Maryland began to enact laws to permit, indeed require, the status of slavery for Africans. The irony was that the English, who prided themselves on being the freest people of all Europe, were hammering out in the New World the legal framework of a novel status of chattel slavery that ran directly counter to English law. By the early 1700s complex slave "codes" had been enacted in the southern colonies. Yet the early years of uncertainty in the seventeenth century produced some leaks in the novel system: at least a few blacks were "free," not legally slaves, no matter how greatly they might otherwise be degraded. From the beginning, race and slavery were never perfectly matched.

The overriding pattern, however, rapidly became clear. There were not a great

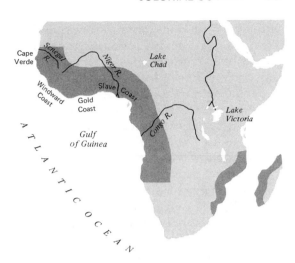

African Origins of the Slave Trade

many blacks in the colonies from Maryland southwards until about 1700. From then until the Revolution, they were imported in massive numbers. A relative trickle reached the Middle and New England colonies. From 1720 to the American Revolution, Africans and Americans of African descent constituted some 20 percent of the population, far higher a proportion than before or since.

In the eighteenth century, the brutality of this forced migration began with wartime capture, judicial condemnation, or kidnaping, usually by other African ethnic groups but sometimes by European raiding parties. During the marches to the sea, many of which spanned hundreds of miles, those least able to bear the ordeal perished or were killed. On the coast, survivors were chained, branded, and segregated by age and sex.

Despite the careful commercial organization of the trade on the African coast, slaving vessels frequently rode idly offshore for weeks before finding a full cargo or a favorable wind. Slaves mutinied most often during these offshore periods. Sometimes, even on the high seas, the miserable captives loosened their fetters and threw themselves into shark-infested waters to seek their liberty. What Europeans saw as suicide was in many cases a thoroughly rational action, since many West Africans believed that Europeans were cannibals and that only through death and spiritual remigration could they return to their African homeland.

Britain was one of the last of the Western powers to enter the African slave trade on a commercial basis, but the British came to predominate in the eighteenth century. A majority of African slaves were shipped to the West Indies. Of the relatively small numbers who were sold to the British mainland colonies, most came directly from Africa.

The early years of the African experience in colonial America will probably always remain a mystery. Africans and their

immediate descendants learned English manners and language rapidly—they had to. In Virginia and Maryland, "new Negroes" from Africa were normally put to work in the fields in units of some sixteen slaves and an overseer, far from the larger home plantation of the owner. Many of the second and third generations were trained or permitted to practice as tradesmen (skilled laborers) on the home plantations, which served as commercial and manufacturing centers because there were no large towns. This pattern prevailed in the Chesapeake.

In South Carolina and Georgia, the rice and indigo plantations contained more Africans and fewer whites. Thus Africans were able there—as nowhere else in North America—to preserve many of the cultural patterns and languages they had known as different ethnic groups in West Africa.

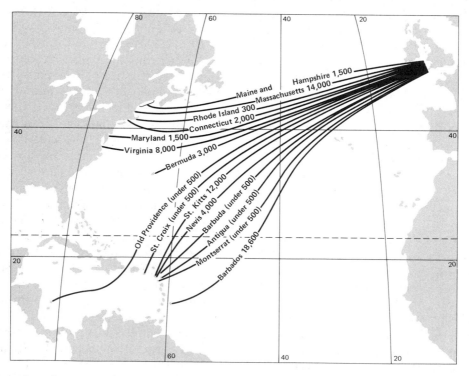

Migrations from England before 1640

Africans were welcomed as slaves. At the same time, their color and status caused English colonials to welcome immigrants from Protestant Europe. White Americans needed white men as protection against potential black rebellion.

The Germans

Continuous German immigration began in 1683, when small groups of Mennonites and Quakers established Germantown, near Philadelphia. These early immigrants were mainly well-educated people who paid their own passage, brought property from the Old World, and bought land on their arrival in the New.

Along with these radical sects, German Lutherans and German Reformed Calvinists were also encouraged to settle in Pennsylvania early in the eighteenth century. These denominations, the Lutherans predominant among them, were by far the most numerous of the German-speaking immigrants to America. Most of these people were too poor to pay their way to America, so they came mainly as *redemptioners*, very much as indentured servants had come earlier to Virginia and Maryland. The redemptioners of the eighteenth century sold themselves to ship captains or "soul brokers" in European ports, in exchange for their transatlantic passage. Many of them died at sea.

Once the redemptioners landed in America, their indentures were sold to the highest bidders. Since the healthiest were sold first, the ship captain kept the sick and old on board for weeks, until they were sold or dead. Parents were often forced to sell their children into service. The usual term was from four to seven years, at the expiration of which the servant was to receive "freedom dues," usually fifty acres of land, tools, and clothing, and perhaps a bit of cash with which to get started. The evidence suggests that these dues were often withheld or, when granted, that the servant sold off his or her land for a small amount of ready money. Not surprisingly, runaways were frequent and many went unapprehended.

German immigration reached its high point between 1749 and 1754. To the dismay of the English colonists, who feared they were being outnumbered, over 5000 Germans arrived in American ports each of those years, most of them in Philadelphia.

While many of the Germans tried to take on English ways, others held to their traditional farming practices and, more than any other immigrant group, to their native language. The Pennsylvania Germans became celebrated throughout the country for their rich gardens, orchards, and well-tended livestock. German artisans developed the famous long rifle, first manufactured in Lancaster and later adopted and improved by frontiersmen everywhere.

The Scotch-Irish

German immigrants in the eighteenth century were outnumbered by the so-called Scotch-Irish. Their ancestors were lowland Scottish Calvinists who moved to Ulster early in the seventeenth century. James I deliberately encouraged this migration in order to strengthen Protestantism in Ireland. At first they prospered as farmers and artisans. After 1696, however, new Navigation Acts hurt the economy of Ireland. Then, in the early years of the eighteenth century, British absentee landlords began doubling rents. The people of Ulster began leaving in thousands.

Poverty in Northern Ireland, as in England, filled the prisons with debtors. In time of war, male prisoners were often thrown into the army. But when poverty and unemployment spread during periods of peace, something was needed to empty the jails.

The common penalties of "burning in the hand and whipping" were inadequate. As a substitute, thousands of English and Scotch-Irish debtors were shipped to Maryland and Virginia to work in the tobacco fields.

Paying passengers probably accounted for no more than one in ten of the Scotch-Irish immigrants. The rest, like most of the Germans, obtained their passage by signing indentures. Many landed in Philadelphia or in nearby Newcastle, Delaware. They continued to arrive by the thousands each year, and as their indentures expired they moved beyond the Germans on Philadelphia's western frontier and then across the Susquehanna to the Cumberland Valley. Here mountain passes led southwest to Maryland, western Virginia, and North Carolina.

CLASSES AND LIFE STYLES

During the eighteenth century the English settlements were turning into more mature societies. They became much more diverse in terms of ethnic makeup, and differences in their economies made for differences in social organization. Although most colonists still farmed, or had servants and slaves to farm for them, an increasing number moved to urban areas. All the colonies maintained social distinctions among people, an arrangement that seemed perfectly ordinary and proper at the time.

Southern Style

Throughout the colonial period, most of the white population of tidewater Virginia and Maryland and parts of North Carolina was of English extraction. Here, although corn and other food crops continued to be grown, the production and export of tobacco was the main focus of economic activity, along with land speculation.

Led by a small elite group, the Chesapeake planters kept close ties with Britain and copied the manners of its aristocracy. They filled their houses with the finest imported furniture or hired artisans to copy the designs of foreign cabinet makers. Yet the Chesapeake gentry were an outdoor people, fonder of fox hunting, horse racing, and prolonged partying than of formal learning.

From the 1730s to the 1750s, when the price of Virginia tobacco soared, the rising profits from their staple put a premium on the planters' land. This was the golden age of the Chesapeake gentry. Yet few could long afford the high life, the expenditures for clothes, carriages, and body slaves, the mansions, parks, and wine. Eventually the Virginians' debts for imported indulgences grew enormously. To those who crashed, the West loomed as a refuge or a new springboard to success.

Of all the settlements, tidewater South Carolina, extending inland about sixty miles and southward to the Savannah River, was closest to the West Indian sugar islands in character. Eighteenth-century South Carolina was the only mainland colony where blacks outnumbered whites. The whites below the 2000 leading families were the most depressed on the continent. They had the lowest literacy rate and some of the strongest antagonisms toward the ruling group. Carolina rice proved to be the single most profitable staple in all the mainland colonies, and the rice barons of South Carolina became the wealthiest of American planters. By midcentury, they were being encouraged to grow indigo, heavily in demand as the source of a dye used in the booming English textile industry. Indigo and rice were less subject than tobacco to price fluctuations, so the Carolina planters, unlike the Chesapeake gentry, had stable incomes and few problems with debt.

Carolina rivers were not deep enough

for seagoing vessels to sail directly to the plantations, as they did in the Chesapeake region, so the colony's produce was brought to Charleston for shipment abroad. Although the Chesapeake region remained virtually without towns for generations, Charleston had become the fourth largest colonial city by the 1750s. Its midcentury population of 10,000 was almost equally divided by color.

By the time of the American Revolution, about 250,000 migrants had come into the Chesapeake back country and much of the "back parts" of the Carolinas and Georgia. Although the entire back country was at first a paradise for hunters and trappers, a mixed subsistence agriculture producing cereals, potatoes, fruits, meat, flax, and hemp gradually developed. In the Chesapeake region, small market centers grew up along the main routes and at ferry crossings.

Northern Style

Life in the North was already different from life in the South. During the eighteenth century the Middle Colonies—New York, New Jersey, Pennsylvania, and Delaware— formed the most heterogeneous part of British North America. Pennsylvania, the newest of these colonies, quickly became the largest and most diversified. By 1755, Philadelphia, with 28,000 inhabitants, had passed Boston to become the most populous colonial city.

Though Quakers were no longer a majority in Philadelphia, Quaker merchants dominated the whole settlement. Their religious beliefs, like the Puritans', inspired the thrift, industry, and reliability essential to business success. By the early years of the eighteenth century, the liberal government Penn had created for his settlement was being corrupted by his absentee successors at the expense of the local assembly. For a time, the assembly enjoyed the confidence of all sections of the colony. But by 1754 it had come under severe criticism for failing to protect the frontier from Indian raids— even though the raids were brought on by the land-grabbing and violence of the frontiersmen. The Pennsylvania frontier, right up to the Revolution, continued to be the scene of bloodshed.

In the eighteenth century, travelers on their way overland from Philadelphia to New York sometimes stopped long enough to comment on New Jersey's natural beauty and prosperity. But they usually hastened to New York City, with its fine harbor, cosmopolitan atmosphere, and 13,000 inhabitants. The colony of New York had developed much more slowly than such colonies as Massachusetts, Connecticut, Pennsylvania, Maryland, and Virginia. The relatively slow growth of New York was caused in large measure by Iroquois control of the interior and by the existence of enormous landed estates in the Hudson River valley.

From the end of the seventeenth century, British governors of New York, like the Dutch, had rewarded their favorites with land grants ranging up to one million acres on either side of the Hudson River. Some of these owners paid small taxes on their vast estates and thus had little incentive to sell or lease them. German, Scotch-Irish, and other squatters, however, took advantage of the unpatrolled country. When in later years owners tried to collect rents from families that had squatted on their lands for generations, they were forcibly resisted. In addition to this class conflict, ethnic tensions, which had their roots as far back as the period of Dutch rule, continued to trouble the colony.

Connecticut, like all New England, was dominated by family farms and Puritan churches. The same was true of rural New Hampshire, Rhode Island, and Massachusetts, except that the latter two each boasted a large town. Newport, Rhode Island, was a favorite summer vacation spot for southern planters. The city also thrived on the slave trade and the distilling of molasses into rum.

Boston was the heart of New England. With more than 17,000 people in 1750, it was a prosperous little town. Its merchants traded at ports throughout the Atlantic world. Fishermen and whalers brought their catches back to Boston as well as dozens of other New England harbors. Shipbuilding, rope manufacturing, and sailmaking were important industries. Wealthy men and women in Boston wore elegant clothes and lived in elegant houses. The early years of plain living were gone.

North, south, and west of Boston, new settlements grew up everywhere in the first part of the eighteenth century. To the outsider, rural New England villages seemed remarkable for their order. Many travelers commented on the relative lack of social distinctions. "They seem to be a good substantial Kind of Farmers," remarked one visitor, "but there is no break in their Society; their Government, Religion, and Manners all tend to support an equality. Whoever brings in your Victuals sits down and chats to you." Here were the makings of a more democratic society than prevailed in many of the other colonies.

Family Farms

From Pennsylvania northward the typical way of life was that of the family farm. Even in the southern colonies, the majority of whites were non-slaveowning farmers. Anyone who has ever lived on a family farm knows that such a life involves long hours and hard work for everyone. Children worked at least some of the time from the age when they could be shown how to shell peas, shuck corn, or fetch firewood. Older

girls and women had an unending round of tasks. They cooked in metal pots hung over the open fireplace, and they baked in the hollow compartment in the chimney that served as an oven. Many of them spun and wove rough cloth and sewed it into clothing for the family. They washed clothes and bedding in wooden tubs, with soap they made themselves, and then hung them out to dry on a fence or anything else that was handy.

Mothers fed their babies at the breast. They used a nursing can with cow's milk only if they had to. When the baby was old enough, he or she was fed a mixture of potatoes or corn meal or wheat meal, mashed with vegetables or fruit. Meat was sometimes available for the family, but not every day. Stringy chicken meat was fresh when available, but pork, beef, and fish were usually salted or smoked. In winter, some foods could be kept cold in an underground compartment; the warmer months were more of a problem.

For the most part, a woman's work outdoors was confined to lighter tasks, such as feeding livestock and slopping the hogs, which ate most of the family's garbage. Only at harvest time did women join in the heavier jobs; even then, their participation was regarded as necessary rather than normal and desirable. There was an important exception: widows worked in the fields because they had to.

The men of farming families did most of the heavy outdoor work. They cleared the fields, steering the plow around boulders and tree stumps behind a horse or ox or mule. They set the seed, prayed for rain, chopped the weeds, and prayed for clear skies at harvest time. After harvest, they had time to build a shed, cut fence rails, mend the harness, trap raccoons, fix the chimney, and help the women teach the children to obey, to work, to read, and to pray.

For all the members of farming families, life was busy but not rushed. Certain things had to be done. If you did not chop firewood, you went hungry and in the winter you froze. As always and everywhere, there were emergencies and sudden strokes of misfortune. If the new baby died, a little grave had to be dug. If lightning struck the house, another had to be built. If Indians gave trouble, they had to be talked to or shot at. If the field just planted for corn was washed out by a thunderstorm, it had to be reseeded. If the planks over the creek on the way to town washed out, they had to be replaced.

In many ways this was a simple life by modern standards. There was very little paperwork—or paper of any kind. There were practically no bills to pay, for exchanges of goods and services were usually done on the spot, often without any cash. Credit normally depended on one's reputation with a peddler or the owner of a tiny general store or with a neighbor. As time went on, however, rents became a problem for the minority of family farmers who did not own their own land.

Taxes, whether from the town, the county, or the colony's government, could also become a problem. But the purpose of such taxes was obvious. The farmer who voted on the local tax rate had a very good idea of what he was paying for. His taxes would help support widows and orphans, become part of the minister's salary, and pay the travel costs of the town's or county's representatives in the colonial assembly.

These farmers were not well off by modern standards: they lived with more hardship and far less leisure than modern Americans. Compared with the farmers of Europe, however, they were prosperous. They had a far better chance of owning land in America than in England. Because land was easy to get, American farmers wasted what they had. Knowing it would be easy to move on to new land, many farming families simply abandoned fields that had been worn out and went elsewhere.

Colonial Cities

All the colonies remained closely tied to the Atlantic Ocean. Water transportation was crucial. As settlers moved westward, they settled the river valleys first, partly because the soil was more fertile, but also because river transportation was easier and cheaper than overland travel. The best roads consisted of twin ruts worn down by the wheels of wagons.

In 1740 Boston was still the largest colonial town, with its population of 17,000. Philadelphia and New York soon grew larger. Charleston and Newport remained the fourth and fifth largest towns. By the time of the American Revolution, Philadelphia had about 35,000 inhabitants. London was more than ten times as large, but Philadelphia was then one of the two or three largest cities in the English-speaking world.

To the country farmers of eighteenth century America, the city was an impressive place. Many country people never saw a city in their entire lives. Those who did were astounded by the crowding and the bustle. The farmer's wagon was only one of many that rattled through the narrow streets, piled with corn or wheat, vegetables and fruits, boards or firewood. Now and then a brightly painted gentleman's carriage made its way through the traffic. Dogs yapped at the horses and oxen; pigs ate the garbage in the streets. Sheep and cattle were herded along to slaughterhouses while screaming sea gulls circled overhead. Hundreds more circled the masts of the sailing vessels tied at the wharves or lying at anchor in the

The bustling harbor of New York, with the forests of Manhattan in the background. (From William Burgis, *A South Prospect of New York*, 1719; New York Historical Society)

harbor, watching for fish heads and garbage from the ships.

The inhabitants of the cities saw these surroundings rather differently. A small group were wealthy enough to live comfortable lives. But the majority of people, even the wealthy, worked hard. Merchants worked long hours supervising their account books. They wrote out instructions for ship captains and corresponded with their agents in other colonies, in the West Indies, and in London.

Already there were urban problems that did not exist in the countryside. All the cities had exhausted their local supplies of firewood. This early energy crisis had to be met by bringing in wood from greater and greater distances. Part-time watchmen dealt with crime, much of which was associated with the large temporary population of sailors. Sanitation remained a problem, but gradually sewers and pipes for drinking water were put into place. Fires were a serious menace because the wooden houses were packed together. Every colonial city experienced fires that wiped out whole sections of town. There was no city fire department. Instead, citizens organized volunteer companies.

Only about 5 percent of the colonial population lived in these tiny cities. As a group, though, the city dwellers were more skilled and better educated than the population as a whole; they also had a somewhat higher standard of living. Most important, they were better informed about politics and about developments in other colonies and in Europe.

COLONIAL POLITICS

When John Adams of Massachusetts went to the Continental Congress in Philadelphia in 1774, he saw for the first time southerners waited on by their slaves. By then it was apparent that such a diverse collection of colonies was not a likely candidate for national unity. Style, customs, and economic interests divided them. Vague boundaries in the colonial charters caused many disputes. Other issues—currency, piracy, smuggling, religion, and politics—made for bad relationships among the colonies.

And yet unifying influences were at work, especially among colonial leaders. Despite their differences, they shared many interests, beliefs, experiences, and hopes. Trade united the merchants. Family ties united distant kin. The colonists read one another's newspapers, sermons, pamphlets, and almanacs. The great majority spoke English. Most important, the colonists shared a common legal and political heritage. They were all committed to the ancient English common law. All of them valued traditional English liberties, such as trial by jury and due process. At the very center of this com-

mon experience was the English tradition of representative government—a tradition colonial politics did a great deal to strengthen.

Governors and Assemblies

Each of the colonies was headed by a governor, occasionally an American but more often an Englishman. In Connecticut and Rhode Island, the governor was elected by the legislature. In Maryland and Pennsylvania, he continued to be appointed by the absentee proprietor in England. In all the other colonies he was appointed by the king upon recommendation by the Board of Trade.

Sharing the responsibility for government were the lower houses of the elected legislatures, the assemblies. These bodies had two principal functions: to make laws and to appropriate money for the colony's expenses. Although either the governor or the Board of Trade could veto such legislation, neither could force the assemblies to pass specific laws. As time went on, the assemblies grew more and more powerful. They used the power of the purse to gain concessions of all kinds from the governors, including approval of legislation he was not supposed to sign. In many cases the assemblies controlled the governor's salary, and they were happy to use this weapon to gain more power for themselves. In almost every colony there were struggles between the assembly and the governor. But by the 1760s it was clear to all concerned that in most colonies the assembly had won.

Votes and Issues

The right to vote was restricted to males twenty-one and older who had a certain amount of land, money, or other property. In most colonies, free black men could not vote. Neither could women.

There were remarkably few objections to the system of property requirements for voting. People simply assumed that servants and poor people did not have enough at stake in society to participate in government. Most people also assumed that it was proper for government offices to be held by gentlemen of wealth, refinement, and education.

In the New England colonies, perhaps as many as 90 percent of white adult males had the right to vote; in the Middle Colonies, the proportion was somewhat lower; and in the southern colonies, the figure was as low as 50 percent. Even that latter proportion, however, was far higher than the percentage in England.

Helping to limit control to the wealthy was the fact that new inland settlements had few representatives in the assemblies. Except in New England, the assemblies often refused to establish new counties and towns in distant regions and to reapportion seats according to changing population patterns. In addition, men on the frontier often did not bother to vote, even when they could. The frontier settlements were sometimes happy not to have to pay for county or town governments or for representation in the assembly. They had few complaints until crises involving Indians, courts, or taxation aroused them.

The most important source of political conflict was money. Farmers were often in debt; urban merchants were usually their creditors. The scarcity of cash in the colonies was aggravated by the mercantilist system, which drained gold and silver to the mother country. It became common for debtors to demand more and more paper money, and their demands were often met. But since there was a tendency to overissue paper money, which then declined in value, easy-money policies were usually reversed during economic downswings.

CONVICTIONS

When we speak of the "mind" of an entire society, we are talking about a concept that we use as an organizing principle. There were, in fact, as many actual minds as there were colonists. But because they shared so many common ideas and assumptions, it seems both fair and useful to treat them as a unit. In doing this we are doing what historians always do: we generalize about the past because we cannot re-create it in all its infinite detail.

Religious Faiths

The early English colonists thought that there could be only one true and lawful church in a Christian society. Yet eventually they had to accept the existence of competing denominations in the colonies. They also had to deal with a general consensus that religion was in a state of decline.

The early decades of the eighteenth century saw a drop in church membership. Many people seemed to be doing so nicely in this world that they paid less attention to the next, and many preachers seemed to lack spiritual warmth and enthusiasm. There was a general feeling that people no longer cared deeply about religious matters.

In 1735 there was a stunning revival in the Congregational church of Northhampton in western Massachusetts, led by the local minister, Jonathan Edwards. Edwards was perhaps the most profound philosopher and theologian ever to live in America. His writings dealt with fundamental and very difficult questions about human existence. He struggled, for instance, with the following problem: Is a person ever free not to do what he or she actually does do? He reemphasized Calvin's original insistence that humankind was helpless in the hands of an all-powerful God. He declared

The charismatic George Whitefield preaching. (Library of Congress)

that people must do more than recognize their own sinfulness. They must feel it, and they must feel the necessity of opening themselves to God. Unless they did so they were doomed. Edwards saw conversion as a profoundly emotional experience of the heart rather than the head. It was this view that led him to active and successful preaching.

It took a different sort of person, however, to bring about a more widespread revival of religion. This revival began in the colonies in 1740, and it produced such excitement that it soon became known as the Great Awakening. The man who sparked it was a remarkable young Englishman named George Whitefield.

When he arrived in the colonies, Whitefield had already gained fame as a popular preacher. No building in all the colo-nies could hold the astonishing numbers of people who flocked to hear him, so he often preached outdoors. At the beginning of 1741 he returned to England, leaving the colonies in a state of general excitement and turmoil. He made subsequent trips to the colonies, but they failed to cause the great stir of 1740. Nonetheless, Whitefield was the first man known to almost everyone in every colony.

Much controversy developed in the wake of Whitefield's passage through the colonies. Some ministers saw his preaching as the work of God. People flocked to join the churches. But some ministers got carried away. In Connecticut, James Davenport made a specialty of torchlit evening meetings where he stripped to the waist and did imitations of the devil. More conservative ministers thought this sort of behavior was more the devil's work than God's. Jonathan Edwards was not disturbed when his preaching caused members of the congregation to fall to the floor and scream aloud for mercy. Other ministers were profoundly shocked.

They were also disturbed that uneducated, unqualified men were wandering about preaching to anyone who would listen. Church members began to take sides. Individual congregations split over the proper qualifications of their ministers. By 1742 the two largest Calvinist groups, the Congregationalists and the Presbyterians, were divided into two camps, which became known as New Lights and Old Lights. As the names implied, Old Lights emphasized the need for learned preaching and a thoroughly educated ministry; New Lights stressed the importance of emotional experience. There were arguments over doctrine and church organization.

The Great Awakening had two other results for the American people. First, the prestige of ministers was undermined, for people were evaluating religious leaders as never before. Members of individual congregations even felt free to debate whether their minister was saved or damned. Then too, the multiplication of churches gave people more choices. If they did not like one church and its minister, they could always choose another. The Great Awakening worked in the direction of spiritual democracy, planting an idea that could easily be applied to politics as well.

Another development was the revival meeting. The huge crowds that came to hear Whitefield and other preachers at the vast outdoor meetings found release for their emotions. Despite the excesses accompanying the Great Awakening and the backsliding that followed, a new social form had been created in America. It was one especially suited to a spiritually and socially lonely rural people.

The general excitement of the Great Awakening was pretty well over by the end of 1742. Yet it never really died out completely, for local revivals kept breaking out from time to time. Revivalism had come to stay in American culture.

Beginnings of Antislavery

Revivalists did not challenge slavery as an institution. But since they preached that every person, no matter what the color, was "conceived and born in sin" (as Whitefield reminded slaveholders), the spiritual equality of blacks could no longer be denied. Thus the Great Awakening had three important impacts on slaves. It marked the beginning of the Christianization of the Afro-American population. A few blacks began attending revival meetings and joining various evangelical churches, especially the Baptist ones. Second, the religious equalitarianism of the Awakening encouraged the rise of preaching by blacks. Eventually this meant development of a separate leadership class within black communities. Finally, by becoming Christians in increasing numbers, blacks were becoming more like whites, who in turn were driven to seek other grounds for distinguishing themselves from blacks.

Pennsylvania Quakers held back from the Great Awakening but underwent their own reforming revival in the mid 1750s. In the process, they became increasingly hostile to slavery. They were led to adopt this novel view by the saintly John Woolman, who was the first American religious leader to realize clearly that whites were "prejudiced" against blacks and that slavery and prejudice were intertwined. The term *prejudice* itself, as it concerned attitudes toward racial groups, was first used in America about 1760.

Forthright action against slavery remained confined to the Society of Friends, which took an increasingly hard line on slaveholding among its members. By the time of the American Revolution, the Society had rid most of its membership of slave owning.

Protestant Religions

The increased number of different religious denominations promoted tolerance and a growing acceptance of what finally came to be the American principle of the separation of church and state.

The following generalizations about colonial religion in the 1750s seem valid. First, Americans were overwhelmingly Protestant. Only about 25,000 Catholics and 2000 Jews were living in America on the eve of the Revolution. Protestant Americans differed among themselves in organization and doctrine, yet stood united in their opposition to Roman Catholicism. England's wars against Catholic France partly explain this anti-Catholic feeling, but the hostility was much older and went far deeper.

Second, American Protestantism was strongly influenced by its Calvinist heritage. That is, the great majority of churches shared, in varying degree, certain common emphases: they tended to favor simple ceremony grounded in biblical theology, and they emphasized individual piety rather than control by a strong clergy.

Third, the doctrine and organization of American churches reflected in a very rough way the social background of their members. The wealthiest denominations in the colonies were the New England Congregationalists, the Presbyterians, and the Anglicans, but these churches had many poor people. A higher proportion of poorer people became Baptists or joined the Methodists, who emerged in the late 1760s. Because of their successes in the South and on the frontier, these two groups eventually became the two largest Protestant denominations in the United States.

Fourth, although the churches of the non English-speaking settlers in the eighteenth century had little influence on the main currents of colonial religion, they served as vital social organizations. It took some time for European immigrants to adjust to American ways, and they often looked to religious leaders for guidance.

Fifth, the tendency throughout the eighteenth century was toward greater religious freedom. Even in orthodox New England, the persecution of Quakers and Baptists had ceased by 1700.

THE ENLIGHTENMENT

Religious belief continued to be of great importance to many Americans of the eighteenth century. Yet new ideas were in the air, ideas closely connected with the beginnings of modern science. Since we have inherited these ideas, they now seem normal and reasonable. At the time, however, they were revolutionary.

Newton and Locke

The relationship between the earth and the sun seems to be a simple matter. Everyday observation clearly suggests that the sun goes around the earth, since the sun rises in the morning, moves through the sky, and disappears on the other side of the earth at night. By ordinary observation, we cannot see or feel the earth rotate. The obvious conclusion is that the sun moves around a stationary earth. Western Europeans took this very sensible view until the sixteenth century. In 1543 the Polish astronomer Copernicus proposed a completely opposite view—that the earth moves once a year around the sun and that the earth itself completes one rotation every twenty-four hours. Copernicus saw things in a new way. His discovery had important consequences for the way people looked at God's universe: now the earth was no longer at the center.

During the next few centuries scientists made many other advances in understanding the natural world. In particular one Englishman dominated the thinking of the eighteenth century: Sir Isaac Newton. His work suggested that the world was not ruled by chance or miracles. Rather, the universe was a perfect machine governed by fixed mathematical laws. The same universal force of gravity, for example, governed both the falling of an apple and the movement of planets around the sun. Newton showed that apparently unrelated facts and events were part of a unified plan.

Human reason seemed to be the key for unlocking the secrets of the natural world. It also seemed to be the key to an understanding of human beings and society. Another great English thinker dominated eighteenth-century views on these subjects. John Locke argued that human beings were born with their minds blank. People learned things, Locke said, by using their eyes, ears, and other senses to gather experience. The mind had the ability to organize this experience into true understanding. This view of human knowledge had important consequences. It was experience that counted, not previous ideas. People could learn about the world through experiments.

Benjamin Franklin: The Enlightened American

One American became a living example of the ideals of the Enlightenment. Benjamin Franklin was born in Boston. At age twelve he worked for his older brother as a printer's assistant. They did not get along together, so the younger Franklin took off for Phila-

delphia, where he set himself up as a printer. This was the beginning of the most varied and successful career in early American history. By the age of forty Franklin had made a small fortune and was able to retire from business. Then he began a half-dozen careers at once, all of them distinguished.

In Philadelphia, Franklin founded the first American public library, the first American volunteer fire company, and the first American scientific society. He made many useful inventions, including a fuel-efficient stove, bifocal eyeglasses, improved carriage wheels, a musical instrument, an improved watering trough for horses, and a fan for his chair to keep off the flies. He worked out accurate ideas about the paths of hurricanes, and he showed ship captains how to shorten the voyage to Europe by taking advantage of the Gulf Stream.

He achieved international fame as a scientist by his work with electricity. Most of that work was a good deal more sophisticated (and less dangerous) than flying a kite in a thunderstorm. He was the first to propose the concept of positive and negative currents. His famous kite experiment was helpful, however, for it showed that lightning and electricity (which was then regarded as a toy) were in fact the same thing. Characteristically, Franklin gave his discovery a practical application—the lightning rod.

Franklin refused to take out patents on his inventions because he felt that the benefits of science should be available to everyone. In the same spirit, he kept his own newspaper open to a wide variety of opinions.

When he was an elderly man, Franklin became the American ambassador to France. By then he was internationally famous. At the very formal court of the French king, Franklin looked odd in his simple clothes. He wore a long-haired wig, as all gentlemen did, but no one else walked the streets of

Benjamin Franklin. (New York Public Library)

Paris wearing a fur cap. At age seventy-five, he charmed the ladies and greatly impressed the gentlemen by his direct, modest, and reasonable manner.

A People of the Written Word

The proportion of colonists who knew how to read was the highest in New England. Even more than most Protestants, the Puritans insisted that members of a godly community had to know how to read the Word of God. The New England pattern of orderly settlement by towns made it possible to set up formal schooling. From the 1640s, Massachusetts law required all towns with more than fifty families to support a schoolmaster. In effect, all children were to be taught to read at public expense.

Often, however, these laws were not observed, especially in small towns or in those exposed to attack by Indians. None of the townspeople liked the expense, but in general they believed in the ideal. Many children were taught to read by their parents and lacked formal schooling. Yet by the 1720s many New England towns found they could maintain schools that ran from the end of harvest until spring planting. New England had a literacy rate of over 90 percent.

In the Middle Colonies, the literacy rate was lower. There were no laws requiring public support of schools, and farms were more scattered. The literacy rate among southern whites was probably about 50 percent—approximately the same as that of adult males in England.

In all the colonies, fewer women learned to read than men. Women were not excluded from education, but they were left behind. Many girls learned to read and write English, a few learned French, but very few were taught Latin and Greek. Sometimes girls were taught the piano and fancy sewing, rather than the fundamentals of arithmetic. Despite these disadvantages, however, the level of women's education was considerably higher in the colonies than in England.

No women attended college, and in comparison with today, very few men did either. The earliest American college was Harvard, founded in 1636 as a training ground for ministers. From the first, however, students there studied the subjects that were traditional at English universities. These included Latin and Greek, mathematics, some sciences, and the philosophy of morals. After about 1700, more than half the graduates of Harvard went into occupations other than the ministry. By that time two other colleges had been established: William and Mary (1693) and Yale (1703). Later, at least five more colleges were founded as a result of the Great Awakening. Most of these colleges remained connected to some church group, though attendance was not restricted to church members.

The largest colleges were smaller than most high schools today. Usually the students came from rather well-to-do families, but there were bright farm boys at all of them. Only one of these little colleges (William and Mary) was located in a southern colony.

Today we tend to contrast our various mass media, such as television, radio, newspapers, and magazines, with formal learning in school, and now computers. Such distinctions made much less sense in the colonies, where transmission of knowledge and information was by face-to-face contact or print. A wide assortment of books was imported from England and reprinted in the northern colonies. Until the political controversies of the 1760s, the most widely printed works were sermons. On many farms there were few books in the house except the Bible, though annual almanacs were popular.

Newspapers were widely read—and read aloud. The first colonial newspaper appeared in Boston at the beginning of the eighteenth century. By 1765, twenty-five newspapers were being published in the colonies. While Franklin was deputy postmaster of the colonies, he managed to reduce mailing rates for newspapers and to speed their circulation. The papers appeared once a week and contained only four pages, the last two devoted mostly to advertisements in very small print.

Colonial newspapers served as the most important public tie among the colonies. Their circulations were small by modern standards. Many backwoods farmers rarely saw one, even if they knew how to read. Yet newspapers were passed from hand to hand and read aloud at crossroads stores. They served as a vital network of communication among a relatively literate people. And as time went on, that communication link became more and more vital to their interests.

THE STRUGGLE FOR A PROTESTANT AMERICA

As time went on, the English settlements occupied more and more territory. The Indians east of the Appalachian mountains were drastically reduced in numbers and in power. To the north and west lay the French settlements, forts along the St. Lawrence Valley, the southern Great Lakes, and the Mississippi River all the way to New Orleans. French Catholic missionaries and fur traders had friendly relations with the Indians, for the fur traders did not take the Indians' land. They often lived in Indian villages and had children by Indian wives. French royal officials tried to encourage settlement by farmers, but they were not very successful. By 1760 there were only about 60,000 French people in all of New France. The English colonists numbered nearly 1,500,000.

English numerical superiority was partly balanced by the weight of Indian power. Whenever there was war between England and France, the colonial French encouraged their Indian friends to raid English settlements. New York became the most crucial battleground because it included the only water-level break in the Appalachian mountain chain. Fortunately for the English, the Iroquois Confederacy controlled the Mohawk Valley. To the north and west of the Iroquois were the Hurons. The French had long ago befriended the Hurons, not knowing they were traditional enemies of the Iroquois.

From 1689 to 1713 there was almost continual warfare between England and France, which by this time were the two most powerful nations in Europe. Europe remained the main scene of the conflict, and neither country sent troops to their colonies. But the English and French settlers in America sent raiding expeditions against each other, and Indians became involved in most of this fighting. By and large, the English won.

The Founding of Georgia

For twenty-five years after the peace of 1713 there was no further warfare between Great Britain and France. But the southern border of the mainland colonies remained in dispute between Spain and the British, who moved to strengthen their position in that region. They did so by founding a new colony, the last of the thirteen that later became the United States.

In 1732 General James Oglethorpe and several other English gentlemen obtained a royal charter for a new colony to be located south of the Savannah River. The charter gave Oglethorpe and the other trustees the right to govern the colony for twenty-one years. Thereafter the colony of Georgia would be administered by the Crown through a royal governor.

Besides the Crown's desire for a military outpost for defense against the Spanish in Florida, there was another reason for the establishment of the new colony. Oglethorpe wanted a refuge for imprisoned debtors. The Georgia trustees laid down certain rules that they hoped would help both aims. Landholdings were limited to 500 acres. Rum and brandy were banned. Slavery was prohibited, not because it was thought to be wrong, but because it would weaken the colony as a military outpost.

Most of these plans for the new colony fell through. The trustees did support settlement of some debtors from England, but these settlers were soon outnumbered by land-hungry men from South Carolina and other established colonies. The trustees withdrew their ban on rum because of thirsty protests. Planters from South Carolina brought in slaves and bought up large tracts of land in the low country. By the time Georgia became a royal colony in 1752,
it was a small copy of its neighbor to the north. At the time of the American Revolution Georgia had fewer people than any of the other twelve colonies.

The Capture of Louisburg

Shortly after the founding of Georgia, hostilities broke out again in Europe. From 1739 to 1748 Britain was at war, first with Spain and then with France. At first there was little action in the American colonies. Then in 1745, something truly amazing happened. For years, the famous fort of Louisburg had stood as the sentry for the St. Lawrence River. Louisburg was the gateway to New France, and it was heavily fortified and armed. That year, Massachusetts and other New England colonies sent militiamen and sailors to assault Louisburg. To almost everyone's surprise the expedition succeeded, with the help of the British Navy.

The victory fired the colonists' imagination. They had proved their own strength. Colonial leaders (especially in Massachusetts) began to think in grander terms. Some began to predict that all of New France would eventually fall to Anglo-American power.

Peace came three years later, in 1748. Yet it was widely believed that the treaty was merely a temporary truce. King George's War had been a sideshow to the main conflict in Europe. France remained more populous and perhaps more powerful than Great Britain. No one was sure on the latter point—but it was clear in London and Paris and the colonial capitals that a showdown was coming.

SUGGESTED READINGS

P.S. Foner, *History of Black Americans: From Africa to the Emergence of the Cotton Kingdom* (1975). W.D. Jordan, *White*

Over Black: American Attitudes Toward the Negro, 1550-1812 (1968). J.G. Leyburn, *The Scotch-Irish: A Social History* (1962). J.A. Henretta, *The Evolution of American Society* (1973). D. Hawks, *The Colonial Experience* (1966). S.E. Ahlstrom, *A Religious History of the American People* (1972). H.F. May, *The Enlightenment in America* (1976). H.H. Peckham, *The Colonial Wars, 1689-1762* (1964).

SUMMARY

As the colonies grew, they developed new forms of politics and new kinds of societies. The population exploded because of easy access to land, and this growth speeded up the economy and raised the standard of living. Since most of the population was young and almost everyone worked, productivity was high. The new settlers were no longer exclusively English. Immigrants came from western Germany and northern Ireland; there were Dutch in New York and West Africans in the South.

Distinctions were drawn between social classes in all the colonies. In the South, the tidewater gentry copied the life style and manners of the English aristocracy; in the North, wealthy Quaker and Puritan merchants lived in elegant homes. Most people, however, lived on family farms, where everyone worked long and hard; almost everything the family needed was made at home. Only about 5 percent of the population actually lived in the small cities.

Colonial politics was marked by both unity and diversity. The colonies were certainly different from one another, but there were interests, such as trade and a common legal and political tradition, that brought them together. Their commitment to representative government made them strong supporters of the colonial assemblies.

In the eighteenth century, the concern about religion that brought so many people to America was still very important. But it was affected by a whole new set of ideas called the Enlightenment—new beliefs about human reason and science.

Because many Americans thought religion was in decline, some ministers began to promote revivalism. The most widespread revival, the Great Awakening, was led by George Whitefield. Many ministers followed his example, and the outdoor meeting at which emotion could be freely expressed became an American institution.

New discoveries about the workings of the natural world changed people's perspectives and increased their confidence to understand and therefore control nature. Benjamin Franklin became a living example of Enlightenment ideas in America through his public service and inventions and his interest in science.

Public education was the rule in New England, and literacy rates there were high. Colleges expanded their teaching to subjects other than religion. Weekly newspapers became an important link among the colonies.

Political events also fostered a spirit of optimism and expansionism. English colonists moving west collided with French settlements. In the south, Georgia was set up as a buffer colony against the Spanish presence in Florida. Another war in Europe between Britain and France was ended by treaty in 1748. But by then it was clear a showdown was coming, which this time would involve the overseas colonies as well as the mother countries.

4

Revolution

When war is expected it usually comes. France and Great Britain slipped into conflict almost as if they had scheduled it in advance. This time North America became a main theater in a worldwide war. British victories resulted in a stunning enlargement of the British empire. In America, most of New France came under British rule.

Officials in London quite naturally thought that an enlarged group of colonies needed better administration and firmer control. They also felt the colonies ought to pay a fair share of the costs of running such an empire. When Parliament decided to raise revenue in the colonies, there were howls of protest.

For a dozen years the colonies and the mother country pushed and shoved each other on the matter. Other issues arose, and self-interest and high principles became so entangled that no one could tell them apart. The two sides staggered from crisis to crisis. Grievances on both sides finally exploded in armed conflict—a conflict neither wanted and both had tried to avoid. Thirteen continental colonies took up arms against their lawful government. From the beginning, a major issue was whether these colonies would act separately or together, and in the long run this problem proved to be as difficult as making the break with Britain. Ideas about self-government helped support the thirteen colonies; so did the values of the Enlightenment and the emotions of the Great Awakening.

VICTORY OVER THE FRENCH

Both sides began to prepare for a showdown. The French constructed a long string of forts from Lake Erie south to the "forks of the Ohio." There they built Fort Duquesne (the site of modern Pittsburgh). Anglo-Americans began to realize that they were being prevented from further westward expansion.

The Ohio Country

The westward pressure of Anglo-American settlement soon came up against the line of French forts. In 1747 a group of wealthy

Virginia planters formed a landowning company. They were interested particularly in western land. In 1754 a young man named George Washington was sent with a small group of men toward Fort Duquesne to find out what the French were doing.

When he learned that the fort was heavily fortified, he and his men built a stockade some fifty miles to the south, naming it Fort Necessity. The French attacked, and the badly outnumbered Virginians surrendered. Because the two nations were not officially at war, the French released the Virginians so that they might return with word that the Ohio country was firmly in the hands of France.

The skirmish at Fort Necessity was, in fact, the opening battle of a great war that lasted until 1763. Anglo-Americans called it the French and Indian War. But since the worldwide conflict was not officially declared until 1756, it became known in Europe as the Seven Years' War.

The Albany Congress

While Washington and his men were returning from Fort Necessity, an important meeting was taking place in Albany, New York. The London government had summoned delegates from all the colonies from Virginia northward to meet with leaders of the Iroquois Confederacy. Officials in London knew that the various colonies would have to cooperate if there was renewed conflict with the French. They also regarded the Iroquois as crucial allies in any such war.

At the Albany Congress, Benjamin Franklin proposed a general "plan of union" for the mainland colonies. The plan provided for a grand council of representatives from all the colonies. The powers of the council would cover western lands and set-

tlement, joint defense, and relations with the Indians. The council would have the power to raise taxes on its own. The presiding officer would be appointed by the king and have a veto over actions by the council. The Albany delegates sent the plan to the various colonies for their approval. In every colony, it was rejected or ignored. The plan aimed to please all parties and ended up pleasing none. Authorities in London were relieved, for they had no desire to see the colonies united on a permanent basis.

Fruits of Victory

After the Albany Congress, the government in London decided for the first time to send regular troops to the colonies. In the spring of 1755 General Edward Braddock arrived at the head of an impressive army of 1400 redcoats. Braddock planned a major expedition to destroy Fort Duquesne and drive the French from the Ohio country. The British troops were joined by 1000 colonial militiamen, but only eight Indian guides could be found. Together they marched off toward the forks of the Ohio. Only eight miles south of the fort they were ambushed by a combined force of French and Indians. Braddock was killed, and his army suffered nearly a thousand casualties. This stunning defeat shook the famous reputation of the British redcoats.

By 1756 the war that had started in the American wilderness spread over the continent of Europe. At first it went very badly for the British, both in Europe and in America. In 1758, however, a new chief minister took charge in London, and within a year he had turned the conflict completely around. William Pitt paid for German armies on the European continent. But he thought the central objective should be the

JOIN, or DIE.

This cartoon compared the squabbles of the colonies to the separated parts of a snake, warning that they must "Join, or Die." (Library of Congress)

conquest of Canada and the American interior. He used British superiority at sea to strike hardest at the city of Quebec.

The climax of the fighting came in 1759, when the brilliant young General James Wolfe brought a large army up the St. Lawrence and successfully stormed Quebec. The next year, British troops captured Montreal. The British continued a long string of victories—at sea, in the West Indies, in Africa, in India, and in the American West.

The Treaty of Paris (1763) was a general settlement of what had become a major world war. France ceded to Britain all of Canada and all the great interior east of the Mississippi River except the crucial port of New Orleans. Spain surrendered East and West Florida to the British in exchange for Cuba, which the British had captured the year before. By a separate treaty, France ceded to Spain all its territories west of the Mississippi, as well as the port of New Orleans.

BRITISH POLICIES: SOURCES OF CONFLICT

After the French and Indian War, Great Britain adopted certain policies toward the colonies that aroused great resentment. The colonists' major grievance was taxes—direct taxes laid upon them by Parliament. But other imperial policies angered various segments of the colonial population. Westerners and land speculators resented London's ideas about how to handle the Indians. Merchants were troubled by enforcement of the Navigation Acts and by new currency regulations. And when the British government decided to station regular troops in the colonies, many Americans grew suspicious.

Two developments added to the deepening sense of alienation that many Americans felt. One was the instability of the English government. In the early years of his reign, which began in 1760, George III could not find a chief minister who really satisfied him. The king was intensely patriotic and intelligent, but so unsure of himself that he dismissed ministers almost as fast as he named them. At that time, the king had the right to choose a first minister, who then chose other members of Parliament to form a *ministry*. For ten years various ministries came and went, and with them Britain's policies toward the colonies. No one could be sure whether or not today's policy would be reversed tomorrow.

Second, many colonists were extraordinarily suspicious—almost paranoid—about British intentions. When officials in London proposed efficiency, officials in the colonies smelled attack. They had grown so attached to self-government that they were inclined, as a British statesman told the House of Commons, to "sniff the approach of tyranny in every tainted breeze."

Problems in the West

As long as France owned Canada, Americans were forced to rely on Britain for protection. The defeat of France removed one menace, but it failed to settle the colonists' relationship with the Indians.

Established fur traders in the colonies and in Canada wanted the West permanently reserved for Indian hunters and trappers. Land speculators, on the other hand, were urging settlers to go west; they wanted the Indians cleared out or "pacified." Both sides had powerful friends in Britain. Colonial land speculators were particularly active in Pennsylvania and Virginia, and many of their claims conflicted with one another as well as with those of rivals abroad.

During the war most of the northwestern Indian tribes, fearful of British expansionism, had chosen to ally themselves with the French. The victory of the British renewed their anxiety. Urged on by French traders who talked of the return of French

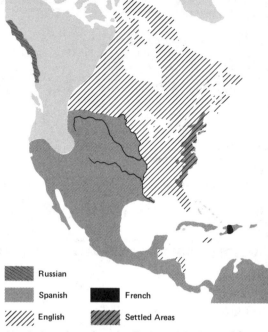

Russian

Spanish

French

English

Settled Areas

North America after the Treaty of Paris, 1763

power to North America, Indians in New York and Pennsylvania launched attacks on British forts. They were led by the Ottawa chief Pontiac.

Shortly after this news reached London, the British government issued the royal Proclamation of 1763. It set boundaries for three new royal colonies: Quebec, East Florida, and West Florida. Most other western territory—from the Alleghenies to the Mississippi and from Florida to fifty degrees north latitude—was reserved for the Indians. The proclamation excluded all white fur traders, land speculators, and settlers. It was intended as a temporary measure to give Britain time to work out a permanent western policy, but it angered the colonists.

No proclamation issued thousands of miles away could keep speculators and frontiersmen out. Opposition to the Proclamation of 1763 grew so strong that within a few years the British revised their western policy. They made a series of treaties with the Indians that would give the speculators room. In each case the treaties pushed the map of English control farther westward, and before long the paper fence of the proclamation was in shreds.

Britain's new policies caused especially strong resentment in Virginia, one of the most populous of all the colonies. By concentrating on one money-making crop, tobacco planters had started to wear out their best soil; cheap lands farther west seemed their only salvation.

Land policy was only one source of planter discontent. British and Scottish merchants served as middlemen for everything the planters bought or sold abroad, and British shipowners charged high rates for carrying the planters' produce and purchases across the ocean. As the return from their lands dwindled, the planters' debts mounted.

Troops and Taxation

The worst problem raised by the French and Indian War was taxation. Britain's long, costly struggles for empire had boosted tax rates sky-high. Now the British had to face the cost of protecting their expanded possessions. Several bureaucrats estimated that 10,000 troops were needed for the colonies, and Parliament felt the colonists should share the cost. There was also a more sinister motive behind the British plan to station regular troops in America: war veterans could be taken care of, and a large army could be maintained without the distrust that would come if it were on home soil. As things turned out, colonial Americans had strong suspicions about what was then known as "a standing army at home."

The colonists had long since learned to manage their home finances without British interference. They began to demand that the British solve their own financial crisis. For one thing, the colonies had piled up a war debt of £2.5 million. In addition, British merchants made profits of at least £2 million a year on colonial commerce.

The Sugar and Currency Acts

The task of handling postwar problems of imperial government and finance fell upon the ministry of George Grenville. His first step was the Sugar Act of 1764.

A duty of six pence a gallon on the importation of foreign molasses for distilling into rum had been passed by Parliament in 1733, but it was weakly enforced. The new act halved the duty but made clear it would be collected to the penny. To insure collection, suits over the payment of the new duties and charges of smuggling on other grounds were removed to the hated admiralty courts, where there were no juries. They had previously been tried in the regular colonial courts, where Americans were usually let off by friendly juries.

But what aroused Americans most of all were the implications of the official title of the act—the Revenue Act—and the preamble, which said the purpose of the measure was to tax the colonists directly. Heretofore, charges placed upon the colonials had been explained as a legitimate part of imperial administration. The Sugar Act was the first law Parliament passed with the stated objective of raising money in the colonies.

The Currency Act, passed in the same month as the unprecedented Sugar Act, worsened the situation. The colonists were faced with one measure designed to draw money from America and another to forbid expansion of American currency. Preparing instructions for its representatives in the General Court at this time, Boston asked a deadly serious question: "If taxes are laid upon us in any shape without ever having a legal representation where they are laid, are we not reduced from the character of free subjects to the miserable state of tributary slaves?" The Massachusetts legislature named a committee of correspondence to write other colonies about the issue. In Boston, New York, and elsewhere, merchants and mechanics pledged not to buy or use certain British goods. The Sugar Act brought on the idea of nonimportation, which soon became an effective revolutionary weapon.

The Stamp Act Crisis

When Grenville announced the Sugar Act, he gave notice that another revenue measure was being prepared. This was the Stamp Act, to go into effect in November 1765. Every time a colonial wanted a legal document, a license, a newspaper, a pamphlet, an almanac, playing cards, or dice, he or she had to purchase a stamp ranging in value from a halfpenny to ten pounds.

One section of the Stamp Act especially alarmed the colonial clergy. This was the section that required stamps on every document from courts "exercising ecclesiastical jurisdiction within the said colonies." As yet, there were no courts in the colonies having such jurisdiction, but there was a justifiable fear that the Church of England might gain the authority to set them up under a bishop for America. The assumption apparent in the Stamp Act that these courts and this royal religious authority would be imposed alarmed the many colonials whose whole tradition was based on congregational self-determination. The Stamp Act provided further that

all violators were to be tried in the hated juryless admiralty courts and fined heavily if found guilty. The Sugar Act had struck mainly at merchants. The Stamp Act hit every influential person in the colonies— lawyers, printers, editors, tavern owners, and Dissenting preachers. Indeed, colonials of all classes, including small shopkeepers and artisans, were outraged by a measure that would cripple their businesses. The Stamp Act set people talking and acting throughout the colonies. Colonial leaders began to develop the revolutionary machinery by which they ultimately separated from Britain.

When news of the Stamp Act reached America the Massachusetts General Court called for a full-scale intercolonial congress. It was the first ever to meet on American initiative. In the meantime groups known as the Sons of Liberty—secret organizations of shopkeepers, mechanics, and laborers, many of them led by men of wealth and standing—formed in most port cities to intimidate stamp agents and others insufficiently rebellious.

In August 1765 a Boston mob burned the records of the admiralty court, ransacked the home of the comptroller of the customs, then wrecked the elegant mansion of Lieutenant Governor Thomas Hutchinson. Even before November 1, when the Stamp Act was to go into effect, every stamp agent in the colonies had been pressured by mobs and rioting into resigning or promising not to execute his commission.

When the Stamp Act Congress met as scheduled, nine colonies were represented. Most of the absentees failed to send delegates only because royal governors would allow none to be selected. It was at this congress that Christopher Gadsden of South Carolina proposed that "there ought to be no New England man, no New Yorker, known on this continent, but all of us Americans." The congress's moderate Declaration of Rights and Grievances began by acknowledging "all due Subordination" to Crown and Parliament, but it went on to sharply advance the American position: "The only Representatives of the People of these Colonies, are Persons chosen therein by themselves, and . . . no taxes ever have been, or can be Constitutionally imposed on them, but by their respective Legislatures."

The Stamp Act Congress was followed by signed agreements among hundreds of merchants in each of the major ports not to buy British goods until the hated law and other objectionable trade regulations had been repealed. Pressure from English merchants who felt the pinch of the American boycott helped bring about repeal of the Stamp Act in March 1766. But along with the repeal came the Declaratory Act, in which Parliament asserted that it had full right to make laws "to bind the . . . people of America . . . in all cases whatsoever."

Parliament did more. Within a few days of passing the Stamp Act it enacted a Quartering Act requiring the colonists to supply barracks and rations for British troops who were to be moved down from Canada. Next year it passed a new Quartering Act, aimed chiefly at New York. This measure listed public inns, alehouses, unoccupied buildings, even private barns, as places where British troops had to be quartered if barracks were inadequate. Both New York's legislature and New York City's residents resisted the new law. Redcoats and residents of the city clashed briefly in the streets, and Isaac Sears, leader of the local Sons of Liberty, was wounded.

The Declaratory Act's assertion of power in London and the mobilization of standing armies were bad signs for the future, despite the rejoicing with which the repeal of the Stamp Act was hailed. Repeal seemed such a fine victory, indeed, that the Declaratory Act was scarcely noticed in the colonies.

The Townshend Acts

The repeal of the Stamp Act had been accomplished by the Rockingham ministry that followed Grenville's. A few months later, Pitt was asked to form a new ministry, but he was forced by gout to retire temporarily. Control then fell to the clever and devious chancellor of the exchequer, Charles Townshend, whose fiscal measures turned the Americans from resistance toward revolution.

Townshend had been led by some American arguments in 1765 and 1766 to believe mistakenly that the colonials would accept revenue-raising acts presented not as "internal taxes" but as traditional "external" trade regulations. In 1767, on his recommendation, Parliament passed the Townshend Acts, imposing new import duties on glass, lead, paints, paper, and tea.

To insure collection of the new duties, the Townshend Acts reasserted the power of imperial courts in the colonies to issue writs of assistance, which were very broad and imprecise search warrants. The acts also provided that violators of the new regulations be tried in admiralty courts. Anger in the colonies about these provisions was heightened by the creation of a new Board of Customs Commissioners, resident in America, whose job was to sniff out the most minute violations. Ominously, the salaries of the king's new commissioners were to be paid out of fines levied by the admiralty courts. The final section of the Townshend Acts hit New York for not observing the Quartering Act: after October 1, 1767, all legislative functions of the New York Assembly were to be suspended.

Many American colonists were outraged by the Townshend Acts. Even before the customs commissioners reached Boston in November 1767, colonial merchants had revived the nonimportation agreements that had cost British merchants so much during the Stamp Act crisis.

In addition, the Sons of Liberty mounted a campaign in the newspapers to persuade the public to give up British-made luxuries. They sang the virtues of homespun cloth and a life of domestic simplicity. In doing so they touched the feelings of a great many people. Simplicity and hard work had long been regarded as virtues by a people with a Calvinist outlook on life; now these traditional virtues could serve the cause of liberty.

As nonimportation grew more and more effective, some colonists grew busy with their pens. Pennsylvania's John Dickinson published a series of *Letters From a Farmer in Pennsylvania,* which gained a wide audience through the newspapers. Dickinson denounced the Townshend duties as a violation of the unwritten constitution of the British empire. He admitted that Parliament had the right to regulate trade with taxes. These taxes might even result in some revenue. But taxes imposed for the purpose of raising money for the English treasury were another matter. They were no more acceptable in the form of import duties than in the form of stamps. Dickinson also pointed out that if Parliament could shut down the New York Assembly, it could shut down others.

Parliament responded with the idea of virtual representation. True, said British government defenders, Americans were not directly represented in Parliament. But neither were the people of Manchester, Birmingham, and other growing industrial cities in England. Yet they willingly paid taxes levied by members elected elsewhere in the kingdom, who virtually represented them, and the colonials should profit from that example. To Americans, 3000 miles from London, "virtual representation" by men who never saw them from one year to the next was no representation at all.

Trouble in Massachusetts

In Boston a clever agitator took advantage of the Townshend Acts. Samuel Adams was a Bostonian who had failed in the brewery business but had then turned to local politics with great success. Adams seized upon every new British measure as evidence of tyranny. For several years he sustained a high level of public indignation and even established a network of cooperation among the thirteen colonies. In the early 1770s, however, British policies seemed to most Americans much less repressive than previously.

Early in 1768, on behalf of the Massachusetts legislature, Adams wrote a circular letter to the other colonies restating Dickinson's points. In retaliation, the British ministry instructed all colonial governors to see to it that their assemblies treated Adams's letter with "the contempt it deserves." Governor Bernard in Boston was told to dissolve the Massachusetts Assembly should it fail to rescind the letter. On June 30, 1768, the Massachusetts House of Representatives voted 92 to 17 not to rescind. Next day, Bernard dissolved the House. Tensions ran high. The streets of Boston were alive with rumors of British troops on the way. In fact, by the end of September two well-equipped regiments dispatched by General Thomas Gage had arrived; the general followed soon after and assumed his post as British commander in chief in America.

But there was no immediate explosion, and when Parliament repealed most of the Townshend Acts in 1770, happy Americans dropped the nonimportation movement. Tension might have lessened had it not been for the "Boston Massacre." The presence of redcoats in Boston, as in New York earlier, made for the possibility of riot, and it is remarkable that serious violence was avoided for eighteen months. One cause of friction was competition for jobs between Massachusetts laborers in the port and redcoats seeking work in their off-duty hours. A fist fight over this issue occurred the afternoon of March 5, 1770, and that night the "massacre" took place. Ten British soldiers, egged on by an unruly crowd, fired at their tormentors despite their officer's efforts to restrain them. They killed five men and injured others. Sam Adams made the "massacre" a popular theme for oratory, pamphleteering, and a famous engraving by Paul Revere.

Further "outrages" provided agitators in Boston and elsewhere with additional fuel. No one knew better how to exploit each new incident than Sam Adams. "I doubt whether there is a greater incendiary in the King's dominion," wrote a conservative opponent, and many moderates came to share this opinion. In 1772, acting on a motion by Adams, a Boston town meeting voted to appoint an official "committee of correspondence. . .to state the rights of the Colonists of this Province, . . .and to communicate the same to the several towns and the world." Virginians were among the first to adopt Adams's suggestion that other colonies form similar committees, and soon a network of seditious organizations had spread over the country.

THE SLIPPERY SLOPE TO WAR

In the early months of 1773, very few American colonists realized they were on the verge of war with Great Britain. Only a handful had the faintest idea about the possibility of American independence. But as often happens, a single and apparently trivial decision in one place started a chain of events that led to outright conflict in another. People in the thirteen colonies rapidly came to realize that they had to establish a united front against Great Britain. In doing so they fell back upon the precedent of cooperation they had established at the time of the Stamp Act, on their representative assemblies, and on their commitment to ideas about English liberties and natural rights.

Tea and the Intolerable Acts

When Charles Townshend died, George III finally found a chief minister he could get along with. The ministry of Lord North began in January 1770 and lasted for twelve years.

Lord North realized that the Townshend Acts were costing much more to enforce than they would ever bring in. English merchants were complaining loudly about the colonial boycott of their goods. So Lord North called upon Parliament to repeal all the duties except the one on tea. He saw two obvious reasons for retaining this one tax. Americans were willing to pay a good price for tea. More important, continuation of this tax would maintain the principle of Parliament's power to tax the colonists. Parliament did as North asked in April 1770.

When word of the repeal reached the colonies, the nonimportation movement

Paul Revere's drawing of "The Bloody Massacre" in Boston. (Metropolitan Museum of Art) collapsed. Sam Adams and the Sons of Liberty in other cities tried but failed to keep the boycott alive. Business boomed. The political atmosphere became more relaxed than at any time since word of the Sugar Act had arrived in 1764. This relative quiet lasted three years.

Then a serious crisis arose in 1773 for reasons that originally had little to do with the American colonies. The East India Company was a gigantic monopoly to which Parliament had entrusted even the government of India. Owing largely to corruption and mismanagement, the company was headed toward bankruptcy, and it turned to Parliament for help in marketing its vast overstock of Indian tea. Parliament passed the Tea Act, which gave the company the right to sell tea in America at reduced prices through its own agents, thereby completely undercutting colonial importers.

By December 1773, East India Company tea had reached Boston harbor. At the end of a large and futile public protest meeting, a group of white American men disguised as Indians proceeded to the wharves under cover of darkness. They boarded the tea ships and threw cask after cask into the murky water after chopping them open.

The North ministry could scarcely ignore such a defiant act as this "Boston Tea Party," nor could many people on either side of the Atlantic approve of the destruction of private property. To punish the Americans, Parliament passed in the spring of 1774 a series of measures called in the colonies the Coercive, or Intolerable, Acts. First, the Port of Boston was closed until the East India Company and the British customs were reimbursed for their losses. Second, any British official indicted by Massachusetts courts for capital offenses committed while enforcing British laws was to be tried

at home, away from hostile colonials. Third, in Massachusetts, the king or his governor was given the power to fill by appointment many heretofore elective offices. Fourth, no town meeting could be held without the governor's permission, and then only on business he approved. Last, a new Quartering Act was imposed on all the colonies.

With coincidentally poor timing, Parliament also passed the Quebec Act, by which it hoped to gain the support of the conquered settlers in Canada by recognizing certain features of French law. These features included trials without juries and political equality for Catholics. English Protestant colonials reacted with alarm, which was heightened by the act's enlargement of the Province of Quebec to include territory north of the Ohio and east of the Mississippi, an enormous region where Massachusetts, Connecticut, and Virginia all had claims.

The First Continental Congress

To voice their united opposition to these acts and to take steps in what they thought of as self-defense, the Massachusetts House of Representatives asked all colonies to send delegates to Philadelphia in September 1774. All but Georgia agreed. Delegates of the twelve, all named by extralegal conventions to perform acts now unthinkable for regular state legislatures and governors, made up the First Continental Congress.

Work began in Philadelphia with the proposal by the conservative Joseph Galloway of Pennsylvania that a grand colonial council be set up to share power with Parliament on colonial matters. But the Congress rejected Galloway's scheme by a single vote and decided on more drastic action.

Just as the First Continental Congress was gathering, a meeting of delegates in Massachusetts towns adopted the Suffolk Resolves, which boldly advocated that the colonies (1) raise their own troops and (2) suspend all trade with Britain, Ireland, and the British West Indies. After bitter debate, the Continental Congress endorsed these proposals. Companies of "minutemen" soon began to drill on New England village greens. To insure complete boycott of British trade, Congress organized a Continental Association, with local enforcement committees in each colony. Although these committees were empowered merely to publish the names of all violators of the boycott as "enemies of American liberty," they soon became little organs of local government. The First Continental Congress was in effect the first national government of what became the United States.

The Fighting Begins

Before adjourning at the end of October, members of the First Continental Congress agreed to reconvene in May 1775 unless their grievances were fully met. By the time they met again, everyone knew that armed conflict had broken out.

On April 19, General Gage, provoked by reports of minutemen gathering around Boston, sent forth 700 redcoats to seize the stores of munitions and supplies that the colonists appeared to be collecting in Concord, about twenty miles northwest. Boston patriots, in turn, sent Paul Revere and two other men to arouse the minutemen along the way. At Lexington green, five miles short of Concord, the redcoats encountered a line of armed farmers and townsmen. Eight minutemen fell there, and the British pressed on to Concord, where they discovered that the patriots had removed their munitions. Frustrated at Concord, Gage's men turned back toward Boston, but by then thousands of minutemen lined the road and sniped effectively at the redcoats as they passed. By the time they reached Boston, the British had suffered 273 casualties. Ninety-three Americans had been killed or wounded.

When the Second Continental Congress gathered hastily in Philadelphia in May 1775, few of the delegates imagined that they would remain officially in session for fourteen years. One of their earliest actions, reported only in an offhand announcement, was to "adopt" the army then congregating around Boston, for "the general defense of the right of America." With an eye toward securing intercolonial backing for the cause of Massachusetts, the delegates voted nearly unanimously for Washington the Virginian as commander in chief of this army.

In July 1775, Congress adopted a Declaration of the Causes and Necessity of Taking up Arms. The delegates said they were "with one mind resolved to die freemen rather than live slaves." Then came an open threat: "Our internal resources are great, and, if necessary, foreign assistance is undoubtedly attainable." But there was also a note of hope: "We have not raised armies with ambitious designs of separating from Great Britain, and establishing independent states."

The same month, Congress adopted the Olive Branch Petition, the work of its most cautious members. This document begged King George to keep Parliament from further tyrannical measures, so that a plan of reconciliation could be worked out. On receiving it in August, however, the incautious king brushed it aside. He proclaimed the Americans rebels and warned all loyal persons not to assist them.

Still, there remained peace-minded individuals in Britain. Lord North himself persuaded Parliament to offer last-ditch concessions. In 1765 these might have helped, but in 1775 they were too late.

By the time North's plan reached Philadelphia, the Battle of Bunker Hill, the bloodiest engagement of the entire war, had been fought. The main battle actually took place on Breed's Hill, overlooking Boston, where American militiamen had gathered soon after the surviving redcoats withdrew from Concord. On June 17, 1775, General Gage, strengthened by fresh troops, decided he would drive the patriots off. He did manage to dislodge them, but at a frightful cost. The Americans lost almost 400 men; Gage lost more than 1000—over 40 percent of those he had moved into battle. Two weeks later, General Washington arrived at Cambridge, outside Boston, to take command.

By this time too, fighting had begun farther to the north. In May 1775, in an effort to win control of Canada, Ethan Allen had captured the British posts at Crown Point and Ticonderoga in New York. Washington decided to follow up this victory with an invasion of Quebec led by Colonel Benedict Arnold. But this effort ended in disaster on December 31, 1775. By then Congress had rejected North's proposals, and for their part Lord North and George III had decided to wage war to the finish.

One of the first problems faced by George's ministers was to mobilize a fighting force. The average Englishman had little desire to cross the ocean to fight his "brothers," and the Crown had to hire German mercenaries. Almost 30,000 Hessians (named after a small part of western Germany) served in the British army during the Revolutionary War.

Independence

It seems astonishing that actual fighting could continue for a year while each side hoped for reconciliation. Yet Americans were deeply attached to their mother country and seemed downright fearful of even whispering the word *independence.* It was an English writer newly arrived in America who broke the log jam of public sentiment. In *Common Sense*, published anonymously in January 1776, Thomas Paine directly attacked the monarchy, not merely the king's ministers, and called for establishment of an independent republic. Having attacked "the Royal *brute* of Britain," he went on to declare, "There is something very absurd in supposing a Continent to be perpetually governed by an island." Paine's *Common Sense* was widely read and widely acclaimed. It was, in fact, one of the most immediately influential political pamphlets ever written.

Public opinion shifted rapidly. On April 6, 1776, Congress opened American ports to the commerce of all nations except Britain. This, in itself, placed America independent of Britain. A month later, Congress advised all colonies to form new state governments if they had not already done so. Nine hours of debate on July 1 helped to bring some reluctant delegates around, and on July 2, Congress adopted a Resolution of Independence: "Resolved, That these United Colonies are, and of right ought to be, free and independent States, . . . and that all political connection between them and the State of Great Britain is, and ought to be, totally dissolved."

Adopting this resolution was crucial, but one further step seemed desirable as a way to enlist the support of foreign powers. As Thomas Jefferson put it, referring to the American action, "a decent respect to the opinions of mankind requires that they should declare the causes which impel them to the separation." On July 4, 1776, having made numerous changes in Jefferson's draft of such a declaration of causes, Congress finally ordered it printed and "proclaimed in each of the united states & at the head of the army."

The Declaration of Independence was an appeal to the world. A brief preamble stated the theory of natural rights, which, after nearly a hundred years of discussion since their classic formulation by John Locke, could well be called "self-evident." Then followed the long list of British transgressions, which supported the right of revolution. The note of moderation remained: "Governments long established should not be changed for light and transient causes." But in the eyes of the Americans, their grievances were heavy and of long duration.

The Declaration's statement that "all men are created equal" may not have seemed to Congress to go beyond the conventional notion of the political equality of free and propertied citizens. But even before the Declaration, many white people were deeply troubled that the institution of slavery continued while they were calling for liberty themselves. When in May 1775 the question of using slaves as soldiers came up in Massachusetts, it was decided that their enlistment would be "inconsistent with the principles that are to be supported," and they were rejected. When the British began to use slaves that November, however, white Americans altered their stand. Many of the slaves among the 5000 black men who

served with the American revolutionary army were freed at the end of the war.

Loyalists

Some Americans opposed independence and the war. These Loyalists—or Tories, as the patriots called them—varied in number from place to place and from time to time. The best modern estimates suggest that the Loyalists never numbered more than a fifth of the white population.

But numbers alone do not tell why some people chose to remain loyal to the British Crown. For many people the decision was a crisis of conscience; for others it was a matter of self-interest. Men who had held positions as royal officials, for example, found it easy to remain loyal to the Crown. Some Loyalists had a distaste for popular rule. Certain ethnic groups tended to become Loyalist because other ethnic groups in the same area were becoming patriots. Quakers and German pacifists could not become active patriots because their principles prevented them from supporting any sort of war.

Probably the most important determinant was the presence of armed men in the immediate neighborhood. British troops in an area could work in two ways: they could make Loyalists out of those who wished to pick the winning side, or they could make patriots out of outraged farmers who watched helplessly as redcoats made off with their corn and livestock. As the fighting moved from one part of the colonies to another, more and more Americans had to make a choice. This pattern placed the Loyalists at a tremendous disadvantage; British troops came and went, while their armed American opponents remained. The patriot majority remained a majority mostly through its long-term control of the countryside.

Committees of patriots, backed with bayonets, drove many Loyalists from their homes and communities. The new states provided legal machinery for taking Loyalist property. There were brutalities on both sides, but few Loyalists lost their lives except in open battle against patriot forces. Throughout the war, the British constantly overestimated the number of Loyalists. Yet at the same time they failed to take full advantage of Loyalist support. Professional British army officers often treated potential allies with the same contempt they had for all colonials.

Many Loyalists left the United States for England or other parts of the British empire. Many even received financial compensation from the British government for their losses during the war.

The departure of so many Loyalists had an important impact on the future of the new country. It meant that the most determined opponents of the Revolution were no longer on the scene when the Americans won. After the war, Americans were able to deal with the problems of nation building without having to worry about a large group of people who opposed the entire enterprise.

WAR AND PEACE

The war had begun in Massachusetts. But the arena of conflict shifted to the Middle Colonies when the British decided to isolate New England by capturing New York. For several years, most of the fighting took place in New York, New Jersey, and Pennsylvania. During the final years, the theater of war shifted to the southern colonies. All in all, the Americans lost more battles than they won, but eventually they achieved a final victory. That triumph would have been impossible without the aid of their old enemies, the French.

Strengths and Weaknesses

During the entire Revolutionary War, the colonists faced enormous military disadvantages. They had a population of about 2.5 million, of whom nearly 20 percent became Loyalists and another 20 percent were slaves. The population of Great Britain was four times as large, and the British could put far more troops on the field. And these were troops who had been trained and seasoned during the Seven Years' War. The British navy was the largest and probably the most efficient in the world.

Yet the British also faced disadvantages. The worst was 3000 miles of Atlantic Ocean. In addition, they had to fight on unfamiliar, badly mapped stretches of territory that seemed to be crawling with hostile farmers. British troops and generals were accustomed to the better roads and more open country of Europe. Any army required good transportation for cannon, troops, and supplies. One British officer complained after the war that transportation difficulties "absolutely prevented us this whole war from going fifteen miles from a navigable river."

The Americans were fighting on their own ground, true. But they did not have a sizable navy. They also had great difficulty in keeping an army together. In any given place, the colonists would turn out in large numbers to fight. But staying in the army and marching off to other colonies was not an attractive prospect for many of them. Long service in the army meant low pay, rigid discipline, cold, hunger, and disease.

There were no pensions for soldiers disabled by wounds, no insurance payments for their widows if they died. So it is scarcely any wonder that many American farmers enlisted for three months and then went back home to their crops.

George Washington's great achievement was that he managed to keep something resembling an army in the field for eight years. He commanded two varieties of soldiers: militiamen from the various states and the men of the Continental Army. The latter were so called because they were drawn from all the states and because they were paid (or supposed to be paid) by the Continental Congress. They served longer periods and therefore became better trained and much more reliable in battle. As the war went on, the Continentals began to take pride in themselves both as professional soldiers and as the truest of patriots. They grew intensely loyal to their tall, somewhat aloof, but always devoted commander.

The Course of Warfare

If the rebels' overall strategy was to disrupt the enemy's resolve, the main purpose of the British became to divide and conquer. After losing Breed's Hill in June 1775, rebel forces successfully occupied Dorchester Heights overlooking Boston. Confronted by this force, Sir William Howe, who had replaced General Gage as the British commander in America, decided in March 1776 to evacuate the Massachusetts capital in favor of New York City. Despite continuing harassment by the patriots, Howe occupied New York late in 1776 and Philadelphia, the rebel capital, in September 1777, thereby virtually separating New England from the South for the duration of the war.

Starving American prisoners on board the prison ship *Jersey*. (Frick Art Reference Library)

When Benjamin Franklin, representing the Continental Congress in Paris, received the news that Howe had captured Philadelphia, he observed, "No, Philadelphia has captured Howe." And so it was, for Howe gave himself over to the delights of Philadelphia's Loyalist society and entertained himself with his mistress. These occupations kept him from joining with "Gentleman Johnny" Burgoyne, the general whose elaborate plan to control the Hudson River valley counted on Howe's troops moving northward from New York City to meet his own moving south from Canada.

With his wine, his fine clothes, his camp-following women, and almost 8000 redcoats, Burgoyne set forth from Canada in June 1777. Misfortune followed him at every step. Bands of frontiersmen riddled his troops and then disappeared into the woods. In August Burgoyne learned that Howe had gone south from New York City instead of north, but he pushed on anyway to the vicinity of Saratoga in New York State. There, heavily outnumbered after a month more of fighting, he surrendered to Benedict Arnold (now a general) on October 17, 1777. Most of his army was shipped back to England with the proviso that they not serve again in the war.

Burgoyne's failure electrified all Europe and helped transform the American War of Independence into a renewal of the international struggle for empire in North America. Before this event France had unofficially aided the Americans with money, guns, and ships. Now, convinced that the rebels might win, the French government formally recognized their independence and in February 1778 made a treaty of alliance with them.

By June, France and Britain were at war; a few months later Spain joined France; and in 1780 Britain declared war on the Netherlands to check her trading in America. Rebel privateers, moreover, now operating safely off the French coast, joined other nations in attacking British shipping even in the English Channel. As early as September 1779, John Paul Jones, commanding a French man-of-war renamed *Bonhomme Richard*, won his famous battle with the British warship *Serapis*. By then, George Rogers Clark, fighting with fewer than 200 men under the authority of Virginia, not Congress, had lifted the pressure of Britain's Indian allies in the Ohio Valley and the Illinois country.

These developments failed to stem a slide in numbers and morale in Washington's main army. Late in 1779 he took this army to winter quarters in Morristown, New Jersey, where its sufferings were even worse than those at Valley Forge the winter before. Desertions soared, and before camp was broken in the spring of 1780 the general had to put down an armed mutiny of Connecticut regiments.

The British tried to take advantage by offering bribes to discontented American officers. Benedict Arnold, who had fought so bravely in the patriot cause, sold out to the British in the summer of 1779, agreeing to turn over the fort at West Point on the Hudson River. The plot collapsed when a British agent, Major John André, was trapped behind rebel lines with incriminating evidence and hanged as a spy. Learning of André's fate, Arnold fled to a British warship in September 1780. There was glory in the Revolutionary cause, but it was easily tarnished.

The final battles of the war were fought in the South, where the British, led now by Lord Cornwallis, believed Loyalist feeling ran deep. After Savannah fell to the redcoats in December 1778, the Americans lost Georgia. Charleston, South Carolina, fell in May 1780, and the British went on to secure that state. The tables were turned in North Carolina, where at King's Mountain in October 1780 an army of 1100 Tories was shot up by back-country patriots. Other costly defeats persuaded Cornwallis in March 1781 to abandon North Carolina for Virginia, where, he supposed, British ships would assure the evacuation of his troops if necessary. But he was unaware of a French fleet on the way, and also of the approach of Washington's army from the north. Pinned down finally between the French fleet and a combined French-American army of 16,000 men, Cornwallis surrendered.

The British surrender at Yorktown in 1781 virtually ended the fighting. As the British troops there stacked their arms, their band played an old song, "The World

English
French
Spanish
United States

North America in 1783

Turned Upside Down." On learning the news, Lord North cried out again and again "Oh God! It is all over!" In March 1782 he resigned, and a new British ministry prepared to grant American independence.

Winning the Peace

Benjamin Franklin, John Adams, and John Jay were the American peace delegates sent to Paris by Congress in 1782. Under the terms of the Treaty of 1778 with France, they were expected to consult closely with that country in their negotiations. Yet as Jay observed, "We can depend upon the French only to see that we are separated from England, but it is not in their interest that we should become a great and formidable people, and therefore they will not help us become so." Jay and his colleagues knew too that Spain had never approved of American independence and opposed the Mississippi River boundary the envoys were seeking. Since it seemed certain that France would support Spain, the three Americans took an independent way. The French foreign minister, Vergennes, was angered by their behind-the-scenes deals, but Franklin soothed him and even won another fat French loan for the United States.

The Treaty of Paris between the United States and Great Britain was signed in September 1783 and ratified in Philadelphia in January 1784. By its terms, (1) Britain recognized American independence; (2) America obtained all the territory bounded by the Mississippi River on the west, the thirty-first parallel on the south (the line agreed upon if Britain ceded Florida to Spain, which it did), and the Great Lakes on the north; and Britain (3) acknowledged America's right to the Newfoundland fisheries, but (4) retained the privilege with America of navigating the Mississippi. The United States agreed (5) to impose "no lawful impediment" to the recovery by British creditors of private debts due them, but (6) consented only to "recommend" that the states restore Loyalist property.

The American negotiators had been remarkably successful. Although the treaty left many important issues unresolved, many commercial agreements uncertain, and some boundaries dangerously inexact, American independence had become a recognized fact, and an enormous stretch of land had been acquired for the new nation.

SOCIAL CHANGES

Historians have often asked an obvious question about the American Revolution. How much change did it produce in American society? We usually think of revolutions as periods of great and rapid social change. Certainly the French Revolution of 1789 and the more recent Russian and Chinese revolutions produced profound changes in those societies. Was the American Revolution, in this sense, really revolutionary? The answer to this apparently simple question is in fact a complicated one.

It is clear that the American Revolution produced considerably less social change than almost any major modern revolution. The main reason for this is obvious: a great deal of change had already taken place during the century before the Revolution. The great majority of white people already had some property and good hopes of getting more. So during the Revolution there were few demands for seizure of property from the wealthy. There was no widespread cry for freedom of religious worship, because that freedom already existed. There were no calls to change the economic system, because that system seemed to be working rather well. By and large, Americans were well off, and prosperous people do not like to rock the foundations of their prosperity.

Slavery

One group of Americans had no share in this freedom and prosperity. Black slaves and slavery itself stood out as the one great exception to the principles of the Revolution. What happened with American slavery was easily the most important social result of the Revolution. The war itself changed the lives of some slaves, for several thousand served in the armed forces of both sides, and many of them gained their freedom by doing so. Thousands of others were carried off by the British when they left Georgia and South Carolina. For the great majority of blacks, though, the war meant continued toil in the fields.

Yet the rationale for the Revolution brought into question the entire institution of slavery, for it was obvious to many white Americans that their claims about liberty and the rights of all men meant that holding slaves was wrong. Yet there were major barriers to freeing the slaves.

First, slaves were property, and for years white Americans had argued that no government could deprive people of their property without their consent. In this case, one principle of the Revolution, the owner's natural right of property, collided directly with another, the slave's natural right of liberty. Second, many white Americans thought that freed slaves would become a drain on society, a hostile group of people who would either rob or starve. Third, many whites simply did not want to live with free blacks. They would have been happy to see them free if they would somehow go away. Finally, many slaveowners opposed emancipation simply because they were profiting from slave labor.

The net result of these feelings was

that some states took steps toward abolishing slavery and others did not. From Pennsylvania northward, where there were few slaves, it was relatively easy to end slavery. In Massachusetts, court decisions found that slavery violated the state constitution's assertion that "all men are born free and equal." Elsewhere in the North, the states passed gradual-emancipation laws. These acts did not abolish slavery outright; they provided that slaves born after passage of the act would become free at a certain age, such as twenty-one or twenty-eight. Many such laws named July 4 as the date when they would go into effect. That date itself pointed to the force of Revolutionary principles. By 1802 all northern states had provided for the gradual end of slavery.

In the southern states, the principles were the same but the number of slaves much greater. In Virginia and Maryland, where slavery was less profitable than farther south, there was much discussion about getting rid of it. The major difficulty was that most whites wanted to get rid of blacks if they were freed, and there was no realistic way of doing this. A number of masters privately freed some or all of their slaves. In doing so they often cited the principles of the Revolution, but just as frequently they referred to principles of Christian brotherhood; in many cases they referred to both.

The Revolution had still another important impact on the pattern of American slavery. The coming of the war brought the importation of slaves from Africa to a halt. For several reasons this change was nearly permanent. A majority of white Americans had begun to recognize the cruelty and injustice of the Atlantic slave trade. Slaves were in great demand only in South Carolina and Georgia; elsewhere in the South, planters had more slaves than they could use. And most whites thought there was already a surplus of black people. They feared and disliked the ones they already had, whether slave or free, and they wanted no more. The great majority of white Americans wanted the new nation to be a white man's country.

Churches and Property

The Revolution gave Americans a chance to make certain changes in the relationship between church and state. In the southern states, the established Anglican church lost its privileged position. Yet most states still continued to tax their citizens for the support of the churches. Usually the taxpayer could name the church he wanted to support. The Congregational churches in Massachusetts and Connecticut kept certain special privileges until the nineteenth century.

Although the principles of the American Revolution strongly supported the idea of private property, the war itself resulted in a slightly more equal distribution of property among white Americans. We do not know exactly how great this change actually was. Widespread printing of paper money resulted in its depreciation, a process that favored poorer people who borrowed money because they were able to repay their debts with inflated currency. Many wealthy merchants suffered great losses during the war. Others did very well by selling supplies to the army. Some farmers profited by selling food supplies to one army or the other and sometimes to both. Others lost most of what they had. The seizure of Loyalist lands by the states resulted in somewhat broader landholding, since the states usually sold these lands at public auction. However, many of these estates were purchased by speculators who then made money from resales to small farmers. The Revolution resulted in somewhat wider possession of land.

The winning of independence and the establishment of new governments caused Americans to examine their society more closely than ever before. By and large, they liked what they saw. Yet there were obvious flaws. Especially in the northern states, efforts were made to make punishments for crime more humane. Many states ended the practice of putting debtors in jail until they had paid their debts. New private schools and colleges were established because Americans thought they needed better-educated citizens for the new republic. These and other reforms were stimulated by the Revolution. Yet they probably would have been undertaken even without it. Most of the constructive energies of the nation's leaders were going into problems of government.

Independence raised pressing political problems that had to be solved somehow. It was in the realm of politics that the American Revolution turned out to be truly revolutionary.

SUGGESTED READINGS

J. Sosin, *The Revolutionary Frontier, 1763-1783* (1967). E.S. and H.M. Morgan, *The Stamp Act Crisis: Prologue to Revolution* (1953). J. Shy, *The Role of the British Army in the Coming of the Revolution* (1965). B. Bailyn, *The Ideological Origins of the American Revolution* (1967). W.H. Nelson, *The American Tory* (1962). R. Middlekauff, *The Glorious Cause: The American Revolution, 1763-1789* (1982). R. Isaac, *The Transformation of Virginia, 1740-1790* (1982).

SUMMARY

The American Revolution had its seeds in the long war between France and England from 1756 to 1763. This conflict began in America and then spread to Europe. The Treaty of Paris, which settled what had been a major world war, gave Britain all of Canada and the lands east of the Mississippi River except for New Orleans, plus Florida.

The Seven Years' War changed the balance of power in America. The British were now in command—but they were also in debt. Royal officials thought the colonists should help pay at least some of the expenses of empire—in particular, those for their own defense. Parliament passed new

taxes, which Americans resented very much.

The first crisis came with the Stamp Act of 1765, which the colonists refused to obey. At a Stamp Act Congress in 1765, delegates from nine colonies drew up a Declaration of Rights and Grievances demanding repeal of the act. Groups called Sons of Liberty began to enforce the protest by mob action.

Repeal of the Stamp Act of 1766 brought the colonists joy, but within a few months British authorities managed to enrage them once again with the so-called Townshend Acts. These measures imposed new import duties on manufactured goods sent to the colonies from the mother country and provided for stricter enforcement.

The American response to Townshend's program was nonimportation—a boycott of British goods—plus a widespread and effective propaganda campaign. The situation was tense, but then for the next three years there was relative quiet. In 1770 the Townshend Acts were repealed, except for the tax on tea. The colonists relaxed their suspicions, although their committees of correspondence remained active.

The passage of the Tea Act was followed by the Boston Tea Party. This brought retaliation in the form of the Intolerable Acts. But to the surprise of the British—and perhaps the colonists themselves—instead of isolating the troublemakers in Boston, the new laws united the colonists.

The First Continental Congress met in September 1774 to find effective ways to combat British policies. Many colonists, especially in New England, began to stockpile firearms and train militiamen. In the spring of 1775, British troops in Boston had their first battle with colonial minutemen. Without anyone quite realizing it, the American Revolution had begun.

In military and political terms, the American Revolution was indeed revolutionary. But in social and economic terms, not very much changed. Slavery continued in the southern areas where it was most profitable, although the Atlantic slave trade nearly ended. The idea of established churches began to fade, although in a few states citizens still paid taxes for church support. Land ownership broadened somewhat as lands taken from the Loyalists were redistributed. But the economic system remained the same. Americans were mainly well off and conscious of their country as a land of opportunity.

5

Problems of Government

In many ways the American revolutionaries were lucky when it came to dealing with problems of government. The idea of natural rights gave them a very clear idea of how governments ought to work. They already shared strong ideas about such matters as representation, taxation, and the dangers of standing armies, courts without juries, and public officials over whom they had no control. And the American rebels had one thing most other revolutionaries lacked. They already possessed certain institutions that embodied their ideas about government. These institutions—notably the courts and representative assemblies—provided a foundation for carrying on the work of change. No other single fact does more to explain the character of the American Revolution.

Yet old institutions and practices can create problems as well. Americans were used to having their forms of government set down in writing. The governments of the colonies had been based on charters issued by the Crown to a joint-stock company, to proprietors, or to an individual colony. Once the king had been rejected, the question arose as to who should write and issue

a new framework of government. Theory suggested that "the people" should draw up the fundamental framework, but here there were obvious difficulties. Exactly how did the people go about drafting and approving a charter of government, a constitution? Given their experience with Great Britain, Americans were anxious to write down not only what their governments could do, but what they could not.

A related problem was the relationship of the various states to one another. At first the Continental Congress called them the United Colonies and then the United States, but it was not at all clear what the "United States" actually was—or were. If the "United States" was to be anything more than a temporary alliance, there had to be some agreement about what it could and could not do.

As the war ended, the touchiest question remained the one that had dominated politics in the 1760s: taxation. Other problems came to the surface. A major one was how to deal with the vast territory Americans had won in the West. Another was the relationships of the new country (or *thirteen countries) with foreign powers. Spain and Britain remained hostile to American interests, and France not overly friendly. Could Americans solve these problems and still remain faithful to the principles of the Revolution? In the modern world, most ex-colonies have ended up as dictatorships. Thanks to their own historical experience, however, Americans were able to find another way.*

STATE CONSTITUTIONS

In 1776 the states were governed by legislative assemblies. Indeed, at first the old assemblies simply transformed themselves into the governing bodies of the newly independent states. Everyone assumed that more permanent arrangements needed to be made and written down in state constitutions. Despite wartime difficulties, every state adopted a written document of fundamental law long before the war ended.

Power to the People

For the most part, the new constitutions continued old forms and practices of government. All the states retained their assemblies.

The new constitutions also broadened the suffrage somewhat by lowering property requirements for voting. Yet Americans did not abandon the old idea that a man ought to possess at least some property in order to vote. In contrast with Europe, however, the suffrage was so broad that the United States seemed really to be ruled by the people.

In most states, the revolutionary provincial congresses drew up and adopted new constitutions without consulting the voters. Massachusetts, however, set a different example, one that was followed by the others when they rewrote their basic law, and by the Republic itself when the Great Convention of 1787 wrote the fundamental law of the land. This new procedure was one of the American Revolution's most important contributions to modern democratic government—the idea that constitutions are derived directly from the will of the people.

In Massachusetts, when the provincial congress asked the towns for power to draw up the new state constitution, the majority agreed but the town of Concord objected. If the provincial legislature makes the constitution, the Concord town meeting asked, what is to prevent it from unmaking it? Concord demanded that a special "Convention . . . be immediately Chosen, to form & establish a Constitution."

The Massachusetts provincial government ignored Concord's proposal and drafted a new constitution. But the Concord notion spread, and when the provincial congress presented its work to the people in 1778, they rejected it by a five-to-one majority. In 1780, under the leadership of John Adams, a specially elected convention wrote a new constitution, which the voters approved.

Bills of Rights

Most state constitutions set forth a bill of rights. These rights included "acquiring, possessing, and protecting property"; freedom of worship, speech, and assembly; moderate bail, trial by jury, and punishments to fit the crime; and protection from general search warrants and from liability to serve in, or support, standing armies.

For some time conservatives found it easy enough to live with these generalizations. Yet the bills of rights gave the people, in the language of the times, "a standing law to live by." Without promises of such bills they almost certainly would have rejected the federal Constitution of 1787.

THE ARTICLES OF CONFEDERATION

It took the Second Continental Congress more than two years to draft an instrument of government that its members would agree to submit to the states. John Dickinson of Pennsylvania, the principal author of the new document, tried to establish a national government without weakening the individual states. The Second Continental Congress then became the formal ruling body of the United States of America.

Foreign Affairs

At the close of the Revolution, an Englishman predicted that the Americans would be "a disunited people till the end of time, suspicious and distrustful of each other." In 1783, there was justification for such a view. For several months, Congress lacked enough members to form a quorum. It proved impossible to gather enough delegates to ratify the peace treaty within the required six months. Eventually, however, it went into effect.

According to the peace treaty, the British were to surrender their military and fur-trading posts in the Northwest "with all convenient speed." But the British held onto the posts in order to protect the rich Canadian fur trade until, as they hoped, the new nation collapsed.

Spain, an ally of France in the Revolutionary War, proved to be as much an enemy to the Americans as Britain. In 1783

the Spanish had received East and West Florida from the British. They established forts there and proceeded to make treaties with the Indians of the region. The treaties obligated the Indians to join in harassing American settlers. Congress was unable to force Spain to stop, and this weakness cost it support in the South and Southwest, just as weakness toward the British angered Americans in the Northwest.

British and Spanish stubbornness over the West was hardened by American failures in other international issues. The peace treaty, for example, declared that no legal barriers should prevent creditors on either side from collecting old debts. Actually the great bulk of the debts was owed by the ex-colonists. Although Congress urged the new states to honor the treaty provision, it had no power to prevent them from passing legislation designed to frustrate collection.

By the terms of the peace treaty, Congress also made "earnest recommendation" to the states to restore confiscated property to former Loyalist owners. Most states chose to ignore this recommendation; even after the war, patriots continued to confiscate Loyalist lands.

Financial Problems

With no power to levy taxes, Congress had to face its problems without a sound financial base. With no money to pay the troops, it was physically menaced by its own army. Many other claims arising from the war poured in. There was the back interest and principal on the debt. Robert Morris, named secretary of finance in 1781, urged Congress to establish a national tariff so that it would no longer have to beg states for funds.

In 1783, Morris decided to quit. When

no successor could be found, he was persuaded to remain until the army had been paid. In June, Washington got the troops to go home, even though they were not to be paid for some months to come. A loan from Holland enabled the government to limp along for a time. When Morris finally left in September 1784, the treasury was empty, as usual.

American shipowners were especially hard hit by the loss of their favored trading position with Britain and the British West Indies. When the Americans tried to get Britain to reopen the West Indian trade to American goods and American ships, they were laughed out of court. The loss of British trade was offset only partially by the new trade opened up with China in 1784.

Just after the war, American importers had a taste of prosperity when the ex-colonists went on a buying splurge. But the market for luxuries was small, and the splurge was quickly over. American manufacturers and artisans, who had had the American market for coarse goods largely to themselves during the Revolution, also suffered from postwar foreign competition. They demanded protective tariffs that would keep foreign goods out and subsidies that would support their own industrial expansion—neither of which Congress could provide.

There was a brighter side. Most Americans were subsistence farmers who did not depend on Congress for their well-being. Even the loudest critics of Congress often found ways to help themselves. Philadelphia, New York, and Baltimore merchants profited from illegal West Indian trade. Public creditors, though unpaid by Congress, apparently still had enough money to sponsor new business ventures. Immediately following the war there was unprecedented activity in river and road improvements,

house building, land transactions, and banking. The resumption of immigration to America also helped the basic soundness of the economy.

The Northwest Ordinance

Settlement of the vast area northwest of the Ohio River was orderly partly because of the New England tradition of controlled settlement and partly because of Thomas Jefferson's liking for planning. Jefferson wrote much of the Northwest Ordinance of 1785, which set the basic pattern. It established the crucial principle that the settled portions of the West would be admitted to the Union on an equal basis with the original provinces. Jefferson's original ordinance was modified two years later by the addition of provisions for the transition from organized territories to full-fledged states.

The Northwest Ordinance of 1787 was probably the Confederation Congress's most important piece of legislation. Under this ordinance, the Northwest Territory became a single unit with a governor appointed by Congress. When 5000 free male inhabitants had settled in the territory, those who owned at least fifty acres were to elect a territorial legislature whose acts would be subject only to a governor's veto.

No less than three and no more than five states were to be carved out of the territory. When a potential state had 60,000 free inhabitants, it was to be admitted to the Union on an equal footing with the original states. The ordinance also prohibited slavery in the territory and in all the states to be carved from it.

Shays's Rebellion

Apart from the Northwest Ordinance, the Confederation Congress had few successes during the postwar years. Even in the Northwest, pioneers were left almost entirely to their own resources in fighting the Indians and the British. Frontier violence and threats of violence weakened the demand for land. Speculators were unhappy.

Other postwar developments aroused the anger of the largest single economic class in the new nation, the farmers. The war had piled up what appeared to be monstrous debts for the states. As a result, the men who were owed money by state governments were in conflict with the general mass of taxpayers, many of whom were debtors. In addition, as in any inflationary situation, private debtors were happy to pay off their debts in currency of reduced value, to the dismay of their creditors. Debtors demanded abundant paper money, lower taxes, and *stay laws* that would delay mortgage foreclosures. Creditors wanted heavy taxes in gold or silver and swift and rigid enforcement of legal contracts.

Seven states issued some form of paper money, often with good effect. But in New England in particular, creditors and conservatives in the coastal commercial towns usually managed to avoid paper money and also to shift a great part of the tax burden onto inland farmers. By 1786, conditions had grown so bad in New Hampshire that the militia had to be called out to disperse a mob of farmers who surrounded the legislative meeting house in an effort to force the members to issue paper money.

It was in Massachusetts, however, where farmers appear to have been taxed as much as one-third of their income, that conservatives received their greatest shock. The legislature there had not only failed to listen to the farmers' demands for relief, but had levied higher taxes. In 1785, farmers in the western part of the state decided to take the same sort of action that Boston merchants had thought legitimate ten years earlier: domestic rebellion.

Daniel Shays was not very different from the thousand men who became his followers. He had seen action at Bunker Hill. "A brave and good soldier," as a subordinate described him, he waited four years for a promised commission to captain. In 1780 he returned home to await payment for his long service to his country. His farming went badly, and his army compensation was delayed.

His neighbors shared his bitterness. Many western-Massachusetts towns were too poor to send delegates to the legislature in Boston. Without any voice in the state government, the debtor leaders resorted to the familiar device of county conventions. Men from neighboring towns gathered to voice their political sentiments by means of resolutions and petitions to the legislature.

After the legislature adjourned in July 1786, having ignored these petitions, more and more county conventions met. Shays and other leaders warned the members to "abstain from all mobs and unlawful assemblies until a constitutional method of redress can be obtained." But mobs soon attacked civil courts where foreclosure proceedings were scheduled.

By October 1786 Shays had somehow become the focus of a whole movement, and the rebels who followed him soon became the targets of state forces gathered by General Benjamin Lincoln. Fighting between the Shays forces and Lincoln's continued from mid January to the end of February 1787, when the rebellion was finally crushed. Shays fled to Vermont.

News of Shays's Rebellion shocked conservatives. They were already alarmed by the weakness of Congress, the discontent of the army, and the vulnerability of government to mob action. Washington himself described Congress as "a half-starved, limping" body "always moving upon crutches and tottering at every step."

THE CONSTITUTION

Only a small group of men worked for a stronger central government. We know now that they succeeded with the Constitution of the United States. At the time, however, they faced enormous obstacles and came extremely close to failure. Some had grown so discouraged about the whole experiment that they thought it should be given up.

Washington, steadfast in his nationalism and republicanism, would not tolerate disunion or despotism. Even before the Articles of Confederation had been ratified, he and other nationalists were calling for their improvement in order to strengthen the union. They carried the day, but only by taking revolutionary steps of their own.

The Constitutional Convention

A strong movement for a new form of government emerged from the efforts of a few practical men to achieve what the Articles could not—a more satisfactory regulation of interstate commerce. Early in 1785, delegates from Maryland and Virginia met to settle their differences over navigation on the Potomac River and Chesapeake Bay. These discussions eventually resulted in a recommendation for a convention in Annapolis, Maryland.

The Annapolis convention adjourned with a call for a new convention to meet in Philadelphia the following May to amend the Articles. Meanwhile, Shays's Rebellion had aroused great concern. All states except Rhode Island sent representatives to Philadelphia.

The men whom the states chose were a remarkably able group. Some prominent political leaders were not available: John Adams and Thomas Jefferson were abroad on diplomatic missions; Sam Adams was not named a delegate; Patrick Henry, appointed by Virginia, refused to attend. Otherwise the famous names of the country were there: Benjamin Franklin and James Wilson from Pennsylvania; James Madison, Edmund Randolph, and Washington from Virginia; and Alexander Hamilton from New York.

Of the seventy-four men named to the convention, only fifty-five actually attended. Their average age was forty-two. Many had been army officers during the Revolution. Only eight were signers of the Declaration of Independence. In an age when few Americans went to college, a majority of the delegates were college graduates. Lawyers, businessmen, and planters were numerous.

On May 25, twenty-nine delegates unanimously elected Washington presiding officer. Next, uneasy about local rumors and the press, they voted unanimously to keep their discussions secret. Debate then took place on their purpose in coming together. Some maintained that they must follow their instructions to amend the Articles. But others, led by Hamilton, argued that they must not "let slip the golden opportunity." The convention decided to replace, not amend, the Articles. It adopted Edmund Randolph's resolution: "That a national government ought to be established, consisting of a supreme legislative, executive, and judiciary."

Guiding Ideas

Although the delegates had many disagreements, almost all shared certain basic assumptions about the nature of humankind and of government. They agreed that people were basically driven by self-interest and that the structure of any government had to deal with this fact. As Madison said, "Ambition must be made to counteract ambition."

The delegates generally acknowledged that the people must have a voice in government. But they felt they knew from both history and experience that the people could be stampeded into following demagogues and dictators. So the people's role must be limited. Although most of the delegates were men of property who distrusted democracy, they had no illusions about the benevolence of the rich. Even a wealthy aristocrat like Gouverneur Morris of Pennsylvania acknowledged that "wealth tends to corrupt the mind," and that rich men as well as poor would use power to their own advantage if given the opportunity. Thus the greed and pride of the rich, like the passions of the poor, must also be held in check.

The delegates were also reluctant to entrust power to special interests. They believed that a landed interest, a slaveholding interest, a creditor interest, a debtor's interest, or a commercial interest would tyrannize the rest of society if given the opportunity. And the danger would be even greater if several interests were to join forces to control the nation. To meet this problem, the advocates of a strong constitution turned to a federal republic. Political selfishness among the parts would offset power grabs by the various interests working together.

The concept of offsetting competing interests was as old as Aristotle. John Adams gave the best statement of the idea:

A legislative, an executive, and a judicial power comprehend the whole of what is meant and understood by government. It is by balancing each of these powers against the other two, that the efforts of human nature toward tyranny can alone be checked and restrained, and any degree of freedom preserved in the constitution.

Traditional American political practices gave the delegates an opportunity to introduce such balancing into the new national government. In the provincial and state legislatures, the lower house usually served as the "democratical branch," elected by a broad suffrage. In the new national legislature, most delegates agreed, there must also be two houses, the democratic one to check and in turn be checked by a second, which would represent the wealthier elements. A few delegates thought that a two-house legislature, by pulling in opposite directions, would be incapable of effective action. But advocates of bicameralism pointed out that a strong and independent executive could prevent this.

Naturally the convention could not agree unanimously even on these general principles. Some delegates were concerned about state Power. Others, certain that the establishment of a national sovereignty would swallow up traditional personal liberties, earned reputations as obstructionists.

Compromise

The first and one of the most divisive controversies concerned the relative power to be granted large and small states. Once the delegates had agreed to go beyond amending the Articles, they took up Edmund Randolph's so-called Virginia Plan for a new government structure. Randolph proposed a two-house National Legislature with membership in both houses given to the states in proportion to their free population. Members of the upper house were to be elected by the members of the lower, who were themselves to be elected by the people. The whole National Legislature was then to elect the National Judiciary. This proposal obviously violated the principle of balancing separate powers, and it aroused considerable opposition. It particularly alarmed the small-state delegates, who feared they would be overwhelmed in the popularly elected house and that some states might have no representatives at all in the upper chamber.

As a counterproposal, the small states offered a plan of their own: Congress would remain a single house, as under the Articles, with each state having one vote. The delegates quickly rejected this suggestion because it continued the current situation and because it based representation on states rather than on people.

Early in July a special committee brought forth a compromise made largely by Benjamin Franklin: there would be a two-house legislature, with membership in the lower house according to population (to satisfy the large states) and membership in the upper house equal for all states (to satisfy the small ones). This arrangement provided the basis for the Great Compromise of the Constitution. It determined the general character of the two bodies that were soon named the House of Representatives and the Senate.

The two-house plan enabled the delegates to establish the lower house as the people's branch of government. Members of this house were to be elected by all voters in each state who were eligible to vote for "the most numerous branch of the State Legislature." Thus the question of voting requirements was left to the states.

The Great Compromise raised two issues that divided the delegates along completely different lines. The first concerned the direct taxes the new government could levy. The convention agreed that such taxes should be apportioned among the states according to population. But the slave states wanted their blacks, if they were counted at all in the apportioning of taxes, to be given less weight than free men. The North wanted blacks to be given less weight only for congressional representation. In the debate, a proportion of three-fifths was proposed many times. But Wilson of Pennsylvania "did not well see on what principle the admission of blacks in the proportion of three-fifths could be explained. Are they admitted as Citizens? Are they admitted as property?" Nevertheless, he admitted the necessity of compromise, and the others yielded on the three-fifths rule. For both direct taxes and representation, five blacks were to be counted as equivalent to three whites.

Delegates from the commercial North urged that the new government be granted full power to regulate interstate and foreign commerce and to make treaties that the states would have to obey. The convention easily agreed on these points. But the South, fearful of being outvoted in the new Congress, demanded that commercial regulations and all treaties require the consent of two-thirds of the Senate. Southerners were concerned about taxes on exports and the possibility of treaties requiring them, for they were dependent on selling tobacco and rice in competitive world markets.

Delegates from the lower South were even more concerned about the slave trade. If Congress had control over commerce, it could ban the slave trade or tax it out of existence. Delegates from South Carolina and Georgia warned that their states would never approve the proposed constitution if the supply of slaves was threatened. From Virginia northward there was no demand for the importation of slaves, and a great many people had decided that the slave trade was unjust and inhumane. In order to placate South Carolina and Georgia, the majority of delegates reluctantly agreed on a compromise: Congress would be prohibited from interfering with the slave trade for a period of twenty years.

The convention next turned to the problem of the executive branch. The delegates discussed the questions of whether it should be composed of one or several men, how long he or they should serve, whether its holder(s) could serve for another term, and what name to give him or them. They decided on an arrangement that prevails to this day (with one exception, concerning reelection): a single executive, elected for four renewable years, called a *president*. The method of the president's election presented one last test. Strong nationalists wanted the president elected directly by the people; state-sovereignty men wanted him chosen by state legislatures. After many arguments, the convention devised the elaborate electoral-college plan (Article II, Section 1). Each state was to have as many electors as it had representatives and senators, and the method of choosing these electors was left up to the state legislatures.

Toward Sovereign Power

Among the flaws of government under the Confederation, two were fatal: Congress had neither the power of the purse nor the power of the sword. Most of the delegates at Philadelphia, though distracted at the outset by the question of apportioning power to the states and the people, had come mainly to solve these problems by giving a new national government such sovereign strength.

Almost every delegate voted to give the new national government power to levy and collect taxes and tariffs. The clause permitting Congress to pay the debts of the United States passed unanimously. No one opposed giving Congress the power to coin money and "regulate the value thereof," or the power to borrow money on the credit of the United States, or the power to regulate commerce among the states and foreign nations, or to deal with Indian tribes. The delegates almost unanimously forbade the states to issue "bills of credit" (paper money); to make anything but gold and silver legal tender for the payment of private or public debts; to interfere with the obligations of contracts; or to tax imports or exports in commercial wars with one another.

The Constitution's provisions for a military establishment also shifted power from the states to the national government. The new government alone was enabled to "provide for the common defense"; "to declare war"; "to raise and support armies"; "to provide and maintain a navy"; "to provide for calling forth the militia to execute the laws of the Union, suppress insurrections and repel invasions"; and more broadly, to provide for the "general welfare of the United States." To insure that national sovereignty would not be impaired by technicalities, the framers added the famous "elastic clause," enabling Congress "to make all laws which shall be necessary and proper for carrying into execution the foregoing powers."

A third flaw in the Confederation had been the absence of an independent executive. In remedying this defect, the Constitution made the president commander in chief of the army and navy and of the state militias when called into federal service. His power of appointing federal officers was extensive, and only for his higher aides was the consent of the Senate required. The power of dismissing such aides, though not specifically mentioned, was later held to be included. With the consent of two-thirds of the Senate, the president could conclude treaties with foreign nations. He could call Congress into extraordinary session and could veto acts of Congress, although his veto could be overridden by a two-thirds vote in both houses. For protection against wrong doing, the convention provided that the president could be impeached by a majority vote in the House and then convicted by a two-thirds vote after a trial in the Senate presided over by the chief justice.

A fourth flaw of the Confederation was its lack of judges who were independent of state courts. The Constitution provided for a national judicial system. At the head of the system stood the Supreme Court of the United States. It could decide cases on appeal from lower federal courts. The Constitution made no specific provision for *judicial review* of federal legislation—that is, the power of federal courts to declare acts of Congress unconstitutional. But the Supreme Court later concluded that any state actions or laws that violated the supreme powers of the federal government must be found unconstitutional by the federal courts. It was a short step for the Supreme Court to decide that it also had the power to declare acts of the federal Congress and the president to be unconstitutional.

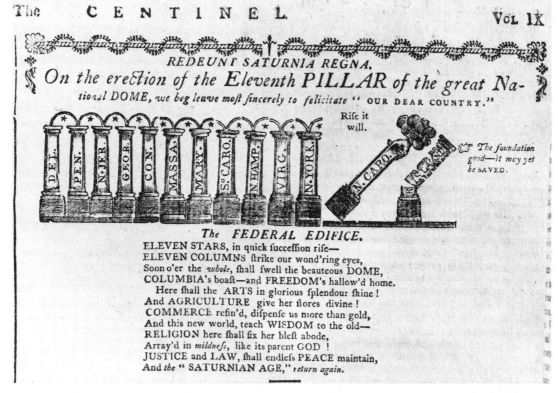

The CENTINEL. VOL IX

REDEUNT SATURNIA REGNA.

On the erection of the Eleventh PILLAR of the great National DOME, we beg leave most sincerely to felicitate "OUR DEAR COUNTRY."

Rise it will.

The foundation good—it may yet be SAVED.

The FEDERAL EDIFICE.

ELEVEN STARS, in quick succession rise—
ELEVEN COLUMNS strike our wond'ring eyes,
Soon o'er the *whole*, shall swell the beauteous DOME,
COLUMBIA's boast—and FREEDOM's hallow'd home.
　Here shall the ARTS in glorious splendour shine!
And AGRICULTURE give her stores divine!
COMMERCE refin'd, dispense us more than gold,
And this new world, teach WISDOM to the old—
RELIGION here shall fix her blest abode,
Array'd in *mildness*, like its parent GOD!
JUSTICE and LAW, shall endless PEACE maintain,
And *the* " SATURNIAN AGE," *return again.*

North Carolina and Rhode Island were needed to help the other "pillars" support the new nation. (New York Historical Society)

A Powerful Government

The Philadelphia convention created a government that could act with speed and strength. The Constitution radically shifted sovereign power away from the states and toward a truly national government. No one knew at the time whether the arrangement would work. It took Americans about forty years before they began to regard the federal government as truly permanent.

If the framers wanted mainly to substitute a strong central government for the weak Articles of Confederation, they also hoped to create a government, as Madison put it, "for the ages." Their success rested in part on features they introduced and on others that were unforeseen but Proved at least as important.

From the framers' point of view, the Constitution's built-in checks and balances were its best safeguards for the Republic. No chief executive could become a dictator. And no temporary surge of popular feeling, reflected in the "democratical branch" of the legislature, could unseat the president or overturn the courts.

A second source of the Constitution's lasting strength was its amending process. Trying to amend the Articles by unanimous consent of the states had been impossible. The easier amending process in the Constitution was at first used sparingly—but only after the first ten amendments, the Bill of Rights, had been adopted.

A third source of the Constitution's long life was the breadth of its wording. The framers avoided fine detail because they assumed that the principles of good government were universal. They left important powers to the states, but they spelled out the powers of the national government so broadly that these powers could later be expanded.

There were also nonconstitutional sources of the Constitution's long life. Among them we may note the two-party system that developed early in the United States, the development of the cabinet, the committee system in the House and Senate, the civil service, and the regulatory agencies of the executive branch.

For all its stress on private property, which in the eighteenth century was thought to be the best foundation for public responsibility, the Constitution required no property qualification for office, not even that of president. It also required "compensation—to be ascertained by law, and paid out of the Treasury of the United States" for all elective posts, so that the poor as well as the rich might hold them. The Constitution forbade religious tests for any federal position.

RATIFICATION

The Constitutional Convention was in session from May 25 to September 16, 1787. Of the fifty-five delegates who took part, forty-two stayed to the end and thirty-nine signed the document. The other three warned there would be a storm when the Constitution was brought to the people for approval.

Antifederalist Arguments

The day after the convention adopted the Constitution, a copy was sent to Congress, largely out of courtesy. "In all our deliberations on this subject," said the signers, "we kept steadily in our view that which appeared to us the greatest interest of every true American—the consolidation of the Union—in which is involved our prosperity, felicity, safety, perhaps our national existence." They did not ask Congress for a vote. Nor would they ask the state legislatures for confirmation. In the Constitution itself they asked for the consent of nine special state conventions like their own.

But the Constitution's critics, named Antifederalists by friends of the Constitution, had many objections. There was no Bill of Rights; state sovereignty would be destroyed; the president might become king; the standing national army would be everywhere; only the rich could afford to hold office; tax collectors would swarm over the countryside; the people could not bear to be taxed by both state and national governments; commercial treaties would sell out the West and the South; debtors would no longer be able to defend themselves with paper money.

Many state politicians feared that a stronger national government would cause them to lose their influence. More important, many ordinary citizens worried about such drastic changes and about centralized political power.

The First Ratifications

At first, ratification went smoothly. In December 1787 and January 1788, five states approved the Constitution. The conventions of Delaware, New Jersey, and Georgia did so without a single opposing vote. Connecticut ratified by 123 to 40. Only in Pennsylvania, among the first five, was there controversy. Federalists seized enough of their opponents and pushed them into the chamber to make a quorum. Pennsylvania voted to ratify, 46 to 23. In the key state of Massachusetts, the next to ratify, the contest was close. Its convention debated for a month. Finally, Massachusetts voted for the Constitution, 187 to 168.

In the less crucial states of Maryland and South Carolina, ratification won easily. In New Hampshire, opposition was powerful. After a first convention failed to reach a vote, a second convention narrowly ratified on June 21, 1788. Technically speaking, the new government could now go into effect, for nine states had accepted it. But no one believed it could function without Virginia and New York, and in these two states the outcome remained doubtful.

Virginia and New York

In Virginia, an extraordinarily thorough and brilliant review of the issues took place, the opposition led by George Mason and Patrick Henry. But four days after New Hampshire ratified, Virginia did also, by a vote of 89 to 79. By arrangement between Madison and Hamilton, messengers were quickly dispatched to New York, where an extremely close struggle was taking place.

In New York, Hamilton led the Federalist fight in support of ratification; Governor Clinton led the opposition. Well aware of Clinton's strength, Hamilton, John Jay, and Madison had undertaken a series of anonymous newspaper articles supporting the Constitution. Later published as *The Federalist*, these articles provide the best commentary on the Constitution by contemporary advocates. But there was no landslide for the Constitution in New York. More important in the voting here was the news of Federalist success in New Hampshire and Virginia. Once again, the promise of a Bill of Rights overcame opposition. Having agreed to support such amendments, Federalists in New York finally won by a narrow margin.

Rhode Island and North Carolina rejected the Constitution. But when the new national government got under way, they had little choice but to join. North Carolina

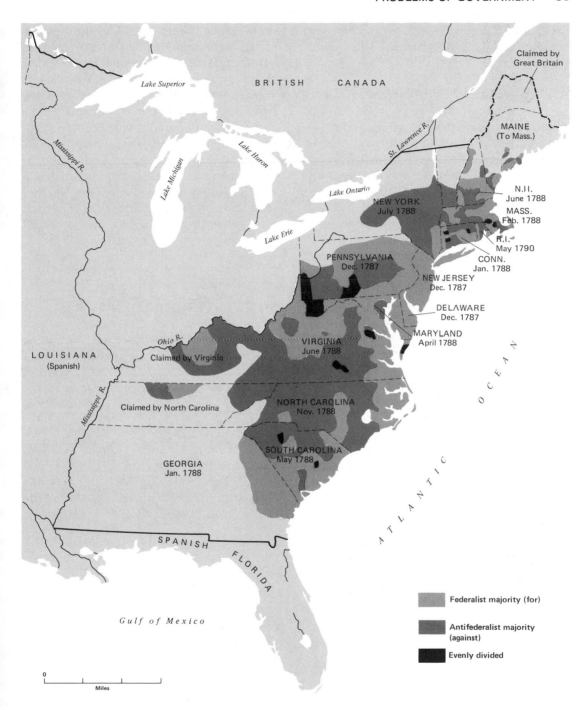

BRITISH   CANADA

Claimed by
Great Britain

Lake Superior

MAINE
(To Mass.)

Lake Michigan

Lake Huron

St. Lawrence R.

Mississippi R.

Lake Ontario

Lake Erie

NEW YORK
July 1788

N.H.
June 1788

MASS.
Feb. 1788

R.I.
May 1790

PENNSYLVANIA
Dec. 1787

CONN.
Jan. 1788

NEW JERSEY
Dec. 1787

DELAWARE
Dec. 1787

Ohio R.

MARYLAND
April 1788

LOUISIANA
(Spanish)

Claimed by Virginia

VIRGINIA
June 1788

Mississippi R.

Claimed by North Carolina

NORTH CAROLINA
Nov. 1788

A T L A N T I C   O C E A N

SOUTH CAROLINA
May 1788

GEORGIA
Jan. 1788

SPANISH   FLORIDA

Gulf of Mexico

Federalist majority (for)

Antifederalist majority
(against)

Evenly divided

0
Miles

Vote on Ratification of the Constitution

decided by a wide margin to join in November. Rhode Island held out for a few more months.

An Appraisal

Among historians there has long been controversy about all these events, and even today there is no full agreement. Interpretations have varied all the way from a coup détat by conservative counterrevolutionaries to the divinely inspired work of intellectual giants bent upon fulfilling the aims of the Revolution. The truth lies not exactly in between, but somewhere off center between these two poles.

At the national level it is clear that leaders who favored the new Constitution had the edge in talent. Men who had previously participated in politics outside their own state tended to favor adoption. Wealthy persons were inclined toward adoption, and some who favored the Constitution knew they would gain financially from a stronger central government. Within each state politics were important, especially the influence of popular local leaders such as John Hancock (who wanted ratification) and Patrick Henry (who did not). Cities and towns and regions of commercial activity tended to be Federalist; small farmers in more isolated areas tended to the Antifederalist. Representation in the ratifying conventions favored the commercial regions, and it is quite clear that a majority of actual voters opposed the Constitution. Finally, had George Washington not favored it, the Federalist cause would have been doomed, It was almost universally assumed that he would be the first president under the new government. He was widely admired and trusted—but it remained to be seen whether a victorious general would make a good president, and whether the new system would work.

SUGGESTED READINGS

J.T. Main, *The Sovereign States, 1775-1783* (1973). G.S. Wood, *The Creation of the American Republic, 1776-1787* (1969). M. Jensen, *The New Nation: A History of the United States during the Confederation, 1781-1789* (1950). J.T. Flexner, *George Washington and the New Nation, 1783-1793* (1970). J. Brant, *James Madison: Father of the Constitution, 1787-1800* (1950). R.A. Rutland, *The Ordeal of the Constitution: The Anti-Federalists and the Ratification Struggle of 1787-1788* (1966).

SUMMARY

The United States had become a country as far as the world was concerned. But as far as Americans were concerned, they had yet to set up the most important institution of all, a national government. New state governments, with written constitutions, had been established during the war. These documents gave governing power to legislatures elected by the people. Fundamental power was reserved to the people themselves, who were protected by bills of rights guaranteeing individual liberties.

The great problem was the national government. The Articles of Confederation, drawn up by the Second Continental Con-

gress, provided for a loose association of states to be governed by a one-house legislature.

The most significant accomplishment of the government under the Articles was the Northwest Ordinance of 1787, which established the terms for the settlement of the Northwest Territory, that vast area northwest of the Ohio River. The ordinance unified the whole territory under a governor, laid out tentative boundaries for new states, and set the terms for their admission. It also prohibited slavery in the territory and in the states to be carved from it.

The worst problem for the government was money and credit. Farmers, who were taxpayers and often also debtors, wanted paper money with which they could ease the pressure of their money payments. Creditors wanted payment in specie—gold or silver coin—so that they would not be paid back with devalued currency. The agitation and discontent over this issue reached a peak in western Massachusetts in the autumn of 1786 in Shays's Rebellion, which the government finally managed to put down in early 1787.

By that year it was clear something had to be done. The Articles had constructed a government that was simply too weak. A convention finally met in Philadelphia in May of 1787.

It was this convention that eventually replaced the Articles with a new federal government. The Constitution set up not only a strong government but a new kind of national structure. By means of checks and balances, it divided power among three branches of government—executive, legislative, and judicial—so that no one class, interest group, or faction could dominate. The balance of power between large and small states was solved by the two-house legislature; that of representation and how taxes were to be divided, by the three-fifths compromise. And the new federal government had two powers the Confederation Congress had lacked: the power to tax and the power to raise an army. It also had an independent executive (a president), and an independent judiciary.

The new Constitution of the United States was ratified only after a long and difficult campaign in the states, and only after immediate amendment by a Bill of Rights was promised. By June of 1788 nine states had ratified. But Virginia and New York, two large and powerful states, had strong opposition groups. Ratification, especially in New York, came late and by a narrow margin. But by the end of 1788, all except Rhode Island and North Carolina had ratified. The new government, with George Washington as the first president, was ready to go to work.

6

The Federal Era

The new national government faced grave problems. For one thing, it had to create parts of itself. At first there were only two members of the executive branch—the president and vice-president—and no judicial system at all. The government was badly in debt. In the West, Spain claimed a huge portion of United States territory, and the British still occupied forts on American soil. Various Indian tribes regarded most of the western lands as their own. The monarchs of Europe hoped to see the new nation fall apart. A major war broke out in Europe in the wake of the French Revolution, and the United States became involved in bitter battles on the high seas.

President Washington hoped for a spirit of unity in the national government. He dis-

liked political factionalism. But he soon discovered that the American people and their leaders disagreed on such critical matters as the powers of the new federal government, its fiscal policies, and the best way to deal with the war in Europe. Despite Washington's intentions, two political parties had come into existence by the time he left office in 1797: the Federalists and the Republicans. (Though the name was the same, the Republican party of that time was completely different from the modern one of the same name.) No one expected or welcomed the development of a system that has proved to be a basic feature of American political life. A long time passed before Americans came to believe that political parties were a legitimate and useful means of working out their differences on public policy.

THE NEW GOVERNMENT AT WORK

The president and Congress had to establish executive offices and a judicial system. They also had to find ways to raise money for operating expenses and for paying off

the debts inherited from the Confederation government. But they dealt first with amendments to the Constitution, amendments that had been widely demanded (and promised) during the campaign for ratification of the Constitution.

The Bill of Rights

Almost everyone agreed that Congress's first business should be to adopt a Bill of Rights. Even a quick reading of the Bill of Rights gives a good glimpse into the distrust of government that prevailed at the time. These first ten amendments to the Constitution protect freedom of religion, freedom of speech and of the press, the right to assemble peacefully with other persons, and the right to petition the federal government to correct wrongs. They require federal officials to obtain search warrants from a court before searching a person's home. The Bill of Rights also provides for trial by jury in criminal cases and prohibits excessive bail and "cruel and unusual punishments." The Fifth Amendment gives individuals the right not to testify against themselves in court. The Ninth and Tenth amendments limit the powers of the federal government to those specifically named in the Constitution. All other powers were, in a phrase that was both clear and ambiguous, "reserved to the States respectively, or to the people."

The Bill of Rights was ratified by the states in December 1791. Like many provisions of the Constitution, its various provisions have undergone considerable interpretation and reinterpretation by the courts.

The Judiciary

The Judiciary Act of 1789 did a great deal to cement the federal system. The first Congress spelled out the procedure by which federal courts could review—and if necessary declare void—state laws and state-court decisions involving powers and duties that the Constitution delegated to the federal government.

Also in 1789, the system of federal courts was completed by three circuit courts and thirteen district courts. Attached to each district court were United States prosecuting attorneys, as well as marshals and deputies who served as federal police. It was the duty of these marshals to supervise the taking of the first federal census in 1790, as required by the Constitution.

The Executive

The executive had been one of the weakest elements in the old Confederation. Nonetheless, Congress was slow to create executive departments. In the summer of 1789 Congress created a Department of State to manage foreign relations, a War Department, and a Department of the Treasury.

While Congress busied itself with these measures, the president gave his attention to appointments. Washington wanted to surround himself with the best men available, but he had other things in mind as well. He was acutely aware of the thinness of the thread that held the states together and of the need not to offend local people in filling even minor posts.

At the same time, Washington was reluctant to appoint an opponent of the Constitution to any office. He also had in mind sectional considerations, and he gave preference when he could to men he had known personally during the war. He appointed General Henry Knox of Massachusetts, his old chief of artillery and one of the army's most outspoken opponents of the old Congress, as the first secretary of war. He named Edmund Randolph of Virginia, one of his wartime aides-de-camp, as attorney general. The Treasury went to Hamilton, another of his military aides. John Jay, also of New York, had been in charge of foreign affairs for the old Congress and had continued to direct them until 1790. Then Thomas Jefferson of Virginia took over as secretary of state, and Jay became the first chief justice of the Supreme Court.

The Constitution made no provision for a presidential cabinet, but early in his administration Washington established the practice of taking action only on matters that had been referred to him by the secretaries of his three departments and the attorney general. Gradually, he began to consult these men on questions that arose outside their departments. After a crisis in foreign affairs in 1793 arising from the wars of the French Revolution, these meetings became regular. The cabinet thus became a feature of the federal machinery.

Hamilton's Fiscal Program

Hamilton was the driving force behind the solution of the new nation's financial difficulties. His goals were political as well as fiscal. He was determined to win the support of wealthy financiers for the new government by giving them a personal stake in its success. In doing so, however, he aroused great opposition, especially from southerners who were not in a position to benefit from his measures. Yet he was largely successful in solving the financial problems that had so badly weakened the old Confederation government.

On Hamilton's urging, the act creating the Treasury Department gave the secretary the right to advise Congress directly on finance. Near the end of the first session, Congress asked the secretary to prepare financial reports, and Hamilton had his first report, "For the Support of Public Credit," ready in January 1790. Later that year he submitted his report on a national bank, and in 1791 he advised the Second Congress on the value of a mint and on means of fostering manufactures.

Thirty-four years old at this time, Hamilton had been close to great men for more than twelve years. He quickly grasped what he called the executive impulse. Even his enemies in Congress acknowledged "the force of his genius," which sometimes misled the secretary himself into supposing nothing was beyond him.

In his report on the public credit, Hamilton recommended (1) that the foreign debt of almost $12 million be repaid by means of a new bond issue; (2) that the domestic debt, made up of many kinds of Revolutionary securities valued in 1789 at about twenty-five cents on the dollar, be exchanged at its face value, plus back interest, for additional new bonds; and (3) that the remaining state debts be assumed by the federal government and refunded on a similar basis. Congress adopted Hamilton's proposal on the foreign debt with little debate. His proposal on the domestic debt found much tougher going. This was largely because his friends, a number of them in Congress and in the treasury itself, had been told about the proposal in advance and were known to have bought up most of the depressed securities, certain they would rise in price. Reports of the activities of this "corrupt squadron" scandalized Madison and his southern followers in Congress, and some northern Federalists as well.

As an alternative to Hamilton's plan, Madison and his followers proposed to discriminate between the original holders of the securities representing the domestic debt and those who purchased them later on speculation. The latter, they held, should not be permitted to profit at the patriotic public's expense. "Discrimination," however, proved too difficult to work out. Madison's hastily written bill failed, and Hamilton's plan won.

The South proved even more hostile

to Hamilton's proposal for federal assumption of the outstanding state debts. Georgia, for example, had few such debts, and Virginia had paid off most of hers. Such states resisted being taxed under federal authority simply for the benefit of northern states such as Massachusetts, whose entire debt was still outstanding. When assumption came up for vote in April 1790, southerners, again led by Madison, helped defeat it by a narrow margin. By taking the lead of the opposition, Madison emphasized his differences with Washington's administration but at the same time strengthened his political position.

Yet like Hamilton and the speculators, Madison was unwilling to upset the whole funding program and hence the credit of the new nation. Jefferson, recently returned from France to take up his duties as secretary of state, agreed. Recognizing that Hamilton was committed to assumption, the two Virginia leaders yielded in exchange for objectives of their own.

At the same time the funding program was being disputed, the subject of the permanent residence of the new government was deeply disturbing Congress. New York City and Philadelphia both wanted it. So, after numerous failures to reverse the House vote on assumption, Hamilton at last proposed to Madison and Jefferson that in exchange for their support of the whole funding program he would undertake to swing enough northern votes behind the proposition to locate the permanent capital in the South. The deal was made. Philadelphia would be the temporary capital for ten years. In the meantime, the commissioners for development of the new "federal city" announced that the capital would be named for the first president.

Hamilton made two more financial proposals—and again stirred factional and sectional strife. First, he called for a Bank of the United States, modeled explicitly on the Bank of England. One-fifth of the capital was to be subscribed by the government, the rest by private investors. Hamilton argued that a commercial bank was needed to supply notes that would serve as currency in business transactions. The bank would also assist the government by lending it money to meet its short-term obligations and by serving as a depository for government funds. Finally, by providing personal loans, the bank would make it easier for individuals to pay their taxes.

"This plan for a national bank," objected Representative James Jackson of Georgia, "is calculated to benefit a small part of the United States, the mercantilist interests only; the farmers, the yeomanry, will derive no advantage from it." But Hamilton's bill passed the House because the commercial North was able to outvote the agrarian South. In 1791 the Bank of the United States was chartered for twenty years, with headquarters in Philadelphia. Ultimately eight branches were established in port cities from Boston to New Orleans.

In the House debate, Madison had argued that a national bank would be unconstitutional. The 1787 Convention, he insisted, had expressly rejected the proposition that the federal government be empowered to charter companies. When the bank bill was sent to Washington, the president asked Jefferson and Hamilton for their opinions on its constitutionality. Jefferson supported Madison, but Hamilton argued that since the government had been delegated the power to regulate currency, it had the *implied power* to establish a bank in order to issue currency. Washington rejected Jefferson and Madison's *strict interpretation* of the Constitution in favor of Hamilton's *broad interpretation*, but his decision was based more on instinct than on constitutional reasoning.

Signs of Crisis

Hamilton's second proposal for raising money was a tax on various commodities, including distilled liquors. It was enacted quietly in 1791, but it soon raised a storm that tested the intentions and vigor of the inexperienced new government.

Opposition to the taxes was especially strong in the West, where whiskey was the most easily transported grain product. The most violent resistance to Hamilton's measure occurred in western Pennsylvania, where government efforts to collect the taxes were resisted with gunfire. Here, as on other frontiers not close to water transportation, whiskey was regarded as an important means of raising cash. It was also thought of as a personal right and necessity.

In 1794, the federal court in Philadelphia issued writs against seventy-five western-Pennsylvania distillers, who would have to travel across the state to answer them in Philadelphia. When federal marshals came west with the writs, a mob attacked them. Hamilton interpreted the uprising against federal collectors as a rebellion against the United States, and he prevailed upon Washington to order 13,000 militiamen to crush the farmers. Characteristically, Hamilton rode west with the troops. Although they found no organized opposition, the militia rounded up about a hundred men. Two were later convicted of treason and sentenced to death, but Washington eventually pardoned them.

In suppressing the Whiskey Insurrection Hamilton felt he had shown European capitalists, who were active investors in the government's new securities, that the Republic could force its free citizens to pay taxes. But frontiersmen grew angry. Wash-

ington's administration made no more progress than the old Confederation in getting Spain to open the Mississippi in the Southwest or in dislodging Britain from the Northwest Territory and the Great Lakes. In the Northwest, Indians solidly defeated U.S. military forces in 1790 and 1791. Finally, however, in the Battle of Fallen Timbers in 1794, General "Mad Anthony" Wayne defeated a major group of Indians in the Northwest Territory. The next year, by the Treaty of Fort Greenville, these tribes agreed to give up most of their lands in what is now Ohio.

PARTY POLITICS

We cannot assign specific dates to the beginnings of political parties in the United States. During the colonial period, factions came and went with little continuity. In the new government Washington regarded factions as unpatriotic, and he was appalled to see opponents of his administration develop into a well-organized, permanent political party. He was unaware of his own contribution to this process, even as he became increasingly influenced by Hamilton. As Jefferson and Madison organized their political forces, he grew more and more upset. He could not know it, but a strange four-handed game was shaping the course of the nation's politics.

Four Politicians

It was their differing visions of the proper future for the new country that separated Hamilton from Madison and Jefferson. Hamilton envisioned a powerful nation resting on a balanced economy of agriculture, trade, finance, and manufacturing. Agriculture, he thought, needed no special encouragement.

Jefferson, on the other hand, thought farmers would always be the chief supporters of the Republic and the eternal guardians of public virtue. More than Madison, he distrusted the world of cities, commerce, and finance. He thought of them as breeding grounds for moral and political corruption. Born to the life of a slaveholding Virginia country gentleman, Jefferson felt a deep attachment to the land and had an unquestioning trust in the common people who tilled it. He was neither the first nor the last public person to hate privilege because he had it himself.

Madison concentrated on the art and practice of politics. Deeply committed to balance and moderation, he thrived on the give and take of political horse trading. But now he saw his own goal of strengthening the national government being pushed too far by Hamilton's program.

For his part, Washington remained deeply attached to country and to duty. Convinced that his proper role was to stand at the head of the new nation, he felt he should take no part in quarreling over details of public policy. Although he was one of the wealthiest planters in the South, he never shared Jefferson's distrust of commercial interests. Unfamiliar with complicated fiscal matters, he was happy to leave them to Hamilton. He tried evenhandedly to soothe the mounting hostility between Hamilton and Jefferson in the cabinet. He intervened more in foreign than in domestic affairs because he thought himself obligated and more competent to do so. When Hamilton assured him that no congressmen were speculating in government securities, Washington believed him. The aging general was slow to recognize that some men could place their own interests above the government's.

Organizing

As tension mounted over Hamilton's financial program in 1791–92, Madison and Jefferson set out to gain support for their position in the country at large as well as in Congress. They toured several New England

George Washington and his family. (John Carter Brown Library, Brown University)

states and especially New York to express their views to political leaders there. Jefferson and Madison also backed a new newspaper, the *National Gazette,* as a vehicle for criticizing Hamilton's policies. Madison wrote several articles for it in which he referred to those who backed his views as "the Republican party."

Hamilton was not a man to sit by while his opponents organized. He and his allies, taking the name Federalists, backed a newspaper of their own. Like the Republicans, the Federalists began organizing local clubs of supporters. The Federalists had several important advantages. They had a well-thought-out, positive program. The great majority of newspaper editors and clergy supported Federalist ideas, and so did a majority of the wealthy. In addition, Federalists in government were able to reward party workers with jobs.

By the time of the 1792 national election, the Republicans were not yet well enough organized to run a candidate for president. It would have been futile to do so anyway, for Washington had reluctantly agreed to serve again. Yet the election returns showed that the Republicans were a new force in American politics. During the next few years, voting in Congress did not take place according to firm party lines. By 1795, however, developments in foreign affairs had clarified and deepened the division into two national political parties.

FOREIGN AFFAIRS UNDER WASHINGTON

During Washington's first administration, party lines had been drawn over financial issues. In his second administration, problems of foreign policy dominated. The French Revolution, which began just a few weeks after Washington first took office in 1789, was the source of most of the trouble.

Citizen Genêt

At first, most Americans welcomed the French Revolution. They felt their own revolutionary principles were spreading to Europe. Within a year, however, the Hamiltonians had aligned themselves against the French Revolution; the Jeffersonians still praised it. The execution of Louis XVI in January 1793 alarmed American conservatives about excessive democracy. In the meantime, the French had gone to war in 1792 against the monarchs on the Continent, who had combined to end the threat of republicanism.

It was not long before the conflict of opinion was deepened by issues of foreign policy. The old treaty of 1778 with France provided that the United States must defend the French West Indies in case of attack upon France and that American ports must receive enemy ships captured at sea by French vessels. Late in 1792, the revolutionaries ruling France sent "Citizen" Edmond Genêt to the United States to see that the treaty obligations were performed. Genêt had other instructions as well. He was to organize expeditions from the American Southwest to detach Louisiana and Florida from Spain and to commission American privateers to prey on British shipping. He began to carry out these instructions immediately upon landing in Charleston, South Carolina, in April 1793, not even waiting to present his credentials to the United States government in Philadelphia. Genêt had one more project: to organize revolutionary clubs in America that would advance the cause of "liberty, equality, and fraternity"—just when Jefferson had begun to sponsor Republican political clubs of his own.

By the time Genêt reached Philadelphia, Washington had consulted with Jefferson and Hamilton and issued his Neutrality Proclamation of April 22, 1793. This document made it clear that the United States would not participate in the French wars. Jefferson had argued that since only Congress could declare war, only Congress could proclaim neutrality, and that a presidential proclamation was unconstitutional. Hamilton held that the French treaty had died with the French king, and in any case that neutrality was the only feasible policy for so weak a nation. Having made his constitutional argument, Jefferson backed off, and Washington's proclamation followed.

Genêt eventually overstepped himself, and the president and the cabinet unanimously demanded his recall. Yet the effects of his mission were considerable. Jefferson's early sympathy with Genêt led the president to be very suspicious of his secretary of state and the new Republican grass-roots clubs. "It is not the cause of France, nor I believe of liberty, which they regard," he wrote in October 1793, but only the "disgrace" of the new nation under Federalist rule. At the end of that year, after months of indecision, Washington accepted Jefferson's resignation from the cabinet.

Neutrality: Profits and Problems

The war in Europe opened the way for a shipping boom in the neutral nations. As a leading maritime nation, the United States was among the greatest gainers. Since the French had only a small fleet and one that was vulnerable to British attack, they desperately needed assistance from the neutrals. Early in the war, France at last surrendered its monopoly of the French West Indian trade and opened its islands' ports to American shipping.

The British retaliated. In 1793 they announced that all ships sailing to or from the French colonies would be subject to British seizure. American vessels had swarmed into the Caribbean. The British seized about 300 United States ships, abused their passengers, and forced many of their sailors into the British navy.

Even so, American trade thrived. Many ships were captured, but many more slipped through. These losses served as an additional stimulus to the shipbuilding industry. By 1794, however, the British had become so brazen that even Federalists expected war. The United States insisted that "neutral ships made neutral goods," but the British enforced their self-proclaimed right to search for enemy supplies anywhere on any ship.

Painful as Federalist shippers found these British measures, the Republicans were the ones who made the most of them, calling them insults to the American flag. Remembering how effective commercial retaliation had been against the British in the great days of the Revolution, the Republicans demanded an embargo in order to keep British ships out of American ports and American ships off the seas, where they were subject to British seizure.

The British in Canada chose this moment to encourage Indians to raid the Ohio country, where thousands of white American farmers were settling. The British also made clear that they still had no intention of giving up their armed posts on American territory, which were aiding the Indians. Public opinion pushed the embargo through Congress early in 1794, but it lasted only three months.

Jay's Treaty

The Federalists decided to try to gain more concessions through diplomacy. In 1794 Washington sent John Jay to Britain with instructions to get the British to surrender their military posts in the Northwest, to pay for American ships that had been captured illegally, and to respect the American position on the rights and privileges of neutrals. Jay was also to negotiate the best commercial treaty he could. If he could not get the British to agree on all these points, he was to try to get the countries of northern Europe to agree with the United States to jointly enforce neutral rights.

By the terms of the treaty Jay brought back, the British agreed again to evacuate their Northwest posts. By 1796 they had done so, but Jay had had to barter away a great deal in return. The British could still carry on the fur trade on the American side of the Canadian border with Indians hostile to advancing American settlement. This concession almost canceled out the surrender of the posts, and it angered western Americans. The issue of British payment for captured ships was left to a future joint commission, which would determine what, if anything, was owed. On the rights of neutrals, Jay failed altogether. His efforts to gain commercial concessions were also unsuccessful.

Jay's Treaty was so unsatisfactory that Washington hesitated a long time before sending it to the Senate. The Senate, in turn, made every effort to hide its terms from the people. But there were leaks. On June 25, 1795, the Senate ratified the treaty by the slenderest possible two-thirds majority. The public outcry was extraordinary. In the months following, "Sir John Jay" was hanged in effigy throughout the country. One person chalked up in large letters on a Boston street wall, "DAMN JOHN JAY! DAMN EVERY ONE WHO WON'T DAMN JOHN JAY!! DAMN EVERY ONE WHO WON'T SIT UP ALL NIGHT DAMNING JOHN JAY!!!"

When Congress met in December 1795, the question was asked whether the House of Representatives, by failing to vote appropriations required under the agreement, could in effect reject the treaty, even though the Senate had accepted it. The House voted 57 to 35 that it had the constitutional right to reject treaties by withholding funds, but it went on to approve the appropriations by a vote of 51 to 48.

Pinckney's Treaty

In June 1795, while the Senate was considering Jay's Treaty, Spain made peace with the revolutionary government in France. This step made Spain fearful of British reprisals, and when Britain and America concluded Jay's Treaty, Spain became fearful of attacks from American frontiersmen. Spain's fears for its empire grew, and the Spanish decided to try to win American friendship. After several proposals failed, the American ambassador, Thomas Pinckney, negotiated a treaty.

Pinckney's Treaty, signed by the Spanish in 1795, was approved unanimously by the United States Senate in 1796. This agreement settled the northern boundary of Florida at the latitude of thirty-one degrees. Much more important, Spain opened the Mississippi "in its whole length from its source to the ocean" to American traffic and allowed Americans to use the port of New Orleans for three years, after which the arrangement could be renewed.

The Election of 1796

The party strife Washington hated was nearing its peak when he retired. Debate in the House over Jay's Treaty had continued well into 1796, and Washington's decision not to run for a third term intensified the conflict by opening up the highest office to the rising political machines. The Federalists brought out a ticket of John Adams of New England and Pinckney of South Carolina. Adams won with seventy-one votes. Jefferson, with sixty-eight votes, was second in the balloting and, according to the constitutional arrangement of that time, thereby defeated Pinckney for the vice-presidency.

THE ADAMS ADMINISTRATION

Americans now take the transition from one presidential administration to another as a matter of course. In 1796 the public was experiencing the first transfer of presidential power from one man to another. Anxiety was deepened by the fact that Washington was about to retire.

Foreign Policy

No statesman in the United States had written more than John Adams about human nature. But Jefferson shrewdly observed that in practice Adams was "a bad calculator" of the "motives of men." He made the mistake of retaining in his cabinet second-rate Hamiltonians. Worse, by being absent frequently from his post, Adams gave these Hamiltonians free rein. In his retirement, Adams counted as one of his major accomplishments his keeping the United States at peace with France, as Washington had. Hamilton's anti-French friends in Adams's virtually independent cabinet, however, carried the administration to the brink of all-out hostilities.

The French took offense at Jay's Treaty. Interpreting it as a British diplomatic victory, they intensified their attacks on American ships bound for British ports and captured about 300 American vessels.

Adams decided to send a three-man mission to Paris to persuade the French to end their raids on American shipping. When Talleyrand, foreign minister of France, refused to negotiate unless the Americans gave a bribe of $250,000 to three subordi-

nates, the mission collapsed. In their reports home, the American envoys referred to Talleyrand's three subordinates as X, Y, and Z.

An uproar broke out within both parties over the so-called XYZ dispatches. Congress voted millions for the expansion of the army and navy in 1798 and 1799. It also created a separate Navy Department and repealed all treaties with France.

In 1798 and 1799, an undeclared naval war raged with France. American ships, operating mainly in the Caribbean, took almost a hundred French vessels and suffered serious losses themselves. But Adams refused to ask Congress to make an official declaration of war.

The Alien and Sedition Acts

At the time of Adams's election, Madison had written to Jefferson, "You know the temper of Mr. A. better than I do, but I have always conceived it to be rather a ticklish one." One thing Adams became ticklish about was the Republican taunt that he was "president by three votes." Other attacks caused him to lash back at his opponents. Many of his most vocal critics were recent immigrants, including Albert Gallatin, the Swiss who became Republican leader of the House when Madison retired. Adams suspected a number of recently arrived French intellectuals of engaging in espionage. He was also troubled by a number of Irish immigrants who, defeated in their fight for Irish freedom, had brought to the United States their hatred of England.

Adams might easily have gotten over his anger if some extremists in his party had not pushed through Congress in 1798 four laws known as the Alien and Sedition Acts.

The first was a Naturalization Act that raised the residence requirement for American citizenship from five to fourteen years. The second, the Alien Act, empowered the president to order any alien from the country and to imprison any who refused to go. The third, the Alien Enemies Act, permitted the president to jail enemy aliens in wartime. No arrests were made under either alien act, but they did frighten hundreds of foreigners from the country. The fourth measure was the Sedition Act. It provided for severe fines and jail penalties for anyone speaking or writing against the government.

A number of Republican editors were actually jailed, and some Republican papers were shut down. The trials were travesties of justice dominated by judges who saw treason everywhere. Juries were hand-picked by Federalist United States marshals.

Madison called the Sedition Act "a monster." He and Jefferson both recognized it as the beginning of the Federalist campaign for the election of 1800. They moved quickly to a broad attack on the whole Federalist philosophy. Their offensive took the form of a series of resolutions in the legislatures of Kentucky (which had become a state in 1792) and Virginia in 1798. The resolutions were then circulated among the other states.

Both sets of resolutions attacked the broad interpretation of the Constitution and developed a state-rights position. In Jefferson's words, "the several states composing the United States of America, are not united on the principle of unlimited submission to their general government." Madison, in the Virginia Resolutions, said that the states together might "interpose" to stop the exercise of unauthorized federal powers. Jefferson went further: he held that the legislature of each state had this right. The Kentucky Resolutions held that the states, as parties to the "compact," had the right to declare what measures went beyond their agreement and were "unauthoritative, void, and of no force," and to decide what remedies were appropriate.

No interpretations of the intent or action of the Great Convention of 1787 could have been more far-fetched than these resolutions. But in pushing their argument this far, Madison and Jefferson at least had a liberalizing goal that was not part of later states'-rights movements.

Federalists in several northern states passed resolutions denouncing Virginia and Kentucky for misinterpreting the nature of the Constitution. They argued that the Constitution was much more than an agreement among independent states and that only the federal courts could decide whether actions of the other two branches violated it. So the Virginia and Kentucky Resolutions had little effect at the time.

The Election of 1800

The XYZ affair and other actions by France had cost the Republicans some strength in the country, but their prospects for the presidential campaign of 1800 were helped by the sharp split in the Federalist ranks between the Adams men and the Hamiltonians. For the campaign of 1800, the Republicans named Jefferson and Aaron Burr of New York as their candidates. The Federalists offered a ticket of Adams and Charles C. Pinckney. The electoral college voted sixty-five for Adams and sixty-four for Pinckney; Jefferson and Burr each received seventy-three votes.

The Republicans had won, but they faced an unexpected difficulty because of the tie between their candidates for president and vice-president. According to the Constitution, the House would have to decide between the two. There the voting was to be by states, and nine states (out of the sixteen) were needed to win. The balloting went on for a week. The deadlock was broken on the thirty-sixth ballot. A few Federalist congressmen took their state out of

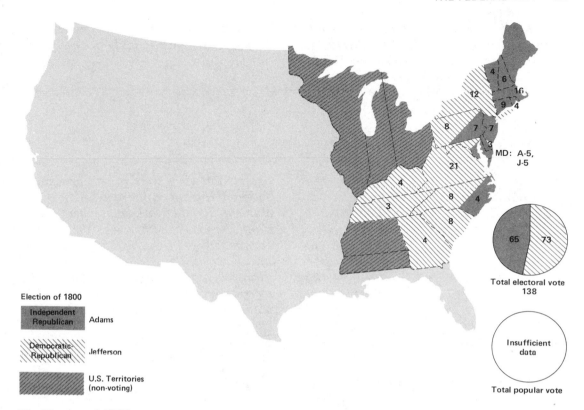

Election of 1800

Independent Republican — Adams

Democratic Republican — Jefferson

U.S. Territories (non-voting)

MD: A-5, J-5

65 | 73

Total electoral vote 138

Insufficient data

Total popular vote

The Election of 1800

Burr's camp by voting blanks. The next Congress put an end to this problem by writing the Twelfth Amendment, ratified by the states in 1804.

Despite the viciousness of the election campaign, the transfer of power from the Federalists to the Republicans was accomplished peaceably. Americans were beginning to realize that an organized political opposition had to be permitted its own free voice and hopes for power. But although the Republicans captured the presidency and control of both the House and the Senate, the country's first great shift in political power was not quite complete. Just before adjourning in March 1801, the retiring Federalist Congress gave Adams a new judiciary act, which created a whole new group of judges. Adams put Federalist sympathizers in these lifetime jobs and other new judicial posts. Most important, he named John Marshall chief justice of the Supreme Court.

Adams was the last Federalist president. After him, as the country became more Republican and expansive, his party became more sectional and narrow. Yet for more than thirty years of Republican rule, the new chief justice handed down Federalist, nationalist interpretations of the law despite continuous crises generated by wars in Europe and an expanding economy.

SUGGESTED READINGS

J.C. Miller, *The Federalist Era, 1789-1800* (1960). L.S. Kaplan, *Colonies into Nation: American Diplomacy, 1763-1801* (1972).

R.H. Kohn, *Eagle and Sword: The Federalists and the Creation of the Military Establishment in America, 1783-1802* (1975). J.E. Cook, *Alexander Hamilton* (1982).

L.W. Levy, *Legacy of Suppression: Freedom of Speech and Press in Early American History* (1960).

SUMMARY

The new Constitution described the United States government; now its leaders had to fill in the framework and make it work. The first item on the new Congress's agenda was passage of a federal Bill of Rights—the first ten amendments to the Constitution. They were ratified by the states late in 1791. The Judiciary Act of 1789 set up the federal court system and spelled out its powers. The building of the executive branch was begun with three departments—State, War, and Treasury.

Congress, meanwhile, turned to the urgent money problems that caused so much trouble under the Articles, and passed the first money-raising law, a tariff. Hamilton proposed a variety of plans for dealing with the public debt and for tying the fate of the new nation to the fortunes of the merchants and the wealthy, whom he saw as its most important citizens. He succeeded in establishing a national bank modeled on the Bank of England.

Hamilton tried taxing liquor, which resulted in the so-called Whiskey Rebellion in western Pennsylvania in 1794. The new government's inability to deal immediately and firmly with the Indians, the British, and the Spanish on the frontiers also added to its troubles.

All these controversies helped to build factions, and eventually political parties. Four men—Hamilton, Madison, Jefferson, and Washington—were the country's leading figures. But they were not in agreement, and from their opposing views of how government should work and where power should reside—whether with the national government or with the states—came political parties. The Federalists, led by Hamilton, favored a strong, wealthy nation led by commercial and financial interests. The Republicans, led by Jefferson and Madison, trusted the farmer and the common people far more than they did the urban merchant. Washington was a patriot, but one firmly against parties and factionalism. As president, he saw it as his duty not to take sides.

Washington's agreeing to serve for a second term meant there was no presidential contest in 1792. But the parties were already active in the vice-presidential race and would run presidential candidates in 1796.

Washington's second term was occupied with foreign affairs, mostly because of the French Revolution. It had begun in 1789, but within a few years its effects spread beyond the French borders and caused war between England and France. The subversive activities of Citizen Genêt, the problem of neutrality on the seas, and the unpopularity of the treaty John Jay negotiated with the British in 1794 all caused discontent in the United States. Thomas Pinckney's treaty with Spain in 1795 had a better reception.

The election of 1796, the first peaceful transfer of power, was won by the Federalist John Adams. Much of his attention was devoted to avoiding war with France and to battling political enemies at home. It was also in his administration that Congress passed the first laws abridging individual freedoms—the Alien and Sedition Acts. The Republican reaction to these measures was sharp. Madison and Jefferson, through the Virginia and Kentucky Resolutions, began a debate over states' rights and federal power that would become part of American politics for many years.

With the Republican capture of the presidency in 1800, the Federalist party faded. But before Adams left office, he appointed a new chief justice of the Supreme Court, John Marshall. The decisions of this Federalist in favor of a broad, nationalist interpretation of the Constitution were to have a permanent influence on the new nation.

7

The Jeffersonian Era

Of all the great figures among the Founding Fathers, Thomas Jefferson was both the most approachable and the most aloof. He dressed casually and informally, even on solemn public occasions. "The people," writes one of Jefferson's biographers, "could have quite taken him to their hearts if they had not felt, as every one felt in his presence, that he was always graciously but firmly holding them off."

Thomas Jefferson called the Republican victory that brought him to office "the revolution of 1800." Few historians today would agree with Jefferson. His election was followed by change, but not as much as he thought or would have liked. Jefferson himself felt that the great majority of Federalists had been led astray by a few wealthy, power-hungry persons, and he wanted to bring them to his own party. He was somewhat successful, for Federalists never again controlled the presidency. Yet they continued for at least fifteen years to be an active political party, and they continued to control the courts.

Jefferson and his hand-picked successors, James Madison and James Monroe, wanted to avoid further involvement in European conflicts. Jefferson's eyes were on America's "continental destiny," a phrase he used even though the rest of the continent was still claimed by European powers and occupied by Indians. As things turned out, Jefferson doubled the size of the United States. But then James Madison allowed the country to drift into involvement in European wars.

JEFFERSON IN POWER

The new president immediately set out to correct what he regarded as the injustices of the previous administration. He also cut the federal budget. He struggled against Federalists in the judiciary, but with very little success. His greatest interest, however, was more positive. Most of the North American continent, he was convinced, was destined to fall into the hands of the young Republic. He gave destiny a helping hand by sending out explorers and by approving the purchase of a territory as large as the existing states.

Cleaning House

The new administration seemed much different from the old Federalist ones. Jefferson's inauguration was the first to take place in the new "federal city" on the Potomac. Grand plans had been made for the city. In 1801, however, it was anything but imposing. The streets were ruts of dust or mud. Pennsylvania Avenue ran from the Capitol through a swamp. Most of the public buildings were still under construction. The rest of the city consisted of one stationery shop, one grocer, one shoemaker, one printer, one washerwoman's shop, one tailor shop, one dry-goods shop, and one oyster house. Elected and appointed officials lived in seven or eight crammed boardinghouses. Members of Congress spent as little time as possible in Washington. Philadelphia had been far more attractive, a real city with paved and lighted streets, established taverns, and even a theater.

Upon taking office, Jefferson and the Republicans immediately set about to nullify the Alien and Sedition Acts. Since these laws were due to expire within a few months, the only positive action needed was Congress's changing the period of naturalization back from fourteen to five years. As a matter of personal and symbolic justice, Jefferson pardoned the men convicted under the Sedition Act and had their fines returned with interest.

Jefferson's first appointment to his cabinet indirectly showed how important Washington's example had been. He appointed Republicans, men who basically agreed with him, but kept a careful eye on geographical balance. James Madison was named secretary of state and Albert Gallatin secretary of the treasury.

The new administration reduced the size of the army, stopped the scheduled expansion of the navy, shrank the diplomatic corps, and cut expenses on government social functions. Such reductions were easier then than they would be today, for the federal bureaucracy was tiny. When Jefferson took office, the State Department had nine employees. Jefferson wanted to achieve a simple style appropriate for a republic.

Struggles with the Judiciary

Jefferson was particularly opposed to the judicial appointments that Adams and the Federalists had slipped through at the last moment. He persuaded Congress to pass another Judiciary Act (1802), which reduced the number of federal judgeships. This was the opening gun of Jefferson's war on the Federalist judiciary.

A minor incident in this struggle was transformed into a major constitutional case by Chief Justice John Marshall. Known as *Marbury* v. *Madison* (1803), the case arose out of Adams's last-minute appointment of William Marbury as a federal justice of the peace. Marbury's commission was signed so late that it could not be delivered to him before Jefferson took office. Madison then refused to deliver it. (In those days the secretary of state had certain domestic duties as well as foreign affairs.) Marbury asked the Supreme Court to order Madison to hand it over. The Court, by the Judiciary Act of 1789, had the power to do as Marbury asked. But Marshall refused to use it. He held that Marbury, despite the Judiciary Act, had no case at all.

The Constitution, Marshall argued, stated explicitly in what actions the Supreme Court had original jurisdiction, and Marbury's complaint was not among them. Only an amendment to the Constitution could extend the Court's jurisdiction to it. That being so, Marshall continued, the provision in the Judiciary Act of 1789 that granted the Supreme Court the authority to issue writs such as Marbury asked for was unconstitutional.

The Constitution, Marshall said, was law, to be enforced by courts. It was, moreover, the supreme law, to which even federal legislation must conform. In conflicts over the meaning of the Constitution, "it is emphatically the province and duty of the judicial department—and not of the states or the legislature—to say what the law is." Thus Marshall started a practice now widely accepted—judicial review.

Marbury v. *Madison* was the first Supreme Court decision to nullify a federal statute. Since it made the entire Republican legislative program vulnerable to Federalist judges who could not be removed except for proven misconduct, Jefferson lost little time in opening war on them. The legislative check to the judiciary, he said, was the power of impeachment. Republicans in the House began looking for vulnerable federal judges to bring to trial in the Senate, as the Constitution provided. Their most conspicuous victim was Supreme Court Justice Samuel Chase, a man of brilliant mind and vicious tongue who had given anti-Republican lectures to juries in trials under the Sedition Act. The House impeached Chase in 1805, but he escaped conviction in the Senate. This failure convinced the Republicans that a better policy would be to look to the growing popular approval of their program to bring the courts into closer harmony with the election returns.

Jefferson and the West

In 1801, though other Europeans were not challenging the Americans' right to settle the region west to the Mississippi, that land

was not vacant, for Indians had lived there for centuries and continued to do so. Over the next forty years, however, they would be systematically evicted from their homelands through government "treaties" and outright annihilation.

In order to encourage white settlement of the "public lands," Congress in 1796 and 1800 had lowered both the minimum acreage a pioneer had to buy and the cash he had to put down. In 1804 Jefferson got Congress to reduce these requirements further: for a down payment of only eighty dollars, a man could get title to a quarter section of 160 acres. These measures speeded settlement of the Northwest Territory, where Ohio, admitted to the Union in 1803, was the first state to be formed.

Jefferson also tried to promote settlement in the Southwest, where conflicting state and federal claims involving huge tracts of land near the Yazoo River in present-day Mississippi had been blocking development since 1789. Jefferson's entry into the conflict in 1803 on behalf of the federal government resulted in splitting off from Republican forces in Congress certain die-hard states'-rights men led by John Randolph of Virginia. These men pointedly reminded Jefferson of his own philosophy stated in the Kentucky Resolutions of 1798. Not until Randolph was temporarily missing from the House in 1814 could Congress take the steps needed to close the Yazoo controversy. Within five years, Alabama and Mississippi, both carved from disputed territory, were admitted as states.

Jefferson had far larger plans for the West. He looked, as he said, "to distant times, when our rapid multiplication will. . . cover the whole northern, if not the southern, continent, with a people speaking the same language" and "governed . . . by similar laws." Early in 1803, Jefferson got

Congress to make a secret appropriation with which he sent Meriwether Lewis and William Clark on an expedition to the Pacific Northwest coast. By 1806 Lewis and Clark had successfully completed their mission. They gathered a great deal of scientific data and demonstrated that the Pacific Coast region could be reached by land. They also established an American claim to the vaguely defined Oregon Country. Jefferson sent two other expeditions, both led by Zebulon Pike, to find the source of the Mississippi River and to explore the Southwest. Pike's second expedition went through territory that clearly belonged to Spain.

The Louisiana Purchase

Lewis and Clark had at first supposed that they too would be traveling through foreign territory. But before they left, an extraordinary series of events put much of the middle of the continent in American hands.

Spain held the vast Louisiana Territory—or New Orleans, as the whole area was often called—from 1762 to 1800. "Till our population can be sufficiently advanced [in numbers] to gain it from them piece by piece," Jefferson thought, it could not "be in better hands." The president grew concerned when he learned that Napoleon, by secret treaty in October 1800, had retaken Louisiana for France. Napoleon intended to develop Louisiana into a breadbasket for the French West Indies. But in Haiti, the western part of the island of Hispaniola, a massive slave insurrection led by the black general Toussaint L'Ouverture threatened to spread and ruin Napoleon's vision of a new American empire. Once Napoleon had conquered much of Europe, he sent some 20,000 men to crush Toussaint and then to occupy the port of New Orleans. But his

campaign in Haiti failed when his troops lost to the rebellious blacks and to tropical diseases.

When Jefferson first learned of the treaty by which Napoleon had reacquired Louisiana he said, "There is on the globe one single spot, the possessor of which is our natural and habitual enemy. It is New Orleans, through which the produce of three-eighths of our territory must pass to market, and from its fertility it will ere long yield more than half our whole produce and contain more than half of our inhabitants." Spain, feeble, pacific, and cooperative, he added, "might have retained it quietly for years. [But] France placing herself in that door assumes to us the attitude of defiance."

The extent of this defiance became clear in October 1802, when the president learned that the Spanish officer still in charge at the port of New Orleans had been instructed by France to close it once more to Americans. To quiet war talk in the West, Jefferson sent James Monroe to France in March 1803 with instructions to buy the territory around the port of New Orleans, and also Florida, which he suspected France might also have taken from Spain.

By the time Monroe reached Paris, defeat in Haiti had completely changed Napoleon's mind about a new American empire, and he had already made a staggering offer to the American minister in Paris: he would sell the entire Louisiana Territory for a mere $15 million. On April 30, 1803, the two Americans closed the deal that doubled their country's territory.

The Constitution did not give the federal government the power to purchase territory. But Jefferson swallowed his strict-constructionist reservations and sent the purchase treaty to the Senate, which ratified it in November 1803. The House then appropriated the money for this "noble bargain." Florida was not included in the deal, Spain never having yielded it to France. But Jefferson was not discouraged. "If we push them strongly with one hand, holding out a price in the other," he said, "We shall certainly obtain the Floridas, and all in good time."

The method, if not the results, of the Louisiana Purchase troubled the Randolph Republicans in the South. But the strongest reaction came from Federalists in New England, who expected their influence in the nation to be destroyed by the acquisition of this enormous new territory. So distraught were some northerners that they proposed to leave the Union. Desperate, they turned for help to Aaron Burr, Jefferson's alienated vice-president, who was running for governor of New York. If victorious, Burr was to take his state into a new northern confederation with New England and thereby escape from the "Virginia dynasty." Hamilton helped defeat Burr, and the projected confederation collapsed. Embittered by this and older offenses, real and imaginary, Burr challenged Hamilton to a duel on July 11, 1804, in which Hamilton was killed.

Like many other discredited Americans, Burr took refuge in the West, where he was allegedly involved in plots to detach Louisiana from the United States and to make war on Spain over Florida and Mexico. Eventually cornered by Jefferson, Burr was tried on both treason and high-misdemeanor charges arising from these activities but acquitted on both after trials famous in American criminal-court annals.

Snared in Europe's Wars

The schemes of Burr's Yankee conspirators so weakened the Federalist party, even in New England, that in the presidential election of 1804 Jefferson carried every state but Connecticut and Delaware. Within a year of his inauguration in March 1805, however, the country was plunged so deeply into the storm of the Napoleonic wars that Jefferson found himself "panting for retirement."

Napoleon's military victory at Austerlitz in 1805 had given France control of much of the European continent, and Nelson's naval victory at Trafalgar the same year had given Britain control of the seas. This "war between the lion and the whale" brought disaster for neutral ships, especially those of the United States. The dominant British fleet was the worst offender.

Between 1804 and 1807, hundreds of American ships were confiscated by the British. Americans were much more angered by the impressment of American seamen. The much expanded British navy was always short of men, and it was British policy that anyone who had ever been a subject of His Majesty was subject to forced service aboard any of His Majesty's naval vessels. This brutal form of what we would call the draft was in fact the normal manner in which most nations manned their naval fleets. Moreover, there were many British subjects sailing aboard United States vessels, attracted by higher pay and less brutal discipline. Given these circumstances, British officers were not overly careful in checking citizenship papers when boarding an American merchantman in search of "British deserters" with whom to fill their undermanned ships.

There was bound to be an international incident. In June 1807, the newly launched U.S. frigate *Chesapeake* was cruising just outside the three-mile limit of Virginia. When H.M.S. *Leopard* ordered her to heave to and permit search for a named deserter, *Chesapeake*'s captain refused. *Leopard* opened fire. *Chesapeake*, her new guns badly mounted and her decks cluttered with as yet undistributed gear, suffered twenty-one casualties before being boarded by *Leopard*'s officers. They found their deserter and also took three Americans who had served in the British navy.

To most Americans, this attack meant war. But the president was desperate to preserve his domestic triumphs, especially the reduction in the national debt and in its tax burden on the people—gains that war was certain to reverse. Accordingly he tried "peaceful coercion." Congress voted this policy on December 27, when it adopted the Embargo Act, which stopped Americans from shipping in or out of the country. By keeping American vessels entirely off the high seas, this act, according to the president, would end incidents that might lead to war. If the warring powers of Europe were deprived of American goods and ships, he thought, they would be forced to acknowledge the rights of America and other neutrals.

The Embargo Act brought ruin not to Britain and France but to American commerce and American ports. In spite of ship losses that ran into the hundreds, American commerce had been highly profitable. Under the Embargo Act it came to a standstill and the industries associated with the maritime trade, such as shipbuilding and sailmaking, also shut down.

Fourteen months of this policy, even though they were fourteen months of peace, proved enough even for many Republicans, and on March 1, 1809, three days before Jefferson's retirement, he was forced to sign an act repealing the Embargo. Jefferson's successor was Secretary of State Madison, who easily won the election of 1808 despite a surge in Federalist strength caused by the Embargo.

The War of 1812

Madison proved temperamentally unsuited for the crisis he inherited. "Our President," freshman congressman John C. Calhoun observed during Madison's first term, "has not I fear those commanding talents which are necessary to control those about him." The lack of unity in the administration was aggravated by the sectional controversies the new president inherited. Under Madison these controversies grew so severe that even a foreign war failed to unite the country.

The Urge to War

Driven from the sea by Jefferson's policies, northern businessmen began to take a greater interest in manufacturing after 1807, especially in cotton and in wool. In the South, meanwhile, cotton growing in the uplands, made practicable by Eli Whitney's invention of the cotton gin in 1793, was further stimulated by northern demand for the staple. These changes in the American economy disturbed British industrialists and exporters. In order to maintain their American markets, they began pressing their own government, as Jefferson had hoped they would, for concessions to American carriers.

The British government, however, was far too deeply committed to the destruction of France to yield to such pressure. To quiet discontent at home, London sent emissaries to Washington, but they were given little authority. In 1810 Madison required the British to recall them while he called home the American minister. Meanwhile the French played their own game with Madison and Congress, conceding little and jockeying them early in 1811 into restoring the ban on trading with Britain. New England merchants were furious.

Popular anger about foreign affairs showed in the elections of 1810 and 1811, in which the voters unseated most of the Eleventh Congress. The replacements arriving in Washington in November 1811 included angry young men from the frontiers. They were not much concerned with attacks on American ships except in the sense that these constituted insults to the American flag. These newcomers had their eyes on enlarging American territory at Europe's expense.

Their first disappointment came early in 1812. Two years before, Madison had turned an uprising of American inhabitants in Spanish West Florida into an occasion to annex that region. Now he sent an armed expedition to take weakly defended East Florida. But when Spain threatened war and New England threatened secession if war came, Madison recalled the expedition. Southwestern Americans thought this was treachery.

Events were even more ominous on the frontier in the Ohio and Mississippi valleys. Between 1801 and 1810, the Indians had been tricked by treaties they did not understand into giving away more than a hundred million acres of prime land to the United States. Soon they were driven off their old lands.

In 1811, the great Shawnee chief Tecumseh attempted to organize an alliance among Indian tribes in this enormous area. His goal was to hold the Ohio River as a permanent border against whites. Governor William Henry Harrison, one of the harshest negotiators of Indian treaties, attacked Tecumseh's headquarters at Tippecanoe while the Shawnee chief was away mobilizing other tribes. Finding the ruins on his return, Tecumseh vowed he would revenge his people. But this military defeat spelled the beginning of the end; from then on Tecumseh's union went steadily downhill.

American frontiersmen were convinced that the British in Canada had been arming Tecumseh and egging him on. They called for the conquest of all Canada and the ejection of the British from "our Continent," and for the conquest of all Florida from Spain. Their spokesmen, who brought this cry to Congress in November 1811, were led by Henry Clay of Kentucky, and were promptly branded War Hawks by easterners.

Taking advantage of personal hostilities among older members of the decaying Republican party, Clay's friends elected him Speaker of the House of Representatives. Soon they had before Congress bills for an enlarged army and navy. Madison found it impossible to resist such pressure, coming as it did on top of the failure of diplomacy and continuing insults to the American flag on the high seas. On June 1, 1812, he reluctantly sent a message to Congress asking for war on Britain; the House and Senate complied. New England and the Middle States opposed the decision mainly because their ships would bear the brunt of the fighting and their commerce the brunt of the cost. The South supported the war. Except in upper New York State and part of upper Vermont, where relations with Canada were close and trade across the border was favorable, the war had vociferous support on the frontiers.

In his war message Madison had named impressment of American seamen by the British navy as the most important cause of the war. He said nothing of Canada and Florida and little of the Indians. But they were all tied together: Andrew Jackson of Tennessee put the matter in these words:

We are going to fight for the reestablishment of our national character, . . . to vindicate our right to an open market for the productions of our soil now perishing on our hands because the *mistress of the ocean* has forbid us to carry them to any foreign nation; in fine, to seek some indemnity for past injuries, some security against future aggression, by the conquest of all the British dominions upon the continent of North America.

War on Land and Sea

Confusion in American minds over the nature and objectives of the war muddied preparations at the outset and strategy throughout. Money, men, ships, and supplies all had to be provided. Yet early in 1811, Congress had allowed the Bank of the United States to die at the expiration of its twenty-year charter, just when it was to be needed most. Despite the urging of Secretary of the Treasury Gallatin, Congress put off consideration of new taxes until 1813, and throughout the war taxes were reluctantly voted and expertly evaded. Government loans raised little money.

Not until six months after war had been declared did Congress appropriate money to enlarge the navy. The army faced a different problem. Early in 1812 Madison was authorized to accept 50,000 volunteers for a year's service. But in six months only about 5000 signed up. Later the president was authorized to call out 100,000 state militia, but few men would follow their officers across the borders of their own states.

Canada, it was universally agreed, was the place to engage the British. But New England, the logical base for an invasion of Canada, opposed the war and withheld its militia. At the opening of the war the United States tried three timid and uncoordinated attacks against Canada, scat-tered over almost a thousand miles of border. These resulted in a court-martial and death sentence (later withdrawn) for the leader of the first for cowardice and neglect of duty, and disgrace for the leaders of the second and third. Far from occupying Canadian territory—"it will be a mere matter of marching," Jefferson had said—after six months of fighting, the United States had surrendered Detroit and found its own frontier pushed southward to Ohio.

At sea, the American navy was no match for the enemy statistically. Yet in the opening months of hostilities, American vessels won startling victories over British warships in single engagements. The winter of 1812–13, however, found most of the American navy back in harbor, where the British succeeded in bottling it up for the rest of the war. But they could not discourage American privateers, who, all told, captured more than 800 British merchantmen, most of them after 1813.

In the election of 1812, De Witt Clinton of New York, named by the "peace party" among the Republicans and supported by the Federalists, carried every northern state except Pennsylvania and Vermont. Madison, however, won with solid support in the South and West.

Perhaps the war party's political victory inspired more successful efforts in the field. The first step was to regain Detroit, and General Harrison and others agreed that control of Lake Erie was essential to success here. The job of capturing the lake was given to young Captain Oliver Hazard Perry. By August 1813 Perry's laboriously constructed lake fleet was ready, and on September 10 he found the British squadron in Put-in-Bay at the western end of the lake. At the end of the engagement Perry reported to Harrison, "We have met the enemy and they are ours."

Harrison followed up immediately by defeating the British at the Thames River in Canada. Tecumseh, who had earlier gone over to the British, was killed in this battle, and his Indian forces ceased to be a factor in the war. To the east, U.S. troops raided York (now Toronto) on Lake Ontario, burned the Parliament houses, and fled.

In April 1814, Napoleon fell and Britain was ready to put the Americans in their place. First, she strengthened her blockade of American ports and even attacked several of them. One British force, landing from Chesapeake Bay, marched on Washington, routed the hastily mobilized defenders, and set the Capitol and the White House afire.

Britain's second major step in the summer of 1814 was to launch a three-pronged attack against the Niagara region, Lake Champlain, and New Orleans. All three failed. Fought to a standstill at Niagara in July, the British landed 10,000 veterans of the Napoleonic campaigns at Montreal in August and prepared to march south toward Lake Champlain. Their objective may have been to detach northern New York and New England from the United States and pull them back into the British empire. Whatever their purpose, they were foiled at the battle of Plattsburg Bay.

Plattsburg Bay was the last battle before the Treaty of Ghent officially ended hostilities, but it was not the last battle of the war. In the Southwest, Andrew Jackson had been campaigning more or less on his own authority against the Indians. After routing the Creeks at the Battle of Horseshoe Bend in Alabama in March 1814, he had forced a treaty by which they gave up thousands of acres of excellent land.

Jackson's actions brought him full command in the southwestern theater and the responsibility for checking the British there. Aware that the British might use Pensacola in Spanish Florida as a base, Jackson invaded the area and burned the town. Then he marched to New Orleans and was ready when the enemy, 8000 strong, arrived in January 1815. The British lost more than one-fourth of their men in this needless battle. Jackson's miscellaneous collection of 4500 militiamen, blacks, sailors, and pirates lost only 21. From this triumph "the Hero of New Orleans" went on to become the nation's most popular figure since George Washington.

A Peace without Peace

Britain had launched her military offensive in the summer of 1814 partly to gain a better bargaining position at the war's end. When her peace commissioners, confident of reports of victories in the new campaign, met formally with the Americans in the Belgian town of Ghent in August 1814, they presented Madison's negotiators with stiff demands. They declared that they must have western territory on the American side of the border in order to provide for an Indian buffer state between the United States and Canada and to give Canada access to the Mississippi River. They seemed determined, at the same time, to concede nothing on maritime matters. There was to be no restoration, for example, of New England's privilege (granted in 1783 but withdrawn in 1812) to fish in Newfoundland and Labrador waters.

Henry Clay, who had joined Gallatin and John Quincy Adams in Europe for the peace conference, was happy to trade off New England's fishing privileges for the territorial demands of the War Hawks. He thought the New Englanders had forfeited all claims on the nation by refusing to support "Mr Madison's War" with men or money.

Indeed, even during the Ghent sessions the most embittered Yankee Federal-

The battle of New Orleans, with the victorious American troops entrenched on the left. (New York Historical Society)

ists, responding to a call from the Massachusetts legislature, were preparing to meet in Hartford, Connecticut, to sever the Union, "amicably if they can, violently if they must." When "this mad project of national suicide" (John Quincy Adams's phrase) convened in December 1814, however, moderates gained control of the proceedings. The meeting ended simply with proposals for amendments to the Constitution aimed at stopping Virginia's domination of the presidency. When news of the signing of the Treaty of Ghent reached America in mid February 1815, even these propositions lost all support.

The treaty had been signed on Christmas Eve 1814. By that time news of Britain's defeats at Niagara and Plattsburg had seriously weakened the British negotiating position. The Americans, in turn, had come to realize that their own quarreling was merely postponing their main objective—to bring hostilities to an end. Despite the in-conclusive military standoff with Great Britain, the United States had, after all, achieved major victories over powerful Indians in the West. Thus, the final treaty with Britain left most issues precisely where they had been at the war's start. At the same time, however, it provided for commissions to be appointed later to negotiate solutions to boundary, fisheries, and commercial issues.

POSTWAR INTERNATIONAL RELATIONS

After the treaty, Henry Clay commented, "We are destined to have war after war with Great Britain, until if one of the two nations be not crushed, all grounds of collision shall have ceased between us." New foreign wars, as it turned out, did not occur, but the many unresolved "grounds of collision" kept the threat of hostilities alive.

Canada and Florida

One of these grounds was the Canadian border. The Treaty of Ghent did not settle the matter of impressment, and after 1815 the British persisted in searching American vessels on the Great Lakes for British sailors. News also reached Madison that the British were building new frigates in Canada for lake service. With an armaments race appearing imminent, Madison and the British foreign secretary agreed early in 1816 to seek a peaceful solution. The result was the

Rush-Bagot agreement of 1817, which virtually demilitarized the Great Lakes for the future.

Another area of potential conflict was Florida. The irrepressible General Jackson helped the War Hawks gain one of their territorial objectives. In 1817 two British adventurers in Florida, Alexander Arbuthnot and Robert Ambrister, convinced the Creeks that they had been robbed of their land by Jackson's wartime treaties. Scalpings of whites followed. Ordered to punish the Indians, Jackson routed their forces, hanged

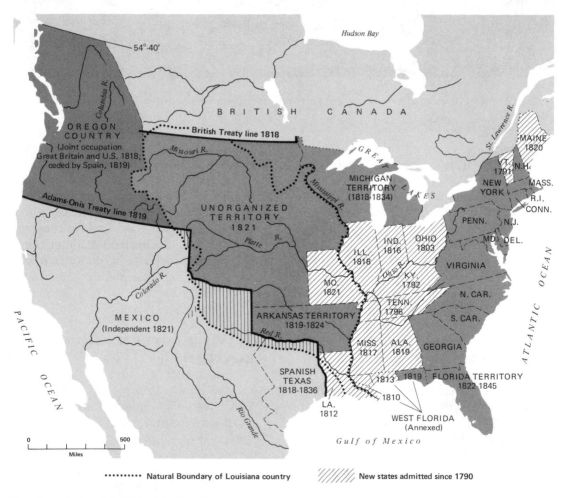

New Boundaries Established by Treaties

their chiefs, and court-martialed and executed Arbuthnot and Ambrister. Next his men marched on Pensacola, where he threw out the Spanish governor, who had given aid to the Indians. Jackson then claimed Florida for the United States. Britain, Spain, and Congress were all up in arms. Peace was kept, but Spain realized that it would be better to sell Florida before the uncontrollable Americans simply took it. In 1819 the United States bought Florida for $5 million by a treaty ratified in the Senate in 1821.

The Florida treaty settled the southern boundary for the time being by drawing a line westward to the Pacific coast. This line, while recognizing Spanish claims to Texas and California, afforded the United States a diplomatic claim to the Oregon Country for the first time. But there were expansionists, even in New England, who remained unsatisfied. For the United States to take all of North America, said John Quincy Adams in 1819, was "as much a law of nature . . as that the Mississippi should flow to the sea." As secretary of state, Adams successfully negotiated a southern limit to Russian claims on the Northwest coast.

The Monroe Doctrine

Revolts against Spain by the last Spanish colonies in the New World sharpened appetites for Latin America as well. By 1823 these revolts had proved almost entirely successful. President Monroe thereupon took the opportunity to assert "that the American continents, by the free and independent condition which they have assumed and maintain, are henceforth not to be considered as subject for future colonization by any European powers."

This pronouncement was one component of what we know as the Monroe Doctrine. The second declared that the United States would consider any interference by European powers with the independence of the new Latin American republics to be a show of "an unfriendly disposition." European countries were thus explicitly warned not to interfere in Central and South America.

SUGGESTED READINGS

M. Smelser, *The Democratic Republic, 1801-1815* (1968). M. D. Peterson, *Jefferson and the New Nation: A Biography* (1970). R. E. Ellis, *The Jeffersonian Crisis: Courts and Politics in the Young Republic* (1971). R. Horsman, *The Causes of the War of 1812* (1962). S.F. Bemis, *John Quincy Adams and the Foundations of American Policy* (1949). S. Livermore, Jr., *The Twilight of Federalism: The Disintegration of the Federalist Party* (1962).

SUMMARY

Thomas Jefferson came to the presidency determined to move the country in a Republican rather than a Federalist direction. His aim was financial economy and a simple style of government.

One way to reach this goal was to try to dismantle the Federalist judiciary. But

Chief Justice Marshall continued to hand down decisions based on a broad interpretation of the Constitution, and in the landmark case Marbury v. Madison, Marshall established the authority of the Supreme Court to nullify federal legislation.

Although a Republican, Jefferson was a

strong nationalist. He believed it was America's destiny to expand over the North American continent. In 1803, he got Congress to sponsor the Lewis and Clark expedition to the Pacific coast and the two Pike expeditions to the source of the Mississippi and to the Southwest. His most ambitious undertaking was the Louisiana Purchase of 1803. For $15 million Napoleon sold the Louisiana Territory—the whole middle of the continent—to the United States.

Jefferson's second administration saw the beginnings of international problems caused by the Napoleonic wars in Europe. American hostility was directed against the British over the issues of the rights of neutral ships, freedom of the seas, and impressment of American seamen into the British navy. An Embargo Act keeping American ships off the seas passed Congress at the end of 1807. It resulted not in keeping the United States out of war, but in ruining American commerce and American ports.

It also brought the revival of the Federalist party, James Madison as president, sec-

tional conflict, and then war with England. The War of 1812 ended in 1814 with the Treaty of Ghent, which left most of the issues—boundaries, fishing rights, and the terms of commerce—to be settled by commissions. The war also made a national figure of Andrew Jackson, the hero of New Orleans.

American-British hostilities continued. But relations eventually improved, and tensions along the Great Lakes were settled peacefully. They became touchy again over the issue of the Floridas, which were ceded to the United States in 1819 after another military adventure by General Jackson. The Florida Treaty also established the southern border of the United States all the way to the Pacific. The Monroe Doctrine of 1823 set forth the principle that in the Western Hemisphere the United States would act alone. The settlement in 1822 of the southern limit of Russian claims in the Pacific Northwest ended American boundary problems for the time being and gave the United States thirty years of peace with foreign powers. The troubles now were to be growing pains at home.

8

A Nation Reborn

The War of 1812 is often called America's second war of independence, and there is much truth in that label. The coming of peace in 1815 set the stage for important developments in the American political system and the American economy. The two-party system fell apart, largely because the Federalists had opposed the war and Republicans had adopted so much of the Federalist program. The nation's economy boomed—and then went bust. John Marshall produced an impressive series of court decisions, many of which had as much to do with economic matters as with federal supremacy. And the issue the Founding Fathers had swept under the rug—slavery—came spilling out and exposed deep sectional hostilities.

THE "ERA OF GOOD FEELINGS"

In 1816, the Republicans nominated Madison's secretary of state, the Virginian James Monroe, as their presidential candidate. The Federalist candidate, the last in history, carried only Massachusetts, Connecticut, and Delaware.

Shortly before his inauguration in March 1817, Monroe accepted an invitation to visit New England. His tour was so successful that even Massachusetts and Virginia seemed ready to get along with each other. A Federalist newspaper published an article titled "Era of Good Feelings" celebrating the event. By then, the Republicans had shown so much concern for manufactures and a protective tariff, for an army and a navy, even for chartering a national bank, that the old issues that had divided them seemed dead. Monroe was reelected in 1820 with only one electoral vote cast against him.

Boom, Bank, and Bust

Once the war ended, most of the "war babies" among American factories lost out to British competition, despite American efforts at tariff protection. Britain's own postwar boom soon promoted another kind of boom in the United States. British textile manufacturing brought an enormous demand for southern cotton. The end of the war also reopened European markets for southern tobacco. Furthermore, poor European harvests in 1816 and 1817 added to the demand for American grain.

The boom in agriculture quickly inspired a boom in land speculation, especially in the West, where the population increased dramatically. By 1820, Ohio had more people than Massachusetts, and the entire West had more people than New England. Settlers and speculators bought and sold land with the aid of several hundred state and private banks that had been established after the charter of the first Bank of the United States expired in 1811. These banks had issued millions in paper money by 1817, much of it unacceptable even in neighboring communities.

Congress established a Second Bank of the United States in 1816. Like the first national bank, the Second Bank was chartered for twenty years as the sole depository for government funds. The Second Bank had the right to establish branches in different parts of the country. But influential local bankers persuaded some states to write into their constitutions provisions against "foreign banks"—that is, branches of the national bank doing business within their borders.

In the summer of 1818, when the postwar boom was at its height, the Second Bank decided to try deflationary measures to control speculation. But the sudden shrinking of credit prevented many people from paying their debts. The boom collapsed before 1819 was over, and the country was gripped by its first major economic depression. The Second Bank became widely unpopular.

Actually, the economic collapse was worldwide. The revival of European agriculture after the Napoleonic wars and the weakening of the postwar textile boom created a glut of wheat and cotton in world markets. But the depression was most severe in the United States and most devastating in the West. The crisis prompted a number of states to abolish the practice of punishing debtors with imprisonment and to pass liberal bankruptcy laws. Congress came to the aid of the West with a new land act in 1820, which permitted a settler to buy an eighty-acre homestead for $100 in cash.

Marshall's Nationalism

Against this background John Marshall issued a series of historic Supreme Court decisions that alarmed state's-rights men. The most important—*Dartmouth College* v. *Woodward* (1819)—dealt with the subject of contracts.

The Dartmouth College case raised this issue: Could the royal charter granted to the college in 1769 and later approved by the New Hampshire legislature be changed by the legislature without the college's consent? In a decision as interesting to business corporations chartered by state legislatures as to colleges, Marshall decided that it could not. A charter, he said, was a contract between two parties, neither of whom could change it without the other. Therefore the state's measure was unconstitutional. In the case of *Sturges* v. *Crowninshield* (1819), Marshall declared unconstitutional a New York bankruptcy law that attempted to relieve debtors of their contractual obligations.

Marshall's court nullified thirteen state laws that it considered contrary to the federal Constitution. One of the most far-reaching of these cases was *McCulloch* v. *Maryland*, also decided in 1819. The state of Maryland, among others, had attempted to tax a branch of the Second Bank of the United States out of existence. In finding the Maryland tax unconstitutional, Marshall observed that "the power to tax involves the power to destroy." If states were permitted to nullify acts of Congress by attacking its agencies, they could "defeat and render useless the power to create." In the broadest possible statement of implied powers, Marshall went on to assert the constitutionality of the act creating the bank: "Let the end be legitimate, let it be within the scope of the Constitution, and all means which are . . . plainly adapted to that end, which are not prohibited, but consist with the letter and spirit of the Constitution, are constitutional."

Finally, in *Gibbons* v. *Ogden* (1824), the Supreme Court prohibited a monopoly of steam navigation between New York and New Jersey that had been granted by the state of New York. Marshall stated the case for the broadest interpretation of the Constitution's commerce clause: the monopoly grant by New York, even if it covered state waters alone, interfered with the exclusive power of Congress to regulate interstate commerce.

In these and other decisions, the Marshall court in effect lessened the powers of the states. Protection of individual and corporate rights meant placing limits on state actions. The enlargement of federal powers had the same effect.

The Missouri Compromise

An important feature of the economic advance of the country was the orderly admission of new states. First there were Vermont (1791), Kentucky (1792), Tennessee (1796), Ohio (1803), and Louisiana (1812). After the war came Indiana (1816), Mississippi (1817), and Illinois (1818). This orderly procession was brought to a halt by controversy over slavery in Missouri, the first territory that applied for statehood in the so-called Upper Louisiana Territory, where many slaveholders had already settled.

There was no question about Missouri's application until February 1819, when Congressman James Tallmadge of New York shocked the South by proposing to ban the introduction of more slaves into the new state. He also proposed that all children born of slaves there be freed at the age of twenty-five.

The Tallmadge Amendment passed the House by a narrow margin, reflecting northern strength in that chamber. The Senate turned it down. Even though free states outnumbered slave states eleven to ten, a number of northern senators had been born and raised in the South, and they voted with the large minority of southern senators.

The deadlock carried over to the next session of Congress which opened in December 1819. Missouri's request for statehood was now joined by one from Alabama. There was no question about admitting Alabama as a slave state. Upon admission Alabama established the balance between slave and free states at eleven each. Missouri now would make a twelfth slave state, giving southern senators a virtual veto of all legislation passed by the northern majority in the House.

Northerners in the House remained firm in their support of the Tallmadge amendment. When the northeastern part of Massachusetts applied for admission as the state of Maine, however, some members of Congress led by Henry Clay seized the chance to compromise. In a series of measures known as the Missouri Compromise, they arranged to keep the sectional balance of power in the Senate by admitting Missouri as a slave state and Maine as a free one. The most significant provision of this compromise permitted slavery in Missouri but prohibited it "forever . . . in all territory ceded by France to the United States" north of the southern border of Missouri.

Under these terms, Missouri become the twenty-fourth state in 1821. There the issue of slavery in the territories rested for

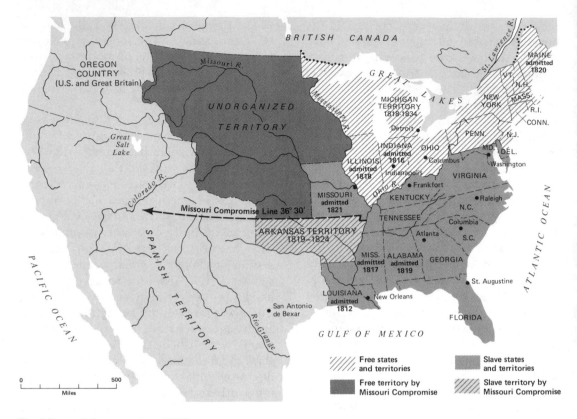

The Missouri Compromise, 1820

a generation. But the Missouri controversy intensified sectionalism and threatened the spirit of national union.

ENTERPRISE AND EMPIRE

For several decades after 1815 the majority of white Americans still lived on family farms. They were not fully aware of the new technology and expanding enterprise that were fundamentally altering American life.

Bounty from the Sea and Land

Some Americans continued to gain an independent existence from fishing as well as farming long after the Revolution. One spec-

ialized occupation—whaling—brought in large profits until kerosene supplanted whale oil for lighting after the Civil War. Whaling remained a conservative industry: the only significant changes since colonial times were that voyages grew longer and crews—paid, like fishermen, with a share of the catch—were exploited more ruthlessly.

In lumbering, as in farming, fishing, and whaling, few changes were made in the first third of the nineteenth century. The industry grew, of course, but until the railroads created a huge demand for wood for fuel, ties, and rolling stock, lumbering remained the occupation of individual loggers who supplied timber to widely scattered and independently owned sawmills.

The Indians had taught the first settlers how to grow corn, harpoon whales, and bring down trees. For more than two centuries, these basic techniques of farming, fishing, and lumbering spread unchanged as the country gradually expanded. Commodities such as flour, leather goods, and ironware were made according to the old methods, generation after generation in the same family. It was a living and a way of life. Until vast new markets were opened up by improved transportation, this traditional system continued to characterize the American economy.

The Rise of the Middle West

Traveling over trails first marked by Indians, thousands of white settlers moved westward. In the Middle West, some were new immigrants from Europe. Many more were second-, third-, and fourth-generation Americans who moved westward in successive steps of a few dozen or a few hundred miles. In 1810 only one-seventh of the American population of 7.2 million lived west of the Alleghenies; by 1840 more than a third of 17.2 million Americans lived there. Production of corn and wheat rose, but not dramatically. The new lands were more fertile than those in the East, which had been worn out by years of repeated cultivation. The result was that many unproductive farms in New England were simply abandoned.

Until settlers reached the more open prairie country in Indiana and Illinois, the supply of trees seemed unlimited. Farmers wanted wood for fuel, fences, tool handles, and house construction. But they also regarded standing trees as a barrier to farming. Piles of fallen trees were burned outdoors just so they would be out of the way. One symbol of this wastefulness was the log-cabin method of constructing houses. First

introduced in the seventeenth century by Swedes and Finns along the Delaware River, this technique was adopted by westward-moving pioneers. It was probably the most labor-efficient way of turning trees into housing: it wasted a lot of wood, but it saved a lot of work. Since wood was far more plentiful than labor, Americans did not think twice about wasting it: when it ran out, settlers could always move on to where there was more. This attitude was part of a general assumption that the abundant natural supplies of the continent would exist forever.

King Cotton

In the Southwest, westward settlement was encouraged by the expansion of upland cotton. Commercial cotton growing had made great strides in the South after 1790, when British East Indian indigo destroyed the market for American indigo. For two generations indigo had been a staple of the South Carolina and Georgia planters, but between 1790 and 1793 the indigo planters turned their land to cotton. Most of this cotton was of the fragile long-staple variety. This was the finest kind, and the only kind that could be cleansed of its oily black seed at reasonable cost. In America, however, the climate and soil requirements of long-staple cotton limited its cultivation to the South Carolina and Georgia sea islands and the coastal plain extending into Spanish Florida. The other type of cotton, the coarser, short-staple, green-seed boll, could be grown on almost any soil, provided the warm season was long enough. Its single drawback was the difficulty of removing the seed: one worker could clean only a single pound in a day.

An invention solved this problem and brought about a major economic revolution in the American South. In 1793 Eli Whitney, a young man from Massachusetts, invented a machine for cleaning the

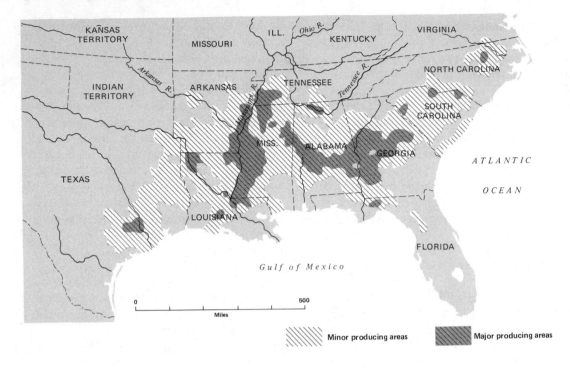

Cotton-Growing Areas

green-seed plant. With adoption of Whitney's innovation, short-staple cotton production began spreading rapidly. One worker operating a single cotton gin by hand could clean fifty pounds a day. Rapid improvements in Whitney's and other gins and the introduction of steam power greatly increased productivity. In 1800 about 75,000 bales of cotton went to market, most of it the short-staple kind.

Within a few years, however, coastal lands were used up. Cotton planters pushed west into Alabama and Mississippi. By 1830 the combined population of these states exceeded 400,000, even though the large planters had bought up many small farms in the best cotton areas. Sections of Tennessee, Arkansas, and Florida suitable for cotton planting also became heavily settled,

as did the Louisiana sugar country. The traffic at New Orleans reflected the rapid growth of the new regions. Most of the cotton went to English textile factories, and some to New England mills.

TRANSPORTATION AND TRADE

In colonial America, the ocean was the easiest means of communication and trade. As farms and plantations spread inland among the eastern rivers, these waterways also began to carry their share of people and goods. Settlement in the West brought the Mississippi River system into the transportation network, and the steamboat made it the foremost inland carrier of all.

Steamboats

The first steamboat on the western waters was the *New Orleans*, built in 1811 by Robert Fulton. Rates between Louisville and New Orleans on the flat-bottom vessels called keelboats had been about five dollars per 100 pounds of freight. By 1820, steamboat rates for this trip had fallen to two dollars per 100 pounds. By 1842, competition had driven them down to twenty-five cents. Western staples now moved down to New Orleans for shipment overseas or for distribution to the rest of the South and Southwest and even to the Northeast. In addition, commodities from abroad or from the Northeast were funneled into New Orleans for transshipment inland.

The Mississippi system, however, was less than ideal. The river itself and most of its tributaries were filled with snags, shifting sandbars, floating trees, and unpredictable currents.

Roads

Road transportation presented even greater challenges. From the earliest times, many Americans chose to settle far from neighbors on land several miles from water routes. Yet somehow they had to travel to grist mills, tobacco warehouses, forges, country stores, country courts, and rivers. As time went on, a crude network of roads spread across the countryside, many of them following old Indian trails and the paths of trappers and traders. Only a few such roads were wide enough for wagons or carts. Rains transformed them into muddy pools, and winter cold froze them into ruts.

Gradually, however, roads were improved. Private investors financed turnpikes on which they collected tolls. Congress appropriated funds for a paved National Highway westward from Cumberland, Maryland.

Canals

New York, Philadelphia, Boston, and the other eastern seaports turned to canals to link the great waterways of the American continent. But canals were far more expensive than turnpikes, and they took not one or two years but seven to ten to build. They presented new problems in finance and management as well as in engineering.

In 1816 the country had only 100 miles of canals. As early as 1810, however, the New York State legislature had appointed a committee to investigate the possibility of digging a canal to the West—a canal that would connect the Hudson River with Lake Erie, a breathtaking 363 miles.

Construction of the Erie Canal began in 1817. By 1823, a 280-mile stretch was in operation from Albany to Rochester. The tolls that came pouring in from traffic helped finance the final leg to Buffalo, completed in 1825. Over the next nine years the Erie was able to pay back its total original cost of $7 million. Two figures tell the story of the Erie's success: it reduced freight rates between Albany and Buffalo from $100 to $15 a ton, and travel time between those points from twenty to eight days.

Throughout the country, but especially in the Northeast and Middle West, canal construction became almost a mania. Various states and cities rushed to get ahead of their competitors.

Internal Improvements

Farmers in the Middle West were also eager for East-West trade. They found that their rich soil produced more wheat and corn, and their corn could fatten more hogs, than southern markets could absorb. In the 1820s westerners turned a sympathetic ear to Henry Clay's program for high tariffs and "internal improvements" that would promote the growth of eastern factory towns as well as provide the means for opening towns to western produce. Internal improvements would also mean that manufactured goods could be shipped more cheaply directly from the East than through New Orleans. Congress never adopted Clay's program. But even without federal assistance, Ohio and other western states started ambitious canal and railroad projects. By 1840 some 3326 miles of canals, most of them in the North and West, had been built in the United States at a cost of $125 million. Private investors supplied only a small part of this money. More than half the total came from state funds or from the sale of state bonds abroad, mainly in England.

The impact of the canals, the first enterprises to receive large-scale public financial backing, proved as beneficial as expected. The South remained a valuable, growing customer of the West, and the Ohio and Mississippi river systems continued to be heavily used. But the West's connection with the Northeast became stronger as the canal system developed. Without that connection, the history of American sectional conflict might have been very different. Travel on canals was much cheaper than on roads, but for about four months of the year northern canals were often frozen. Railroads soon freed shippers from the weather and

The bustling New York City waterfront, 1828. (New York Public Library)

from the slow pace of oxen and tow horses. By 1840, the United States had 3328 miles of railroad, almost exactly the canal mileage. Only 200 of these railroad miles were in the West. For some time after 1840, rivers, canals, and roads remained the principal paths of inland commerce.

THE INDUSTRIAL REVOLUTION

The expansion of commercial agriculture in the West, the rapid growth of population, and access to western markets all gave a strong push to the development of eastern industry. Concentration on cotton in the South also made that region a market for the coarse textiles worn by slaves and for other manufactures. Until western and southern markets were opened, however, factory industry had difficulty getting started in America.

Factories and Capital

The first successful full-time factory in America was the cotton-spinning plant of Almy and Brown. Under the direction of an experienced Englishman, Samuel Slater, this factory began operations in Rhode Island in 1791. This early factory employed only children at twelve to twenty-five cents a day—wages unacceptable to adult males. After the outbreak of the Napoleonic wars in Europe, Americans found it more and more difficult to get British products. To supply their needs, Slater's mill expanded operations, and many hopeful imitators started up to enjoy a share of the market.

The first textile mills were small operations rarely capitalized at more than $10,000. Since their managers had little experience in keeping accounts, handling money and workers, and supplying markets, conservative banks would having nothing to

do with them. But in 1813 a group of wealthy Boston investors headed by Francis Cabot Lowell organized the Boston Manufacturing Company. This company built the first cotton manufacturing plant in the world in which *all* operations—from the unbaling of the raw cotton to the dyeing and printing of the finished cloth—were contained under one roof.

The Early Labor Movement

Many of the new textile mills found a cheap and eager source of labor in young women from rural areas. A paying job in town looked attractive to farm girls, and they flocked to factories in Lowell, Waltham, Lawrence, and Dover. They had to deal with long hours on the job and a completely controlled environment in boardinghouses off the job. They were required to attend church and forbidden to discuss grievances. At the mills, their wages were kept low and they were subject to fines for the slightest violations of factory rules.

American workers in the seventy years before the Civil War slowly came to learn that their interests were best served if they joined together. Skilled artisans first broke away from their employers in the 1790s by joining mutual-aid societies. By the beginning of the nineteenth century, improvements in transportation had opened larger markets to master artisans. Some of these individuals became businessmen who gathered up larger orders than one artisan and a few helpers could fill and who employed others to work for them. By the 1820s, as competition became keen, artisans' wages were cut. Artisans were further embittered by the loss of their independent status. Worse still, the integrity of their work and their product was being destroyed as skills were broken down into simpler tasks to be performed by lower-paid apprentices.

The first labor unions were formed in America in protest against these conditions. From the start, businessmen, with the aid of the government, made it dangerous for workers to join these alliances. Until 1842 labor unions were frequently declared by the courts to be "conspiratorial combinations."

Neither court decisions nor coercion could prevent laborers from organizing. Economic depressions, however, slowed the labor movement considerably during the first half of the nineteenth century. In the 1819–22 depression, 40,000 laborers were thrown out of work in Philadelphia and New York alone. Most labor unions were crushed, and no relief for the unemployed was offered by the government.

The business collapse of 1837 virtually destroyed the early labor movement. Unemployment threatened all workers. Layoffs were becoming harsher for industrial workers, since many families had moved off the farm and become dependent on the factory for their living. Many of the more recent European immigrants were also tied to the factories. Having arrived penniless, they had to remain in the cities. Industrialization did provide jobs for these new Americans as well as for many poor farmers. But the cost in the quality of life was great. Farm work did not disrupt families or put individuals in lonely, alienating, and dangerous jobs.

These changes in the life of American workers, as well as changes in the lives of farmers and businessmen, were not so obvious then as they are now. Many Americans were conscious that something was going on, but they were not sure what. They welcomed what they called the age of improvement. But they grew vaguely anxious about the direction of social change. There was an inherent tension between these reactions, a tension that easily spilled over into politics.

SUGGESTED READINGS

G. Moore, *The Missouri Compromise* (1953). D.C. North, *Economic Growth of the United States, 1790-1860* (1960). S. Bruchey, *Growth of the Modern American Economy* (1975). L. Baker, *John Marshall: A Life in Law* (1974). G.R. Taylor, *The Transportation Revolution, 1815-1860* (1951). N. Rosenberg, *Technology and American Economic Growth* (1972). B.M. Wertheimer, *We Were There: The Story of Working Women in America* (1977).

SUMMARY

America experienced a boom after the War of 1812, and then a bust in 1819. The Second Bank of the United States was chartered for twenty years. Federal power was strengthened by a series of decisions by John Marshall.

The problem of slave versus free states was settled for a time by the Missouri Compromise of 1820. Slavery was permitted in Mis-souri, but prohibited "forever" in all territory ceded by France north of a certain line.

The economy began to grow and change. Farming and fishing were still the most common occupations. Thousands of settlers moved onto the lands of the Middle West. At first their lives were hard, but it was clear the land was fertile and could be a source of agricultural wealth. The demand for cotton in world markets, especially that of Britain, led the southern plantation system to expand westward into Alabama and Mississippi. Steamboats and canals revolutionized inland water transport. By 1840 the United States had about 3000 miles of canals and an equal amount of railroad track.

The first successful full-time factory in America was a textile plant in Rhode Island. Most of the early factories were small, but in 1813 a group of wealthy Boston investors organized not only textile plants but also insurance companies and banks in order to maintain and concentrate capital.

A labor movement began during this period, and the first unions were formed. The women and children who worked in the textile factories were the first to go out on strike. But labor was vulnerable to employers, government, and the business cycle. The business collapse of 1837 crushed the early movement for a number of years. Labor protest made Americans conscious that material progress might have a price, and that social change might not always be all good. These ideas, however, were still dim and shadowy; most Americans focused their attention on growth and national politics.

9

Jacksonian Politics for a New Age

When James Monroe left the White House in 1825, the nation was free from difficulties with foreign nations. His successor was in many ways a transitional figure. John Quincy Adams inherited his position in diplomacy and politics from his distinguished father. He himself was the last president until the twentieth century who could possibly be called an intellectual.

Americans returned to political bickering in an extremely nasty campaign for the presidency in 1828. The outlines of two new political parties were beginning to emerge, and the next few years saw the development of what has been called the second political-party system. The voters elected an old war hero, Andrew Jackson, who loved having political opposition so he could fight it.

The American people were in a changed mood. They no longer turned for leadership to aristocratic gentlemen of wealth and breeding. Many of them praised the virtues of the common people even while they admired those who forged ahead in the world of business. They welcomed the new age yet wanted to return to the simpler days of the early Republic.

Yet there was more to Jacksonian politics than a change in mood and style. A new economy presented Americans with significant issues. Westward expansion raised the problems of how to treat Indians and whether to construct internal improvements. The complexity of the economy raised questions about the National Bank and tariffs. These matters in turn often raised important questions about the proper interpretation of the Constitution. At the center of these controversies stood the figure of Andrew Jackson, who stamped the era with his iron will and vigorous style.

THE BEGINNINGS OF THE NEW POLITICS

The Age of Jackson may be said to have begun in 1824, when he won the popular vote, lost the election, and had friends pushing him for the presidency all during the administration of John Quincy Adams. One important development often associated with Jackson—the expansion of the electorate—actually took place before he was a political candidate and owed nothing to his ideas or actions. Oddly enough, the extension of the franchise through the elimination of property requirements was one of the few important political developments that did *not* arouse debate about constitutional issues.

Expanding the Electorate

During the first quarter of the nineteenth century most states quietly eliminated property qualifications for voting, thus opening up the franchise to almost all adult white males. In Europe, particularly in Great Britain, broadening the suffrage was a major public issue throughout much of the nineteenth century. The United States escaped quarrels on the matter because the Founding Fathers had left suffrage requirements to the states. Americans did not have to deal with the matter as a national issue. Nonetheless, it is clear that public feeling was in favor of giving the vote to "all men."

The democratic spirit failed to carry over to one significant class of the population—free blacks. As late as 1820 a number of northern states permitted black men to vote, but after that many states deprived them of that right. After 1837 blacks could vote only in the states of northern New England.

The loss of the right to vote was only one of the lengthening list of restrictions on blacks in the free states. They were cooped up in miserable alley slums, confined by curfews, placed outside the judicial and educational systems, and barred from all but the most menial occupations and from the land as well. By the 1850s many western states would not allow free blacks even to enter.

For the "political community of white persons," on the other hand, even more important than the suffrage was the greater interest of men in exercising that right on the national level. Although up to 70 percent of the electorate had voted in hot local contests, presidential elections before 1828 seem to have left most voters cold. Even in 1824, when Jackson was first a candidate, only 27 percent of those eligible voted. Popular enthusiasm for presidential elections reached its peak in 1840, after Jackson had retired, when 78 percent of the eligible voters went to the polls. That proportion was new in American politics and has never been equaled. One reason for the new interest was the gradual emergence of a new two-party system after 1824 and sharper party differences on issues. Another was voter participation in the selection of the candidates.

In most states, presidential electors had been chosen by the legislatures. But by 1828, almost every state had provided for popular election of members of the electoral college. The change forced presidential candidates to appeal to the people rather than to a small group of politicians. Jackson, as he often reminded his opponents, was the first president who could claim to have been elected directly by the voters. The claim was not altogether justified, since members of the electoral college could cast their ballots as they wished. Governors also began to be popularly elected, and property qualifications for that office and others were swept away. Finally, by the 1840s state judges were being elected rather than appointed.

This trend toward popular participation did not, of course, bring many plain folk to high political office. A man still needed standing in the community, achievement, or at least a certain eloquence to win office. But popular participation in politics remained more broadly based in the United States than in any other country in the world. It would not be long before it would occur to a few reformers that women too should be included in the political process.

The Election of 1824

Four contenders for the presidency emerged in 1824, all of them claiming rather vaguely to be Republicans. One was Andrew Jackson of Tennessee, who had little government experience but a great reputation as an Indian fighter and especially as "the Hero of New Orleans." Another candidate was John Quincy Adams of Massachusetts, the heir apparent because by this time it was assumed that the secretary of state would succeed to the presidency. William Crawford of Georgia was a personally attractive man who presented himself as the true heir of Thomas Jefferson. Finally, Kentucky's Henry Clay had built a strong power base as Speaker of the House, as well as a broad popular following for his American System.

Clay's American System was one of the most thoroughly worked out platforms ever devised by a presidential candidate. Clay pictured an industrial East providing a growing home market for southern cotton and western grain and meat. An agricultural West and South would provide an expanding market for eastern factory goods. For the East he would supply protective tariffs; for the West and South, internal improvements such as canals and turnpikes to reduce transportation costs. Trade between the sections was to be aided by a stable credit system underwritten by a national bank.

Jackson won a heavy plurality of the popular vote. In the electoral college, however, his 99 votes fell short of the required majority, so the contest was thrown into the House of Representatives. Here Clay, having polled the lowest electoral total, was eliminated under the terms of the Twelfth Amendment. Of the top three, Crawford was ill. The contest was left to Jackson and Adams. After a private talk with Adams, Clay swung his supporters to him. Clay's influence was largely responsible for Ad-

ams's election. One of Adams's first presidential acts was to name Clay as secretary of state. To most people this was like naming him as his successor. The Jackson men lost little time in charging that a "corrupt bargain" had been made at the Clay-Adams talk. The charge was not really fair, since Clay and Adams agreed on most matters. But "bargain and corruption" became the Jacksonians' slogan for the 1828 campaign, which they opened as soon as they learned of their defeat in 1824.

John Quincy Adams in Office

The alleged deal was not the only issue that haunted Adams in the White House. A sensitive and high-minded man, he regretted having to accept the presidency with, as he said, "perhaps two-thirds of the whole people" opposed to him. Popular opinion, however, did not stop Adams from launching a program he considered right for the country. With stubborn courage but without political skill he argued for an active national government and for internal improvements. He was warned by Clay and most of his cabinet that at a time when states'-rights feelings were rising and sectional jealousies were strong, it was all but suicidal for a president—and a minority president at that—to urge such a policy.

Adams proposed a highly nationalistic program, much of which his opponents thought overreached federal powers as stated in the Constitution. He urged the establishment of a national university, financing of scientific expeditions, construction of astronomical observatories, reform of the patent system, and development of a national transportation system. This comprehensive program for centralized economic and cultural development, and Adams's failure to push it through, encouraged states'-rights opponents everywhere to mobilize their machines behind Jackson.

Jackson's Election

By the time of the congressional elections of 1826, Adams's program had gained for his followers the name of National Republicans. His opponents became known as the Democratic Republicans (before long their party was known simply as the Democratic party). In these elections, for the first time in the history of the country a president lost his majority in Congress after two years in office. On convening under Jacksonian leadership, the new Congress made its single purpose the advancement of the general's presidential prospects. In 1828, the hero of New Orleans, the victim of the Adams-Clay "corrupt bargain," the most visible old soldier in the country for four solid years, polled 647,000 votes. The surprise, if any, was that Adams, with 508,000 votes, was far from destroyed.

Andrew Jackson. (Library of Congress)

OLD HICKORY IN THE WHITE HOUSE

Jackson's inauguration attracted an immense crowd to Washington. They surged through the unpaved streets, pressed into the White House, stood on sofas, smashed glasses, and generally convinced observers that the presidency had somehow been brought to the masses. Jackson himself did nothing to discourage this mood. He thought of himself as a man of humble background, a man of the common people. He had been born in poverty in the southern back country, and both he and his supporters made a great deal of this. He was, however, scarcely one of the common people. He had built a highly successful career in Tennessee, in law, politics, land speculation, cotton planting, and soldiering. His home was a mansion, not a log cabin. Anyone who owned more than 100 slaves, as Jackson did, was a very wealthy man.

He was also a man of strong convictions but few ideas. As president he saw himself as the one government official who had been elected by all the people, and he therefore regarded himself as representing the national interest. Always suspicious, Jackson disliked special-interest groups and men whose power came from privilege. Lurking just beneath the surface of his iron will was a deep streak of anger. When crossed he lashed back, whether at the British army, Indians, Spanish officials, judges, bank officers, or political opponents. He was the only president ever to have killed a man in a duel. He seemed to symbolize the virtues of the new America—a common man successfully on the make, ready to tackle and destroy aristocratic privilege wherever he found it. His opponents thought that he had all the qualities of a democratic emperor. The National Republicans soon began calling themselves Whigs to symbolize their resistance to "King Andrew I." As president Jackson moved quickly to defend the political spoils system, to veto internal improvements, and to challenge the Supreme Court.

The Spoils System

The new chief executive's most important cabinet appointment went to Martin Van Buren of New York who was named secretary of state. But Jackson liked to rely on the advice of personal friends. His administration was marked by the rise to power of men who became known as the Kitchen Cabinet—a small group of what we would call White House advisers. They all shared his feelings about the need for a strong presidency.

Jackson's policy toward the executive civil service was consistent with his independent view of his high office. The president fired about 900 jobholders from among the 10,000 he found on the payroll. His party chiefs, having made many commitments in two campaigns, wanted even more heads to roll, but Jackson restrained them.

In the long run it was the president's defense of the spoils system, rather than the particular replacements he made, that so firmly associated his name with it. Earlier presidents had removed opposition people from office without raising many eyebrows. Jackson was the first to make the spoils system seem a social and moral as well as a political "reform." In his first annual message to Congress, he defended "that rotation [in office] which constitutes a leading principle in the republican creed." "The duties of public offices," he declared, are "plain

and simple," and plain and simple men could best perform them in the people's interest.

The Rights of the States

In his relations with Congress and the courts, Old Hickory proved equally aggressive. Earlier presidents had been content to administer the laws passed by Congress. But Jackson took the constitutional power given the executive to participate in making (or unmaking) the law as well as executing it. In his two terms, Jackson vetoed more legislation than all former presidents combined.

One of his most famous vetoes killed the Maysville Road Bill in 1830, which would have required the federal government to buy stock in a private corporation. The company was to build an internal improvement, a road in Clay's home state of Kentucky. Because the road would lie only within a single state, Jackson's stand was easy to justify. He was well aware that he would be strongly supported in such states as New York and Pennsylvania, for they had helped elect him and had developed transportation systems at their own expense. He knew he would also find support in the South Atlantic states, which were committed to slavery and states' rights. These states were also becoming opposed to protective tariffs, which supplied most of the federal money for internal improvements. Jackson told Congress, "The great mass of legislation relating to our internal affairs was intended to be left where the Federal Convention found it—in the State governments."

Jackson viewed the presidency as the only direct reflection of the people's will. Almost inevitably this view resulted in a clash with the Supreme Court as well as with Congress. Again he based his stand on the rights of the states.

The Cherokee Indians

In 1803, after Georgia had ceded its western lands to the United States, the federal government agreed to settle Creek and Cherokee claims to the region. Federal action was slow, however, and as cotton growing spread in the state the planters' patience ran out. Georgia's militant governor ordered a state survey of Creek lands in 1826. When President Adams threatened to stop the survey with federal forces, Governor George Troup said he would resist force with force. Conflict was avoided only by the Creeks' surrender and their forced removal beyond the Mississippi.

Far more than most Indian ethnic groups, the Cherokees, like the Creeks, had embraced the white man's ways. They had established farms and factories, built schools, and begun a newspaper. They also adopted a constitution. In 1827 they decided to form an independent state on the American model. Georgia responded by nullifying all federal Indian laws and ordering the seizure of Cherokee lands. When Georgia courts convicted a Cherokee of murder the Supreme Court of the United States ordered the conviction set aside. Governor Troup and the state legislature ignored the federal government's "interference" and executed the prisoner.

By then, Jackson had become president. He had no sympathy for Indians. The Cherokees asked the Supreme Court to prohibit the extension of Georgia law to Indian residents and to negate Georgia's seizure of Indian lands. In 1832 Marshall declared in *Worcester* v. *Georgia* that the Cherokee nation was a legitimate political community, with clearly defined territories, where "the laws of Georgia can have no force, and which the citizens of Georgia have no right to enter" without Cherokee consent. In effect, Marshall was saying that the Cherokee nation would exist or not at the pleasure of the federal government, not that of any single state. Nevertheless, Georgia ignored the Court's decision.

The Jackson-dominated House of Representatives tabled an order restraining Georgia from evicting the Cherokees. This meant that no federal troops would be made available to support Marshall's decision, and the takeover of the Indian lands continued. By 1835 only a few southwestern Indians retained their lands. After the subjugation of the Florida Seminoles (1835–42), millions of acres were thrown open to whites. The Indians, meanwhile, were forced onto a westward trek that became known as the Trail of Tears. A fourth or more of them died on the journey. Officials overseeing them robbed them of their money; what was left went for burial rites.

The Webster–Hayne Debate

From time to time agreements like the Missouri Compromise of 1820 cemented up sectional breaches over slavery. But new issues in the rapidly developing country soon reopened the sectional controversy. The protective tariff was one such issue. A second, related to it, involved the disposal of federal lands. The Webster-Hayne congressional debate in January 1830 plumbed the sectional depths of both. It also led to a profound test of the states'-rights philosophy of the White House.

Westerners made certain demands on the government. They wanted to guarantee the ownership of land settled by squatters by requiring the government to sell them the land at the minimum rate of $1.25 an acre when it came up for sale. This right, known as *preemption*, was finally enacted in 1841. Senator Thomas Hart Benton, the spokesman for western interests, proposed further that the price of land not sold within a specified period be gradually reduced, first to $.75, then to $.50, and finally, if no buyers appeared, to nothing. This proposal came to be known as *graduation.*

Easterners regarded Benton's plan as one more scheme to tap their labor supply and to raise their wage costs. They also saw the quickening of western development as a further threat to their political strength in the nation. On the other hand, it was obvious that continuation of land sales at the established prices would bring the Treasury so much money that it would invalidate one of their principal arguments for high tariffs—the need for additional revenue to pay off the national debt and support government services. In an effort to eat their cake and have it too, some easterners offered the policy of *distribution*—keep up the price of land and the tariff, and distribute the surplus revenue among the states to help them improve public education and business morality. When nothing came of this, they resorted to the rather desperate proposal that the West be closed to settlement altogether.

In December 1829, Senator Samuel A. Foot of Connecticut offered a resolution to this effect. Senator Benton, speaking for the West, angrily denounced Foot's resolution as a manufacturer's plot. Spokesmen for the slave South, in turn, supported Benton in the hope that they could aggravate differences between the free East and the free West.

Senator Robert Y. Hayne of South Carolina presented the South's case. His most divisive remarks were derived from an anti-tariff essay published anonymously by Vice-President John C. Calhoun in 1828. According to Calhoun, the Tariff of 1828 made southerners serfs to northern industrialists. No free government, Calhoun argued, would permit the transfer of "power and property from one class or section to another." The tyranny of the majority could

be met by the constitutional right of each state to nullify any unconstitutional act of Congress.

In an address regarded for many years as a model of eloquence, Daniel Webster of Massachusetts replied that the Union was no mere compact among state legislatures; it was "the creature of the people." They had erected it; they alone were sovereign. It was for the Supreme Court, not the states, to decide whether laws passed by Congress were in keeping with the Constitution. If a single state had that right, the Union was in effect dissolved. After speaking for four hours Webster concluded with the famous words "Liberty *and* Union, now and forever, one and inseparable."

Once the debate ended, the first question everyone asked was where Jackson stood. He was for states' rights; about that there was to be no mistake. But he was for states' rights within the Union. There was to be no mistake about that either.

In April 1830, when the leading Democrats gathered at a Jefferson birthday dinner, Old Hickory looked Calhoun in the eye and proposed this toast: "Our Union—it must be preserved!" Calhoun was unrepentant. He rose to reply, "The Union—next to our liberty, the most dear."

Nullification Attempted

In the following months old personal grudges, deliberately raked up, and new personal conflicts, some of them trivial but telling, speeded Calhoun's decline and Van Buren's rise. But Calhoun still had more moves to make.

The tariff once more provided the decisive issue. Receipts from existing duties and other sources had become so high by 1830 that the national debt had been almost entirely paid off. Jackson believed protective (as against revenue) tariffs to be as unconstitutional as federal appropriations for internal improvements. In December 1831, therefore, he urged Congress to revise the Tariff of 1828 downward. If he hoped to appease the South by this proposal, he also sufficiently modified the requested reductions so as not to antagonize the industrial Northeast. In July 1832 Congress passed a tariff bill that met Jackson's specifications. It hardly satisfied Calhoun, however, and the vice-president rushed home from Washington to mobilize southern opposition.

In South Carolina a legislature overwhelmingly favorable to nullification ordered the election of delegates to a special convention. In November 1832 this body adopted by a vote of 136 to 26 an ordinance declaring the 1828 and 1832 tariffs void. It also ordered the state legislature to prohibit collection of duties in state ports after February 1, 1833, and asserted that the use of federal troops to collect the duties would be followed by secession.

Jackson, more assertive than ever after his smashing success in the election of 1832, replied on December 10 with his ringing Nullification Proclamation:

> I consider . . . the power to annul a law of the United States, assumed by one State, incompatible with the existence of the Union, contradicted expressly by the letter of the Constitution, unauthorized by its spirit, inconsistent with every principle on which it was founded, and destructive of the great object for which it was formed.

Jackson warned that the laws of the United States compelled him to meet treason with force.

In February 1833 the Senate passed a Force Bill empowering the President to use the army and navy if South Carolina resisted federal customs officials. At the same time, Henry Clay sponsored a new tariff bill calling for gradual reduction of the 1832 duties.

South Carolina leaders, having learned that other southern states had repudiated nullification and that a vigorous Unionist faction inside their own borders would continue to fight it, anxiously awaited the decision on these two measures.

On the day (March 2) that the Force Act became law, Jackson also signed Clay's Tariff of 1833. Even Calhoun, who had resigned as vice-president in order to be named a member of the Senate by the Carolina legislature, voted for this bill, and South Carolina showed its satisfaction by withdrawing its nullification ordinance. At the same time, the South Carolina legislature adopted a new ordinance nullifying Jackson's Force Act. Since he no longer needed that act, Jackson wisely ignored this face-saving step.

THE BANK WAR

Not long before the election of 1832, President Jackson settled into brooding hostility toward the Bank of the United States. The bank's rechartering was not due for another four years, but its continuation came up during the election campaign. Although significant financial issues were involved, the fact that Jackson carried on a war against "the monster" bank even after he had won the election suggests that his opposition came from what the bank symbolized as much as from what it actually did. Many of the political developments of the 1830s had a symbolic quality. Nullification, for example, suggested South Carolina's growing sense of isolation from the rest of the nation.

Jackson versus Biddle

For ten years prior to the election of 1832, the Second Bank had been managed by the able Philadelphian Nicholas Biddle. Cautious about issuing the notes of his own Bank, he refused to accept at face value the notes of state and local banks that had issued more paper than their specie reserves warranted. He thereby forced upon such banks an element of caution that they and their clients came to resent. The West particularly, growing faster than the rest of the country, felt stunted by Biddle's policies. The Second Bank, in addition, was an enormous institution with far-reaching powers. It had considerable control over the private economy as well as privileged custodianship of government funds. Its enemies were apparently justified in denouncing it as a monopoly.

The Bank's services to the country made Jackson reluctant to attack it. But Biddle's measures in defense of the Bank soon convinced the president that the "monster" must go. What especially nettled him was Biddle's attempt to buy support in Congress and the press with Bank favors, such as interest-free personal loans.

Increasingly angry, Jackson was confronted in July 1832 with a bill from Congress that rechartered the Bank. Convinced that the "monster" was out to destroy him and his mandate from "the people", Jackson vetoed it. The characteristic closing remarks of the veto message were admirably suited to the election campaign:

> Distinctions in society will always exist under every just government. Equality of talents, of education, or of wealth, cannot be produced by human institutions . . . but when the laws undertake to add to these natural and just advantages artificial distinctions . . . to make the rich richer and the potent more powerful, the humble members of society . . . have a right to complain of the injustice of their Government.

Biddle thought so little of Jackson's "manifesto of anarchy" that he had it circulated as pro-Bank propaganda. But Jackson swept the election and interpreted his triumph as a mandate to press his war against Biddle's "Hydra of corruption."

Boom and Bust

The president's opening shot was to order the removal of government deposits from the Bank's branches and to place them in selected state institutions that came to be known as Jackson's "pet banks." These orders were more easily issued than performed. The secretary of the treasury alone had the power to withdraw government deposits, and Jackson's secretary was a friend of the Bank. Such obstacles did not deter Old Hickory, however. He fired two such secretaries before he found the man who would do his bidding—Roger B. Taney of Maryland.

Biddle counterattacked. If the Bank was to be forced to close, it must begin to call in its loans and restrict its new business. Soon after the federal deposits had been removed, Biddle embarked on this policy with zeal. His object was to create a business panic so widespread that public opinion would force Jackson to reverse his stand on the charter. For some months in 1833 and 1834, a panic indeed seemed imminent. But once again Biddle miscalculated the political effects of his actions. In time even segments of the business community appealed to Biddle to relent, and finally he gave in.

Relief over Biddle's capitulation promptly turned the near panic into a soaring boom. This was especially true in the South and West, where land was in great demand and speculators used each purchase as collateral for loans to buy still more land. The administration accelerated the dizzy pace by throwing millions of acres of public lands onto the market. Where the land was opened, moreover, there arose an immediate cry for internal improvements. As a consequence, the land boom was accompanied by reckless investments in turnpike, canal, and railroad schemes. Many of these projects were financed in part by foreign capitalists who would not risk their money in private American corporations but were willing to purchase state bonds backed by state revenues.

Optimistic state programs multiplied in the summer of 1836 when it became clear that the federal government was about to distribute to the states some of the $35-million Treasury surplus on hand from tariff revenues and land sales. This surplus disappeared, however, before distribution could be completed. What dissipated the surplus was the collapse of the boom itself, hastened by another government measure, Jackson's Specie Circular. Issued in mid July 1836, this famous document required that all land purchased from the federal government after August 15 be paid for in silver or gold.

This drastic reversal of policy turned land sales sharply downward. In the spring of 1837, stock and commodity prices also broke, and soon the Panic of 1837 was on in earnest. Like other panics, that of 1837 had worldwide as well as American causes and effects. Especially hard hit were British investors in American securities and British banks engaged in financing American trade, particularly trade in cotton. Their calls on American merchants forced many to the wall. A serious depression set in for six years.

Uncomprehending Americans blamed everyone—British capitalists, American bankers, their state governments, the federal government, President Van Buren, ex-president Jackson, Nicholas Biddle, the new Whig party, the Democratic party, alcohol and the moral fiber of the American people. When a man worked hard and then lost his farm, his business, his job, his plantation— who else was there to blame? No one fully realized that large, impersonal, international market forces were at work. Van Buren himself could only offer the suggestion that the depression was caused by "overbanking" and "overtrading."

He was not altogether wrong, but the dimensions and nature of the problem were not well understood. The national and international market economy was far more complex and interwoven than it had been a generation before, but it was not easy to see the relationships. It was not yet obvious that a bank failure in New Orleans might be connected with the failure of a New York cotton merchant, a bank in Boston, and a cotton factory in Manchester, England. It was even more difficult to see the relevance of a rise in silver exports from Mexico or a temporary interruption of the opium trade in China. Such developments, in fact, could affect a farmer in Illinois or Alabama. It was easier to find the cause of one's own difficulties closer to home. It is no wonder that many Americans in this era turned inward to reform their own society, not realizing that it was rapidly becoming part of a much larger and more impersonal world.

JACKSONIAN POLITICS WITHOUT JACKSON

President Jackson barely escaped the economic storm and its political consequences. The election of 1836 took place before financial panic set in, and Van Buren's nomination was assured by Jackson's support. Having failed four years earlier with Henry Clay, the Whigs were unable to decide on a candidate. At their national convention they resolved matters by selecting four regional candidates in the hope of depriving Van Buren of a majority and throwing the election into the House of Representatives. With national prosperity at its height, Van Buren won. But his popular and electoral majorities were far smaller than his predecessor's. In the election of 1840, he paid the political price of presiding over a depression. The Whigs out-ballyhooed the Democrats and finally won control of the presidency— only to lose it a month later because their candidate caught a chill at his inauguration.

Little Van

Soon after Van Buren took office in March 1837, the business panic was in full swing. The president received plenty of advice on how to reverse the trend, most of it centering on the Specie Circular, which business leaders claimed "had produced a wider desolation" than a recent cholera epidemic. Easy-money Democrats urged the president to recall the Specie Circular but to continue the pet-bank system. Financial conservatives, though, proposed that the government go even further than the Circular in its hard-money crusade. They also demanded that Van Buren remove public funds from all banks, so that federal fiscal operations might no longer be "embarrassed by the doings of speculators."

The president favored the hard-money approach to banks, and finally in 1840 Congress passed an independent treasury bill. This measure created depositories for government funds around the country from which government obligations would be paid in cash. The "divorce of bank and state," as the independent-treasury victory was called, did little for economic recovery.

"Tippecanoe and Tyler Too"

As the election of 1840 drew near, Whig leaders scented victory. Clay, defeated for the nomination on the bank issue in 1832

and by-passed in 1836 for strategic reasons, now hoped to gain the elusive prize. This time, however, he failed to receive the support of Webster, who looked upon him as a rival. With little hope of winning the nomination himself, Webster backed William Henry Harrison. At the Whig convention, old "Tippecanoe" was nominated. John Tyler of Virginia was named the general's running mate, in the hope he would strengthen Whig chances in the South. The Democrats renominated Van Buren. But since Jackson's retirement, they had become so divided that they were not able to agree on a candidate for vice-president and were forced to leave the choice to the states.

In the campaign the Whigs made much of Harrison's victory over Tecumseh at Tippecanoe all of thirty years earlier. They also derided the persisting "regal splendor of the President's Palace" during the prevailing hard times and the "Turkish divan" on which Little Van was said to repose. When a Baltimore paper taunted the Whigs by saying that "old clod-hopper" Harrison would be perfectly satisfied with a log cabin and a good supply of cider, his managers capitalized on the intended slur and picked up the log cabin as a party symbol. In fact, the log cabin was as foreign to Harrison's gentlemanly origins and life-style as the Turkish divan was to Van Buren's White House, but the frontier symbol helped elect old "Tippecanoe." The record vote represented an extraordinary 78 percent of those eligible. Of these votes, Harrison won 53 percent. Unfortunately for the Whigs, Harrison died after only one month in office and John Tyler became president.

Harrison had humbly accepted the guidance of Webster and Clay, but stubborn John Tyler went his own way. A congressional veteran who had favored nullification, he also had made no secret of his anti-Bank, antitariff, anti–internal improvements views. As president he signed the law terminating Van Buren's independent-treasury system, but he also twice vetoed Clay's bill for a third national bank, one of the Whigs' great objectives. After the second veto, almost the entire cabinet quit at Clay's behest. Only Webster, in the midst of delicate negotiations with Britain, stayed at his post as secretary of state. When Webster resigned in 1843, he was soon succeeded by Calhoun—further evidence of the nominally Whig administration's new Democratic orientation, and confirmation that the Democratic party had become the standard-bearer of the slave states.

SUGGESTED READINGS

R.V. Remini, *Andrew Jackson* (1966). E. Pessen, *Riches, Class, and Power before the Civil War* (1973). M. Feldberg, *The Turbulent Era: Riot and Disorder in Jacksonian America* (1980). W.W. Freehling, *Prelude to Civil War: The Nullification Controversy in South Carolina, 1816-1836* (1966). D. Howe, *The Political Culture of the American Whigs* (1979). R. Seager, II, *And Tyler Too* (1963).

SUMMARY

The political tone of the Age of Jackson began even before Andrew Jackson became president in 1828. During the first quarter of the nineteenth century, most states opened up the vote to almost all adult white males. Interest in national politics grew as government seemed to become more accessible to the people. A new two-party system gradually emerged after 1824. By 1828, every state except two had popular election of members of the electoral college.

The election of 1824 had brought John Quincy Adams to the presidency, with Henry Clay as secretary of state. But Adams's program for centralized economic and cultural development failed, and he lost his congressional majority in the midterm elections. In 1828 Andrew Jackson—Old Hickory and the hero of New Orleans in the War of 1812—became president.

Jackson's name became linked with the spoils system, the right of a president to

put his own people in the executive branch. Jackson greatly enlarged the power of the presidency. He clashed with Congress and with the Supreme Court and warred on the Second Bank of the United States. During his administration, the various regional heads in Congress introduced sectional debate on several issues. The Webster-Hayne debate of 1829 was one instance; the debate over South Carolina's nullification was another.

Almost immediately after his reelection, Jackson continued his war with the Second Bank of the United States, whose rechartering was now due. He had vetoed the bill for rechartering before the election, and saw his victory as a sign that the public approved. In 1836 the bank expired. Jackson had been successful in removing the government's money from the bank and placing it in selected state banks. The shaky economic boom became a panic in 1837. The country went into a severe depression that lasted until the mid 1840s.

Andrew Jackson cast a long shadow over American politics. His enlargement of presidential power aroused fears of a strong executive. His successor, Martin Van Buren, had to cope with an economic depression. As a result he lost the election of 1840 to a Whig, William Henry Harrison. Harrison died within a month of his inauguration, and John Tyler of Virginia became president. Tyler was a supporter of nullification and of states' rights. He vetoed the legislation of his own party, and Congress came almost to a standstill.

During the 1830s the Whigs and the Democrats emerged as two distinct groups, and a two-party system came to be seen as beneficial to the functioning of national government. Both parties had to deal with economic problems they did not fully understand, and with social changes that seemed to come from nowhere.

10 *Manifest Destiny*

Throughout the 1820s, and 1830s, and 1840s, Americans were very much on the move—not only into new states in the Louisiana Purchase but all the way to the Pacific coast. Within little more than a quarter of a century, the unbroken expanse of the United States had been extended to its present limits. Both Canada and Cuba still looked tempting to those who thought the United States was destined to rule the North American continent.

The term "Manifest Destiny" became identified with American expansionism about 1845, but the idea of a divine mission was much older. This notion, which had begun to tempt some Americans when they captured Louisburg, suggested that God had set aside the American continent and nearby islands as reservations "for the free development of our yearly multiplying millions."

Practical politicians promoted more tangible objectives. They kept running into serious border conflicts with Canada. They had to deal with the question of the Oregon Country, an area claimed by both Great Britain and the United States. In the Southwest, a new republic emerged as the result of American westward settlement. For a time Texas remained independent, but there was strong sentiment for annexing it.

In the mid 1840s an aggressive American president provoked a war with Mexico. That conflict brought great territorial gains for Americans. But it also raised the question of whether those territories should be open to slavery. That issue came close to tearing the nation apart, but it was patched over by a complex compromise in 1850. The compromise produced both relief and anger. Many people began to doubt whether it would last.

THE CANADIAN BORDER

Tensions between Britain and America increased in the late 1830s. Three incidents in particular brought the two countries close to war.

In 1837, insurrections against the Crown flared up in Canada but were quickly suppressed by loyal forces. During the uprising certain Americans who sympathized with the rebels' cause supplied them with provisions. One evening an American steamer, the *Caroline*, which had been supplying the rebels, was set afire by loyal Canadians, and in the scuffle one American was killed.

The United States first demanded an apology from the British. Then they arrested one of the participants, a Canadian named Alexander McLeod, and charged him with murder and arson. At the insistence of Britain's truculent foreign secretary, Lord Palmerston, the British government refused to apologize. It argued that McLeod had merely been obeying orders, and threatened war if he were not released. Fortunately for both sides, McLeod was acquitted of the charges.

The next incident involved the Aroostook River valley, an area rich in lumber and claimed by both the state of Maine and the province of New Brunswick. Trouble broke out between the two sides when Canadian lumberjacks began clearing the forests. Although the "Aroostook War" was a bloodless affair, Congress was prepared to fight before diplomatic efforts cooled tempers.

The *Creole* incident, though it did not concern the border, further strained Anglo-American relations. In her attempts to stop the slave traffic on the high seas, Britain had made treaties with many countries allowing her navy to search suspected merchantmen. The United States, however, had refused to sign such a treaty, and slave ships often escaped search and seizure by flying the American flag.

In 1841, slaves being transported from Virginia to New Orleans aboard the American brig *Creole* revolted. Led by a man with the ironic name of Madison Washington, they sailed to the British port of Nassau. The slaves were freed upon reaching the port, and the British resisted efforts by American officials to have them returned. It was the most successful slave insurrection

in American history. It also looked like another step toward international conflict.

There were sighs of relief on both sides of the Atlantic when a change of ministries threw the combative Palmerston out of office in 1841. The new foreign secretary was far more friendly, and he appointed as special envoy to the United States Lord Ashburton, the husband of an American heiress.

The principal object of the Webster-Ashburton talks was the Canadian-American border. Ultimately, Daniel Webster compromised on the Maine boundary. The two diplomats also agreed on the still inaccurately surveyed boundary that ran along northern Vermont and New York and westward to Minnesota and Ontario. Going further still, they smoothed over the *Caroline* and the *Creole* affairs with such skillful language that both sides were made to seem in the right. In addition, the Americans agreed to help the British patrol the African coast in order to suppress illegal slave running.

These results did much to enhance the two negotiators' historical reputations, though not their popularity at the time. The Webster-Ashburton Treaty, signed in 1842, was a model of compromise that paved the way for other peaceful settlements between Britain and the United States during the next two decades.

ISSUES IN THE WEST

Texas

American claims to the Mexican province of Texas were based upon the carefree geography of the Louisiana Purchase treaty. When the United States obtained Florida from Spain in 1819, she surrendered those dubious claims. American traders and military adventurers nevertheless continued the illicit commercial relations they had already established with the Mexicans, despite Spain's many warnings. When Mexico, with the assistance of such traders and fighters, won her independence from Spain in 1821, she promptly put American commerce on a legitimate footing and invited additional Americans to settle in Texas and develop its resources.

Mexican officials had hoped that the settlement of Texas by white Americans would protect their country from Indian raids and from possible aggression by the United States. But they soon realized they had miscalculated. Between 1820 and 1830 about 20,000 Americans with approximately 2000 slaves had crossed into Texas, largely from the lower Mississippi frontier. The Texas-Americans soon began to complain about lack of self-government.

In 1830 the Mexican government sent troops to occupy Texas, called a halt to further American immigration, and passed other restrictive measures, including the abolition of slavery. Texas-Americans began to hold anti-Mexico meetings. Shortly thereafter, General A. L. de Santa Anna emerged as Mexico's strong man, instituted a centralist program, and abolished all local rights. Early in 1836 he led an army of several thousand men into Texas to bring the rebellious Americans to book. Confronted with this threat, Americans in Texas declared their independence, set up a provisional government under a constitution that sanctioned slavery, and appointed Sam Houston commander in chief.

Before the Texans could formulate military strategy, two of their companies were wiped out: 187 men died defending the Alamo mission in San Antonio (among them such legendary figures as Davy Crockett and Jim Bowie), and more than 300 were massacred at Goliad after they had surrendered. A month later, on April 21, 1836, General Houston surprised Santa Anna at San Jacinto Creek. Fired up by the cry "Remember the Alamo," his Texans defeated the Mexicans and captured Santa Anna, who signed a treaty pledging Texas independence. The Mexican Congress repudiated the general's pledge but could do nothing to reverse it.

Sympathy for the Texas rebels had been strong in the South and also in the Northwest, where their cause was identified with the struggles of frontiersmen. There was far less support for the Texans' cause in the Northeast. Whig leaders in particular viewed the Texans' request to enter the Union as a slave owner's plot. Anywhere from five to seven states, they pointed out, might be carved from the huge Texas domain, and that would insure southern control of Congress. Opponents of annexation protested so vehemently that President Jackson held off even recognizing the Lone Star Republic until just before he left office in 1837. Van Buren also withstood growing annexationist pressure.

Denied admission to the United States and menaced by an unforgiving Mexico, the Lone Star Republic sought protection elsewhere. Britain in particular, though it opposed slavery, welcomed an independent Texas that would export cotton and import British manufactured goods.

That Texas might link herself with Britain was a frightening prospect to northern businessmen and slave-owning planters alike, and Sam Houston, now president of Texas, played so cleverly on the fears of both that annexationists were ready to do almost anything to bring Texas in.

In April 1844, seeking credit for attaching this virtual empire to the United States before his successor reached the White House, President Tyler submitted a Texas statehood treaty to the Senate, only to see northern opposition kill it. In February 1845, after the annexationists had triumphed in the 1844 election, Tyler tried again, this time by means of a joint resolution of both houses, which needed only a majority vote in each, not the two-thirds vote needed for treaties in the Senate. This resolution squeaked by the Senate, 27 to 25; the House tally was 132 to 76. In October, Texas voters ratified the annexation terms, which explicitly permitted slavery under Missouri Compromise provisions. When, on December 29, 1845, Texas became the twenty-eighth state, Mexico recalled her minister from Washington.

The Oregon Country

The future of Oregon as well as that of Texas had reached a critical point when Americans rallied to their party standards for the presidential campaign of 1844. Distant though it was from the mainstream of European and American politics and business, the Oregon Country had long been the scene of competition among France, Spain, Russia, Britain, and the United States. Early in the nineteenth century, France and Spain had surrendered their claims and the Russians had agreed to fix their own southern boundary at 54°40'. This left Britain and the United States free to contest ownership of the remainder of Oregon.

Following the Lewis and Clark expedition of 1803–6, American fur traders led by John Jacob Astor had pushed into the Oregon Country both overland and around Cape Horn to the mouth of the Columbia River. Their business collapsed when the War of 1812 began, and the British in Canada kept Oregon closed to Americans for a generation. By the 1830s, however, American missionaries were seeking to reach the Indians there, and soon the Oregon Trail became a familiar if dangerous path of American enterprise.

The fertility and beauty of Oregon's Willamette Valley so captivated these men that farming quickly took precedence over conversion of the Indians. The home church in the East soon washed its hands of the enterprise, but settlement flourished.

While American leaders in Oregon struggled to organize a provisional government, expansionists back east began to thunder about America's right to the territory. They rejected the old boundary at the forty-ninth parallel, the limit of American claims in earlier discussions with Britain. The Democrats' campaign slogan for 1844 was "fifty-four forty or fight."

No other United States presidential election was fought so clearly over the issue of national expansion. By opposing the annexation of Texas, Van Buren had forfeited his chance of renomination by the Democrats. The Democratic convention finally settled upon a single-minded planter from Tennessee, expansionist by conviction though as yet not widely known. James K. Polk promptly endorsed "the reoccupation of Oregon and the reannexation of Texas."

Having passed him over in previous years, the Whigs were almost forced to choose their idolized Henry Clay as standard-bearer. But Clay had openly opposed the annexation of Texas, on which the Whig platform remained silent. The more he hedged during the campaign, the worse off he became, and Polk, clearly a "dark horse" against the glamorous "Harry of the West," won by an electoral margin of 170 to 105. The Democrats enlarged their House majority and gained a majority in the Senate.

The election results were widely interpreted as a mandate for expansion, especially by Polk himself. Yet his triumph was hardly decisive, and the closeness of the popular vote in the election was a sign that expansionism as much as slavery might en-

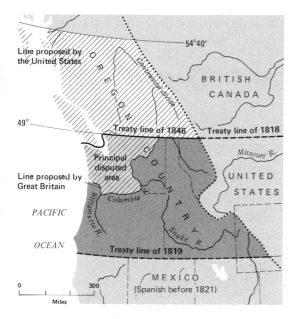

Line proposed by the United States

54°40'

BRITISH CANADA

49°

Treaty line of 1846 — Treaty line of 1818

Principal disputed area

Missouri R.

Line proposed by Great Britain

Columbia

UNITED STATES

PACIFIC

Willamette R.

OCEAN

Snake R.

Treaty line of 1819

0   300

Miles

MEXICO (Spanish before 1821)

The Oregon Controversy

danger national unity. As president, Polk opposed protectionism, and in 1846 he signed the Walker Tariff, which put the country back on low duties for revenue only. He opposed a national debt and meant to keep it low enough to be serviced (and reduced when possible) by the revenues available. He opposed banks and restored Van Buren's independent treasury system for handling federal funds. He gave nullifiers no comfort. Above all, he was as expansionist and isolationist as Jefferson.

Aware of the threat of war against Mexico over Texas, Polk also kept his eye on the tempting Oregon territory. "Fifty-four forty" was a fine campaign slogan, but perhaps it had served its purpose. Oregon above the forty-ninth parallel, Polk had been reliably advised, was ill suited to agriculture. Below the forty-ninth parallel, he said, lay "fine harbors and rich surrounding soils." Three times before, the United States had offered to divide the territory at this line, which in fact was a direct extension of

the northern boundary fixed in 1818 as far as the Rockies. Now, in an atmosphere free from election pressures, negotiations were resumed, and on June 15, 1846, they were successfully concluded. The territory north of the Columbia River, though clearly British by right of settlement, fell into the American sphere, later to become the state of Washington; over present-day Oregon there was no conflict. Britain retained Vancouver Island and navigation rights on the Columbia.

Mormons in Utah

While thousands of Americans from the North and the South were moving west to "perfect," as Polk said, American title to North America, one group moved west to escape rather than embrace the American government.

In 1823 Joseph Smith, a visionary from Vermont, claimed to have been led by angels to a hill in upper New York, where "there was a book deposited, written upon gold plates," and "two stones in silver bows" to guide the book's translation. As God's helper, Smith used the stones to reveal the Book of Mormon, a composite of mythology and prophecy recalling an ancient legend that the Indians were descendants of the lost tribes of Israel and enjoining Smith's followers to convert them.

On the basis of this revelation, Smith in 1830 founded the Church of Jesus Christ of Latter-Day Saints and published his book. Along with other messianic movements of the times, Mormonism spread into the Western Reserve in Ohio. There the distinctive pattern of Mormon community living—markedly similar to the seventeenth-century New England settlements centered on the church—first took shape.

Thereafter, trouble dogged the Mormons. Smith was murdered in Nauvoo, Illinois, in 1844 over the issue of the plural marriages practiced by some of his sect but abhorred by others. Two years later, provided now with a martyr, the Mormon church began to recover under the leadership of Brigham Young, a follower of Smith, who became the new "Lion of the Lord."

Forced out of Illinois after the Prophet's assassination, Young led the Mormons on a tortuous exodus westward in the winter of 1846. The found in the Salt Lake Valley a Zion isolated on a barren Mexican plateau, remote from the lands of the gentiles. Here, encircled by dusty mountains and a smoking desert, the Mormon leaders created a theocracy superbly organized for survival.

Owing both to geography and ideology, the Salt Lake community was cooperative rather than competitive. The Mormon desert state (eventually named Utah) was probably the most successful communitarian project every established in America.

On to California

The present state of California had first been opened to European expansion by Spanish Franciscan missions, protected by small garrisons. The purpose of these settlements had been to convert Indians and to prevent British and Russian penetration on the California coast. In theory, the missions were temporary: they were set up to teach the Indians agriculture and household arts and to Christianize them. But gradually, mission lands fell into private hands. By the time of the Mexican War in 1846, the Indians were hopelessly dependent remnants, and few active missions remained.

During the preceding twenty-five years, Yankee whalers from Nantucket and New Bedford had begun stopping at Monterey and San Francisco, leaving behind them deserters and adventurers. Other emigrants came from the Oregon and Missis-

sippi frontiers. Bitter conflicts arose over wealth, territory, and cultural differences.

Although California had not been an issue in the 1844 campaign, it soon became identified with Oregon. San Francisco, all agreed, was the great prize. It was twenty times more valuable, thought Daniel Webster, than the whole of Texas. San Diego harbor, according to many observers, would outweigh Oregon.

The United States had no claim to California except desire. During the administrations of Jackson and Tyler, government efforts to buy California merely deepened Mexican hostility. Anglo-Californians were eager to break away from Mexican control. When they learned of the outbreak of war with Mexico in 1846, they raised the standard for a Bear Flag Republic, which they hoped would be annexed to the United States.

WAR AGAINST MEXICO

The Mexican-American War was one of the most patently aggressive wars in American history. President Polk first ordered General Zachary Taylor to occupy disputed territory on the southern boundary of Texas. Taylor had carried out his orders by the end of March 1846. That show of force, thought Polk, might push the Mexicans to reconsider their refusal to negotiate. Failing that, it might cause an incident that would serve as an excuse for war. Almost inevitably there was a clash of troops at the disputed border. Polk had already prepared a war message for Congress, which overwhelmingly voted to back his request. The shedding of American blood on what the United States claimed to be its own soil put the legislators in a mood to act without lengthy debate.

The size of his congressional majorities may have raised Polk's hopes for bipar-

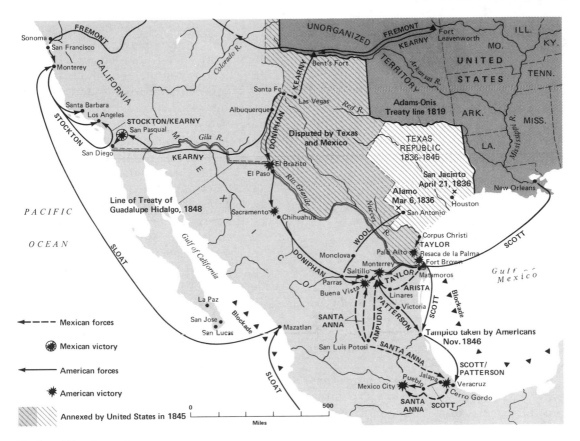

Mexican War Campaigns

tisan support of the war, but these hopes were soon dashed. His refusal to openly declare his war aims (the seizure of New Mexico and California) encouraged southern as well as northern Whigs to attack his entire Mexican policy. On the other hand, some expansionists were calling for the annexation of all Mexico.

Moral and political dissatisfaction with the war was most strident in the Northeast, where New England Whigs and anti-slavery spokesmen caustically denounced Polk's adventurism. The populous Northeast supplied only 7900 recruits for the army; some 20,000 southerners and 40,000 westerners enlisted.

General Taylor captured Monterrey, Mexico, on September 24, 1846, and defeated a Mexican force of 15,000 men at Buena Vista early in 1847. General Winfield Scott overcame stout resistance on the coast of Vera Cruz and went on to take Mexico City on September 14, 1847. Troops commanded by Colonel Stephen W. Kearny, starting from Fort Leavenworth, Kansas, captured Santa Fe and pushed through to California. Commodore Robert F. Stockton and a battalion under General John C. Frémont had already proclaimed the annexation of California in August 1846.

On February 2, 1848, Polk signed the Treaty of Guadalupe Hidalgo. He thereby secured the Rio Grande boundary; Upper California, including the ports of San Diego and San Francisco; and New Mexico. In return, Polk agreed to pay some $13 million to Mexico. Several years after Polk left office, the United States paid Mexico an additional $10 million—the Gadsden Purchase of 1853—for 54,000 square miles of territory, which would facilitate building a transcontinental railroad.

THE SLAVERY ISSUE

The "Free-Soil" Election

As American soldiers stormed into Mexico, a New England essayist wrote in his journal, "The United States will conquer Mexico, but it will be as the man who swallows the arsenic, which brings him down in turn. Mexico will poison us."

The symptoms of poisoning came swiftly. As early as August 1846, David Wilmot, a Democrat from Pennsylvania, offered an amendment to an appropriation bill in the House: "neither slavery nor involuntary servitude shall ever exist in any part" of the territory that might be acquired from Mexico. The House adopted the amendment; the Senate defeated it. But that was far from the end of the matter. The Wilmot Proviso was added to bill after bill in Congress and was hotly debated there and in the country generally. At the same time, admission of Iowa and Wisconsin to the Union was pending; Minnesota was soon to apply for statehood; and even Oregon Territory was readying its petition. For all these inevitably free states to enter the Union while the South was deprived of slave states in the new southern territory was an intolerable prospect for many southern spokesmen. But growing numbers of northerners saw slavery as an evil that had to be contained.

Did Congress indeed have the authority to determine whether or not slavery might exist in territory obtained by the United States? Southerners who first raised this question claimed that since the Constitution recognized and protected property in slaves, owners of such property could not lawfully be prohibited from carrying such property wherever they went, even across the Missouri Compromise line. Antislavery northerners replied that the Constitution (Article IV, Section 3) plainly gave Congress control over the territories. Congress had exercised its right first by confirming the exclusion of slavery from the Northwest Territory. Then—and especially—it had adopted the Missouri Compromise in 1820.

A third position on slavery in the territories was squatter sovereignty, or popular sovereignty, set forth by Lewis Cass of Michigan and Stephen A. Douglas of Illinois. Let the new territories be set up with the question of slavery left open, and then permit the people to decide for themselves. Plausible though it was, this doctrine was disastrously vague on an important matter of timing. Precisely when should a territory decide the momentous question—after slaves had been brought in or before? What if free settlers had arrived before slave owners? By leaving resolution of the question open to zealots of both camps, popular sovereignty also left it open to violence.

By 1848 the issue of the extension of slavery to new territories had become so poisonous that both major parties avoided it while preparing for the presidential campaign. On taking office, Polk had pledged himself to a single term. "Regular" Democrats, convening in Baltimore, therefore nominated Lewis Cass on a platform that ignored slavery. The "regular" Whigs, convening in Philadelphia, hoped to silence talk of all issues by nominating the "hero of Buena Vista," General Taylor.

The watchword of the regulars in both parties was party harmony. But they reckoned without determined antislavery northern Democrats. In New York and New England these Democrats became known as Barnburners because they were said to be willing to burn down the Democratic "barn" in order to get rid of the proslavery "rats." The regulars also reckoned without the "conscience" (as against the "cotton") Whigs. In August 1848 antislavery Democrats and Whigs, who had bolted from their regular party conventions, met in Buffalo with other antislavery leaders and formed the Free-Soil party, adopting the slogan "free soil, free speech, free labor, and free men." They named as their standard-bearer Martin Van Buren, who had won their sympathy by his forthright stand against the annexation of Texas.

The 1848 election itself aroused little popular enthusiasm. Neither Taylor nor Cass possessed much popular appeal, and Van Buren—despite his repudiation of slavery—could not live down his long-standing reputation as a slippery political fox. Moreover, he had no nationwide machine behind him. In the balloting, Taylor won. The Free-Soilers polled only 291,000 votes, but they absorbed enough Democratic ballots in New York to give that state's electoral vote to Taylor, and enough Whig votes in Ohio and Indiana to throw those states to Cass. Most important, the Free-Soilers had demonstrated the potential strength and disruptive power of a purely sectional party based on the issue of slavery.

Sectional tensions relaxed for a moment when the news of gold in California spread across the nation early in 1848.

These ships in the San Francisco harbor were abandoned by their crews, who took off to dig in the gold fields. (Smithsonian Institution)

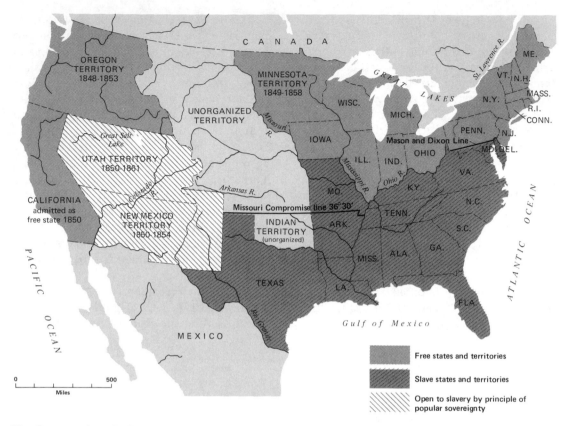

The Compromise of 1850

The Compromise of 1850

Americans of every class and occupation headed for the Pacific Coast. Men from all over the world joined them.

The Compromise of 1850

By 1849, California possessed an unruly population of over 100,000—and an inadequate military government. President Taylor recommended that California (and New Mexico and Utah as well) draw up constitutions and decide without congressional direction whether or not slavery should be excluded. Congress, however, was in no mood to let the new president decide such an important matter on his own.

The fears of proslavery spokesmen were soon confirmed. The constitutions of all three territories banned slavery, but would Congress agree to this violation of the Missouri Compromise? Amidst talk of secession, many southern congressmen prepared an uncompromising stand on all sectional issues. It was becoming increasingly clear that the South might indeed secede from the Union rather than accept exclusion of slavery from the southwestern territories.

Yet Congress was still controlled by older men who loved Union more than section. Henry Clay in particular remained at age seventy-three a powerful and persuasive orator who understood the truly desperate mood of the South. On January 29, 1850, Clay won consideration in the Senate for a series of resolutions, of which these were the most important: (1) that California be admitted as a free state; (2) that the territorial governments in New Mexico and Utah decide for themselves to permit or to prohibit slavery; (3) that slave trading be abolished in the District of Columbia but (4) that slavery itself not be outlawed there without the consent of the District's inhabitants and the state of Maryland, nor without "just compensation" for slave owners; (5) that a stricter fugitive-slave law be adopted by Congress; and (6) that Congress acknowledge that it "has no power to promote or obstruct the trade in slaves between the slaveholding states."

The battle over the Compromise of 1850 was one of the most hotly contested in congressional history. Arrayed against Clay were an angry, suspicious president, secessionists, antislavery men, and Free-Soilers. President Taylor was firm in his conviction that California had to be admitted to the Union without any reservations.

But Clay's resolutions were sufficiently broad and conciliatory to win over the many moderate Unionists in both sections. Among the staunchest of these was Webster, who in a moving speech in the Senate supported Clay's compromise, including even the strict new Fugitive Slave Law. In the North there was an immediate outcry against Webster. But for the moment at least, his efforts strengthened the Unionist position, to which other eloquent men rallied. Outstanding among them was Stephen A. Douglas, who brought many in Congress around to the view that the Southwest was geographically unsuitable for slave labor. After the exhausted Clay retired from the fray, Douglas whipped through the separate measures that made up the Compromise of 1850. His cause was helped by the sudden death of President Taylor early in July and the ascent of Vice-President Mil-

lard Fillmore, a Free-Soiler who nevertheless supported the compromise.

Under the compromise, California entered the Union as a free state. The rest of the region given up by Mexico in 1848 was to be organized as the territories of New Mexico and Utah, where squatter sovereignty would resolve the slavery issue. Slave trading, but not slavery, was banned in the District of Columbia. And, with many northern members of Congress abstaining, the newly tightened Fugitive Slave Law was adopted.

Several northern states soon virtually nullified the Fugitive Slave Law by reenacting and strengthening "personal-liberty laws." These enabled alleged fugitives in those states to have legal counsel, jury trials, and other means of defending their freedom. Northern blacks themselves also took up the defense of fugitives. Blacks, they said, had too long been characterized as meek and yielding. "This reproach must be wiped out," declared the famous escaped slave and abolitionist Frederick Douglass. "Every slavehunter who meets a bloody death in his infernal business, is an argument in favor of the manhood of our race."

The Election of 1852

The nation as a whole, nevertheless, applauded the compromise. In the presidential election of 1852 the national yearning for sectional tranquility and moderation seemed to persist. Franklin Pierce, the Democratic candidate, easily defeated General Scott, the Whig candidate. The Free-Soil party made a poorer showing than in 1848, as northern Democrats in particular returned to the fold.

In the long run the issue of slavery and its extension could not be compromised so easily. Politics was not the only realm of sectional division. The slave South had become profoundly conscious of its differences from the burgeoning free North and West in all phases of life.

SUGGESTED READINGS

W.C. Binkley, *The Texas Revolution* (1952). W. Stegner, *The Gathering of Zion: The Story of the Mormon Trail* (1964). W.E. Bean, *California: An Interpretive History* (1968). D.M. Pletcher, *The Diplomacy of Annexation: Texas, Oregon, and the Mexican War* (1973). K.J. Bauer, *The Mexican War, 1846-1848* (1974). W.J. Cooper, *The South and the Politics of Slavery, 1828-1856* (1978). H. Hamilton, *Prologue to Conflict: The Crisis and Compromise of 1850* (1964).

SUMMARY

Along with slavery, the issue that dominated American politics during the 1840s was Manifest Destiny—the idea that America was destined to rule the entire continent.

The conflict with Britain over the Canadian border, aggravated by events such as the Caroline *affair, the Aroostook War, and the* Creole *incident, was settled peacefully by the Webster-Ashburton Treaty of 1842, which fixed the boundary as far west as Minnesota and Ontario.*

In the Southwest, Texas became an independent republic in 1836 and a state in 1845. In the Far West, Americans looked to the Oregon Country and to California.

The election of James Polk in 1844 was a victory for expansionists. Polk promptly settled the Oregon boundary with Britain, since war with Mexico over Texas was still a possibility. By treaty in 1846, the Canadian–United States border was finally drawn to the Pacific.

The same year, Americans who had settled in California declared themselves the independent Bear Flag Republic. Polk declared war on Mexico, aiming to win New Mexico and California. Obviously a war of aggression, it did not receive bipartisan support. The Treaty of Guadalupe Hidalgo

in 1848 established the Rio Grande boundary and gave Upper California and the Utah and New Mexico territories to the United States in return for a payment of $13 million to Mexico.

The joy over these new territories was marred by the urgency of the slavery issue. The questions now were whether the new states to be carved out of the territories would be slave or free, and whether Congress or the people who settled the new states would decide. The issue of the extension of slavery became poisonous in the election of 1848.

Open conflict was postponed another ten years with the Compromise of 1850, by which California entered the Union as a free state. In two new territories—New Mexico and Utah—the question of slavery was left to the people to decide. Slave trading, but not slavery, was prohibited in the District of Columbia. A strong Fugitive Slave Law was passed to satisfy the South.

The Fugitive Slave Law deeply angered many northerners. Yet for a few years politics went on as usual, and in 1852 the Democratic candidate, Franklin Pierce, was elected president. At the time, no one knew whether the great compromise had permanently solved the issue of slavery in the territories.

11

Society and Thought in Two Nations

During the first half of the nineteenth century American society was undergoing change at an unprecedented rate. The most basic root of this change was economic. Sparked in part by important technological developments, the North especially underwent a revolution in transportation and agriculture as well as beginning a modern factory system. The South had its own revolution as it became increasingly committed to a single cash crop—cotton. These developments were accompanied by wide- spread interest in evangelical religion, by a flowering of literature in the North, and by a spirit of social reform that, again, was confined largely to the North. It was becoming increasingly apparent that the North and the South were developing very different societies characterized by very different values and ideologies. What is especially striking is the relationship between socioeconomic developments and prevailing modes of thought.

THE NEW NORTHERN ECONOMY

New Settlements and New People

Mechanized agriculture first became wide-spread in the United States on the family farms of the northern prairies and the eastern edges of the unforested Great Plains. This fertile country stretched from upper Indiana and Illinois northward to central Wisconsin and Minnesota, and westward through Iowa and upper Missouri to the townships of eastern Kansas and Nebraska.

Even more than the southern coastal plains, this flat and lush terrain invited the large-scale farming that characterizes the twentieth century. At the outset, most of its settlers were independent small farmers from the British Isles and continental Europe or from neighboring states to the east.

During the 1840s a wave of economic distress, accompanied by political repression and religious persecution, spread across western Europe. Irish Catholics were especially hard hit by potato-crop failure and famine in 1845. During the next ten years about 1.3 million Irish fled their Emerald Isle for the United States. Usually they were too poor to move inland from the northern coastal cities in which they landed, though some traveled west as laborers with canal- and railroad-building crews. Second in numbers to the Catholic Irish were some 940,000 Germans (both Catholic and Lutheran), many of whom settled in such midwestern cities as Cincinnati, St. Louis, and Milwaukee. During the same decade, immigrant English, Welsh, and Scots numbered about 375,000. A few thousand Scandinavians also came, heralds of a large migration later in the nineteenth century, along with smaller contingents from other countries in western Europe.

All told, between 1844 and 1854 almost three million European immigrants braved the harrowing Atlantic crossing to America. Most of these newcomers shunned the land of slavery and cotton. As long as southern planters kept their labor system to themselves, away from the Lord's free soil, these western pioneers felt no interest in meddling with the institution of slavery. They had a sufficient supply of labor in their own large families. They kept their sons and daughters on the land, and they invested in machines to augment their productivity.

Farming by Machine

For most of the fifteen years before the Civil War, settlement of the free West ran well ahead of the railroads. Pioneer families traveled on foot, in wagons, and in boats on the rivers, canals, and the Great Lakes.

From the beginning of this westward movement, corn was always the frontier farmer's first marketable crop. Easily converted into fattened hogs, corn could be made to walk to market when other transportation was lacking. Corn also served as winter feed for cattle. For human consump-

tion, corn could be distilled into "likker," eaten off the cob, baked into bread, and prepared in many other ways.

Acre for acre, wheat paid better than corn, over which it had advantages both in marketing and in production. Unlike corn, wheat was eaten all over the world. Less bulky than corn in relation to value, it could bear high transportation costs more easily. It also withstood shipment more successfully. Finally, on the open prairies and plains, where land was plentiful but hired labor scarce, wheat production responded magnificently to improved tools and labor-saving machinery.

In 1837 John Deere, an Illinois blacksmith, produced the first American steel plow. By 1858, after making many improvements on his original design, he was manufacturing 13,000 a year. The most important early farm machine was the steel-toothed reaper, which Cyrus McCormick of Virginia patented in 1834. Sales lagged until 1848, when McCormick moved his plant to Chicago and headed his sales demonstrators toward the western frontier. Ten years later, by means of interchangeable parts, McCormick was manufacturing 500 reapers a month and still failing to meet the demand. By then, mechanical binders and threshers were already being used to harvest and clean the vast quantities of wheat the reapers cut down.

Once the northwestern farmer had committed himself to investing in machines, he found his life greatly altered. The most disturbing change was that he was suddenly in the grip of forces over which he had less and less control. His costly machines could not be turned to other crops if the wheat market faltered, as it did in 1854 and 1857. His worldwide markets, in turn, created problems that seemed to multiply with distance. Marketing, especially,

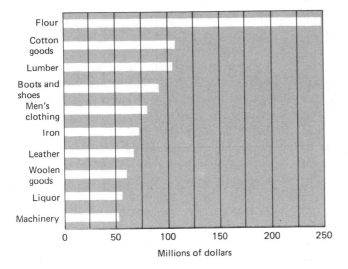

Flour
Cotton goods
Lumber
Boots and shoes
Men's clothing
Iron
Leather
Woolen goods
Liquor
Machinery

0   50   100   150   200   250

Millions of dollars

The ten leading American industries as listed in the 1860 census of manufactures are ranked here by value of product. (From John A. Garraty, *The American Nation*, 4th ed., p. 291. Copyright © 1966, 1971, 1975, 1979 by Harper & Row, Publishers, Inc. Reprinted by permission of the publisher.)

left him at the mercy of graders, storage-elevator operators, rail and water carriers, insurers, and speculators.

The worldwide collapse of prices in 1857 staggered these wheat farmers. In 1858 they began attending meetings other than religious revivals. From these meetings arose broad denunciations of conspiratorial "trading combinations," monopolistic elevator and railroad operators, and grasping money-lenders.

Rather quickly came a demand for two specific programs. One was for agricultural colleges, financed by federal land grants, that would educate farm youth in the new "science" of agriculture. The second demand, which had far broader backing among farmers, was for free homesteads—free of payment and free of slaves—on the remainder of the public domain. Over southern opposition, Congress enacted a land-grant-college bill in 1859, only to have President James Buchanan veto it. In 1860 Buchanan vetoed a homestead bill that would have made western lands available at twenty-five cents an acre. In the elections later that year,

the farmers of the West, rallying around the slogan "vote yourself a farm," helped carry the country for Abraham Lincoln.

The Peak of Water Transportation

In 1860 American foreign trade was five and a half times what it was in 1843, when the ravages of the Panic of 1837 had passed. Domestic trade, however, was ten times as great. By 1860, domestic carriers were hauling goods worth at least fifteen times the combined value of exports and imports. By then the railroad was dominating the economy of the free North and had become a powerful influence on the general welfare of the entire nation. But the railroad had to fight for ascendancy, and during its rise, other forms of transport were fully as important.

Before the railroad boom of the 1850s, domestic commerce was almost monopolized by water carriers. Of these, the oldest—and for a long time the most successful—were the coastal sailing ships. In 1852, the value of goods carried by these vessels was three times the combined value of goods hauled by the railroads and on canals.

The most glamorous of the sailing vessels were the clipper ships, which in the early 1850s were making the New York–San Francisco run around Cape Horn in the then incredible time of ninety days. Their importance, however, lay elsewhere than in the small fraction of American commerce they carried. The clippers helped to tie the East and West coasts to each other and to connect the free states.

When canals between East and West were first built, river men hoped that the artificial waterways would serve as feeders to river craft, just as the rivers fed the coastal carriers. Yet in the long run the Erie Canal, together with the Ohio canals and others, took trade away from the western rivers. More and more of the western trade went from the Mississippi system toward the North and the East.

Perhaps the most dramatic shift was brought about by the completion in 1848 of the canal linking Chicago on Lake Michigan with the Illinois River. The Illinois, which joined the Mississippi north of St. Louis, quickly siphoned off so much Mississippi traffic that by 1850 Chicago had become a major port even though it still lacked a single railroad connection.

In the fifteen years before the Civil War, a struggle for control of western commerce took place between the Mississippi River system and the Great Lakes—a struggle that paralleled the rivalry between the free and slave states for control of the West. By reversing the direction of southbound traffic on the Ohio, Illinois, and northern part of the Mississippi rivers, the canals transformed these former main arteries into

1850

1860

The Railroad Network, 1850–1860

mere feeder streams. By midcentury, the canals had swung the victory irrevocably to the Lakes.

The Triumph of the Railroad

The striking extension of the canal system when railroads had already proved their practicality serves as a reminder that rails were not so obvious an improvement over other means of transportation. Yet by 1860 Americans had built a railroad network of 30,000 miles—one of the world's marvels. As late as 1850, most of the completed railroads were in the Northeast or else connected that section with *waterways* beyond the Appalachians. With few exceptions, these railroads started in great cities, ran through rich and populous territory, and promised considerable profits for those who had invested in them early in the game. Although most of the roads had received state and local government assistance, they were financed largely by the purchase of corporation stock.

During the 1850s the nation's network of railroads expanded dramatically, especially within a 500-mile radius of Chicago. These middle western roads faced more difficult conditions than those in the East: private investment capital was scarce beyond the Appalachian mountains, distances were great, and population was sparse.

By 1860 Congress had granted 18 million acres in ten states for the benefit of forty-five different railroads. With these lands as collateral, the roads were able to market bonds through Wall Street investment bankers to American and foreign investors. During the 1850s, indeed, such bonds became so voluminous that many New York mercantile firms gave up handling goods and became investment bankers specializing in the distribution of railroad securities.

All over the West in the 1850s, railroad construction knocked out canal systems and decimated river traffic. Railroad trains were faster than canal barges or steamboats, and railroad spurs could be laid to factory doors and warehouses. The competitive practices of railroad managers hastened their triumph. Where they encountered water rivals, the railroads cut rates below cost in order to capture the available traffic. They recouped losses by charging all that the traffic would bear at noncompetitive terminals.

Yet two waterways survived railroad competition. One was the Great Lakes route, over which heavy freight such as wheat and iron ore could still be carried more efficiently by barge than by freight trains. The second was the Erie Canal. The continued use of these two waterways reflected the massive volume of the East-West trade, which needed every carrier available to meet the demands of the rising population of western farms and eastern cities.

The New Industrialism

In the 1850s, southern businessmen were among the last to yield to their section's secessionist agitators. They remained a tiny minority in an overwhelmingly agrarian society.

Northern businessmen, for their part, valued their southern business connections. Almost without exception, they deplored the abolitionists in their own section. Yet few of them wished to restore to New Orleans or St. Louis the commerce that New York and Chicago had captured. Fewer still were willing to grant the slave states the first transcontinental railroad or the western lands it would traverse.

The first reasonably accurate census of American manufactures was taken in 1850. Its results were dramatic, for they showed that the annual output of American industry had just surpassed the value of all agricultural products, including cotton.

The growth of manufacturing and of agriculture reinforced each other. As the industrial cities grew, their landless people needed to be fed, and as the number of farms increased, farm families provided an expanding market for domestic manufactures.

What characterized the new economy was its *organization*. Lumber mills, for example, began to *specialize* in the production of barrel staves or shingles or railroad ties, and to use single-purpose machines for the work. Specialization and mechanization appeared in other industries as well. In meat-packing, for example, the hams and shoulders of hogs were packed for eating, and the rest of the flesh was rendered into oil for lubricants and shortening. The hog's bristles went into brushes, the blood into chemicals, the hooves into glue. What remained of the animal was ground into fertilizer. It is no wonder Americans thought of themselves as epitomizing a "newly efficient" age.

Nonagricultural inventions remained far fewer than agricultural ones, but they helped swell the number of patents issued by the United States Patent Office, which had opened in 1790. In 1835 a record number of patents (752) were issued. More than six times that number were issued fifteen years later.

One of the great inventions of the nineteenth century was the electric telegraph, for which the talented painter Samuel F. B. Morse received the first American patent in 1840. Americans first used the telegraph for transmission of business messages and public information. Its effect on the newspaper business was immediate. The "penny press" already dominated American journalism, and printing machinery could produce 1000 newspapers an hour. But news telegraphy caused the demand for newspapers to rise sharply; presses needed to turn out at least 10,000 papers an hour. This huge volume was achieved in 1847 by the cylindrical press developed by Richard March Hoe.

An equally important invention was Elias Howe's sewing machine. I. M. Singer was probably an equally talented inventor, but his long-term success lay in his innovative marketing. He contrived the notion of installment selling backed by advertising. Having worked up an impressive demand for his sewing machines, Singer proceeded to mass-produce them by assembly-line methods. In doing so, he made possible mass manufacture of shoes and clothing.

An Age of Iron

The whole cycle of invention—from the simple steel plow to the sewing machine—gave powerful impetus to the American iron industry. Most of the new agricultural machinery was made from iron and steel parts.

In the 1850s the railroad was by far the biggest single user of iron—for rails, locomotives, wheels, axles, and hundreds of other parts of equipment and rolling stock. Railroads ran the most extensive machine shops in the country, undertaking repairs and manufacturing their own iron and steel tools, parts, and machinery.

It is difficult for us today to recapture the exhilaration that this new metal provided. To all the industrial peoples of the world, iron seemed the staff of life. America's leading iron manufacturer observed, "The consumption of iron is a social barometer by which to estimate the relative height of civilization among nations."

In 1860 invention and industry had just begun to transform the face of America and the character of its people. Nobody knew exactly what was taking place, but everyone was acutely aware that the world was being transformed with unprecedented rapidity. By and large, people felt invigorated by the opening horizons. It seemed to many Americans in midcentury that the generous promise of their continent was coming to fruition.

Others were able to see only the seamy underside of the process. Even when fully employed and receiving regular wages, the members of the new industrial proletariat endured the worst working and living conditions yet found in white America. Bad as working conditions had become, living conditions in the segregated slums of industrial cities were worse.

A PROTESTANT PEOPLE?

Revivalism

In the nineteenth century there was no burst of revivalism such as had swept the colonies during the Great Awakening, though a massive outdoor camp meeting at Cane Ridge, Kentucky, in 1800 led some people to speak hopefully of a second great awakening. Yet revivals occurred frequently at various times and various places. Outdoor camp meetings, often lasting for days at a time, attracted people from hundreds of miles. At these gatherings audiences could listen to a dozen different preachers of nearly as many denominations. Revivals could occur in unexpected places: letters from students at the University of North Carolina, for example, indicate that out-

breaks of religious enthusiasm sometimes swept that college. Upper New York State, settled largely by New Englanders, was swept so frequently by the fires of religious passion that it became known as the "burned-over district." Revivals were not confined to rural areas: in 1857 there was an outbreak in several eastern cities.

Perhaps the most astute comment on revivalism was made by Alexis de Tocqueville, the famous French analyst of American society in the early 1830s. Tocqueville found a "fanatical and almost wild spiritualism" in America and decided that religious enthusiasm was probably natural in a society "exclusively bent upon the pursuit of material objects."

Sectarianism

But one major weakness in a country of churches was sectarian rivalry. Americans seemed to be the most religious of peoples, and yet the most torn by denominational conflicts. The United States had always provided a fertile soil for new sects. But in the 1830s and 1840s the splintering of dissenting churches, each claiming to have the true faith, reached a new peak. Baptists and Methodists, the fastest-growing denominations, were most susceptible to schisms. New cults sprang up everywhere, and the competition for the souls of immigrants pouring into the Mississippi Valley was often uncharitable. Doctrinal differences created a good deal of friction, and different denominations catered to different social classes. Presbyterians, Congregationalists, Episcopalians, and Unitarians differed in theology and in church organization, but drew their membership especially from the well-to-do. Baptists, Methodists, Campbellites, and Universalists were held to be a cut lower socially. The churches for immigrant

Catholics and free Negroes stood, so people thought, at the bottom.

Anti-Catholicism

Most Protestants shared a common hatred of the Roman Catholic church. Even to sophisticated ministers such as Lyman Beecher, the father of Harriet Beecher Stowe and president of Lane Seminary in Cincinnati, Catholicism still meant religious tyranny. Gullible Americans swallowed stories about Catholic atrocities and sensational "exposés" of Catholic depravity. Anti-Catholic prejudice deepened after 1830, when immigration began to rise. In the following twenty years, 2.5 million newcomers arrived, many of them Catholics from Ireland and Germany. In 1830 there were 500 priests in the United States and about 500,000 Catholics. Twenty years later, 1500 priests served 1.75 million of their faith. In addition, the Roman Catholic church had established seminaries, schools, colleges, monasteries, convents, hospitals, and other institutions.

The great majority of Americans, however, regarded themselves as Protestants and the United States itself as fundamentally a Protestant nation. Although a majority of Americans were not church members, evangelical Protestantism (of whatever denomination) formed the basis of much American thought and style, in the South as well as the North.

INTELLECTUAL FERMENT IN THE NORTH

An American Literature

These years of economic change and expansion in the United States were also a time of literary and intellectual flowering scarcely equaled by any other generation in American history.

In the arena of formal literature, Washington Irving, a New Yorker, was the first professional man of letters to win wide popularity at home and applause abroad. When still in his twenties he wrote his *History of New York* (1809), a rousing burlesque of the early Dutch and later backwoods Democrats. It had the whole country laughing. Even more popular among his works was *The Sketch Book* (1819–20), which made Rip Van Winkle and Ichabod Crane vivid American characters in the rural and village setting of his native state.

An even more illustrious member of the New York group was the novelist and moralist James Fenimore Cooper (1789–1851). In Europe, where he lived and wrote for a number of years, Cooper aggressively defended the government and institutions of his native land. In America, he scolded his countrymen for bad manners, chauvinism, contempt for privacy, and slavish submission to public opinion.

A prolific writer, Cooper remains best known for his celebrated Leatherstocking series, which included *The Last of the Mohicans* (1826)—the romance of a white hunter, Natty Bumppo, who lived among the Indians. In his first incarnation, Natty was but a composite of some of the types Cooper had known during a boyhood spent in a pioneer settlement in New York. In successive appearances, however, he grew into a mythic figure, a kind of forest philosopher-king who mediated between white people and red and was immune both to the viciousness of civilization and the barbarism of the frontier.

A surer gauge of American taste in this early period of American literature was the phenomenal success of the New England poet Henry Wadsworth Longfellow (1807–1882). Sitting in his Cambridge study, Longfellow composed volume after volume of flowing verse that made him famous throughout the world. *Hiawatha* (1855), for example, delighted perhaps the largest audience that any American poet ever commanded. His sentimentality and optimism satisfied popular taste.

Although born in Boston, Edgar Allan Poe (1809–1849), regarded himself as a Virginian. He was of humble background, and his actor parents died during his infancy. Poe was no apostle of progress. He had no taste for middle-class truths or democracy. As a literary critic, he wrote cruel reviews of bad books and performed a tremendous service by attacking American provincialism. His own poetry and fiction contained most of the weaknesses he detected in his inferiors: theatricality, bombast, and sentimentality. But in stories like "The Fall of the House of Usher" and "The Imp of the Perverse"—tales of murders, neurotics, and the near-insane—his vulgarity was redeemed by an extraordinary intelligence and intensity.

Transcendentalism

The most wide-ranging literary mind of his generation was Ralph Waldo Emerson (1803–1882). Boston-born and Harvard-educated, he entered the ministry but resigned his pastorate in 1832 because he found church formality meaningless.

Like many other Boston intellectuals of his day, Emerson rebelled against the coldness of the Unitarian faith. While repudiating the harsh Calvinist doctrine of human depravity and a vengeful God, Unitarianism had become passionless in the process. Emerson wanted to revive old-time Puritan fervor without the rigidities of Puritan theology. Quakerism, with its doctrine of the inner light, its gentleness, and its humanitarianism, moved him deeply.

Half Yankee and half yogi, Emerson embodied the warring tendencies of his age. Part of him belonged to the practical American world of banks and railroads. At the same time, Emerson was a mystic and an idealist who looked upon the external world as a passing show and detected an unchanging reality behind it. This shrewd and canny man declared himself to be "part and particle" of God and rejoiced in the unsettling effect his theories had on other Americans.

Transcendentalism, the philosophy associated with Emerson and his sympathizers, was not a systematic faith. It had no creed and could not easily be defined. To some, the word *transcendentalist* covered "all those who contend for perfect freedom, who look for progress in philosophy and theology, and who sympathize with each other in the hope that the future will not always be as the past."

Although vague in its outlines, transcendental doctrine was nobly formulated in Emerson's essays and lectures, in which he announced to his fellow Americans that they too could speak to God directly without churches and creeds. He urged them to be self-reliant, to get their experience at first hand. The ability to communicate with God, or the "Over-Soul," was everyone's gift. But only a few poets, scholars, and philosophers had developed this inborn capacity. From them, others might learn that only the idea is real, that evil is negative (the mere absence of good), and that a kindly destiny awaited them.

Thoreau and Whitman

Henry David Thoreau (1817–1862), like Emerson, his friend and mentor, was a graduate of Harvard and a resident of Concord, Massachusetts. Thoreau gave all his time to self-cultivation and self-exploration. He carefully entered the results in his literary medium, the diarylike record of his experiences. As he once wrote, "I have traveled much in Concord."

In *Civil Disobedience* (1849) and especially *Walden, or Life in the Woods* (1854), Thoreau expressed his tart and unconventional conclusions about literature, religion, government, and social relations. Many of the reformers were his friends, but he distrusted their work. What do the practicalities of life amount to, he asked a generation geared to practicalities. The wealth of the world, he said, is less a reward than one true vision.

Thoreau advised his countrymen to simplify their private lives and their government. He regarded the state as a threat to true independence. Abolitionist, naturalist, poet, rebel, and a down-to-earth but subtle writer, he did not attract much notice while he lived. In our day, *Walden* is justly considered a literary masterpiece, and its author—who discovered a universe in Concord—is regarded as one of the most original minds of the New England literary flowering.

Walt Whitman (1819–1892) was born on Long Island and was a lifelong New Yorker. During his formative years, Whitman worked as schoolteacher, printer, carpenter, journalist, publisher, and editor. When *Leaves of Grass*, his first volume of poems, appeared in 1855, its undisguised references to the body and sex caused him to be denounced as the "dirtiest beast of his age."

Whitman's poems, like Emerson's essays, embody the idea of progress, celebrate the innate goodness of man, and idealize nature. They insist on the spiritual reality underlying the material world. But Whitman looked more to the people than to his own soul for inspiration. Whitman imagined ranks, races, and civilizations commingling, and it was to be America's mission,

he held, to promote this final fellowship of peoples.

Hawthorne and Melville

Emerson and Whitman made many telling criticisms of American society, but their optimism never flagged. Some of their fellow writers, however, were less sure.

Nathaniel Hawthorne (1804–1864) was one who could not shake off the pessimistic doctrines of his Puritan forefathers. In his tales, sketches, and novels—*The Scarlet Letter* (1850), for example—Hawthorne painted a somber moral landscape where men and women were devoured by vices they felt they had to keep secret, but that he exposed. These terrible facts of life mocked the claims of progress. In his works, schemes for human improvement came to nothing; reformers and scientists were changed into monstrous villains who were thwarted in their search for perfection.

Hawthorne's New York friend Herman Melville (1819–1891) held even more strongly to the idea of original sin. An ardent nationalist and celebrator of "the great democratic God," Melville nevertheless cautioned against a freedom that sanctioned barbarism. He pronounced slavery "a blot, foul as the craterpool of hell" and predicted that "these South savannahs may yet prove battlefields." A saddened observer of the war he envisaged, he wrote in *Battle-Pieces* (1866) some of the noblest poetry on the tragic war.

Melville rejected transcendental optimism. Evil, he believed, not only resided in the tainted heart but hung over the world like a curtain. In *Moby Dick* (1851), one of the greatest American novels, Melville struck through the "mask" of life to confront this eternal menace. Ahab, a Yankee whaling captain, the doomed hero of this deep book, spends himself in pursuit of

Moby Dick, a gigantic white whale that symbolizes the beauty, wickedness, and mystery of nature. The pursuit fails, Ahab dies. If humans were half divine, as the transcendentalists insisted, they nonetheless faced a tragic destiny, according to Melville. God remained unknowable; progress, an illusion.

Popular Reading

Although many front-ranking literary figures such as these were achieving recognition, American reading habits were moving in a different direction. During the first third of the century, the number of newspapers rose from 200 to 1200, most of them weeklies. The larger cities boasted numerous daily papers, and competition grew ferocious. In 1830 New York City had 47 papers; only one daily among them claimed as many as 4000 subscribers. Enterprising editors reduced the price of their papers to a penny and sought to lure readers by featuring "robberies, thefts, murders, awful catastrophes and wonderful escapes." New printing presses and improved delivery methods helped meet the rising demand.

Magazines sprang up by the dozens in the middle decades of the century, but few survived for long" With no generally accepted literary standards to rely upon, always in danger of offending the prudish, and yet aware of the "vulgar" preferences of their public, harassed magazine editors found it hard to know which way to turn.

Perhaps the most significant change in popular writing—with novels as well as magazines—was its increasing orientation toward women. After about 1820, more than half the novels published in the United States were written by women. New magazines were published for a specifically female audience. The two most widely circulated of these were *The Ladies Magazine* and *Godey's Lady's Book*, which merged under the editorship of Sarah Josepha Hale in 1836.

Education in Lower Schools

The religious spirit that had such a powerful effect on literature and the family in America was felt even more strongly in the field of education. Most Americans, southern as well as northern, favored Bible teaching in the schools. But despite the lip service paid to Christian, democratic, and practical education, crusaders for free public schools faced an apathetic and often hostile populace. Those who could afford to educate their children in private academies saw no reason why they should be taxed to educate children of the poor. Administrators of private and parochial schools, farmers, and non-English-speaking groups joined the conservatives in fighting the free-school movement.

Yet the advocates of free public schools had strong arguments, and they began to win their battle. By 1860, most northern states had installed a tax-supported elementary-school program. One motivation behind this basically middle-class movement was the hope that free public schools would help assimilate the great numbers of immigrants coming to America in the mid-nineteenth century. But upon their arrival many of these Europeans joined the ranks of the urban poor, whose children could not afford to stop working to attend school. Even after the institution of free public schools, it was chiefly the middle class and not the poorer workers or farmers whose children benefited. Education on all levels continued to suffer because of low teacher salaries, poor equipment, primitive teaching methods, unmanageably large classes, and a short school term.

By the 1840s, private academies were

providing elementary and secondary education for girls. In 1833, Oberlin became the first coeducational college. Twenty-five years later, the University of Iowa became the first coeducational state university. For the most part, girls' seminaries concentrated on ornamental attainments. The learned lady was considered an undesirable oddity, "an unsexed woman" who "does not fill her true place in the world."

Public high schools were rare until 1840, but during the next two decades their number increased substantially, especially in Massachusetts, New York, and Ohio. Such schools offered a more practical kind of education than private schools and were open to both girls and boys.

Higher Education

The number of so-called colleges grew from 16 in 1799 to 182 in 1860. This increase resulted in part from the difficulties and expenses of travel, but sectarian rivalry and local pride were probably the principal causes. Each important religious denomination and many minor ones supported one or more colleges that hoped to rekindle the spirit of piety. Most of them were hardly more than dressed-up academies that students might enter at fourteen or fifteen. So-called universities were hardly more than large colleges. Most professional schools in this period, law and medical schools in particular, were separate institutions.

The most popular and informal educational institution was the lyceum, a private system of public lectures on the arts and sciences. By 1835 lyceums could be found in fifteen states, their activities coordinated by a national lyceum organization. By 1860 no less than 3000 lyceums had been set up, mainly in New England, New York, and the upper Mississippi Valley, where public-school sentiment was strong.

The lyceums sponsored talks on every conceivable topic; scientific and practical subjects aroused the greatest interest.

THE SPIRIT OF REFORM

Temperance and Humanitarianism

The spirit of reform of which the free-school and lyceum movements were reflections pervaded America during the ante-bellum years. Most reformers were motivated by religious zeal to promote pet projects, many of them eccentric, such as seeking salvation through dress and diet practices or the abandonment of money. But reform had its less visionary side as well. During the 1830s and 1840s, a number of men and women devoted their lives to stamping out specific social evils or to supporting defensible social innovations. They advocated temperance with alcohol; kindness for the insane and the criminal; education for the deaf, dumb, and blind; world peace; equality for women; and the abolition of slavery.

Until abolitionism aroused the country after 1830, the temperance movement was the most intense reform enterprise. What caused the rising consumption of liquor is hard to say, but the social scapegoats most frequently pointed to were the excessive mobility of the American population, the attendant disruption of community life, and the long hours of the industrial worker newly arrived in the impersonal city from the country or from abroad. The campaign against demon rum probably reduced the consumption of alcohol. More people participated in this reform movement than in any other. The temperance movement also afforded a training ground for supporters of other reform movements.

One of the most salutary was the crusade for humane hospital treatment of the insane and feeble-minded, led by Dorothea Dix (1802–1887). Her *Memorial to the Legislature of Massachusetts* (1834), the result of painstaking investigation, depicted conditions in asylums throughout the state as medieval in their barbarity. To the popular mind, insanity was a hideous moral regression into animality. Its victims were whipped, caged, and neglected as if they were indeed dangerous beasts. Dix played an important part in establishing mental hospitals in more than thirty states.

Abolition

From the 1830s on, the issue of antislavery grew larger and more ominous until it overshadowed all others. Its origins lay in the mid eighteenth century, when some Quakers denounced the buying and selling of slaves by their coreligionists. Leaders in Revolutionary and post-Revolutionary America deplored slavery. They also deplored the presence of blacks. This conviction inspired the American Colonization Society— founded in 1817 with private, state, and federal support—to establish Liberia in 1822 as a colony for ex-slaves. Yet no more than 1000 free blacks were transported to Africa between 1822 and 1830, and the others showed little desire to emigrate. The failure of the colonization plan and the ineffectiveness of those who backed gradual liberation encouraged radical abolitionists to start their campaign for immediate emancipation.

In 1831 William Lloyd Garrison began publishing *The Liberator,* an uncompromisingly abolitionist periodical. Its appearance marked the beginning of a great antislavery offensive. Garrison was a Massachusetts journalist, neurotic or at least eccentric, tolerant on occasion, yet uncompromising in his cherished beliefs. As with

many of his followers, abolition was only one of Garrison's causes. He eventually became an ardent worker for women's rights and international peace, and a fervent opponent of capital punishment and imprisonment for debt. Yet it was slavery that most absorbed him. He denounced it not because it was inefficient or undemocratic, but because it was unjust and sinful. He damned the Constitution, which guaranteed slavery, and publicly burned copies.

Garrison's vituperative attacks on the "Southern oppressors" did much to intensify antiabolition sentiment in the South, and his fanaticism frightened moderate antislavery people everywhere. His refusal to resort to political action also reduced his effectiveness. A different approach was taken by Theodore Dwight Weld of Ohio, who organized and directed the activities of abolitionist societies in the Northwest. Weld preferred patient organization to flamboyant pronouncements, and his devoted followers, well versed in the techniques of revival meetings, converted thousands to the abolitionist cause. By 1850 almost 2000 abolitionist societies comprising close to 200,000 members had been formed.

Emerson, Thoreau, Whitman, Longfellow, and Melville all condemned slavery. Boston's eloquent Wendell Phillips thundered against it, as did reputable ministers such as Theodore Parker, William Ellery Channing, and the Quaker Lucretia Mott. Southerners such as James G. Birney and the Grimké sisters renounced their slave property and joined the forces of antislavery. Many blacks—Frederick Douglass and Sojourner Truth were only the most famous—worked as effective advocates of the cause.

The abolitionists' strength lay in their unselfish dedication to their appeal to Christian principles. Their weakness lay in their insufficient reckoning with social barriers that blacks had to overcome once they were free. Practically all abolitionists abhorred the idea of violent revolution by the slaves, a fact seldom recognized in the South. They did not envisage or want a civil war over slavery.

At first, abolitionist reformers met massive opposition. In the mid 1830s public opinion, even in the North, stigmatized the abolitionists as a band of misguided bigots whose activities on behalf of a hopelessly inferior people would destroy the Union if left unchecked. Many northern cities were swept by antiabolition riots and mobbings that took place in defiance, or with the connivance, of local authorities.

Despite the stern repression of the abolitionists in the North and the constant (and correct) assurances given to southern leaders that the majority of people in the free states detested the ideas of *The Liberator*, the South grew ever more uneasy. Southern postmasters confiscated suspected abolitionist literature. Fears of slave insurrections and resentment against atrocity stories in abolitionist propaganda made the South magnify the strength of the antislavery movement in the North. This southern response only increased northern antislavery sentiment. As the sectional conflict deepened, the dream of the millenium that had stirred the hearts of reformers in the 1830s and 1840s faded.

The Condition of Women

To many contemporaries, one of the most startling (and alarming) aspects of the abolition movement was the active involvement of women. Reform-minded members of "the female sex" soon saw a connection between the condition of the slave and their own legal and social disabilities.

At first, in the 1830s, the women's-rights movement took aim at laws and social practices that reinforced prevailing ideas about male superiority. A major issue was the participation of women in "promiscuous assemblies" —public meetings attended by both sexes. Angelina and Sarah Grimké were probably the best-known public speakers. They came under fierce attack from members of the clergy, some of whom resolved in 1838 that when a woman "assumes the place and tone of a man as a public reformer, . . . her character becomes unnatural."

Such opposition was widespread. The number of men willing to back the cause of women's rights was very small. Thus it was left to a small but growing number of bold women to speak out on their own behalf. They did so with vigor and eloquence. Sarah Grimké declared in 1838, "I ask no favors for my sex. . . . All I ask of our brethren is that they take their feet from off our necks."

As time went on, women's rights became a campaign in its own right, independent from, yet still connected with, the abolition movement. In 1848 Lucretia Mott and Elizabeth Cady Stanton organized a Woman's Rights Convention at Seneca Falls, New York. The resulting Declaration of Sentiments was deliberately modeled on an earlier declaration: "We hold these truths to be self-evident: that all men and women are created equal . . . ." The convention was attended by sixty-eight women and thirty-two men. It was characteristic of the movement as a whole that the only resolution *not* passed unanimously was a demand for women's suffrage. Everyone agreed that women should be able to control their own property after they married.

These middle-class women were bucking not only forthright opposition but very common cultural assumptions about their proper place in society. During no other period of American history was so much writ-

The Beecher family, the nation's most famous family of preachers. Lyman Beecher, the father, is seated center, with Harriet Beecher Stowe on his left and Catherine Beecher on his right; Henry Ward Beecher is standing at the far right. (Library of Congress)

ten about woman's proper character and sphere of influence. Her place was in the home, where she was to reign supreme in the realm of moral excellence. In this prevailing view, her naturally refined nature made her first duty the moral nurture of her children and the gentle encouragement of her husband, who was said to be overly busy at the countinghouse or even, alas, at the tavern. Most women accepted this role, but the demands of a vocal minority suggested that there was growing discontent on the pedestal.

For working-class women the issues were very different. A grueling fourteen-hour day in a factory was an issue in itself. In 1844 five women workers organized the Lowell Female Labor Reform Association, which then joined with the growing movement of male workers for the ten-hour day. Within a year 600 women in Lowell had joined the association.

Perhaps the most remarkable perspective on the problems faced by women was provided by Sojourner Truth, the ex-slave who became a popular speaker for abolition and women's rights. She told a women's-rights convention in 1851,

That man over there says that women need to be helped into carriages, and lifted over ditches, and to have the best place everywhere. Nobody ever helps me into carriages, or over mud-puddles, or gives me any best place! And ain't I a woman? . . . I have borne thirteen children, and seen them most all sold off to slavery, and when I cried out with my mother's grief, none but Jesus heard me! And ain't I a woman?

SOUTHERN SOCIETY

White People of the South

White society in the South was more homogeneous than in the North, more conservative in its ways, less exposed to social and intellectual ferment. In 1860 three-fourths of white southerners owned no slaves at all. Almost half the slaveholding families owned fewer than six slaves, and only 12 percent of all slave owners possessed twenty or more. The real "planting class" was thus a very small minority. A mere 8000 planters owned fifty or more slaves. There were, in addition, important regional differences in slaveholdings. In the six states of the lower South (except Texas) between one-third and one-half of the white families owned slaves. Elsewhere the proportions ranged from only one-thirteenth to one-fourth. Within each state, moreover, large plantations were concentrated in areas possessing the most fertile soil and access to water transportation.

Some large planters lived the high life of saber-rattling, fire-breathing "cavaliers." In the older South many of the gentry lived well—some extravagantly. But most of them bore the cares that went with ownership of property, and they had little time to enjoy more than the simple pleasures of rustic society: hunting, horse racing, card playing, visiting, and perhaps an annual summer pilgrimage to the mountains or the sea to escape the heat.

The farms of the plain yeomen of the South might be discovered tucked away among the large plantations in the cotton and tobacco country, but they predominated in the upland South—in eastern Tennessee, western North Carolina, and northern Georgia, Alabama, and Mississippi. Here, although some produced the southern staples, most of the plain folk grew subsistence crops and raised livestock. The plain folk also included the storekeepers, the mechanics, and other artisans in the villages and towns.

Seen through the perceptive eyes of Frederick Law Olmsted, the Connecticut Yankee who traveled through the South in the early 1850s, yeoman living standards seemed distinctly below those of northern farmers. Olmsted reported riding through an area of thin, sandy soil "thickly populated by poor farmers. . . . They are very ignorant; the agriculture is wretched and the work hard." Yet although Olmsted complained of wretched cooking, vermin-filled beds, and rude manners, he also noted that the yeomen in general were a sturdy, hospitable people. "If you want to fare well in this country," he was told in northern Alabama, "you stop to poor folks' housen; they try to enjoy what they've got while they ken, but these yer big planters they don' care for nothing but for to save."

The "bottom sill" of southern white society were the so-called poor white trash. Once lumped indiscriminately by outsiders with all nonslaveholding whites, they made up a minority reduced by disease to what subsistence they could scratch from unwanted land, as well as from fish and game. Many of them worked as little as possible because they associated hard labor in the fields with black slaves. Of the poor whites, the discerning Olmsted wrote "They are said to 'corrupt' the negroes, and to encourage them to steal, and to pay them with liquor, and to constantly associate licentiously with them. They seem, nevertheless, more than any other portion of the community, to hate and despise the negroes."

The Black Population

Prior to the invention of the cotton gin (1793), slaves were concentrated in eastern Virginia and lowland South Carolina and Georgia. With the westward expansion of upland cotton and with the official closing of the international slave traffic in 1808, there began a massive forced movement of slaves into Alabama, Mississippi, Louisiana, and beyond. This domestic slave trade meant that hundreds of thousands of blacks were uprooted from their homes in Virginia and in the East and forced into the role of land-clearing western pioneers.

A considerable majority were thrown onto large cotton and sugar plantations. Indeed, the slaves (unlike whites) typically lived on the factorylike plantation unit. On the eve of the Civil War, appreciably more than half the slave population lived on units with more than twenty slaves; about one-quarter, on units of more than fifty. Slaves were concentrated in the richest agricultural regions. In some counties of the lower South, they greatly outnumbered whites. Only about 10 percent lived in cities and towns. Slaves were also employed in factories and in river commerce. In fact, just before the Civil War, about 6 percent of the blacks in the South were technically not chattel slaves at all, though these "free Negroes" remained legally and socially downtrodden.

This demographic pattern profoundly affected the lives of both blacks and whites. It meant that the principal social contacts of many blacks were with other blacks. And it meant that the families of the wealthy planting class, more than other whites, had direct contact with masses of slaves. On the one hand, many blacks thus grew up somewhat isolated in their own Afro-American subculture; on the other, the South's ruling class was raised in intimate contact with the actual workings of the peculiar institution, with all its ambiguities of daily contact, distrust, and fear.

Another characteristic of the black population immediately preceding the Civil War had important consequences for both peoples. By 1860, despite some smuggling of slaves from Africa, the overwhelming majority of American slaves were native-born, as they emphatically had not been a century earlier. Thus the black population was Afro-American, not African. From birth, for example, slaves spoke English, though in their own dialect. All this meant that the cultural distance between blacks and whites had narrowed considerably.

The Slave Experience

On the characteristic Black Belt plantation, as elsewhere, the field hand's routine varied little from day to day, year to year. The day's work lasted, as the saying went, from "can see, til can't." There were short breaks for the breakfast and lunch rations, which were brought to the men and women in the fields. Plowing behind a stubborn mule, weeding or "chopping" the endless rows of cotton, and finally picking the bolls of their white fibers without including in one's bag much in the way of brown leaves and stalks—this routine, twelve to sixteen hours a day, was the slave's life. And no matter whether the master or overseer was brutal or kindly, this labor was *forced*.

The treatment of slaves ranged enormously, all the way from sadism to gentle paternalism. On some plantations, slaves found themselves continually beaten; on others, never. Some slaves were always hungry; others ate nearly as well as the white folks. The principal cause of this variation in treatment was not so much the region or plantation size as the personalities involved. On large plantations, the slave's principal contact with authority was usually with the white overseer, whose personality made a great difference. But at least in the long run, the owner and the slaves decided what kind of overseer they would tolerate. The weight of power, of course, lay with whites, but they rarely had complete control.

Generalizations about "the slave experience" keep breaking down along these lines, but it remains possible to make certain general statements. Slaves in the old frontier Southwest were treated with greater severity than in the older South. Slaves on large plantations were confronted with more impersonal, though not necessarily more severe, discipline than slaves on small plantations. There were greater class and occupational distinctions on large plantations than on small ones. The distinction between house servants and field hands was never absolute, but as time went on, there was a tendency for slave children to inherit the skills and status of their parents. Slaves in the old upper South and on small farms were more likely than others to have their lives disrupted by sale away from their homes and families.

The family life of slaves has been a matter of controversy among historians. In the eyes of the law there was no such thing as a binding marriage between slaves, and slave children might be sold away from their parents. In practice, however, although a great many slave families were broken up, a far larger number managed to survive as much intact as other nineteenth-century families. Slaves wanted, and many masters actively encouraged, a stable family life, including children raised by their parents under the same roof. On large plantations this was the usual pattern. Especially on smaller units, however, the husband was likely to live on a neighboring plantation and be able to see his family only once or twice a week, under protection of a written pass from his owner. Thus despite the absence of legal protection and the informality of marriage ceremonies—often mere "jumping over the broomstick," as it was called—many slaves were able to maintain loving and nurturing family relationships.

Many of these families lived under the threat of disruption by sexual advances by white men. Black men could do little, of course, to defend their sexual interests, and they knew better than to approach white women. The restrictions on white women were equally clear: they had all the advantages and disadvantages of being confined atop a pedestal.

The Slaves' Inner World

Hemmed in as they were on so many sides, slaves struggled to create a measure of precarious independence. In their work, some took fierce pride in productivity while others took an equal satisfaction in their skillfullness at malingering. Some boasted of their capacity for bearing punishment; others claimed skill at avoiding it. A great many sought the comforts of religion. It was an ambiguous refuge. Christianity could be used as an escape from the toils of this world, or it could be used as a handbook for revolutionary action. For the most part, though, slaves adopted Christianity in order to make their own world comprehensible and their own communities partially independent of the white world.

Music was frequently used by slaves as a means to heighten shared feelings within the community. In no other arena of activity was their common African background more pervasive and obvious. Singing and dancing formed an integral part of a wide variety of activities: prayer meetings, quilting bees, corn shuckings. There were ax songs, boat songs, and children's ring games. What is perhaps most remarkable about the words of these songs is that there is no clear dividing line between the sacred and the secular. One common theme runs through a great many of the songs: a desire for a better life.

Slave Resistance and White Response

Slaves also dealt with the circumstances of their lives by actively resisting the system. Throughout two centuries of slavery, slaves malingered, broke tools, abused farm animals, feigned illness, and otherwise struck out at the principal requirements of the system: hard work and productivity. Slaveholders responded with some combination of punishments and rewards, but they disagreed about which was more effective, a thorough lashing or gifts of tobacco and clothing at Christmas.

An early photograph of living quarters of slaves on a South Carolina plantation. (New York Historical Society)

From the planters' point of view the worst problem was running away. After about 1800, slaves in the upper South sometimes headed for freedom in the northern states. A far more common pattern was for slaves to run off for a few days or weeks in the woods and then return to face a whipping. Many runaways did not run "away" at all. Rather, they left their owner's plantation in an attempt to rejoin a spouse or other relatives.

Slavery rested on a base of violence, and slaves sometimes responded in kind. There were just enough instances to keep the white population thoroughly on edge. Two of the most effective and drastic means at the slaves' disposal were arson and poisoning. Probably more common were the numerous instances when a slave suddenly decided that he would rather fight and die than be whipped.

Despite the overwhelming odds against them, slaves also conspired to mount armed rebellions. Most of these uprisings involved a half a dozen to twenty-five slaves, and most were aborted when whites were tipped off ahead of time by a slave unwilling to go along with the rebels. The most important rebellions (as opposed to baseless panics and rumors among whites) occurred during a forty-year period following the successful slave uprising in Haiti in the 1790s.

Nat Turner, a Virginia slave preacher, led the most drastic slave revolt. He took his followers on a route of killings through Southampton County in 1831 that left some sixty white persons dead. Terrified whites, who regarded Turner as a fanatic, lashed back by tracking down the rebels and killing many on the spot. In the process, many blacks who had no connection with the rebellion were also slaughtered, probably over one hundred in all. Turner himself re-mained at large for a month but was finally captured and hanged.

The impact of Turner's revolt was immediate and long-lasting. The reports of suppression and bloody reprisals carried a disheartening message across the black South. The white South, meanwhile, sharpened its defenses as abolitionist propaganda spread. In the towns and cities, police costs "for the purpose of 'keeping down the niggers,' " as one traveler reported, made up the largest municipal-budget item. "Free people of color," along with abolitionists, came increasingly under suspicion in the South, and many black preachers among the slaves were silenced. Indeed, the religious language in which slave rebels exhorted their followers convinced many planters that Bible reading—in fact any reading—was downright incendiary. Many states outlawed teaching slaves to read and write. Yet many slaves persisted in study and in individual strikes for freedom despite the growing hostility of their environment.

The Plantation Economy

Everyone in the South, whatever color, sex, or status, was affected by the workings of the plantation economy. The first southern agricultural staple had of course been tobacco in the Maryland and Virginia tidewater region. After 1800, tobacco culture spread westward across the upper South, where by midcentury more tobacco was being grown than on the older plantations. Yet, compared with cotton, tobacco remained a relatively minor southern crop.

Only the wealthier planters could successfully embark upon production of rice or sugar, the South's two other significant, lesser staples. Both crops required large-gang labor, easily drawn from the dense black populations of South Carolina, Georgia, and southern Louisiana. The size of these plantations was unmatched by those of even the Gulf states of the Cotton Kingdom.

As early as 1820, the South's cotton crop had become more valuable than all its other crops combined. Just before the Civil War, cotton accounted for two-thirds of the *nation's* exports.

With a little capital, small acreage, and a few slaves, a cotton farmer could make a profit. Cotton could survive rough handling when shipped to market, and it did not spoil when stored—important considerations where poor transportation and warehousing caused marketing delays. Much of the American cotton crop, even on the frontier, was in fact grown by small farmers. Yet its huge market and great adaptability to slave-gang labor made cotton the ideal staple for the big planters who spread over the virgin lands of the Southwest. By 1860, slave gangs were growing more than 93 percent of the Mississippi crop.

Where land was plentiful and cheap but labor was dear, the essence of good plantation management was high production per slave, not per acre. Assuming a planter had effective overseers and slave drivers, the more slaves he had, the greater his margin of success with cotton.

White southerners were familiar with the invidious contrasts drawn even by their own spokesmen between the busy North—enterprising, public-spirited, prosperous—and the indolent, poverty-stricken South. Many of them feared the impact of factories upon an agrarian slave society. Some felt (though there was evidence in southern factories to the contrary) that slaves working in a factory were already half free.

In spite of such doubts and apprehensions, a favorable attitude toward manufacturing developed during the 1820s and early 1830s when tariff controversies made the South acutely conscious of its dependence on northern industry. Yet although there were some attempts to establish cotton mills, the South remained overwhelmingly agricultural. On the eve of the Civil War, the South was producing less than 10 percent of the nation's manufactured goods.

The South showed even greater aversion to commerce than to manufacturing. At the numerous commercial conventions held in the South between 1830 and 1860, the southern imagination was fired with rhetorical visions of teeming cities, happy artisans, and bustling marketplaces—the rewards of recapturing the cotton-carrying trade from the North. But control of cotton marketing remained in the hands of outsiders. It was not southerners who held the reins of insurance, shipping, brokerage, and banking. The financial capital of the Cotton Kingdom was New York City!

THE MIND OF THE DOMINANT SOUTH

Race and Slavery

After 1830 the allegiance of the vast majority of southerners to the slave-plantation system deepened measurably. Their attachment to the "peculiar institution" varied according to class, region, and occupation, but the following considerations help to explain why slavery received such overwhelming support in the decades preceding the Civil War. First, the extremely heavy concentration of slaves in parts of the South generated deep-seated fears. Southern spokesmen declared that antislavery northerners had no inkling of what it was like to live in South Carolina or Mississippi communities where blacks far outnumbered whites. Second, it was widely held in the

South that blacks would only be harmed by abolition, a belief strengthened by reports about the deteriorating condition of free blacks in the North. Finally, impoverished southern whites ardently supported slavery as a way of preserving what little status they had. When the time came, they fought for slave property and for a slave-owning class.

As early as the Revolutionary period, many leaders in the upper South had seen the incongruity of slavery in a republic dedicated to the principles of the Declaration of Independence, but they had done little about it. About the beginning of the 1830s, however, a number of events triggered a crisis in southern thinking about slavery. In 1829 David Walker, a black man from Boston, published his impassioned *Appeal* to southern slaves for a full-scale revolt. A shudder of horror and outrage went through the white South. In January 1831, Garrison brought out the first issue of *The Liberator*. Abolitionism seemed to shift into high gear, and soon a price had been placed upon Garrison's head. That summer Nat Turner's rebellion horrified the nation, and the following winter, the Virginia legislature not only debated gradual emancipation bills but came close to passing one. And of course the nation was in the midst of the nullification controversy, in which South Carolina's defiance of national tariff duties rested ultimately on that state's commitment to chattel slavery.

The response to these events was immediate and drastic. Whereas southerners had previously claimed that slavery was a necessary evil, they now turned eagerly to embrace the proposition that slavery was a positive good. The Bible and the Constitution as well as political science, biology, and classical requirements for high culture were arrayed in favor of the peculiar institution. Slavery, southern writers claimed, fostered the classical form of democracy with all the Greek virtues, as distinct from the "mongrelized" industrial democracy of the North.

The Reform Spirit in a Strait Jacket

The claim of impassioned proponents of slavery that the South had erected a superior civilization on a slave base was staked on shaky ground. Intellectual novelties were not welcomed in the ante-bellum South, and in education and literacy the South lagged behind the North. In the southern mind, all isms—feminism, transcendentalism, and the rest—quickly became tinged with abolitionism. Feminism in particular outraged the southern ideal of womanhood.

Yet the humanitarian influences and reform spirit that flowed through the country in the 1830s and 1840s did not leave the South untouched. Criminal codes were humanized, at least for whites; prisons were improved, and treatment of the insane was made more humane. Temperance was perhaps the most enthusiastically supported reform movement in the prewar South. Backed by religious and political leaders, temperance societies sprang up everywhere to the accompaniment of parades, petitions, and the publicized testimony of reformed drunkards.

Even before the abolitionist campaign began, suffrage was being extended, though not as broadly as in the North. But the South faced a more serious problem. Public education remained almost nonexistent. Some 2700 small private academies could be found in the South by 1850, but students were few and the quality of education was lower than in the North. The 1850 census showed 20 percent of southern whites illiterate, 3 percent in the Middle states, and 1 percent in New England. Southern higher education compared more favorably, but wealthy southern families continued to send their sons to northern institutions rather than to their own state universities and denominational colleges.

Antinorthern sentiment intensified in the 1840s and 1850s, and southern leaders made strenuous efforts to throw off the intellectual yoke of the Yankees. It was particularly galling for southern students to be given northern texts. One book, for example, described slavery as "that stain on the human race, which corrupts the master as much as it debases the slave." Agitation against the importation of poisonous alien doctrines, however, apparently did not halt the sale of northern books or keep many southern students from northern schools.

Political and religious liberalism, so marked in the Jeffersonian South, declined after the 1820s. The skeptical spirit fostered by the Enlightenment among the aristocracy gave way to religious fundamentalism among the common folk. Religious revivals of the early 1800s converted thousands to the Methodist and Baptist faiths, and ministers of such evangelical denominations acquired powerful influence. Moral reform went hand in hand with intellectual orthodoxy. From southern pulpits came thunderous denunciations of infidelity, alcohol, atheism, and "northern enthusiasms."

Intellectual repressiveness was by no means confined to the South. Heresy hunts and anti-infidel crusades also flickered through the North and West. But in the South the skeptical minority was more thoroughly pressured into silence by those who felt called to denounce what they saw as regiments of "profane sinners, downright skeptics, and God-defying wretches."

Even though a number of talented writers published fiction, poetry, and essays of high quality during the ante-bellum period, there was no literary flowering comparable to New England's. As long as the older and better-educated families dominated southern culture, literary tastes and standards were those of cultivated amateurs who believed professional writing to be unsuitable for gentlemen and ladies.

As sectional animosities deepened after 1830, southern writers found themselves in a dilemma. According to a Charleston poet, any truthful account of the South antagonized northern readers, while southern readers were quick to detect any lapse in local pride. Southern authors were expected to fight with their pens to uphold their culture against criticisms from the North.

As we view their efforts now, it seems clear that they knew in their hearts that the society they were defending was at bottom indefensible in the face of world opinion. So much of southern energy was absorbed by the defense of slavery that little remained for other outlets. Racial slavery lay at the base of the southern economy; it also preoccupied the southern mind.

SUGGESTED READINGS

R.D. Brown, *Modernization: The Transformation of American Life, 1600-1865* (1976). R.O. Matthiessen, *American Renaissance: Art and Expression in the Age of Emerson and Whitman* (1941). G. Frederickson, *The Black Image in the White Mind: The Debate on Afro-American Character and Destiny, 1817-1914* (1971). R.G. Walters, *American Reformers, 1815-1860* (1978). A.F. Scott, *The Southern Lady: From Pedestal to Politics* (1970). L.A. Cremin, *American Education: The National Experience* (1980). K.M. Stampp, *The Peculiar Institution: Slavery in the Antebellum South* (1956). J. Oakes, *The Ruling Race: A History of American Slaveholders* (1982).

SUMMARY

The ante-bellum era saw the development of a new economy in the North. There was massive new migration from Europe—especially from Ireland and Germany—mechanization of agriculture, a revolution in transportation, the beginnings of a factory system, and increased reliance on iron and mechanical inventions. Throughout the country a spirit of evangelical Protestantism held sway. At the same time, in the North there was a flowering of literature that produced many minor and a few major works. More people were influenced, however, by popular newspapers and magazines and by the spread of education at all levels.

These developments were accompanied by a virtual fire storm of social reform in the North. Temperance was the first and most popular, but there were many other worthy causes. After 1830 abolition increasingly took center stage, though a very small minority began turning their attention to the status of women.

Finally, it was becoming increasingly clear that the South was different— in its social structure and in its concerns about slavery and race. Blacks and whites in the South lived very different lives and inevitably had very different outlooks. One can sense not only a split between the two races, which had always been present, but the potentiality for a split between two societies, southern and northern.

12

The Union Comes Apart

In the early 1850s, slavery was brought home to northerners who had previously regarded it as a distant problem. Two developments were largely responsible: The new Fugitive Slave Law created widespread anger in the North. A series of incidents where fugitives were forcibly seized and returned to slavery created a vivid impression. The second factor was, of all things, publication of a novel. Uncle Tom's Cabin had an enormous impact on northern public opinion.

Yet it was slavery in the territories that became the most divisive issue. The Democrats in Congress pushed through the Kansas-Nebraska Act, which repealed the Missouri Compromise and put the future of the "free" territories in doubt. The question became cancerous. Many northerners concluded that there really was a "slave-power conspiracy" to extend slavery throughout the West and perhaps eventually to the free states as well.

The collapse of the Whig party after 1852 left a political vacuum that was filled at first by the Know-Nothings, a new party dedicated to countering the great wave of Roman Catholic immigration. But dedication to free soil proved even stronger, and the new Republican party emerged as the major counterweight to the Democrats almost overnight. By insisting that slavery expand no farther, the Republicans made themselves a purely sectional party. In 1860, many southern spokesmen made it clear that the election of a Republican president would mean secession.

Lincoln was elected as a minority president in a four-way contest. The states of the cotton South thereupon began to secede and organize a government of their own. The upper South remained on the fence until Lincoln maneuvered South Carolina authorities into firing the first shot, at Fort Sumter in Charleston harbor. That action forced the states of the upper South to a decision. They split evenly, four joining the Confederacy and four remaining with the Union. Lincoln moved to suppress the "rebellion." Southerners rallied to the cause of their newly independent nation. The United States had finally come apart on the one issue that the Founding Fathers had tried so hard to avoid.

THE SLAVERY ISSUE

The Democrat Franklin Pierce of New Hampshire took office as president on March 4, 1853. A contemporary described him as a "vain, showy, and pliant man." Unfortunately, the description was close to being correct. Most Americans, including the president, still hoped that the Compromise of 1850 would stop the agitation over slavery once and for all. But the subject would not drop. The weakness of the president did not help matters, but even a much stronger man would probably have been overwhelmed.

Slavery Comes Home to the North

The Fugitive Slave Law of 1850 provided southern slaveholders with considerable powers for recovering runaways. Its provisions were so broad that it made some free northern blacks move to Canada in fear of being legally kidnapped into slavery. Any slaveholder or his or her hired agent was empowered to seize a "runaway" slave, to ask for assistance from any federal marshal in the process, and then to go before a federal judge. Judges received $10 if they ruled that a Negro was a slave or $5 if they ruled that the person was free. The law also provided for a fine of $1000 and six months in jail for anyone convicted of aiding a fugitive slave.

These provisions outraged abolitionists. They also angered a good many people in the North who had been hostile to abolition. Black leaders like Frederick Douglass called upon the black community to resist with force. Many northern states passed "personal-liberty" laws that attempted to nullify the effects of the new federal statute.

A series of incidents brought state and federal officials and mobs into conflict. A black man named Frederick Wilkins was working quietly as a waiter in a Boston coffeehouse when he was suddenly seized by a Virginia slave catcher, who knew him as Shadrach, a runaway slave. While Wilkins was being held for return to Virginia, a crowd of blacks burst in and took him away. In New York City, James Hamlet was grabbed and packed off to Maryland so fast that his wife and children had no chance to say goodbye to him.

Only a few years later, the streets of Boston were lined with federal troops and marshals when the fugitive Anthony Burns was marched from the courthouse down to the ship waiting to carry him back to slavery in Virginia. That force held back an estimated 50,000 people—a crowd larger than the entire population of Boston at the time of the Stamp Act crisis—who hissed and shouted in protest. It cost the federal government the enormous sum of $100,000 to return Burns to slavery. About 300 blacks were dragged back to slavery under the Fugitive Slave Act. For every slave returned, however, thousands of northerners changed their minds about slavery.

Slavery was brought even closer to home by a vivid antislavery book, *Uncle Tom's Cabin* by Harriet Beecher Stowe. It was probably the most influential novel ever published in the United States. It was printed in 1852 in an edition of only 5000 copies because the publisher had no great expectations for heavy sales. The first printing sold out in two days. Within a year the novel sold 300,000 copies. In order to meet demand, the publisher kept eight of the new rotary steam presses going around the clock and bought the entire stock of three paper mills. Throughout the North, Mrs. Stowe was hailed for lifting the veil of the peculiar institution. In the South, she was denounced for having painted it in false colors.

Poster advertising *Uncle Tom's Cabin*. (New York Historical Society)

The Kansas-Nebraska Act

These developments led southern planters to seek countermeasures. A small minority unsuccessfully demanded the reopening of the African slave trade. A more influential group, supported by Pierce himself, urged the acquisition of Spain's Cuba, where slavery was flourishing. Enough public support for annexation might have been gotten if not for the Kansas-Nebraska Act, passed by Congress in 1854. In reopening the question of slavery in the western territories, this measure strengthened northern determination to stop the spread of slavery everywhere.

Many issues, open and concealed, lay behind the Kansas-Nebraska Act. Railroad extension, private political ambitions, sectional bargaining, slavery, and the aspirations of western settlers were all involved. The central figure in the drama was Senator Stephen A. Douglas, New England-born but by 1850 the idol of his Illinois constituents.

An ardent supporter of land-grant aid to western railroads, Douglas had become the leading spokesman for a northern route that would link the Pacific coast with Chicago, where he had large real-estate investments. Before such a railroad could be built, however, the vast Nebraska Territory would have to be organized for settlement. The transcontinental railroad was too much of a prize for the South to simply let go. In order to win support for a bill to organize the Nebraska Territory, Douglas therefore had to make concessions both to a southern group who wanted the railroad line to run along the Mexican border, and to a proslavery group in Missouri who advocated a central route to the Pacific from St. Louis. On January 23, 1854, after extended discussions with proslavery senators that led to his making the required concessions, Douglas introduced his bill to organize the Nebraska Territory.

In its final form Douglas's Kansas-Nebraska Act called for the organization not of one but of two territories, Kansas and Nebraska, the two to be divided at the fortieth parallel. The act also repealed the Missouri Compromise (since both territories lay above 36°30′, where that compromise had prohibited slavery) and stated that the residents of the two territories, and not Congress, should determine by "popular sovereignty" whether they would permit slavery when they became states. But the act was silent on the old question of just when on the road to statehood this decision on slavery should be made. The first transcontinental railroad, moreover, remained a dream until the Civil War had begun.

Douglas himself had predicted that his measure would raise "the hell of a storm," but the storm proved to be far more serious than even he had anticipated. Instead of mobilizing reasonable men behind the progress of the country and his own career, Douglas's bill sharpened sectional differences and weakened his personal appeal. In the Senate, which was less subject than the House

to political storms, the Kansas-Nebraska bill passed 37 to 14. In the House, which in 1854 was up for election, the bill squeaked through 113 to 100. Every one of the forty-five northern Whigs in the House voted against the bill. This group received the support of almost half the northern Democrats, thereby fracturing the principal national party, on whose unity Douglas had staked his future as well as that of the Union. A solid bloc of southern Democrats and half the northern Democrats, on the other hand, together with the majority of the southern Whigs, had put the measure across. Thus the Whig party was split as well. Repeal of the Missouri Compromise sent an especially strong wave of resentment throughout the North.

Bleeding Kansas

The Kansas-Nebraska Act failed its first test in the new Kansas Territory. Did a new territory under popular sovereignty have the power to prohibit or legalize slavery before framing its constitution and before seeking statehood? Douglas said yes; southern spokesmen said no. Only a state could decide this question, southerners maintained; a territory could not keep slaves out. As settlers moved into Kansas, the issue quickly passed beyond debate.

Most of the settlers were slaveless farmers from adjacent states, but Missourians moved to Kansas to head off the Yankees. Hotheads spurred on by partisan newspapers and politicians soon turned Kansas into a battleground. On election day in March 1855, slightly more than 2000 Kansans were registered to vote for members of the territorial legislature. But over 6000 ballots were cast, most of them by Missourians who had come into Kansas just for the day.

The governor of the Kansas Territory tried to disqualify eight of the thirty-one members who had been elected irregularly, but President Pierce refused to back the governor and eventually recalled him.

The new legislature adopted a series of savagely repressive laws that, among other punishments, prescribed the death penalty for aiding a fugitive slave. But Free-Soilers in Kansas were not intimidated. In the fall of 1855 they met in Topeka and drew up their own constitution. In January 1856 they elected their own legislature and governor. Kansas now had two rival administrations and was ripe for war.

While Pierce procrastinated, war came. A force of hard-drinking proslavery men raided Lawrence in search of some Free-Soil leaders whom the proslavery legislature had indicted for treason. The raiders burned the hotel, destroyed homes, and smashed Free-Soil printing presses.

The "sack of Lawrence," exaggerated by northern newspapers, spawned a bloodier sequel. John Brown, a fanatical abolitionist who was soon to become better known, gathered six followers, rode into the proslavery settlement at Pottawatomie Creek, and hacked five men to death. He acted, so he said, under God's authority. But his sacred vengeance started a guerrilla war in which over 200 persons died.

Violence over Kansas spread to the very halls of Congress. Charles Sumner of Massachusetts, speaking in the Senate, carried on for two days about the "harlot slavery." He aimed his most vicious criticisms at Senator Andrew P. Butler of South Carolina. Two days later Butler's nephew, a congressman, entered the floor of the Senate and beat Sumner over the head with a cane, making him an invalid for several years. The assault on Sumner by "Bully" Brooks, together with the news from Kansas, came as

preparations were being made for the presidential campaign of 1856.

POLITICAL TURMOIL

A New Party Alignment

The breakup of the Whigs and Democrats, evident before the Kansas-Nebraska Act but speeded up by that measure, sent politicians scurrying for new homes. The first of the new parties, the short-lived American party, took its name in 1852 from its opposition to the unprecedented number of Irish Catholic immigrants and others pouring into the country. This party was so concerned over its Americanist bias that it required its members to pretend to know nothing when pressed for information. Thus it soon became known as the Know-Nothing party. Politicians in both sections were drawn to the Know-Nothings, hoping that immigration might help deflate slavery as an issue. But the party made strong enemies as well, one of them Abe Lincoln. Slower than most to disown his long Whig allegiance, Lincoln wrote in 1855,

> Our progress in degeneracy appears to me to be pretty rapid. As a nation, we began by declaring that "all men are created equal." We now practically read it "all men are created equal except negroes." When the Know-Nothings get control, it will read "all men are created equal except negroes and foreigners and Catholics." When it comes to this I should prefer emigrating to some country where they make no pretense of loving liberty.

When the American party's 1854 national convention voted to support the Kansas-Nebraska Act, most of its southern following joined the Democrats; northern

Know-Nothings moved to the new Republican party.

One firm principle first brought the makers of the new Republican party together in 1854: the belief that Congress had the right to keep slavery out of the territories. Free-Soilers, of course, flocked to the Republican camp. So did "conscience Whigs," who hated any further compromise with slavery. Democrats opposed to the Kansas-Nebraska Act also joined in goodly numbers, as did some outright abolitionists. A prohibitionist wave was sweeping the country, and the ranks of the so-called temperance movement furnished many Republican recruits. Oddly enough, the Republicans also attracted a considerable number of German immigrants, who might have been put off by the Know-Nothings but whose taste for free land proved stronger than their distaste for teetotalers and "nativist" Americans.

Although the Republicans opposed the extension of slavery, no more than a small minority had any interest in the well-being of blacks. North or South, blacks remained outside the land of opportunity. Most Republicans wanted free soil—not freed slaves—and the advancement of the common white man rather than the welfare of the black.

The Election of 1856

In preparing for the 1856 presidential campaign the Democrats avoided both the discredited Pierce and the controversial Douglas. Instead, they nominated a veteran of forty inconsequential years in politics who had had the good fortune to serve abroad during the recent administration—the conservative Pennsylvanian James Buchanan.

Although "Old Buck" soon came to be despised as a northern man with southern principles, this combination of characteristics helped the efficient Democratic machine bring him victory over glamorous soldier-explorer John C. Frémont, the nominee of the new Republican party. The American party's candidate, former president Millard Fillmore, finished third.

Dred Scott

Buchanan had been in office only a few days when he was confronted with the first great crisis of his administration. The trouble arose over the Supreme Court decision in *Dred Scott* v. *Sandford* (1857), which confirmed the contention of southerners that Congress had no right under the Constitution to exclude slavery from the territories.

Dred Scott, a slave, had been taken by his master in 1834 from Missouri to the free state of Illinois, and from there to Wisconsin Territory, where he stayed until his return to Missouri several years later. The antislavery group who backed his suit for freedom hoped to prove that Dred Scott's residence in free Illinois and in a territory where slavery was illegal under the Missouri Compromise had made him a free man.

In speaking for the Court for more than two hours, Chief Justice Taney spent half his time arguing that since blacks had been viewed as inferior beings at the time the Constitution was adopted, its framers did not intend to include them within the meaning of the term *citizens.* Therefore, the right of citizens of different states to sue in the federal courts could never apply to a former slave or descendant of a slave.

Only two justices would concur with Taney's racial concepts and his interpretation of American history. But these two and four others joined Taney in a majority finding that Scott, even had he become free, had become a slave once again when he returned to the slave state of Missouri, and had no right to sue in a federal court.

Four justices joined the chief justice in going further. "No word can be found in the Constitution," Taney wrote, "which gives Congress a greater power over slave property . . . than [over] property of any other description." According to the Fifth Amendment, Congress could not deprive any person of property, including slave property, "without due process of law." Thus Congress had no right to exclude slavery from the territories, and the Missouri Compromise, by which Scott's backers claimed his freedom in territory north of 36°30', had always been unconstitutional.

The Kansas-Nebraska Act had already declared the Missouri Compromise "inoperative and void." If, as the Court now held, the attempt of the compromise to legislate slavery out of the territories was also unconstitutional, then the fundamental objective for which the Republican party had been formed was unconstitutional. Even the Douglas Democrats were troubled by the decision. For if slaves were property untouchable by law under the Constitution, Douglas's program for popular sovereignty on the slavery question in the territories was dead.

The Lincoln-Douglas Debates

The issue of slavery in the territories was examined most thoroughly during the contest for Douglas's Senate seat in 1858. The rising Republican candidate, Abraham Lincoln, challenged his Democratic opponent to a series of debates. Before they began, however, two events hurt the hopes of the South.

The first was the business panic of August 1857. The depression that followed gave antislavery Republicans strong allies in two groups of the free economy. Businessmen and their employees favored the Republican plank for high tariffs, which were intended to stimulate free industry and industrial employment. Farmers liked the Republican plank for free homesteads.

The second event was the state constitutional convention at Lecompton, Kansas, in October 1857. Here proslavery delegates, named in a rigged election, not only wrote a constitution explicitly guaranteeing slavery but refused to permit the whole body of voters to ballot on it. Under severe pressure, they did offer the electorate a proposition restricting the entry of new slaves but protecting slave property already in the state. The dominant antislavery voters abstained from balloting on this proposition, and the proslavery party thereby carried it.

After considerable maneuvering, Congress offered Kansas its statehood immediately, along with a federal land grant, should her voters decide to accept the Lecompton Constitution, or continuing territorial status if they rejected it. Kansans overwhelmingly rejected the Lecompton Constitution. Kansas remained a territory until 1861, when it entered the Union as a free state.

The Illinois Republican convention that was to nominate Lincoln for the Senate met in Springfield in June 1858. In accepting the nomination, Lincoln observed that the slavery issue had grown worse each year. "In my opinion," he declared, "it will not cease until a crisis shall have been reached and passed. A house divided against itself cannot stand."

This speech was carefully studied by Douglas and furnished the basis for his attacks on Lincoln in the seven debates that followed. Douglas, who admired Lincoln personally, denounced him during the debates as a sectionalist whose "house divided" philosophy would end in "a war of extermination." Why, Douglas asked, did the Republicans say that slavery and freedom could not peaceably coexist? Lincoln replied that his party did not propose to interfere with slavery where it existed, nor did he wish to enforce social equality between blacks and whites, as Douglas alleged. But in keeping with the Republican program, he flatly opposed any further extension of slavery.

In the debate at Freeport, Illinois, Lincoln asked Douglas a momentous question: "Can the people of a United States territory, in any lawful way, against the wish of any citizen of the United States, exclude slavery from its limits prior to the formation of a State constitution?" In order to answer, Douglas had to either abandon his popular-sovereignty concept or defy the *Dred Scott* decision. If the people could not exclude slavery, popular sovereignty meant little. If they could exclude it, popular sovereignty was as much in conflict with the *Dred Scott* decision as the Republican principle of congressional exclusion. Douglas answered that the people of a territory could take this step, in spite of the *Dred Scott* decision. Slavery could not exist for a day, he explained, if the local legislature did not pass the necessary laws to protect and police slave property. Therefore, merely by failing to arrange for slavery a territorial legislature, without formally barring it, could make its existence impossible.

Douglas's realistic answer—his Freeport Doctrine—broadened the opposition to him in the South and widened the split in the Democratic party as Lincoln had anticipated. Douglas won the senatorial election, but the Democratic party and the Union were more divided than ever.

John Brown's Raid

The most ominous event in the sectional struggle was John Brown's raid on the federal arsenal at Harpers Ferry, Virginia (now West Virginia), in 1859. Brown and his seventeen black and white men captured the arsenal and its millions of dollars' worth of arms. That night he sent a detachment to take nearby planters and some of their slaves as hostages. This mission accomplished, he awaited news of the slave uprisings he hoped would follow.

Instead, by dawn Monday news of his exploit had spread across the countryside and to Washington. On Tuesday federal troops in the region under the command of Colonel Robert E. Lee, were dispatched by Buchanan to take charge. They regained the arsenal, captured Brown and five others, and left eleven of Brown's men dead.

Although they did not incite Brown to violence, prominent abolitionists had known of his project and provided him with money and weapons. Such collaboration raised the fury of southerners, who launched vigilante groups to assault anyone suspected of antislavery sympathies and publicly burned dangerous books. In New York, Boston, and elsewhere, meanwhile, huge meetings organized by northern conservatives attacked Brown and his methods. Both Lincoln and Douglas—and men of all parties—joined in the condemnation. But when Virginia's governor rejected the plea of Brown's relatives and friends that the raider was insane and ordered him hanged, he insured Brown's martyrdom. Brown's dignity on the scaffold touched millions who had abhorred his deeds.

SECESSION

Lincoln's Election

In April 1860 the Democratic national convention met at Charleston, South Carolina, the heartland of secession sentiment. Southern extremists had resolved to insist on a platform plank declaring that neither Congress nor a territorial government could do away with the right to own slaves. Northern Democrats, hoping to nominate Douglas without alienating the southerners, expressed willingness to accept the *Dred Scott* ruling. Yet they stood equally firm for popular sovereignty. "We cannot recede from this doctrine," a Douglas spokesman insisted, "without personal dishonor." When it became evident that the extremists' plank would fail, most of the delegates from eight southern states withdrew and the convention adjourned.

When the Democrats reconvened in Baltimore in June, the southern delegates bolted once more, but this convention proceeded to nominate Douglas on a popular-sovereignty platform. Ten days later, the southern Democrats met independently in Baltimore and chose John C. Breckinridge of Kentucky, himself a moderate, to represent their position on slavery in the territories.

The Republicans, buoyed up by the Democratic disaster at Charleston, met in Chicago in May. Their front runner was William S. Seward, of New York. But Seward, among other handicaps, had a perhaps undeserved reputation for being irreconcilable because he had once spoken of the "irrepressible conflict" between North and South. The patient Lincoln, a national figure now, was strongly supported by the Illinois and Indiana delegations and acceptable to both East and West. By allowing the other hopefuls to offset one another, he won the nomination.

The Republicans made a shrewd appeal to powerful economic interests by building a platform containing planks for a protective tariff, free homesteads, and a Pacific railroad. The platform also denied "the authority of Congress, of a territorial legislature, or of any individuals to give legal existence to Slavery in any Territory of the United States."

A fourth group, composed largely of old-line Whigs in the border states and calling itself the Constitutional Union party, met at Baltimore on May 9 and chose John Bell of Tennessee for the presidency.

The 1860 election presented the remarkable picture of a divided nation simultaneously carrying out two separate contests for a single office: one between Breckinridge and Bell in the South, the other between Lincoln and Douglas in the North. Ten southern states did not even place Lincoln's name on the ballot. Of his 1,866,000 popular votes, Lincoln won a mere 26,000 in the entire South. Douglas also ran poorly there. In the North, neither Breckinridge nor Bell found support.

Unionist sentiment, nevertheless, was far from dead. Bell, the Unionist candidate, won Kentucky, Tennessee, and Virginia and barely lost Maryland and Missouri. Although Lincoln had a decisive majority in the electoral college, he carried less than 40 percent of the popular vote. A minority sectional candidate had become president of the United States.

The Deep South Moves Out

Southern leaders had repeatedly warned after Lincoln's nomination that a Republican victory would be followed by secession— for, as the governor of South Carolina put it, the election of a sectional northern candidate would "ultimately reduce the southern states to mere provinces of a consolidated despotism . . . fatally bent upon our ruin." Such expectations perhaps best answer the question of why the South moved out. But it must also be realized that

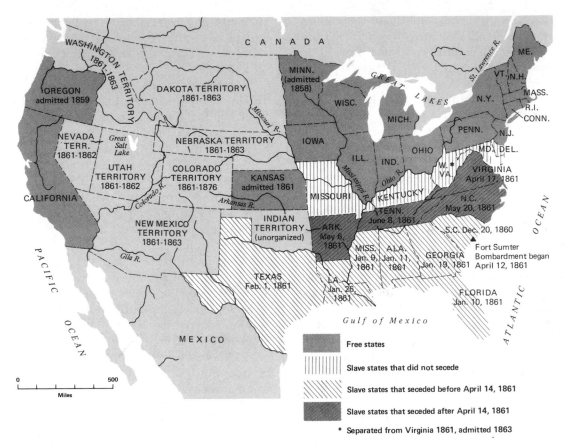

The United States on the Eve of the Civil War

few in the South anticipated the awful after-math of secession and war. The commercial power of King Cotton and the probable sympathy of foreign aristocrats and the numerous southern sympathizers above the Mason-Dixon line permitted a degree of hopefulness.

On December 20, 1860, South Carolina took the initiative. A convention voted to formally repeal the state's ratification of the Constitution and withdraw from the Union. By February 1, 1861, six other commonwealths of the cotton belt—Mississippi, Florida, Alabama, Georgia, Louisiana, and Texas—had followed her example, in almost every case over local opponents who were ready to give Lincoln a chance to show whether he would really enforce the Fugitive Slave Act and meet other southern demands. Pockets of Unionism, moreover, persisted even in the lower South.

On February 4, 1861, delegates from six departing states (with Texas absent) met at Montgomery, Alabama, to form a new government, which they called the Confederate States of America.

Secession, having begun with Lincoln's election, took place while Buchanan, a lame duck lacking will and power, occupied the White House. While the president wondered what to do, border-state people in particular, aware that secession followed by war would make their land a battleground, still sought to avoid disaster. The proposals considered the most seriously were put forward by Senator John J. Crittenden of Kentucky, two days before South Carolina's formal departure from the Union. But these proposals only hashed over old ground. By offering to permit popular sovereignty below the Missouri Compromise line of 36°30' (while suggesting that territories above that line be free), they were bound to be rejected by Lincoln and his party.

ONSET OF HOSTILITIES

Lincoln's Inaugural

By March 4, 1861, when Lincoln stood up to take the oath of office, secession of the Cotton South was an accomplished fact and important federal properties had fallen into rebel hands. Yet a far greater territory than the existing Confederacy remained very much at issue. The upper South—Virginia, Maryland, North Carolina, even Delaware—was in deep conflict. Farther west, in the border states of Tennessee, Kentucky, Arkansas, and Missouri, battles were fought before allegiance to North or South could be established. In all these states the president's inaugural address was eagerly awaited.

Early in his oration Lincoln stressed the unchanging character of "the more perfect Union" established by the Constitution. Then followed his sharpest words to the rebels: "No State upon its mere motion can lawfully get out of the Union; . . . acts of violence . . . against the authority of the

United States, are insurrectionary or revolutionary, according to circumstance."

The president was as conciliatory as his office and his nature allowed. As chief executive, he said, he was bound to enforce federal regulations, including those requiring the return of fugitive slaves, in all the states. Other constitutional obligations, on the other hand, required that he "hold, occupy, and possess the property and places belonging to the Government, and to collect the duties and imposts" in every American port. But in performing these acts, "there needs be no bloodshed or violence; and there shall be none, unless it be forced upon the national authority."

Few if any inaugural orations in United States history bore the burden of Lincoln's first. Few if any played so deliberately for time. Though pressed by zealots of every political creed, Lincoln electrified the nation by putting off action: "My countrymen, one and all, think calmly and well upon this whole subject. Nothing valuable can be lost by taking time."

Sumter: The First Shot

And yet there was action required immediately of the president. In defiance of Buchanan's administration, the Confederacy had seized federal forts, post offices, and custom houses throughout the South in the early months of 1861 without reprisal from the commander in chief. Only Fort Sumter in Charleston harbor and three forts off the coast of Florida now remained in federal hands. The day after his inauguration, Lincoln was handed a letter from Major Robert Anderson, the commander at Sumter, reporting that he could hold the fort only with the immediate aid of 20,000 men, a large naval force, and ample provisions.

Anderson in effect recommended

evacuation. But if Lincoln retreated, as his advisers urged, he would have taken the first step toward recognizing the power if not the legality of the Confederacy. If, on the other hand, he attempted to strengthen Sumter by force, he would be made to appear the aggressor. Lincoln cautiously steered a middle course. He notified South Carolina authorities that he would attempt to provision Sumter peacefully. "If such attempt be not resisted," he wrote the governor, "no effort to throw in men, arms, or ammunition will be made."

Lincoln's decision shifted the burden to Confederate authorities. If they permitted provisioning of Sumter, the fort would remain indefinitely in the mouth of one of their few good harbors, a reproach to their prestige throughout the world. If they attacked a peaceful expedition bringing food, *they* would have fired the first shot.

When requested by Confederate authorities to surrender Sumter before the supply ships arrived, Major Anderson promised to evacuate by April 15, unless relieved or ordered to remain. But the Confederacy dared not risk so long a delay. On April 12, as Union supply ships tried unsuccessfully to land, the batteries on the Charleston shore began a thirty-four-hour bombardment. When Anderson at last ran down the flag, Sumter was virtually consumed in flames, her ammunition spent.

Before Sumter, northern opinion had divided sharply on the proper response to secession. Abolitionists like Garrison thought it futile to enforce union "where one section is pinned to the residue by bayonets." For once, the business community, concerned over collecting southern debts and holding southern markets, fully agreed with abolitionist policy to let the "erring sisters go in peace." Hatred of disunion, on the other hand, was especially widespread

in the Northwest. There, freedom for white people on the land was extremely popular, and free use of the Mississippi to its mouth below New Orleans was important to economic life. After Sumter, peace partisans still were heard here and there in the North. But with the Confederacy branded before the world as the aggressor, it became easier than before to portray hostilities as a defense of the Union and to mobilize Union strength.

The Upper South and Border States Decide

On April 15 Lincoln issued the fateful proclamation that "combinations too powerful to be suppressed" by ordinary means existed in the seven Confederate states; he called "forth the militia of the several States of the Union, to the aggregate number of seventy-five thousand, in order to suppress such combinations." His proclamation was widely hailed in the North. But throughout the upper South and the border states it came like the toll of death. Should Virginia and the rest answer the president's call and yield their militia to the Union cause? Should they stand by while the deep South was invaded?

More than Lincoln's election, more than his inaugural, more even than the attempt to provision Sumter, Lincoln's proclamation of April 15 sealed the issue of war and peace. Two days later Virginia passed an ordinance of secession, eighty-eight to fifty-five. The provisional Confederate government named Richmond its permanent capital and prepared to move from Montgomery. At the end of May a referendum in Virginia sanctioned secession, though people in the western portion of the state disagreed so strongly that they began to organize to secede from the new Confederate state.

Only then did the president acknowledge that all hope was gone: "The people of Virginia have thus allowed this giant insurrection to make its nest within her borders; and this government has no choice left but to deal with it where it finds it."

Lincoln had supplemented his proclamation calling out the militia with an order to the navy to blockade the ports of the first seven Confederate commonwealths. Later he extended the blockade to Virginia and North Carolina. The Supreme Court was eventually to rule that the war legally began with these blockade orders, which officially recognized that a state of "belligerency" existed between two powers. Lincoln himself never recognized the Confederacy as a nation, or secession as anything but "insurrection."

Other states soon followed Virginia's example. Nevertheless, Unionist regions could still be found in the upper South and on the border. Like the western Virginians, the yeomen of eastern Tennessee would probably have rejoined the Union had Confederate troops not prevented them. Four border slave states—Kentucky, Missouri, Maryland, and Delaware—remained in the Union.

SUGGESTED READINGS

J.H. Silbey, *The Transformation of American Politics, 1840-1867* (1967). M.F. Holt, *The Political Crisis of the 1850s* (1978). D.M. Potter, *The Impending Crisis, 1848-1861* (1976). S.W. Campbell, *The Slave Catchers: Enforcement of the Fugitive Slave Law* (1968). R.W. Johannsen, *Stephen A. Douglas* (1973). D.F. Fehrenbacher, *The Dred Scott Case* (1978). G.H. Knoles, ed., *The Crisis of the Union, 1860-1861* (1965).

SUMMARY

By the late 1850s, tension over slavery had led to violence and threats of violence in Congress itself. The crisis arose over the extension of slavery to the new territories and intensified as earlier compromises fell apart. Enforcement of the Fugitive Slave Law of 1850, part of the compromise, and Harriet Beecher Stowe's fictional account of slavery, Uncle Tom's Cabin, *gave northerners a view of slavery they had never had before.*

In 1854 Congress passed the Kansas-Nebraska Act, which reopened the question of slavery in the western territories and nullified the Missouri Compromise. Kansas was marked for slavery by the South, but *not by the North. The territory was turned into a battleground, and for a period there was civil war there.*

After 1852 the Whig party fell apart. The election of 1856 brought new political parties: the Know-Nothings, opposed to Catholic immigrants, and the Republicans, who opposed extension of slavery to the western territories. The Democrats were now largely the party of the South and slavery. Their candidate, James Buchanan, won, but the Republican party ran strongly in the North.

Buchanan hoped the Supreme Court would settle the question of slavery in the terri-

tories. In the Dred Scott decision, the Court decided the Missouri Compromise was unconstitutional. The issue then became the focus of the Lincoln-Douglas debates of 1858, which made Abraham Lincoln a national figure. The next year John Brown's raid on the federal arsenal at Harpers Ferry, Virginia, shocked the entire country. Brown, a fervent abolitionist, was hanged—but then became a legend to abolitionists in the North.

Four candidates ran in the election of 1860. The winner was Abraham Lincoln of the sectional Republican party. The South took his election as a signal for secession. By February 1, 1861, even before Lincoln's inauguration, seven states—South Carolina, Mississippi, Florida, Alabama, Georgia, Louisiana, and Texas—had withdrawn from the Union. On February 4, delegates from six states met at Montgomery, Alabama, to form a new government, the Confederate States of America. When Lincoln took the oath of office on March 4, secession was a fact.

The taking of Fort Sumter in Charleston harbor on April 12 began the war. On April 15 Lincoln issued a call for 75,000 three-month volunteers to "suppress" the Confederacy. At that point the upper South and the border states were forced to make a decision: Virginia, Arkansas, North Carolina, and Tennessee seceded. Kentucky, Missouri, Maryland, and Delaware remained in the Union. Both sides prepared for what neither thought would be a long war.

13 *Civil War*

At the start, both sides seemed paralyzed. Both fervently wished that the fighting, once begun, would soon be over. The Civil War became the deadliest war ever fought on this continent, yet it was very slow in gathering momentum. And when it was finally over, little seemed to have been accomplished by the slaughter. Not that it was in vain. Lincoln made that clear in the Gettysburg Address: "From these honored dead we take increased devotion to that cause for which they gave the last full measure of devotion—that . . . this nation, under God, shall have a new birth of freedom—and that government of the people, by the people, for the people, shall not perish from the earth."

For Confederate leaders, the war became a lost but glorious cause. For Lincoln, the unfinished task was restoration of the Union. But in the back of his mind he knew very well that the condition of black people was fundamental to the entire conflict. Their future was altered but scarcely settled by the war in which roughly one white man died for every six slaves "freed."

ENEMIES FACE TO FACE

On paper the North was far stronger than the South. It had two and a half times as many people, and it possessed far more ships, miles of railroad, and manufacturing enterprises. Southerners, however, had the advantage of fighting on home ground with better military leadership. Civilian authority was another matter. The new Confederate government ran into trouble because of one of the principles it was fighting for—states' rights. In the North, moreover, Abraham Lincoln was self-confident enough to assemble a cabinet of exceptionally strong and able men. He himself assumed powers that made him as close to being a dictator as anyone in United States history.

Soldiers and Supplies

At the beginning of the conflict, about 22 million persons lived in loyal states and territories. There were as well an unknown number of Indians in the West. Nine million (5.5 million whites and 3.5 million blacks) lived in the South. But Union superiority in manpower was not as great as the gross figures suggest.

Half a million persons, scattered from Dakota to California, could make no substantial contribution to Union strength. And every year during the Civil War, Union regiments were sent to the West to fight Indians.

Hundreds of thousands of Americans in loyal border states and in southern Ohio, Indiana, and Illinois worked or fought for southern independence. Many southerners, of course, remained loyal to the Union, but there is little doubt that more Federals than Confederates crossed over.

Other considerations favored the Confederacy. One was the South's superior officers. For twenty years before Lincoln's inauguration, southern officers dominated the United States Army. Another source of southern confidence was cotton. Secession leaders expected to exchange that staple for the foreign manufactured goods they needed, without having to sacrifice fighting men to factory work. Probably the South's most important advantage was that it had to defend only relatively short interior lines against invaders who had to deal with long lines of communication and attack on a broad front. The Confederacy also had no need to divert fighting men to tasks such as garrisoning captured cities and holding conquered territory.

The South's armies contained a considerably larger proportion of the region's white men than the North's. Taking the two white populations as separate wholes, it is clear that the war was supported more widely in the Confederacy than in the Union. In addition, thousands of slaves were made to perform menial tasks and construct fortifications. On the other side, blacks were not welcomed in the early stages. After 1862, however, abolitionists succeeded in gaining approval for black regiments staffed by white officers. Some of these units were recruited from the Free black population in the North; others came into the Union army directly from slavery in border states or in areas captured by Union forces. They suffered discrimination in pay and quarters, but their performance in battle encouraged those—black and white—who hoped to disprove the assumption that blacks were not good fighting men.

In a short war, northern numerical superiority would not have made much of a difference. As the war continued, however, numerical strength became a psychological as well as a physical weapon. During the closing years of the conflict Union armies, massed at last against critical strongholds, suffered terrible casualties but seemed to grow stronger with every defeat. At the same time, staggering Confederate losses sapped the southern will to fight. That the Civil War stretched over years instead of months magnified every material advantage of the North—money and credit, factories, food production, transport. It took time for the North to redirect its economy to the requirements of the battlefield, especially since these requirements were underestimated because of wishful thinking about the length of the war. But the South found it even more difficult to convert to a war footing.

As the war lengthened, southern troops suffered from short rations, ragged clothing, and no boots. Until the end, though, the Confederacy had the basic materials of war—small arms, artillery, ammunition, and horses. Every rural home in the South had weapons. Large quantities of munitions were also taken from captured federal forts and run in through the blockade. Under the brilliant administration of its chief of ordinance, the Confederacy also developed its own munitions plants, which supplemented the output of the giant Tredegar Iron Works in Richmond.

The Confederate Government

Delegates from the first seceding states met at Montgomery, Alabama, in February 1861 to draft a frame of government. By not departing too greatly from the familiar federal document, they hoped to attract their neighbors in the upper South. Because they were so committed to states' rights, however, they wrote in certain weaknesses that had been kept out of the Constitution in 1787. Its preamble declared that the Confederacy was established not by "We, the people" but by "the people of the Confederate states, each state acting in its sovereign and independent character." Of course the new constitution "recognized and protected . . . the right of property in negro slaves."

Although the Confederate Congress was granted power "to . . . provide for the common defense," no mention was made of promoting the "general welfare." "The judicial power of the Confederate States" was placed in a Supreme Court and certain lower tribunals. But no Supreme Court was ever established. The old federal district courts continued to sit, many under their old judges, who applied the old rules and precedents. The president's term was extended to six years. Whatever advantage in stability this brought was lost by the provision barring his reelection. The Montgomery Constitutional Convention named Jefferson Davis of Mississippi and Alexander H. Stephens of Georgia as provisional president and vice-president. Neither man wanted his job, but in the first Confederate elections in November 1861, voters confirmed the convention's choices.

A West Pointer of the class of 1828, Jeff Davis was at heart a soldier, hungry for honor in the field. Convinced that he had been born to generalship, he nevertheless proved to be a miserable military strategist. Davis was especially hard pressed by states'-rights enthusiasts who saw almost no justification for central government. His military strategy came under intensifying criticism. Reverses on the battlefield made his life increasingly miserable.

Lincoln and the Divided Nation

Lincoln was temperamentally far better suited for a protracted struggle than Davis was. Patient, tolerant, flexible, and crafty to the point of deviousness, Lincoln had a genius for giving people enough rope to hang themselves.

Throughout the war he was savagely abused in the press. Many people thought him insufficiently dignified for high office, a bungler as commander in chief, devious, and spineless yet out for himself. Lincoln absorbed much of this abuse quietly, often with wry self-satisfaction. Regarded by many people at the time as petty and oafish, he now seems much more an embodiment of both the narrowness and greatness of the Puritan ethic. His reputation rests largely on his talent at statecraft, his decent magnanimity, and his stunning mastery of English prose. Even to those who knew him longest, he remained something of a mystery, enlivening meetings with his stories yet melancholy, aloof, in counsel with his inner self.

Lincoln seldom acted until he felt that public opinion would sustain him. His delay in getting on with the fighting encouraged the ambitious egotists around him—for example, Secretary of State Seward and Secretary of the Treasury Salmon Chase—each to strive for "a sort of dictatorship for the national defense." They all learned sooner or later. as Seward acknowledged after an early brush with the Rail-Splitter's ego, that "the President is the best of us. There is only one vote in the Cabinet and it belongs to him."

He was tested early from all sides. In 1861 the federal government was filled with secessionists. Lincoln, even more than Jackson, cleaned house indiscriminately, but he chose replacements with care. Outside his administration he faced two principal groups of opponents. Some abolitionists were pacifists, and in the early years of the war they argued that the Union would be better off without the slave South. "Peace" was also the goal of many northern Democrats. Often called Copperheads, they thought the war was needless. To them, the Union seemed nothing in comparison with the thriving North.

As the war proceeded, many abolitionists began to sense the impending end to slavery. At the same time, Copperheads in the North pressed their demands for compromise and were more active in obstructing Union enlistments. As abolitionists gradually came around to conceding the rightness of the fighting, they threw their support to those within the Republican party who were most in sympathy with emancipation as a war objective. This faction bcame known as the Radicals. The Regulars, or Conservatives, wanted only to suppress the "insurrection" and to restore the Union. The Radicals had a formidable array of talent in both houses of Congress. They were led in the Senate by Sumner of Massachusetts, and Benjamin Wade of Ohio, and in the House by Thaddeus Stevens of Pennsylvania, chairman of the Ways and Means Committee. Stevens regarded slavery as "a curse, a shame, and a crime." As a lawyer and businessman, he had defended fugitive slaves without fee.

Lincoln allowed nearly a whole year to pass after the first act of secession before he would even acknowledge that the gulf between the two sections could be closed only by mutual slaughter. He hated bloodshed. But he lost no time in getting the Union ready for survival. In doing so, he earned the labels *despot, tyrant,* and *dictator* more than any other president.

On May 3, without precedent or legislative authority, Lincoln issued a call for forty regiments of three-year United States volunteers to supplement the state militia he had called out in April. On no firmer constitutional grounds, he ordered a rapid expansion of the fleet for blockade service. The Constitution had stated, "No money shall be drawn from the Treasury, but in Consequence of Appropriations made by Law." Without any law, Lincoln ordered Chase to get funds to pay for the new army and navy. Chase obliged.

Lincoln also trampled traditional safeguards of personal rights. Neither private letters nor telegrams were safe from prying federal eyes. Military commanders were empowered to make arrests without warrants and "in the extremest necessity," in Lincoln's words, to suspend the writ of habeas corpus. Eventually, at least 15,000 Americans were jailed. Despite his gestures of clemency, many remained in prison until the war's end without trial or even accusation.

Lincoln's highhanded tactics fell most heavily on citizens of the border states, which had immense strategic importance. Maryland virtually surrounded Washington and could make the national capital captive. Baltimore, Maryland's leading port and railroad center, was also Washington's main link with the outside world. Kentucky controlled the use of the Ohio River. Missouri, with Kentucky, controlled the use of the Mississippi River. In the end none of these

War	Total Population	Total Deaths	
Civil War	31.4 million (1860)	618,000	North 360,000 / South 258,000 — 1,967
World War II	131.7 million (1940)	318,000	241
Revolutionary War	2.8 million (1780, est)	4,044	144
World War I	105.7 million (1920)	115,000	109
Mexican War	23.2 million (1850)	13,270	57
War of 1812	7.2 million (1810)	2,200	31
Vietnam War	203.2 million (1970)	56,227 (Including deaths from "nonhostile causes")	28
Korean War	150.7 million (1950)	33,000	22
Spanish-American War and Philippine Insurrection	76.0 million (1900)	9,700	Spanish-American War 5,400 / Philippine Insurrection 4,300 — 13

Scale: 0 — 200 — 400 — 600 — 800 — 1,000 — 1,200 — 1,400 — 1,600 — 1,800 — 2,000

Deaths in the Civil War as compared to other wars. The death toll for American soldiers was considerably higher in the Civil War than in any other war in which the United States has taken part. The ratio of deaths to the total population at the time gives a truer picture of the losses than do the absolute figures. (From Richard Current, T. Harry Williams, and Frank Freidel, *American History: A Survey*, 3rd ed., vol. II, p. 393. Copyright © by Richard Current, T. Harry Williams, and Frank Freidel. Reprinted by permission of Alfred A. Knopf, Inc.)

four slave states left the Union, so Lincoln's use of troops and trampling of civil liberties there was successful from his point of view.

There was widespread sympathy with the southern cause in the border states, but throughout the mountainous Appalachian regions of the Confederacy, where plantation slavery had never taken hold, there was considerable Unionist sentiment. With the encouragement of the federal government, the western counties of Virginia broke with authorities in Richmond and formed a separate government, which was admitted to the Union in 1863 as the state of West Virginia.

THE STRUGGLE FOR RICHMOND

The North's strategy was to strangle the South with a naval blockade, gain control of the Mississippi River, and take the Confederate capital. Very few people anticipated that it would take four years of bloody warfare before all these aims were realized. The North lost many of the important battles, but finally, at Antietam, Union forces produced a victory that was to have important nonmilitary consequences.

Strategies and Early Battles

Lincoln's principal military adviser during the early months was a holdover from the Mexican War, the elderly general in chief of the United States Army Winfield Scott. His strategy called for the North to clamp a vise on the border states, take the entire length of the Mississippi, and tighten the blockade of every rebel port. This policy would gain time for raising and equipping armies. Lincoln's early success in the border states provided a favorable start. The blockade further improved prospects. In a few

months, most rebel seaports were almost closed. The South's foreign trade had been cut at least 80 percent.

Jefferson Davis had a war plan of his own that played right into Scott's hands. The South, Davis said, had seceded to get away from, not to conquer, the North. He saw a "natural frontier" stretching from the line between Maryland and Pennsylvania to the Dakota Territory. Along this border he proposed to plant a line of forts, then to look for naval assistance from cotton-hungry Britain and France.

Davis's assumption that King Cotton would win the war was badly misplaced, for Britain had filled her warehouses in anticipation of the war. In addition, the Old South was not the only region in the world that produced cotton, and Britain quickly developed other sources of supply.

While Davis opted for an overly ambitious defensive strategy that would protect the entire Confederacy, many other Confederate leaders urged a relentless offensive without delay. This presupposed the superior valor of southern troops. More realistically, they sensed that if the South did not win quickly, she was not likely to win at all.

In June 1861 the main Rebel army under General P. G. T. de Beauregard was stationed at Manassas Junction in Virginia, a critical railroad crossing between Washington and Richmond. Wipe out this army, sweep triumphantly down to the rebel capital, and crush the insurrection in one stroke—this was the plan that Lincoln, nursing a fantasy of a ninety-day war, had adopted.

At last, in mid July, with the "three-months men" nearing the end of their service, General Scott, on Lincoln's authorization, ordered General Irvin McDowell to move. The 30,000 Federal troops had had little training, as had Beauregard's force, estimated at 24,000. Rebel troops dug in on the southern side of the little stream of Bull Run, and there, the next morning, the Federals found them. After several hours of fighting, a Union triumph seemed certain. But General Thomas J. Jackson's "stonewall" stand in one sector, followed by a succession of counterattacks, halted the Union offensive. The southern army received reinforcements that afternoon. McDowell, disappointed at not receiving reinforcements of his own, soon thought it better to retire.

"Give me 10,000 fresh troops, and I will be in Washington tomorrow," Stonewall Jackson is reported to have stated after Bull Run. But President Davis remained committed to his defensive plan.

"All Quiet on the Potomac"

The defeat of its forces alarmed Congress into action. Radicals pushed through the so-called First Confiscation Act, which made it the duty of the president to seize all property used in aiding the insurrection. Although it was hateful for the Radicals to identify blacks as property, the act nevertheless made slaves subject to forfeit if they were employed in building fortifications and in other military and naval work.

Also in the wake of the Bull Run disaster, Lincoln relieved McDowell, created a new Division of the Potomac, and placed General George McClellan, then a cocky thirty-four-year-old, at its head. McClellan's initial orders were to forge the Army of the Potomac into a mighty sword and with it to bring the Rebels to their knees. He was, in fact, a masterly organizer. His failings were his pride in smart execution of the drill and his exasperating reluctance to risk his troops in battle. By the time Congress reconvened for its regular session in December 1861, McClellan was still grandly housed in Washington, still marching his men on parade, and beginning to tax even Lincoln's patience. Radicals began to suspect that McClellan was unwilling to fight the rebels, a view the president shared.

His patience at an end, Lincoln issued General Order Number 1, which named Washington's Birthday, February 22, as "the day for a general movement of the land and naval forces of the United States against the insurgent forces." But McClellan ignored even this unmistakable command. "In ten days I shall be in Richmond," he boasted on February 13, 1862. Union soldiers, in fact, reached Richmond in 1865.

War in the West

While the federal city remained preoccupied with the long silence on the Potomac, the war was far from quiet in the West. There subordinate Union officers took things more or less into their own hands. Early in 1862, Commodore Andrew H. Foote, commanding a small fleet of gunboats under General Ulysses S. Grant's supervision, captured Fort Henry on the Tennessee River and then took nearby Fort Donelson on the Cumberland.

The following month, Confederate General Albert Sidney Johnston led his men across the whole of Tennessee to the strategic railroad center of Corinth, Mississippi. On April 6, Johnston led an attack on Grant's exposed encampment across the Tennessee at Shiloh. With the advantage of surprise, his forces pushed the Federals back the first day. On the next, the Union armies drove off the Rebels, now led by Beauregard. General Henry W. Halleck, recently placed in command of the Department of the West, took charge of pressing the Union counteroffensive into Corinth. But he delayed for weeks, and the rebels got away with their army intact.

Neither side could take much satisfaction from the bloody Shiloh engagement, yet it gave each side greater respect for the other. A total of 23,000 men were killed or wounded. Grant wrote in his *Memoirs,* "I gave up all idea of saving the Union except by complete conquest." Robert E. Lee, still sitting in Richmond as a presidential advisor, warned Davis that unless he held the lower Mississippi and kept the Confederacy from being split, Grant's conquest would not be far off.

Lee's warning was underscored soon after Shiloh by more decisive Union operations farther west. At the end of April, a Union fleet led by Captain David G. Farragut smashed through Confederate fortifications below New Orleans and forced the great Mississippi port to surrender. Baton Rouge fell soon after to a force under General Benjamin F. Butler. In the meantime, Foote's gunboats had pressed down the Mississippi to Memphis, where it destroyed a Confederate fleet. Between Memphis and New Orleans only Vicksburg, Mississippi, and Port Hudson, Louisiana, now blocked Union control of the entire river.

The Peninsular Campaign

Union operations in the West early in 1862 received only the barest notice in Washington, where protection of the capital and preparation of the grand assault on Richmond were the main concerns. Lincoln, who had taken to studying books on military strategy—to compensate for the inadequacy of his advisers—had formed definite opinions about how Richmond might be taken. He was for a new frontal attack, which would have the advantage of keeping the Army of the Potomac between the Confederates and Washington. Largely because he had not been consulted about it, McClellan opposed Lincoln's plan. The Confederate capital, the general argued, should be approached by way of the peninsula formed by the York River on the north and the James River on the south. The peninsular plan involved a hazardous amphibious operation dangerously distant from Washington. The Confederates controlled the Norfolk navy yard at the mouth of the James. At Norfolk, moreover, lay the Confederate ironclad *Virginia,* formerly the United States frigate *Merrimac,* which only a month before McClellan began his campaign had fought the Union's ironclad *Monitor* to a standstill.

The first contingents of McClellan's force—all told, 110,000 strong—landed on the peninsula on April 4, 1862. Yorktown, the first Confederate stronghold on the way to Richmond, might have been overrun in a day. But McClellan, still fearful of a new Bull Run, took a month to enter the town. Almost another month was lost while the general, vainly awaiting expected reinforcements, advanced at a snail's pace up the peninsula. What kept McClellan's reinforcements away was Stonewall Jackson's brilliant foray up the Shenandoah Valley, where, as Lincoln had anticipated, he menaced Washington from the rear. Having unnerved the Union capital sufficiently to force Lincoln to keep an even stronger army there than he had planned, Jackson dashed back to the main theater of fighting to confront McClellan.

Before Jackson arrived, McClellan had been drawn to within five miles of Richmond, where on May 31 he narrowly averted disaster at Seven Pines. McClellan might have taken advantage of the Confederates' loss of General Johnston at Seven Pines. Instead, he left 25,000 men under General Fitz-John Porter in the vicinity of Richmond and returned with the rest to his base at the town of White House, some twenty miles to the east. Here he waited once again for additional men to oppose the vast host that he imagined stood before the Confederate capital. While McClellan waited, Robert E. Lee at last returned to the field.

Lee possessed the capacities as well as the appearance of a hero. His many admirers regarded him as the greatest military genius of the war. His soldiers came to look upon him as a man who "communed with the angels of Heaven." Some military historians have argued that Lee was so concerned with defending his native state that he never developed a coordinated overall strategy. But for most of the war the Virginia front was his only command, and he used it effectively, along with forays into the North, to relieve Union pressure elsewhere.

On learning how McClellan had split his army, Lee sent a small force "looking numerous and aggressive" to intimidate the susceptible general while he himself moved in to crush Porter.

Porter and McClellan were prepared, however. McClellan regrouped his forces and surprised the Confederates. Having done this much, however, he turned again to the strategy of retreat. In the Seven Days' Battle, between June 26 and July 2, McClellan inflicted very heavy losses on Lee's advancing troops, but his own objective was merely Harrison's Landing on the James River, where the Union navy could evacuate his men if necessary.

Second Bull Run and Antietam

Lincoln visited McClellan at Harrison's Landing on July 9 and called off the whole Peninsular Campaign. He also named Halleck commander of all the Union armies. In McClellan's place as commander of the Army of the Potomac, Halleck placed the rash and boastful John Pope. These men were ordered to try to take Richmond at last. But Lee disclosed the full scope of their inadequacies when he routed Pope's army in

the momentous Second Battle of Bull Run, August 29–30, 1862.

This fresh setback left Union soldiers bitter and discouraged. In desperation, Lincoln again entrusted McClellan with temporary command of the disorganized army in the East.

Lee, on the other hand, felt confident enough to send a force across the Potomac to the refurbished federal arsenal at Harpers Ferry in quest of supplies for his ragged veterans. If this daring operation succeeded, he hoped, Maryland and perhaps the other border states might yet cast their lot with the Confederacy. France and England, moreover, might recognize the southern republic and perhaps even intervene on its behalf.

But Lee's plans again miscarried. On September 15, 1862, Stonewall Jackson with 25,000 men did take Harpers Ferry and all they wanted there. They also learned that McClellan had got wind of this adventure in time to have smashed Lee's divided army. But for two days McClellan did nothing. When he did attack Lee on September 17 at Antietam Creek, he almost engulfed the far outnumbered Rebels. But by then Jackson had returned to help check the Federal momentum, and Lee's battered army was permitted to slip away.

Antietam has been called a defeat for both armies. But the Union, at least, had repulsed an invasion on which the South had spent perhaps too much. "Our maximum strength has been mobilized," Jefferson Davis told his secretary of war after the battle, "while the enemy is just beginning to put forth his might."

WAR ON THE HOME FRONTS

The brutal, inconclusive engagement at Antietam was an appropriate symbol of the entire war. The seemingly aimless slaughter badly damaged civilian morale on both

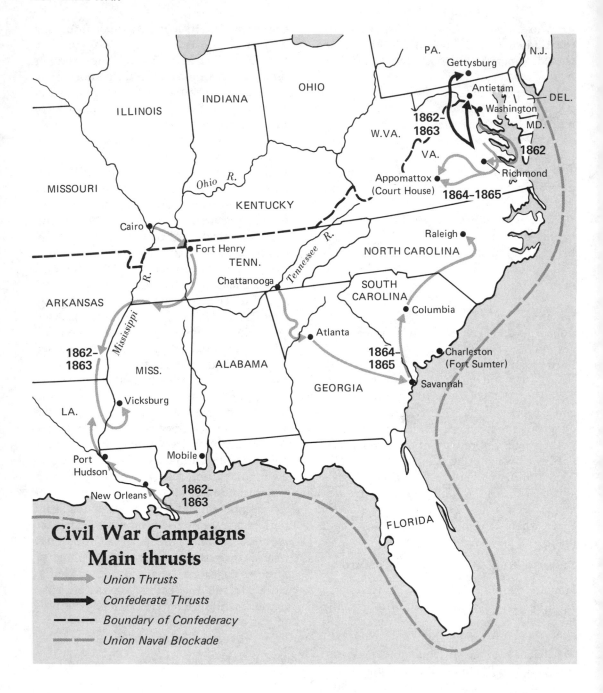

PA.

N.J.

Gettysburg

Antietam

DEL.

OHIO

Washington

1862– 1863

MD.

ILLINOIS

INDIANA

W.VA.

1862

VA.

Richmond

Appomattox
(Court House)

1864–1865

MISSOURI

Ohio R.

KENTUCKY

Cairo

Raleigh

Fort Henry

NORTH CAROLINA

TENN.

Tennessee R.

Chattanooga

SOUTH CAROLINA

ARKANSAS

Mississippi

R.

Columbia

Atlanta

1862– 1863

MISS.

ALABAMA

1864– 1865

Charleston
(Fort Sumter)

GEORGIA

Savannah

Vicksburg

LA.

Mobile

Port
Hudson

New Orleans

1862– 1863

FLORIDA

Civil War Campaigns
Main thrusts

→	*Union Thrusts*
➤	*Confederate Thrusts*
– – –	*Boundary of Confederacy*
‒ ‒ ‒	*Union Naval Blockade*

sides. As the war dragged on, its effects were felt far behind the battle lines. The South tried desperately to win aid and recognition from Great Britain; the North made every effort to keep that country neutral. And Lincoln had an important card to play in the war of nerves between the two sections—the Emancipation Proclamation.

The Confederacy in Wartime

As early as April 1862, the Confederate Congress was obliged to enact the first conscription act in American history, calling up for three years' service all white men eighteen to thirty-five. Later acts raised the age limit to fifty. But anyone could escape the draft by paying for a substitute, and occupational exemptions were numerous. The purchasing of substitutes seemed to confirm the slogan "a rich man's war and a poor man's fight." Desertions soared to well over 100,000—only a third, perhaps, of Union desertions, but much more keenly felt.

Symptoms of economic difficulties could be detected in the South even during the first year of the war. Loans in specie were virtually impossible to make in a country where wealth was traditionally tied up in land and slaves. The Confederacy's luck with taxes was little better. Like other frustrated governments, it began to print paper money. Three years later, in 1864, a Confederate paper dollar was worth, on average, a cent and a half in specie. Prices soared; speculation and hoarding became rampant. Widespread food shortages, made more difficult to fight by the breakdown of transportation, sapped Confederate morale even more than setbacks in the field.

Failure of Southern Diplomacy

Confederate difficulties at home were aggravated by the collapse of southern diplomacy abroad. There had been some early successes. The ruling classes in Europe had no love for slavery, but as aristocrats they would have been pleased with the failure of the "American experiment" in democratic government. Their attitude was reflected in the decision of Britain and France early in 1861 to recognize the Confederacy as a belligerent power if not as a sovereign government.

Britain, moreover, threatened Lincoln's administration with war in November 1861 after a Union cruiser stopped the British mail steamer *Trent* on the high seas and removed two Confederate diplomats who were on their way to London and Paris. War was averted when Secretary of State Seward released the two Rebels.

Confederate hopes for foreign military assistance, high after the *Trent* affair, died a year later with military failure at Antietam. Lincoln took this occasion to announce his Emancipation Proclamation, and the resulting surge of Union sentiment among foreign middle- and working-class elements made it even more unlikely that foreign rulers would risk discontent at home by backing the wrong side in America.

Britain's willingness to build sea raiders for the Confederacy, however, seemed to invalidate her official policy of nonintervention. All told, eighteen such "brigands of the sea" (*Alabama* was the most successful) preyed on northern shipping. Union threats in 1863 to loose a "flood of privateers" against Britain's nominally neutral trade had the desired effect. No new Confederate raiders were launched.

The North in Wartime

Some important measures enacted by the Republican Congress had little to do with the war and a great deal to do with economic goals of the Republican party.

First, in order to satisfy the protectionist interests, Congress passed the Morrill Tariff in 1861. This measure raised duties to their 1846 levels, from which they soared steadily during and after the war. Second, in 1862 Congress voted to build the long-debated transcontinental railroad over a central route and to help finance it with lavish grants of public lands and generous cash loans. Finally, in 1863 Congress created a national banking system that was congenial to northern capitalists, revising it in 1864.

Nor did Republican leaders neglect their Free-Soil supporters. The Homestead Act of May 1862 made available to adult "citizens of the United States" (meaning whites), and to those who declared their intention of becoming citizens, 160 acres of the public domain. The land was free of charge, but its prompt "settlement and cultivation" was required. Farmers also benefited from the Morrill Land-Grant Act of 1862, under which public lands were given to states and territories for the establishment of colleges of agricultural science and mechanical arts.

After a short depression in 1861–62 caused by the loss of $300 million in uncollectible southern debts and uncertainty about the war, the North enjoyed a substantial boom based on the production of war goods. "Shoddy" millionaires made fortunes foisting off useless material on the government. Other millionaires of the future—Rockefeller, Carnegie, Mellon, Morgan—laid the foundations of their fortunes in wartime business activity.

Wartime prosperity had its harsh aspects, of course. Industrial wages, for example, rose far more slowly than living costs; this caused much hardship in cities where food speculators flourished. Families living on fixed incomes were especially hurt by the wartime inflation. Yet few northerners suffered the privations that became all but universal in the Confederacy.

Despite the boom, Lincoln's government had a difficult time financing the war, partly because it failed to realize how long the war would last. In 1862 Secretary of the Treasury Chase was obliged to begin printing paper money. That year and the next, the Treasury issued $450 million of certificates soon to be known as greenbacks. In the summer of 1864, when Union armies were still in trouble, greenbacks fell to a low of thirty-nine cents on the gold dollar, but thereafter their value rose steadily.

Despite the sizable emigration from Europe to the North during the war, shortages of manpower hurt the Union military effort at certain junctures almost as much as they hurt the Confederacy. By March 1863 conscription could no longer be put off, and that month Congress voted the first Union draft. Far from helping the manpower situation, the act lit a torch to social discontent. One of its provisions permitted a man to escape military service simply by paying $300 to the authorities, who were then responsible for finding substitutes ready to serve for a bounty. Clearly the poor were going to be saddled with the rich man's duty in what seemed to be a struggle only to elevate the black worker. In July 1863 a New York City mob gave sinister expression to widespread resentment toward the act by setting fire to buildings and attacking blacks. Valuable military manpower had to be drawn from the battlefield to suppress the violence, which left at least twelve dead, hundreds injured, and $1.5 million in property destroyed.

The Emancipation Proclamation

While Lee sought to end the war's slaughter by breaking the North's morale through invasion, Lincoln attempted to end the dreadful stalemate through political action.

From the day he took office, Lincoln had "struggled," as he said, against every kind of pressure—religious, journalistic, political, personal—to declare the slaves free without compensating their owners and without undertaking to "colonize" freed blacks outside the country. Even had he sympathized with such demands, the sensitivity of slaveholding border states within the Union and northern sentiment in general would have made him hold back.

At first, generals in the field were left to their own discretion in dealing with the increasing numbers of slaves who sought security behind Union lines as the fighting spread. Then in March 1862 Congress adopted "an additional article of war" forbidding the army to return fugitive slaves to their owners. Shortly thereafter, the War Department specifically authorized recruitment of fugitive slaves as soldiers. The authorization was accompanied by an admonition that it "must never see daylight because it is so much in advance of public opinion."

Congress added more rungs to the ladder of freedom. In April 1862 it passed and Lincoln signed a measure abolishing slavery in the District of Columbia. Former owners were to be paid, on average, $300 per slave. Two months later, another act abolished slavery in United States territories, this time with no financial compensation. Congress then adopted the so-called Second Confiscation Act, which provided for the conviction for treason of all persons engaged in rebellion, "or who shall in any way give aid . . . thereto." Among its penalties was the stipulation that "all slaves" of such persons "shall be forever free of their servitude."

In the meantime, Lincoln mounted his own efforts to use emancipation as an instrument to end the war and restore the Union. He cautiously awaited good news from the battlefield before taking public action. On September 22, in the wake of indecisive Antietam, he read to the Cabinet a draft of a proclamation that the papers published the next day.

Lincoln declared that at the next meeting of Congress in December he would recommend enactment "of a practical measure" offering financial aid to all slave states that were not then in rebellion against the United States and that had "voluntarily adopt[ed] immediate, or gradual abolishment of slavery within their limits." He also promised to continue his efforts to "colonize persons of African descent, with their consent." On January 1, 1863, the September proclamation went on, he would designate which states still were in rebellion, and in them, "all persons held as slaves . . shall be then, thenceforward, and forever free"; there would be no financial compensation whatever. Moreover, "the military and naval authority" of the United States would make no effort to suppress any attempts slaves might then make to effect their freedom. On the contrary, this authority would do whatever necessary to shelter them.

Conservatives in the North, sick of the military stalemate and fearful that any tampering with slavery would only prolong the South's resistance, registered their disapproval of the preliminary emancipation proclamation in the fall elections of 1862, when the Democrats cut deeply into the Republican majority in the House. The Radicals, on the other hand, deplored Lincoln's tortuous and tolerant maneuverings and demanded that he get on with the "revolutionary struggle."

Lincoln, nevertheless, held to his plan. The one hundred days of grace following his September announcement expired with no takers among the rebellious commonwealths (who viewed the proclamation as little short of an invitation to slave revolts), and on January 1, 1863, Lincoln issued his final Emancipation Proclamation:

I, Abraham Lincoln, . . . in time of actual armed rebellion against the . . . United States, and as a fit and necessary war measure for suppressing said rebellion, do . . . order and declare that all persons held as slaves within . . . states and parts of states wherein the people . . . are . . . in rebellion . . . are and henceforward shall be free. . . . And I further declare . . . that such persons . . . will be received into the armed service of the United States.

The proclamation neither freed any slaves nor shortened the war. But it ensured the death of slavery when the war was won.

TO APPOMATTOX

No matter how great the difficulties on the home fronts, the two armies staggered from battle to battle in the field. Men died in horrifying numbers, more than in any war of the nineteenth century except the Taiping Rebellion in China. As was true of all major wars until the twentieth century, more men died of disease than in battle. For the first time, women participated near the front lines in army hospitals, nursing wounded and dying men amid the screaming and the stench of body filth, blood, and gangrene.

The Long Road to Gettysburg

Observing that McClellan had the "slows" after Antietam, Lincoln replaced him with General Ambrose E. Burnside. At the battle of Fredericksburg in December 1862 the new commander showed that he was far worse than his predecessor. Lincoln replaced Burnside with General Joseph Hooker, who decided to fake a movement of troops that would draw Lee's from their dug-in positions outside Fredericksburg. His tactic nearly worked, but early in May when Hooker caught up with Lee at Chancellorsville, he, like so many of his predecessors, lost his nerve and almost his army.

Victory at Chancellorsville cost Lee 12,000 men and the life of Stonewall Jack-

A young Confederate soldier lies dead in the trenches of Fort Mahone on April 2, 1865. (Library of Congress)

son. But Lee now thought he saw the path open to an invasion of the North itself and to final victory. When Davis refused to pull men from the western theater in support of a grand assault, Lee decided to go ahead with the nearly 75,000 men in his Virginia command. "General Lee," one of his lieutenants said at this time, "believed that the Army of Northern Virginia, as it then existed, could accomplish anything." He was wrong.

By June 29 Lee's advance corps had reached a point a mere ten miles from Harrisburg, Pennsylvania—the deepest Confederate penetration of the war. Concerned now about the lengthening of his communications, Lee began to look for favorable terrain onto which to lure and confront the "Yanks." By then, Hooker had been replaced by General George Gordon Meade, who was making his own plans to invite attack on favorable ground. Both generals were to be disappointed. On June 30 some of Lee's foragers encountered Meade's most northerly watch at the crossroads town of Gettysburg, Pennsylvania, and on July 1 the Battle of Gettysburg began.

The setting was almost perfect for a fight to the death. On July 3, the Federals on Cemetery Ridge broke General George E. Pickett's famous last charge, and the great battle ended. "Call no council of war. . . . Do not let the enemy escape," Lincoln wired Meade. But Meade called a council while Lee made good his retreat. "Our army held the war in the hollow of its hand," Lincoln said later, "and would not close it."

A seasoned Union officer described the slaughter at Gettysburg, which characterized so many battles of the war:

> We see the poor fellows hobbling back from the crest, or unable to do so, pale and weak, lying on the ground with the mangled stump of an arm or leg, dripping their life-blood away; or with a cheek torn open, or a shoulder mashed. And many, alas!

hear not the roar as they stretch upon the ground with upturned faces and open eyes, though a shell should burst at their very ears. Their ears and their bodies this instant are only mud.

Many months afterwards, the bodies of thousands who there "gave their lives" still lay unburied. The degrading sight led to a call for a national cemetery in their honor. It was at the dedication ceremonies for this cemetery that Lincoln delivered the Gettysburg Address, promising "that these dead shall not have died in vain."

Grant Takes Command

On July 4, 1863, on the heels of Gettysburg, came the thrilling report of a great Union triumph in the West. After a year of struggle, Grant had taken Vicksburg, the key to the Mississippi.

Grant's victory in the western theater focused the attention of the entire nation on this veteran of the Mexican War who had resigned his army captaincy in 1854 so that he could better support his family. "The art of war is simple enough," went his military theory. "Find out where your enemy is. Get him as soon as you can. Strike at him as hard as you can and keep moving on."

After Vicksburg, one Confederate army and part of the Confederacy itself were isolated west of the Mississippi. But another Confederate army, commanded by General Braxton Bragg, was still operating in central Tennessee. In September 1863, under Grant's orders, General William Rosecrans began to pursue Bragg in earnest. But after being outmaneuvered at Chickamauga, Rosecrans's army found itself bottled up in nearby Chattanooga. To raise the siege, Grant called on armies from the east and west. He received them because of northern railroad efficiency. On November 25 these combined forces won a spectacular victory at Chattanooga, splitting the Confederacy north and south as well as east and west.

Following further victories in the West, Lincoln rewarded Grant by appointing him commander of all the Union armies. Grant quickly set to work. His victory program was for the Army of the Potomac to so occupy Lee's army that it could not link up with any other Rebel force—and to bleed it daily in the bargain. At the same time, William Sherman's army was to push eastward from Tennessee into Georgia and take Atlanta, thereby striking into the heart of Rebel territory.

The first reports of Grant's campaigns were disheartening. Throughout May 1864, the Army of the Potomac, under Meade and Grant himself, engaged Lee's forces in murderous but indecisive battles north of Richmond. Enormous Federal casualties in the Wilderness and at Cold Harbor—Grant is said to have lost 55,000 men in his first month—aroused strong resentment in the Union. Newspapers began to refer to him as "the butcher." But Lincoln, with deepening sadness, stood by him, and Grant decided to swing down to the peninsula to get at Richmond once more from the south and to send General Philip Sheridan to counter Confederate thrusts northward in the Shenandoah Valley. For nearly a year there was continual slaughter and devastation in the valley and in the Tidewater region of Virginia. Sheridan executed Grant's order to leave the valley "a barren waste."

The course of war in the Deep South was much less ambiguous. Starting in Tennessee, Sherman's army thrust through Georgia against weakening Confederate resistance. Announcing that "war is hell," Sherman pursued a policy of devastating the countryside, of deliberately aiming at the civilian as well as the military morale of his opponents. His famous "march to the sea" was in fact a major turning point in the modern history of warfare. It was, indeed, a new strategy to aim not only at an opposing army but at the society supporting it. His army left a wake of burning and pillaging among a civilian population that had not expected it. The chaos was complicated by the enormous number of slaves suddenly loosed from ruined plantations.

On September 3 Sherman wired Washington, "Atlanta is ours, and fairly won." Having left that city "smouldering and in ruins," Sherman's "bummers" thrust toward Savannah. "To realize what war is," Sherman said, "one should follow in our tracks."

The End in Sight

Sherman's victory at Atlanta in September 1864 had more than military significance. Only bitter rivalry among the Radicals had enabled Lincoln to win the Union party (Republicans and War Democrats) renomination for the presidency the preceding June. In August the Democrats nominated as their standard-bearer the peace-minded General McClellan. Until September the Democratic theme of war failure seemed to meet the mood of the country. Then came the stirring news of Atlanta's fall and a revival of confidence not only in Lincoln's generals but in the president himself. In November Lincoln won a smashing victory. With 55 percent of the popular vote, he outdistanced McClellan in the electoral college 212 to 21. Victory, not negotiated peace, now became the military theme as well.

In February 1865 Sherman headed north from Savannah toward the "hellhole of secession," South Carolina, where as he said, "the devil himself could not restrain his men." The "pitiless march" brought him to Columbia, South Carolina's capital, and soon, whether by accident or by design, one of the most beautiful cities in the country was consumed in flames. Charleston, outflanked, was occupied the next day by Union forces blockading the harbor after the defending Rebels had fled. Sherman, meanwhile, pounded on into North Carolina.

Gettysburg, Vicksburg, Atlanta, the humiliating failure of cotton diplomacy, the bruising wall of the blockade—none of these had quite managed to undermine the Confederacy's capacity for war. But in the face of Sherman's devastation, the southern spirit drooped. As early as September 1864, Davis acknowledged that "two thirds of our men are absent . . most of them absent without leave."

In March 1865 the Confederacy took the fateful step of recruiting men "irrespective of color," slaves "who might volunteer to fight for their freedom." The measure was a signal of desperation.

By then Grant's 115,000 blues outnumbered Lee's 54,000 grays in Virginia. The time had come for Lee to pull out of his hateful trenches while he still had so formidable a force and to try to join up with Johnston in North Carolina. But under cover of darkness, and while Davis and his government fled from their capital, contingents of Grant's army poured into Richmond. On April 7, his path to North Carolina irretrievably sealed off, Lee asked for terms. On April 9, impeccable in a new uniform, he met the mud-spattered Grant in a farmhouse at Appomattox Court House, a village some 95 miles west of Richmond. "Give them the most liberal terms," Lincoln had ordered Grant. "Let them have their horses to plow with, and, if you like, their guns to shoot crows with. I want no one punished." Grant complied.

On April 26 Johnston surrendered his

The devastated city of Richmond in April 1865. (Library of Congress)

army to Sherman at Durham Station, North Carolina. On May 10 the fleeing Davis was caught in Georgia and imprisoned for two years.

Lincoln's Death

When news of Richmond's fall reached Washington on April 3, the city exploded with joy. But then on April 14 a fanatic actor, John Wilkes Booth, shot Lincoln as the president sat in his box at Ford's Theatre in Washington, watching a performance of *Our American Cousin.* At 7:20 the next morning Lincoln died. It was the first assassination of a United States president.

The victorious president had charged the nation to act "with malice towards none, with charity for all." He had acknowledged the guilt of the North as well as the South for "the bondsman's two hundred and fifty years of unrequited toil." At first Robert E. Lee would not believe the news

of Lincoln's death. Then, on that Sunday, he told a visitor that he had "surrendered as much to [Lincoln's] goodness as to Grant's artillery." Now Lincoln and "goodness" were removed, with consequences foretold by Herman Melville when he wrote in "The Martyr":

> They have killed him, the Forgiver—
> The Avenger takes his place. . . .

SUGGESTED READINGS

J.M. McPherson, *Ordeal by Fire: The Civil War and Reconstruction* (1982). A. Nevins, *The War for the Union,* 4 vols. (1959-71).Stephen Crane, *The Red Badge of Courage* (1895). B.P. Thomas, *Abraham Lincoln* (1952). E.M. Thomas, *The Confederate Nation* (1979). W.L. Rose, *Rehearsal for Reconstruction: The Port Royal Experiment* (1964).

SUMMARY

The Civil War became the deadliest war Americans have ever fought. It lasted four years, killed a generation of young men, and left the South devastated.

It began slowly. At first it was thought that the war would be quick, that the South, fighting on its home ground and led by talented officers, would win. In a long war, the North's advantages in numerical strength and industrial resources were overwhelming. The North had other advantages in its government, which was strong and centralized, and in its political leader, Abraham Lincoln. The South, dedicated to states' rights, had difficulty contending even with the idea of strong central government.

The North's strategy was to strangle the South with a naval blockade, gain control of the Mississippi, and take Richmond, the Confederate capital. The first two steps went well; the third did not.

Even with direct orders from Lincoln, the army did not move in the East and the campaign for Richmond went nowhere. Under more vigorous commanders, Union forces in the West gained control of the Mississippi except for Vicksburg in Mississippi and Port Hudson in Louisiana. The grand assault on Richmond in the spring and summer of 1862 failed utterly because of the generals' incompetence. The North was again defeated in the second battle of Bull Run in August. But at Antietam in

September, the Confederate attempt to penetrate the North failed.

This was to be the turning point, for now the South's resources were being used up, and victory was still nowhere in sight. In its brutality and inconclusiveness, Antietam was also symbolic of a war that seemed to produce only aimless mutual slaughter.

By this time there were clear signs of economic difficulties in the South. The frustrated Confederate government had begun to print paper money in 1861. The result was drastic inflation. Cotton diplomacy failed. In the North, there was economic boom and wartime prosperity as mechanized agriculture and expanding factories poured out huge amounts of food and supplies.

By 1862 Lincoln was ready to end the military stalemate by a bold political action— freeing the slaves. The Emancipation Proclamation took effect on January 1, 1863. It did not shorten the war or free any slaves immediately, but it ensured the death of slavery when the war was over.

After Antietam the military pace of the war picked up. The North lost at Chancellorsville in May of 1863. But then came Gettysburg, July 1–4, and the end of Confederate hopes. On the same day the battle at Gettysburg ended, news came of Grant's victory at Vicksburg. Grant was made supreme commander of the Union armies in the spring of 1864, but another year of terrible fighting followed as Union armies advanced toward Richmond in a great pincer movement. Sherman's army moved relentlessly from Tennessee toward the sea, laying waste the area over which it traveled and burning Atlanta in September 1864.

In November Lincoln was reelected on the strength of the military victories and the clear signs that the end was in sight. By the end of March 1865, Grant's army was ready to enter Richmond. On April 9, General Robert E. Lee surrendered for the Confederacy at the village of Appomattox Court House. But then on April 14, Lincoln was shot in Washington; he died the next day. The war was over. It had cost the life of an American president, in addition to more other American lives than any war before or since.

14

After the War: Reconstruction and Restoration

After four years of warfare, the Union had withstood its most serious challenge. Measured in physical devastation and human lives, the Civil War remains the costliest war in the experience of the American people. When it ended in April 1865, 620,000 men (in a nation of 35 million) had been killed, at least that many more had been wounded, and large portions of the South lay in ruins. Two questions were firmly settled: the right of a state to secede and the right to own slaves. But new problems soon surfaced that would plunge the nation into still another period of turmoil and uncertainty. Under what conditions should the ex-Confederate states be permitted to return to the Union? What was the status of those southerners who had led their states out of the Union? Were the nearly 4 million newly freed slaves entitled to the same rights as white citizens? Finally, where did the responsibility lie for resolving these questions—with the president or with Congress?

President Lincoln's view of reconstruction was consistent with his theory of secession

and rebellion. He held from the outset that states could not break away from the Union. The Civil War, then, had been an illegal rebellion waged by disloyal men. Now that the rebellion was over, the task of reconstruction consisted of restoring loyal governments to the ex-Confederate states. After agreeing to repudiate secession and to recognize the abolition of slavery, the newly restored states would retain the same powers of decision enjoyed by all states, including the right to determine the status of their black residents.

The Radical Republicans, a faction within the party, believed that Lincoln's program would hamper their objective—to rebuild southern society around the equality of newly freed slaves and whites. The rebel states, they argued, were reduced to the status of territories because of their "rebellion." In seeking statehood once again, they came under the jurisdiction not of the president but of Congress, which governed territorial affairs. This was not simply an argument over the respective powers of the legislative and executive branches of gov-

ernment; it was a battle over the very objectives and content of southern Reconstruction.

President Lincoln hoped to build a Republican party in the South based on the votes of white men and on the leadership of those who had initially opposed secession. The Radicals, on the other hand, viewed the black vote as the means of winning the South for the Republicans and ensuring the party's national strength. Lincoln and his successor, Andrew Johnson, were willing to entrust the fate of the newly freed slaves to the defeated whites. The Radicals tried to develop a program of civil rights and education that would afford some protection to the freed blacks. The refusal of the white South to grant such protection strengthened the Radical position and helped to make possible Radical or congressional Reconstruction.

Radical rule in the South ended in 1877 (much sooner in most states), having failed to achieve the objective of a democratic, biracial society. That failure does not mean Lincoln's or Johnson's programs would have worked any better. Whatever its shortcomings, Radical Reconstruction enabled blacks to gain political experience as voters and officeholders. It also laid the legal foundations for a "second reconstruction" in the 1950s and 1960s, when black leaders and movements would seek to complete the work of emancipation.

THE DEFEATED SOUTH

The task of physical reconstruction proved no less challenging than that of political reconstruction. To rebuild the devastated areas and to restore agricultural production required outlays of capital and labor that were not readily available. The planters' land, worth $1.5 billion in 1860, was evaluated at half that amount ten years later. The South's banking capital had been wiped out, and the credit system on which the planters had depended for all essential purchases was paralyzed. Finally, the planters' $2.5-billion investment in slave labor had vanished, along with many of the black workers.

Aftermath of Slavery

In throwing off a lifetime of bondage, black men and women adopted different priorities, ranging from dramatic breaks with the past to subtle though no less significant changes in demeanor and behavior. For some, the first need was to test their freedom, to take some kind of action to prove to themselves that they were really free. The most direct and the quickest test was to leave the plantation. By leaving, some also expected to improve their economic prospects; still others hoped to locate family members from whom they had been separated during slavery. Many did not move at all, choosing to remain in familiar surroundings and to find ways of exercising their freedom even as they worked in the same fields and kitchens.

That freedmen and freedwomen in many instances changed their lives, displayed feelings of independence, deserted their former owners, seized the land of absentee owners, engaged in work stoppages, sat where they pleased in public places and vehicles, and no longer felt the need to humble themselves in the presence of whites should not obscure the extent to which life went on very much as it had before the war.

As long as whites had political and economic dominance, they were in a position to control black freedom. In March 1865 Congress tried to ease the transition from slavery to freedom by creating the Freedmen's Bureau. It was authorized to furnish food, clothing, and transportation to refugees and freed blacks, to oversee labor contracts, and to settle freedmen on abandoned or confiscated lands. Although the bureau provided relief to many freedmen, it never fulfilled its potential. Most of the land worked by freed black laborers was returned to its original owners, and the freedmen's goal of becoming landowning farmers remained unrealized. To survive, most ex-slaves would need to negotiate working agreements with white planters.

Despite the war and emancipation, the white South's racial attitudes remained the same. The need to maintain white supremacy took on an even greater urgency now that the slaves had been freed. The former slaveholding class seemed less equipped, mentally and physically, to make the transition from slave to free labor than their former slaves. "Can not freedmen be organized and disciplined as well as slaves?" a South Carolina planter asked. "Is not the dollar as potent as the lash? The belly as tender as the back?" No matter how hard a few of them tried, whites seemed incapable of learning new ways and shaking off old attitudes. That failure was demonstrated during presidential Reconstruction, when the white South was given the opportunity to reconstruct itself with a minimum of federal interference.

Lincoln's Plan

On December 8, 1863, with several rebel states already overrun, President Lincoln issued his proclamation of Amnesty and Reconstruction. Known as the "10-percent plan," it set forth the terms by which the southern states would be restored to the Union. Except for high military and civil officers of the Confederacy, any southern citizen would be granted an amnesty by the president after taking an oath of loyalty to the Constitution and the laws of the Union. Confiscated property other than slaves would be restored. As soon as 10 percent of those who had voted in the presidential election of 1860 had taken the oath and sworn allegiance to the Union, that state could proceed to write a new constitution, elect new state officers, and send members to the United States Congress. The House and Senate, of course, retained their constitutional privilege of seating or rejecting such members.

The president failed to confront the social realities of emancipation. Lincoln assured the states to which his proclamation applied that he would not object to "any provision" they might wish to make regarding the freed slaves "which may yet be consistent with their present condition as a laboring, landless, and homeless class." This was nothing short of an invitation to the ex-Confederate states to adopt the repressive Black Codes they enacted in 1865 and 1866. Until late in the war, Lincoln still held that the best way to deal with "the Negro problem" was to persuade blacks to leave the country. But black leaders rejected Lincoln's colonization scheme, even as Radical Republicans would reject his reconstruction program.

The Radical Plan

Lincoln had urged a minimum of federal interference in the ex-Confederate states. The Radical Republicans, most prominently Thaddeus Stevens of Pennsylvania in the

House and Charles Sumner of Massachusetts in the Senate, urged a more thorough reconstruction of southern society. The Wade-Davis bill, adopted by Congress a few days before it adjourned in July 1864, set forth the first Radical response to Lincoln's program. It required a majority of the citizens of a state, not just 10 percent, to swear loyalty to the Union before a provisional governor could call an election for a state constitutional convention. Only those southerners able to swear that they had *always* been loyal to the Union and had not "voluntarily borne arms against the United States" were entitled to vote for delegates to the constitutional conventions. The bill also prescribed that new state constitutions in the South must abolish slavery, repudiate state debts, and deprive ex-Confederate leaders of the right to vote.

Radical strategists hoped to commit the Republican party to their program in the 1864 presidential campaign. Lincoln attempted to stop them by permitting the Wade-Davis bill to die by a pocket veto. Defending his action, Lincoln said rebel states might follow the Wade-Davis provisions if they wished, but he refused to make them mandatory. Most Radical leaders supported Lincoln in the 1864 campaign because they did not want to disrupt the party and endanger the war effort. Once the election was over, they pressed again for their program. In January 1865 they adopted the Thirteenth Amendment, which abolished slavery throughout the United States. (It was ratified in December 1865.) In February Congress refused to admit members from Louisiana, which Lincoln had declared reconstructed under the 10-percent plan. In March Congress created the Freedmen's Bureau. With these measures, Congress adjourned. When it reconvened in December, it would have to deal with a new president

and with a South that had been reconstructed under the president's plan.

Johnsonian Restoration

When Lincoln died, Andrew Johnson of Tennessee became president. Like Lincoln, he had been born in poverty. Unlike Lincoln, he was tactless and inflexible, possessing neither humility nor the capacity for compromise. Even though Johnson attacked special privilege and the planter aristocracy, he never became a vocal opponent of slavery and he held traditional southern views on race relations.

Alone among southern senators, Johnson refused to give up his seat after his state had left the Union. In March 1862, while still a senator, he was appointed by Lincoln as military governor of Tennessee, and under him the state became a kind of laboratory for the president's Reconstruction policy. As a demonstration of wartime unity, the Republican party nominated Johnson for the vice-presidency in 1864, even though he had been a Democrat all his life. During the campaign, Johnson made himself attractive to many Radicals by his fierce denunications of Rebel leaders as traitors. But the enthusiasm with which these Radicals greeted Johnson's becoming president proved short-lived.

With Congress still in recess, the new president set out to complete Lincoln's restoration of the South to the Union. Early in May 1865, he recognized Lincoln's "10-percent" governments in Louisiana, Tennessee, Arkansas, and Virginia. He next appointed military governors in the seven states that had not yet complied. On May 29 he offered executive amnesty to all citizens of these states except high Confederate military and civil officers and those owning more than $20,000 worth of property. These people had to apply for amnesty to the president. In each state the "whitewashed" electorate—that is, those who benefited by the amnesty offer—was then to elect members to a constitutional convention. The convention was to abolish slavery, rescind the state's secession ordinance, adopt the Thirteenth Amendment, repudiate the state war debt, and call an election for a new state government. The suffrage for this election was to be determined by each state rather than by Congress, and that clearly meant blacks would be denied participation in southern political life.

By the winter of 1865, all the seceding states but Texas had complied with Johnson's terms. Given the opportunity to reconstruct themselves, the ex-Confederate states moved quickly to restore the old planter class to political power. The president cooperated fully in this move. For all his dislike of the southern Old Guard, Johnson's personal grants of amnesty exceeded all bounds. He pardoned the heroes of the Lost Cause, whom the whitewashed voters proceeded to elect to national, state, and local offices.

While ratifying the Thirteenth Amendment, as required, the reconstructed states warned Congress almost as a unit to leave the status of the freedmen and freedwomen to those who knew them best—the white southerners. In the Black Codes adopted in 1865 and 1866, the fact of emancipation was recognized in some of the rights accorded to blacks for the first time. Although still universally forbidden to serve on juries, even in cases involving blacks, freedmen could now swear out affidavits in criminal cases, sue and be sued in civil actions, appear as witnesses, and otherwise give testimony. Marriages among blacks were to be sancti-fied under law, but interracial marriages carried sentences of up to life imprisonment for both parties. Blacks could make wills and pass on personal property. Their children could go to school and were to be protected from abuse if they were apprenticed.

But nowhere could blacks bear arms, vote, hold public office, or assemble freely. In some states they could work at any jobs and quit jobs freely. Most of the states, however, forbade them to leave their jobs except under stated conditions. Nor could they work as artisans, mechanics, or in other capacities in which they competed with white labor. The Mississippi code forbade freedmen to rent or lease land or houses. The idea behind these codes was that blacks would not work except under compulsion and proper supervision, and with the vigorous enforcement of contracts and vagrancy laws. The vagrancy provisions were the worst. In Georgia, for example, the law said that "all persons wandering or strolling about in idleness, who are able to work and who have no property to support them," could be picked up and tried. If convicted, they could be set to work on state chain gangs or contracted out to planters and other employers who would pay their fines and their upkeep for a stated period.

The Johnson government confirmed the worst fears and predictions of the Radicals and even shocked many moderates. The rapid return to power of the Confederate leadership suggested an unwillingness by the South to accept defeat. By defining the freedman's role in a way that was bound to keep him propertyless and voteless, the Black Codes attempted to deny the fact of black freedom. In the North, the conviction grew that the white South was preparing to regain what it had supposedly lost on the battlefield. By their actions the South and

President Johnson had set the stage for congressional Reconstruction.

THE RADICAL CONGRESS

When Congress met in December 1865, it was faced with Johnson's actions and the South's responses. As their first counter-move, Radicals set up the Joint Committee of Fifteen—six senators and nine representatives—to review the work of presidential reconstruction and the qualifications of those elected in the southern states to serve in Congress. Exercising its constitutional power, Congress refused to seat them. Early in 1866 it enacted a bill continuing the Freedmen's Bureau; Johnson vetoed the bill because he believed that care of the freedmen was better left to the states.

In March 1866 Johnson also vetoed a civil-rights bill that forbade states to discriminate among citizens on the basis of color or race, as they had in the Black Codes. By now a sufficient number of conservative senators were ready to join the Radicals in defense of congressional power, if not of Radical principles, and both houses overrode the president. In July Radicals pushed through a second Freedmen's Bureau bill over Johnson's veto.

Even if many Republicans, like their constituents, remained divided over the proper place of blacks in American society, they could agree that the newly freed slaves should be protected in their basic rights and given the opportunity to advance themselves economically. In their view, the actions of the southern governments and the president's vetoes were undermining those possibilities. Enjoying a growing consensus, Republicans now moved to provide a constitutional basis for black freedom.

The Fourteenth Amendment

To provide a constitutional basis for black freedom, Radicals introduced the Fourteenth Amendment in June 1866, perhaps the most far-reaching amendment ever added to the Constitution. By identifying as citizens "all persons born or naturalized in the United States," it automatically extended citizenship to American-born blacks. It also forbade any state to abridge "the privileges and immunities" of United States citizens, to "deprive any person of life, liberty, or property, without due process of law" or to "deny to any person within its jurisdiction the equal protection of the laws."

The second section of the amendment did not give blacks the vote, as many Radicals hoped it would, but penalized any state for withholding it. (The penalty was never imposed and was ultimately replaced by the Fifteenth Amendment.) The third section disqualified from federal or state office all Confederates who had taken a federal oath of office before the war, unless Congress specifically lifted the disqualification by a two-thirds vote. Finally, the amendment guaranteed the Union debt but outlawed the Confederate debt and any claims for compensation for loss of slaves.

The Fourteenth Amendment had a stormy history before it was finally ratified in July 1868. Many years later, the use of the word *person* in the first section of the amendment was interpreted by the federal courts as applying to "legal persons" such as business corporations as well as to blacks, who were the only persons its framers had in mind. It thus supplied legal grounds for the courts to declare unconstitutional state regulation of railroads and trusts. Still later, the phrase in Section 1 prohibiting the denial of "equal protection of the laws" supplied legal grounds for the Supreme Court's school-desegregation decision in 1954.

Dissatisfaction with the amendment was voiced by Susan B. Anthony and other agitators for women's suffrage, who had hoped to win the franchise because of their contributions to victory in the Civil War. They fought valiantly to delete the word *male* from the voting provisions of the Fourteenth Amendment (and, before long, to add the word *sex* to "race, color, or previous condition of servitude" in the Fifteenth Amendment). But Radical leaders believed that merging women's rights with blacks' rights would weaken the chances of both.

Radicals demanded that southern states ratify the Fourteenth Amendment in order to regain representation in Congress. Johnson advised them not to. By mid February 1867, all but Tennessee—that is, ten of eleven ex-Confederate states—had followed his advice. Without the required three-fourths majority of the states, the amendment was dead. But the rejection of the amendment, along with the president's defiance, only reinforced in the minds of Republicans the need to take over the process of reconstruction.

The Reconstruction Acts and Impeachment

The Fourteenth Amendment had drawn the issue clearly between president and Congress. In the congressional campaign of 1866, Johnson visited key cities on behalf of candidates who favored his policy. Many people considered such active campaigning wrong for a president. In any event, the more Johnson talked, the more he antagonized northern voters. At the same time, racial clashes in New Orleans and Memphis

appeared to confirm Radical warnings about the consequences of Johnson's southern policy. Stung by the South's rejection of the Fourteenth Amendment, the Radicals sought and won a sweeping victory. With a two-thirds majority in Congress, they would be able to impose even sterner measures and carry them over presidential vetoes.

The Radicals began with the First Reconstruction Act, passed over Johnson's veto on March 2, 1867. Tennessee had been accepted back into the Union in 1866, but all other southern state governments were declared illegal. The South was organized into five military districts, each under a general to be named by the president. The general's main task was to call a new constitutional convention in each state, its delegates to be elected by universal adult male suffrage, black and white, except for those deprived of the vote under the proposed Fourteenth Amendment. The new conventions would establish state governments in which blacks could vote and hold office. These governments were to ratify the Fourteenth Amendment as a condition for their return to the Union and the acceptance of their representatives by Congress. By June 1868 all but three states—Mississippi, Texas, and Virginia—had complied with these requirements, and in July the ratification of the Fourteenth Amendment was completed. The three reluctant states were readmitted in 1870.

The Radicals' next step was to protect their program from any possible presidential sabotage. The Tenure of Office Act, passed along with the First Reconstruction Act, declared that the president could not remove federal officers who had been appointed with the consent of the Senate unless the Senate agreed. The second, the Command of the Army Act, forbade the president to issue orders to the army except through the General of the Army (Ulysses S. Grant). These measures were designed to prevent the president from using patronage or control of the army to undermine the Radical program.

The conflict between Congress and Johnson ended in a move to impeach the president. Radicals held that as long as he remained in office, their Reconstruction program could never be fully or fairly implemented. Although Johnson had no real choice but to enforce the acts of Congress, he had used his executive powers to weaken them. But there was no evidence directly implicating the President in any "high crimes and misdemeanors"—the only constitutional grounds for impeachment.

By attempting to remove Secretary of War Stanton, the remaining Radical in his cabinet, and thereby also testing the validity of the Tenure of Office Act, President Johnson gave his congressional opponents the legal grounds to move against him. On February 21, 1868, Stanton was formally removed. Three days later, the Committee on Reconstruction, of which Thaddeus Stevens was chairman, recommended impeachment to the House. By March 2, eleven charges had been drawn up, all but one of them referring to the Tenure of Office Act. The exception was the tenth article, which charged that Johnson had been "unmindful of the high duties of his office" and had attempted to bring Congress into "disgrace, ridicule, hatred, contempt and reproach." This proved to be the major thrust of the impeachment move.

To convict Johnson, two-thirds of the Senate would have to be convinced that the charges against him amounted to "high crimes and misdemeanors" or that impeachment could be broadened to include polit-ical conduct that rendered a president unfit to hold office. But seven Republicans could not be persuaded, and that was enough. By the barest possible margin—only one vote—the Senate refused to remove the president.

The Election of 1868: Grant

Although they had done everything possible to block the president before the election of 1868, the Radicals were determined to secure the office for themselves that year. Their choice was General Grant, who had no known political allegiances—or, for that matter, any known political ambitions. He had served the Radicals in the controversy over Stanton's removal, and his war record appeared to make him a certain winner. At the Republican convention Grant was nominated on the first ballot. Johnson sought the Democratic nomination. But after twenty-two ballots the Democratic convention chose former New York governor Horatio Seymour.

In the campaign, Democrats sought to divert attention from their Reconstruction record by making an issue of cheap money. In 1866 Congress had passed a measure providing for the gradual retirement of the wartime greenbacks, whose dollar value always remained below that of gold. In the next two years, almost $100 million worth were withdrawn from circulation, much to the disappointment of businessmen as well as farmers. Western farmers, although emotionally attached to the Republican party for its liberal land policy, wanted cheap money with which to meet mortgage obligations and other debts. The Democrats' platform made a bid for their support by advocating the reissue of greenbacks for the purpose of retiring war bonds that did not specifically require repayment in gold. The leading proponent of this "soft-money" plank was an early aspirant for the 1868 Democratic nomination, George H. Pendleton of Ohio. It became the "Ohio Idea." The Republicans had another idea. War bonds, they said, should be redeemed in gold; anything else would be a repudiation of a sacred debt. At the same time, they promised businessmen they would extend redemption "over a fair period" so as not to disturb the credit structure. When the time came, all bondholders would be paid in gold.

The Radicals kept the main political issue before the voters—Radical Reconstruction versus Democratic dishonor. The Democratic party, cried Republicans, was the standard-bearer of rebellion, black repression, and financial repudiation. But the campaign did not overwhelm the opposition. In 1868, against a weak opponent, Grant was elected with about 52.7 percent of the popular vote and a popular plurality of only 310,000. If not for the seven reconstructed southern states and the black vote, he might have lost.

The part blacks played in winning the election—and, more important, the fact that blacks in states such as Louisiana and Georgia had been prevented from casting what might have been much-needed Republican votes—led Radicals to attempt to strengthen the Fourteenth Amendment's protection of black suffrage. When Congress convened early in 1869, it promptly passed the Fifteenth Amendment: "The right of citizens of the United States to vote shall not be denied or abridged by the United States or by any State on account of race, color, or previous condition of servitude." This amendment was ratified in March 1870. By then, blacks had already made their presence and influence known in the newly established southern governments.

RADICAL RECONSTRUCTION: LEGEND AND REALITY

With the passage of the Reconstruction Act in 1867, Congress began a new era in southern political history. The new state governments were the first to be organized on the basis of universal male suffrage and to operate on the premise that all men, white and black, were entitled to equal legal protection. For whites as well as blacks, this proved to be an extraordinary experience.

Contrary to legend, blacks did not dominate any of the new governments; federal military occupation was never extensive; and only in South Carolina, Florida, and Louisiana did Radical rule last as long as eight years. The impressions that survived Reconstruction, however, and that generations of Americans would believe, added up to a "tragic era" in which corrupt carpetbaggers, poor white scalawags, and illiterate blacks ran wild in an unprecedented and outrageous orgy of misrule.

Like most stereotypes, this picture is simplified, distorted, and falsified. The carpetbagger was a northerner who moved to the South after the Civil War and supported or participated in the Radical state governments. His reasons for settling in the South were as varied as his personal character. For some, legitimate business opportunities and the availability of land and natural resources provided the incentive. Others were Union veterans who had found the South an attractive place in which to live. Still others were teachers, clergy, and agents of charitable societies who had committed themselves to the task of educating and converting the ex-slaves. Finally, there were political adventurers, but their numbers were small. To the white South, however, the fact that some carpetbaggers supported

Andrew Johnson. (Library of Congress)

John R. Lynch, Speaker of the Mississippi House of Representatives and a U.S. Congressman. (Library of Congress)

black voting and office holding was enough to make them all guilty by association.

Like the carpetbaggers, the scalawags— native white Republicans who supported Radical rule—were a varied lot. In no state were they a majority of southern whites. They were not necessarily poor whites, nor did they all welcome or support black participation in political life. To those who had been Whigs before the war, the Republican party appeared to offer the best hope for promoting the industrial and economic interests of a new South. To those who had opposed secession, the Radical program was a way to neutralize the dominant planters and a chance at political power.

Although carpetbaggers and scalawags aroused white hatred, black voters and officeholders symbolized the changes in postwar southern society far more dramatically. The scene of black men, many of them only recently slaves, now voting and holding public office was a change so drastic and so fearful in its implications that few white southerners could accept it. Their very presence in the government was enough to condemn them, and their successes were in many ways more threatening to whites than their failures.

Radical Rule in the South

Although blacks voted in large numbers, they did not, in fact, dominate any of the southern states. Of the 1.35 million citizens qualified to vote in the ex-Confederate states at the beginning of Radical Reconstruction, about half were black. In Alabama, Florida, Louisiana, Mississippi, and South Carolina, black voters were a majority. Only in South Carolina, however, did black legislators outnumber whites, 88 to

67. In other state legislatures, blacks made up sizable minorities. But in no state did blacks control the senate or the executive mansion.

There were black lieutenant governors, secretaries of state, state treasurers, speakers of the house, and superintendents of education. Fourteen blacks were elected to the United States House of Representatives between 1869 and 1877, and two (Hiram Revels and Blanche K. Bruce of Mississippi) to the United States Senate. The majority of black officeholders had local positions, such as justice of the peace, sheriff, and county supervisor, which were important at a time of much local decision-making. Most were young men, generally in their twenties and thirties at the outset of Reconstruction. Some were illiterate, some were self-educated, and a few were graduates of northern colleges. Many were ministers, teachers, artisans, and farmers who had managed to accumulate small landholdings. Before the war, a number of them had been members of the free-black class in the South. Still others had resided in the North, either northern-born or self-imposed exiles from their homeland. Most impressive,

Campaigning in the South, with blacks seeking public office for the first time. (Library of Congress)

however, were those who had been slaves only recently. The skills they had gained from learning how to survive as slaves may explain why many of them proved to be successful politicians.

Under Radical rule, both races made political and social advances in the South. The new state constitutions eliminated property qualifications for voting and officeholding among whites as well as blacks. They apportioned representation in state legislatures and in Congress more fairly. Judicial systems were revised, and juries were opened to blacks. Above all, constitutions in many southern states provided for public schools for whites and blacks for the first time.

The Radical governments displayed restraint when dealing with economic matters. Even black legislators refused to interfere with the rights of private property, though land ownership remained the principal goal of their black constituents. Rather than experiment with land redistribution, most black leaders argued for legal equality and urged their people to be thrifty and industrious and buy property. But as black sharecroppers knew only too well, legal equality and the vote could not feed hungry mouths or end economic hardship and dependency. They needed land of their own and the means to farm that land. However, although the Radical legislatures and Congress liberally funded the railroads, neither was willing to make that kind of commitment to ex-slaves—even as a token payment for years of unpaid labor.

The black officeholder gained experience in governing during an era in which corruption marked much of American political life. Although corruption in the Radical governments was not as bad as painted, there was enough to tarnish them and to confirm the skepticism in the North about

the entire experiment. Between 1868 and 1874, the bonded debt of the eleven ex-Conferedate states grew by over $100 million. This enormous sum was not itself evidence of corruption. Many of the social reforms of the Reconstruction legislatures were costly, and taxes to pay for such new "luxuries" as public schools fell heavily on the planters, who before the war had been able to pass taxes on to other groups. Still, much of the debt was incurred corruptly, though carpetbaggers, scalawags, and blacks were not necessarily the principal beneficiaries. Like the rest of the nation, the South suffered at the hands of railroad interests, business speculators, and contractors who sought legislative favors and were willing to pay for them. Corruption in the South, as elsewhere, tended to be bipartisan, involving men of both races and all classes, including some of the most distinguished families of the South. It had been under way before Radical rule, and it lasted long after the overthrow of Reconstruction. A black legislator might quickly learn from white colleagues of both parties that payoffs were a natural part of the political process and often a necessary supplement to an otherwise meager income. One black legislator, an ex-slave, offered this moral perspective after accepting a bribe: "I've been sold in my life eleven times. And this is the first time I ever got the money."

The ability of black officeholders varied considerably. But most important, blacks were learning the uses of political power and gaining confidence in their ability to rule. As they did, and as they began to demand political power on a par with their electoral strength and proven competence, the shaky alliance on which Radical rule rested began to fall apart. The idea of black success, independence, and power drove numerous whites out of the party, accelerated internal divisions, and gave the Democrats the opportunity for which they had carefully prepared. If anything about "black reconstruction" truly alarmed the white South, it was not so much the evidence of corruption but the very substantial possibility that this unique experiment in biracial government might succeed! As W. E. B. DuBois wrote, "There was one thing that the white South feared more than negro dishonesty, ignorance, and incompetency, and that was negro honesty, knowledge, and efficiency."

The End of Reconstruction: The Shotgun Policy

From the beginning of Radical rule, before any evidence of corruption had come to light, the white South was determined to use every method at its disposal to restore the rightful heirs of political power—the "natural leaders"—to the positions they deserved. Nothing less was at stake than the survival of Anglo-Saxon civilization: "If the negro is fit to make laws for the control of our conduct and property," a southern educator warned, "he is certainly fit to eat with us at our tables, to sleep in our beds, to be invited to our parlors, and to do all acts and things which a white man may do."

To overthrow Radical rule and the black vote on which it rested, thousands of even the most respectable people in the South banded together in the Ku Klux Klan, the Knights of the White Camellia, and other secret groups. Hooded or otherwise disguised, between 1867 and 1877 they roamed the land, shot, flogged, and terrorized blacks and their supporters, burned homes and public buildings, and assaulted Reconstruction officials.

The Mississippi Plan (sometimes called the Shotgun Policy), by which Democrats regained power in that state in 1875, proved to be a model of repression. It consisted of organized violence and threats, the systematic breakup of Republican gatherings, and the incitement of riots. Its aim was to force all whites into the Democratic party, and at the same time to eliminate black leadership and political participation. In communities where blacks were a majority or nearly so, the plan was carried out with full white support. Where persuasion failed, violence and terrorism were used by well-armed paramilitary units. White Republicans who resisted were driven from their homes and their communities. Defiant black sharecroppers were denied credit by southern merchants, evicted from the land, denied other employment, assaulted, and murdered.

White terrorism, economic coercion, federal indifference, and factionalism in the Radical governments had brought Radical Reconstruction to an end by 1877—much earlier in some states. After 1871 President Grant refused to call upon federal troops to support troubled Republican regimes. In May 1872 Congress passed a liberal Amnesty Act, which restored voting and officeholding privileges to all white southerners except a few hundred of the highest surviving Confederate dignitaries. That same year, the Freedmen's Bureau was permitted to expire. Disillusioned with the reconstruction experiment, northern whites turned to their own pressing economic problems and allowed traditional racist views to rationalize abandonment of the southern blacks.

The white southern response to Reconstruction is hardly surprising. Even honest and capable carpetbaggers came to symbolize alien rule, and even if corruption was fashionable, Radical corruption was not. Most important, if the black man were to succeed, he would no longer be content with a lower place in southern society. That was a difficult proposition to accept.

The tragedy of Radical Reconstruction is that it failed to reconstruct the racial attitudes of southern whites. From the outset, this unique experiment in biracial government rested on a weak base. The commitment of the federal government was limited, and even Republicans did not seek any long-term federal intervention in southern affairs. The commitment of blacks was limited by their economic weakness and dependence. If many of them chose to withdraw from political activism altogether, this reflected not only white intimidation but the recognition that politics had not significantly altered the quality of their day-to-day lives. The end of Reconstruction solidified white supremacy in the South. For blacks, the expectations raised by emancipation remained unfulfilled, and the range of choices open to them had been narrowed considerably. There was no way to assimilate, nor was there any way to separate.

THE GRANT PRESIDENCY

When Ulysses S. Grant became president in 1869, the American people expected him to exercise the same qualities of leadership he had shown in the Civil War. He would, many believed, organize a strong government, staffed by able aides, much as he had mobilized a victorious army. But the problems Grant faced as president—turmoil in the South, the tariff, falling farm prices, and business speculation—were of a far different kind from those he had confronted on the battlefield. He entered the White House with no political experience and few polit-

Ulysses S. Grant—the military hero as President. (New York Public Library)

ical convictions. By this time, moreover, corruption had become fashionable in the highest places, and lobbyists were often prowling the floor of the House and Senate to keep their legislators in line.

The Corruptionists

Inexperienced in the ways of politics and business, President Grant permitted himself and his office to be used by self-seeking politicians and businessmen. He found it difficult to believe that many of those who befriended him were interested only in personal profit. Two scandals hit Grant personally. One was the Whiskey Ring in St. Louis, which had defrauded the government of millions of dollars in taxes. Deeply involved in this, as in other frauds, was Grant's secretary, Orville Babcock, whom the president saved from imprisonment only by interfering in his trial. The second affair led to the impeachment of Grant's third secretary of war, W. W. Belknap, who since his appointment in 1870 had been "kept" by traders in the Indian territory under his jurisdiction. Belknap offered his resignation, and Grant, with characteristic loyalty, accepted "with great regret."

But these scandals were hardly comparable to the profiteering made possible by protective tariffs, land grants, and the money system. Few political plums were more valuable than the tariff, which by 1870 had added to the profits of eastern manufacturing and industrial interests. Railroads also shared in congressional handouts, not only in land grants but in lavish government loans. Revelations that company stock was distributed among legislators produced the famous scandal in 1868 involving the Crédit Mobilier, the construction company that built the Union Pacific, and helped destroy many political reputations. Nor were northern financiers ignored. In March 1869 both houses of Congress, fulfilling Republican campaign promises made the year before, pledged the government to redeem the entire war debt in gold or in new gold bonds. This pledge and the laws that soon implemented it sent the value of war bonds soaring and brought substantial profits to speculators.

In the 1872 presidential campaign, disenchantment with the Grant regime prompted a group of Republican reformers to organize the Liberal Republican party, adopt a platform stressing civil-service reform, and nominate the aging Horace Greeley for president. Editor of the *New York Tribune* for more than thirty years, Greeley had taken so many contradictory political positions that he was known as a crackpot. Seeking to regain national power, the Democratic party swallowed its pride and also nominated Greeley, although in 1866 he had publicly branded Democrats as "the traitorous section of Northern politics." Grant easily won reelection, carrying all but six states.

But the Democrats' hopes were by no means shattered. The scandals of the Grant administration increased public disillusionment with the Republican party and those who profited by its corrupt dealings and its control of patronage. The Crédit Mobilier affair, the first major Grant scandal, broke while the 1872 campaign was in progress. After the business crash of 1873, each new revelation struck with added force; once the Democrats captured the House in 1874, the revelations and prosecutions snowballed.

Grant deserved a better fate. He had been a great military leader with a genuine hatred of war and a compassion for its victims. But he showed little aptitude for the complex machinery of government, politics, and party. His personal honesty, trust, and naiveté made him an easy victim of interests that even the wisest politician found difficult to control.

The Election of 1876: Hayes

As convention time approached in 1876, Democrats were making an issue of corruption and Republicans were deeply divided on the best way to answer them. The Grand Old Party, as Republicans were calling themselves, separated into Stalwarts and Half-Breeds. Stalwarts were the hard-core political professionals, who put politics first: if business wanted favors, let them pay up. Half-Breeds were Republican reformers who had not deserted to the Liberal Republicans in 1872. Stalwarts, closest to Grant, wanted him to run for a third term. Half-Breeds lined up behind Congressman James G. Blaine of Maine, despite the dramatic disclosure of his shady relations with the Union Pacific Railroad while serving as Speaker of the House. When the movement to renominate Grant failed to materialize, the nomination went to Rutherford B. Hayes, the reform governor of Ohio.

The Democratic surge in the South, meanwhile, and the vicious repression on which it was based, accented the sectional differences in that party on every issue. Hunger for the presidency, long denied them, led the Democrats to close ranks behind Samuel J. Tilden, a rich corporation lawyer and hard-money man who had won a national reputation as a reform governor of New York. The presidential scandals, the severity of the economic depression of the mid 1870s, and the rising demand for reform all seemed to work to the Democrats' advantage. No one was certain, however, how the "redeemed" white South would vote. Many southern leaders were the former Whigs to whom Lincoln had looked. They

had never been at home in the Democratic party, into which secession and war had forced them. As representatives of a new industrialized and business-minded South, they found Republican economic policies attractive, and they especially resented the failure of northern Democrats to support land grants and other federal aid to southern railroads.

The attitudes of these southern Democrats were not lost on Hayes's political managers. They wanted to create a white southern Republican wing to offset the losses the party had suffered because of corruption in the North and repression of black voters in the South. But once he had the nomination, Hayes went along with the Republicans whose "southern strategy" was to damn the Democrats, old and new. The Democratic campaign stressed the need to end misrule in the South and to weed out corruption in the federal government. On economic issues, there was little to differentiate Tilden from Hayes; both were conservatives who proclaimed their belief in "sound money" and in limited government.

First reports of the election results suggested a Democratic victory. Tilden had a plurality of 250,000 votes, and the press proclaimed him the certain winner. But returns from Louisiana, Florida, and South Carolina, three states still under Radical control, had not yet come in because of election irregularities. Tilden needed only one electoral vote from these states to win; Hayes needed every one. Any accurate count in the disputed states was complicated by the threats and fraud used by Democrats to keep blacks from voting. Both parties claimed to have won. Congress would have to determine which of the double sets of returns from the three states should be accepted, the Democratic count or the Republican. The two parties agreed to the extraordinary device of deciding the election by turning the problem over to a commission of five representatives, five senators, and five Supreme Court justices. One of the justices, David Davis, presumably was independent in politics. The remaining fourteen members of the commission were equally divided between Democrats and Republicans. Unfortunately for Tilden, Davis quit the commission before it met and was replaced by a Republican justice. The Republican majority of eight then voted unanimously for Hayes.

One step that helped calm an angry South was the pledge exacted from the Stalwarts by their "southern compromise" party colleagues to vote federal subsidies to southern railroads. In exchange, southern leaders, nominally Democrats, agreed to vote for the Republican James A. Garfield as Speaker of the House—a position through which the whole course of legislation could be controlled at that time. But perhaps the critical component of the "Compromise of 1877" was the Republican assurance that Hayes "would deal justly and generously with the South." That was understood to mean the withdrawal of the remaining federal troops and no more interference in the restoration of white political supremacy.

Although the compromise broke down soon after Hayes's inauguration, the new president pursued a conciliatory policy toward the white South. He chose David M. Key of Tennessee, a high-ranking former Confederate officer and a Democrat, as postmaster general. By the end of April 1877 he had withdrawn the last federal troops from the South; with their departure, the last Radical state governments collapsed. That autumn, Hayes set forth on a good-will tour of the South during which he assured blacks that their "rights and interests would be safer if this great mass of intelligent white

men were let alone by the general government."

THE NEW SOUTH

With the collapse of the remaining Radical governments, politics in the South came to be dominated by a new class of men—industrialists, merchants, bankers, and railroad promoters. Calling themselves Conservatives or Redeemers, for having "redeemed" their states from "carpetbag rule," they envisioned a New South devoted to material progress and based on the profitable use of the region's natural resources and abundant labor supply. The old planter class found its prewar power diminished. The heavy voting strength it commanded in the rural sections, however, particularly the Black Belt, enabled it to exert considerable influence. These two classes were generally able to resolve their differences, ruling by coalition if necessary, and thus maintain the supremacy of their political, economic, and social values.

The new state governments set out to cut spending. The principal victims were the public schools and other state-supported services left over from the Radical years. But the same governments that cut taxes and made a virtue of economy proved to be most generous in their encouragement of economic enterprises, bestowing on them liberal charters and tax exemptions. Corruption was no less widespread under the Redeemer governments than under the previous Radical regimes, but somehow it seemed less offensive when committed by whites.

Although blacks continued to vote, they were able to exert little if any political influence. The race relations of the New

South were based on the suppression of black hopes—political, economic, and social.

The Economics of Dependency: Agriculture

Even before the overthrow of Radical rule in the South, freed blacks remained economically dependent on whites. After the war, many planters tried to hold on to their newly freed workers by offering them cash wages or a share of the crop. The wage system failed, largely because there was too little money in the southern economy as a whole. But whether paid in cash or shares, black workers claimed the amount was never commensurate with the labor performed. Many of them also resented working under arrangements scarcely better than those of the old slave system.

Sharecropping gradually stabilized labor relations in the cash-poor South. It also helped preserve the plantation system. The plantation was divided into small plots, which the landowner rented to blacks. In the typical arrangement, the freedman agreed to pay a share of the forthcoming crop, usually one-third, for use of the land, and still another share, again about one-third, for the necessary tools, seed, and work animals. Once the ex-slave realized the government was not about to grant him any land, sharecropping seemed better than working in gangs under an overseer or foreman.

But if sharecropping seemed to give blacks some kind of economic independence and the hope of eventually buying the land on which they worked, the financial realities of the postwar South soon turned the arrangement into a form of economic bondage. The sharecropper had to borrow continually on future crops in order to pay his debts to the planter and supply merchant. He was caught in a web of debt from which there was seldom any escape. Under the sharecropping system, moreover, which emphasized the single cash crop, overproduction soon caused cotton prices to fall.

The devastation of the war also caught up with the small white farmer. He too needed credit from the local merchants in order to get his land back into production and his home and barns repaired. And as in the case of the sharecroppers, the merchants dictated that the whites grow little but cotton. At first, the white farmer might give the merchant a lien on forthcoming crops. As debts mounted, the merchant demanded a mortgage on the land as well. And as the cotton market deteriorated, the merchant foreclosed. Some white farmers managed to beat the trend and became substantial land owners, even merchants. But by the 1880s, most of them had gone under and become sharecroppers or were left with the poorest land.

The Economics of Dependency: Industry

After the South freed itself from Radical rule, many people expected it to share in the type of industrialization that was booming in the North. The idea of a New South was based on industrial development like that of the North. Comparable business institutions and captains of industry were anticipated, as well as an end to the dependency that had characterized North-South relationships until now.

The movement to save the South through industry became a crusade. After 1880 white doctors, preachers, lawyers, and professors and an army of old generals and colonels gave their names and reputations, their energy and their capital, to the mission. The textile industry, already restored, continued to grow rapidly. During the depression of the mid 1880s, southern iron began to compete successfully with Pittsburgh's. The North Carolina tobacco industry responded to the new fad of cigarette smoking, and a bit later the cottonseed-oil industry spurted. Another and more important goal of the crusade was to draw northern capital southward with promises of low taxes, legislative favors, and a cheap labor force said to be immune to trade unions and strikes.

But the invasion of the South by northern capital and industry was far more gradual than the New South promoters had envisioned. As late as 1900, the New South produced a smaller proportion of American manufactures than the Old South had in 1860. Where new industries established themselves, they did so largely as branches of northern-owned enterprises. The labor conditions that prevailed in those industries, moreover, suggested that an enormous social price was being exacted from the southern people.

For those who envisioned a New South, black laborers would "keep their place," growing staples in the hot sun, while whites found employment in the mills and factories. Industry would redeem the South, and the cotton mills would be the salvation of the poor whites. But when a white farming family gave up their struggle with the land to accept work in the mills, they found that little had changed. They lived in villages that resembled the old slave quarters. They now owed their allegiance to the company store, the company landlord, and the company church. They labored long hours, rarely saw sunlight or breathed fresh air, and fell victim to a variety of diseases. The wages paid to adult male workers varied from forty

to fifty cents a day; women and children worked for still lower pay in order to supplement a meager family income. But there was one compensation: the mill villages were the exclusive domain of whites. And that, said an Alabama promoter, lent considerable dignity to their labor.

A Closed Society: Disfranchisement, Jim Crow, and Repression

Although Radical Reconstruction ended in 1877 and white violence at the polls persisted, black voting had not been eliminated altogether. But any time the black vote posed a threat, reviving the specter of "Negro domination," whites returned to the tactics of repression, which ranged from crude election frauds to threats of loss of land, credit, or jobs. These same tactics might also be employed by the ruling Conservative regimes to thwart the challenge of white independents.

In the late 1880s and early 1890s, an agricultural depression caused discontented staple farmers to organize in the Populist movement to challenge the entrenched Conservative regimes. It seemed possible in the South that poor whites and black farmers might be able to form a political alliance. Populist leaders like Thomas E. Watson of Georgia preached cooperation among small farmers and sharecroppers, on the grounds that their economic grievances crossed racial lines. He asked them to recognize their common plight and to subordinate race consciousness to class consciousness. At the same time, Watson made it clear that he did not believe in race mixing, nor would he tolerate black domination.

In several states the Populists openly courted the black vote, entered into political coalitions with blacks, and named some blacks to party posts. But the degree of Populist commitment varied considerably. Many Populists refused to compromise on white supremacy, and the blacks themselves remained skeptical about the motives of white farmers, their traditional enemies. When Populists ultimately succumbed to the rampant racism of this period, they often did so with frightening enthusiasm.

The Conservatives had appealed for racial solidarity among the whites as a means of preventing a return to "Negro domination." Their effective use of this issue had, in fact, helped to blunt the Populist challenge. However, it was becoming difficult to maintain such solidarity when political and economic issues increasingly divided whites. What better way to eliminate black domination as an issue among whites than to eliminate Negro suffrage and officeholding? Mississippi had set the pattern in 1890. Some twenty years later, as a result of such devices as the poll tax, residence requirements, and literacy tests, black voting in the South virtually ceased. Because the new laws "did not on their face discriminate between the races," which was forbidden by the Fifteenth Amendment, the Supreme Court, in the case of *Williams* v. *Mississippi* in 1898, upheld the Mississippi scheme.

Where southern custom and etiquette had previously set the races apart, in the 1890s and early 1900s Jim Crow laws made segregation even more systematic and extensive. Few places where the two races might come into social contact were unaffected. The Supreme Court ruled in 1883 that the federal government had no jurisdiction over discrimination practiced by private persons or organizations. Later on, the Court sanctioned state segregation laws requiring separate public facilities for whites and blacks. In *Plessy* v. *Ferguson* (1896), the Court decided that blacks' equal rights under the Fourteenth Amendment were not violated if the separate facilities on railroads (and, by implication, in schools and other public places) were equal. In *Cumming* v. *County Board of Education* (1899), the Court formally extended the philosophy of "separate but equal" to schools.

The pattern of race relations established in the aftermath of Reconstruction, reinforced by the triumph of Jim Crow and disfranchisement, persisted until the 1950s and 1960s. The concept of a New South proclaimed by industrialists, promoters, and editors had little meaning for the great mass of southerners—white or black. Sunk in poverty, debt, and ignorance, ravaged by diseases of various kinds, many resigned themselves to a dreary and hopeless way of life. The southern white's fear of black domination effectively stifled dissent, class consciousness was subordinated to race consciousness, the Democrats established virtual one-party rule, and race baiting remained a necessary vehicle for every aspiring southern politician. Such was the legacy of the New South.

SUGGESTED READINGS

E. Foner, *Nothing but Freedom: Emancipation and Its Legacy* (1983). L.F. Litwack, *Been in the Storm So Long: The Aftermath of Slavery* (1979). W.L. Rose, *Rehearsal for Reconstruction: The Port Royal Experiment* (1964). K.M. Stampp, *The Era of Reconstruction, 1865-1877* (1965). W.S. McFeely, *Grant* (1981). C.V. Woodward, *Origins of the New South, 1877-1913* (1951). T. Rosengarten, *All God's Dangers: The Life of Nate Shaw* (1974).

SUMMARY

The Civil War settled two important questions—secession and slavery—but it raised a great many new ones. What was to happen to the South? How were freed blacks to be treated? And who would decide, the president or Congress?

Lincoln's policy of presidential Reconstruction, based on the idea that the southern states had rebelled and should now be restored to the Union, free again to govern themselves like all other states, was one solution. In Congress, Radical Republicans proposed quite another. They considered the South a conquered territory under the jurisdiction of Congress and wanted to create a new southern society based on the equality of blacks and whites.

Presidential Reconstruction failed, and not only because of Lincoln's assassination. The new president, Andrew Johnson, believed in white supremacy and followed policies designed to restore the old planter class to power. His liberal pardon policy and the sanctioning of the Black Codes, which kept the freed slaves from participating in economic and political life, brought northern public opinion and the Radicals in Congress to a boil. The war seemed to have been fought for nothing.

In December 1865 the Radicals began a legislative counterattack. A bill continuing the Freedmen's Bureau was pushed through Congress over Johnson's veto, and the Fourteenth Amendment was introduced in June 1866. When it was finally ratified in July 1868, the question of civil rights was legally settled.

The Radical program was written into a series of laws. The First Reconstruction Act was passed over the president's veto in March 1867. It divided the South into five military districts, put each under a general to be named by the president, and directed the generals to call a constitutional convention in each former state. Delegates were to be elected by universal adult male suffrage, black and white, and the conventions were to set up new state governments in which blacks could vote and hold office. By 1870, Reconstruction under this plan was complete.

Radical Reconstruction, with its carpetbaggers and scalawags, brought blacks into government for the first time and gave them valuable experience in politics. But it also brought corruption, white backlash, and repression—fueled by fear that blacks, given education and opportunity, might actually became equal to whites. The Shotgun Policy—terror and violence—brought Radical Reconstruction to an end. By 1877, the federal government had retreated from its commitment to civil rights, and the Republican party in the South was almost destroyed.

The "New South" that emerged after 1877 was marked by characteristics that have begun to change only recently: white supremacy and repression of blacks; one-party rule; a small and wealthy ruling class holding both blacks and poor whites in economic bondage; and a weak industrial base very much dependent on northern capital.

15

The Last American West

Since the first settlements on the Atlantic coast, Americans had learned to conquer new frontiers. They had moved westward, carving out of forest and plain new towns, plantations, and farm sites. By the 1840s this movement had reached the Missouri River. From there the pioneers had to cross forbidding plains, mountains, and deserts until they reached the West Coast. As late as 1860, not a single state besides Texas had been set up between the Missouri River and the Rocky Mountains. Farther west, in the mountain country of the Rockies and the Sierra Nevada and in the Great Basin between these ranges, settlement was still sparse.

On the eve of the Civil War, about 175,000 whites and a sprinkling of blacks were in the future Dakota country: Montana, Idaho, Wyoming, Colorado, New Mexico, Arizona, Utah, and Nevada. Except for the 25,000 Mormons who settled in Utah, almost all of them kept on the move, like most of the Indian inhabitants of this territory. They prospected for precious metals, hunted buffalo, trapped marten and beaver, drove cattle and sheep, guided emigrant trains bound for California and Oregon, scouted for the army, hauled overland freight and mail, and traded and fought with the Indians.

The real invasion came after the war. Miners, cattlemen, farmers, land speculators, railroad men, and businessmen were drawn by newly perceived opportunities in the region. By 1890 all of the Wild West except Utah, Arizona, New Mexico, and Oklahoma had been cut up into states. Railroads spanned the continent and opened connecting lines to the mines, ranches, and farms that great corporations now controlled. The Indian wars were over. The army had been withdrawn from the western forts, and the Indian nations had been reduced, dispersed, and humbled. The frontier was officially closed.

INDIANS: CONCENTRATION AND REPRESSION

When Columbus discovered America, far more than a million people lived on the continent north of Mexico. They were grouped in more than 600 distinct tribes, few of which numbered more than 2000 persons. By the Civil War, only about 300,000 "Indians" remained in the United States, more than two-thirds of them on the Great Plains. Although differing in languages and customs, the Plains Indians tended to share a common culture. Most were nomadic and nonagricultural, and all depended for survival on hunting the bison, or buffalo.

Americans had deemed the Great American Desert uninhabitable and economically useless, and the Plains Indians had been left relatively free to roam in the vast area west of the Missouri River. But then whites came. The western Indians soon came to sense that their world was ending.

The Indian Wars

In the 1840s and 1850s, when traders, travelers, and explorers demanded protection against Indians, the army established a line

of forts on the Plains. But even before the Civil War, the advance of the mining and agricultural frontier forced the federal government to reconsider the policy of maintaining "one big reservation." Determined to restrict if not destroy the Indians altogether, the government adopted a policy of "concentration." Individual tribes would be confined to smaller reserves, and the government would deal with each tribe separately. But it proved one thing to set aside reservations, quite another to force Indians onto them and keep them there.

The first of the Indian wars on the Plains broke out in 1862. After five years, the vigorous resistance especially of the Sioux in the North and the Cheyenne in the South convinced Congress that the cost of controlling the Indians was too great and

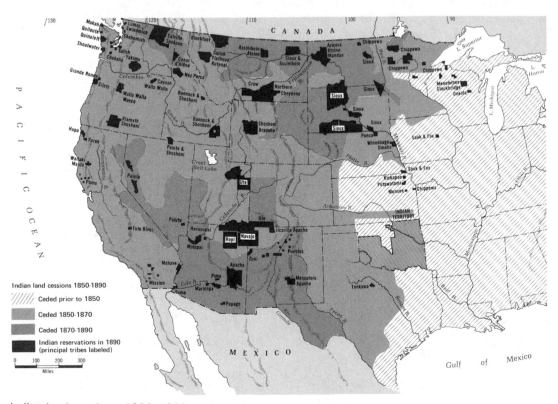

Indian land cessions, 1850–1890

progress too slow. In 1868 treaties setting up new reservations were forced on the war-weary tribes. Not only were they given inferior land, but they were told to submit to white rule and give up many of their traditions. The Indians, however, had no intention of keeping pledges they had no reason to believe the whites themselves would honor. They refused to give up their way of life, and the conflict became constant. Between 1869 and 1875, over 200 pitched battles were fought between the army and the Indians. Although the Sioux under Crazy Horse and Sitting Bull managed to annihilate the incorrigible Colonel Custer in the Battle of the Little Big Horn (June 25, 1876), shortages of ammunition and food forced the Indians to scatter.

What finished the Plains Indians was the end of the buffalo herds. The building of the Union Pacific in the late 1860s left the animals at the mercy of every railroad worker, miner, adventurer, and traveler. Since a stampeding herd could overturn a train, buffalo hunting became a part of railroad building. In 1871 the fate of the buffalo was sealed when a Pennsylvania tannery discovered it could process buffalo skins into commercial leather. Between 1872 and 1874, 3 million head a year were killed; by 1878 the southern herd had been wiped out.

In 1890 a messianic faith threatened to revive resistance among northern Sioux, and federal troops were called in. Confronted with heavily armed cavalry, the Indians fled. The troops followed, and in December 1890 at Wounded Knee they massacred the half-starved remnants of the tribe. The slaughter was the final, tragic chapter in the military conquest of the American Indians. Despite the pride, military prowess, and superb horsemanship of the Plains Indians, despite their willingness to defend their land, families, and traditions, in the end the army's superior fire-

The two men who came to symbolize the "Wild West"—Sitting Bull, a Sioux medicine man, and William F. (Buffalo Bill) Cody, a scout and buffalo hunter—toured the East in Buffalo Bill's Wild West Exhibition. (Library of Congress)

power and technology ensured the triumph of whites on the Great Plains.

The Dawes Act and After

In 1887, three years before Wounded Knee, Congress passed the Dawes Act, which defined the federal government's Indian policy until 1934. The act broke up the tribe as a basic unit of Indian society. Reservation land was divided, and each family head was given 160 acres to cultivate. After a probation period of twenty-five years, the family head was to be granted full rights of ownership and citizenship in the United States. In 1924 the United States granted citizenship to all Indians.

The Dawes Act was the result of growing opposition to the policy of the army and the Interior Department. The alternative was to force the Indians to become settled farmers and to adapt themselves to white ways. But the Dawes Act did the Indians little good. In dividing the land, the government usually gave them the poorest; the best was sold to white settlers. Even when an Indian obtained good land, inexperience in legal matters left him open to the same kind of cheating that had marked the making of the tribal treaties. Again and again, Indians were tricked into selling their best holdings to white speculators. Worse still, they lacked the cultural tradition, the necessary training, and the competitive incentive to cultivate the land they kept. Deprived of the kind of support the tribe had once provided, most became paupers. Some found outlets in alcohol or petty crime. The year the Dawes Act passed, the Indian tribes still had title to about 138 million acres of land. By 1932 some 90 million acres had found their way into white ownership.

The Indian Reorganization Act of 1934 again reversed Indian policy. Under men such as John Collier, a social reformer who had worked for ten years with the American Indian Defense Association, the Office of Indian Affairs succeeded in restoring tribal landholding, self-government, and incentive. At the same time, Indians were permitted to practice their own religions, educational facilities were improved, and cultural programs were encouraged. The government had not abandoned the objective of assimilating Indians into white society, but it appeared to be willing to permit them to have a greater say in the speed and conditions of such assimilation.

THE GREAT AMERICAN WEST: MINERS, RANCHERS, FARMERS

With a thoroughness equaled only by their extermination of the buffalo and the Indians, Americans after the Civil War exploited the natural wealth of the West. The Plains and mountains, it was discovered, were rich in agricultural and mineral wealth. The most productive of the earth's wheat lands stretched across the Dakotas and eastern Montana. In large areas of Wyoming, Colorado, and Texas, and even in sections of Nevada, Utah, and Arizona, there were grazing lands for cattle and sheep that would supply much of the world's beef, mutton, hides, and wool. Other parts of the Plains and mountains held some of the world's largest and purest veins of copper and iron ore, some of the world's greatest deposits of lead and zinc, valuable seams of coal, and gold and silver. Beneath the earth in Texas (and elsewhere in the West) lay incredible reserves of crude petroleum and natural gas.

For generations Americans had had even less use for these resources than the Indians who roamed the western lands. But the demands of the booming cities and expanding industry in the postwar years rapidly changed the western landscape. Within a generation this vast area was providing essential raw materials, meat, and grain for eastern and midwestern markets. By 1890, many individual enterprises had been replaced by corporations, frontier boom camps had been converted into company towns, and prospectors and small businessmen had been reduced to wage laborers.

The Mining Frontier

Although gold had brought miners to the West in the 1840s, the era of the prospector was actually short, from the mid 1850s to

The James gang. Jesse James is seated left, with Frank James seated right; standing are Cole Younger (left) and Bob Younger (right). The Youngers were captured in 1876 and sentenced to life imprisonment. "We were drove to it, sir," Cole Younger told the judge. "Circumstances sometimes makes men what they are." Six years later Jesse James was shot in the head by a fellow gang member for the $10,000 reward money. (Library of Congress)

the mid 1870s. But during those twenty years, speculation was wild. The mining frontier changed with every new rumor of a strike: as soon as one boom ended, another developed. Towns sprang up overnight, and many of them disappeared soon after the prospectors rushed off to still another find.

When the fabulous gold discoveries in California began to run thin, prospectors followed rumors of still newer and richer strikes in Colorado and Nevada. The Colorado discoveries, together with the growth of Denver as a commercial center, made statehood certain, and in 1876 Colorado was admitted to the Union as the Centennial State. Nevada had gained statehood even earlier, in 1864—testimony to the far richer discoveries there, including the spectacular Comstock Lode on Mount Davidson. In 1874, rumors of gold on the Sioux reservation in the Black Hills of southwestern Dakota Territory induced still another stampede of prospectors.

The first copper seam was discovered

in 1881 in Montana. By the end of the decade annual copper production—sparked by the booming demand for copper wire, a more efficient carrier of electric power than iron or steel—had passed that of gold in value. At the same time, big business moved in to dominate the development of the West. Exploitation of the new metals and minerals required heavy investment in plants, machinery, and hired workers, and financiers such as Henry H. Rogers and the Rockefellers of New York, the Guggenheims of Philadelphia, and the Mellons of Pittsburgh took charge. With their arrival,

the open mining frontier of the prospector came to a close.

The Cattle Frontier

Even as prospectors were seeking their fortunes in precious metals, cattlemen were moving into the Great Plains, turning the vast open ranges of unclaimed grassland into grazing lands for increasingly valuable herds. The incentives for reaching northern markets with these cattle multiplied along with the rapid growth of the population and the fantastic prices offered for steers. The fortunes that could be made equaled those

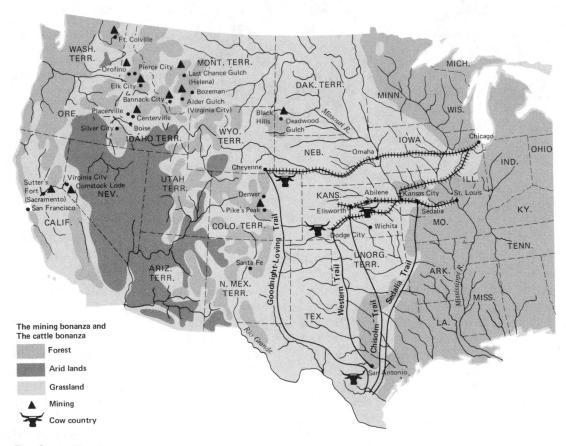

The mining bonanza and
The cattle bonanza

Forest

Arid lands

Grassland

▲ Mining

Cow country

The Cattle Kingdom

of many of the more successful prospectors.

In the 1850s, some Texas ranchers tried to drive their cattle westward to the Colorado and California markets or northward to Illinois. But the surviving steers reached their destination too thin and tough to bring a good price. The ranchers waited out the Civil War, and then began looking again for markets. In the spring of 1866, they were ready for the first of the "long drives" to a railroad town (Sedalia, Missouri, on the Missouri Pacific) from which the cars would haul cattle to great city markets.

As a business venture this first drive was a failure. But some Texas steers survived the unfamiliar forests and the guns of Indians and farmers and brought a price at Sedalia that encouraged many ranchers to try again or to find some other route. An Illinois meat dealer, Joseph G. McCoy, realized he could make a fortune if he could set up a convenient meeting point for northern buyers and western breeders. McCoy chose Abilene, Kansas, on the Kansas Pacific, which (with some other lines) connected Abilene with Chicago. At Abilene, McCoy built a hotel, barns, stables, pens, and loading chutes, and by 1871 this railroad town had become the capital of the cattle frontier.

As the railroads extended westward and southward, new trails developed and new railroad towns nearer the cattle range were used. But since the drive to even the nearest railhead was not good for steers ready for market, in the 1870s ranchers began to drive Texas yearlings to the northern range—western Kansas, Nebraska, Colorado, Wyoming, Montana, and the Dakotas. Northern "feeders" bought the young cattle and fattened them for free on public lands until they were ready for market. The best cows and bulls were taken from the herds, and breeds were constantly improved. The open-range cattle industry came into its own after 1878, when the business depression of the mid 1870s ended and beef prices revived.

On the open range, water was vital. "Range rights" along a stream became the most precious part of any ranch, and often had to be backed up with a gun. Even when ranchers respected one another's territory, the cattle did not. Rules had to be established for recording brands, and ranchers needed protection from rustlers, who found it easy to spirit cattle away on the wide-open spaces. The enforcement of rude justice was one of the main objectives of the numerous stock growers' associations organized in the 1870s. One of their more important business objectives was to prevent competition by making it difficult for newcomers to become members and dangerous for them to operate without joining up. The ranchers were aware of the speed with which the range, endless though it seemed, could be overstocked.

News of immense profits drew so many prospective ranchers to the range each year that by 1885 grazing lands had in fact become overcrowded. The disastrous winter of 1885–86, followed by a blistering summer, destroyed most of the feed and cattle. The steers that found their way to market were of such poor quality that beef prices crashed despite the shortage. To add to the stock growers' misery, farmers began homesteading in larger numbers and fencing in the open range. Many farmers kept herds of their own on fenced fields, where they could control breeding more carefully and regulate the feed. The beef they produced was superior to that grown on the open range. In 1882 range beef sold for $9.35 per hundred pounds in Chicago; by 1887 the price had fallen to $1.90. The end of the open range hastened the end of the last frontier.

The Agricultural Frontier

Although the farmers' frontier had been steadily moving westward, the expansion of agriculture in the post–Civil War decades was extraordinary. Immigration from abroad and the revolution in farm machinery, transportation, and marketing were contributing factors. Between 1870 and 1900, American farmers more than doubled their landholdings—from 407 to 841 million acres—and placed more new land under cultivation than had been farmed in the entire country since 1607. Much of the new acreage lay in the Great Plains, which tens of thousands of homesteaders were helping to convert to an agricultural economy.

Although the Homestead Act of 1862 had opened the land by making available to farmers free 160-acre plots, certain defects in the act restricted its usefulness. For the small settler, the cost of working enough of his 160 acres to get a paying crop on the arid, treeless Plains was prohibitive. For the large farmer or farming corporation, on the other hand, a mere 160 acres hardly justified the investment in new machinery suitable to the broad expanse of the plains.

In the 1870s, belated recognition of these problems led Congress to enact new laws offering larger tracts of land to settlers. But these laws had their own drawbacks. The result was that although 80 million acres were registered under the Homestead Act between 1862 and 1900, at least five times as much land was bought by settlers from railroads, land companies, and states at prices ranging from two dollars to ten dollars an acre. These were fair prices for sites near transportation facilities. The sellers, moreover, often assisted the settlers with credit for equipment as well as for the land.

In a region blasted by hailstorms, windstorms, and sudden frosts, production was limited not by how much farmers could plant, but by how much they could harvest. With the mechanization of farming and the inventions of the 1870s and 1880s, two men and a team of horses could harvest 20 acres of wheat a day. Eastern farmers dared not plant more than 8 acres of wheat a *season*. At the end of the century, a Great Plains farmer with a cord binder (a machine that reaps and ties grain in bundles) could count on harvesting 135 acres. In 1879 Illinois, the leading wheat state for twenty years, still held first place; by 1899 it had fallen out of the first ten, which were now led by Minnesota, the Dakotas, Kansas, California, and Nebraska.

During the 1870s, plains farmers began to insist that ranchers fence in their cattle. The ranchers, in turn, urged the "nesters" to move away or else pay for the fences. Hostility between the two groups led to gunfights, but cheap fencing, not guns, eventually won the plains for the farmers. In 1874 barbed wire was patented. Available in large quantities at low cost, barbed-wire fencing provided farmers with the means to enclose and protect their lands. By 1890, much of the farmland had been fenced.

The improvements in American farm technology coincided with the rapid enlargement of the European market as countries overseas turned from farming to industry. Despite soaring production, then, demand kept prices high. Good prices encouraged expansion, mainly by farmers mortgaging their land to the limit in order to raise money to acquire more land before the next person claimed it. But the agricultural West was riding for a fall. Overproduction in the United States by the mid 1880s, the entry of India and Australia into the world wheat market, the revival of Russian wheat exports—all were bad signs. By the 1870s the commercial farmers of the Plains country, like farmers elsewhere, found their freedom declining, almost in proportion to their increasing dependence on impersonal forces (markets, railroads, and middlemen) over which they had no control.

SUGGESTED READINGS

H.N. Smith, *Virgin Land: The American West as Symbol and Myth* (1950). W.P. Webb, *The Great Plains* (1931). R.K. Andrist, *The Long Death: The Last Days of the Plains Indians* (1964). M.H. Brown, *The Flight of the Nez Percé* (1967). W.E. Washburn, *The Indian in America* (1975). L. Atherton, *The Cattle Kings* (1961). E. Dick, *The Sod-House Frontier* (1937). J.R. Jeffrey, *Frontier Women* (1979).

SUMMARY

After the Civil War, Americans began to move in earnest into the Great Plains and to settle the land between the Mississippi and the Rockies. As they did so, they displaced and overwhelmed the Indian tribes whose home it was. But this time the Indians did not go peacefully—perhaps because there was nowhere to go. The Plains Indians were hunters and fighters, and for twenty years they battled settlers, prospectors, miners, and the United States Cavalry to keep their home.

The reservation system was no solution, for the lands given the Indians were the poorest and most barren, and could not support a population. Eventually, by the late 1880s, the Indians were crushed. Those that remained became wards of the federal government and a forgotten part of American society. What the army had not been able to do by force, government bureaucrats did by regulations and policies that systematically stripped the Indians of their culture, their self-respect, and their independence.

As the Indians were killed or driven onto barren reservations, white settlers poured in to exploit the resources of the West. Mines yielded great quantities of copper and iron, lead and zinc, gold and silver. The rush of prospectors to areas where ore had been found created boom towns overnight—and the raw, rough culture of legend.

The building of a cattle empire on the Plains did the same for other areas. Growing markets for meat in the booming cities of the East made ranching profitable, and the railroad made a western cattle industry possible. Towns like Abilene, Dodge City, Tombstone, and Deadwood, where cattle were driven to be shipped to market, roared to life and contributed to the legend that was the Wild West.

New farming techniques and technology, the availability of land through such government programs as the Homestead Act, and the growing flood of European immigrants willing to work hard for a better life gnaled the end of the last frontier. By the 1880s the settlement boom and the Wild West were over. The open range was fenced in, and the Great Plains became one of the greatest grain-producing areas in the world. Mining, cattle ranching, and farming were now businesses that entailed the risk of failure when prices dropped during swings of the business cycle.

16

The New Industrial Society

With the closing of the land frontier, Americans crossed new frontiers in science, technology, and business management. By the turn of the century, the nation had undergone a massive economic transformation. The population had increased 132 percent between 1870 and 1910. The proportion of Americans living in rural and urban areas, like the proportion engaged in agriculture and industry, had shifted. Tens of thousands of farm youths joined equal numbers of European immigrants in urban and industrial centers. And with rapidly expanding markets, improved transportation, technological breakthroughs, a large and willing labor force, and a responsive federal government, the productivity of American industry seemed limitless—as did its profits.

But even as the conquests on the new frontiers pushed the United States to world industrial supremacy, Americans began to assess the price they had paid for success. The history of industrialization in the last decades of the nineteenth century yields impressive statistics on manufacturing growth. But the personal ordeals and dislocations that made growth possible defy measurement. For scores of American workers, the dream of economic success gave way to a concern for day-to-day survival.

THE GOSPEL OF SUCCESS

During and after the Civil War, the lure of success became stronger than ever, the focus on materialism even sharper. The dominant economic, political, and educational institutions embraced a Gospel of Success which justified the accumulation of wealth and excused the human costs of industrialization. To accumulate wealth was natural, Christian, and progressive, and he who succeeded had proved himself the fittest.

The popularity in the United States of the English philosopher Herbert Spencer (1820–1903) lent intellectual respectability to this doctrine. Applying Darwin's notion of the "struggle for life" to the system of unregulated business competition, the Social Darwinists, as Spencer's followers became known, contended that human society too evolved by the survival of the fittest. If industrialists like John D. Rockefeller and Andrew Carnegie overcame their competitors, if their companies swallowed up

This Currier and Ives lithograph illustrated lessons taught in the *McGuffey Readers*. (Library of Congress)

smaller and weaker businesses, they had simply proved themselves the fittest to enjoy wealth and power. The progress of society demanded that business be left free to operate, just as nature was in selecting and "rejecting" species. Government intervention in economic affairs, such as the regulation of business or social legislation designed to assist the weak and less fortunate, only interfered with the process of natural selection.

Few American capitalists required Social Darwinism in order to rationalize the ways in which they accumulated their wealth. Like most Americans, they had been raised in the spirit of the Protestant ethic to think of worldly success as a sign of God's favor, as outward evidence of inward moral and religious character. And they had been taught at school and at home, as were at least three generations of Americans, the simple moral code set forth in *McGuffey's Reader.* The qualities of character and moral virtues stressed in these widely read text books were precisely those to which the average businessman attributed his success—frugality, sobriety, industry, and piety. Those who fell by the wayside, whatever their circumstances, had failed to make the most of their opportunities. The failure lay in their own weaknesses, not in any defects in the economic system.

The philosophy of success hid the realities of a stratified economic society. Enough examples of rags-to-riches success stories helped to sustain the idea of upward mobility and an essentially good social system. The experiences of tens of thousands of Americans, however, contradicted this theory. No matter how hard some people worked, no matter how hard they practiced all the necessary moral virtues, their success was by no means assured. What their experiences dramatized was a basic conflict between the value of economic growth and the human cost of such growth. In nearly every phase of American industrial life, that conflict would become strikingly clear.

THE RAILROAD: MASS TRANSPORTATION AND BIG MONEY

As America began to become an industrial giant, few enterprises were more important than the railroad. The United States would be joined together as never before: distant markets would be tapped, vast new regions would be opened for settlement and exploitation, mass production and mass consumption would be stimulated, and efficient distribution of goods would affect every sector of the economy. For many industries, the railroad was the key to development. For many towns and cities, the railroad was the most critical factor in growth or decline.

In 1865 approximately 35,000 miles of railroad track served the country. By the time of the Panic of 1873 this figure had been doubled, largely by construction in the East and the Old Northwest. Almost all the new construction was privately financed through the sale of securities to individuals and banks. By clever financing and their control of strategic routes, individuals could make fortunes. Competition among the railroad promoters was fierce and ruthless. Like feudal chieftains, they fought for control of territories, leaving behind them a trail of ruined competitors, bribed public officials, mortgaged cities and towns, and heavily indebted and poorly constructed railroads.

The Battle for the East

As important as new roads and routes was the consolidation of independent lines into large companies that then controlled wide areas. Cornelius Vanderbilt, the shipping magnate who began investing in railroads in 1862, became one of the greatest operators of the postwar period. By 1869, through a series of stock manipulations, he had secured control of the New York Central and connecting lines that gave him a direct route from New York City to Buffalo. Through a series of acquisitions and agreements with other roads, Vanderbilt subsequently extended the railroad into Chicago and beyond, all the way to Omaha, Nebraska.

In the 1870s the Pennsylvania Rail Road, guided by its vice-president, Thomas A. Scott, gained wholly owned routes from Philadelphia to Chicago and St. Louis by building and buying up lines. In 1871 the Pennsylvania at last gained access to New York City, and it soon would reach Baltimore and Washington. In the cutthroat competition of the postwar decades, Chicago, Cleveland, New York, and other cities that were served by rival railroads enjoyed low rates and fine service. But where one railroad had a monopoly of the traffic, as in Pittsburgh, the public was treated with contempt. The lines felt free to charge what the traffic would bear, and shippers had little choice but to pay.

The Transcontinental Railroads

Much more spectacular than railroad building in the older sections was the construction of the first transcontinental roads, which Congress chartered during the Civil War. The Union Pacific was to build westward from Omaha, and the Central Pacific eastward from Sacramento. Both companies received huge land grants and generous loans from Congress.

The Union Pacific and the Central Pacific were not built by the railroad corporations, but by separate construction companies. These companies were handsomely paid by the railroads. And since they were owned largely by the directors of the railroads they served, it was through construction rather than rail service that the promoters made their fortunes. Part of these fortunes also found their way into the pockets of congressmen and senators who looked after the railroads' legislative business.

The engineering problems of this construction had been at least as difficult as the financial ones. Although both roads had to be rebuilt almost completely some years later, the feat of crossing the broad plains and the forbidding mountain ranges remains one of the great engineering accomplishments in history. All told, the Union Pacific construction company laid 1086 miles of track, most of it the work of Civil War veterans and Irish immigrants. The Central Pacific, its construction crews made up largely of Chinese, laid 689 miles. With both companies competing for government subsidies (which were granted according to each mile of track laid), speed outweighed all other considerations. In the spring of 1869 the two lines approached each other, and on May 10 they were joined by golden spikes at Promontory Point, near Ogden, Utah.

The Battle for the West

Before the Panic of 1873, three other transcontinentals were chartered and enriched by the federal government—the Northern Pacific in 1864, the Atlantic and Pacific in 1866, and the Texas and Pacific in 1871. Of the three, only the Northern Pacific reached the coast. By 1872, the other two, along with their land grants, had fallen under the control of the promoters of the Central Pacific and formed part of their Southern Pacific Railroad system, by which they aimed to control all California railroading and the enterprises dependent upon it. In planning their monopoly, however, they reckoned without the ambitious Jay Gould. By 1881 Gould had pieced together a series of lines in the Southwest that so menaced the Southern Pacific that Collis Huntington, the leader of the California group, felt obliged to make a traffic-sharing and rate-fixing agreement with him. From that time on, Gould played an increasingly important role in the development of the Southern Pacific's power in California. By 1890 he controlled about 9000 miles of railroad in the Southwest, nearly half the total mileage of the section. The shippers of the area were at his mercy.

Huntington and Gould came to consider the entire West Coast, if not the entire West, as their private empire. In the North, however, they were confronted with vast transcontinental enterprises they could not quite control. James J. Hill had his own ideas about the Pacific Northwest and how to build and run railroads. With the support of Canadian financiers, he acquired the St. Paul and Pacific. In 1889 this line took the name Great Northern. By then, with very little government assistance, Hill and his backers had pushed construction 2775 miles west through Minnesota, North Dakota, and Montana and north to Winnipeg, Canada. In 1893 the Great Northern reached Puget Sound.

From the start, Hill insisted on constructing Great Northern track and roadbed with the best materials. He also chose to build around mountains rather than over them. Not only did this approach greatly reduce construction costs, it also reduced operating costs once a road was built. The proof of Hill's policies came in 1893, when only the Great Northern among the transcontinentals survived the business crash that year.

During the next decade, Hill acquired the Northern Pacific, which had been financially reorganized with the aid of J. P. Morgan and Company in 1898. In 1901, with Morgan's help, Hill won control of the Chicago, Burlington and Quincy, the best entry to Chicago from the west, and began a bitter fight with Edward H. Harriman. The year before, Collis Huntington had died and Harriman had acquired 45 percent of Southern Pacific's stock. (Gould was already dead.) Harriman's backer, Jacob H. Schiff, was head of Kuhn, Loeb and Company, Morgan's main banking rival. Harriman also enjoyed the financial confidence of the Rockefeller Standard Oil group, always on the lookout for a place to put their millions. Thus the stage was set and the parts assigned for one of the great financial contests of the twentieth century: Harriman, Rockefeller, the National City Bank, and Kuhn, Loeb versus Hill, the First National Bank, and Morgan. Control of the western—and the national—railroad network was the prize.

In November 1901, after a titanic Wall Street battle that ruined many investors but settled nothing, the antagonists finally decided to merge their interests. For this purpose they formed the Northern Securities Company. In 1904 this company was broken up by a Supreme Court decision that was one of the highlights of Theodore Roosevelt's administration. The contestants quickly made new financial arrangements to keep from killing each other off.

By the turn of the century the American railroad network of about 200,000 miles had been virtually completed. There was nothing like it anywhere else in the world. Technological advances—steel rails, heavier and faster locomotives, larger freight and passenger cars, and the double-tracking and quadruple-tracking of thousands of miles of routes in the West and the East—had also assured safer and more efficient rail service.

THE AGE OF ENTERPRISE: HEAVY INDUSTRY

Railroad expansion and improvement had a great deal to do with the growth of northern industry after the war. New construction had expanded the market for all kinds of goods, from iron and steel for rails to meat and blankets for construction crews. Railroad financing attracted large amounts of foreign capital to America and helped make the public familiar with investment procedures that corporations could use to sell securities in the growing money markets of the country. Industrialists like Carnegie and Rockefeller could use their profits to expand their own businesses and to exploit profitable by-products.

Railroad development added to the spirit of optimism that dominated the northern economy after the war. With the opening of the industrial frontier, new men emerged to vie for economic leadership. Most of them were possessed by ambition; they were aggressive, self-confident, and ruthless, willing to manipulate public officials or businessmen who stood in their way. But at the same time they were imaginative and talented. They crushed their competitors, used the government, and ignored the human cost of their operations. But they were conscious of themselves as industrial pioneers conquering new frontiers. Few showed these qualities more vividly than John D. Rockefeller and Andrew Carnegie. The enterprises they directed—Standard Oil and Carnegie Steel—became models for the new wave of economic organization and consolidation.

Petroleum: Rockefeller and Standard Oil

In the 1850s whale oil, then the world's chief fuel for commercial lighting, had become so scarce that its price was almost two dollars a gallon. Seepages of surface petroleum had been detected in many parts of the world for centuries. As "rock oil" it had gradually gained a reputation as a medical cure-all. Some chemical pioneers had also begun to refine petroleum into kerosene, to design lamps for burning it conveniently, and to promote it as a cheap source of lighting.

What no one knew was how to find enough petroleum to meet the rising demand. Then in 1857 a young New York lawyer, George H. Bissell, and his associates sent Edwin L. Drake to Titusville, Pennsylvania, to make the first real attempt to drill for oil. Two years later "Drake's Folly" gushed in. By 1872 oil fields covered 2000 square miles in Pennsylvania, West Virginia, and Ohio, and annual production had soared to 40 million barrels. Of this massive total, John D. Rockefeller's Standard Oil Company was already refining no less than one-fifth.

Born in 1839 in Richford, New York,

Rockefeller made a wartime fortune of $50,000 in a grain and meat partnership in Cleveland. In 1863 he had invested in a small Cleveland oil refinery, to which he was now ready to devote all his time. In 1870 Rockefeller organized the Standard Oil Company, using its capital of $1 million for an all-out attack on the competition, which was located mainly in the oil region and in Cleveland, Pittsburgh, and New York.

First, Rockefeller spent heavily to make his plants the most efficient in the country so that he could undersell competitors and still make a profit. He would often sell his products well below cost in selected markets to ruin a competitor—a practice known as cutthroat competition. To make up his losses, he would charge more than ever once he had the market to himself. With his volume of business soaring, Rockefeller then demanded that the railroads grant him lower freight rates than his competitors. Railroad rates were required by law to be public and equal, so Rockefeller devised a system of *rebates*. Standard Oil would pay the regular charges "on the books" and then get money back secretly. Since Cleveland was a city where competition was intense, the railroads had to agree to Rockefeller's demands in order to keep his business. Having eliminated almost all his competition in Cleveland, Rockefeller applied the same techniques—rebates and discriminatory freight rates on oil shipments—to railroads in other areas and enlarged his industrial empire.

By 1879 Rockefeller held about 95 percent of the refining capacity of the country and had captured almost the entire world market for his products. But by then the oil pipeline was well on the way to replacing the railroad tank car as the major oil carrier. Before long, Standard Oil had used its power to gain a monopoly of pipeline transportation. Consolidating his control of the industry, Rockefeller divided the country into sales districts and sent out executives and agents to sell the products of Standard Oil.

Steel: Andrew Carnegie

Before the Civil War, steel had been a rare and costly metal that could be made only in quantities of twenty-five to fifty pounds by processes that took weeks. In 1847, William Kelly of Kentucky discovered a simple method by which tons of steel could be produced in a matter of minutes. Nothing much was heard of his discovery until ten years later, when Kelly contested the application of an Englishman, Henry Bessemer, for an American patent on a process similar to his own and on an efficient converter. The patent dispute was soon straightened out, but it was not until the early 1870s that what has since become known as Bessemer steel began to be produced in quantity in the United States.

Having had long experience in railroading and the building of steel railroad bridges, Andrew Carnegie entered the steel-making industry in 1872. He put off adopting the Bessemer process, but a trip to England the next year convinced him to use the new method. He came back and built the biggest steel mill in the world near Pittsburgh. On good terms with the railroad kings, Carnegie ignored the depression that began in 1873 and "went out and persuaded them to give us orders." By 1879 American steel production had risen to 930,000 tons, three-fourths of it in the form of steel rails, almost all manufactured by the Carnegie company. By 1890 American steel production had taken another spectacular leap, to an annual figure of over 4 million tons. Carnegie's success came in part from his ability as a salesman. But he also had a far better grasp of management than his competitors. Other steel men often used their profits to live in grand style; Carnegie, like Rockefeller, plowed back his own and the company's earnings, to expand, integrate, and modernize. Before he retired in 1901, Carnegie acquired immense holdings in the fabulous Mesabi Range in Minnesota, from which as much as 85 percent of America's iron ore in the first half of the twentieth century was to come. He also bought up Pennsylvania coal fields, some limestone quarries, and the coke business of Henry Clay Frick, who became his partner. Ore, coal, limestone, and coke are the basic raw materials for the manufacture of steel; to ensure their regular delivery to his plants, Carnegie also invested heavily in ships and railroad cars.

From the mines to the market, Carnegie controlled every phase in the processing of steel. That was the meaning of integration and modernization. By 1890 three other giant steel enterprises had grown up in the South and West, but the Pittsburgh district continued to lead the industry. Carnegie maintained control until he sold out in 1901 to the newly formed United States Steel Corporation. With the Carnegie empire as its base, U.S. Steel became the world's leading steel producer. It controlled 70 percent of the steel business and was capitalized at nearly $1.5 billion.

The New Technology: Telephone, Telegraph, Electric Light

Many of the new management problems in the giant enterprises emerging after the Civil War were mechanical ones, such as communication and record keeping. Simple mechanical devices—the typewriter, first used in business in 1867, and the adding machine, made practical by 1888—set in motion the mechanization of the office. Now record keeping could keep up with the flow of products and the volume of sales.

Two other advances were the electric

telegraph and the telephone. In 1876 Alexander Graham Bell patented the telephone he had invented the year before. The next year Western Union, which already controlled most of the telegraph business, decided it had better enter the telephone field. But the Bell Company sued Western Union for patent infringement and won, and during the 1880s it bought out its remaining rivals. Thereafter, patented improvements kept the Bell Company protected from competition. To expand long-distance service, which had begun in 1885, the Bell directors set up a new corporation, the American Telephone and Telegraph Company. In 1900 AT&T became the overall holding company of the entire Bell system. That year, 1.35 million Bell telephones were in use in the United States.

While Bell and others were improving the telephone, Thomas A. Edison was experimenting with electric lighting. In 1879 he perfected a reasonably priced incandescent bulb. Three years later, in New York City, he built the first central power station, from which he distributed direct current to eighty-five buildings. But direct current could be transmitted great distances only at great cost. With the use of transformers, alternating current could take direct current from a power plant, cheaply increase the voltage for distant transmission, and then lower it again for ordinary purposes. George Westinghouse and William Stanley developed the first generators and transformers for alternating current, and in 1893 Westinghouse made alternating current famous by using it to light up the Chicago world's fair. The great era of electricity, however, was yet to come. Until the twentieth century the United States, as well as the rest of the world, looked to water and steam for power.

With the move toward consolidation in public utilities as well as in steel and

petroleum, the American economy had changed. Now fewer and fewer industrial and financial organizations had greater and greater influence and power. In one industry after another, small enterprises disappeared. By the turn of the century, in a number of industries only one enterprise controlled more than 50 percent of the total product. The concentration of so much economic power in the hands of so few was bound to have an effect on a society that believed in free competition and the idea that anyone who was willing to work hard could succeed.

PANICS, TRUSTS, AND THE BANKS: CONGLOMERATION

By 1860, $1 billion had been invested in American industry; that year the factories and shops that made up the industrial community produced goods valued at about $1.8 billion. By 1890, the investment had soared to $6.5 billion and the annual output had approached $10 billion in value. These are crude indicators of the transformation of the United States in only thirty years from a nation of farmers to one of the leading industrial powers of the world. In refining crude oil, making steel and lumber, packing meat, and extracting gold, silver, coal, and iron, the United States had passed all its rivals. In specialties such as hardware, machine tools, and small arms and ammunition, it retained the leadership it had assumed before the Civil War.

In any age this would have been a towering performance. In an age that worshiped bigness, it meant the achievement of the ideal. Despite frequent complaints of hard times, very few Americans blamed business or questioned "the system." Boom and depression were assumed to be natural. In the nineteenth century, and even up to the crash of 1929, depressions continued to be seen simply as the results of errors in judgment, to be followed soon by recovery. Instead of destroying hope, depressions paid dividends for faith. They presented opportunities to expand and modernize plants at low cost, to corner raw materials at bottom prices, to capture customers by offering attractive schedules, rates, and deliveries. It was during the depression of the 1870s that Rockefeller organized his oil monopoly, Carnegie built his first great steel plant, Philip D. Armour, Gustavus Swift, and Nelson Morris built their meat-packing empires, and Boston capitalists began to finance Bell's telephone.

The Panic of 1873: Consolidation

Signs of trouble during the postwar boom soon became apparent. The number of business failures increased, and from 1868 to 1873 the volume of bank loans grew seven times as fast as that of deposits. The Panic of 1873 began on September 8, when a New York securities company went into bankruptcy, carrying many of its creditors down with it. The greatest shock came ten days later with the failure of Jay Cooke and Company, the most famous banking house in the country. Shock then gave way to depression: railroads halted construction, mills closed down, trade suffered, and Americans experienced unprecedented unemployment, poverty, and labor violence.

Once the depression had run its course, production boomed again and prices fell rapidly. These changes suggested the need for greater industrial efficiency. To keep production costs down, manufacturers were forced to use the most efficient machinery in the most efficient way. In the 1870s and after, the use of interchangeable parts and their assembly along a continuous line became common in many new industries. By mechanizing factories and simplifying workers' tasks, the new techniques made it possible for business to reduce production costs. But the machinery cost so much that the reduction in the cost of individual items was possible only when plants operated at or near full capacity. If plants produced fewer items than they were geared for, the cost of each item rose remarkably; on the other hand, if plants ran at capacity, so much was produced that the markets were flooded and prices sank.

To survive the competition in the mechanized industries, many companies moved toward industrial pools and trusts. *Pools* or *pooling agreements* administered by trade associations were essentially secret agreements among competitors to restrict their output, maintain prices, and divide up the markets. They were a temporary device. Far more permanent—and also far more secure—was the *trust*. The first trust, which became a model for all the others, was organized by Rockefeller in 1879 and reorganized in 1882.

In forming a trust, companies turn over their stock to a group of trustees they have chosen. Trustee certificates are issued in exchange for stock, which remains in the original hands. Management of the enterprises is concentrated in the hands of a single board of trustees. After the Standard Oil trust came the cottonseed-oil trust, the salt trust, the whiskey trust, the sugar trust, and others. Not all were actually trust arrangements, but the label was given to any large combination whose purpose was to restrain competition.

The power of a trust was enormous: it could shut down every one of its plants at will, or close some and keep others open. It could cut purchases of raw materials, artificially limit production, raise prices to enrich itself at the public expense, and lower prices to get rid of a competitor. For business, the trust was an attractive solution to the uncertainties of competition. For the economy, however, it could be a problem.

The Panic of 1893: Banker Control

For a long time the government did nothing about the consolidations and the tendency toward monopoly. The Sherman Anti-Trust Act of 1890, the first attempt at federal control, was the result of growing public anger at the artificially raised prices and artificially closed opportunities the trusts brought about. Competition, however, grew more intense than ever after the passage of the Sherman Act and especially after the Panic of 1893, when thousands of industrial firms failed, banks closed, one railroad out of every six went into receivership, and unemployment soared.

Just as the Panic of 1873 had given Carnegie and Rockefeller opportunities for expansion at bargain rates, the Panic of 1893 gave Morgan and a few other investment bankers their opportunity. Their first objective was to bring order out of chaos in railroad finance. By 1904 they had consolidated 1040 railroad lines into six huge combinations. Each in turn was allied to either the Morgan or the Kuhn, Loeb interests. After this success, the investment bankers moved into manufacturing and public utilities.

The power of the investment bankers came from their ability to supply the capital for growing companies. Having gotten the money from investors who gave it largely because of confidence in the bankers themselves, the bankers felt it necessary to place their own men on the companies' boards of directors and take a hand in management. In this way the bankers' economic power, and Morgan's especially, spread from the financial community to the heart of the big-business system. A second feature of the Morgan method was the bankers' control of, or close alliance with, other sources of capital, such as commercial banks, trust companies that administered large estates and other properties, and huge life-insurance companies that collected payments from millions of small policyholders. The bankers' influence thus eventually extended over almost the entire population.

THE WORKERS

The impact of industrialization on American life in the decades after the Civil War is clearly shown in a 300-percent rise in non-agricultural employment, compared with a rise of only 50 percent in the number of

Pittsburgh coal miner, 1910. (Photograph by Lewis Hine, Library of Congress)

persons working on farms. The working class was by no means an exclusively male domain: by 1900 nearly one out every five workers was female. In such industries as textiles, shoes, and clothing, women might make up as much as 40 to 60 percent of the work force. The 10 million immigrants who poured into the United States between 1870 and 1900 added to the rapidly growing labor force. But these statistics only begin to suggest what industrialization meant. Even though many workers still aspired to middle-class status and managerial positions, the facts of industrial capitalism resulted in a loss of personal autonomy, new work patterns, and a new life style to fit the new surroundings and conditions of labor.

Advances in technology speeded up the pace of production, and the worker was expected to keep up. Work weeks ranging from sixty to over eighty hours were common; the seven-day week was the rule in steel and paper mills, oil refineries, and other mechanized plants. Fast machines greatly increased the physical danger of factory work; long hours and fatigue increased accidents, injuries, and deaths.

Another result of technology was that the machines did more and more of the skilled work, draining much of the personal satisfaction from labor. Proud craftsmen were reduced to the status and pay of menials. This steady lowering of the skilled craftsman's position not only made it difficult for him to support his family, but forced him to change many of his work habits. The informality of the old work establishments was replaced by rigid discipline.

The Great Strike of 1877

Working conditions on the railroads grew so bad during the depression of the 1870s that spontaneous strikes spread across the country in 1877, largely in response to further wage cuts. The leaderless revolt began on July 16, when firemen on the Baltimore and Ohio quit work; the strike soon spread to the Pennsylvania Rail Road, along the Erie and New York Central, and all the way to St. Louis. Coal miners, stevedores, farmers, small businessmen, and thousands of the unemployed joined in demonstrations supporting the railroad workers' cause. President Hayes repeatedly had to order out federal troops when local militia units proved unreliable.

What made this first national strike so ominous was the speed with which it spread and its unplanned character—the workers lacked any real leadership or organization. Nothing like this had happened before: street fighting in Baltimore, Pittsburgh, and Chicago; widespread destruction of railroad equipment; the president of the United States forced to dispatch troops. By August 2, after hundreds of strikers and others had been killed and thousands injured, railroad service had been forcibly restored on all lines. But the workers had made their point. They had succeeded in shutting down two-thirds of the nation's 75,000 miles of track. Some railroad managers wisely moved to halt further wage cuts or to take back those made earlier. But at the same time, the employer class moved to firm up their defenses.

National Unions

After the Civil War, efforts were made to organize labor nationally. The Noble Order of the Knights of Labor, formed in Philadelphia in 1869, achieved little until Terence V. Powderly, a Scranton machinist, became grand master in 1878. The Knights' principal aim was to unite all those who worked (except for liquor dealers, lawyers, gamblers, and bankers) into one huge union that would produce and distribute goods on a cooperative basis. Although Powderly opposed strikes and violence, his organization benefited from a successful strike against the Missouri Pacific Railroad in 1885. Certain unions affiliated with the Knights forced Jay Gould to restore a wage cut and rehire hundreds of union men he had fired. This victory so raised the Knights' standing that within a year membership had grown from about 100,000 to more than 700,000.

The American Federation of Labor, given its modern form in 1886 by the "business unionists," was a very different kind of national labor organization. Led by Samuel Gompers, its members were not individual workers but national craft unions. The AFL imposed certain standards on its members. It insisted on regular dues, which would provide members and the federation (which took a share) with strike funds. It hired full-time organizers. It settled all issues of jurisdiction that arose when two or more member unions tried to organize workers in similar fields, and it sought to protect its members from raids by nonaffiliated rivals.

Because it avoided politics and radical ideology, the AFL under Gompers appealed to the elite of the working class, the skilled workers, and focused on economic gains. It accepted modern capitalism and the reality of a fixed working class. It proposed to protect workers from the worst abuses of the economic system, and to improve the standard of living of those who would most likely remain in the working class for the remainder of their lives. The primary aim of the AFL was to force employers to engage in collective bargaining with member unions on everyday issues such as wages, hours, and working conditions. An essential goal was the establishment of the *closed shop*—that is, a shop that would agree to

employ only AFL members. Between 1886 and 1892, the AFL gained the affiliation of unions having some 250,000 members.

In the entire history of the American labor movement, no organization provoked as much hostility, controversy, and commitment as the Industrial Workers of the World—the Wobblies—between 1905 and 1924. Unlike the AFL, the Wobblies appealed to the forgotten, unskilled, casual, and marginal laborers, including the most degraded segments of the working class: lumberjacks; western gold, lead, silver, and copper miners; construction, cannery, and dock workers; and migratory field hands. Like the AFL, the Wobblies believed in direct action to improve the workers' lives. But by direct action, the IWW meant not simply strikes but massive work slowdowns ending in a general strike that would force the capitalist class to surrender its power and replace the state with an industrial syndicate directed by the workers.

The IWW never attracted more than 5 percent of all trade unionists, and probably never exceeded 150,000 members. It won its most notable strike victory in 1912 at Lawrence, Massachusetts, among previously unorganized textile workers. Like so many IWW-led strikes, this one captured the nation's attention with its combination of giant rallies, massive picket lines, flaming oratory, and revolutionary songs. But this success marked the peak of IWW influence. Failure to consolidate strike victories and to build stable local organizations deprived it of lasting effectiveness. Under the growing pressure of patriotism and conformity after the entry of the United States into World War I in 1917, the IWW came under vigilante attack, federal prosecution, and harassment.

For the immediate future at least, the AFL clearly dominated the portion of labor that was organized. The workers it ignored would have to wait for the emergence of the Congress of Industrial Organizations in the 1930s.

Strikes and Confrontation: Haymarket, Homestead, Pullman

On May Day 1886, Knights of Labor unions and other groups sponsored a massive demonstration to promote the eight-hour day. In Chicago, where an independent strike against the McCormick Harvester Company was in progress, the Knights' demonstration was followed by outdoor meetings addressed by anarchists. At a meeting in Haymarket Square on May 4, a bomb thrown at the police killed an officer. Seven more officers and four civilians died in a riot that followed. The bomb thrower was never found, but seven of the eight anarchists arrested and accused of murder were sentenced to death. Four of the seven were executed and one committed suicide. The sentence of the other two was changed to life imprisonment. Six years later, accusing the sentencing judge of "malicious ferocity," Governor John P. Altgeld courageously and unconditionally pardoned them.

The Haymarket riot outraged the general public, intensified their fears of radicalism, and broke the back of the eight-hour-day movement. Although the Knights of Labor had nothing to do with the incident, newspapers and employers exploited Haymarket in an attempt to ruin the entire labor movement. Within a few years, because of Haymarket and growing internal dissension, the Knights had just about disappeared.

Two massive confrontations between capital and labor in the 1890s—Homestead and Pullman—revived fears of revolution. Only two years after Gompers had negotiated a contract with the Carnegie Steel Company, the Homestead strike dealt a terrible blow to the iron and steel workers. The strike was incited by the company itself when Henry Clay Frick tried to cut wages while Carnegie was in Europe. The powerful Amalgamated Association of Iron and Steel Workers, an AFL affiliate, refused to accept the cut. On July 1, 1892, Frick closed down the huge Homestead plant and hired 300 Pinkerton guards to protect it. When the Pinkertons arrived by barge several days later, they were met by an army of angry workers. Frick then requested the governor of Pennsylvania to call out the state militia. Only after five months did the workers begin to go back to their jobs on company terms. Fifteen years later, an investigation of conditions at Homestead revealed that wages remained low. Most of the men worked a twelve-hour day, and had a twenty-four-hour stretch every two weeks when they changed day and night shifts.

The second great strike of the 1890s broke out at a Pullman company town near Chicago but soon spread to most of the western railroads. The control George Pullman had over the lives of the workers in his "model" town was virtually complete. With the coming of the depression in 1893, the Pullman Company began laying off workers and cutting the pay of those who were kept on. In May 1894 the workers asked for some reductions in rent and store prices; they were refused and their negotiators were fired. The workers then walked out and appealed for help from the American Railway Union, which many of them had joined. This was the union of all levels of railroad workers that Eugene V. Debs had begun to organize in 1893, when he found that the individual railroad craft unions could not fight the companies. In late June 1894, Pullman refused to arbitrate with Debs and 120,000 railroad workers thereupon joined the Pullman strikers. The western roads were paralyzed.

The General Managers Association, an employer organization representing all the railroads terminating in Chicago, had earlier appealed to Attorney General Richard Olney for federal troops to get the trains rolling. Olney, a former railroad lawyer, was more than willing. Using the Sherman Antitrust Act, which forbade "combinations in restraint of trade," he obtained a series of orders in federal courts enjoining the union and "all other persons" to stop virtually every kind of activity impeding railroad operations, even the "persuasion" of workers to quit their jobs.

Somehow violence broke out. Using as his excuse the need to move the mail (railroad owners made a point of attaching Pullman cars to the mail trains), President Cleveland ordered in federal troops, making a bad situation worse. Workers resisted military efforts to move the trains and had to be driven from the tracks.

To obey the federal injunctions was to break the strike. Rather than do so, Debs and three other union officers allowed themselves to be arrested on charges of contempt of court. Harassment of union leaders soon disorganized the strikers. The American Railway Union itself disintegrated. Pullman workers who had not played an active role in the strike straggled back to work under the old conditions. In December the United States Circuit Court convicted Debs of the contempt charge and sentenced him to six months in jail. The Supreme Court subsequently upheld the sentence. The decision had enormous consequences for organized labor. Injunctions gave employers a powerful weapon with which to fight strikes and boycotts, and they used them widely and effectively until they were outlawed by the Norris-LaGuardia Act of 1932.

Despite the publicity given to labor warfare and organization, the vast majority of the work force remained unorganized. By 1898 there were more than 17 million factory workers, but only 500,000 were in unions. Even as the United States became the leading industrial power in the world, millions of workers did not share in its prosperity.

THE RISE OF THE CITY

Although urban growth had proceeded rapidly before the Civil War, in 1840 only one-twelfth of the American people lived in cities of 8000 or more. By 1860 the proportion had grown to one-sixth, and by 1900 to one-third. By 1910, nearly one person in two lived in the city. The number of cities with more than 100,000 people had increased since 1860 from 9 to 50, and the number of cities holding between 10,000 and 25,000 people had increased from 58 to 369. America was well on its way to becoming one of the most urbanized nations in the world.

In 1900 more than 25 million Americans were living in cities, most of which had grown in the preceding fifty years. In 1850 New York City and independent Brooklyn together boasted a population of 1.2 million. By 1900 (two years after the five boroughs were consolidated) it was over 3 million; by 1910 it was approaching 5 million. In the same period, Philadelphia grew from 560,000 to over 1.5 million, again partly by annexing neighboring communities. No other city quite matched Chicago's

Mulberry Street, in the heart of New York City's immigrant area on the Lower East Side, in the early 1900s.
(Library of Congress)

rise from a muddy trading post with twelve families in 1831, to an urban center of 100,000 people in 1860, to the second largest city in the United States, with 2 million people, in the early 1900s. The sudden growth of places that hardly existed in 1860 was equally striking. By the turn of the century Denver, Minneapolis, Los Angeles, and Birmingham were not towns; they were cities.

The rapid growth of American cities after the Civil War was just one sign of the enormous increase in the scale and the pace of American business. The expansion of Pittsburgh and the development of Birmingham were directly related to the modernization and growth of the iron and steel industry. Minneapolis attained city status because of its importance in the grain trade and flour milling. Denver capitalized on the mining boom. Chicago was first a wheat port, next a railroad hub, then the meatpacking center of the world. Its industry and

trade so boosted business activity that it became the financial capital of the West as well. Philadelphia and New York, still building the commercial life that had been established earlier in their histories, also grew with new industries. One was the manufacture of ready-to-wear clothing, given a great push by the demand for uniforms during the Civil War.

Although tens of thousands of urban residents found employment as industrial workers and laborers, new opportunities were also opening up in white-collar and service occupations. Between 1870 and 1910, the number of wholesalers and retailers tripled. The number of salespeople and clerks in stores increased eleven fold. Almost equally spectacular was the growth in the number of domestics and persons employed in laundries, restaurants, boarding houses and hotels, barbershops, real-estate offices, and banks. But most newcomers were drawn into the factories and work-shops. And many of these were new not only to the city but to America as well.

The Lure of the City: Immigration

Of the 42 million city residents in 1910, some 11 million had migrated after 1880 from rural homes in the United States. A similar movement from rural to urban life was under way in Europe, and millions would cross the Atlantic in the belief that they could realize a better life for themselves and their children in the cities of the United States. The migration overwhelmed

the native-born families. By 1900 more than one-third of Chicago's population was for-eign-born. The proportion in New York City was higher. New York had more foreign-born residents than any city in the world. Its Italian population in the 1890s equaled that of Naples; its German population, that of Hamburg. Twice as many Irish lived in New York as in Dublin. And yet the real surge of the "new" immigration had hardly begun.

Many of the new immigrants—Ital-ians, Slavs, Magyars, Croats, Serbs, Slovaks, Greeks, and Jews—came from cultures strik-ingly different from those of the "natives" who had preceded them. Of the 15 million

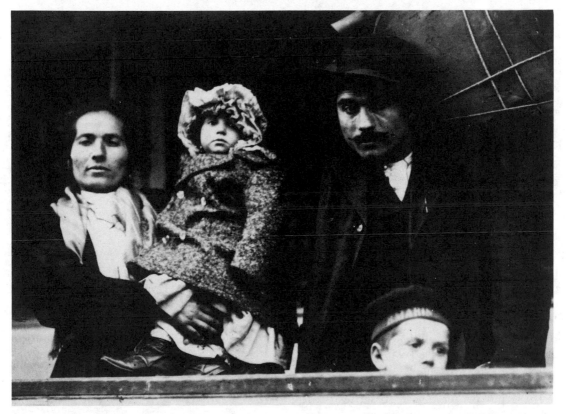

An Italian family on board the Immigration Service boat that carried new arrivals to Ellis Island. (Photograph by Lewis W. Hine, Library of Congress)

Newly arrived Russian Jewish immigrants in New York City, 1908.

newcomers to the United States between 1890 and 1920, 80 percent were from eastern and southern Europe. Between 1900 and 1914, for example, more than 3.1 million Austro-Hungarians entered the United States, more than 3 million Italians, more than 2.5 million from Russia, and nearly 900,000 from the Balkan countries of Europe and the Middle East. Four out of five of these newcomers chose to settle in the industrial cities of the Northeast and Midwest, where economic opportunities were the best.

The spectacle of cities congested with newcomers whose languages, religions, and cultures differed from their own caused considerable debate among "natives" about unrestricted immigration. Race prejudice in the West had already resulted in agitation directed at Chinese immigrants, who first came in large numbers in the 1860s to help build the Central Pacific Railroad. The earliest federal law to restrict immigration was passed in May 1882. It forbade Chinese to enter the United States for a decade; in 1902, another act made this exclusion per-

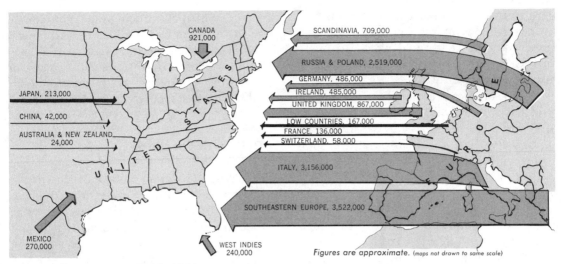

CANADA
921,000

SCANDINAVIA, 709,000

RUSSIA & POLAND, 2,519,000

GERMANY, 486,000

JAPAN, 213,000

IRELAND, 485,000

UNITED KINGDOM, 867,000

CHINA, 42,000

LOW COUNTRIES, 167,000

AUSTRALIA & NEW ZEALAND
24,000

FRANCE, 136,000

SWITZERLAND, 58,000

ITALY, 3,156,000

SOUTHEASTERN EUROPE, 3,522,000

MEXICO
270,000

WEST INDIES
240,000

Figures are approximate. (maps not drawn to same scale)

Sources of Immigrants, 1900–1920

manent. In 1885 the Knights of Labor, reflecting concern over job competition, persuaded Congress to forbid the importation of contract laborers. How to respond to the growing tide of new immigrants remained a source of agitation until Congress responded in the 1920s with restrictive legislation.

City Life: Growth and Decay

The full impact of urban growth was not felt in America until early in the twentieth century. Yet even in the previous century American cities, for all their wealth, accumulated ills and evils. In the nineteenth century, hardships were made worse by ignorance and inexperience. But a major part of the blame goes to the indifference to others that the idea of "success" encouraged.

Most city dwellers took only a halfhearted interest in civic projects that did not immediately affect their own pocketbooks or pleasure. Leaders of older nineteenth-century cities looked with satisfaction on the rising value of the urban land they owned or managed, and left those who were less well off to look after themselves.

The industrialists who dominated the newer cities viewed them simply as sites for factories and tenements for the factory workers. Certain areas might be reserved for the industrialists, general managers, superintendents, and other ranking officials. The rest of the populace got miserable housing and almost no public facilities.

To accommodate the surge in population, real-estate operators cut up city land into blocks of rectangular lots divided by a grid of roads. The lots themselves were divided simply by lines on a layout. Enjoying few restrictions on their operations, builders and landlords made maximum use of the available lots, wiping out all open space. Urban congestion fed upon itself. As sections of a city became thickly populated, more and more transportation was directed there. Water, gas, and electrical utilities might be brought in. Factories, most of them noisy and dirty, then moved in. Eventually, neighboring residential areas were overrun and land values soared. Under such pressures, private dwellings that had housed single families were remodeled into tenements that housed eight or twelve families or else were torn down to make room for business structures. As living conditions deteriorated, families that could afford to do so moved away. The richer ones went to nearby suburban towns.

The problems created by the fast pace of urban growth were enormous. Cities had to respond to demands for expanded services: water, gas, sewage disposal, transportation, and electricity were now the responsibility of municipal departments that had access to large sums of tax money. But the existing and often antiquated city governments were simply not equipped to undertake such imposing tasks. In the absence of any developed science of public administration, political machines run by bosses accepted the challenge and reaped the financial benefits.

In most American cities, power resided in the mayor, the city council, and independent boards. These people determined how municipal funds should be raised and spent. They granted the franchises for street railways, awarded contracts for laying sewers and paving streets, constructed public buildings, bought fire-fighting equipment, and contracted for other services and supplies. Since most of these activities were entrusted to committees drawn from elected aldermen or council members who had no training in city management, political bosses found it easy to place their people in positions where they could dip into city treasuries and enter into profitable alliances with local businessmen.

Despite the absence of professional managers, the political machines somehow made the cities work. They may not have done it efficiently or inexpensively, but there was some order and service. Only when the activities of the political rings became too outrageous did upper- and middle-class residents organize for "good govern-ment." But it was their usual indifference to the needs of city dwellers that had given the bosses their electoral base, particularly among newly arrived immigrants, many of whom were indebted to the machines for jobs and assistance in their new surroundings.

Urban Reformers

Between 1880 and 1900, cleaner streets, purer water, and more efficient methods of fire fighting made the American metropolis more livable. Yet it retained many ugly and brutal features. The very poor, constituting half and more of the metropolitan population, lived under conditions that were scarcely endurable. Whole families, sometimes more than one, lived in airless one-room tenement apartments, usually without sanitary facilities, lighting, or heat, and were victimized by flourishing populations of rats and other vermin.

Municipal reformers confined themselves largely to developing a science of public administration that would staff city departments with university-trained experts. At the same time, however, social workers, philanthropists, and clergy began to deal more directly with the social ills of urbanization. Moved by moral considerations and sometimes by fear of social upheaval, they concerned themselves not so much with altering the structure of city government as with making life more bearable for slum dwellers.

Traditional explanations of poverty and misfortune had blamed the victims. The virtuous succeeded; the immoral did not. But by the 1870s urban reformers realized that the causes of poverty were far more complex. Illness, death of the breadwinner, low wages, and unemployment clearly produced more paupers and criminals than laziness and alcoholism. What was the point of advice to be frugal if unemployment and miserable wages did not permit even the most thrifty families to accumulate any savings? The new view placed more emphasis on the weaknesses of the economy and on the need to do something concrete to assist the victims.

Hoping to narrow the gulf between the privileged and the underprivileged, middle-class reformers and social workers, most of them women, moved into the immigrant ghettos. They learned through direct experience of the lives of the poor; in the poorest neighborhoods they opened settlement houses that offered guidance, recreation, and companionship. The idea of the settlement house originated in London in the 1870s, and the opening of Toynbee Hall in the East London slums in 1884 provided a model. Jane Addams (1860–1935) became the leader of the settlement-house movement in America. In 1889 she and her friend Helen Gates Starr converted the old Hull mansion in Chicago into a settlement house called Hull House. In Boston, Cleveland, Pittsburgh, and elsewhere, college men and women formed clubs for boys and girls, established playgrounds and libraries, conducted classes, transformed settlement houses into a combination nursery, gymnasium, and employment bureau, and campaigned for sanitary regulations, better housing, and penal reform.

The Social Gospel movement emerged during the last quarter of the nineteenth century. Organized by socially conscious ministers of various Protestant denominations, and concerned over the church's failure to reach large numbers of urban dwellers, the movement attacked the social consequences of urbanization and industrialization. Examining conditions in their own neighborhoods, the clergy who made up the movement concluded that environmental forces, not immorality, lay at the root of urban social problems. Some clergy went no further than to advocate moderate reforms in wages, housing, and working conditions. The more radical insisted that the nation's business system be reformed from the bottom up. Ministers like Washington Gladden and Walter Rauschenbusch defended labor unions and expressed the Social Gospel ideal that Christian solutions existed for all social problems. By the 1880s, theological seminaries were offering courses in social Christianity and social ethics.

But most churches did not quarrel with society as they found it. Baptist, Methodist, and other churches whose membership consisted largely of artisans, shopkeepers, and farmers preferred to keep the old emphasis on individual responsibility for sin and the church's need to deal only with religious salvation. The Social Gospel movement was confined to a minority. Despite the efforts of clerics and social workers, the conditions that bred poverty, unemployment, and urban congestion persisted. For those who took up the reform standard in the Progressive Era, urban government and urban living remained a formidable challenge.

SUGGESTED READINGS

A. Trachtenberg, *The Incorporation of America, 1865–1893* (1980). A.D. Chandler, Jr., *The Visible Hand: The Managerial Revolution in American Business* (1977). J. Wall, *Andrew Carnegie* (1970). H.G. Gutman, *Work, Culture, and Society in Industrializing America* (1976). N. Salvatore, *Eugene V. Debs* (1982). C.N. Glaab and A.T. Brown, *A History of Urban America* (1967). O. Handlin, *The Uprooted* (1951). J. Higham, *Strangers in the Land* (1955).

SUMMARY

By the turn of the twentieth century, America had undergone a massive economic transformation and become an urban, industrial giant. Settlement of the whole continent had been followed by an industrial boom in the North that turned the United States into a world power. And although economic success had great costs in terms of the dreary, miserable lives of those who labored in the factories, that cost was at first ignored.

What fueled and supported growth was the Gospel of Success, the idea that anyone could become rich if he or she were willing and able to work hard enough. Darwin's theory of the survival of the fittest was translated into social terms: those who succeeded and won out over competitors, no matter what methods they used, were those who were fit to survive and therefore deserved rewards. Those who failed did so through their own fault. These ideas justified the careers and the methods of such industrialists as Andrew Carnegie and John D. Rockefeller; they also supported the monopolies and trusts and the strangling of competition.

The first step in this economic revolution was the development of a nationwide mass-transportation system—the railroads. Railroads offered a way to move vast quantities of goods easily and quickly to markets. They also offered opportunities for enormous profits, especially where there was only one line for producers of goods to use. Great fortunes were made—but the cloud of suspicion raised by shady business practices and titanic paper battles among financiers led eventually to calls for reform and for government regulation. Despite the corruption and the "deals," however, by 1900 the American railroad network of 200,000 miles was the best, the most efficient, and the safest transportation system in the world.

The great expansion of northern industry after the Civil War was built on the railroads, which drew European capital to America and familarized Americans with money markets and the idea of great corporations. Outstanding examples of the new industrial giants were Andrew Carnegie and John D. Rockefeller, whose steel and petroleum empires swallowed competitors like flies and who pioneered new kinds of vertical as well as horizontal expansion. Not only did Carnegie and Rockefeller buy up competitors, but they also bought out processors, distributors, and users of by-products; the Standard Oil Company and the Carnegie Corporation were, in fact, self-sufficient systems controlling every aspect of the making, distribution, and sale of their products.

The organization and management problems of these new giant corporations were solved by new technology: the telephone, the telegraph, the electric light, the typewriter, the adding machine. Public utilities in large cities also profited from economies of scale and became big enterprises. Together with the financiers and the bankers, the heads of these large businesses came almost to control the American economy. For they had soon found ways to make even bigger combinations in the form of trusts, pools, and cartels.

Workers in particular began to realize their position in this new economic structure.

They could be made to work long hours under unsafe conditions; they could be hired and fired at will; their wages could be lowered when business was bad—and there was nothing they could do about it. Furthermore, they were completely dependent upon their salaries for survival: almost no one in a city owned a house or a piece of land, and there was no such thing as welfare or unemployment insurance.

After 1870, labor conflict in the United States was intense and massive. The Great Strike of 1877 on the railroads, a spontaneous, unorganized work stoppage, set the tone for much of the labor strife that followed—the Homestead and Pullman strikes and the great Haymarket riot. Workers striking for better conditions or just against a wage cut found themselves at war not only with their employers but with society as a whole. Governments called out troops to fire upon them, employers hired goon squads to beat them up, and sometimes they would have to give in after months of struggle and go back to work under conditions worse than those before the strike.

Efforts to organize national unions met with mixed success. The Knights of Labor, organized in 1869, was ruined by the Haymarket riot in Chicago in 1886. The only union that grew and survived, the American Federation of Labor under Samuel Gompers, did so in part because it confined itself to economic issues such as hours and wages, and in part because it avoided the radical social and political activities of such movements as the IWW. But the AFL grew at the expense of real labor solidarity, and the kind of influence that European labor, with its political activism, was to

have on major issues confronting industrial society.

After the Civil War, America became an urban nation as well as an industrial one. By 1910 almost one person in two lived in a city. New York had nearly 5 million people, Chicago nearly 2 million. The cities grew because industry and trade grew: there were thousands of new jobs as factory workers and laborers, as salespeople, office workers, and clerks. The people who filled these jobs were migrants from rural American seeking success; they were also immigrants from Europe seeking a better life. Between 1866 and 1915, about 25 million people immigrated to the United States.

The exploding nineteenth-century American city had all the problems of rapid, unplanned growth—poor sewage disposal, bad water, inadequate housing, tangled transporation. These difficulties were compounded by the absence of people who really knew how to run a large city, and by the prevailing idea that poverty and misery were the victim's fault. Such attitudes led to many opportunities for political corruption, and to the growth of the political machine and the boss.

Although the basic urban social problems were not solved, between 1880 and 1900 the American city became a slightly more livable place. Technical advances in transporation, street cleaning and lighting, and sanitation and the water supply helped. So did the activities of the editors, architects, and reformers who planted the idea of a planned city governed in a humane way. Housing, however, remained a mess.

The problems and evils of city life were attacked by social reformers, who tried to help those who lived in the slums and worked in the sweatshops. The challenge was great, and they could do little about the underlying conditions that caused poverty and ignorance. But they did begin to change the attitude of blaming the victim,

and they involved some churches in social work. Nothing substantial would happen, however, until the twentieth century, when government would come to see social legislation and the solution or urban problems as part of its duties.

17

Parties, Politics, and Reform

When Mark Twain and Charles Dudley Warner coined the expression "The Gilded Age" for their novel of 1873, they wanted to suggest that the corruption of American life had made politics a sordid and shabby affair. But the politics of the Gilded Age, like that of any period in the nation's history, was many-sided. It was critical and creative as well as callous and corrupt, and the interplay of political, economic, and cultural interests was often complex. If the political candidates were mediocre, the turnout on election day was impressive. If the parties seemed hardly distinguishable on national issues, clear differences emerged on the state and local level and over cultural, religious, and ethnic issues. If bosses, lobbyists, and the spoils system dominated politics, these abuses also stimulated reform movements. Narrow though these movements were in concept, and limited though they proved to be in action, they still reflected a public willingness to stop corruption. They helped to establish a merit system in the civil service, and public regulation in big business. The emergence of the Populist movement in the 1890s began a debate about the distribution of power and the role of government that would persist well into the next century.

THE PARTIES

Even today, when public relations and the media are at their command, political parties do not arouse the electorate as the Democrats and Republicans did in the last three decades of the nineteenth century. The percentage of voter turnout exceeded those of the earlier period and the succeeding Progressive Era. What voters responded to was not necessarily the ballyhoo—speeches, torchlight parades, rallies, and picnics—or the political machine. The outcome of many elections was determined instead by issues and tensions important on the state and precinct level.

PUCK.

Joseph Keppler's cartoon, "The Bosses of the Senate," 1889. (Library of Congress)

Republicans: Stalwarts, Half-Breeds, and Mugwumps

For a long time the Republicans lived off the issues of the past. They waved the "bloody shirt" of the Civil War with success for a quarter of a century. They reinforced party loyalty by attacking the Democrats as traitors and by providing liberal pensions for former Union soldiers and their dependents. By identifying Democrats with secession and the Confederate cause, Republicans were able to avoid the problem of "hard times"—the economic and social issues of industrialization and the growth of the cities.

As the party of high tariffs for industry, liberal aid to railroads, and conservative

monetary policies, the Republicans had the support of much of the business community—especially manufacturers, bankers, and the holders of government bonds. Factionalism, however, continued to work against party unity. The Stalwarts, led by Roscoe Conkling of New York, remained the hard-core machine politicians who put party success and the distribution of offices above any issue or principle. The Half-Breeds, led by James G. Blaine of Maine, gave the appearance of trying to balance party needs against the cries for reform. Essentially, however, the Stalwarts and Half-Breeds differed not over principles and policies but rather over which group would inherit the spoils of an election victory. Neither cared to be associated with the Independents (later called the Mugwumps), who had deserted the party in 1872 and were prepared to do so again in order to advance the crusade for good government. On economic questions such as the tariff and sound money, there was little disagreement among the factions. They divided sharply, however, over their commitment to civil-service reform and occasionally over the quality of the presidential candidate.

Democrats: Southern Conservatives and City Bosses

The Democrats, despite the treason label, were strong contenders in national elections. After the overthrow of Radical Reconstruction and the defeat of black political aspirations, the South became solidly Democratic. White politicians waved their own kind of bloody shirt, reminding constituents of the "horrors" of "black rule" during Reconstruction and of the need to maintain party unity in the name of white supremacy. In northern industrial cities, where Irish bosses organized the immigrant population, the Democrats developed powerful political machines. They had less support from northern industry than the Republicans, but they did have some business backers, mostly northern merchants in the import trade and commercial bankers who had southern business ties.

Conservative southern Democrats sometimes joined with western Republicans to support laws favorable to farm constituents. But for the most part they sided with the representatives of eastern commercial and financial interests against the more independent Democrats of the West and against movements of economic radicalism. For a share of the spoils, southern Democrats would also vote in Congress with northern Republicans—a political alliance

of convenience and conservatism that lasted well into the twentieth century.

Party Unity

The Democrats lost the presidency when Lincoln was elected in 1860 and regained it only temporarily with Cleveland's two victories in 1884 and 1892. Yet the two parties showed almost equal postwar strength in numbers. In no election from 1876 to 1896 was the winning side's share of the popular vote greater than 50.8 percent. In two elections, 1876 and 1888, the Republican candidate won with fewer popular votes than his Democratic rival. In the thirteen Congresses elected between 1870 and 1894, the Democrats controlled the House nine times. Such balanced voting made party unity important.

Determined to hold their loose coalitions together, neither Democrats nor Republicans encouraged the kind of debate on issues that might sharpen internal differences. On such questions as the tariff, monetary policy, and regulation of railroads and corporations, both parties worded their positions vaguely so that they could attract the widest range of voters. Neither suggested any fundamental dissatisfaction with the pace or cost of industrialization. Nor could they conceive of a need for the federal government to play a major role in the economy. No matter which party won, the industrial sector could feel reasonably secure.

The efforts of the two parties to blur their differences on national economic issues in no way discouraged voter participation. In many sections of the country, party identification and voting reflected cultural values and ethnic and religious loyalties. The Democrats drew large numbers of urban Catholics and immigrants. Republicans drew support from native-born,

The issue of state aid to private Catholic schools divided the electorate. In this cartoon by Thomas Nast, crocodiles in the regalia of bishops are viewed as menacing the traditional public school system. (Library of Congress)

Anglo-Saxon Protestants. The differences and conflicts between these two blocs of voters were often expressed politically and took on added dimensions in a political campaign. The Democrats, in representing their immigrant constituents, were more likely to oppose prohibition, Sunday-closing laws, and any interference with the right of parents to send their children to parochial schools. The Republicans, reflecting the strong evangelical Protestantism that had helped to start the party during the anti-slavery conflict, were more sympathetic to using government to regulate morals and personal conduct: they favored *blue laws* (statutes regulating work, commerce, amusements, and recreation on Sunday), re-

strictions on the sale and consumption of alcoholic beverages, and the prohibition of the use of public funds for parochial schools. At the same time, a revival of nativist agitation in the 1880s and 1890s found a warmer welcome in Republican ranks.

When any of these issues surfaced at election time, the campaigns on the local and state levels would be bitterly fought. These elections determined not only the fate of the issues themselves, but the outcome of presidential and congressional races. Although the voter might find it difficult to understand how the tariff and currency reform could affect his daily life, he could easily see affronts to his cultural values and threats to his personal and religious freedom. And he could be expected to vote accordingly.

The Reformers

The reform politics of the period were dominated for a time by a group of men variously called Independents, Liberal Republicans, or Mugwumps. To them, the primary source of the nation's moral decline was the corruption of political power and the poor quality of government. The democratic ideals and heritage of the country were threatened because those who had once been given power on the basis of intellect, culture, and experience were no longer in command. They resented the political and economic power of the newly rich industrialists, who flaunted their wealth and influence. They expressed equal resentment toward the masses of immigrants in the urban centers, the political bosses who used them, and the patronage system that kept those bosses in power.

Elitist, of high social standing, and university-trained, the liberal reformers prided themselves on being independents in politics. They were prepared to cross party lines to advance their cause and return government to the hands of the virtuous. But they were committed to orthodox, laissez-faire economics and disliked those who operated outside the mainstream of American politics, particularly socialists and trade unionists. What these liberal reformers worked for was civil-service reform and the end of the spoils system. They wanted honest and efficient public service, and that meant government run by men who were sufficiently disinterested and dedicated to act in the public interest—in other words, men like themselves.

THE REPUBLICAN YEARS: HARD TIMES AND CIVIL-SERVICE REFORM

No matter how hard political leaders worked for party unity, the issues simply refused to disappear. In a period of economic fluctuations, rapid industrialization, and growing labor strife, it was difficult to keep issues such as "hard times" and currency inflation out of the political arena. The alliance of businessmen and politicians also kept alive the agitation to eliminate the spoils system. If that movement required a further push, it was soon supplied by a disappointed office seeker who assassinated a newly elected president.

Hayes and Monetary Policy

When Rutherford B. Hayes won the Republican nomination for president in June 1876, the depression of the seventies was nearing its lowest point. Unrest was widespread. Although the federal government would not assume direct responsibility for individuals, there were traditional political steps to be taken to reverse the downward course of the economy. Most popular with debtors, especially long-term debtors such as western farmers with mortgages, were proposals to inflate the money supply and thereby cheapen the currency and raise prices. Creditors took the opposite view: they wanted to be paid back in currency at least equal in value in gold to the currency available at the time the debts were incurred. The changing status of the paper money (greenbacks) issued during the Civil War intensified the conflict.

With the end of the Civil War, advocates of "hard" or "sound" money wanted the government to withdraw the greenbacks from circulation and return to a standard in which money was redeemable in and backed by gold. But the supporters of "soft" money argued that an expanding economy required an expanding currency; contraction of the currency made no sense to them. There was a particular urgency about this question. The nation was experiencing deflation, and the prices of agricultural products were declining. Farmers who had gone into debt during the war to increase production found themselves with obligations that had been incurred when prices were high and money was cheap.

The end of the long depression of the seventies momentarily lessened the agitation for currency inflation. The United States returned to the gold standard, and all federal issues were redeemable in gold on demand. But the demand to increase the volume of money in circulation would soon gather new strength and take a different form.

A drive for unlimited coinage of silver grew in political importance during the Hayes administration, ending finally in the depression of the nineties and the election of 1896. It had the support of silver-mining interests as well as farmers. Its promoters could be found in both political parties, along with its critics. Some argued that if the government coined large amounts of silver, the economy would be stimulated, interest rates would drop, and the prices farmers received would rise. But to hard-money people, this course of action was an invitation to fiscal irresponsibility that would undermine credit and wreck the economic system. The battle lines were drawn early, and each new "crisis" made the conflict worse.

In 1834 Congress had established a ratio of sixteen to one for the silver and gold that backed up the dollar. That is, silver could be legally exchanged for gold at a ratio of sixteen ounces of silver to one of gold. Until 1849, this ratio reflected the market value of the two metals. Then gold came pouring in from the mines of California and other parts of the West, and its value in terms of silver declined. Owners of silver found it more profitable to sell on the open market than to present silver to the mint for coinage. So no one protested when in 1873 Congress adopted a new law ending both the minting of silver dollars and the legal-tender status of the existing supply. In the depression seventies, however, western silver mines began to yield their own enormous wealth. Silver quickly fell in value in terms of gold, and it became worthwhile again to offer it to the mint. With silver overvalued at the ratio of sixteen to one, it was the cheaper metal with which to meet financial obligations. And there was an abundant supply of it.

On discovering the law against silver coinage, inflationists charged that a sinister group of bankers had engineered the "Crime of '73." In 1877 the silverites pressed for passage in the House of the Bland bill, which would permit unlimited coinage of silver at sixteen to one. At that time, the silver dollar was worth about eighty-nine cents and was falling. Bankers advised President Hayes that passage would amount to debt repudiation. If silver became legal tender, capitalists would never again buy government bonds for gold; their confidence in the government's credit would be badly shaken. The gold-standard advocates managed to hold off the silver inflationists with the amended Bland-Allison Act of 1878, which substituted limited for unlimited coinage of silver. It required the Treasury to buy not less than $2 million and not more than $4 million of silver every month and coin it into silver dollars at the old ratio of sixteen to one. Until 1890, silver purchases did not drive gold out of circulation or produce the kind of expanded currency that soft-money people wanted. The agitation persisted.

Garfield and Arthur: Civil-Service Reform

When Hayes refused to run for a second term, the Stalwarts—led by Roscoe Conkling of New York—tried unsuccessfully to bring back Grant. They finally agreed to the nomination of a dark-horse compromise candidate, James A. Garfield, a veteran Ohio congressman. For vice-president the Republican convention backed Conkling's patronage chief in New York, Chester A. Arthur. The delegates then proceeded to write a platform in favor of veterans' pensions and exclusion of the Chinese, but little else. The platform expressed pride in the party's accomplishments, and carefully hedged its position on civil-service reform, the protective tariff, and other important issues. The Democrats chose Winfield Scott Hancock of Pennsylvania, whose major accomplishment was that he had been a hero of the Battle of Gettysburg. He came close to winning. Garfield squeaked into office with a plurality of 39,000 votes out of more than 9 million cast. His large electoral majority was the result of narrow victories in Indiana and New York, which had been carried by Republican discipline and plenty of hard cash.

After the election, Conkling and his Stalwart friends expected recognition for their support. But the new president had other ideas. He broke with Conkling right after his inauguration by giving the best patronage post in the United States, Chester Arthur's old job as the collector of the Port of New York, to an anti-Conkling Republican. Before the controversy had subsided,

however, the nation suffered the second assassination of a president in less than twenty years. On July 2, 1881, Garfield entered the Washington railroad depot and was shot by a deranged job seeker. The president died two months later.

Although President Arthur filled his cabinet with Stalwarts, his administration saw the beginning of civil-service reform. The assassination had dramatized in the minds of many Americans the evils of a patronage and spoils system that had become entrenched in American government and politics. The first real step toward the merit system was the Pendleton Act of 1883. This act gave three civil-service commissioners, to be named by the president, the authority to draw up practical, competitive examinations. It forbade assessing federal employees for campaign funds or firing them for political reasons. It required that Treasury and postal employees be classified in civil-service categories within sixty days, and it permitted the president to extend civil-service classification to other federal employees. During Arthur's administration, about 12 percent of federal employees (compared with 85 percent in the mid twentieth century) were classified.

THE DEMOCRATIC YEARS: REGULATION AND PROTECTION

Both Democrats and Republicans claimed credit for civil-service reform. But more divisive issues now demanded attention. No longer could the federal government afford to ignore corporate abuses, whether these took the form of unreasonably high tariff rates, unfair methods of competition, or industrial combinations that prevented competition. Farmers organized by the Patrons of Husbandry (the Grange) pushed for laws against misconduct by the railroads. The Great Strike of 1877 had dramatized not only the plight of railroad workers but the degree to which the public shared their grievances against the railroad companies. If nothing else, public concern about the growth and use of corporate power had to be satisfied. At the same time, the government did not want to tamper with "natural" economic forces by imposing restraints on industrialization. The inhabitants of the White House—Democratic or Republican— believed that the least amount of government was best. They would cling to that belief even as the nation headed into another depression.

The Campaign of 1884: Cleveland

Although Chester A. Arthur did a fair job as president, he pleased neither the reformers nor the old guard. The Republican convention in 1884 passed him by in favor of the perennial candidate, James G. Blaine. Blaine had most of the qualities that make a successful presidential candidate. But his many years in the House had marked him: he had grown rich without any visible means of outside income and had not allowed anyone to uncover the sources of his wealth. With his nomination, the Mugwumps left the party and supported the Democratic nominee, Grover Cleveland. Cleveland had attracted notice as a reform mayor of Buffalo and as governor of New York. His defense of sound money and property rights earned him industrial and banking support.

In the campaign, the parties treated the public to sensational disclosures about the private lives and personal morals of the two candidates. Blaine was tied to railroad scandals, and Cleveland, a bachelor, was shown to be the father of a seven-year-old child. Each party claimed not to be opposed to tariff revision, as long as it did not endanger any domestic industry. Both parties also agreed that something had to be done about corporate abuses.

Blaine lost New York by 1149 votes, and that state turned out to be decisive in the electoral college, where Cleveland squeaked through 219 to 182. His popular plurality was only 23,000 out of 10 million votes. But it was enough to bring the Democrats back to the White House after a quarter of a century.

Cleveland's idea of government was almost entirely negative. He especially disliked what he called paternalism. Early in 1887, in vetoing an act to distribute seeds in drought-stricken Texas counties, he used a phrase that returned to haunt him during the depression of the nineties: "The lesson should be constantly enforced that though the people support the Government, the Government should not support the people." In destroying paternalism, he also foiled pension grabs by veterans and tariff grabs by industry, and even retrieved 81 million acres of the public domain from the railroads. Cleveland fought federal regulation of business in the public interest, but lost that fight to public pressure. By the end of his term, railroads, tariffs, and big business were all the subjects of new legislation.

Railroad Regulation

After the panics of 1873 and 1884 had forced many speculators to the wall, the movement for railroad regulation and reform increased. Rate and dividend policies came under bitter attack from shippers and investors. When the railroads fought back by spending money to make political friends and hire the best legal talent, they made more enemies.

In the late 1870s and throughout the 1880s, average railroad freight rates went down steadily because of the competition for traffic. The trouble was that average rates included suicidally low ones for railroads at junctions where two or more lines crossed, and murderously high ones for shippers at monopoly points. This situation satisfied no one, least of all the railroads, which were under pressure for special consideration from all sides. Shippers at monopoly points along railroads that ended at competitive points were the worst off. They were often required to pay more for short hauls along a small portion of the road than shippers at the terminals paid for long hauls over the road's entire length. Rebates and other special favors to powerful shippers such as Standard Oil were also a source of anger.

The first regulatory commission was a state effort in Massachusetts in 1869, and it could only investigate railroad abuses and make its findings public. But by 1880, despite railroad opposition, fourteen states had set up railroad commissions; some had taken more severe measures. Urban manufacturers and distributors and their banker allies sometimes began the fight, but the most persistent organization was the Patrons of Husbandry, which began organizing farmers into local granges in 1867. A year after the Panic of 1873, the Grangers had 1.5 million members, mostly in Iowa, Wisconsin, Minnesota, and Illinois. Here they won legislation setting statewide maximum rates for railroad traffic and maximum charges for the use of grain elevators, where farmers had to store their crops while awaiting shipment.

Railroad management fought Granger legislation in the courts: they attacked rate fixing by public bodies as legalized confiscation. In 1877, in *Munn* v. *Illinois,* the most important of the Granger cases to reach the Supreme Court, a majority of the justices found against the railroads and grain-elevator operators. Owners of property "in which the public has an interest," said the Court, must "submit to be controlled by the public for the common good."

But single states could not regulate corporations chartered by other states and carrying on most of their business across state borders. Pressure for federal regulation mounted in the early 1880s. After the Supreme Court decision in the *Wabash* case (1886), which reflected conservative attitudes, the federal government could not postpone action any longer. The *Wabash* decision took much of the strength from *Munn* v. *Illinois* by forbidding any state to set rates even within its borders on railroad traffic entering from, or bound for, another state. With the states thus removed from the regulatory process, any effective control of the railroads now rested with the federal government.

The Interstate Commerce Act, signed by President Cleveland on February 4, 1887, provided that all charges made by railroads should be "reasonable and just." It forbade higher rates on noncompetitive short hauls than on competitive long ones and outlawed rebates to favored shippers. It also prohibited self-regulating practices, such as agreements to pool traffic and maintain high rates. Of particular importance was the establishment of the Interstate Commerce Commission, the first federal regulatory board. But its powers proved inadequate to the tasks it faced. The "cease-and-desist" orders the ICC was empowered to issue could be made to stick only by court action, which the railroads found easy to delay. And in the end the railroads almost always won. In the first ten years of its existence, 90 percent of the commission's orders on rate charges were overruled by the courts. Of the sixteen cases heard by the Supreme Court between 1887 and 1905, the carrier was upheld in fifteen.

The Interstate Commerce Act did not reduce rates significantly. Nor did it put an end to cutthroat competition. Like so many regulatory commissions, the ICC would eventually be dominated by the very forces it had been created to control. Yet the act was not a complete failure. It clearly affirmed the right of the federal government to regulate private interstate business, and it provided the foundation on which a system of effective regulation could be built in the twentieth century.

Protection: The Tariff

Although Democratic politicians advised him to soft-pedal the tariff issue, Cleveland was determined to achieve some reforms in this sensitive area. Beginning with the wartime duties of 1864, protection of domestic industries had increased until it covered at least 4000 items in 1887. Cleveland did not oppose those who sought to nurse "infant industries." But he saw some of the tariff rates as excessive, and he felt that such "unnecessary taxation" only encouraged Congress to spend the annual surplus that accumulated in the Treasury.

Responding to Cleveland's call for tariff reform, the House adopted the Mills bill early in 1888. The measure reflected deep study of industry's genuine needs and recommended the moderate tariff reductions that mild revisionists like the president wanted. The Senate responded with a sub-stitute bill, which called as usual for a general rise in the tariff. With Congress deadlocked, resolution of the issue was postponed until after the presidential election of 1888.

Republican Interlude

The Democrats renominated Cleveland by acclamation; the Republicans selected Benjamin Harrison, a dreary corporation lawyer from Indiana, and the grandson of President William Henry Harrison. The Republicans charged that Cleveland's "free-trade" policy would ruin American manufacturing and betray the American worker to the "pauper labor of Europe." Even the Knights of Labor believed this argument and endorsed Harrison.

Although Cleveland's popular vote topped Harrison's by more than 100,000, Harrison won an electoral majority of 65. A switch of only 6500 votes in New York would have given Cleveland that state and the election. Since Cleveland did surprisingly well in protariff regions, the effect of that issue on the election is questionable. Like so many elections in this period, the national campaign was run largely on personalities and on the ability of party organizers to mobilize supporters.

After the election, Congress took care of the industrial contributors to the campaign with the McKinley tariff (1890), the highest and broadest in the nation's history. By raising already high duties even higher, the new tariff not only protected domestic industries but made it virtually impossible for foreigners to compete. Secretary of State Blaine feared that exporting nations hit by the new duties would refuse to buy American farm surpluses. He got Congress to hold a club over resisting nations by inserting a "reciprocity" clause in the new tariff act:

the president had the authority to remove remaining items from the free list in retaliation for any discriminatory duties on American produce.

In return for western votes on the McKinley tariff, Congress passed the Sherman Silver Purchase Act in 1890. This act authorized the Treasury to issue notes redeemable in gold or silver coin in exchange for greater amounts of silver than had been pemitted under the Bland-Allison Act of 1878. Virtually a gift to the silver mining companies, the Silver Purchase Act was defended as an agrarian cheap-money measure. But the issue was not settled; inflationists wanted unlimited silver coinage.

One more sop offered to the public was the Sherman Anti-Trust Act, which passed Congress in July 1890. Many states had passed antitrust statutes, but they were no more effective against trusts chartered in other states than state regulation of interstate railroads had been. After the *Wabash* decision of 1886 cut the ground away from stronger state measures against private corporations, the demand for federal trust regulation grew stronger. The Sherman Anti-Trust Act sounded severe. It made combinations in restraint of trade illegal, subjected offenders to heavy fines and jail sentences, and ordered that triple damages be paid to persons who could prove injury by such combinations. Few courts, however, upheld any of the actions brought under the measure.

The Sherman Act did push certain groups of companies to change specific trust arrangements and to merge into huge corporations. Without having to act together, these companies succeeded in dominating industries at least as thoroughly as the trusts had. In other industries, the holding-company device was employed. The *holding company* was an independent corporation that owned enough stock in other companies to control their policies. Dodges such as these neutralized the Sherman Act for a while, but in the twentieth century political administrations and the courts gradually began to enforce it. Although business consolidation and centralization continued, antitrust legislation did serve as a brake on many combinations considered harmful to the public interest.

The Election of 1892: Cleveland Again

Running against Cleveland in 1892, Harrison this time got 5,176,000 votes. But Cleveland got 5,556,000. Narrow though this margin was, it was the most decisive victory since 1872. The electoral college count was Cleveland 277, Harrison 145. After viewing the results, politicians of both parties had something new to think about—the showing of the People's party (familiarly known as the Populists), especially in the new wheat states.

THE POPULISTS AND THE SILVER CRUSADE

The economic crisis of the 1890s and the emergence of a strong third political party made it increasingly difficult for the two major parties to avoid the issues. Much of the unrest of the decade focused on the farmers, who, like so many industrial workers, sensed that they were no longer in control of the products of their labor. Farmers protested declining prices for their products and the growing percentage of their incomes falling into the hands of middlemen. They were joined by other groups experiencing economic hardship and concerned over corporate power and government unresponsiveness. These concerns found expression at all levels of society and soon took on political significance. Whatever the ultimate fate of Populism as the basis of a third party and as an economic and cultural movement, it managed to raise critical questions that would outlast both the party and the movement.

The Farmers

Broadly speaking, the farmers faced four major problems: the high cost of transportation, heavy taxes and tariffs, falling prices, and the high cost of credit. It was said that Nebraska annually produced three principal crops—corn, freight rates, and interest—and that the last two were harvested by those who farmed the farmer.

Few enterprises had received more civic support than the railroads of the West. In return, farmers felt that the railroads owed the community moderate rates. But the farther west one moved, the worse conditions grew. In 1887, for instance, the ton-mile charge on the Pennsylvania Rail Road east of Chicago was $.95. On the Burlington from Chicago to the Missouri River it was $1.32; on the Burlington west of the Missouri it jumped to $4.80. According to railroad officials, they had to charge high rates in sparsely populated regions. The farmers, dependent on the railroads for getting their crops to market, could hardly agree.

Heavy taxes made the high railroad rates harder to bear. Personal property then consisted chiefly of land and livestock, on which it was relatively simple to assess a personal-property tax. Railroads and other corporations created new kinds of personal property—stocks and bonds—that were far easier to conceal. Since the railroads also pushed the politicians for tax exemptions or low rates on their own huge landholdings and other real property, taxes fell more and more heavily on the middle-class farmer. Involved in a competitive market, he could not pass these taxes along to the consumer, as could many monopolistic industrial corporations, which did not have to worry about losing business to the competition by doing so.

The protective tariff was still another kind of discriminatory tax that angered farmers. In their opinion, it protected the trusts, which had the power to force down the prices for raw materials produced on the farms and to force up the prices of farm machinery and other manufactures.

Falling farm prices, of course, made heavy taxes seem even worse. The price of staples began to fall in the 1880s and hit bottom in the depression years of the nineties. Wheat brought $1.20 a bushel in 1881 and $.50 in 1895, and cotton $.10.5 a pound in 1881 and $.04.5 in 1894. Of course, prices of nonfarm products fell too. But the fall in farm prices hit the grower particularly hard because he was a debtor with fixed *money* obligations. His constant concern with the currency came from his need to keep these obligations stable in terms of the amount of *commodities* needed to pay them. Critics told the farmers they received low prices because they produced too much. But the only way the individual farmer could think of to make more money when prices were falling was to raise even bigger crops. To him, the price decline reflected a cold-blooded Wall Street conspiracy to squeeze the settlers of the West.

The high cost of credit seemed to confirm this view. The credit system helped force the landless southern farmer, and eventually the small southern landholder as well, into the vicious circle of sharecropping and crop lien. Tenancy came later in the West, where land was more easily obtained and more easily mortgaged. But when mortgage money cost 15 percent or more a year, as it did in Kansas and states farther west in the 1880s, the foreclosures began and farmers faced the prospect of being evicted from the lands on which they lived and worked.

The Origins of Populism

The roots of the People's party of the 1890s were firmly planted in American history. Its direct ancestors were the organizations, unions, and alliances that sprang up in the 1880s to replace the Grange. By 1890 many of these had consolidated into two regional groups, the Southern Alliance, which claimed over a million members, and the somewhat smaller National Farmers' Alliance in the Northwest, mainly on the Great Plains. The Colored Farmers' Alliance, begun in 1886 by a white Baptist preacher, reportedly recruited over a million blacks, but it had neither the power nor the influence of the two white organizations.

 The Southern and National Farmers' alliances gave a strong stimulus to the social life and the thinking of their members. Like the Granges, they held picnics, conventions, and rallies to help overcome the isolation and bleakness of farm life. They gave out agricultural information and tried to teach their members better business methods. They sponsored economic and political discussions and established circulating libraries, which enabled members to read books of social criticism. At one time perhaps as many as a thousand local newspapers were connected with the movement. What emerged was both a political and a cultural movement, in which farmers came together to share their experiences and to propose and act upon measures that would improve their working lives and free them of the credit system. "People commenced to think who had never thought before," one alli-

Populist leader Mary E. Lease. (Library of Congress)

ance sympathizer wrote, "and people talked who had seldom spoken."

 Despite organizational differences, the reform programs of the National and Southern alliances proved to be very much alike, except that northerners gave greater emphasis to the railroad issue, southerners to farm finances and farm credit. The most important proposal for solving the credit problem came from C. W. Macune, organizer of the Texas Alliance. Macune suggested that the federal government set up a subtreasury office and warehouse in every county that would offer for sale more than $500,000 worth of farm products annually. Farmers who placed nonperishable crops in these warehouses would receive as a loan Treasury notes in amounts of up to 80 percent of the local market value of their stored crops. This loan was to be repaid when the crop was sold. Macune's plan, later incorporated into the agricultural programs of the 1930s, had the double advantage of allowing the farmer to hold a crop for the best price and of increasing the money supply.

Eastern conservatives laughed off the alliance proposals as "hayseed socialism." But they could not laugh off the political force behind them. Between 1887 and 1890, Southern Alliance people, working at first through the Democratic party, elected three governors and won control of the legislatures of eight states. National Alliance candidates, in the major parties or in local third parties in the grain states of the Northwest, made impressive gains. It was in Kansas that the third party was first called the People's party. Its members there became known as Populists.

The People's Party

Encouraged by their entrance into politics, northern and southern alliance members came together in 1890 to form a third party and to seek wider support for their program. In their first national convention, which was held in Omaha in 1892, the Populists drew up a platform calling for a flexible currency system based on free and unlimited coinage of silver, which would increase the money supply and enable farmers to pay their debts more easily; nationalization of railroads and the telegraph and telephone industries; prohibition of foreign ownership of land; direct election of senators (who were still elected by state legislatures); a graduated income tax; immigration restriction; and an eight-hour day for workers. What the Populist platform made clear—and this marked an important break with laissez-faire ideas—was that the federal government would henceforth need to play a far more significant role in the economic life of the nation. But first that government would have to be redeemed, so that it could act on behalf of the masses and not the special interests.

The party ran General James B. Weaver of Iowa in 1892 in its first bid for the presidency. The general got over a million votes, more than 8 percent of the total. The Populists succeeded in capturing four states and brought the silver issue and the needs of the farmers to national attention. With the exception of the Republicans in 1856, no third party had done nearly as well in its first national effort. The Populists showed enough strength in 1892 to worry the major parties, but no more than that. The next year, though, one of the worst depressions in American history began. Discontent spread across the land, setting the stage for a campaign in which the Populists would alarm every conservative.

The Crash of 1893

As Cleveland took office, the nation experienced the severest economic collapse thus far in its history. Overexpansion and overinvestment in railroads and industry, along with a decline in exports, were partly responsible. At the same time, falling farm prices had reduced the purchasing power of large numbers of Americans. Some placed the blame on the Silver Purchase Act, charging that it destroyed business confidence. The withdrawal of foreign capital, they argued, had been prompted by fears that America was going off the gold standard. This move seemed imminent by April 1893, when the Treasury's gold reserve dropped below $100 million.

Cleveland's first thought was to repeal the Silver Purchase Act, which permitted holders of silver certificates to exchange them for gold. He called a special session of Congress in the summer of 1893, and "Gold Democrats" and Republicans closed ranks and enacted the repeal in October. By then, however, a run on the Treasury was gaining momentum. After the failure of other measures to stop it, Cleveland was forced to borrow $62 million in gold from the Morgan and Belmont banking syndicate in February 1895 on terms decidedly unfavorable to the government. The inflationists denounced the president as a tool of Wall Street. But the bankers, by bringing gold from Europe, succeeded in reversing the drain on the Treasury. Having restored confidence, in January 1896 the government floated another loan that ended this crisis.

Cleveland's defense of the gold standard aggravated discontent in the West and South as much as it encouraged eastern financiers. It probably destroyed any hope of getting mass support for the tariff reform he had promised once again. Cleveland regarded the tariff act Congress finally passed in August 1894 (the Wilson-Gorman Tariff) as a disgrace to the party, and it became law without his signature. This act did contain one provision that the Populists wanted, a 2-percent tax on incomes over $4000. But in 1895 the Supreme Court declared the income tax unconstitutional by a five-to-four decision, on the ground that "direct taxes" could be apportioned among the states only on the basis of population, not personal wealth. (In 1913, the Sixteenth Amendment made the federal income tax constitutional.)

As the depression deepened, the public mood grew worse. Thousands of unemployed roamed the country, sometimes in large gangs. Since the government offered them nothing, agitators proposed schemes of their own. In 1894 General Jacob S. Coxey of Massillon, Ohio, a rich man himself, convinced frightened property holders that a revolution had actually begun. Coxey proposed that Congress authorize a half-billion-dollar public-works program. To dramatize his plan, he organized a march on Washington. Soon "armies" all over the country were heading for the capital. Not all the marchers made it: of the thousands who started out, only Coxey's Army of about 300 men managed to reach Washington. Police speedily dispersed them after arresting Coxey and a few of his aides for illegally carrying banners on the Capitol grounds and for trampling the grass. But Coxey's march helped make an issue of unemployment, one the Populists hoped to use in the election of 1896. The silver issue, however, soon became the focus of the campaign and of public attention.

The Election of 1896: The Cross of Gold

The Republican party nominated William McKinley of Ohio, sponsor of the high tariff of 1890. McKinley was hand-picked by his fellow Ohioan Mark Hanna, the shipping and traction magnate who was emerging as the Republican national boss. The platform pledged the party to maintain the gold standard and to oppose the free coinage of silver. Silverite Republicans walked out of the convention.

In the Democratic convention, the silverites beat the "goldbugs." The platform repudiated Cleveland's policies and came out flatly for unlimited coinage of silver at the ratio of sixteen ounces of silver to one ounce of gold. A sharp debate over the adoption of the silver plank was resolved once a thirty-six-year-old Nebraskan, William Jennings Bryan, had spoken in its favor. "You shall not press down upon the brow of labor this crown of thorns," he said in closing. "You shall not crucify mankind upon a cross of gold." The Democratic nomination was also resolved by his memorable speech, for Bryan was voted the candidate on the fifth ballot.

When the Populists convened they confronted this sad dilemma: to wage a Populist campaign would be to split the silver

William Jennings Bryan (left) and William McKinley (right), opponents in the fiercely fought election campaign of 1896. (Library of Congress)

vote and hand the election to the Republicans; to join the Democrats in support of Bryan would mean the end of their party. Fusionists pointed out that the Democratic platform, besides demanding the unlimited coinage of silver, did attack Cleveland's deals with the bankers, did recommend stricter railroad regulation, and did support a constitutional amendment that would make an income tax possible. The Populist convention finally nominated Bryan for president.

The campaign of 1896 was one of the most dramatic in American history. Bryan concentrated on free silver. Hanna, in the meantime, extracted millions for McKinley from those eager to sink the silver ship. Bryan traveled more than 18,000 miles and delivered over 600 speeches. McKinley stayed on the front porch of the family home in Canton, reading carefully drafted statements to delegations brought there by party leaders. Although Bryan won more popular votes than any previous loser,

McKinley's plurality of over 600,000 was the largest of any candidate since Grant defeated Greeley in 1872. McKinley won 271 electoral votes to Bryan's 176. Even such farm strongholds as Iowa, Minnesota, and North Dakota went Republican.

No doubt the flood of propaganda, the pressure employers put on industrial workers, and the identification of Bryanism with anarchy and revolution had something to do with McKinley's success. But there were more obvious causes. Republicans argued, with justice, that an inflationary price movement would leave wages far behind and that workers would be the losers. Urban workers failed to provide the mass support Bryan had hoped for. Nor did he do well with the traditional Democratic Catholic vote. In the midwestern farm states, where the agricultural depression had been less severe than in the prairie states and the South, distrust of free silver lessened Bryan's appeal. And every middle-class American who had invested in stocks, bonds, or insurance

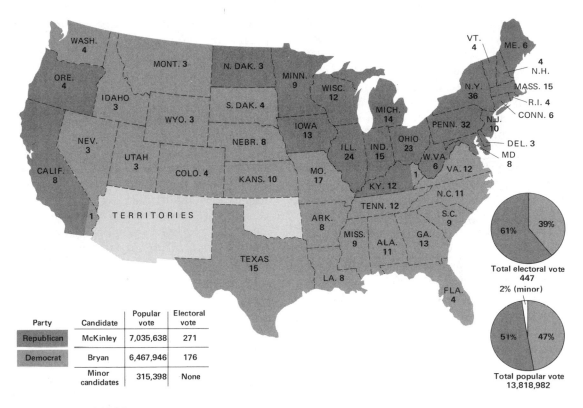

Party	Candidate	Popular vote	Electoral vote
Republican	McKinley	7,035,638	271
Democrat	Bryan	6,467,946	176
	Minor candidates	315,398	None

Total electoral vote 447
2% (minor)

Total popular vote 13,818,982

The Election of 1896.

was in a small way a creditor. So it was easy to see the point of the Republican argument that inflation would reduce the value of personal holdings. Finally, the Republican party, learning from past mistakes, succeeded in selling itself to the voters, particularly the growing middle class, as the party of stability, political flexibility, and ethnic and cultural diversity.

Republican "Good Times"

McKinley's election in 1896 did not restore prosperity, as the Republicans claimed. But Bryan's defeat did raise the confidence of those who stood to gain the most from sound currency and protective tariffs. The Republican administration quickly adopted

the Dingley Tariff of 1897, which raised schedules even above those of the McKinley Tariff of 1890. Three years later McKinley signed a Currency Act that made the gold dollar the sole standard of currency and required all paper money to be redeemable in gold.

To the losers, the results were disheartening. The Populist party was finished. The silver issue had brought the Democrats their worst defeat in many years, leaving the party more divided than ever. But history takes strange turns. The joy of the victors may have been justified; the despair of the losers was not. Soon the money supply was enlarged by new flows of gold, from the Klondike, South Africa, and Australia, and by greater United States production due to a new process for extracting gold from lower-grade ores. Ironically, the inflation the agrarian reformers had failed to win through silver came through gold. Good harvests and good prices also became the rule. In the election of 1900 McKinley, boasting of "Republican prosperity," again defeated Bryan, this time even more decisively than in 1896.

At the same time, several of the radical planks in the Populist program that Bryan and the Democrats had neglected in favor of silver in 1896 soon became law: direct election of senators, the income tax, an improved national currency and credit structure, postal savings banks, and certain features of the subtreasury plan. The doctrines of Populism outlived the party, and Mc-

Kinley's victory did not stop the forces of protest and reform.

SUGGESTED READINGS

J.A. Garraty, *The New Commonwealth* (1968). M. Keller, *Affairs of State* (1977). M. Josephson, *The Politicos* (1938). J.G. Sproat, *"The Best Men": Liberal Reformers in the Gilded Age* (1968). R. Hofstadter, *The Age of Reform* (1955). L. Goodwyn, *Democratic Promise* (1976). S. Hahn, *The Roots of Southern Populism: Yeoman Farmers and the Transformation of the Georgia Upcountry, 1850–1890* (1983). P.W. Glad, *McKinley, Bryan, and the People* (1964).

SUMMARY

The Gilded Age in America was a time of corrupt politics, but it was also a time of reform.

Voters came out in record numbers between 1870 and 1900; campaigns were lively events in which most people were interested. Their interest, however, was generated primarily by local issues. At the national level, both parties used rhetoric and personal attacks to avoid dealing with the hard issues that faced the country. This was the heyday of the machine and the political boss. It was also a time of considerable intraparty division. Republicans were split among Stalwarts, Half-Breeds, and Mugwumps; Democrats between southern conservatives and city bosses. But all disagreements were papered over for elections. The Democrats had the Solid South, and the Republicans New England and part of the Middle West. The rest of

the country was a battleground for votes, and party unity was necessary to win.

Opposed to the parties, which were dominated by conservatives, were the liberal reformers. Their goal was to check abuses of economic and political power. But they could not unite among themselves; class and political differences kept them apart. The liberal Republican reformers (the Mugwumps) worked for civil-service reform. But they had no patience with economic or social reform and thought labor agitation dangerous to society. So the reformers mostly failed—though the government did take some steps toward enlarging its role in the economic and social spheres—but the problems they raised did not go away.

Under the Republican presidents Rutherford B. Hayes, James Garfield, and Chester

A. Arthur (1876–84) the issue of monetary policy again became central. The old argument over paper money surfaced again because greenbacks had been issued during the Civil War to expand the money supply and keep the government going. Once again, debtors wanted cheap money and creditors did not. Although the United States went back to the gold standard, the issue of expanding the money supply did not die. It reappeared next in the drive for unlimited coinage of silver.

The election of 1880 brought James Garfield and, after his assassination in 1881, Chester A. Arthur to the presidency. It also brought the first step in civil-service reform and the end of the patronage system—the Pendleton Act of 1883. The Democrats who took power with Grover Cleveland in 1884 faced another explosive issue: corporate abuses, especially by the railroads. Farmers organized into granges to push for laws against discriminatory practices and high rates. Railroad workers went out on strike to protest salary cuts and unsafe working conditions. Cleveland, opposed to government paternalism of any kind, fought the trend for federal regulation. But he was not successful: by the end of his term, the first steps had been taken to regulate railroads. The Interstate Commerce Act of 1887 created not only federal rules but an Interstate Commerce Commisson to oversee them.

The 1890s brought new agitation over the currency and a new third party, the Populists. Formed by farmers, who were again in economic trouble because of high transportation costs, heavy taxes, falling prices, and expensive credit, the party was joined by other groups experiencing hardship and angry about the government's unresponsiveness. The Panic of 1893 brought depression and widespread unemployment. Workers fought Carnegie steel at Homestead in 1892, and railroad workers went on another nationwide strike in 1894. The Populists grew strong enough to elect a number of congressmen and senators in the elections of 1894 and to worry conservatives.

All these forces gathered momentum as the 1896 election approached. But then they were sidetracked in favor of silver, which became the focus of the campaign and of public attention. The Republicans, favoring the gold standard, nominated William McKinley of Ohio. The Democrats, taking advantage of the support for silver, chose William Jennings Bryan, whose "cross of gold" speech had swayed the convention. Despite Bryan's skill as a speaker and a campaigner, the Democrats lost. The Populists, who had backed Bryan, lost as well: their party was finished. But some of the Populist program eventually became law— direct election of senators, the income tax, and a better currency and credit structure.

18

Intellectual Life in the Gilded Age

For many Americans, the impressive advances in American technology and industry confirmed the superiority of their society and the pioneering tradition. Both intellectuals and political leaders extolled the virtues of a nation and an economic system that would be a model for the world. Educators and editors, economists and sociologists praised the laws of competition; historians confirmed the superiority of Anglo-Saxon institutions; popular ministers talked of money-making as the highest form of public service. Defenders of society drew on every kind of belief and knowledge to support their arguments. Some even adapted the new Darwinian ideas to their purposes.

But they did not go unchallenged. Nor did the business ethic, the inequalities, the ostentation, and the vulgarity that were so characteristic of the age. A growing number of respected critics began to question and condemn business values. And in raising critical questions about the changing nature of American civilization, the work of these critics would have a lasting impact on such twentieth-century developments as the Progressive movement and the New Deal. In literature too, writers dealt more realistically with their society and offered different models of behavior. Mark Twain's Huck Finn, battling the tyranny of the village, would long outlast the boys in the Horatio Alger novels, who succeeded only by losing their identity in the urban business world.

SOCIAL DARWINISM

When Charles Darwin published *Origin of Species* in 1859, the age of the earth, the process of its formation, and the origins of its inhabitants had long been discussed by philosophers, naturalists, and other scientists. But none had reached such firm conclusions from such convincing evidence. Darwin argued that the species of life all around us, far from having been created by separate acts of God in seven days, had gradually evolved over millions of years through the operation of natural selection. According to Darwin, all forms of life were engaged in an unceasing "struggle for existence" in a constantly changing natural environment. Although some species died, the "fittest" had survived and passed on to their offspring their favorable characteristics. Over long ages, successive adaptations had produced entirely new species, including humans.

Darwin's ideas outraged biblical fundamentalists and offended some leading scientists. More remarkable, however, was the readiness of Americans to embrace the new views, which rapidly gained popularity in intellectual circles. Darwin's popularizers in the United States found nothing antireligious in the belief that humans were the product of a long evolutionary process. On the contrary, they viewed that process as nothing less than "God's handiwork." In this way, religion and science could be made perfectly compatible.

Darwin's Popularizers

By combining scientific Darwinism with American optimism, the English philosopher Herbert Spencer achieved an impressive following in the United States. His synthetic philosophy, as he called it, explained the new biology in moral terms easily translated by journalists and other publicists. By ensuring the survival of the fittest, who would in turn pass on their characteristics to their offspring, the evolutionary process promised constant progress. The physical and intellectual power of the fittest would become ever greater. For God, Spencer substituted the "Unknowable." This satisfied the many Americans who no longer interpreted the Bible literally yet clung to a faith in a supernatural agency.

By 1900 about 350,000 copies of Spencer's books had been bought in America—a remarkable sale for sociological and philosophical works. Harvard in 1869 and Yale, Johns Hopkins, and other universities in the 1870s adopted the Spencerian view in teaching religion as well as the biological and social sciences. William Graham Sumner (1840–1910) of Yale, the most independent thinker among American Social Darwinists, stressed inevitability more than optimism. Sumner, like Darwin and Spencer, accepted the theory of the English economist T. R. Malthus that population increase outstrips food supply. But he rejected the idea that progress arose out of the resulting struggle for existence. He saw reformers as meddlers engaged in an absurd attempt to make over the world.

Critics and Dissenters

To accept Darwin's ideas was not necessarily to accept the social implications stressed by many of his popularizers. Among the most outspoken opponents of Spencer and his American followers was the sociologist Lester Ward (1841–1913). He rejected the theory that "neither physical nor social phenomena are capable of human control" and pointed to the superiority of selectivity over natural breeding in agriculture. Ward believed in social planning and welcomed government intervention in social matters. A democratic government operating in the interests of all, he said, would permit a truer individualism by breaking up monopolies that strangled opportunity.

Henry George (1839–1897), more of an activist than Ward, reached a far larger audience. He rejected Spencer's talk of the "survival of the fittest." Progress, he said, depended on human association and social equality, which unleashed a person's creative powers. When inequality prevailed, civilization declined. George felt that poverty went with progress because of the system of private land ownership. The value of land, he said, was largely a matter of accident. Since land grew in value because of the people who lived on it, George argued, the profit ought to return to the public in the form of a tax on the unearned increase in land values resulting from favorable location, improvements in transportation and production, and community development. He would leave the ownership of land in private hands, but socialize the rent. The single tax on land would make other taxes unnecessary and bring funds to the government for many useful social purposes. George's ideas, set down in *Progress and Poverty* (1879), attracted worldwide attention. He narrowly missed being elected mayor of New York City in 1886.

Edward Bellamy (1850–1898), George's contemporary, also rejected the fatalism of the Social Darwinists. But unlike George, he concentrated on the competitive system itself. Bellamy's radicalism had something in common with the utopian experiments of the 1840s and with the Social Gospel movement of the 1880s. In *Looking Backward*, a novel published in 1888, Bellamy offered a vision of an ideal society in the year 2000 whose beauty, tranquillity, and efficiency contrasted vividly with the smoky, striving, strike-ridden America of his day. This Golden Age dawned after the nationalizing of the great trusts and the replacement of private with public capitalism.

The social ideas of George and Bellamy found little support in the universities, where conservatism was firmly fixed. American students learned that inequality in wealth produced the incentives for progress; that labor's wages depended on the number of workers competing for jobs; and that competition was the only way for free individuals to work for "the greatest good of the greatest number." Only in an unregulated society could "natural" economic laws function properly.

These ideas began to be challenged in the mid 1880s by a group of younger schol-ars, many of them trained in German universities. Although they differed in their economic and political programs, by and large these younger social scientists all distrusted a static view of the universe, absolute laws, and fixed conceptions. Society, they felt, was constantly changing and had to be examined in terms of process and growth. They turned to the past in order to understand the present and looked in other disciplines for relevant facts that would help illuminate their own.

Foremost among the academic rebels was the economist Thorstein Veblen (1857–1929), who believed that millionaires were not, as Sumner had insisted, products of natural selection. Nor were they socially useful. Captains of enterprise, he said, actually sabotaged industry through monopolistic practices. Their concern, unlike that of the engineer, was profit, not production. In his most widely read book, *The Theory of the Leisure Class* (1899), and in other volumes, Veblen discussed the habits and thoughts of the rich—for instance, their showing off of their wealth—as if they were a primitive tribe. He introduced ethical, psychological, biological, and anthropological material new to economic studies. He visualized an economic community organized under a technical elite who would use their mastery of the machine for the good of society. Veblen's ideas seemed odd in the early 1900s, but his influence grew steadily as events made it clear that neither American society nor its economic system was perfect.

PHILOSOPHY: PRAGMATISM

Although Darwinian ideas won acceptance in academic circles, the ways in which American scholars and intellectuals would choose to apply those ideas differed widely. Rather than use the theory of evolution to defend the economic system and laissez faire, some used it as a basis for questioning everything. Darwinism opened up new areas for exploration and speculation in philosophy, the social sciences, and education. Traditional findings and interpretations underwent much revision. Most important, the development of pragmatic philosophy, which emphasized ideas as tools for solving practical problems, gave social thinkers confidence in their attack on the evils of industrial and urban society.

Before the Civil War, the standard philosophy taught in the more liberal colleges was Scottish or "common-sense" realism. It assumed that individuals possessed a natural faculty—common sense—that enabled them to arrive at the truth. In much the same way that Sir Isaac Newton had formulated the natural laws of the universe, it was possible for others to formulate the natural laws of politics, economics, and ethics.

Toward the end of the century, a new school of philosophy appeared: the pragmatists. They rejected the notion of an ideal or eternally fixed system in an evolving society and chose to evaluate ideas and theories in terms of their practical results. William James and John Dewey extended pragmatic thinking into a philosophy of action that would have a profound effect on social and educational reformers.

In rejecting absolute truths, William James (1842–1910) argued for free will and the ability of individuals and societies to arrive at their own truths. The only way to examine those truths was to test them in the real world and see how they worked. Pragmatism, he wrote, prefers to see theories as instruments rather than as answers to problems. As a philosopher and psychologist at Harvard, James developed his case against the "awfully monotonous" Spencerian universe, wrote a brilliant exposition on the active role of the mind that helped establish

psychology as an academic discipline, and preached his views on pragmatism.

Like James, John Dewey (1859–1952) argued the importance of practice rather than theory; he looked on philosophy as providing an agenda for action. Like Ward, George, and other dissenters, Dewey became an early critic of laissez faire and Social Darwinism in politics and business. He applied his ideas to education, which he felt must be related to the rest of life and made into a tool for social reform. Dewey saw the school as an institution through which the child would prepare for citizenship in modern society by learning to criticize the customs and beliefs of that society. The child would acquire this knowledge not by absorbing the teacher's words or a specific body of information, but by developing a scientific approach to solving problems. Dewey wanted students to participate directly in the issues or situations that concerned them, to learn by doing. At the same time, he felt strongly that the school should help build the child's character and teach him or her to be a good citizen.

EDUCATION

Once farm families and the society of small towns had shaped the character of American youth and taught them how to survive. Now this task fell more and more to educators. Public schools, colleges, and universities experienced a phenomenal growth after the Civil War, the result of urbanization and increased support. That the average American received only about five years of schooling at the turn of the century suggests how recent the commitment to public education has been. But illiteracy declined from 17 percent of the population in 1880 to 7.7 percent in 1910. And the educational system was undergoing significant changes not

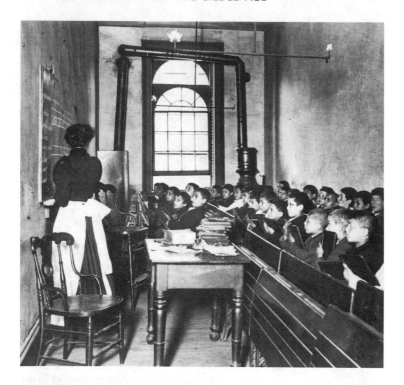

Contrasting classroom scenes at the turn of the century: (top) immigrant children in a public school in New York City, and (bottom) a private school for boys in New England. (Top photograph by Jacob A. Riis, the Jacob A. Riis Collection, Museum of the City of New York; bottom photograph by Charles Currier, Library of Congress)

only in the number of students, but in curriculum and methods of instruction. Along with the increase in public libraries and the immense popularity of public lectures, the expanding school system reflected a growing hunger for education.

Public Education

By 1865 about 50 million acres of the public domain had been set aside for the support of public schools and colleges. With the end of the Civil War, the drive for a nationally supported system of public education became stronger. Impressive advances could be seen after 1865 in the lengthening of the school term, the higher dollar expenditure per pupil, the declining illiteracy rate, and the compulsory-school-attendance laws. The old prewar academy that once monopolized American secondary education gave way after 1870 to the public high school. A broadened curriculum included history and literature as well as vocational and commercial courses designed to prepare students for work. Between 1870 and 1910, the number of public high schools grew from 500 to more than 10,000. A high-school education had begun to be the normal expectation of great numbers of young Americans, especially white youths in towns and cities.

After the Emancipation Proclamation, education acquired almost a religious meaning for the ex-slave. Not only did northern missionary societies and the Freedmen's Bureau assist them in their quest for knowledge, but blacks themselves organized educational associations, built schools, and hired teachers. But the educational gains made during Radical Reconstruction were undermined in the New South. Where schools continued to be provided for blacks, vocational training suitable to their low economic position dominated the curriculum. Northern philanthropists, many of whom

shared prevailing racist attitudes, funneled their contributions to vocationally oriented black colleges. The best known of these institutions was at Tuskegee, Alabama, and its principal, Booker T. Washington, achieved a national reputation by advising his people to accommodate to the racial caste system. He believed that for an indeterminate future the southern black majority would be confined to agricultural, domestic, or menial work. The best way to assure their welfare and the tolerance of the master caste, he reasoned, was to train them in useful pursuits.

Public schools for blacks in the South floundered. By 1910, despite the legal mandate for separate but equal schools, in most of the South twice as much was being spent on each white student as on each black student; the minimum salary for white teachers was nearly twice the maximum salary for black teachers. In the North, most cities had found a dual educational system too expensive and had abolished segregated schools. But the belief persisted that black children were less capable intellectually than white children. As a result, few blacks reached high school and still fewer got to college.

Higher Education

Since 1860, American colleges and universities had increased in numbers and enrollments and had grown larger and more bureaucratized in administration. At the same time, they improved steadily in quality. Public and private donations helped finance the expansion. Within a decade of the Morrill Act of 1862, Wisconsin, Minnesota, California, Texas, Massachusetts, and New York had established land-grant colleges, many of them coeducational. Private money was responsible for other colleges and universities. Ezra Cornell, who made a fortune from the electric telegraph, founded Cornell, which opened in 1868. Vanderbilt University (1873) and Stanford (1891) were the beneficiaries of two railroad millionaires, and the University of Chicago (1891) received $34 million from the oil magnate John D. Rockefeller.

Prewar colleges had confined themselves largely to traditional subjects—the classics, mathematics, and theology. The postwar institutions responded to the demand for professional, business, and technical education. The prestige of science had risen so high that such practical additions to the curriculum had to be accepted. By the end of the century, a number of American university scientists had won international reputations, and the number of schools of medicine, law, business, and other specialities had increased substantially.

Under the direction of Charles W. Eliot, president of Harvard, a new kind of university emerged. Undergraduates elected courses from an expanded curriculum, instead of being limited to required courses. Graduate schools grew, and faculties were assembled. Not all the changes in university and college life were intellectual or administrative. The introduction of baseball, football, and other organized sports aroused an almost fanatical concern with school rivalries. By the 1890s, intercollegiate football had become a spectacle attended by crowds of 30,000 or 40,000 and critics were protesting its professional emphasis.

Although there was much evidence to the contrary, many people continued to doubt women's intellectual or physical capacity to profit from college education. The founding of Vassar College at Poughkeepsie, New York, in 1861 did much to dispel such antiquated ideas. The course of study at Vassar became as demanding as that of any men's college of the day, and Vassar graduates quickly distinguished themselves among scholars, in the professions, and in social reform. By 1880, most of the important midwestern universities admitted women. Smith, Bryn Mawr, and Wellesley—founded shortly after Vassar—and other women's colleges offered professional training. The number of women enrolled as undergraduates rose from about 8000 in 1869 to more than 20,000 in 1894, and soared in the twentieth century. But for the graduates of the women's colleges, improvements in educational opportunities were not translated into improvements in economic opportunities. They were expected not to aspire to careers but rather to find economic salvation in a well-chosen husband and cultural satisfaction in women's clubs and in the romantic novels that dominated the best-seller lists.

LITERATURE IN THE GILDED AGE

The best-informed postwar critics remarked on the poor quality of American literature. Romance, sentimentality, and tales of success reflected the values, tastes, and stereotypes of middle-class readers. Neither the world depicted in such literature nor the characters themselves suggested that American society was being transformed.

Already partly visible by the 1870s, however, was a surge of fresh talent. Young new writers, many of them influenced by industrialism, Darwinian ideas, and pragmatism, explored subjects largely excluded from polite literature: slums, crime, class conflict, violence, divorce, racism, political corruption, drunkenness, adultery. To be sure, the dominant romantic mood had not disappeared even by the end of the century. But a new realism had given fresh life to literature, making the final break with the "genteel tradition" easier.

Mark Twain

In many respects, Mark Twain (1835–1910)—the pen name of Samuel L. Clemens—was the most revealing figure in postwar American literature, the one who best combined the virtues and defects of the society he analyzed. Born in Hannibal, Missouri, he had been a reporter, river pilot, and popular lecturer before his first literary success. Twain wrote about everything from jumping frogs to Andrew Carnegie, but his best works, *The Adventures of Tom Sawyer* (1876), *Life on the Mississippi* (1883), and *The Adventures of Huckleberry Finn* (1884), all derive from his river-boat days. It was his loyalty to the simple America of his boyhood that partly accounts for his rage over the betrayal of democratic ideals in the Gilded Age. "In my youth," wrote Twain, "there was nothing resembling a worship of money or of its possessor, in our region." It took people of the Jay Gould variety, he said, "to make a God of money and the man." And yet Twain enjoyed striking it rich as much as anyone, speculated recklessly, and wrote always with an eye on his large audience.

In his own way, Mark Twain was a moralist who looked upon humanity with exasperation because of its cruelty, credulity, and pigheadedness, and with compassion because it was not to blame. *Huckleberry Finn* remains an assault on social hypocrisy, false respectability, and the Gospel of Success. In renouncing civilization, Huck remains true to his natural goodness, yet without denying human depravity or his kinship with the wicked.

Realists and Naturalists

William Dean Howells (1837–1920), a friend of Twain, became the leader of the

Mark Twain. (Library of Congress)

postwar school of realists. *Realism*, as Howells used the term, simply meant "the truthful treatment of commonplace material." The romanticism of the popular literature of his day was immoral, in Howell's opinion, because it corrupted American taste and falsified life. He wanted fiction of "fidelity, not merely to the possible, but to the probable and ordinary course of man's experience." Let the novelist, he said through one of his fictional characters, paint "life as it is, and human feelings in their true proportion and relation." His best-known novels are *The Rise of Silas Lapham* (1885), the story of a self-made businessman, and *A Hazard of New Fortunes* (1890), which reflected his New York experience—the mindless struggle for wealth, the paradox of Fifth Avenue luxury and East Side squalor, the degradation of the republican dream.

Because he visited his native land so seldom, and because so many of his novels and short stories have a European setting, many critics put Henry James (1843–1916) outside the main current of American literature. Actually, his international plots deal almost exclusively with Americans, and from his vantage point he saw much about the American character that escaped writers who remained too close to home. James liked to place his Americans in what he called morally interesting situations. He subjected his traveling businessman (*The American*, 1877), his sensitive and intellectually curious heiresses (*The Portrait of a Lady*, 1881), his artist heroes, hungry for culture (*Roderick Hudson*, 1876), to moral tests. America remained for him a land of innocence and promise; Europe was beautiful but decadent. A superb technician and psychologist, James was also a social historian who faithfully recorded the moral gaps and strains he detected in upper-class society.

As a result of the realists' efforts, the young writers who came of age in the last two decades of the century could experiment even more boldly than their predecessors with unvarnished truth. Although it no longer took courage to expose a society committed to railroads, stockyards, real estate, and Wall Street, the new literary school went much further than the realists in uncovering the seamy and brutal aspects of American life. Naturalism, as the new movement was called, was inspired by French novelists like Emile Zola, who believed that literature should be governed by the same scientific laws that guided the physiologist. Human fate was determined by heredity and environment, by inner drives and external circumstances over which people had no control. Theoretically, the naturalist writer put down what he or she saw, no matter how disgusting or shocking it might be.

In America, naturalists such as Stephen Crane (1871–1900) and Frank Norris (1870–1902) never matched the frankness of the French school. But they dealt with themes from which even Howells flinched. In *Maggie: A Girl of the Streets* (1893) Crane wrote of the seduction and suicide of a New York slum girl; in *The Red Badge of Courage* (1895) he reproduced the animal fear of a young Civil War recruit under fire and his psychological recovery. In all his tales and sketches of derelicts and soldiers, of frightened, abandoned people, Crane suggests that human beings must confront nature without help from the supernatural.

Norris, a less able writer than Crane and more given to melodrama, disliked Howells's realism because it smelled so much of the ordinary, "the tragedy of the broken tea cup." Norris liked huge supermen clashing with titanic natural forces. Many of his books suffer from violence and sensationalism, but in *McTeague* (1899), the story of a man's reversion to brutishness, he displayed a power new in American fiction. In his best-known novel, *The Octopus* (1901), Norris depicted an epic struggle between California wheat growers and the railroad. The apparent radicalism of this book was considerably diluted by Norris's message that wheat and the railroad represented natural forces, each governed by the law of supply and demand.

In the works of Jack London (1876–1916), many of Norris's themes are repeated, especially the tendency to exalt the brutal while condemning the brutality of the social order. Born in 1876 and thrown on his own resources at an early age in the waterfront environment of Oakland, California, London became a hobo and a seaman, among other things, before settling down to write. While preaching the doctrine of the awful power of the forces of nature, London embraced the hopeful teachings of socialism. He never reconciled these ideas, but his work expressed one or the other well enough to make him one of the most widely read writers of his time. London's most interesting books are his autobiographical novel *Martin Eden* (1909) and *The Iron Heel* (1907), which concerns a fight to the death between the exploited classes and an oligarchy.

The writings of Theodore Dreiser (1871–1945) reflect a naturalism even more uncompromising than that of Crane, Norris, or London. But in Dreiser, the replacement of the good and the bad by the strong and the weak was accompanied by a deeper feeling for character and a profound, almost maternal tenderness. His first novel, *Sister Carrie* (1900), tells of a girl who comes to Chicago from a small western town and succumbs to a vulgar but generous salesman and then to a restaurant manager. The best chapters of the book trace the gradual downward drift of her second seducer, Hurstwood, who moves toward ruin while Carrie becomes a successful actress.

The Romantics

Although realists and naturalists tried to deal honestly with life and gained a following among liberals who wanted to improve social and economic conditions, they failed to outsell the sentimental school among the reading public. With love stories, cloak-and-dagger romances, and tales of exotic lands, the sentimentalists helped their middle-class audience, the largest in the world, avoid the raw society around them.

During the last three decades of the nineteenth century, the romanticists and the realists engaged in a kind of journalistic warfare. The realists, said their critics, "taught pessimism in every line of their work. They taught that marriage is a failure, that home is a brothel, that courtship is lewd, that society is an aggregation of animals." The romanticists, replied the realists, supplied flimsy illusions to adults who evaded the issues of the day. In practice, however, both schools made concessions to popular taste and interests. Since romantic fiction outsold realistic novels four to one, it is hardly surprising that the realists and naturalists injected a little exotic color, mysticism, and pseudoscientific information into their work. At the same time, the romantics could not ignore the social turmoil that soon involved so many of their women readers in social reform. By 1900 romantics and realists were appearing together in the pages of the *Saturday Evening Post* and the *Ladies' Home Journal*—and it was not always easy to distinguish one from the other.

SUGGESTED READINGS

R. Hofstadter, *Social Darwinism in American Thought* (1955). E. Goldman, *Rendezvous with Destiny: A History of Modern American Reform* (1952). J.L. Thomas, *Alternative America: Henry George, Edward Bellamy, Henry Demarest Lloyd, and the Adversary Tradition* (1983). B. Kuklick, *The Rise of American Philosophy: Cambridge, Massachusetts, 1860–1930* (1977). L.A. Cremin, *The Transformation of the School: Progressivism in American Education* (1961). L.R. Veysey, *The Emergence of the American University* (1965). A. Kazin, *On Native Grounds* (1942).

SUMMARY

If economic life during the Gilded Age was dominated by laissez faire and the Gospel of Success, cultural life was dominated by Social Darwinism and the Gospel of Progress.

Darwin's Origin of Species, *published in 1859, introduced the ideas of evolution and the survival of the fittest into biology. These concepts were soon popularized and translated into social terms. The Social Darwinism proposed by the English philosopher Herbert Spencer became another support for the Gospel of Success and brought a new creed—the Gospel of Progress. All the changes of industrialization and urbanization were not only good, they were all for the better.*

Some thinkers—Lester Ward, Henry George, and Edward Bellamy—challenged these ideas and rejected the fatalism of the Social Darwinists. In the universities, younger social scientists began to break out of the conservative strait jacket and to question systems such as laissez faire. Among these rebels was Thorstein Veblen, whose Theory of the Leisure Class *(1899) became one of the most influential works of social criticism of his time.*

Darwinism also opened up new ways of thinking in philosophy, law, education, and history. Pragmatism aimed to make philosophy useful by looking at ideas as tools for solving practical problems. Pragmatists such as William James and John Dewey had great influence on the new discipline of psychology and the older one of education.

All these changing ideas found wider and wider audiences as the American people became more educated and more literate. Public schools, colleges, and universities grew rapidly in number and size after the Civil War as government made a genuine commitment to education for all. The public school system for elementary and secondary education, though always remaining under local control, became nationwide, especially in the cities. Compulsory-school-attendance laws were passed, and illiteracy declined rapidly. A separate system of black education began to develop in the South, but with an emphasis on technical and vocational training.

Higher education also expanded and changed. Many new colleges were established, and under Charles W. Eliot, Harvard pioneered a new kind of university. Students chose courses from an expanded curriculum, major scholars were recruited to teach at graduate schools, and practical training was required for certification in the professions.

Women gained access to higher education and to professional training. By 1880 most major midwestern state universities admitted women. Vassar College for women had been founded in 1861; Smith, Bryn Mawr, and Wellesley were established soon afterward. The number of women enrolled as undergraduates rose from 8000 in 1869 to 20,000 by 1894. But education for women still did not mean independence and equal opportunity. It would not be until well into the twentieth century that women would join the labor force on a permanent, though still unequal, basis.

American literature between 1860 and 1900 was dominated by romanticism and sentimentality, and designed to be read mainly by middle- and upper-class women who had too much leisure time. But by 1876 a new literature of realism that dealt with the evils and problems of society was surfacing. The works written in this tradition would establish American literature as a separate, mature cultural expression.

19

The American Empire

For more than 500 years before the space age, the history of Europeans was the history of expansion overseas. The European discovery of America was a single chapter—the prologue, really—for more than three centuries of rivalry among European nations for dominance in the New World, and in Africa and Asia as well. The wealth and productivity created by the Industrial Revolution stimulated the competition for world markets. England, France, Belgium, Holland, and Russia, along with Bismarck's newly unified Germany and the newly westernized Japan, sought a share of the spoils. What they wanted were the same areas the United States would come to look upon with growing interest: Latin America, the islands of the Pacific, and China.

The 1890s had been a difficult decade in the United States: there were economic depression, labor conflict, divisive politics, "new" immigrants, racial violence, corporate abuses. Most Americans, confident about the destiny of their nation, still needed some reassurance, particularly with the closing of the frontier, that the power, the vigor, the pioneering character of the society remained intact. At the same time, the rapid transformation of the economy

had a great impact on foreign relations. With the United States now producing large quantities of manufactured goods, more than the domestic economy could absorb at profitable prices, the need to find foreign markets became urgent. With American investments abroad soaring between 1900 and 1914—from $455 million to $2.5 billion—there was also the need to protect those investments. With American manufacturers dependent on raw materials from abroad, it became imperative to try to control the sources of those supplies. Concern mounted as European competitors, motivated by the same needs, became more and more active overseas.

Confident of the superiority of its institutions and values, the United States was ready by the 1890s to shoulder the "expansionist destiny" of the Anglo-Saxon race, to join "the Christian nations," as an American missionary said, who "are subduing the world, in order to make mankind free." Having established the "fittest" of all political systems, why not bestow the blessings of American civilization on the less fortunate? In the minds of policy makers and the American public, economic and humanitarian considerations reinforced *each other. The idea that the United States should plant its institutions and values in the "waste places of the world" and at the* *same time exploit their economic potential helped shape American policy in the Caribbean, Mexico, Latin America, and Asia.*

THE NEW EXPANSIONISM

Expansion was hardly a new idea in the United States in the 1890s. Even before the Revolution, American colonists had resisted England's policy of restricting settlement to an area east of the Appalachians. Once independent, the United States rapidly spread westward across the continent. And Mexico to the south and Canada to the north were always part of expansionist plans.

Mexico and Alaska

While the United States was involved in the Civil War, Napoleon III of France attempted to establish a Catholic monarchy in Mexico. He installed his puppet, Maximilian of Austria, on a Mexican throne and backed him with the French military. In 1866 Secretary of State Seward told France that its presence in Mexico was unacceptable, and 50,000 American troops were sent to the Rio Grande. That was enough, along with new problems in Europe, to persuade France to withdraw. Although Maximilian tried to reign without the French, he was quickly seized, court-martialed, and executed by Mexican nationalists. In his communications with France, Seward never mentioned the Monroe Doctrine. But it had become apparent that the United States now had the strength to enforce its will in the Western Hemisphere.

   While avoiding armed conflict with foreign enemies, Andrew Johnson's administration carried out successful negotiations with foreign friends. Among these was Russia, one of the few European states that had not unofficially sided with the Confeder-

ates. Russia hoped to build up the United States as a counterweight to Britain, and in March 1867 the Russian minister in Washington offered to unload distant and costly Alaska. Secretary Seward, an expansionist, jumped at the chance and negotiated a purchase treaty. Despite opposition to what the press soon called Seward's Folly, the opportunity to expand America's frontier was enough to win congressional approval. The purchase price was $7.2 million. On completing the negotiations with Russia, Seward expressed the hope that Alaska would form the northern arm of a giant pincer movement that would bring Canada into the American fold. "I know that Nature," he said, "designs that this whole continent, not merely these thiry-six states, shall be sooner or later, within the magic circle of the American Union."

THE PACIFIC: TRADE AND EMPIRE

American ambitions did not end with North America or at the water's edge. The construction of the transcontinental railroads after the Civil War, along with rapid industrialization, sharpened interest in the economic possibilities of the Far East. In the 1840s and 1850s the United States had acquired most-favored-nation treaty rights in China. These rights gave American traders terms equal to those granted any other country. After Commodore Matthew Perry had forcibly opened Japan in 1854, the American consul negotiated a treaty of friendship by which he became the chief adviser on international relations to the Japanese gov-

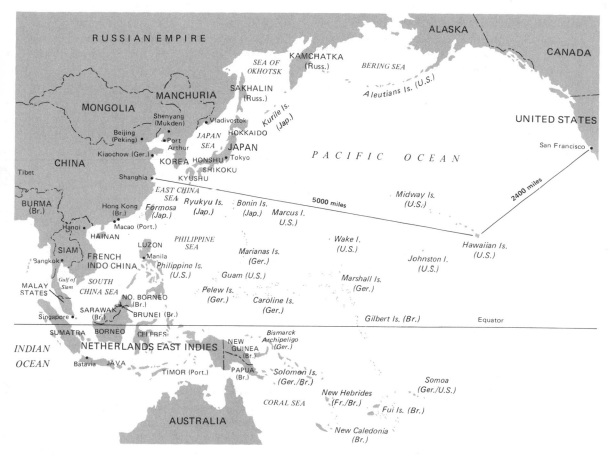

Imperialism in Asia

ernment. Seeking coaling stations for American ships, the United States obtained the use of an excellent harbor, Pago Pago, in Samoa in the southern Pacific in 1878; the port and surrounding territory were acquired outright in the division of Samoa with Germany in 1899.

Hawaii

The Hawaiian Islands, closer than Samoa and a natural strategic outpost of the North American continent, had long been known to American traders. As early as 1820, Yankee missionaries had settled in the islands; by 1860, many American citizens owned

permanent homes there, and a growing local faction sought annexation. Meanwhile, sugar cane had replaced whaling as Hawaii's main industry, and problems of land tenure and labor supply were added to the issues standing between the government and outside capitalists.

Until 1875, American sugar producers in the Louisiana area had succeeded in keeping Hawaiian sugar out of United States ports. That year, however, a reciprocity treaty between the United States and the islands (negotiated under threats by Hawaiian growers to look to Britain for markets and political support) admitted Hawaiian sugar into the United States and American commodities into Hawaii, both duty-free. At the same time, the islands pledged not to give any territory to foreign governments or to extend to them the commercial privileges won by the United States. Sugar growing boomed under the treaty, and with it the rest of the business community. Native Hawaiians, however, saw more and more of their land controlled by white planters, and themselves submerged by a flood of Chinese workers.

When the United States negotiated a new reciprocity agreement in 1887, it gained exclusive use of Pearl Harbor as a coaling station and repair base for naval vessels. The same year, Hawaiian-born white businessmen forced King Kalakaua to accept a new framework of government—the Bayonet Constitution, Hawaiians called it—giving themselves control of the government and extending the franchise to white foreigners. Property qualifications, on the other hand, disfranchised most native citizens.

Hawaii was becoming more dependent on the United States. In 1890, sugar for the American mainland made up 99 percent of Hawaiian exports. At the same time, Hawaiians were growing more and more angry about the new constitution. Discontent spread after 1891, when King Kalakaua died and was succeeded by his sister, Queen Liliuokalani, a firm opponent of white rule. By 1893, "Queen Lil's" disregard of constitutional restraints and her efforts to throw off the constitution altogether had driven white businessmen into a second rebellion. They had the support of the American minister to Hawaii, John L. Stevens, who helped protect them with American troops landed from a cruiser. Stevens promptly recognized the provisional government set up by the rebels, who lost no time in sending a commission to Washington to negotiate a treaty of annexation. The retiring President Harrison favored the treaty and sent it to the

Senate, where it met Democratic opposition. It was still under discussion when Grover Cleveland was inaugurated. Suspicious of Stevens's activities in Hawaii, Cleveland recalled the treaty and sent a special commissioner to the islands to investigate. His report charged that Stevens, by his abuse of the authority of the United States, had done a great wrong to a "feeble but independent State." Cleveland tried to restore Queen Lil under a constitutional regime, but the provisional government would not let go. In 1894 it wrote still another constitution, proclaimed the Republic of Hawaii, and confirmed Sanford B. Dole as its first president.

Realizing he would have to use force to unseat the new government, Cleveland decided to recognize it instead. But he refused its urgent requests for annexation. Feelings changed during the Spanish-American War, when Hawaii's strategic value became more evident. In July 1898, Congress approved by joint resolution a new treaty making Hawaii "a part of the territory of the United States." In August 1959, about seven months after Alaska had become the forty-ninth state, Hawaii became the fiftieth.

DIPLOMACY AND POWER

After the Civil War, Americans were so intent on developing domestic resources and home markets that the United States merchant marine was almost allowed to disappear. For nearly a century it had been one of the largest in the world. The navy, once as strong as the merchant marine, had shrunk by the 1880s to a small number of wooden sailing ships worse than useless in an age of steel and stream. The United States, especially in competition with a naval power such as Great Britain, hardly appeared ready to establish and maintain its influence anywhere abroad.

The need for the United States to assert itself more aggressively in its foreign relations won more support in the 1880s and 1890s. A group of spokesmen emerged to provide the necessary direction and momentum. Two were particularly important: James G. Blaine, secretary of state in 1881 under Garfield and again from 1889 to 1892 under Harrison, and Captain (later Admiral) Alfred T. Mahan, the gifted propagandist who became the model for a later generation of imperialists. Both believed in an aggressive and spirited diplomacy. Blaine focused his energies on Latin America, Mahan concerned himself with making certain the United States had the power to carry out an aggressive diplomacy.

Latin America

Latin America still had strong cultural ties with Spain and Portugal and commercial ties with Britain. In the 1870s Germany began to seek Latin American outlets for its goods and capital. To deflect Latin American trade and development toward the United States, Blaine issued invitations to a Pan-American Conference in 1889. Delegates from eighteen nations met in Washington and formed the Pan-American Union, but accomplished little else.

Although Latin Americans bought largely from Europeans, they sold mainly to the United States, and mainly items that were duty-free. When the Latin American delegates to the 1889 conference failed to grant tariff concessions to United States exporters, Blaine threatened to respond with tariffs on Latin American goods. The so-called reciprocity provision of the McKinley Tariff in 1890, which said the United States would respond to favorable treatment, was Blaine's weapon. But his tactics did not

work very well. Latin Americans remained hostile and uncooperative.

Sea Power and Trade

As secretary of state, Blaine also advocated a powerful American navy, and in 1881 Congress set up a Naval Advisory Board to agitate for larger appropriations. Though Blaine was soon out of office, this first step led to others, among them the establishment of the Naval War College at Newport, Rhode Island, in 1884. Just before he was made president of the college in 1886, Captain Mahan gave the lectures that eventually became the heart of his famous series of books on sea power in history. Britain, he said, had grown great on sea power. The United States should profit from Britain's example not simply by rebuilding its merchant marine and its navy, but by adding colonies and naval bases throughout the world. In particular the United States must have naval bases in the Caribbean, to protect a potential canal across the Isthmus of Panama, and in the Pacific, not only to guard American trade but to take part in the coming struggle between Western and Oriental civilizations. Between 1883 and 1890, Congress authorized the building of nine cruisers. Construction began on the first modern American battleship, the *Maine.* After additional pressure from naval expansionists, Congress authorized construction of so many battleships, cruisers, gunboats, and torpedo boats that by 1898 only Britain and France outranked the United States as a naval power.

Toward the end of the century the position of the United States in world trade improved greatly, as Blaine had hoped. Valued at $462 million in 1870, American imports almost doubled in the next thirty years, reaching $850 million in 1900. In the same period, American exports almost tri-

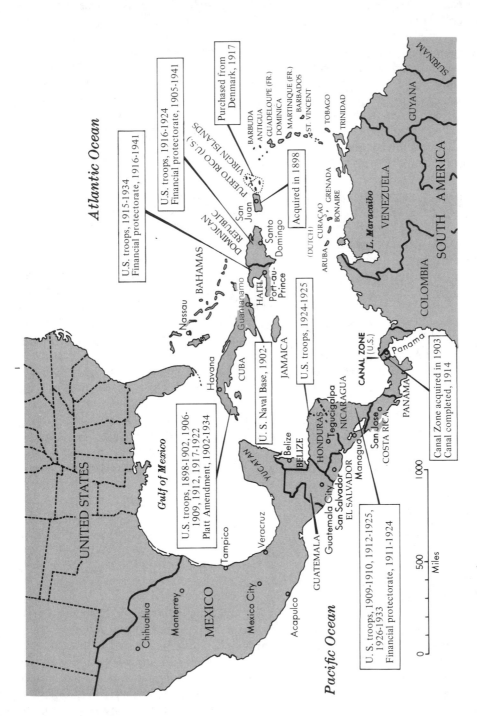

Imperialism in Latin America

UNITED STATES

Gulf of Mexico

Chihuahua
Monterrey
MEXICO
Mexico City
Acapulco

Tampico
Veracruz

Atlantic Ocean

Pacific Ocean

U.S. troops, 1898–1902, 1906–1909, 1912, 1917–1922
Platt Amendment, 1902–1934

U. S. Naval Base, 1902–

U.S. troops, 1924–1925

U.S. troops, 1909–1910, 1912–1925, 1926–1933
Financial protectorate, 1911–1924

Canal Zone acquired in 1903
Canal completed, 1914

U.S. troops, 1915–1934
Financial protectorate, 1916–1941

U.S. troops, 1916–1924
Financial protectorate, 1905–1941

Purchased from Denmark, 1917

Acquired in 1898

BAHAMAS
Nassau

CUBA
Havana

VIRGIN ISLANDS (U.S.)
PUERTO RICO (U.S.)
San Juan

DOMINICAN REPUBLIC
Santo Domingo

HAITI
Port-au-Prince

Guantánamo

JAMAICA

YUCATAN
Belize
BELIZE
GUATEMALA
Guatemala City
San Salvador
EL SALVADOR
HONDURAS
Tegucigalpa
NICARAGUA
Managua
San José
COSTA RICA

CANAL ZONE (U.S.)
Panama
PANAMA

BARBUDA
ANTIGUA
GUADELOUPE (FR.)
DOMINICA
MARTINIQUE (FR.)
ST. VINCENT
BARBADOS
GRENADA
TOBAGO
TRINIDAD

(DUTCH)
ARUBA
CURAÇAO
BONAIRE

L. Maracaibo

VENEZUELA

COLOMBIA

SOUTH AMERICA

GUYANA

SURINAM

0   500   1000
        Miles

pled, rising from $530 million to approximately $1.4 billion. The Panic of 1893, which shrank markets at home, pushed the quest for markets abroad.

Hemispheric Diplomacy

While the United States was using its resources to promote the growth of foreign trade and world power, a series of diplomatic incidents in the Western Hemisphere triggered talk of war and revived the Monroe Doctrine.

The most serious incident involved disputed territory between British Guiana and neighboring Venezuela, where gold was discovered in the 1880s. The United States offered to mediate the dispute, but Britain rejected the idea. In July 1895, Richard Olney, Cleveland's secretary of state, sent a virtual ultimatum to Lord Salisbury, the British foreign minister. He urged him to agree to arbitration and charged that Great Britain had violated the Monroe Doctrine by interfering in hemispheric affairs. "Today," said Olney, "the United States is practically sovereign on this continent, and its fiat is law upon the subjects to which it confines its interposition."

Salisbury rejected Olney's offer and reminded the United States that the Monroe Doctrine was not recognized in international law and did not apply to boundary disputes. Cleveland made the Olney-Salisbury correspondence public and asked Congress for funds to finance a commission to determine the actual boundary between British Guiana and Venezuela. He pledged at the same time that the United States would "resist by every means in its power as a willful aggression upon its rights and interests" any efforts by Great Britain to take territory that the United States, after investigation, found to be Venezuela's.

Although Congress cheered Cleveland's message, the peace parties eventually won out in the United States and Britain. Cleveland's proposal for a boundary commission gave Americans time to simmer down, since nothing could be done until such a commission reported. Britain, meanwhile, was growing more nervous over German rivalry, and therefore more interested in American friendship. In February 1897, at America's suggestion, Britain and Venezuela negotiated a treaty whereby the boundary dispute was turned over to international arbitration. In 1899 a final settlement was made.

THE SPANISH-AMERICAN WAR

To secure American markets and sources of raw materials, to protect the national interest, and to increase the influence of the United States in the world community had become principal objectives of American policy makers by the 1890s. Such objectives were also consistent with the American mission of spreading American institutions and ways of thinking. The ways in which strong diplomacy, commercial imperialism, and missionary idealism could be combined were best exemplified in the growing American concern over Spanish-held Cuba—a concern that ended in a war and in the debut of the United States as a world imperial power.

The Cuban Crisis

When the Cubans rebelled against the Spanish in 1868, Americans had not cared much. The rebellion dragged on for ten years before Spain finally agreed to undertake serious reforms. The Cubans made two major demands: emancipation of the slaves on the island and self-government for the island's inhabitants. Spain took another ten years to free the slaves, and postponed granting self-government indefinitely. In the meantime, it saddled the ruined Cuban economy with all the costs of the rebellion.

After the emancipation of the slaves, large amounts of European and American capital were invested in Cuba. Modern business practices were introduced, especially in the production of cane sugar. The United States gradually became Cuba's principal market and source of capital. After the removal of the American duty on Cuban sugar in 1884, production of that export reached new highs and almost all of it went to the United States. Events then suddenly worked against Cuban prosperity. Europe's production of beet sugar became so great that the world price of sugar fell. The worldwide depression of the 1890s further weakened prices. Finally, the Wilson-Gorman Tariff of 1894 restored a 40-percent duty on raw sugar. The acute economic distress that followed, combined with the continuing political trouble, brought another revolt against Spanish rule in 1895. American interests were of course threatened.

Spain sent its best general and 200,000 men to suppress the uprising. But the Spaniards could not cope with the rebel leaders and their guerrilla followers, who had taken to the hills. The rebels destroyed property in order to exhaust the government and force the withdrawal of the troops. Much American property was also deliberately destroyed in an effort to push the United States to intervene. During all this time a *junta*, or council, of Cuban exiles in New York kept pressing for American intervention and Cuban independence. Joseph Pulitzer of the *New York World* and William Randolph Hearst of the *New York Journal* engaged in a circulation battle, each trying to outdo the other in printing sensational accounts of Spanish atrocities. Mahan, Theodore Roosevelt, Senator Henry Cabot Lodge, and other expansionists also whipped up the war spirit. Unlike the American public, however, which focused on the Cuban struggle for liberty, the expansionists sensed there were higher stakes involved. The Spanish Philippines were a potential stronghold of American power in the Far East and a gateway to the China trade.

Presidents Cleveland and McKinley refused to be stampeded into war. Early in 1898, however, pressure mounted for American intervention. On February 15, the visiting American battleship *Maine* apparently hit a mine in Havana harbor, which destroyed the ship and killed 2 officers and 258 of the crew. Although an official inquiry left the causes of the explosion uncertain, Congress promptly granted the president's request for $50 million for national defense and Americans rallied under the slogan "Remember the *Maine*!" But many Americans still wanted peace. The business community believed that the economic revival that had followed the long depression would be endangered by war costs and war taxes. For a time, at least, it thought it could protect its investments in Cuban sugar plantations and iron mines without armed intervention. There was considerable doubt, moreover, about the ability of the Cuban rebels to set up a stable government in case of independence.

Even a great leader might have found it impossible to reduce the growing war fever of the American people. On March 27, 1898, President McKinley consulted with his cabinet and then made a series of demands on Spain. He called for an armistice on the island, during which the United States would act as a mediator between the contestants. But he also made it clear that Cuban independence would be the only satisfactory outcome. Spain was willing to make many concessions, but Premier Sagasta, fearing the end of his government and even the demise of the Spanish monarchy if Cuban independence were granted, refused to accept any armistice that the rebels did not ask for first. The pope agreed to suggest an armistice, however, saving Spain the humiliation of yielding to the United States, and Sagasta gratefully took the offer. The American minister in Madrid promptly cabled home Spain's consent to "immediate and unconditional suspension of hostilities."

But it was too late. The public, the press, the Protestant clergy, and expansionist politicians in both parties created an atmosphere in which negotiation seemed to mean giving in. On April 11, 1898, President McKinley, "in the name of humanity, in the name of civilization, in behalf of endangered American interests," sent a war message to Congress. He asked for authority to use military and naval force to end the hostilities in Cuba. On April 20, by a joint resolution, Congress declared Cuba "free and independent," demanded that Spain withdraw from the island, and authorized the president to use military force to assure compliance. Congress added to the resolution the Teller Amendment, which stated that the United States had no intention to annex Cuba and would "leave the government and control of the Island to its people." Within a week of the resolution, the United States and Spain formally declared themselves in a state of war.

Theodore Roosevelt and his Rough Riders on San Juan Hill in 1898. (Library of Congress)

The "Splendid Little War"

The war with Spain was almost too short for those who wanted to display American power, but the results were gratifying. In the Philippines, Commodore Dewey sailed into Manila Bay on April 30. The next day he blasted the antiquated Spanish fleet sitting there, and by July 25 about 11,000 American troops under General Wesley Merritt had landed. Supported by Filipino insurrectionists under Emilio Aguinaldo, whom Dewey had befriended and helped arm, Merritt took Manila on August 13. By then, the "splendid little war," as the American ambassador to Britain called it, had already ended in the West Indies. On April 29, a Spanish fleet under Admiral Cervera had sailed west from the Cape Verde Islands. A patrol fleet tried to find Cervera before he reached Cuba, where they decided he was headed. They did not locate him, however, until he was safely in Santiago harbor, where American ships bottled him up. A military expedition was now planned to capture Santiago and force Cervera out under the American fleet's waiting guns.

In June a poorly equipped expeditionary force of 17,000 men under General William R. Shafter reached the Cuban coast near Santiago. After a two-day battle, which saw Theodore Roosevelt lead the Rough Riders (the First Volunteer Cavalry Regiment) up San Juan Hill, the American attack petered out. Luckily for Shafter, the Spaniards were in even worse shape. On July 3 Cervera decided to escape. American firepower, however, destroyed his ships. On July 16 General Linares surrendered Santiago to the Americans, and on July 25 a second American expeditionary force made a triumphant march through Puerto Rico. The Spanish government had already begun to seek a peace treaty, and on August 12 hostilities were declared over. All told, the United States lost 5462 men in the four-month war, but only 379 in combat. The rest died from disease and other causes. Spain's losses in the fighting were much higher, and in addition it lost the last of a once great New World empire.

The Peace and the Philippines

Few Americans doubted the nobility of their mission in helping an oppressed native people achieve freedom. But there was far less agreement about what the United States should do with some of the spoils of the victory. Did the "liberation" of Cuba require the annexation of the Philippines? While American negotiators worked on the treaty, hunger for the Philippines kept growing. The fear that Germany would seize the islands no doubt fed American demands, as did economic and strategic considerations.

The final treaty, insuring the freedom of Cuba and granting the United States the Philippines (for a payment of $20 million), Puerto Rico, and Guam, was signed in Paris on December 10. In the debate on ratification in the Senate, the annexation of the Philippines became the principal issue. To acquire the Philippines and not admit the Filipinos to full citizenship, argued critics, violated a principle in which this nation had long believed—government by consent of the governed. But to admit Filipinos as citizens posed still other dangers. They would be entitled to vote, to send representatives to Congress, and to migrate to the United States, where they would become a source of cheap labor. (That specter helped to line up Samuel Gompers of the AFL with the anti-imperialists.) Finally, both southern and northern opponents of annexation agreed that annexation would make even worse an already critical race problem. The Anti-Imperialist League, organized in November 1898, grew rapidly as the administration's expansionist policies developed. The league's supporters included many of the leading thinkers and writers of the time, some of them horrified by the behavior of American occupation forces in the Philippines, some of them fearful that imperial expansion would involve the United States in an armaments race, foreign alliances, and wars of intervention.

On February 6, 1899, the Senate ratified the treaty fifty-seven to twenty-seven, only two votes above the required two-thirds majority. The decision might have gone the other way had it not been for the Filipinos themselves. On December 21, 1898, with the debate in the Senate at its peak, McKinley had ordered the War Department to extend the military occupation of Manila to the entire archipelago. This move promptly touched off armed Filipino resistance under Aguinaldo, who headed a group that had suffered imprisonment, exile, and death in its years of struggle for independence from Spain. When the Senate learned that American lives had been lost in the fighting, enough votes were generated for the treaty to squeak by. The commitment to liberate the Cubans now became a war to conquer the Filipinos. There was nothing splendid about this war. The Filipino rebels held off the Americans for three years in a conflict that cost more men and money than the war with Spain. The United States was forced to use the same brutal methods for which it had condemned the Spanish in Cuba.

In Cuba, meanwhile, General Leonard Wood ruled as military governor until May 20, 1902, when the Cubans were compelled to accept the so-called Platt Amendment. This amendment to an army appropriation bill limited Cuba's treaty-making powers, its right to borrow money, and other rights of sovereignty. Moreover, Cuba could not withhold lands wanted by the United States

for coaling or naval stations, or give territory to any other power. Finally, the amendment permitted the United States to intervene in Cuba "for the protection of life, property, and individual liberty." The United States required the incorporation of the Platt Amendment in any constitution drawn up by Cuba. It also demanded that Cuba make a permanent treaty with the United States that used the terms of the amendment. The Platt Amendment remained in force until 1934, when it and related treaties were canceled by agreement.

In the middle of public discussion of the new imperialism, the election of 1900 took place. Though not a supporter of the peace treaty, William Jennings Bryan, the Democratic candidate, had secured some Democratic votes for it in the Senate. He had done this to guard his party from charges of wanting the war renewed, and to carry the whole issue of overseas expansion into the campaign. McKinley won relection, and his victory was interpreted by many as a victory for the new policy. McKinley was assassinated a few months after his inauguration in 1901, and when Theodore Roosevelt became commander in chief, the imperialists expected further expansion.

In May 1901, the Supreme Court added its approval to that of the president and the people. In the so-called Insular cases, the Court held that the Constitution did not follow the flag, that the rights of United States citizens did not automatically belong to the people of the territories. By 1907, however, the Filipinos had gained the right to elect the lower house of their legislature, and in 1916 the Jones Act gave them virtual control over their domestic affairs. Some of this ground was lost during the 1920s. But in 1934 the Tydings-McDuffie Act provided for independence after ten years. The Filipinos agreed to the ten-year provision in 1936. After the islands were recovered from Japan during World War II, Filipinos achieved independence, as planned, on July 4, 1946.

POWER POLITICS

With the acquisitions of the Spanish-American War and with its industrial supremacy, the United States had become a major world power. It was a role that almost immediately demanded new commitments and entanglements. Other imperial powers were carving out spheres of influence in China. Japan was embarking on an imperial policy very much Western in inspiration. The dominant influence exercised by the United States in Cuba made its presence in the Caribbean and Central America more visible and its meddling more frequent. Expanding American interests in Latin America and the Far East also pointed up the need to construct a canal across Central America to make intercoastal shipping easier and the American navy more maneuverable. Whether by the Open Door policy in the Far East or by the Monroe Doctrine in the Western Hemisphere, the United States reserved to itself the right to intervene to preserve stability and counteract discrimination by rival powers. These were the principles that would guide twentieth-century foreign relations—principles that bridged the political parties and the occupants of the White House.

China and the Open Door

In the Far East, the United States faced a serious dilemma. The Western powers—France, Germany, Britain, and Russia—and Japan were staking out spheres of influence in the weak and still passive China. Partition of China might well ruin American hopes for further trade with that country. The problem was to find a way to gain and main-

tain equal trading rights without risking war and without becoming a party to further partition. In September 1899 McKinley's new secretary of state, John Hay, sent notes to the imperial powers inviting them to respect the principle of equal trade opportunity—an Open Door—and to impose no discriminatory duties within their spheres of influence. Although none of the powers would make such concessions, Hay refused to accept their vague rejections. He calmly announced on March 20, 1900, that all had given "final and definitive" consent to his request. Only Japan challenged his bluff.

Hardly were negotiations over the Open Door notes finished when a group of Chinese nationalists—Westerners called them Boxers—rose up against foreigners in their country. Before they were put down by an international force, to which the United States contributed 2500 men, they had killed hundreds of persons and destroyed much property. Only swift action by Britain and the United States prevented the other powers from retaliating by taking more Chinese territory.

Hay advised the imperial rivals that American policy was to work to preserve China's territorial and administrative integrity and to "safeguard for the world the principle of equal and impartial trade with all parts of the Chinese Empire." This announcement went further than the Open Door notes and had more effect. Eventually, the nations accepted a money indemnity from China rather than new grants of territory. Most important, though, the Open Door policy had laid the basis for greater American influence in the affairs of China and the rest of Asia.

Japan: The Russo-Japanese War

Theodore Roosevelt's preaching about the importance of what he called "soldierly virtues" frightened many people when he became president at the age of forty-three in September 1901. But his first major international venture did not come until his second term, and then he was a peacemaker. The Japanese had beaten the Russians in the Russo-Japanese War of 1904, and in the spring of 1905, temporarily exhausted by their efforts, they secretly asked the American president to mediate. Fearful of the growing unrest at home, which was to end in the Revolution of October 1905, the Russians were easily persuaded to agree. But Roosevelt would take no steps until Japan consented to respect the principles of the Open Door policy. When this happened, the president invited the Japanese and the Russians to meet at Portsmouth, New Hampshire, in August. Here, among other claims, the Japanese demanded a huge money indemnity to offset their war costs. When the Russians balked, Roosevelt warned the Japanese against pressing their demand. They accepted some small territorial grants instead, along with Russia's promise to leave Manchuria.

The Japanese people had counted on the Russian indemnity for tax relief and did not quickly forget America's role in cheating them of it. Meanwhile, Japan's emergence as a great power increased anxiety on the West Coast about the "yellow peril." In October 1906 the San Francisco Board of Education ordered that the ninety-three Japanese children in the city be segregated in a separate school. Only after bringing a great deal of pressure on local authorities did Roosevelt succeed in getting the action reversed. At the same time, he promised Californians that Japanese immigration would be curbed. In the Gentlemen's Agreement, a series of notes made up in 1907 and 1908, Japan promised to issue no more passports to workers seeking to emigrate to the United States.

Having pacified the Japanese, Roosevelt was anxious, as he wrote to a friend, "that they . . . realize that I am not afraid of them." In 1907, as a demonstration of strength, he decided to send the American fleet around the world on a practice cruise. Japan welcomed the visit of the fleet as a friendly gesture, and for a time Japanese-American relations improved. The Root-Takahira Agreement of November 1908 reflected the better feeling. An executive agreement, not a treaty, the terms bound only Roosevelt's administration and its counterpart in Japan. Both powers agreed to maintain the status quo in the Pacific area, to uphold the Open Door in China, and to support that country's "independence and integrity."

Roosevelt's Far Eastern policy was upset by his successor as president, William Howard Taft, and Taft's secretary of state, the corporation lawyer Philander C. Knox. They favored a policy of promoting American investment and trade abroad, a policy that became known as Dollar Diplomacy. With the full support of the State Department, Taft encouraged investments by American bankers in China and Manchuria, which included financing China's purchase of Manchurian railroads in which Russia and Japan were interested. This effort only aroused the suspicion of Russia and Japan, driving together the two nations Roosevelt had sought to keep apart.

The Panama Canal

Having become a world power with interests in the Pacific as well as the Caribbean, the United States began to look toward the construction of a canal to link these two great waters. Back in 1850, the United States and Britain had agreed in the Clayton-Bulwer Treaty that they would enjoy equal rights in any canal. Now, the United States pressed Britain to surrender its rights. At last, in 1901, following a new policy of keeping America as a friend, Britain gave in. The Hay-Pauncefote Treaty of that year gave the United States a free hand to build, control, and fortify an Isthmian canal. The United States promised to open the canal without discrimination to the commercial and fighting ships of all nations.

Two routes were possible for this canal—one through Panama in the Republic of Columbia, the other through Nicaragua. The United States decided to use the Panama route. By holding the alternative of a Nicaraguan canal over the heads of Colombia's negotiators, Secretary of State Hay was able to drive a hard bargain in a treaty approved by the United States Senate in March 1903. When the Colombian Senate rejected the treaty, a furious President Roosevelt encouraged Panamanian rebels to declare their independence from Colombia and ordered a warship to the Isthmus to intimidate Colombian forces. With the "revolution" a success, Washington promptly recognized the new Republic of Panama and negotiated a treaty that gave the United States the desired strip of territory for the canal zone for $10 million and $250,000 a year. Roosevelt's behavior created many enemies for the United States throughout Latin America. But the canal was completed, and on August 15, 1914, the first ocean-going steamship passed through it.

The Caribbean

The Panama Canal, by giving the United States a great new enterprise to protect, broadened American involvement in the Caribbean. The political and financial instability of the smaller republics in that region was an especially touchy problem. Al-

most all their public financing had been done in Europe. If any country failed to pay interest due on its bonds, its European creditor, eager for empire, might move in with the idea of staying indefinitely—as France did in Mexico in 1863. To avert this danger, Roosevelt set forth the Roosevelt Corollary to the Monroe Doctrine in a message to Congress on December 6, 1904: in the event of "flagrant cases of . . . wrongdoing or impotence" in Latin America that required outside intervention to set matters right, the United States, "however reluctantly," would undertake the necessary exercise of "international police power."

The first application of the Roosevelt Corollary came in 1905, when the Dominican Republic was unable to pay its debts. After an American show of force, the Dominican government had to invite the United States to step in. The Dominican foreign debt was then scaled down and transferred from European to American bankers. A percentage of Dominican customs collections was allocated to pay future interest and to reduce the principal. Cuba drew the attention of the Roosevelt administration in 1906, when revolutionary disturbances led the United States to send troops to impose order. They were not withdrawn until 1909. The most provocative case of Dollar Diplomacy took place in 1911, when a revolution in Nicaragua led American bankers to take charge of that country's finances. In 1912, American marines followed the bankers in to prevent further upheavals.

These almost routine displays of force naturally deepened Latin American hostility toward the United States. When Woodrow Wilson succeeded Taft as president in 1913, he promised to correct matters. But Caribbean diplomacy remained essentially the same. American marines entered Haiti in response to revolutionary disturbances in 1915 and stayed there until 1934. American forces occupied the Dominican Republic again in 1916 and intervened once more in Cuba in 1917. By then, Wilson had become embroiled in a painful adventure in Mexico.

Wilson in Mexico

In May 1911 President Porfirio Diaz, dictator of Mexico since 1877, was overthrown by a revolutionary coalition led by the liberal idealist Francisco Madero. Unable to organize a new government rapidly enough, the revolutionaries were themselves suppressed in February 1913 by General Victoriano Huerta, who arranged Madero's assassination. Most European governments recognized the Huerta regime. American business interests, which had made large investments in Mexican industry, urged Wilson to do likewise. Wilson refused on the ground that Huerta's was not a free government resting on the consent of the governed. This departure from the American policy of recognizing all governments in power gave the United States the responsibility of deciding which governments were pure and which were not. When Huerta's government failed to collapse, as Wilson hoped it would, he offered to help the anti-Huerta Constitutionalist forces under Venustiano Carranza. But Carranza wanted no support from Yankees, and Huerta's regime stood up.

An incident on April 9, 1914, gave Wilson an excuse for direct intervention. One of Huerta's officers arrested the crew of an American vessel that had landed behind the government's lines at Tampico. Although the Americans were promptly released with expressions of regret, the com-

mander of the American squadron demanded a more formal apology. This Huerta refused to make. Wilson took Huerta's action as an insult to the United States and asked Congress for authority to win an apology by force. Even before Congress could act, Wilson learned of a German steamer about to arrive at Vera Cruz with a load of ammunition for the Huerta government. To stop the delivery of armaments that might be used against American forces, Wilson ordered the navy to occupy the port. This action cost 126 Mexican lives. Even Carranza's Constitutionalists were so angered, that they threatened war.

At this crucial point, the ABC powers—Argentina, Brazil, and Chile—offered to mediate. Wilson welcomed the chance to crawl away from his difficulties. Mediation failed, but Huerta's regime soon collapsed anyway. It was unable to secure arms from European nations, who in 1914 were strengthening their own forces. Carranza took over the presidency, but his regime quickly became embroiled in civil war with one of his best generals, Francisco (Pancho) Villa. Disorder spread, and in March 1915 Wilson sent General John J. Pershing across the border on a "punitive expedition" against Villa, who had repeatedly raided American territory and killed American citizens. Carranza replied to this American "invasion" by mobilizing his army. Preoccupied with the war in Europe, Wilson withdrew Pershing's forces and in March 1917 recognized the Carranza regime. Peace was maintained, but only after Wilson had aroused the lasting distrust of a people he meant to help.

The Mexican policy, though pursued with the best of intentions, suggested a tendency that would persist throughout much of the century. Whether the United

States chose to use its growing power for reasons of idealism or for self-interest, the assumption persisted that it had an obligation to improve and shape the lives of other peoples. Such an assumption was perfectly consistent with the triumph of progressivism in the first decade of the twentieth century. Many of those who became Progressives were expansionists who supported a strong navy and an aggressive foreign policy. To redeem "the waste places of the world" and the slums of American cities were expressions of the same missionary impulse, and both progressivism and imperialism recognized the need to impose order and stability on societies threatened with social upheaval.

SUGGESTED READINGS

W. LaFeber, *The New Empire: An Interpretation of American Expansion, 1860–1898* (1963). W.A. Williams, *The Tragedy of American Diplomacy*, 2nd ed. (1972). E.R. May, *Imperial Democracy: The Emergence of America as a Great Power* (1961). H.K. Beale, *Theodore Roosevelt and the Rise of America as a Great Power* (1961). R.L. Beisner, *Twelve Against Empire: The Anti-Imperialists, 1898–1900* (1968). D.G. Munro, *Intervention and Dollar Diplomacy in the Caribbean, 1900–1921* (1964) and *The United States and the Caribbean 1921–33* (1975). A. Iriye, *Across the Pacific* (1969) and *Pacific Estrangement* (1972).

SUMMARY

In the 1890s the United States joined the European powers in a new drive for world empire. Americans concentrated on areas of interest to them: the Caribbean and Latin America, the islands of the South Pacific, and the Philippines and China abroad; Canada and Mexico nearer home.

In the Pacific, America looked for new markets for manufactured goods, for new sources of raw materials, and for control over its own system of harbors and coaling stations for its ships. In 1854 Commodore Perry had forcibly opened Japan. In 1899 Samoa was divided between the United States and Germany. The Hawaiian Islands had been visited by traders in the 1790s and by missionaries as early as 1820, and had a large American colony by 1860. After much political turmoil, the islands were annexed by the United States in 1898.

Part of the push for expansion came from politicians and industrialists eager for world power and wealth. Expansion was supported by the new idea that to be a world power, a nation needed a large and strong military establishment, and particularly a strong navy. The ways in which strong diplomacy, commercial imperialism, and missionary idealism were combined were best shown in American actions toward Spanish-held Cuba. The result of these actions was a war with Spain, the independence of Cuba, and the debut of the United States as a world imperial power. By the end of April 1898 the war was over in the Caribbean but not in the Pacific. There the American fleet under Admiral Dewey sailed into the Philippines, which was still a Spanish possession. Like Cuba, it was in revolt and seeking independence. Hostilities were declared over on August 12. The peace treaty ensured the freedom of Cuba and gave the United States the Philippines (for $20 million), Puerto Rico, and Guam.

Now a world power, the United States naturally became involved in the competition over China, where the European powers and Japan were staking out spheres of influence. To gain entry into what everyone thought would be a rich trade, the United States proposed the Open Door policy, which was in fact a proposal that each nation take its share but not poach on the shares of others. This policy, although it created an impression of disinterested neutrality, laid the foundation for greater American influence in the affairs of China and the rest of Asia.

Theodore Roosevelt was a supporter of expansionism and American power. During Roosevelt's presidency, the United States began to build the Panama Canal, which was opened to traffic in August 1914. But the president's heavy-handed methods of gaining the consent of the Central American nations and getting rid of British interest earned the United States many enemies in Latin America. The Roosevelt Corollary of 1904 to the Monroe Doctrine set up the United States as the police officer for Latin America. In 1905 the United States took over the debt of the Dominican Republic to prevent a European creditor from moving in. Troops were sent to Cuba

in 1906 to keep order and protect American investments. In 1911 a revolution in Nicaragua led American bankers to take charge of that country's finances, and in 1912 American marines followed the bankers in to maintain order. American marines went to Haiti because of revolutionary disturbances in 1915 and stayed until 1934. Cuba and the Dominican Republic were the object of interventions in 1916 and 1917.

Although none of this made the United States popular in the Western Hemisphere, perhaps the worst blunder was Wilson's intervention in Mexico in 1914 and 1915. The troops he sent were not withdrawn until 1917, when the United States entered the war in Europe. By that time Wilson had succeeded in arousing the lasting distrust of the Mexicans, though he had proceeded with the best of intentions.

The idea that the United States had a mission to improve and shape the lives of other peoples was to haunt American foreign policy throughout much of the twentieth century. That the results were usually resentment rather than gratitude never seemed to make a dent in the thinking and actions of American presidents and policy makers.

20

People and Politics: The Progressive Era

Although the Progressive Era generally means the years between 1900 and World War I, the roots of progressivism may be found in the concern with government and business abuses in the post–Civil War decades, and its influence remained apparent as late as the New Deal of the 1930s. But the period of its most intensive growth and expression was clearly the first two decades of the twentieth century. The return of prosperity seemed an ideal time for Americans to measure the damage done to their society by the rapid growth of industries and cities. Prosperity had a way of making that damage more obvious by forcing middle-class families to see and compare their comforts and advantages with those of the people trying to survive below the subsistence level.

Progressive reformers looked for ways to make American society a more decent place in which to live. Within two decades, progressivism had touched nearly every aspect of American life: the structure of city government and the conduct of corporations and trade unions; the education of children and the interpretation of laws; the conservation of natural resources and the socialization of immigrants; the status of women and the labor of children; the qual-

ity of food and the content of magazines. Where progressivism did not touch people's lives was also significant: black Americans were relatively unaffected, as were the rural poverty of tenant farmers and migrant workers and the quality of labor of most unorganized workers. And Progressive efforts to reform humankind included some odd policies: restricting the consumption of alcoholic beverages, limiting the number of immigrants, and directing the relations of peoples in other parts of the world.

So varied were the makeup of the Progressive movement and its concerns that programs differed widely in the degree to which they marked new departures in thinking and in applying ideas. But despite their differences, Progressives did share a certain optimism. National confidence, reinforced by international triumphs and an upswing in the economy, appeared to put nothing beyond the reach of good will. And Progressive reformers expected to tap that good will for the benefit of all classes. The United States, although flawed in places, remained in their estimation a model to inspire the world. To improve their society and its institutions, in fact, was to make them all the more exportable.

308

THE PROGRESSIVE SPIRIT

The early decades of the twentieth century were marked by the vitality and breadth of the Progressive spirit. Since their purpose was not simply to make changes in society but also to free it from the past, Progressives naturally looked for support among those willing to question fixed systems of belief. They did not have far to seek. In the study of law and political science, in economics, education, philosophy, and the interpretation of history, Progressives found helpers at home and abroad. The new ideas of the social scientists and philosophers, along with the Protestant clerics who embraced the Social Gospel, provided a good atmosphere for reform. Progressives had only to test those ideas by applying them to actual situations.

The Reform Commitment

The men and women who assumed leadership roles in the Progressive movement emerged largely from the urban Protestant middle class at a time when the nation seemed divided along class lines more than ever before. The conflict between capital and labor, the changes in the sources of immigration, the squalor of the slums, the corruption of politics, the growing appeal of the Socialist party in the early twentieth century—all deeply concerned the Progressives. If most of them could agree on the need to counter the Socialist challenge by eliminating abuses in American society, they were less agreed on which were the worst abuses and how best to get rid of them.

The Progressive movement was a coalition of many different movements, and Progressives were men and women who had different degrees of commitment to reform and different priorities. Some businessmen were attracted to progressivism as a safe and practical way to satisfy the popular demand for reform. Crusaders for good government thought their cause was critical to progressivism, if only because reform depended on success in making government more responsive and more efficient. Women Progressives seeking to eliminate bias based on sex expanded their struggle to include those who were oppressed by poverty and the conditions of their employment. They brought to the movement new attitudes toward poverty and a commitment, shown most vividly by the settlement-house workers, to reach the people most affected by it. Protestant clerics who joined the movement did so in the spirit of the Social Gospel, convinced that to save humankind, they must save society first. Many journalists came to progressivism as a result of investigations they had conducted into abuses in almost every phase of American life. Some of the politicians who responded to the exposés with legislation also claimed to be Progressives.

Most Progressives shared a commitment to restore opportunities for the common person, broaden income distribution, rescue the poor, and clean up politics. To achieve these goals, the federal government would have to assume a major responsibility. The New Nationalism propounded by the Progressive theorist Herbert Croly in his influential book *The Promise of American Life* (1909) set much of the tone of the period. What he advocated was a positive and strong state that used professional expertise and social planning.

Although progressivism was a new departure in attitudes and practices, it did not result in any far-reaching redistribution of wealth or power. The legacy of progressivism was not the reorganization of society but rather the public disclosure of social and political abuses and corrective legislation to minimize those abuses.

The Muckrakers

To progressives, disclosure of social and political evils was critical to the success of their efforts. If only the facts were known, the people would demand action. The new muckraking magazines and books supplied the facts in abundance. They exposed malpractices everywhere: city, state, and national government; corporations; the medical profession; patent medicines; life insurance; the police; the preparation of food products; the banks. Theodore Roosevelt first pinned the label *muckrakers* on the young journalists who were exposing the worst aspects of American society. "In Bunyan's *Pilgrim's Progress*," he said, "you may recall the description of . . . the man who . . . was offered the celestial crown for his muckrake . . . but continued to rake the filth on the floor." Roosevelt agreed that many of the revelations were true, but argued that their effect was simply to make discontent worse. He felt his own Square Deal and other programs could satisfy the clamor for reform. Muckrakers argued that the American people would not fight for reform until they had been stirred up.

For many years, reporters had written stories of the kind that made the muckrakers famous. What was new after the turn of the century were the popular magazines— *McClure's, Cosmopolitan, Everybody's, Arena*, and others, heavily illustrated and selling for as little as ten cents—that provided research funds and nationwide audiences. Very little that was wrong in America escaped their attention. Perhaps the muckrakers' most sensational accomplishment was Lincoln Steffens's series on corruption in the cities. Ida Tarbell's almost equally popular exposé of Standard Oil retold the story of the methods by which that huge combine had been built. David Graham

Phillips wrote a lively series of articles called "The Treason of the Senate," exposing that body as a millionaires' club acting for special interests. Upton Sinclair, a Socialist rather than a muckraker, wrote a devastating exposé of the meat-packing industry in his novel *The Jungle* (1906).

What muckrakers offered the public were sensational disclosures rather than any solutions to the abuses they described. Few had any real quarrel with the basic economic institutions, only with the way some people abused them. "We muckraked," Ray Stannard Baker recalled, "not because we hated our world, but because we loved it. We were not hopeless, we were not cynical, we were not bitter."

PROGRESSIVISM IN POLITICS: LOCAL, STATE, NATIONAL

If the revelations of the muckrakers were to be translated into action, Progressive reformers needed to detach government at all levels from the special interests and make it more responsive to the public. Until that had been done, they could not, for example, expect to improve living conditions for slum dwellers, eliminate child labor, regulate the working hours and conditions of women workers, and enforce safety regulations in factories. Though often frustrated in their efforts, the reformers persisted. The new attitudes and policies they introduced eventually worked themselves into the political bloodstream and became permanent features of American government.

City Politics

By the turn of the century, municipal reform efforts had been going on for almost fifty years. The problems of corruption, inefficiency, and special privilege seemed worst on the local level, and so cities were among the first objects of Progressive attack.

Progressive mayors fought the effects of bossism and persuaded good men to work in city government. Tom L. Johnson of Cleveland stressed public involvement in decision making and forced street railways to cut their fares. In neighboring Toledo, Samuel M. Jones, who ruled from 1899 until his death in 1904, opened free kindergartens, free playgrounds, and free golf courses. He also established a minimum wage for city employees and checked the often arbitrary power of city police.

Many Progressives were reluctant to depend on the chance availability of good and energetic men like Johnson and Jones. They wanted institutional safeguards as well. This meant changing the structure of municipal government, removing it from state control through "home-rule" charters, and creating a permanent professional staff that would run the city on a nonpartisan basis. It took a hurricane and tidal wave in Galveston, Texas, in 1900 to point a way. The politicians who made up the city council so botched the administration of relief and reconstruction that in 1901 the state appointed a five-man commission of experts in their place. This commission did so well in rebuilding the city, restoring its credit, and rehabilitating services that Galveston kept it to run the city.

By 1914 over 400 American cities, most of them small or middle-sized, had adopted the commission form. Most city commissioners, however, were required to run for office. More changes in the name of greater democracy resulted in political authority being vested in a small body of elected commissioners who in turn appointed a professionally qualified city manager to run the city departments. By 1923 more than 300 cities had adopted this system.

Through the various reforms, the Progressives claimed to have democratized city government. But the evidence might also suggest the contrary. What they had introduced into municipal government was expert management based in part on corporate models. With decision making centralized in a city manager, commission, or professional staff, city government became more efficient—but not necessarily more responsive. The urban poor, at least, seemed to have enjoyed more influence in city affairs under the boss than under the efficiency expert. And with the declining influence of the political-party machine, fewer voters turned out for elections.

State Government

No less entrenched than the local bosses were the powerful state machines. Legally, cities are creatures of the states, operating under charters or other limited grants of power from state legislatures. In order to prevent municipal reforms from being undone by the political allies of city bosses, urban Progressives extended their attack to the state machines and the business interests they served.

Perhaps the innovation they expected to be the most beneficial was the *direct primary*. Reformers hoped that this device, which left the choice of candidates to the people rather than to the party machines, would ensure the selection of abler and more independent officeholders. By 1916 some form of the direct primary had been adopted by almost every state. Several states also adopted the *initiative*, a reform that permitted the public to propose legislation, and the *referendum*, which enabled voters to approve or reject measures passed by the legislatures. The *recall* of public officers through popular votes, another reform device, received wide support as a means of getting rid of officials before their terms expired.

The kingpins of a state's party machine was its United States senators, much of whose power came from their access to federal patronage. United States senators, according to the Constitution, were elected by the state legislatures. One of the reforms most in demand by Progressives was direct election of senators by the people. The Seventeenth Amendment, passed by Congress in 1912 and ratified in May 1913, provided for this change. But although the reformers succeeded in translating a great many of their political reforms into law, the results often disappointed them. The direct primary, for example, made party funds unavailable to those who wanted to run for office. That seemed to favor wealthy candidates over poor ones. Party bosses also

soon discovered how to manipulate the political process despite the direct primary. The initiative and referendum became political devices that often misfired, permitting special-interest groups to saddle the public with their pet projects. Recall was used only rarely. All too often, outbursts of reform lasted only a short time, rising or falling with the enthusiasm of one outstanding leader. The professional, full-time bosses usually outlasted the amateurs; they became somewhat more careful, perhaps, but they were still powerful. The reformers held that their occasional victories might at least prevent the machines from doing greater harm.

Business Interests

Progressives also attacked business interests. Particular targets were the railroads and other public utilites, which relied heavily on government grants of power and political privilege. The state that provided a model

A young mill worker in 1909.
Photograph by Lewis W. Hine, Library of Congress)

for what could be done was Wisconsin, where Robert M. La Follette was elected governor in 1900. La Follette's first step was to replace his party's strong state machine with a Progressive machine of his own. With expert advice from his "brain trust," he proceeded to please his farm constituents by establishing an effective railroad commission. Within a few years, this commission brought other utilities under its umbrella. La Follette's career as a reformer in Wisconsin carried him to the United States Senate in 1906 and almost to the Progressive presidential candidacy in 1912.

Social Legislation

Much of the credit for what was accomplished in social legislation belongs to Progressive women. Like Progressive groups in other fields, they based their campaigns on solid study and research, wide publicity, and the use of trained lobbyists in state capitals and Washington. Under the leadership of the National Child Labor Committee, new child-labor laws or amendments to old ones were adopted in nearly every state between 1902 and 1914. Most of these prohibited the employment of young children (often defined as under fourteen), at least for factory work. Enforcement was made simpler in many states by laws requiring school attendance until the minimum working age. Other measures prohibited the employment of minors at night and in dangerous occupations. In 1916 Congress passed the Keating-Owen Act, which prohibited interstate commerce in goods made in factories, mines, or quarries that employed children under specific ages. Two years later, in *Hammer* v. *Dagenhart*, the Supreme Court declared this act unconstitutional on the grounds that it invaded the police powers of the states and attempted to use federal control

of interstate commerce to attain unrelated ends. But the state laws survived.

Although the courts permitted state regulation of child labor as part of the states' police powers, they ruled that control over working conditions of women infringed upon their freedom of contract. But then in 1908, in *Muller* v. *Oregon*, the United States Supreme Court reversed its position and upheld Oregon's ten-hour law for women. This was another triumph for Progressive research, which was reflected in the 112-page brief submitted by Louis D. Brandeis for the state. Brandeis offered the Court a mere two pages of the usual argument buttressed by "authorities." The rest of his brief consisted of historical, sociological, economic, and medical facts providing "some fair ground, reasonable in and of itself," on which the Court might find excessively long hours of work for women injurious enough to "the public health, safety, or welfare" to justify limitations. Brandeis's social facts swayed even the most conservative justices. In 1917, on the basis of a 1000-page brief modeled on Brandeis's, the Supreme Court upheld a ten-hour law for men in *Bunting* v. *Oregon*. Many state laws were enacted on the basis of these decisions, but in 1923 the Supreme Court again reversed itself and rejected hours legislation for women as well as men.

Progressives also won state laws providing insurance for families of workers killed or injured on the job and succeeded in establishing a certain amount of public responsibility for the support of children and old people. Mothers-assistance acts, which granted financial aid to working mothers, helped widows with dependent children, as well as families left destitute by divorce, desertion, or incapacity of the breadwinner. And in 1914, states began to provide home relief for the aged poor.

Progressive social legislation, especially legislation covering working conditions, was soon challenged, especially by those who would have to foot the bill and who were otherwise affected by bureaucratic interference. After 1900 employer associations, some of them established years earlier to combat unionization, turned their attention to politics. The effectiveness of the propaganda and pressure politics used by business interests contributed to the decline of progressivism in the states. To satisfy the voters, legislators often found they had no alternative but to enact reform measures. But they did not have to provide funds and machinery for enforcement. Progressive faith in legislation was often doomed to bitter disappointment.

PROGRESSIVISM AND THE PARTIES

To Progressive reformers, who looked more and more to the national government to realize many of their objectives, the president had to be a person who shared their principles. That included a commitment to positive government as a tool of social and economic change. In the first two decades of the twentieth century, three presidents—Roosevelt, Taft, and Wilson—all shared that commitment. The differences among them pointed up some of the differences within the movement itself.

The Republicans: Roosevelt

If anyone personified progressivism, it had to be Theodore Roosevelt. He was a master politician; he knew how to respond to and manipulate public sentiment; and he had a dramatic flair that had long been missing from the presidency. His identification with the outdoors, his relentless pursuit of the "strenuous life," his exploits in the Spanish-American War, and his colorful style excited the public. To conservatives and liberals, Roosevelt was a paradox. Although he came to symbolize Progressive reform, he was often a reluctant reformer. He made no effort to hide his dislike for the men and women who made up the radical and labor movements of his time. But like many Progressives, he saw the need to confront the abuses of the social and industrial system and to adopt reforms that would satisfy public fears and demands.

A Republican by family tradition, an aristocrat by temperament, Roosevelt rose through the political ranks. McKinley appointed him assistant secretary of the navy just before the Spanish-American War. His feats as the Rough Rider added to his popularity, and in the fall of 1898 he was elected governor of New York with full party support. He soon showed himself so independent of the Republican machine, however, that the state boss, Tom Platt, determined to bury Roosevelt in the vice-presidency in the election of 1900. This strategy backfired when an assassin shot McKinley at Buffalo in September 1901.

Roosevelt and Big Business

Not since the days of Andrew Jackson had the White House been occupied by a president so devoted to the expansion of the role of the chief executive. But where Jackson used his position to strengthen states' rights, Roosevelt used the presidency to build federal power. In confronting private power, however, Roosevelt was always cautious. His attack on the trusts was a case in point. Despite his speeches, Roosevelt aimed not at breaking up the trusts but at satisfying public concern about corporate power. On March 10, 1902, he ordered Attorney General Philander C. Knox to bring suit to dissolve the Northern Securities Company under the Sherman Anti-Trust Act. This was the company created by the country's greatest bankers to combine the holdings of the country's greatest railroad barons. So stunning was Roosevelt's attack that J.P. Morgan himself went to Washington to find out what the president had in mind. Two years later the Supreme Court, by a five-to-four vote, gave its verdict: the Northern Securities Company must be broken up. The company's directors gained their consolidation goals by other means, but this did not hurt the president's public image or his opinion of himself. The decision, he said, was "one of the great achievements of my administration. The most powerful men in this country were held to accountability before the law."

The *Northern Securities* verdict was followed by prosecutions of the beef trust, the oil trust, and the tobacco trust. Despite these actions, the wave of consolidations continued, corporate power remained as strong as ever, the same men remained in control, and competition became no freer. The president had simply given notice that *unfair* combinations would be held accountable for their actions. He wanted to make clear to the American public that the government stood ready if necessary to exert its authority over big capital. Roosevelt also made it clear that big labor was no different from big business.

In October 1902, workers in the Pennsylvania anthracite pits had been on strike for months in protest against conditions in the mines and in the company-owned mining towns. The operators, led by George F. Baer, the Morgan-appointed head of the Reading Railroad, remained unwilling to listen to the complaints. With winter coming and coal bins empty, coal riots broke out in northern cities. When Roosevelt demanded that the strike be arbitrated, the operators refused until the workers went back to the pits. John Mitchell of the United Mine Workers voiced the workers' determination to stay out until their demands were met. Finally, Morgan and Roosevelt were able to agree on an arbitration commission satisfactory also to Mitchell. The settlement awarded the mine workers a nine-hour day and a 10-percent wage increase, which left them only partially satisfied. The union failed to gain recognition as labor's bargaining agent in the coal industry, and the miners were prohibited from striking for another three years. The public, however, was grateful to the president for the prospect of winter heat, and Roosevelt no doubt felt the coal operators should have been equally grateful. "I was anxious," he recalled, "to save the great coal operators and all of the class of big propertied men, of which they were members, from the dreadful punishment which their folly would have brought on them if I had not acted." After all, as he saw it, he had stood "between them and socialistic action."

The Square Deal

In reviewing his intervention in the coal strike, Roosevelt felt he had given a "square deal" to all sides. That phrase became a hallmark of his presidency, and it seemed calculated to overwhelm any opposition to him in the election of 1904. Judge Alton B. Parker, the Democratic candidate, proved colorless, and Roosevelt's huge majority (7,623,000 popular votes to 5,077,000) took even him by surprise. President at last in his own right, Roosevelt now pursued a broader reform program on the national level. His major achievements were in railroad regulation, protection of consumers, and conservation of natural resources.

By 1904 the Interstate Commerce Act of 1887, which had been designed to regulate the railroads, was practically dead. This was largely because of the Supreme Court's narrow interpretation of the Interstate Commerce Commission's powers. In 1903, in response to pressure from the railroads themselves, Congress had passed the Elkins Act. This measure made it illegal for railroads to depart from their published freight rates and made shippers as well as railroads liable for punishment for infractions. The act struck at the practice of rebating, which the railroad companies had come to regard as a major nuisance. The Elkins Act, however, failed to give the Interstate Commerce Commission any power to fix rates, which was what farmers and other shippers wanted.

Roosevelt now prodded Congress to strengthen and enlarge the ICC's powers. In response, Congress passed the Hepburn Act in 1906. The commission had been able to order alterations in railroad rates, but the roads did not have to comply until the courts ordered them to do so. Under the Hepburn Act, the commission was authorized to set maximum rates when complaints from shippers were received and to order the roads to comply within thirty days. The roads might still go to court, but in the meantime the new rates were to be in force. In two years, shippers made more than 9000 appeals to the commission and a great many rates were revised downward. With the Hepburn Act, Roosevelt felt he had helped blunt the demand for government ownership of the railroads.

In 1905 Roosevelt responded to growing public pressure by asking Congress for an act that would protect consumers from undesirable adulterants and preservatives in food packaging. His request was based in part on the public indignation aroused by Upton Sinclair's exposé of the meat-packing industry and by subsequent investigations. The packing interests fought TR's proposal.

But in June 1906, Congress passed the first federal meat-inspection law. The same year, it enacted a Pure Food and Drug Act in response to a muckraking exposure of the patent-medicine industry and its misleading advertising. This law did not ensure full protection for consumers, but it attacked some of the worst abuses and prepared the way for stricter regulation later on.

As an amateur naturalist and an outdoor person with a taste for natural beauty, Roosevelt took an early interest in conservation. Under the Forest Reserve Act, which had been passed in 1891, he set aside almost 150 million acres of unsold government timberland. He also closed to public entry about 85 million additional acres in Alaska and the Northwest in order to give the United States Geological Survey a chance to study mineral and water resources in these areas. He turned over the supervision of the national forests to the secretary of agriculture, who put a professional conservationist, Gifford Pinchot, in charge.

But the "good times" that had helped sustain the Roosevelt presidency and Progressive reform received a rude jolt in 1907 when a financial panic, brought on by speculation and mismanagement, forced a number of New York banks to the wall. Anxious to avoid a long depression, Roosevelt, by his actions, brought into question his earlier insistence that the federal government could always assert its authority over large corporations. When industrialists and Wall Street representatives advised him that business would recover sooner if he permitted the United States Steel Corporation to acquire control of the Tennessee Iron and Coal Company, a firm whose shaky securities were held by many shaky brokerage houses, Roosevelt nervously approved. Whether his action saved the country from a business collapse remains doubtful.

The day after the election of 1904,

Roosevelt had announced that he would not seek a third term. As the 1908 campaign neared, Roosevelt stood well enough with his party to name its next candidate, his friend William Howard Taft of Ohio, the first civil governor of the Philippines and Roosevelt's secretary of war since 1904. The president also stood well enough with the people to put Taft over. The Democrats returned to William Jennings Bryan, but Progressive reforms under Roosevelt left Bryan issueless. Taft swept in by a vote of 7,679,000 to 6,409,000; his margin in the electoral college was 321 to 162.

Taft and Progressivism

Like Roosevelt, Taft recognized the need for social legislation and regulation of the trusts. He supported Roosevelt's "square deal." He shared Roosevelt's ideas on most questions, and he fully expected to follow Roosevelt's policies. But he was not Roosevelt. He had no charismatic qualities and none of Roosevelt's flair. His administrative skills could not make up for his lack of political skills. His loyalty to the party was not enough to hold the party together. And Taft himself helped to bring the split in party ranks when he chose to raise an issue Roosevelt had wisely evaded—the protective tariff.

By 1908, the call for a reduction of tariff duties was reflecting both urban and rural concern over the steadily rising cost of living. By protecting the trusts from foreign competition, critics charged, the tariff forced the public to pay higher prices. Responding to pressures within the party, particularly from midwestern Progressives, Taft promised early action. In March 1909, he called Congress into special session to deal with the tariff question. Although Taft may have been genuinely interested in lowering tariff duties, the Old Guard in the party

fought as always. Moderate reductions were adopted in the House. But by the time Nelson Aldrich and his conservative friends in the Senate were finished with the measure, it not only failed to reduce the levies but actually raised them. Taft had done nothing to stop Aldrich, and this betrayal of a platform pledge so enraged certain western senators that they attacked their own party leaders. They lost the battle, but their revolt shook the Old Guard to its foundations.

With the Republican party increasingly divided between the Old Guard and Progressives, the battle shifted from the tariff issue to the sweeping powers exercised in the House by the Speaker, Joseph G. (Uncle Joe) Cannon, who had repeatedly blocked consideration of reform legislation. Taft backed the Old Guard; Roosevelt indicated his sympathy for the rebels; and the rebels won when they got enough votes to restrict the Speaker's appointive power. They followed up this victory with new railroad legislation that went beyond Taft's wishes. In the Mann-Elkins Act of 1910, Congress empowered the Interstate Commerce Commission to suspend general rate increases (enlarging the power granted by the Hepburn Act to suspend specific increases) and to take the initiative in revising such rates. These terms were in line with Taft's desires. But the Progressives also pushed through a provision forbidding railroads from acquiring competing lines, and added another that put telephone, telegraph, cable, and wireless companies under ICC control.

What may have remained of Republican unity was nearly wrecked by the Pinchot-Ballinger affair. The trouble began when Pinchot heard that Secretary of the Interior Richard A. Ballinger had agreed to let private interests take over the reserved coal lands in Alaska. Pinchot attacked Ballinger, but Taft chose to believe his secretary's denials. When Pinchot continued the attack he was removed. Progressives in Congress now investigated the Interior Department and showed that Ballinger, though not guilty of misconduct, had no sympathy with conservation policies. Somehow Taft gained the same reputation.

Taft did not disappoint the Progressives at every turn. Important measures passed during his tenure included the Sixteenth Amendment, which made the federal income tax constitutional, and the Seventeenth Amendment, providing for the direct election of United States senators. Both were ratified in 1913. He also initiated about twice as many prosecutions under the Sherman Act in his one administration as Roosevelt had in two. But Taft's two leading cases, against International Harvester and United States Steel, turned out to be worse than failures. The U.S. Steel prosecution, coming after Roosevelt's virtual guarantee of immunity to the corporation, ended hope for reconciliation between Roosevelt and Taft. The Harvester action alienated the company's promoter and director, the former Morgan partner George W. Perkins, who was to become one of Roosevelt's leading backers in 1912.

The Bull Moose Party

By June 1910, strife in Republican ranks had broken into open warfare over Taft's use of presidential patronage to build up conservative strength for congressional elections later in the year. At first, Roosevelt made no move that would publicize his difficulties with Taft. But then in August he set out in a swing through the West for a series of speeches in which he endorsed the concept of the welfare state under the slogan New Nationalism. In 1911, Republican insurgents helped form the National Progressive Republican League in order to promote

Robert La Follette. As governor of Wisconsin, La Follette was the most successful Progressive; as United States senator, he was the most militant. Roosevelt, though pressed to head off La Follette as well as Taft, waited almost a year to make up his mind. After La Follette, worn down by campaigning, collapsed during a major speech early in 1912, Roosevelt publicly announced, "My hat is in the ring." A savage fight followed, and by the time of the Republican convention in Chicago in June, Taft's supporters were in control. Roosevelt and his followers, charging that the president had gained his delegates by fraud, stormed out.

In response to questions about his own physical energy, Roosevelt said upon arriving in Chicago that he felt "fit as a bull moose." His supporters now hastily organized a Progressive-party convention of their own in that city, hoping to send him back to the White House. The delegates adopted a platform calling for the initiative, referendum, and recall, women's suffrage, workmen's compensation and social insurance, minimum wages for women, child-labor legislation, and federal trade and tariff commissions to regulate business.

The Democrats: Wilson

Encouraged by the Republican split in 1912, the Democrats turned to a political newcomer, nominating the Progressive Democratic governor of New Jersey, Woodrow Wilson, on the forty-sixth ballot. Fifty-five years old at the time of his nomination, Wilson had had little political experience. While president of Princeton University from 1902 to 1910, he had been known as an educational reformer. He proved attractive to the Democratic bosses of New Jersey, who in 1910 were seeking a respectable candidate for governor, preferably one they could control. But when he won the governorship, Wilson broke with the bosses and promoted reforms that earned him Progressive support.

The stage was now set for a dramatic political showdown within the ranks of Progressivism. Taft soon lagged, and the battle narrowed down to Wilson and Roosevelt and the central issue of the trusts. Brandeis said that Wilson was for regulated competition, Roosevelt for regulated monopoly. Wilson held that the business combinations were too powerful to be regulated, "that monopoly can be broken up. If I didn't believe it, I would know that all of the roads of free development were shut in this country." A "new freedom" for the individual was more important than a "square deal" from the government. In the election, the two overwhelmed Taft, who got only 8 electoral votes. Roosevelt won 88, Wilson 435. Eugene V. Debs, running on the Socialist ticket, won no electoral votes, yet his popular vote of over 900,000 was impressive. Although Wilson's popular vote was slightly less than 42 percent of the electorate, the Democratic party captured the House and Senate as well as the presidency. Armed with the additional support of a bloc of Progressive Republicans, Wilson took office with excellent prospects for a Progressive administration.

Differences on the trust issue may have dominated the election, but other subjects now demanded the president's attention. First on the list was the tariff. In 1913 Wilson called a special session of Congress on this issue. With strong support from Senator La Follette and other Republican Progressives, the Democrats that year passed the Underwood Act, the first satisfactory downward revision since the Civil War. To supply the revenue that would presumably be lost through tariff reduction, this act also placed a tax of 1 percent on personal incomes of $4000 and graduated surtaxes of from 1 to 6 percent on higher incomes.

Financial reform came next. The Panic of 1907 had revealed a poorly functioning financial system and the need for a more flexible currency. A commission set up in 1908 under Senator Aldrich had suggested establishing a great central bank with branches dominated by the leading banking interests. Progressives led by La Follette responded with proposals for more public control: remove financial power from the hands of private banking houses and place it in the hands of experts who would be more responsive to the public. As finally passed on December 23, 1913, the Federal Reserve Act set up twelve regional banking districts, each with a Federal Reserve bank. The Federal Reserve banks were owned by the member banks of the Federal Reserve system. All national banks were required to join; state banks were eligible. Member banks were required to subscribe 6 percent of their capital to the Federal Reserve bank in their region. On the security of this subscription and commercial and agricultural paper, the Federal Reserve banks would create a new currency, Federal Reserve notes, issued by the Reserve banks to member banks and circulated by them to borrowers. The Federal Reserve system was placed under the direction of the Federal Reserve Board, consisting of the secretary of the treasury and seven other persons appointed by the president.

By 1923, the Federal Reserve system covered 70 percent of the nation's banking. It created a flexible and sound currency and made it available to all sections of the country through the regional Reserve banks. It also left banking a private business under federal supervision and did not really reduce the power of the great New York financial institutions. To improve the farmer's access to funds, Congress passed the Federal Farm Loan Act in May 1916, which created a Federal Farm Loan Board of twelve regional Farm Loan banks patterned after the Federal Reserve system. The banks were authorized to lend money to cooperative farm-loan associations on the security of farm lands, buildings, and improvements; up to 70 percent of the value of these assets could be borrowed.

Like his predecessors, Wilson trusted the regulatory agencies to deal with corporate abuses and punish individual wrongdoers. The first Wilsonian antitrust measure, the Federal Trade Commission Act of September 1914, undertook to prevent unfair trade practices rather than punish their perpetrators. This act created a five-person Federal Trade Commission authorized to investigate alleged violations of antitrust laws. The commission was empowered to issue cease-and-desist orders against corporations found guilty of unfair practices. If this failed, the commission could bring the corporations to court. During Wilson's administration, 379 cease-and-desist orders were issued and a few dissolutions of trusts were initiated in cooperation with the Department of Justice. Even so, Progressives soon came to feel that the commission was not using its powers vigorously enough.

A second antitrust law, the Clayton Act, was passed in October 1914. It prohibited a number of business practices: price discrimination that might lessen or destroy competition; *tying contracts* (contracts that forced purchasers not to buy the product of competitors); the acquisition by corporations of stock in competing firms; and the creation of interlocking directorates in corporations and banks over a specified size, as measured by capitalization. Officers of corporations were made subject to prosecution if they violated these provisions. Labor unions as such were not to be considered illegal combinations or conspiracies in restraint of trade. Labor injunctions were forbidden except when necessary to prevent "irreparable injury to property, or to a property right."

The domestic record of Wilson's first administration also included legislation designed to control child labor (the Keating-Owen Child Labor Act of 1916), to improve the condition of merchant seamen (the Seaman's Act of 1915), and to establish an eight-hour day for interstate-railway workers (the Adamson Act of 1916). Like much of the social legislation passed during the Progressive era, however, many of these measures proved difficult to enforce—because of the way they were written, because of administrative neglect, or because of the hostility of the courts. And two groups in particular continued to struggle on their own: women and blacks.

WOMEN AND PROGRESSIVISM

In attacking glaring inequalities in American life, women played a particularly active role in the Progressive movement. By the turn of the century, the General Federation of Women's Clubs, organized in 1889, had grown into a militant organization, especially in the fight for women's suffrage and even for birth control. The discovery that some 5 million women and nearly 1 million children under the age of fifteen were now in the labor force (as reported in the census of 1900) soon pushed the General Federation and similar organizations into new fields of activity and agitation. Although the vote remained the first priority for many women activists, it was viewed not as an end in itself but as a means for attacking a broad range of social problems.

The Suffrage

Since the 1840s, a small advance guard under the leadership of Elizabeth Cady Stanton, a graduate of Emma Willard's Female

Seminary in Troy, New York, had argued that women as well as men deserved the right to vote. Angered by their failure to win the vote under the Fourteenth Amendment, suffrage groups formed the American Woman Suffrage Association in 1869, with Lucy Stone and Julia Ward Howe of Boston at its head. A more radical contingent favoring easy divorce and other social reforms soon split off. This group, led by Susan B. Anthony and Stanton, then organized the National Woman Suffrage Association. By 1898, Wyoming, Colorado, Utah, and Idaho had given women full voting rights. Other states permitted them to vote for certain offices, such as school-board members. But no federal amendment was passed, despite agitation throughout the nation.

The role of women in bringing about so many Progressive reforms encouraged them to demand political rights for themselves. One of the strongest arguments for giving women the vote was their participation in business. By 1910 nearly 8 million American women were working, many of them in offices and stores as well as in factories. Some had entered the professions of law and medicine. Their number in education, even at the college level, had soared. Although Taft and Wilson evaded it, women's suffrage became an issue in the presidential campaign of 1912. The election of Wilson, who held conservative southern views on the place of women in society, was a setback. But women went right on agitating, and by 1914 they had won the franchise in eleven states.

Such limited gains dissatisfied many

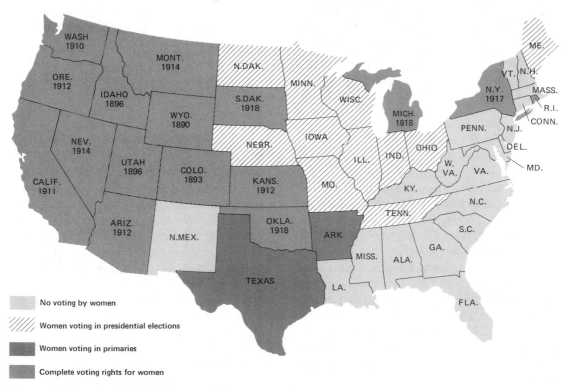

No voting by women

Women voting in presidential elections

Women voting in primaries

Complete voting rights for women

Woman Suffrage before the Nineteenth Amendment

An Italian mother carries home work to be finished by the family. (Photograph by Lewis W. Hine, Library of Congress)

suffragists many new male supporters. In June 1919 Congress passed the Nineteenth Amendment by a narrow margin, giving them the vote. The amendment was ratified in August 1920; women throughout the country took part in the presidential election that fall.

Feminists and Suffragists

"All feminists are suffragists, but all suffragists are not feminists," Winnifred Harper Cooley correctly observed in 1913. The "younger feminists," she explained, often digressed from their "elders within the fold," refusing to believe that the ballot alone, like some kind of "magician's wand," would solve the problems confronting women in American society. "They claim the vote as 'wives and mothers,' as 'homemakers,'" she said of the suffragists. "Just why wives should be happier, as *wives*, because they vote, is difficult to see."

Once the vote had been won, feminists argued, the ballot would amount to very little unless women waged equally vigorous battles to improve their legal position, obtain equal economic and educational opportunities, and redefine their roles in the social system. Nor should middle-class women, who dominated the suffrage movement, ignore the oppression of their working-class "sisters," to whom the ballot was far less important than the conditions of life and labor. The campaign for improvement in women's working conditions, whose slogan was "Let us be our sisters' keepers," reflected the broadened interests of women's organizations.

Few working-class women belonged to any of the feminist or suffragist organizations, but they fought their own significant struggles to improve the quality of their lives. The most dramatic protest was the

women, who now decided to concentrate on a federal amendment. They prepared a huge petition for Congress with 400,000 signatures and opened a lobby in Washington. Some, like Carrie Chapman Catt and Anna Howard Shaw, preferred gradual education and propaganda. Others, who followed the lead of Alice Paul, patterned their strategy after the English suffragists and engaged in dramatic demonstrations and picketing. Eventually, even Wilson was persuaded to give the women some encouragement, and the role of women in World War I won the

Women picketing during "The Uprising of the Twenty Thousand," a general strike by shirtwaist workers in New York City, February 1910. (Library of Congress)

Uprising of the Twenty Thousand, a general strike by shirtwaist workers in New York City. It was the largest strike of women in the nation's history, involving a rapidly expanding industry in which 80 percent of the workers were female. The young strikers, most of them between sixteen and twenty-five, proved themselves as resourceful as male workers in confronting police harassment, mass arrests, violence, and three hard months on picket lines during the winter of 1909. Although the women failed to win a clear victory, they did lay the groundwork for the successful organizing campaign of the International Ladies' Garment Workers' Union. Two years after the strike, a tragic fire at the Triangle Shirtwaist Company took the lives of 146 women and revealed the conditions that still prevailed in the industry (most of the fire escapes had been locked).

Although the women's organizations lent some support to the struggles of working-class women, the question of priorites was never satisfactorily resolved. Some suffragists still insisted that their cause should not be mixed up "with outside interests." Nor did the constructive activities of social workers in the emerging urban ghettos lessen the suspicion with which black women tended to regard the largely white, middle-class women's movement. Many of the suffragists had themselves emerged from the ranks of the abolitionists, but by the turn of the century the women's organizations had broadened their appeal and constituency to include thousands of southern white women. To preserve national unity, these organizations were forced to make a series of crippling compromises on the explosive issue of race relations. Like so many Progressives, women reformers were not always able to overcome their own racial and class biases. To some, in fact, female suffrage promised to counter the growing influence of illiterate European immigrants and preserve white supremacy in the South.

After 1920, women would vote in substantial numbers. Despite their access to the polling place, however, women were as reluctant as men to use the ballot as a tool for social regeneration. Despite their growing access to the work place, women tended to hold the lowest-paying jobs, deferred to male bosses and foremen, and found few opportunities for advancement in their positions.

BLACKS AND PROGRESSIVISM

Progressivism coincided with the worst period of race relations in the nation's history. During the last decade of the nineteenth century, the South moved systematically to disfranchise and segregate its black population. Although the Progressive movement also took root in the South, blacks were excluded. More often than not, Progressive and racist leaders were the same, and the two movements were barely distinguishable. With few exceptions, northern Progressives did nothing about the steady deterioration of race relations throughout the country. The new academic sciences such as psychology and sociology, which had become quite fashionable in intellectual and Progressive circles, tended to reinforce racist assumptions. Progressive-minded historians praised the achievements of Anglo-Saxon civilizations and documented the failure of blacks to become intelligent and useful citizens.

Booker T. Washington: Strategy for Survival

Against a background of white violence, disfranchisement, and segregation, Booker T. Washington followed a policy of realistic accommodation: "In all things that are purely social we can be as separate as the

Booker T. Washington. (Brown Brothers)

W.E.B. DuBois. (Brown Brothers)

fingers, yet one as the hand in all things essential to mutual progress." Rather than agitate, black people should accumulate property: "The trouble with the Negro is that he is all the time trying to get recognition, whereas what he should do is to get something to recognize." Rather than intrude where they were not wanted, black people should look to their own communities. Once black people had proved themselves, largely by measuring up to white middle-class standards, their constitutional rights would be recognized. After all, Washington observed, "There is little race prejudice in the American dollar."

Whites—North and South—supported Washington's ideas. The financial support whites funneled through Washington enabled him to monopolize black leadership and virtually control black colleges, churches, and newspapers. The success of this self-made man, who had risen from slavery, also won for him the admiration of many of his own people. To a small but growing black business class, most of them self-made people with a vested interest in serving a segregated black community, Washington's emphasis on pride and enterprise, rather than political agitation, simply made good sense.

W. E. B. DuBois: The Talented Tenth

Although Washington remained the dominant personality in black America for nearly two decades, his leadership did not go unchallenged. His principal critics, such as W. E. B. DuBois, proved to be black intellectuals and professionals. Almost all of them were northerners who thought Washington had carried accommodation too far and who resented the enormous power "King Booker" wielded.

Unlike Washington, DuBois had not experienced slavery, poverty, or personal struggle. Highly regarded as an authority on black social and industrial life, largely because of his research at Atlanta University, DuBois did not openly attack the Washington gospel until 1901, nor did he actively oppose the disfranchisement of the illiterate black farm worker. But he bitterly resented denial of the ballot and other elements of equality to the educated black, "the talented tenth" destined to lead their people.

Between 1901 and 1903, DuBois set down his ideas on the dual heritage of black people. They were at once black and American, inheriting a national culture, yet exhibiting unique gifts. Racial differences were beneficial; racial inequalities were insufferable. The black "would not Africanize America," DuBois wrote in *The Souls of Black Folk* (1903), "for America has too much to teach the world and Africa. He would not bleach his Negro soul in a flood of white Americanism, for he knows that Negro blood has a message for the world. He simply wishes to make it possible for a man to be both a Negro and an American." Although DuBois acknowledged that industrial training was important, he thought blacks should also have the kind of liberating education Washington's philosophy denied them. Black advancement, he felt, depended ultimately on civil equality. Protest was essential if blacks were to maintain self-respect.

The Niagara movement, launched by DuBois and his intellectual black friends in 1905, advocated agitation rather than accommodation. But few people, black or white, listened, and the movement had little impact. In 1909 a group of white and black Progressives organized the National Association for the Advancement of Colored People (NAACP). As editor of its official journal, *The Crisis*, DuBois became the organization's most militant spokesman.

But the NAACP's most practical work from the start was legal action designed to protect civil rights and challenge disfranchisement. The organization appealed largely to college-educated, professional blacks; its following among the great mass of working-class blacks remained minimal.

Betrayal of Expectations

Despite their differences over strategies priorities, and the value of agitation, DuBois and Washington both urged black people to cultivate middle-class virtues: thrift, sobriety, orderliness, cleanliness, and morality. Contrary to their expectations, however, economic advancement failed to stop the wave of lynchings and riots that took such a dreadful toll of black lives. Even Washington had to concede in 1904 that "the custom of burning human beings has become so common as scarcely to excite in-

terest." What Washington must have found difficult to comprehend was the fact that blacks who proved themselves economically often generated white fear and resentment rather than applause. When white mobs took to the streets, as in the Atlanta race riots of 1906, much of the violence fell on the respectable, law-abiding middle-class blacks—the ones whites referred to as the "uppity, aloof, smart-ass niggers."

Frustration confronted DuBois when he tried to make a choice in th 1912 election among Roosevelt, Taft, and Wilson. Neither Roosevelt nor Taft had shown any particular regard for the rights of blacks. Both had gone out of their way, in fact, to demonstrate their feeling for the white South. DuBois finally cast his ballot for Wilson, thinking such "a cultivated scholar" would be more sympathetic to black grievances. But that proved to be a mistaken assumption. In 1914 a black delegation registered its out-

Between 1889 and 1941 an estimated 3811 blacks were lynched in this country, frequently with thousands of spectators. (UPI/Bettmann Archive)

rage over the actions of the new administration, particularly segregation in federal departments; Wilson took offense at their language and all but ordered the black leaders out of his office. Progressivism was apparently for white folks only.

SUGGESTED READINGS

R. Hofstadter, *The Age of Reform* (1955). R.H. Wicbe, *The Search for Order* (1967). J.M. Blum, *The Republican Roosevelt* (1977). A.S. Link, *Woodrow Wilson and the Progressive Era* (1954). A.S. Kraditor, *The Ideas of the Woman Suffrage Movement, 1890–1920* (1965). L. Gordon, *Woman's Body, Woman's Right: A Social History of Birth Control in America* (1976). R. Rosenberg, *Beyond Separate Spheres: Intellectual Roots of Modern Feminism* (1982). W.E.B. DuBois, *The Souls of Black Folk* (1903). L.R. Harlan, *Booker T. Washington,* 2 vols. (1972, 1983).

SUMMARY

America in the early twentieth century was the America of the Progressives as well as the America of big business. The middle-class reformers, mostly urban and Protestant, confronted a broad range of problems: conflict between capital and labor, immigration, the terrible slums, corrupt politics. But although all could agree that there were problems to be solved, they did not agree on which to attack first and how. The movement itself was a coalition of different groups with different aims. No group tried to revolutionize society. The basic aim was to correct the evils of the system but keep the system itself intact.

Publicity was important for the Progressives, who believed that arousing the people was the way to bring pressure for change. Muckraking, the disclosure of social and political evils in the popular press, was part of the Progressive campaign.

One of the first targets of the Progressives was government at all levels. In municipal government Progressives fought for and introduced the ideas of the commission form of administration and the city manager. To protect these reforms, Progressives attacked state machines as well, advocating such innovations as the direct primary, the initiative, the referendum, and the recall. They also pushed to have United States senators elected by the people rather than by the legislatures (The Seventeenth Amendment, ratified in 1913, accomplished this.) Other targets were the business interests, particularly the railroads and the other public utilities which depended on government grants and political privilege.

In the area of social legislation, Progressives worked for child-labor laws, for laws limiting work hours, for industrial-accident insurance (compensation), and for public responsibility for the support of children and old people.

Three presidents shared the Progressive commitment, although all in different ways: Theodore Roosevelt, Taft, and Wilson. Roosevelt moved against big business by using the Sherman Anti-Trust Act to bring companies to court and to prosecute the beef trust, the oil trust, and the tobacco trust. He considered "big labor" the same as big business, and intervened in the Pennsylvania coal strike of 1902. His theme was the "square deal"—justice for all law-abiding citizens, whether rich or poor. His major achievements were in railroad regulation, protection of consumers, and conservation of natural resources.

Taft, who took office in 1908, attacked the protective tariff, but had a vision of reform different from that of many of the Progressives in his own party. Some reforms were passed during his administration— the Sixteenth Amendment, establishing the federal income tax, and the Seventeenth. But some of his actions led to a split in the Republican party and the rise of a third party for the election of 1912. Taft was the Republican candidate, Wilson ran for the Democrats, and TR was the candidate of the Bull Moose (Progressive) party. Wilson won, and now the country got a Democratic version of progressivism.

Among Wilson's domestic achievements were tariff and financial reforms, the latter designed to correct abuses in the financial system that had led to the Panic of 1907. A Federal Reserve system, created in 1913, led to a flexible and sound currency and national supervision of banking, which remained a private business. The Federal Farm Loan Act of 1916 created a financial system for farmers like the Federal Reserve for banking. Antitrust laws such as the Federal Trade Commission Act of 1914 and the Clayton Act of the same year continued the policy of relying on regulatory commissions to deal with business practices. There was also legislation to control child labor, to improve the condition of merchant seamen, and to establish an eight-hour day for interstate-railway workers.

But like much of the social legislation passed during the Progressive era, these laws were seldom enforced. The Progressives' major accomplishment seems to have been to satisfy public opinion. Very few structural changes were actually made. And not all segments of society were included: women and blacks continued to struggle along on their own. Neither the women's desire for the vote nor black desires for equality of opportunity and civil rights received much attention. The two major black strategies—Booker T. Washington's "survival" and W. E. B. DuBois's "talented tenth"—were doomed to betrayal by the continuation of virulent racism and by lack of interest on the part of the nation's leaders.

21

World War and World Revolution

The incident meant little to most Americans, but it would have great consequences for them and for much of the world. On June 18, 1914, Archduke Franz Ferdinand, heir to the throne of the Austro-Hungarian Empire, was shot and killed by a young Serbian nationalist at Sarajevo in the Austrian province of Bosnia. For more than a generation, the European nations had been living in fear of one another. They had been engaged in an intense competition for world markets and sources of investments and raw materials. As their suspicions and rivalries grew, so did their haste to accumulate arms and allies.

When Ferdinand died, Europe was divided roughly into two camps: the Central Powers (Germany and Austria-Hungary) and the Allied Powers (Great Britain, France, and Russia). Within six weeks, these powerful coalitions were engaged in an armed conflict that would soon engulf the rest of Europe and much of the world—the Great War, or World War I.

Few Americans in 1914 could have conceived that national or economic interest might force them into the war. When Wilson won reelection in 1916, his followers shouting "He kept us out of war," he could hardly have imagined that in only five months he would be before Congress to ask for a declaration of war. When the United States entered the European conflict, which then became a world war, Wilson justified American intervention as a necessary step to make the world safe for democracy.

When it came to constructing a peace, Wilson was moved by the same moral considerations. But the world after the Great War was far different from that of 1914. The Bolshevik Revolution in Russia, social upheavals elsewhere, and colonial and nationalist stirrings complicated and frustrated his peace mission. He would be victimized not only by the legacy of Europe's long history of national jealousies, but by his own self-righteousness and sense of mission. In the end, the Allies denied him the "just" peace he had sought. The Senate denied him the means by which he had hoped to impose a kind of Progressive order on humankind. And the American people seemed to have grown weary of his rhetoric and his crusade.

TOWARD INTERVENTION

Preoccupied with domestic problems, most Americans were startled by the outbreak of fighting in Europe. When the president appealed to them in the early days of the war to be "impartial in thought as well as in act," they saw no reason why they should be drawn into an overseas war they barely understood. In the propaganda battle for the hearts and minds of Americans, however, the Allies clearly had the advantage. Allied propagandists turned the conflict into a war to preserve the basic values of civilization from the German "Huns." Reports of German atrocities in Belgium seemed to confirm this view. The sea war also worked in favor of Allied public relations. The Allied blockade of Central Europe brought hunger and malnutrition to women and children in 1916, but such slow cruelty was hard to dramatize. The German submarine, on the other hand, was a relatively new weapon of war, and evoked shocking images of ships lost at sea with no chance for survivors. That warfare took on added significance when it threatened to undermine the American economy.

The Economy and Freedom of the Seas

When war broke out in Europe in 1914, the disruption of international trade and exchange threatened the United States with an economic depression. The Allied blockade so interfered with American trade with the Central Powers that it fell in value from almost $170 million in 1914 to virtually nothing in 1916. But the Allies looked to the United States for manufactured goods and food, the British Navy controlled the seas, and in 1914 and 1915 orders poured into the United States. American trade with the Allies soared from $825 million in 1914 to about $3.2 billion in 1916. The surge rescued the economy from a recession and started a boom that lasted until 1919.

Even more important was the transformation of the United States from a debtor to a creditor nation. The large amounts of American bond issues and corporate securities held by British investors were sold to pay for war materials. To finance further buying, on which Allied success in the war depended, the British and their friends had to borrow. The State Department discouraged American bankers from making loans to Allied governments, for fear the American stake in an Allied victory would become so great it would draw the country into war. But in June 1915, with Allied gold and dollar resources nearly gone, the administration reversed its position. To maintain American prosperity, wrote Secretary of the Treasury William G. McAdoo to the president, "we must finance it." The United States, then, despite its neutrality, came to have an enormous stake in the Allies' ability to pay for the goods and loans they acquired. The United States had become in effect the principal source of supplies of the Allied Powers.

The more deeply the United States became involved with the Allies, the more likely it was that American ships would be affected by German submarine warfare. To Wilson, however, the rights of neutrals were fully protected under international law, including the right to engage in trade with a belligerent power. Despite his sympathy for the British, Wilson insisted that both sides observe the rights of neutrals. To the European powers, engaged in a struggle for survival, modern methods of warfare had made much of international law obsolete. Wilson soon found himself in conflict with both sides over the rights of neutral carriers. The critical difference between British and German violations of those rights was that German violations destroyed American lives and property; British violations did not.

In November 1914, the British declared the entire North Sea a military area and mined it so thoroughly that no neutral vessel could cross it without first receiving directions from them. If the United States had chosen to challenge the British action by sending its ships unescorted into the North Sea, no doubt American ships would have been sunk. But the Wilson administration decided instead to protest the British practice through a formal note.

On February 4, 1915, the German government announced its intention of establishing a war area around the British Isles in which all enemy ships would be destroyed without warning. It was clear that neutral vessels would not be safe. Americans traveling on belligerent ships would also be in grave danger. On May 7, 1915, a German submarine sank the unarmed British liner *Lusitania;* 1198 passengers were lost, 128 of them Americans. Although the ship was carrying rifle cartridges and other war goods, the toll of lives dramatized the submarine issue. In March 1916 a submarine torpedoed the unarmed French ship *Sussex,* injuring Americans aboard. Wilson warned Germany that if it did not immediately abandon these tactics, the United States would sever diplomatic relations. This threat drew from the Germans the *Sussex* pledge of May 4, 1916: no more merchant vessels would be sunk without warning, *provided* the United States held Britain accountable for *its* violations of international law. By ignoring this proviso but accepting the pledge, Wilson succeeded in forcing Germany to place crippling restrictions on its principal maritime weapon.

The Decision to Fight

Wilson became convinced early in the war that the best way to keep the United States at peace was to bring an end to the fighting. In January 1915 and again a year later, he sent his personal advisor, Colonel Edward M. House, on peace missions to Europe. These visits came to nothing. Discouraged by the failure, Wilson at last gave in to the agitation for preparedness that had been organized by Roosevelt, Lodge, and others almost from the moment Belgium had been overrun. Late in January 1916 he took off on a nationwide tour to promote the preparedness idea. By June, Congress had adopted his proposals for enlarging the army, navy, and merchant marine and opening officer-training centers at universities and elsewhere. Plans also were made for industrial mobilization.

In taking these steps, Wilson took over what might have become a useful Republican issue in the 1916 presidential campaign. Although some Progressives felt that much-needed domestic reforms were being sacrificed for military preparedness, they were few in number, even in the Progressive party. Urged to accept the Progressive presidential nomination, Roosevelt asked the party to back the Republican nominee, Supreme Court Justice Charles Evans Hughes, instead. Hughes, he said, stood for the "clean-cut, straight-out Americanism" Progressives themselves admired. This the Progressives agreed to do, although some were disillusioned enough to vote for Wilson.

The Democrats renominated Wilson. Four years earlier Wilson had been elected only because Republican strength had been

U.S.A.
1917

NORTH
SEA

NORWAY

SWEDEN

Oslo

Stockholm

FINLAND
Indep. July, 1917

Lake
Ladoga

Helsinki

Petrograd

Edinburgh

ESTONIA
Indep.
Feb. 1918

Battle of Jutland
May-June, 1916

DENMARK

Copenhagen

Kiel

BALTIC SEA

LATVIA
Indep.
Nov. 1918

Riga

RUSSIA
1914

Riga offensive
Sept, 1917

Smolensk

GREAT
BRITAIN
1914

NETH.

Hamburg

Memel

Konigsberg

LITHUANIA
Indep. Feb. 1918

Vilna

Minsk

London

Amsterdam

Danzig

Masurian Lakes
Sept, 1914

Brussels

BELG.
1914

Cologne

Berlin

Tannenberg
Aug, 1914

POLAND
Indep. Nov. 1918

Pinsk

Paris

LUX.

Metz

Mainz

GERMANY
1914

Leipzig

Dresden

GERMAN INVASION
AUG-SEPT, 1914

Prague

Warsaw

Brest-Litovsk

Lublin

Kiev

Cracow

Lemberg

GALICIA

FRANCE
1914

Strasbourg

Berne

SWITZ.

BAVARIA

Munich

Danube R.

Vienna

Pressburg

UKRAINE

Vittorio-Veneto
Oct-Nov, 1918

Graz

Budapest

Milan

Piave June, 1918

Trieste

AUSTRIA-HUNGARY
1914

Odessa

Genoa

Venice

Marseilles

ITALY
1915

BOSNIA

Belgrade

Bucharest

RUMANIA
1916

BLACK
SEA

SPAIN

Withdrew from
Triple Alliance 1914

Sarajevo

Danube R.

CORSICA

MONTENEGRO
1915

SERBIA
1914

BULGARIA
1915

Rome

Sofia

Constantinople

SARDINIA

Naples

ALBANIA

OTTOMAN EMPIRE
1914

PORTUGAL
1916

MEDITERRANEAN

Salonika

Gallipoli

GREECE
1916

Dardanelles campaign
1915-1916

Smyrna

Athens

SICILY

SEA

CRETE

1916 Date of entry into the war

—————— Maximum advance of the Central Powers

— — — — Maximum Russian advance

•••••••••• Line of the Brest-Litovsk Treaty Mar, 1918

—————— Armistice lines, eastern front Dec., 1917

0   500

Miles

Central Powers

Allied Powers

Neutral Powers

World War I

split between Roosevelt and Taft. This time, with Roosevelt campaigning for Hughes, it was hard to see how Wilson could win. Hughes, however, straddled the issue of peace and war and failed to excite the voters. Wilson, on the other hand, could boast of the *Sussex* pledge, which he had wrung from the Germans while keeping the United States out of war. Wilson's domestic reforms—the child-labor law, the eight-hour day for railroad workers, and low-cost loans for farmers—also helped him. But in the end, the election was close enough to hang for the first time on western ballots. Wilson carried California by a mere 4000 votes and with it enough states in the electoral college to give him a majority of 277 to 254. In the popular vote, he received 9,129,000, to 8,538,000 for Hughes.

Wilson now renewed his attempts to bring the war to an end through mediation. He sent notes asking all the powers to state acceptable terms of peace. When nothing came of this gesture, Wilson followed with another. In a speech before the Senate on January 22, 1917, he announced to the world his own conception of a just and lasting peace and outlined ideas for a league of nations to maintain it. "It must be a peace without victory," he said, based on the self-determination of all peoples, freedom of the seas, and disarmament.

Unfortunately for Wilson, his gestures came at a time when Germany's military fortunes were high. The bloody stalemate that characterized the fighting was wearing down the Allies. Within ten days of Wilson's speech, in fact, the Germans felt confident enough to revoke the *Sussex* pledge and strike for complete victory. On January 31, 1917, Germany announced that its submarines would again sink all vessels on sight, armed or unarmed, within a specified zone around the British Isles and in the Mediterranean. The Germans realized they now risked almost certain war with the United States, but they hoped to knock Britain out by cutting off its food supply before American forces reached the battlefields. They almost won the gamble.

As Wilson had promised, he now broke off diplomatic relations with Germany. He next called on Congress to authorize the arming of American merchant vessels. Wilson thought he still might avoid war, but several factors made this highly unlikely. Suspicion of Germany grew in January 1917, when British naval intelligence intercepted a message in code from German foreign secretary Alfred Zimmerman to the German minister in Mexico, instructing him to propose an alliance with Mexico in case of war with the United States. In return, Germany promised to help Mexico recover "her lost territory in New Mexico, Texas, and Arizona." Wilson disclosed the message on March 1 in order to create further support for his armed-ship bill. Two weeks later, the March revolution in Russia replaced the czarist regime with a provisional representative government, making it easier to describe the war against the Central Powers as a war for democracy and against autocracies. Finally, German submarine warfare in the Atlantic, which resulted in three American ships being torpedoed in March, clarified the issue in the minds of most Americans as a question of defending national honor.

On April 2 Wilson asked Congress for a declaration of war, condemning German submarine warfare as "a warfare against mankind." But he placed the conflict on even higher moral grounds. By going to war, the United States intended to fight for the liberation of all peoples, including the German people: "The world must be made safe for democracy." Distinguishing between the "military masters of Germany" and their subjects, Wilson declared that the United States entered the war "not as a partisan" but as everybody's friend; it would defend not only neutrals' rights but the rights of all people. On April 4 the Senate voted for war against Germany, 82 to 6. Two days later the House concurred, 373 to 50. Not until December 7, 1917, was war declared against Austria-Hungary.

THE WAR AT HOME AND OVERSEAS

The decision of the United States to join the fighting against Germany came when the Allies were doing badly almost everywhere. Losses in the Russian armies already exceeded a million men, and the Russian people were prepared to oppose any government that would not call a halt to the slaughter. The Bolshevik Revolution in November 1917 took Russia out of the war altogether, permitting the Germans to move men and supplies from the eastern to the western front. Worst of all, the new German submarine campaign was a great success; 880,000 tons of Allied shipping were sunk in April alone.

The United States entered the war in April 1917. The American navy almost immediately reduced the amount of tonnage lost to submarines. American ground troops ultimately helped turn back the German armies. And the continuing flow of American supplies and money sustained the entire war effort. To make all of this possible, the United States needed to mobilize its government, people, economy, and society on a new scale. Americans had to be conditioned to make the necessary sacrifices and commitments. For a nation that had grown accustomed to Progressive ways of thinking, much of this planned effort was only a shift in goals rather than in means.

U·S·NAVY RECRUITING STATION
(Library of Congress)

Mobilization

Even before Congress declared war, thousands of Americans had volunteered to serve with the Allies, and many of them saw the full four years of fighting. When the United States entered the war, the combined strength of the regular army and the National Guard was about 372,000 men, from whom were drawn the officers and noncoms of the new army to be created under the Selective Service Act of May 18, 1917. This act required all men between the ages of twenty-one and thirty (later extended to eighteen and forty-five) to register for military service. Registrants were placed in five classes, headed by able-bodied unmarried men without dependents. From this group alone the nation drew all the 2,810,000 men actually drafted, although by the end of the war as many as 4,800,000 persons had been enrolled in the army, navy, and marine corps.

Of the nearly $33 billion spent on the war between April 1917 and June 1920 about half was raised by taxation. The rest was borrowed mainly through four Liberty Loan drives in 1917 and 1918. Backed by rallies, parades, and posters, volunteers sold the bonds directly to the public rather than to the banking community. To mobilize the nation's other resources, Wilson created the Council of National Defense, made up of six cabinet members and an advisory commission of seven additional civilians. Under the council's supervision, huge agencies performed specific wartime tasks. The Emergency Fleet Corporation had been created as early as April 1916 to enlarge the merchant marine. The Food Administration, headed by Herbert Hoover, undertook to supply civilians and combatants. The Fuel Administration doled out coal and oil. The Railroad Administration consolidated the nation's railroads and, without removing them from private ownership, operated them as a single system. In March 1918 the Council of National Defense placed the War Industries Board under the direction of Bernard Baruch, a Wall Street broker, and gave him dictatorial powers over American business. Great savings were effected by coordinating the national economy and the standardization of products.

AFL president Samuel Gompers, on becoming one of the civilian advisors of the Council of National Defense, declared that American workers backed the war, but that he hoped the government would prevent exploitation and profiteering at their expense. Early in 1918, in return for its pledge not to strike, organized labor was assured the right of collective bargaining, maintenance

of the eight-hour day where it existed, and other privileges. A National War Labor Board was created to mediate labor disputes, and a War Labor Policies Board to deal with grievances. The wartime demand for labor pushed wages up as much as 20 percent in purchasing power in key military industries and approximately 4 percent overall. At the same time, salaried employees suffered from wartime inflation, losing as much as one-third of their prewar purchasing power.

Businessmen and farmers fared best of all. Baruch's War Industries Board, unwilling to delay production, gave up the traditional practice of competitive bidding and made war purchases on the basis of *cost-plus contracts*. Such contracts guaranteed sellers profits ranging from 2.5 to 15 percent of production costs. By padding costs, some contractors made enough to increase dividend payments and executive salaries and still pile up profits, despite huge taxes. Hoover's Food Administration, meanwhile, set such a high government price on wheat and other staples that farmers stretched their resources to acquire more land. Farm operators' real income was 29 percent higher in 1918 than in 1915. Soon after the wartime demand ended, however, the farmers found themselves in deeper financial trouble than ever before.

Propaganda and Civil Liberties

To mobilize public thinking, Congress established the Committee on Public Information within two weeks of the declaration of war. Wilson named George Creel, once a prominent muckraker, to head it. Creel enlisted journalists, scholars, and clergy to convince the country that the Germans were depraved. Although the vast majority of German-Americans accepted the necessity of war once the United States joined the Allies, they became the most obvious targets of abuse. But pacifists, Socialists, and left-wing workers suffered the worst repression. Congress made intolerance official by adopting the Espionage Act of June 1917 and the Sedition Act of May 1918. The Espionage Act set a fine of up to $10,000 and a prison term of twenty years for anyone who interfered with the draft or encouraged disloyalty. The Sedition Act set the same penalties for anyone who obstructed the sale of government bonds, discouraged recruiting, or did "willfully utter, print, write, or publish any disloyal, profane, scurrilous, or abusive language" about the American form of government, the Constitution, the flag, or service uniforms, or "advocate any curtailment of production . . . of anything necessary or essential to the prosecution of the war."

President Wilson maintained a discreet silence on the widespread violation of civil liberties. Under the Espionage and Sedition laws, over 1500 persons were imprisoned, including Socialist leader Eugene Debs. Several antiwar newspapers lost their mailing privileges, Department of Justice agents conducted illegal raids on antiwar organizations, judges gave harsh sentences to war critics, and patriotic mobs took out their fury in the streets. The House of Representatives voted 309 to 1 not to seat Victor Berger, a Socialist congressman from Wisconsin, because of his antiwar views and consequent indictment under the Espionage Act. "The one and only issue in this case," one congressman made clear, "is that of Americanism."

The Army in Action

The first American troops, under General John J. Pershing, arrived in France in June 1917 and were fed into the sagging Allied lines largely to bolster morale. When the Germans launched a massive offensive in March 1918, hoping to end the war, about 300,000 American soldiers had reached France and more were arriving every day. By the war's end, of the more than 2 million men who had been carried to Europe, about 1.4 million had become actively engaged, mostly on the Western Front. In April 1918 the Germans had a numerical superiority of perhaps 320,000 on this front. By November, fresh American troops had given the Allies the advantage by 600,000.

Pershing's men faced their first major test when assigned to help repulse a German thrust toward Paris. By May 30, 1918, the Germans had reached Château-Thierry on the Marne, only fifty miles from the French capital. The Americans drove them back, and from June 6 to June 25 cleared nearby Belleau Wood of enemy forces. In July, when the German General Staff made its last great effort to break through to Paris, between Rheims and Soissons, 85,000 Americans helped check the assault. In its first major offensive assignment, in September 1918, the American army launched an attack on the St. Mihiel salient, a German bulge protruding into the Allied lines across the Meuse River southeast of Verdun. Pershing sent American troops against both flanks of the salient and with some French support reduced it in two days. The Meuse-Argonne offensive, from late September to early November, became one of the fiercest battles in American military history. Together with the French forces on that front, Americans captured more than 25,000 prisoners and a great deal of equipment, but at a high cost in casualties. This offensive, part of a coordinated drive against the Central Powers all along the Western Front, helped defeat Germany and its allies. By early November, German armies everywhere were in retreat, the navy was on the verge of general mu-

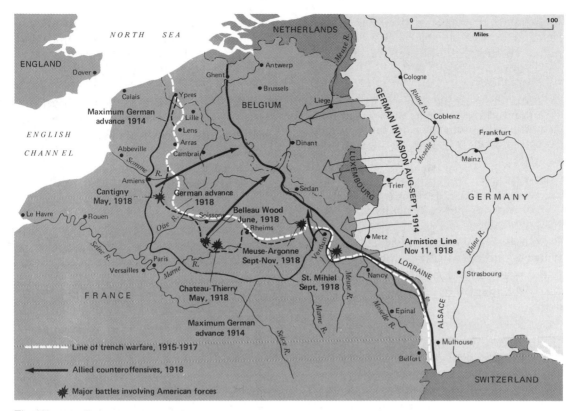

The Western Front

tiny, and the civilian population was hungry, exhausted, and dangerously discontented. On November 11, Germany gave up and signed an armistice.

The war was not over, since terms of peace had yet to be worked out. But fighting on the major fronts had ceased at last. American losses—48,000 killed in battle, 2900 missing in action, 56,000 dead of disease—were light in comparison with those the other nations had suffered since 1914. Before pulling out of the war early in 1918, Russia counted 1,700,000 battle deaths. Germany lost 1,800,000 men, France 1,385,000, Britain 947,000 and Austria-Hungary 1,200,000. The war had come close to wiping out an entire generation.

PEACEMAKING AND REVOLUTION

While his administration waged a militant propaganda campaign on the home front, Wilson was seeking to clarify the objectives of the war. Still unaware of the secret treaties among the Allies, the president held that neither punitive damages nor territorial gains were the real objectives, but rather the end of autocratic government and a settlement that would ensure permanent peace.

In the peace treaty he helped to negotiate, as in his proposal for a league of nations, Wilson hoped to translate his idea of the war's objectives into reality. What sustained him in that hope was the conviction that the peoples of the world, if not their governments, shared his views and looked to the United States for leadership and inspiration:

> My dream is that as the years go by and the world knows more and more of America it will turn to America for those moral inspirations which lie at the basis of all freedom and that America will come into the full light of day when all shall know that she puts human rights above all other rights, and that her flag is the flag not only of America, but of humanity.

In an age of power politics, nationalist rivalries, and Socialist revolution, to have such a vision of the world was at best a risk and at worst a dangerously foolish denial of reality.

The Fourteen Points

Soon after the United States entered the war, Wilson finally learned of the secret agreements. The Allies had already agreed to certain territorial readjustments and to the seizure of enormous indemnities from the defeated enemy. To Wilson, such agreements violated his "peace without victory" as well as the principle of self-determination. The existence of the secret treaties, moreover, encouraged Wilson to make even clearer the American and the Allied objectives. Events in Russia added to the need for clarification.

After the Bolshevik Revolution of November 1917, the new Russian government invited all belligerents to end the entire war almost on Wilson's terms—no territorial changes and no indemnities. No response came from the Allies. The Bolsheviks saw their silence as proof of the imperialist nature of the war. Within three weeks, Vladimir Lenin, the Bolshevik leader, began ne-

gotiations with the Central Powers to close down the Eastern Front. This step the Allies viewed as a stab in the back. The Bolsheviks next threatened to publish the secret treaties. (The deposed czar had signed them for Russia.) Wilson, having failed again to win Allied agreement to his peace plan, thought it essential to meet the Bolshevik challenge with a statement of his own. This he did in a message to Congress on January 8, 1918, in which he set forth in his Fourteen Points all the ideas he had been proposing during the past two years.

The first five points consisted of general principles aimed at removing the fundamental causes of conflict. Peace agreements should be arrived at openly, not secretly. Free use of the seas should be guaranteed to all nations, in peace as well as in war. Economic barriers to free trade ought to be removed, and armaments reduced "to the lowest point consistent with domestic safety." The conflicting claims of the colonial powers should be settled in a way that reflected the interests of the native peoples. The next eight points dealt with territorial readjustments, which should be based, Wilson argued, on the principle of self-determination along "historically established lines of nationality." The fourteenth point, the most important in Wilson's eyes, would establish "a general association of nations" to guarantee "political independence and territorial integrity to great and small states alike."

To Wilson, the Fourteen Points were "the moral climax of this final war for human liberty." The Allies were less certain. Some of them expressed anger over points that appeared to affect their national honor and imperial ambitions; others found Wilson's proclamation hopelessly naive. Whatever their feelings, however, the Allied leaders saw the propaganda value of Wilson's effort. It was for this reason that they agreed to use the Fourteen Points as at least a basis for the peace negotiations.

Intervention in Russia

When finally forced to sign a separate peace with Germany (the Treaty of Brest-Litovsk) some eight months before the armistice ended the war, the Bolsheviks yielded all of Poland, Lithuania, the Ukraine, the Baltic provinces, Finland, and neighboring territories. By May 1918, the British and French had begun to send troops into Arctic Russia by way of Murmansk on the Barents Sea. Americans soon followed. If they had intended the overthrow of the Bolshevik regime—their primary goal, in the opinion of some historians—their more immediate objective was to keep the German military machine busy enough to prevent the transfer of troops to France. Ideological concerns probably reinforced strategic considerations. If the Bolshevik government collapsed as a result of the intervention, that would have been an added bonus.

The Allied and American presence in Russia encouraged those who opposed the Bolshevik regime. By August 1918, the Westerners had helped set up an anti-Bolshevik puppet government in northern Russia. Anti-Bolshevik groups in Siberia were aided by the arrival there of British, French, American, and Japanese forces. In this way, the Western powers became involved in the Great Civil War of 1918–20, which raged across the entire Russian Empire. When the Germans collapsed in the west in November 1918 the Bolsheviks promptly renounced the Treaty of Brest-Litovsk and tried to reclaim the surrendered territories.

Although the Soviet Union would not be invited to the Paris Peace Conference, the fear of Bolshevism played a prominent role in the deliberations. If they disagreed in other matters, the United States and the Allies shared a common alarm over the effect of the Russian Revolution. They continued to support anti-Bolshevik activity within Russia. Allied and American troops remained in northern Russia until late in 1919. The Bolshevik regime survived, however, and the Allies' intervention and subsequent policy of economic blockade and nonrecognition won for them the enduring suspicion of the Soviet government and many of the Russian people.

The Versailles Treaty

Although Wilson's statements on peace were vague enough to be interpreted in various ways, he became a hero to people everywhere who were eager for a better world and thought the president could lead them to it. But Wilson confronted mounting opposition at home. In October 1917, facing off-year elections, he issued a fatal appeal to voters to express their approval of his leadership by returning a Democratic Congress. His appeal not only failed, it also embittered the Republicans who had supported the war effort. At the polls, the voters elected Republican majorities to both houses of Congress. When Wilson went to Paris in December 1918, he seemed to have been rejected by his own country. By then, he had further angered the opposition by failing to appoint a single Republican leader or a single United States senator, even from his own party, to the commission that accompanied him to the peace talks.

The Paris Peace Conference, a meeting of victors to decide the fate of Germany, sat at the Versailles Palace from January to June 1919. Representing Britain was its prime minister, David Lloyd George, who had called for the punishment of Germany in a general election the preceding December and had triumphed. Representing France was Georges Clemenceau, its premier, a determined promoter of French interests and French security. Wilson had come to Paris with three cardinal goals: (1) political self-determination for the peoples of Europe and to some extent even the peoples of colonial countries; (2) free trade; and (3) a league of nations. He left Paris with his goals only partially attained. Unfortunately, his concessions were made largely to secure the League of Nations, which the United States Senate was to forbid the United States to join. Wilson did succeed in moderating the Allied demands on Germany. But here too he was far from attaining his goal of "peace without victory." The terms of the final treaty were harsh enough to almost guarantee that the Germans would make every effort to break the peace when they felt strong enough to do so.

The Treaty of Versailles, signed by the Germans on June 28, 1919, stripped Germany of its colonies in Africa and the Far East, and of Alsace-Lorraine and the Saar Basin north of Lorraine. France won all rights in the coal-rich Saar for fifteen years, after which its future was to be decided by plebiscite. To the east, German territory was given to Poland, becoming the Polish Corridor to the Baltic Sea. The huge indemnity of $5 billion levied on the Germans and the provision for additional "reparations" later on made them look upon the Allies as vultures. Perhaps most distressing was the article that attempted to justify the indemnity and reparations by forcing Germany to acknowledge responsibility for starting the war. In an effort to prevent future aggression, the treaty deprived Germany of a navy and merchant marine and limited its army to 100,000 men. Other treaties in conjunction with the Versailles Treaty established

New independent nations   Plebiscite area

Allied occupation zone

Europe after Versailles

such new states as Czechoslovakia and Yugoslavia by taking apart the Austro-Hungarian Empire.

For all its harshness, the Versailles Treaty was no worse than the terms Germany would have imposed on the Allies had it won. Wilson placed his confidence in the League of Nations Covenant, which had been inserted into the treaty. Under the covenant, responsibility for maintaining peace rested with an assembly (in which every member nation would be represented), a council (which would include the major powers), and a Permanent Court of International Justice. Each member nation pledged to respect the territorial integrity and political independence of other members; to recognize the right of any nation to bring any threat to peace to the league's attention and to submit dangerous disputes to arbitration; and, as a last resort, to use military and economic sanctions against aggressor nations.

PEACE AT HOME: WILSON, THE LEAGUE, AND THE SENATE

When Wilson returned to the United States he faced a difficult battle. He needed to persuade a divided Senate to ratify the treaty, and he needed to keep the support of the American people, who were now concerned with unemployment and inflation. The president was confident. He had fought for the people of Europe over the heads of their rulers; he would now wage a similar struggle for the minds of Americans.

The Senate Debate

On July 10, 1919, two days after Wilson's return from Paris, he formally presented the Versailles Treaty, including the League Covenant, to the Senate. He was confronted by the Republican majority elected in 1918 and especially by his enemy, Henry Cabot Lodge, now chairman of the Foreign Relations Committee. In addition, a strong group of "irreconcilables," including such western Progressives as William E. Borah, Hiram Johnson, and Robert La Follette, were determined to resist the treaty and the league. Nevertheless, more than the needed two-thirds of the Senate seemed ready to vote for the Versailles Treaty, with some form of league membership, and there is every evidence that the majority of the people would have backed them. As the Senate and the people debated the league through the summer of 1919, Wilson grew more and more stubborn about even minor changes in the covenant and more tactless in defense of his all-or-nothing stand. When the irreconcilables opened a tremendous propaganda barrage, the president, although exhausted by work and illness, decided to take his case to the country. In more than forty speeches delivered in some twenty-two days, he pressed home his point. For what had American youths died? he asked. "For the redemption of America? America was not directly attacked. For the salvation of America? America was not immediately in danger. No; for the salavation of mankind. It is the noblest errand that troops ever went on." If the United States rejected the treaty and league membership, it turned its back on those troops.

While the president was gone, Lodge proposed a series of reservations to the covenant, which he knew Wilson would reject and over which the Senate might talk the whole treaty to death. Lodge's strategy worked. By the time his reservations were introduced in the Senate, Wilson had had a physical breakdown, forcing him to cancel the rest of his trip. Early in October he suffered a stroke that left him half-paralyzed. His sickbed appeal to "all true friends of the treaty" to reject the Lodge reservations helped defeat them in the Senate in November. But a resolution to ratify the treaty and the league without reservations also failed, by 38 to 55, with every Republican but one voting against it. Enough support for the league remained even in the Senate for the treaty to be brought up again, in March 1920. Although a majority (49 to 35) voted for the treaty with the modified Lodge reservations, that was seven short of the necessary two-thirds. Wilson supporters remained opposed to compromise. The treaty and league membership were both dead.

The Election of 1920

Even with the treaty dead in the Senate, Wilson did not give up hope. The election of 1920, he announced, must be "a great and solemn referendum." The people would now vote directly on the issue. But it has rarely been possible in peacetime to make an American presidential election a clear referendum on foreign policy, and 1920 was no exception.

Deprived of their most popular leader by Roosevelt's death early in 1919, the Republicans at their national convention nominated the largely unknown Senator Warren G. Harding of Ohio. This small-town newspaperman, owner and editor of the *Marion Daily Star*, had been elected United States senator in 1914. The equally surprising nominee for vice-president, Calvin Coolidge, was governor of Massachusetts when he suddenly came to national fame by breaking the Boston police strike in 1919. To run against Harding, the Democrats named another Ohioan, Governor James M. Cox, who had not been closely identified with Wilson's policies. As his running mate they chose Franklin Delano Roosevelt, Wilson's assistant secretary of the navy. Meanwhile, the Socialists decided to offer an alternative by again nominating Eugene Debs. Since the president had refused to pardon him, Debs would have to conduct his campaign from behind prison walls.

Although Cox strongly favored the league, he wavered on what amendments he might be willing to accept. The Republicans caught the mood of the public by evading this and all other issues. On election day, the American people reacted not so much to the league as to the rising cost of living, the number of people out of work, high taxes, and labor violence. Cox was crushed at the polls, 16 million to 9 million. No major-party candidate had ever been defeated so badly. Harding had said little during the campaign. But what he did say may have been the key to his overwhelming success at the polls. He promised the American people no new crusades, no calls for self-sacrifice to save humanity, but simply a return to "normalcy." After eight years of Wilson's drives, that in itself was a welcome change.

SUGGESTED READINGS

A.S. Link, *Woodrow Wilson and the Progressive Era* (1954). E.R. May, *The World War and American Isolation* (1959). D.M. Kennedy, *Over Here: The First World War and American Society* (1980). N.G. Levin, Jr., *Woodrow Wilson and World Politics: America's Response to War and Revolution* (1968). A.J. Mayer, *Politics and Diplomacy of Peacemaking* (1967).

SUMMARY

World War I brought the United States into European power politics. The entry of the United States also made the European war into a world war. At first, Americans did not understand why they should be involved. But the Allies (Britain and

France) soon won the public-relations campaign. In addition, the Allies' wartime demand for goods rescued the American economy and started a boom that lasted until 1919. Even more important, the United States was transformed from a debtor to a creditor nation. And since the debtors were the Allied countries, America now had a huge economic stake in the outcome of the conflict.

At first, problems of neutral shipping brought the United States into conflict with both Britain and Germany, since both were battling for control of the seas and their source of supplies. The climax came in January 1917, when Germany broke its pledge on submarine warfare in a gamble to win the war before America could come to the Allies' rescue. The Allies were in deep trouble, and their defeat would have meant an economic disaster for the United States. In April 1917 the United States declared war on Germany. Nineteen months later, the Germans were forced to agree to an armistice.

The American navy reduced the amount of tonnage lost to submarines. American ground troops helped to turn back the German armies, and the flow of American supplies and money sustained the entire war effort. These achievements required the United States to mobilize its resources on a vast new scale. A new army was created by the Selective Service Act of May 1917. A Council of National Defense supervised huge federal agencies that managed the merchant marine, food and fuel supplies, transportation, and industry. The war also brought some loss of civil liberties and official intolerance in the form of the Espi-

onage Act of June 1917 and the Sedition Act of May 1918.

When it was over, Wilson noped to realize in the peace treaty his dream of "making the world safe for democracy." But in an age of power politics, national rivalries, and Socialist revolution, such ideas were hopelessly and dangerously naive. His Fourteen Points were an effective propaganda device, but the Allies, bound by secret agreements, had no intention of negotiating anything but a punitive peace. This they did in the Treaty of Versailles, drawn up at the Paris Peace Conference from January to June 1919. It stripped Germany of its colonies abroad and its territory in Europe, saddled it with a $5-billion indemnity, deprived the Germans of military forces, and declared the Germans responsible for the war.

Wilson did get his League of Nations, for which he had sacrificed all his other objectives. But then the United States Senate, in a bitter campaign, refused to ratify the treaty and allow the United States to become a member of the league. Wilson, exhausted and ill, suffered a stroke that left him paralyzed and removed him from politics. In the election of 1920, Republican Warren Harding of Ohio became the new president. His slogan was a return to "normalcy"—to stability and to minding America's own business.

22 *The Twenties: Business and Culture*

Few decades evoke as many different colorful images as the twenties, and few have been subjected to more distortion and exaggeration. High-spirited college students and flappers, emboldened by bootleg gin, danced the Charleston and the Black Bottom and went to petting parties. Marathon dancers competed with flagpole sitters for public attention. Sophisticated urbanites violated Prohibition in speak-easies; young and old alike satisfied their fantasies in the movie houses; the small-town elites found their outlets in Rotary, Kiwanis, or Lions clubs. Advertising became a major industry in its own right, and the automobile became a necessity, along with the radio, the washing machine, and the refrigerator. Easy credit made these and countless other commodities available to millions of Americans.

But there is another side to the twenties that tends to get lost in the nostalgia Americans still feel for the Jazz Age. If the decade was a carefree fling for some, many sections of the population experienced none of the "good times." While ad men made a virtue out of conspicuous consumption, a lopsided distribution of in-

come made reduced consumption necessary for millions of Americans. While the twenties tolerated bobbed hair, short skirts, cosmetics, and a relaxation of sexual rules—the trademarks of a new subculture based on age—they were intolerant of radicals, union organizers, immigrants, and blacks. More often than not, even the "flaming youth" reflected and reinforced the dominant business culture. The same decade in which some Americans flaunted their liberation also witnessed a revival of the Ku Klux Klan, the Red Scare, racial violence, a court test of the right to teach evolution in the public schools, and the first restriction on the number of immigrants admitted to the United States.

The family underwent much change, as did the role of women in the household. The size of urban middle-class families continued to decline, and in the 1920s the impact of this change became more obvious. The smaller family and labor-saving devices enabled mothers to spend more time on the personality and education of their children. Knowledge of birth control, advances in the technology of contraception, and more open discussion of sex not only re-

sulted in earlier marriages but influenced the dominant middle-class sexual ethic. Women were encouraged to be more sexually responsive and to expect sexual gratification in marriage. While this improved the quality of sexual relationships, it may also have contributed to the rapid increase in the divorce rate. In 1890, 6 out of every 100 marriages ended in divorce; in 1930, it was 18 out of every 100. The number of working women increased, as did the number of women attending college. On the other hand, the percentage of women in the work force and in professional employment declined. For middle-class women,

college and career were still an interval before marriage. The ideal woman of the 1920s was encouraged to be more feminine in order to further her husband's career, not her own.

The White House in this decade was occupied by Harding, Coolidge, and Hoover. They differed widely in talent, but were united in the conviction that "the chief business of the American people is business." The 1920s closed, however, in a mood of panic and desperation. The unemployed and the depressed of the twenties suddenly found themselves with plenty of company.

AFTER THE WAR: REPRESSION AND INTOLERANCE

The kind of planning that had enabled the United States to go to war was not used for demobilization afterward. With controls on the economy suddenly lifted and several million soldiers returning to civilian life, the nation found itself in a brief recession. Inflation and unemployment took their toll. Lingering wartime emotions and tensions found new outlets in hysteria over radicalism, in immigration restriction, and in racial violence. At the same time, the rapid pace of urbanization (the 1920 census revealed that for the first time most Americans lived in urban areas) fed traditional rural-urban antagonisms. And many of the 19 million Americans who moved from the farms to the cities in the twenties brought rural ways of thinking with them.

The Red Scare

During the war, Americans had grown used to the suppression of dissent. With the war's end, the intolerance that had been directed

mainly against those suspected of sympathizing with Germany came to cover a wider range of persons—foreigners in general, Catholics, Jews, blacks, radicals, strikers. The new wave of fear found a scapegoat in the Bolshevik Revolution in Russia and the threats of worldwide revolution against capitalism. Actually, Socialists were split over the virtues of the new Soviet government. The Russian Revolution had fragmented rather than united an already demoralized American radicalism. The number of Communists in the United States did not exceed half of 1 percent of the population—and most of them were intellectuals, not workers. But violence in labor relations right after the war deepened concern about the safety of the social order.

No longer bound by wartime no-strike pledges, trade unions made new wage demands after the armistice. They were seeking not only to keep previous gains, but to keep up with the soaring cost of living. In 1919 alone there were 3630 strikes involving about 4 million workers. The most spectacular strike pitted workers against the powerful U.S. Steel Corporation. Hours, shop conditions, and union recognition, as well as wages, were at issue. But the corporation blamed the strike on Communist agitators. Using its own "security" forces along with state militia and federal troops, it broke the strike after eighteen workers had been killed and hundreds beaten. Meanwhile, employer associations, using as their excuse the influence of foreign ideologies in the labor movement, spent large sums of money promoting the American Plan. This was a set of attitudes, the most important of which was that collective bargaining and the closed or union shop were un-American.

In 1919 and 1920 a bomb scare, climaxed by an explosion in Wall Street that killed thirty-eight persons, intensified the Red Scare. Although the work of only a handful of anarchists, the bombs lent support to fears of a massive conspiracy to overthrow the government. Wilson's attorney general, A. Mitchell Palmer, did nothing to discourage such fears. On New Year's Day 1920, Palmer ordered simultaneous raids on every suspected Communist cell in the country; more than 6000 persons were arrested and their property confiscated. The raids were followed by the eventual deportation of 556 aliens convicted of no crime. Vigilantism spread across the nation. Students, professors, editors, writers, actors, and others suspected of harboring subversive ideas or engaging in un-American activities were the victims.

A few months after the Palmer raids, two Italian anarchists, Nicola Sacco and Bartolomeo Vanzetti, were arrested for a murder committed in connection with a payroll robbery in South Braintree, Massachusetts. Upon the jury's finding them guilty, Judge Webster Thayer sentenced the two defendants to death. The evidence against them was not conclusive, and the suspicion grew that they had been convicted not because they had committed the crime but because

of their political beliefs. Judge Thayer's conduct of the trial, in which he made little secret of his feelings about anarchists, only deepened suspicion of the verdict. Appeal motions delayed the execution of the two men for years. Vanzetti's dignity and both men's quiet persistence in their anarchist beliefs while their lives hung in the balance won them additional sympathy. When they were electrocuted in 1927, despite worldwide protest, millions were convinced they were innocent. Millions more were convinced that, guilty or innocent, they had not been given a fair trial.

The "Race-Suicide" Alarm: Immigration

Antiforeign feeling after the war brought to a head the anti-immigration sentiment that had been growing in the United States since the 1880s. The flood of "new" immigrants from southern and eastern Europe in the fifteen years before World War I brought some Americans to the verge of panic over "race suicide" and the survival of the "American character." Such fears helped to pave the way for a complete reversal of the old, easygoing terms of admission to the United States.

The Immigration Restriction Act of 1921 established a quota system based on national origin. Each European nation was assigned an annual quota equal to 3 percent of the number of its nationals resident in the United States in 1910. Most Asians were already barred. The National Origins Act of 1924 cut quotas to 2 percent and made the base year 1890, when the proportion of "Nordics" in the American population had been much higher than in 1910. The National Origins Act also shut the door completely on Japanese immigrants. It was a national humiliation for Japan, which warned that the act would have "grave consequences." The 1924 act was to last only until 1927. Afterward, no more than 150,000 immigrants were to be admitted annually, according to quotas based on the ratio of each country's nationals to the whole American population in 1920.

With the restrictive legislation enacted in the 1920s, the idea of America as the promised land or the refuge for the oppressed came to an abrupt end. Only in the 1960s and 1970s—when the doors were opened to thousands of political refugees from Southeast Asia, Cuba, and Haiti—would that idea be momentarily revived.

The Great Black Migration

Although restrictions on immigrants affected the ethnic makeup of the nation, the movement of southern blacks to northern cities during and after World War I altered the racial map of the United States and introduced new tensions. Between 1910 and 1940, more than 1,750,000 black people left the South, nearly 500,000 during the war and another 800,000 in the twenties. By 1940, the black population outside the South had more than doubled. In cities such as New York, Chicago, Detroit, Cleveland, and Buffalo, the percentage of blacks in the population grew by 100 to 250 percent. Within only a few decades, a largely rural black population had become more urban than the white population. The Jim Crow restrictions, the alarming rate of lynchings and beatings, the absence of adequate educational facilities, and the impossible tenantry and credit systems led large numbers of southern blacks to look for a better life elsewhere.

Until 1915, the North had offered the southern black migrant very little. The labor demands created by World War I and the decline in European immigration changed that situation and opened up opportunities in northern industry—munitions plants,

A black family from the South arrives in Chicago in 1910. (Historical Pictures Service, Chicago)

steel mills, stockyards, auto factories—at wages unknown in the South.

Encouraged at first by labor agents, black newspapers, and the letters of friends, the Great Migration soon had a momentum all its own. It was not uncommon for entire communities to transplant themselves. Although all classes of blacks made up the movement, many in the early waves were young, unskilled, and unmarried, the sons and daughters of sharecroppers and tenants. The chances for a rewarding life in the South had seemed increasingly dismal to these migrants, and they hoped for something beyond what their parents and grandparents had been forced to accept.

The Great Migration took place in an atmosphere of growing racial intolerance. Despite the optimism with which many blacks had participated in World War I, in the first year of the armistice 70 blacks were lynched, 10 of them soldiers still wearing their uniforms. Between 1918 and 1927, more than 416 blacks were lynched; 42 of them were burned alive. Nor was this brutality confined to the old Confederacy. As the black migration to the North grew, so did white fears, resistance, and discrimination. On July 2, 1917, East St. Louis, Illinois, was the scene of a savage attack on the black community in which 39 blacks and 9 whites died. Fear of black competition for white jobs and the use of black strikebreakers triggered the riot, but ignorance and bigotry accounted for its ferocity.

During the Red Summer of 1919, as it came to be called, there were more than twenty-five riots in various parts of the country. On July 27, the worst race riot in the nation's history erupted in Chicago; it lasted for six days and nights. Before the state milita restored some order, 38 persons (15 whites and 23 blacks) had died, 537 had been hurt, and more than a thousand were homeless. Several of the postwar outbreaks,

including the Chicago riot, were provoked by incidents involving urban police, which brought the charge that law-enforcement officers practiced a double standard when dealing with white and black communities. The residents of the black urban enclaves known as ghettos also faced high rents for substandard housing, high prices, poor municipal services, and white economic control. As many migrants came to discover, racial oppression did not always show itself in lynchings, Jim Crow laws, or disfranchisement.

The Ku Klux Klan and Fundamentalism

The revival of the Ku Klux Klan in the 1920s reflected a concern not about blacks alone, but about the general erosion of the nation's moral fiber. The Klan of Reconstruction days had almost died out in the 1870s. The new Klan, founded in Georgia in 1915, grew rapidly after 1920. At its peak in 1924, no fewer than 4.5 million "white male persons, native-born Gentile citizens," as they said, had joined the hooded group. On its night rides, the Klan burned fiery crosses to advertise its presence. It flogged or kidnapped blacks and whites, acted as a moral censor, especially as the enforcement arm for Prohibition, made and unmade local politicians, and frightened union organizers.

This time around, the Klan had a much wider appeal, both geographically and ideologically. It did well in portions of the Midwest and Far West, broadening its targets to include Jews and Catholics as well as blacks. It found support among people who felt most threatened and frustrated by the changes in American society. The Klan revival, however, was short-lived. The conviction of its Indiana leader on a murder charge and exposés of Klan corruption con-

The Ku Klux Klan marching in full regalia past the White House in 1925. (Library of Congress)

tributed to a rapid decline in membership and influence.

The repression of foreigners and foreign ideologies and habits carried over to the repression of thought and speech. Protestant fundamentalists, demanding an absolutely literal reading of the Bible and resisting all modifications of theology in the light of modern science and biblical criticism, led the assault. The object of their attack became the public schools, where, they insisted, Darwin's theory of evolution should not be taught. The fundamentalists gained a victory in Tennessee in 1925 with the passage of a law forbidding the teaching of evolution in the state's schools and colleges. The American Civil Liberties Union was eager to test the law, and the same year, John T. Scopes, a young high-school teacher in the country town of Dayton, violated the law and was arrested. Reporters from all over the country swarmed into Dayton (population 1700) to cover the court proceedings.

To defend the Bible, William Jennings Bryan joined the prosecution. Clarence Darrow, perhaps the most brilliant trial lawyer in the country, headed the defense. The climax came when Darrow subjected Bryan to questioning that exposed his ignorance and inconsistencies. Scopes was found guilty, but fined only $100. More significant, Darrow's defense and the national publicity took much of the strength from fundamentalist efforts to retain a system of values by legal compulsion.

Prohibition: The Dry Decade

The reform impulse scored one of its greatest and more questionable successes in the Prohibition Amendment, the end of more than half a century of agitation to control the production and sale of alcoholic beverages. Much of the strength of the movement lay in the rural, fundamentalist South and Midwest, but during the Progressive Era it also gained urban support, particularly among middle-class women reformers who saw alcohol as a social disease.

With the formation of the Anti-Saloon League in 1893, the "drys" at last built up an agency strong enough to combat the saloon and distiller interests and the machine politicians associated with them. The league kept the pressure on both major parties, and after 1907 state after state in the West and South fell into the "dry" ranks. In December 1913 the "drys" introduced a prohibition amendment in Congress. Four years later, when wartime conditions brought resentment against German brewers and there was need for the materials used in distilling, Congress passed the Eighteenth Amendment. In October 1919, in anticipation of the amendment's becoming law in 1920, Congress passed the Volstead Act to implement it. This act defined intoxicating liquor as any beverage containing more than one-half of 1 percent of alcohol. It forbade any person, except for religious and medical purposes, to "manufacture, sell, barter, transport, import, export, deliver, furnish, or possess" such beverage without a license.

Making liquor illegal nationwide had two immediate results. The old saloon was replaced by the speak-easy, where drinking soon took on a new glamour. At the same time, by putting outside the law a personal habit millions of Americans would not give up, Prohibition opened up a new field for city gangs—control of the undercover liquor business. The proceeds from bootlegging, smuggling, speak-easies, and gambling also strengthened gang domination of local police and local politics.

Criticism of the noble experiment, as Prohibition was called, gradually mounted. After the Democratic landslide in the election of 1932, Congress adopted the Twenty-first Amendment, repealing the Eighteenth,

in February 1933. By the end of the year it had been ratified. With control of liquor returned to the states, only seven chose to continue Prohibition. In 1966 Mississippi became the last of the seven to go wet.

THE CULTURE OF DISSENT

The literary and artistic expression of the 1920s reflected the conviction that America had lost not only its innocence but its promise. The invasions of civil liberties, Prohibition, fundamentalism, Klansmen, Rotarians, the triumph of business values, the small-town and service-club mentality of the White House—all confirmed the belief of many intellectuals, writers, and artists that materialism, intolerance, and hypocrisy were making a shambles of American civilization. These individuals did not look for a political solution. The problem with America was simply too deep to be resolved by legislation. Though the nation could boast of mass consumption on an unparalleled scale, its people, in their view, were suffering from emotional and aesthetic poverty.

The spirit of freedom and experimentation taken up so eagerly by writers and artists in the 1920s had found outlets for expression in the prewar years. Across the country, in large cities and in small towns, intellectually liberated Americans, as they liked to think of themselves, began to meet and exchange ideas. They included political radicals as well as experimental poets and painters. Some preferred to live abroad, convinced that individual artistic fulfillment could never be realized in the machine culture of America. Still others flocked to New York's Greenwich Village, which by 1914 had become a mecca for youthful rebels, the fashionable place in which to flout convention and to debate all the "new" ideas, from penology and poetry to birth control and sexual liberation.

The prewar writers and artists had a certain confidence and optimism about themselves and their ability to change society. Although some were committed to socialism, the prevailing spirit was more often anarchistic or free-thinking. But even before America entered the war, much of the optimism had gone. And what remained failed to survive the war and the postwar repression.

Disillusion and Disenchantment

The *lost generation* was the term Gertrude Stein used to describe the postwar writers and artists, because in their youth the war had broken the continuity of their lives. But Malcolm Cowley (born in 1898) said of himself and his literary and artistic contemporaries that they had actually lost their innocence before the war. To come of age in the America of the Progressive Era was to suffer from "a sense of oppression." He and his friends could feel little passion or optimism. Progressive reform threatened to create only "an intolerable utopia of dull citizens"; morality was "a lie told to our bodies"; what they learned in school was "useless or misdirected"; and "society in general was terribly secure, unexciting, middle-class, a vast reflection of the families from which we came."

Many of the young writers and artists participated in World War I, and it had a deep effect on their lives, leaving them bitter, resentful, and thoroughly disillusioned. To the question of what men had died for in the war, the poet Ezra Pound delivered the classic response of the "rebel" generation:

For an old bitch gone in the teeth,
For a botched civilization.

Ernest Hemingway (1899–1961) had only recently graduated from high school when he enlisted in a volunteer ambulance unit in France. What he experienced of the war convinced him of its senseless brutality, stupidity, and insensitivity, and in *A Farwell to Arms* (1929) he conveyed that view most effectively. Like Hemingway, who settled in Paris after the war, many of those who fought found it difficult to return to an America that had, in their eyes, betrayed and deceived them. In *The Sun Also Rises* (1926), Hemingway described one such group of expatriates, broken by the war, amusing themselves in a postwar wasteland—drinking, boxing, watching bullfights, making love, all to no purpose.

What made postwar America such a stifling place for the rebel writers and artists who made up the lost generation was its business mentality, its machine standardization, and its spiritual sterility. To these critics, the businessman was the symbol of bourgeois culture. They mocked and condemned him not as an exploiter of labor or a corrupter of politics, but for his blind conformity and emotional emptiness. His motto was "Gotta hustle," and he spoke in clichés, worried about trivia, and practiced bigotry and moral censorship. George Folansbee Babbitt, the creation of Sinclair Lewis (1885–1951) for his novel *Babbitt* (1922), entered the American vocabulary as a way of defining business or professional men who conform unthinkingly to middle-class standards. Babbitt was the end product of standardization and mass marketing; his very character was shaped by the goods he consumed and the material objects he worshiped.

The need to probe the sources of America's troubles required many of the writers of the twenties to analyze the very places in which they had been born and nurtured—the small towns of Middle America and the Bible Belt, where "dullness is made God." In *Main Street* (1920), Sinclair Lewis, whose birthplace was Sauk Center, Minnesota, drew caricatures of small-town types obsessed with material success and standardized in their thoughts and emotions. With more compassion, Sherwood Anderson (1876-1941), born in Ohio, tried in *Winesburg, Ohio* (1919) to convey how the industrial machine had destroyed the community and poetry of the village and alienated its inhabitants from each other. More concerned with a region than a small town, William Faulkner (1897–1962), a native of Mississippi, broke with conventional literary forms in novels such as *The Sound and the Fury* (1929). He described the decadence, violence, and terror that marked the transition from the old values and civilization to the New South.

Few writers came closer to symbolizing the lost generation than F. Scott Fitzgerald (1896–1940). He emerged as the principal spokesman for a generation "grown up to find all Gods dead, all wars fought, all faiths in man shaken." Fitzgerald, along with his wife Zelda, followed a life style of reckless and decadent abandon. *This Side of Paradise*, published in 1920 when Fitzgerald was twenty-four, made him a celebrity overnight with its vivid and daring depiction of "flaming youth." But in his best novel, *The Great Gatsby* (1925), Fitzgerald managed to suggest both the glitter of American prosperity and the treacherous foundations on which it rested. With particular skill, he exposed the success ethic for the ways in which it consumed and destroyed individuals. Jay Gatsby, the romantic bootlegger who believes every dream can come true simply by wishing for it hard enough, is betrayed by his gangster friends and by the privileged rich who "smashed up things and then retreated back into their money and their vast carelessness."

Once the prosperity of the 1920s vanished, intellectual disenchantment and personal and artistic rebellion became transformed into social and political awareness. Writers in the Great Depression thought less about criticizing their country, more about trying to save it.

The Harlem Renaissance

While seeking equality in white America, W.E. B. DuBois had advised his people in *The Souls of Black Folk* (1903) that blacks should not sacrifice their racial heritage or their individuality. For too long, he felt, blacks had been forced to look at themselves through white eyes, calculating every move and word in terms of white expectations. In the 1920s, the rapid urbanization of blacks in the North, along with the postward racial violence and the new cultural influences, helped to promote a movement in which black writers and artists attempted to express the "true self-consciousness" DuBois had urged.

As Greenwich Village lured white artists, so Harlem—that part of northern Manhattan formerly occupied by the Dutch, the Irish, and the Jews—became the center of black America, and an exotic attraction for the white pleasure seeker. Black people flocked to Harlem because that was the only place to be. To young, aspiring black writers and artists, many of whom came there in the 1920s, Harlem was less a social problem than a remarkable place that deserved to be celebrated and loved for what it was.

Like the young white rebels, Harlem intellectuals and artists, in large part the children of middle-class parents, rejected many of the values and standards of their seniors. What had stood in the way of "true Negro art in America," Langston Hughes (1902–1967) insisted, was that unfortunate "urge within the race toward whiteness, the desire to pour racial individuality into the mold of American standardization, and to be as little Negro and as much American as possible." Having arrived in Harlem in 1921, Hughes would spend the remainder of his life there celebrating in his poetry, novels, and humor the beauty and spontaneity he found.

The Harlem artists were intent on revealing the freshness and variety of black culture. They found inspiration and spiritual identity in their African origins. They rediscovered the spirituals, the work songs, the sermons, and the rich plantation folklore. They sought to describe, honestly and realistically, the lives and troubles of their people, both in the slave past and the urban present. Perhaps the most brilliant single achievement of the renaissance was Jean Toomer's (1894–1967) novel *Cane* (1923), a series of black portraits that ranged over unexplored parts of black life in the South.

The twenties, Langston Hughes recalled, was a period "when the Negro was in vogue." That is, white publishers courted black writers, and downtown whites and tourists went to Harlem to see the action, to listen to the music, to drop their inhibitions and find emotional release. The only renaissance novel to make the best-seller charts, Claude McKay's (1890–1948) *Home to Harlem* (1928), celebrated those qualities of Harlem. Once the Great Depression struck, however, the white patrons departed, as did the publishers. "How could a large and enthusiastic number of people be crazy about Negroes forever?" Hughes noted. "The ordinary Negroes hadn't heard of the Negro Renaissance. And if they had, it hadn't raised their wages any."

THE POPULAR ARTS

Applied to the popular or "lively" arts, technology had an enormous impact in the twenties. It shaped American attitudes and tastes in ways that few if any books could. Radio reached into the homes of millions, and similar numbers flocked to the movie houses and listened to phonograph records. The effects were both liberating and conditioning. Rural isolation broke down. Americans everywhere were introduced to make-believe worlds, new styles of music, new levels of sophistication, different life styles, and new models to imitate. Movies and radio programs nationalized popular culture, revolutionized people's expectations, and standardized society even more. With their vast potential for influencing and molding the habits and tastes of Americans, the popular arts had become big businesses in their own right by the end of the decade.

The Movies

The movies began as a peep show in a penny arcade. The viewer put a nickel in a device called a kinetoscope (invented by Thomas A. Edison about 1896) and saw tiny figures moving against blurred backgrounds. Edison thought little of his invention, but others took it up and soon succeeded in projecting images on a screen for large audiences. By 1905 more than 5000 "nickelodeons," housed in converted stores and warehouses, were showing films for a five-cent admission.

Peep shows had prospered by showing short comic action. The new films introduced many inventions, most of them endless variations on the chase: cowboys after rustlers; sheriffs after badmen; city cops after bank robbers. Comedians threw pies at one another, slipped on banana peels, fell into manholes. David W. Griffith liberated the movie camera from nickelodeon themes and the limitations of the stage set. In *The Birth of a Nation* (1915), a partisan and distorted film about the Civil War and Reconstruction, Griffith showed sweeping panoramas of massed armies, fade-outs, close-ups, and other kinds of shots revealing the scope and flexibility of camera and screen. The most successful of Griffith's imitators was Cecil B. De Mille, whose religious spectacles—*The Ten Commandments* (1923) and *The King of Kings* (1927), for example—exploited the mechanical possibilities of the camera and the ways that sex could be worked into almost any subject.

Besides sex and spectacles, slapstick comedy quickly became a movie staple featuring such stars as Roscoe (Fatty) Arbuckle, Harold Lloyd, and Buster Keaton. The greatest comic of all, Charlie Chaplin, achieved an international reputation with his brilliant characterization of the wistful little tramp with the battered derby hat, cane, and funny walk.

By 1917 the movies had become a multimillion-dollar industry, and Hollywood, California, the film capital. Luxurious movie theaters were rapidly replacing the nickelodeons, and Americans were spending $175 million a year on admissions. The first stars—Mary Pickford, Douglas Fairbanks, Marie Dressler—earned fabulous salaries, lived glamorous lives, and attracted incredible newspaper and magazine attention.

With the opening of Al Jolson's *The Jazz Singer* in 1927, the era of sound films began. Within two years, "talkies" had replaced silents, and Hollywood, with what John Dos Passos called "its great bargain sale of five and ten cent lusts and dreams," was reaching even larger audiences.

The Phonograph: Ragtime and Jazz

What the film projector did for motion, the phonograph, another Edison invention, did for sound. By 1905 the phonograph had become a successful commercial device. Comedians, actors, singers, and musicians could be heard in the home or in places of public entertainment. By 1914 more than half a million phonographs were being manufactured each year, and soon it was nearly a million.

Before radio, the phonograph gave the greatest impetus to the spread of popular music, much of it ragtime and jazz. Ragtime had emerged in the 1890s. Scott Joplin was its best-known composer, and it borrowed heavily from black work songs and both black and white minstrel songs. With the wartime and postwar migration of blacks, jazz and blues spread northward, especially to Chicago's South Side and New York's Harlem. Dixieland bands first played in these cities around 1915, the year W.C. Handy wrote his "St. Louis Blues." In 1920, the Okeh Record Company made the dramatic decision to permit a black singer to make a commercial recording. With Mamie Smith's rendition of "Crazy Blues," race records, as they were called, made a successful debut. In the next several years, blues and jazz recordings multiplied, and attending jazz concerts became fashionable.

Radio

Unlike the movies, whose commercial possibilities were obvious from the first, the early development of radio was haphazard and accidental. In 1920, perhaps 20,000 amateur "hams" listened on homemade sets to wireless messages sent mainly from ships at sea. That year, the Westinghouse Electric and Manufacturing Company in Pittsburgh began to broadcast musical programs as an experiment. Amateurs in the area responded enthusiastically, and soon popular demand induced Westinghouse to air the programs on a regular basis and to introduce reports of baseball scores. In 1920 the first commercial broadcasting station, KDKA, was set up in Pittsburgh in time to broadcast the results of the Harding-Cox election.

Overnight, radio became big business. Within four years, 562 stations were sending out music, stock-market and news reports, bedtime stories, church services, and sports events. Sales of radio sets boomed. Radio stations covered the country, approximately a fourth of them controlled by newspapers or newspaper chains bent on dominating news outlets. Stations were combined into networks so that programs could reach mass audiences simultaneously.

Now that Americans could listen to nominating conventions and campaign speeches in their homes, interest in politics increased. But that did not appear to affect the quality of politics in the twenties. Radio did enable millions to follow the Smith-Hoover campaign of 1928. Millions more would hear Franklin Delano Roosevelt seek to calm fears over the collapse of the economic order.

THE POLITICS OF COMPLACENCY

The American people responded favorably to Warren G. Harding. He was an easy man to like, a public favorite as long as he held office. He embodied the nation's small-town virtues. He belonged to the right clubs; he was a self-made man; he exuded a deep sense of civic responsibility; and he impressed people as a man of moderation and good will. Unlike Wilson, Harding had no difficulty pardoning Eugene Debs for his wartime statements. If Harding made a virtue of humility and small-town Americanism, Calvin Coolidge, his successor, made one of dedication to the principle that "civilization and profits go hand and hand." Both men reflected the dominant business culture of the decade. And in their policies both of them helped promote the maldistribution of wealth and the speculation that were speeding the nation toward economic disaster.

The Tragedy of Harding

When Harding said "We must strive for normalcy to reach stability," he had in mind his campaign promise to encourage less government in business and more business in government. To help him in that task, he said he would bring the "best minds" to Washington. He kept this promise in part by making such able men as Charles Evans Hughes secretary of state, Herbert Hoover secretary of commerce, and Henry C. Wallace secretary of agriculture. But he also brought with him some lesser minds, his small-town "Ohio gang," and they would exploit their friendship with Harding for personal gain.

At the head of the Ohio gang was Harry M. Daugherty, a small-town lobbyist for tobacco, meat, and utility interests, who helped to launch the Harding presidential boom. Rewarded with the attorney generalship, he held the position until dismissed by President Coolidge in 1924, when his activities were revealed. While in office, Daugherty had made a business of selling liquor permits, pardons, and paroles to criminals at fancy prices. Two divided juries in 1926 enabled him to escape prison. But a number of administration insiders did spend time in prison. The director of the Veterans Bureau and the alien-property custodian were convicted of defrauding the government. Albert B. Fall, the secretary of the interior, had secretly leased government oil reserves in Teapot Dome, Wyoming, and Elk Hills, California to private operators in return for over a quarter of a million dollars. A congressional committee untangled the story, the Supreme Court voided the leases, and Fall was sentenced to a year in prison for accepting bribes.

To Harding, normalcy was linked to prosperity and the triumph of business values. However, he would have rejected any notion that he was a servant of business. In furthering the interests of the business community, he viewed himself as a spokesman for the aspirations of most Americans. He could not understand why radicals and some trade unionists persisted in their agitation rather than place their faith, as he had, in the American Dream. He had made it, and he assumed any American who had the right kind of hustle and determination would also succeed.

While on a speaking tour in the West, Harding became ill; he died on August 2, 1923. Still ignorant of the worst scandals of his administration (as the president himself had been to the end), the public went into mourning as deep as that for any leader since Lincoln. It was as though they had lost a personal friend. Disclosures of corruption after his death only slowly eroded his popularity.

Normalcy in Government: Economic Policies

The transition from Harding to Coolidge was bound to be smooth. To Coolidge, as to the man he replaced, business values were sacred. "The man who builds a factory builds a temple," Coolidge observed. "The man who works there worships there." The government justified itself by its success in encouraging the business community. Beyond that objective, it needed only to cut expenses and reduce taxes.

The beginning of a business revival for which the Republicans took full credit permitted them to confront the electorate in 1924 with the slogan "Keep Cool With Coolidge." The Democrats were badly divided between the rural Protestant segment of the party and a segment that drew its support from the city machines and the "wets." After a furious struggle over the presidential candidate, the delegates turned to John W. Davis, a conservative New York corporation lawyer, as their standard-bearer. Convinced that the American people needed a choice in the election, Robert M. La Follette ran as a third-party candidate on a revived Progressive ticket. The platform called for nationalization of railroads, recognition of labor's right to bargain collectively, and a popular referendum for any declaration of war in cases other than invasion of the United States. Although attacked by both major-party candidates as a dangerous radical, La Follette managed to poll nearly 5 million votes. Davis received over 8 million, and Coolidge well over 15 million. The vote ensured the Republican party's virtually free hand during his administration.

"No one can contemplate current conditions," said Coolidge in his inaugural address of March 1925, "without finding much that is satisfying and still more that is encouraging." The good times seemed to have justified the economic measures already taken during Harding's term. Many were the inspiration of Andrew W. Mellon, the immensely wealthy head of the aluminum trust, owner of oil companies, steel mills, utilities, and banks, and a lavish contributor to the party, who became secretary of the treasury in 1921. He believed that government should promote private enterprise. He would seek to reduce the national debt by reducing government expenses and by insisting that the Allies repay the United States in full. At the same time, he wanted to lower taxes for the upper-income groups in order to provide incentives for the wealthy to become even wealthier. Adopting his ideas, Congress repealed the wartime excess-profits tax in 1921, and in a series of acts from 1924 to 1929 made major cuts in the maximum income tax.

As taxes went down, tariffs went up. As early as 1916, Americans had feared a postwar domestic market flooded by European manufactures. Primed by this threat, Congress raised duties to high levels in the Fordney-McCumber Act (1922). This prevented the Allies from reducing their war debts by exporting goods to the United States. It also caused many nations to adopt tariffs against American imports. Nevertheless, protectionism remained an essential part of Republican economic policy in the twenties. During the Hoover administration, duties would be raised even higher, in the Hawley-Smoot Tariff (1930).

Under Harding and Coolidge, the principal regulatory agencies—the Interstate Commerce Commission, the Federal Trade Commission, and the Federal Reserve Board—were staffed by men who shared the belief that government serves the people best by serving the needs of business. The FTC, for example, encouraged business conferences in which industrywide agreements for corporate benefit were negotiated. Hoover directed this policy as secretary of commerce under both presidents. Through trade associations in which companies shared product and market information, Hoover hoped to achieve his goal of industrial cooperation and standardization. In addition, the Commerce Department helped businesses find overseas markets for materials and investments. Encouraged by a favorable judicial atmosphere, as well as by federal agencies and cabinet-level departments, business went on a new merger spree in the 1920s. In the field of public utilities, 3744 firms were swallowed up. Comparable consolidations occurred in manufacturing, banking, transportation, and wholesale and retail trade.

Organized labor, in contrast, lost ground. Between 1919 and 1922, strikes failed against the great steel, coal, and railroad industries. Employers pushed workers into subservient company unions, whose members numbered more than 1.5 million by 1929. AFL membership, at a peak of over 4 million in 1920, had fallen to under 3 million by 1923 and continued to fall thereafter. Most workers, particularly in the new mass-production industries, remained unorganized. Employers used various methods, including paid informers and blacklists, to keep it that way. Although workers gained modest annual improvements in real wages during the decade, the average annual income for many of them fell below the $1800 thought necessary to maintain a minimum decent standard of living.

The economic problem most troublesome to the Republicans was the distress of farmers deeply in debt from wartime overexpansion. Dairy, vegetable, and fruit farmers prospered from nearby city markets. Staple farmers had to sell in world markets, where increased competition after the war worsened the problem of overproduction. Net farm income, including that of prosperous dairy and truck farmers, fell by nearly 50 percent in the 1920s. A strong farm bloc in Congress responded with the McNary-Haugen bill for federal-government support of staple prices. It passed in 1927 and again in 1928, but the president vetoed it both times. "Farmers have never made money," Coolidge said; "I don't believe we can do much about it."

"Coolidge Prosperity"

Despite weaknesses in the economy, the country at large seemed content. New production techniques and new consumer industries gave a golden glow to "Coolidge prosperity." By the end of the decade, 70 percent of American factory machinery was operated by electricity, compared with 30 percent fifteen years before. Electrochemical processes tripled the quantity of gasoline that could be refined from a gallon of crude oil, resulted in higher-quality parts for internal-combustion engines, and brought gains in the manufacture of phonographs, refrigerators, radios, washing machines, vacuum cleaners, and other adjuncts of the good life.

No industry was rooted more firmly in the technological and managerial changes of the postwar years than automobiles. For the rubber, glass, and alloys of which body and engine parts were made, automobile manufacturers depended on the new chemical and electrical knowledge and the new electrochemical processes. Automobile manufacturers became the greatest users of each of the commodities that went into their product, and work on auto assembly lines became highly mechanized and repetitive.

Many attempts had been made to build a horseless carriage run by steam, electricity, alcohol, or some other fuel. After a series of experiments with a gasoline engine, the automobile became commercially feasible about 1903. In 1909 Henry Ford introduced the Model T, and in 1914 he opened his revolutionary plant at Highland Park, Michigan. It was equipped with the first electric conveyor belt, which carried the gradually assembled car at a uniform—and rapid—speed past stationary workers. Each worker used materials and tools to perform one simple mechanical task. In 1913 it had taken fourteen hours, on the average, to assemble a Model T. In the new plant it could be done in ninety-three minutes. In 1914 Ford built 248,000 cars—45 percent of the total automobile output—at a base price of $490. By 1925 Ford was turning out a complete car every ten seconds.

In 1920 about 9 million automobiles were registered in the United States. Ten years later it was nearly 30 million. Millions of Americans came to see the automobile as part of the minimum standard of living. It broke down distances and encouraged a movement into the suburbs, created a new kind of tourist industry, and stimulated government expenditures for street and highway construction.

Between 1921 and 1929, industrial output in the United States almost doubled, even though the size of the labor force remained stable. At the same time, population and economic growth, as well as the wartime construction lag, pushed the demand for housing to record levels. This stimulated the private-construction industry, which traditionally used more capital and labor than any other. But Coolidge prosperity rested on a slippery footing. Workers did not share adequately in the profits of increased production, and this resulted in an unequal distribution of purchasing power. Technological unemployment increased, and farmers failed to recover from the postwar recession. For a time, the construction and auto booms, along with speculation in real estate and securities, sustained the "good times." And as long as the prosperity lasted, the

Republicans would maintain control of the White House.

The Election of 1928

When Coolidge let slip the announcement that he did not choose to run in 1928, Republican leaders turned to his secretary of commerce. Born in modest circumstances on an Iowa farm, Herbert Hoover had had a rewarding career as an engineer and promoter. He won acclaim for his relief work in Europe during the war. After the war, he was credited with having used American wealth to stop the advance of communism. These activities gave him a reputation for practicality and humanitarianism. His attacks on the many unwise aspects of peace-making also gave him standing as a statesman.

To oppose Hoover, the Democrats this time united behind Al Smith. As governor of New York, Smith had an outstanding record of backing liberal legislation and ideas. But that record meant nothing to the nation at large. An Irishman, a Catholic, a New Yorker, and a "wet," Smith was the incarnation of everything that aroused rural and small-town suspicions.

With Hoover's initial advantages, it seems unlikely that any Democrat could have beaten him. His popular *majority* exceeded 6 million votes, and he carried all but eight states, including, for the first time since Reconstruction, five in the Solid South. Many Catholics blamed bigotry for Smith's defeat. But Coolidge prosperity and Hoover's promise of more to come were more likely the decisive factors. Even as the new president took the oath of office, however, the shaky foundations on which Coolidge prosperity had rested were cracking. When the collapse came, there was little left but the dreary statistics of depression.

SUGGESTED READINGS

W.E. Leuchtenburg, *The Perils of Prosperity, 1914–1932* (1958). W. Preston, *Aliens and Dissenters: Federal Suppression of Radicals, 1903–1933* (1963). R.K. Murray, *Red Scare* (1955). R. Wright, *Black Boy* (1945). N.I. Huggins, *Harlem Renaissance* (1971). P.S. Fass, *The Damned and the Beautiful* (1977). W.H. Chafe, *The American Woman: Her Changing Social, Economic, and Political Role* (1972). F.J. Hoffman, *The Twenties* (1955).

SUMMARY

The twenties were an extraordinary decade in America—a time when life and culture changed rapidly, when the "good times" and the prosperity of some contrasted sharply with the struggles and poverty of others.

The decade began with postwar depression and repression. Wartime tensions carried

over into hysteria over radicalism, the restriction of immigration, and racial violence. The Ku Klux Klan was revived; a great Red Scare engulfed and defeated a labor movement once again pushing for better wages and working conditions. The murder trial of two Italian anarchists and their execution brought worldwide protest from millions convinced of their inno-

cence. The race-suicide alarm resulted in the Immigration Restriction Act of 1921 and the National Origins Act of 1924.

In the South, Jim Crow laws, lynchings and beatings, lack of educational facilities, and the misery of the sharecropper's life brought thousands of blacks to northern cities. Between 1910 and 1940, more than 1.7 million blacks left the South; by 1940, the black population outside the South had more than doubled. But the Great Migration took place in an atmosphere of growing racial intolerance in the North as well as in the South. The worst race riot in the nation's history took place in Chicago in July 1919.

Prohibition was another aspect of the twenties. Making liquor illegal nationwide had two immediate results: drinking moved from the old saloon to the speakeasy, where it took on a new glamour, and a new field was opened up for organized crime. Not until 1933 did Congress, with a new Democratic majority, finally pass the Twenty-first Amendment to repeal the Eighteenth.

For American intellectuals, writers, and artists, the Twenties were enormously productive. In their willingness to question the sanity of their society and to experiment with new ideas and forms, this generation stood out. These were the writers and artists of the lost generation, some of whom became expatriates for a while because they felt they could not work at home. Among them were Ernest Hemingway, Ezra Pound, Malcolm Cowley, Sinclair Lewis, Sherwood Anderson, William Faulkner, and F. Scott Fitzgerald.

This was also the time of the Harlem Renaissance, a flowering of black culture that was to spread to the white world as well. New York's Harlem became the center of culture for blacks, the "place to be." Black music—jazz, ragtime, and blues—became known worldwide. Among the black writers and intellectuals of this period were Langston Hughes, Claude McKay, and Jean Toomer.

The new popular arts—movies, radio, records—were all the result of technology. They shaped American attitudes and tastes in new ways. They reached mass audiences, nationalized popular culture, and speeded up the standardization of society.

Politics during the twenties were marked by a return to the American Dream—that anyone who had the right kind of ambition and determination could succeed. It was a politics of complacency, shaken but not shattered by the scandals of the Harding administration. To Harding, as to Coolidge, business values were sacred. Taxes were lowered, tariffs raised. The regulatory agencies and the Supreme Court cooperated to make life easier for business. But organized labor lost ground, social legislation had a hard time in the courts, and staple farmers were in deep trouble.

"Coolidge prosperity" was marked by new production techniques and new consumer industries. Electrochemical technology made possible a revolution in the petroleum industry and the mass production of consumer goods such as phonographs, refrigerators, radios, washing machines, and vacuum cleaners. Factory organization and operation changed because of the availability of electric power. And the automobile became part of every American's life. In 1920, about 9 million automobiles were registered in the United States; ten years later, it was nearly 30 million.

This prosperity rested on a shaky foundation. The workers' share in the profits of increased production was not enough to raise their purchasing power; technological unemployment grew; the farmers did not recover; and wild speculation on the stock market blew the bubble up to the bursting point. The election of 1928 brought Herbert Hoover to the presidency, along with promises of continued Republican prosperity. But the good times were not to last much beyond his inauguration in March of 1929.

23

The Great Depression and the New Deal

The presidential inaugurations of 1929 and 1933 provided a striking contrast in personalities, issues, and the state of the Union. In his somewhat muffled, droning voice, Herbert Hoover spoke with confidence of America's future. "In no nation are the fruits of accomplishment more secure." Less than eight months later, on Black Tuesday, October 29, 1929, stock prices at the New York Stock Exchange fell in the most disastrous trading day in the history of the market. Within a few hours, more than $10 billion of America's "fruits of accomplishment" were gone. In the next three years, consumer purchasing declined and manufacturers closed plants or reduced the work force. Some 100,000 workers, on the average, were fired each week. The number of unemployed stood at 2 million in 1929, 4 million in 1930, 8 million in 1931, and 12 million in 1932. National income was cut more than half. Over 5000 banks and 9 million savings accounts were wiped out; tens of thousands of mortgages were foreclosed. Families found themselves evicted from their homes and barely able to exist. More than a million homeless people took to the road or settled in "Hoo-

vervilles," shantytowns made of old packing cartons and car bodies. They came to symbolize not only the depths of the Depression but the president's inability to do anything about it.

By March 4, 1933, when Frankin D. Roosevelt took the oath of office as president, three and a half years had passed since the crash of October 1929, the number of unemployed had reached 13 million, and the nation was experiencing failure on a scale unprecedented in its history. But the new president, even as he described "the dark realities of the moment," conveyed a sense of confidence and determination in his voice and manner that comforted his audience.

The American people would respond to FDR's appeal for confidence—"the only thing we have to fear is fear itself"—with an enthusiasm matched only by the contempt they had shown for Hoover's plea for confidence—"All the evidences indicate that the worst effects of the crash . . . will have been passed during the next 60 days." But the Great Depression, as both Hoover and Roosevelt would learn from *their attempts to deal with it, could not be solved with psychology. Confidence alone could not feed hungry people or create jobs for the unemployed, and there was much more to fear than fear itself. Amer-* *icans were thrilled by FDR's pledge to treat the economic crisis "as we would treat the emergency of a war." Few had any reason to suspect that only a war would ultimately bring them out of the crisis.*

THE CRASH

The crash centered in the New York Stock Exchange on Wall Street, the scene in 1929 of an enormous amount of activity in stock securities. Overnight success stories, the assurances of business and political leaders, and easy credit terms fed the fever. Thousands of small investors, along with the wealthy, poured their savings into common stocks. The warning signs went unheeded: cutbacks in private construction, large business inventories, the decline in consumer purchasing. Industry was not making enough profit to justify the soaring stock prices. The market wavered, and on October 29, 1929, it came crashing down. President Hoover tried to assure the public that there was no reason to panic. But with every new assurance that the worst had passed, the depression deepened.

A Flawed Economy

The stock-market crash dramatized fundamental weaknesses in the economy. It revealed more pockets of economic hardship than had been acknowledged, larger ones than had been supposed, and their tendency to grow. Farm receipts had already bottomed out, and farmers throughout the twenties had to deal with large surpluses, declining prices, and higher expenses. For many years chronic unemployment had characterized uncertain industries, in particular textiles and coal mining. In the twenties, the un-

even distribution of income should have suggested that the nation was risking economic disaster. The slowly rising real wages of industrial workers were outdistanced by the salaries, savings, and profits of those higher on the economic ladder. In 1929, the 24,000 richest families had an aggregate income more than three times as large as that of the nearly 6 million poorest families. Forty percent of all families had incomes under $1500. No wonder the purchasing power of Americans did not keep up with the production potential of the industrial plant and the flood of commerical advertising. Those who were getting rich, meanwhile, found their savings piled up out of all proportion to need. Looking for opportunities for sound investment, they turned to speculation in real estate and securities, both blown up into a bubble sure to burst.

The federal government had failed to deal with these matters. Tax policies favored the rich, making even more unequal the distribution of income. Labor policies were antiunion. The economic situation abroad only aggravated the domestic crisis. European nations needed goods and credit from America to restore their economies and stabilize their currencies. But American tariffs like the Hawley-Smoot Tariff, passed during the Hoover administration, presented obstacles to exports and limited Europe's buying power. American manufacturers found it ever more difficult to sell abroad. And the American and European economies were so closely linked that the Depression soon became worldwide.

In 1932, when the number of unemployed went above four million, job-hunting lines such as this were a common sight. (Library of Congress)

Hoover and the Depression

For all his stress on confidence, Hoover acknowledged the need for direct federal intervention. That decision in itself marked a significant break with the past. In 1930, when the slide of wheat and cotton prices became catastrophic, Hoover tried to use the extension of agricultural credit and the new Federal Farm Board to reverse the price trend by open-market purchases. It was not long, however, before government warehouses bulged with surpluses that might be released at any time; prices felt the pressure and resumed their slide.

To help labor and industry, Congress granted the president $700 million early in 1930 for public works, the start of a new program that saw Hoover spend almost $3 billion on public construction. The president also tried to get companies to delay firing workers and cutting wages. But even the best-willed industrialists could not keep people at work at a living wage when there were no markets for products. By 1932, wages had plummeted and 12 million were unemployed. Great companies faced bankruptcy. In an effort to save insurance companies and the philanthropic organizations that had invested in their securities, Congress created the Reconstruction Finance Corporation. By the end of 1932, the RFC had loaned $1.5 billion to about 5000 shaky firms. But this shot in the arm did little to help the economy.

No previous administration had ever taken such extensive measures to revive the private economy or help the victims of its collapse. Yet they proved wholly inadequate. The crisis became even more acute when local and private welfare agencies also crashed. But Hoover's principles—his belief in the market forces, voluntarism, and self-help—did not permit him to undertake the massive federal intervention the crisis demanded. Even as the Depression deepened, he clung to the belief that the only function of government was "to bring about a condition of affairs favorable to the beneficial development of private enterprise."

The Election of 1932

With unemployment increasing and local and state welfare funds nearly exhausted, Hoover faced a grim electorate in 1932 and a formidable Democratic opponent. Aware that they had to renominate Hoover or accept the charge of a Hoover Depression, the Republicans did so on the first ballot. The Democrats named Franklin D. Roosevelt, governor of New York. On receiving the nomination, Roosevelt flew to Chicago to accept the honor in person, something no candidate had done before. "I pledge you, I pledge myself," he told the delegates, "to a new deal for the American people."

Despite the urgency of the Depression, neither the platforms of the two major political parties nor the candidates themselves suggested that the federal government might need to play a central role in the industrial society. Hoover stressed international economic difficulties as the main causes of the crash. Roosevelt zeroed in on the flaws the crash revealed in the American economy. Hoover warned that too much government intervention would destroy individual liberty. Roosevelt called for novel methods to meet novel conditions—"bold and persistent experimentation." But his few specific commitments were conventional, and his pledge to assist the victims of the Depression while reducing government expenditures and balancing the budget must have baffled economic analysts. Yet more voters were heartened by his promises, however vague, than were impressed by Hoover's warnings. Roosevelt

carried all but six states and won a popular majority of more than 7 million votes. The Democratic party, moreover, won overwhelming majorities in both houses of Congress.

FDR'S NEW DEAL

Charming, self-assured, energetic, and fearless, FDR was the New Deal's greatest asset. Unlike Hoover, the new president seemed to have both compassion and confidence, and the people responded. However erratic his actions, and despite the uncertainty with which he moved sometimes, Roosevelt knew how to communicate. In his radio "fireside chats," he made the people feel that he was discussing important national questions with them directly, that he understood their problems and frustrations. Few expressed that reaction more clearly than the North Carolina millworker who explained to an anti–New Deal journalist why he stood by the president: "Mr. Roosevelt is the only man we ever had in the White House who would understand that my boss is a sonofabitch."

Roosevelt was deeply moved by the plight of the poor. Unlike Cleveland and Hoover, he believed the underprivileged had a legitimate claim on the federal government. During the early years of the New Deal, many people spoke of it as an attempt at economic planning. Economic experimentation would be a more accurate description. No one knew of a single solution. Hoover's approach to the problem of recovery had been largely the traditional one of allowing the deflation to run its course. The New Dealers experimented with currency inflation and with heavy government spending to prime the pump of business. Led by the president, they moved to rescue the banks, stabilize business and agriculture, re-

Franklin D. Roosevelt. (Wide World Photos)

duce unemployment, and provide assistance for the victims of the Depression.

Banking and Currency Reform

One of the most dangerous developments of the Depression—the headlong plunge of the nation's banks toward bankruptcy—was the first to be attacked. The first steps were taken within a day or two of Roosevelt's inauguration and gave the public a welcome taste of energetic new leadership.

So many banks had failed that even solvent institutions were menaced by frightened depositors rushing to withdraw their money. To stop the panic, the governors of almost half the states had declared "bank holidays," and most of the banks were closed when Roosevelt took office. By proclamation on March 6, Roosevelt suspended all banking operations and gold transactions. Three days later Congress was called into special session, where it passed the Emergency Banking Act, ratifying the president's actions and establishing procedures

for getting sound banks back in business. Roosevelt then went on the air with his first fireside chat, a brilliant effort to reassure people that a sound banking system was about to emerge from the reorganization. Before the end of March, most of the sound banks had reopened and the unsound ones were on the way to being permanently closed. Within another month, more than 12,000 banks, containing 90 percent of the country's deposits, were functioning normally.

"In one week," wrote columnist Walter Lippmann of the bank crisis, "the nation, which had lost confidence in everything and everybody, has regained confidence in the government and in itself." Roosevelt's avoidance of the more radical solution to which he could have turned—nationalizing the banks—quieted conservative suspicions. His action also made it clear that the New Deal intended to patch up the old order rather than replace it—that is, he would keep intact the basic structure of American capitalism. But to do so he would have the federal government play a major and unprecedented role.

Bank reform soon followed. One of the best reform measures was the Glass-Steagall Act of June 1933, which created the Federal Deposit Insurance Corporation (FDIC) and authorized it to guarantee bank deposits up to $5000 per depositor. Many banks had got into trouble using depositors' money to speculate in the stock market. The banks had invested through their affiliates in the securities business. The Glass-Steagall Act forbade national banks to maintain such affiliates, and it contained other reforms intended to divorce commercial from investment banking. Finally, the Banking Act of 1935 greatly increased federal authority over the banking system by empowering the Federal Reserve Board to regulate interest rates.

The administration also pressed for closer supervision of the stock market. The Securities Act of 1933 required greater publicity for the details of stock promotion and closed the mails to sellers failing to provide it. This measure was followed by the Securities Exchange Act of June 1934, which created the Securities and Exchange Commission. The SEC was authorized to require registration of all securities traded on the stock exchanges and to cooperate with the Federal Reserve Board in regulating the purchase of securities.

The New Deal experimented with various plans to stimulate industrial activity, mostly with no success. One of the earliest ideas was to cheapen the dollar. That would reduce the burden of fixed debts, which had become a drag on expansion. At the same time, it would raise domestic prices and encourage output. Cheapening the dollar was also expected to stimulate exports, because foreign currency would buy more goods. In May 1933 Congress authorized the president to issue greenbacks, reduce the gold

content of the dollar, and provide for unlimited coinage of both gold and silver at a ratio that he could set.

The president used his new authority with great caution. In a new effort to increase the money supply and boost commodity prices by currency manipulation, Roosevelt ordered the purchase of gold on the open market. This action, he hoped, would raise the price of gold, which in turn would help to raise the general price level. But despite these experiments, the price level did not rise. Business recovery proved far more difficult than banking reform.

Business: The NRA

The idea behind currency experiments was that under favorable monetary conditions, ordinary market mechanisms might push prices up. But the New Dealers were not alone in realizing that the market mechanisms themselves needed artificial respiration and probably a permanent iron lung. To help the economy breathe once more, Congress passed the National Industrial Recovery Act (NIRA) in June 1933. The president hailed it as "the most important and far-reaching legislation ever enacted by the American Congress."

The point of the NIRA was not so much to expand the economy as to ration the nation's business among the surviving corporations. It had the support, and in some cases the sponsorship, of businessmen and leaders of the United States Chamber of Commerce. Under its provisions, the antitrust laws were in effect suspended. Trade associations and other business groups were permitted to draw up "codes of fair competition," which would include comprehensive price agreements, firm production quotas, and wage scales high enough to improve the condition of the lowest-paid workers. Each type of business was empowered to draw up its own code. The government reserved the right to accept or reject the codes, to set up its own when companies in any industry failed to agree, and to enforce them. Section 7(a) of the NIRA guaranteed labor the right of collective bargaining. A National Recovery Administration (NRA) was formed to administer the codes. It was chaired by General Hugh Johnson, who had worked on the War Industries Board during World War I.

In order to make the NRA comparable to mobilization for war, administrators organized parades and mass meetings. They adopted a placard with a blue eagle as a symbol to be awarded for display to businessmen and even to consumers who cooperated. One of their hoped-for effects was to stir up boycotts of uncooperative firms, substituting public pressure for legal enforcement.

No less than 746 NRA codes were adopted by businessmen eager to get started again. But there were problems. The paperwork required to supply needed information to the government quickly reached fantastic proportions and was resented. Big corporations resisted all further signs of bureaucratic interference. Small firms complained that the codes, which were drawn up by the larger firms in each industry, discriminated against small business. Workers, who at first supported the NRA, soon nicknamed it the National Run Around. Code administrators, they said, sided with antiunion employers in labor disputes. Employers detested the very existence of Section 7(a) and the expansion of organized labor it would allow. Moreover, when the codes succeeded in reviving production by raising prices, they aroused consumer discontent.

The NRA had reached a low point in popularity when the Supreme Court killed it in May 1935. In the case of *Schecter Poultry Corporation* v. *United States*, the Court unanimously found that the National Recovery Act was unconstitutional on two counts. First, it improperly delegated legislative powers to the executive. Second, the provisions of the poultry code constituted a regulation of intrastate, not interstate, commerce.

The NRA had not been entirely worthless. It established the principle of maximum hours and minimum wages on a national basis. It reduced child labor. It made collective bargaining a national policy. In many instances cancellation of a code brought a return to poor working conditions, to which the labor movement soon turned its attention.

Agriculture: The AAA

Two months before Roosevelt's inauguration, the normally conservative head of the Farm Bureau Federation, Edward A. O'Neal, warned a Senate committee, "Unless something is done for the American farmer we will have revolution in the countryside within less than 12 months." Even as he spoke, farmers were beginning to take matters into their own hands. They forced a stoppage of eviction sales and mortgage foreclosures. They intimidated and assaulted public officials and agents of banks and insurance companies. Violence became so widespread in Iowa by April 1933 that the governor put several counties under martial law and called out the National Guard.

The New Dealers were well aware of the need for quick action to raise the prices of agricultural products to a level that would increase farmers' purchasing power. When they acted, they approached the farm problem in the same mood with which they approached the problems of industry. The farm plan was incorporated in the Agricultural Adjustment Act of May 1933, which established the Agricultural Adjustment Administration.

Abandoning all hope of regaining lost foreign markets for staples, the AAA hoped to raise farm prices by cutting back production to domestic needs and rationing the domestic market among producers. In this way it planned to bring farm prices up to parity with those of the prosperous prewar years of 1909 to 1914. To compensate farmers for cooperating with the government plan, the AAA was authorized to pay various subsidies for acreage withdrawn from production and for certain marketing practices. Funds to finance the program were to come from taxes on the processors of farm products, such as millers, cotton ginners, and meat packers. At first, the act provided for reductions only in cotton, wheat, corn, hogs, rice, tobacco, and milk. Later, other products were included.

To cut production when people were hungry was bound to bring criticism. But farm spokesmen insisted that if the profit system meant anything, then the farmers had the same right as businessmen to do this. To make matters worse, the AAA did not begin to function until after the spring planting of 1933. Where acreage had not been sufficiently reduced, farmers were ordered to plow under a large part of their crops. With people reportedly starving in the cities, the AAA's action seemed heartless. It also fell short of its goal. Many farmers accepted government checks for reducing acreage and then calmly cultivated their remaining acres more intensively. In 1934 Congress added production quotas to acreage restriction and imposed taxes on violators. The new and old laws helped double and triple farm staple prices. Total net income of farm operators rose dramatically.

The Supreme Court ruled in January 1936 that it was unconstitutional for Congress to impose a tax on processors for the purpose of regulating farm production. Congress responded with the Soil Conservation and Domestic Allotment Act, which put crop restriction on a sounder constitutional basis. When prices tumbled again in 1937, Congress passed a second Agricultural Adjustment Act. The price fall in 1937 had come from bumper crops produced in 1936. The new act aimed to keep such bumper crops off the market by compensating farmers for storing them. Large amounts were paid to farmers, but staple growers did not really do well until wartime demand in the 1940s pushed prices up.

Millions of farm families gained nothing from legislation designed to help commercial, landowning farmers. By 1935, an estimated 46 percent of all white farmers were tenants, as well as some 77 percent of black farmers. Rarely did the benefits of the AAA seep down to the tenants and sharecroppers; 90 percent of the government payments went to the planters and landlords, and these same people usually controlled the local and county committees to which the tenants would have to appeal their case. And with acreage being removed from cultivation so that planters could qualify for AAA payments, landlords evicted many tenants rather than split the payments with them. They thereby stimulated a movement of tenants to the cities, where they could join the army of unemployed.

As the Depression wore on, concern for sharecroppers, farm tenants, and hired farm laborers grew. The New Deal's response was the Resettlement Administration, created in 1935. It withdrew 9 million acres of wasteland from cultivation and moved the families on them to resettlement areas. It extended loans to farmers who could not obtain credit elsewhere, and it

Migratory worker, 1940. "When they need us, they call us migrants. When we've picked their crops, we're called bums and we've got to get out." (Photograph by Dorothea Lange, Library of Congress)

encouraged cooperation among farmers who had always insisted on going it alone. In response to the report of a presidential committee on rural poverty, Congress passed the Farm Tenancy Act in 1937 in order to provide loans to sharecroppers, tenant farmers, and farm laborers for the purchase of land, livestock, supplies, and equipment. By June 1944, 870,000 rural families had been helped.

Although it recognized the problem of rural poverty, the New Deal had still done very little about it. When sharecroppers and farm laborers—white and black—began to attack their troubles through the newly formed Southern Tenant Farmers' Union, they found violent resistance from the farming interests that had benefited most from New Deal legislation. The union's newspaper finally concluded that under President Roosevelt, "too often the progressive word has been the clothing for a conservative act. Too often he has talked like a cropper and acted like a planter."

Rural Redevelopment: The TVA

One of the poorest of all American farm areas was the Tennessee Valley, which was immensely rich in natural resources. Government projects to harness the mighty Tennessee River were begun at Muscle Shoals in northwestern Alabama during World War I. But the private power companies opposed all efforts to keep Muscle Shoals a public project, and Coolidge and Hoover vetoed the necessary legislation.

After his election, Roosevelt visited Muscle Shoals and soon had a grand plan for the whole valley. On May 18, 1933, Congress created the Tennessee Valley Authority and empowered it to buy, build, and operate dams in the valley. It would generate and sell electric power, and plan re-

Migratory worker's wife. "If you die, you're dead—that's all." (Photograph by Dorothea Lange, Library of Congress)

forestation and flood control. The TVA could withdraw marginal lands from cultivation and undertake regional planning to improve the standard of living of the people who lived in the valley.

Of all the New Deal experiments in government, the TVA was probably the boldest and most original. It was an independent public corporation, and its area of responsibility embraced 40,000 square miles in seven states. The TVA built sixteen new dams and took over five others. By 1940, four dams were generating electric power in the TVA region. Over 40,000 users, many of them farmers who had no previous access to electricity, were directly or indirectly served. TVA rates were kept low, and served as a yardstick by which to measure private rates. The result was to force private companies in the area to keep rates down. Land redeemed by the TVA from flooding was made productive for the first time. Like earlier valley plans, the TVA was fought by the power companies. They gained the support of disinterested conservatives who saw in the experiment a threat to the private-enterprise system. Like other New Deal measures, the TVA was soon taken to court. But unlike some other measures, it survived.

Unemployment: CCC, PWA, WPA

When Roosevelt took office, at least 13 million workers were unemployed. With their families, they added up to about 50 million persons, many of them on the verge of starvation. The issue was no longer whether the federal government should act, but how. Should it give handouts to the poverty-stricken, which was the cheapest plan, or should it provide work, which seemed less wasteful and more humane?

The first New Deal assistance to the unemployed was the Civilian Conservation Corps for the youth of the country. At one point the CCC had on its rolls 500,000 young men, eighteen to twenty-five. Recruited from cities to live in camps built by the War Department, they worked on reforestation, road and dam construction, control of mosquitoes and other pests, and similar tasks. Of the thirty dollars a month in wages, twenty-two dollars was sent to the young men's families. By the end of 1941, some 2,750,000 youths had spent some part of their lives in CCC camps.

The first comprehensive New Deal relief measure was the act of May 1933 creating the Federal Emergency Relief Administration (FERA). Under Harry Hopkins, the FERA had half a billion dollars to use for direct emergency relief. Although the federal government provided the money, the relief itself was to be administered by the states. Cash payments were distributed at first, but Hopkins thought work relief was psychologically and economically superior. In time, almost half of those receiving relief were put to work on jobs that presumably did not compete with private business. Pay began at thirty cents an hour.

The Public Works Administration (PWA), under Secretary of the Interior Harold Ickes, was more a pump-priming than a relief agency. Its duties included planning bridges, dams, hospitals, and other public projects and contracting private companies to construct them.

Many people complained that New Deal relief agencies, besides duplicating one another's tasks, made no effort to distinguish between employable persons who needed relief and "unemployables," who could not have found work even in good times. Early in 1935 Roosevelt proposed a reorganization of the entire relief program.

The federal government would aid employables only. The care of others would be left to the states and municipalities. The Emergency Relief Act of 1935 put these proposals into effect. The CCC and the PWA were continued. All other federal relief was brought under a new agency, the Works Progress Administration, directed by Harry Hopkins. When its operations ended in July 1941, the WPA had spent $11.3 billion. At its peak, in November 1938, nearly 3.3 million persons were on its payroll, and all told WPA provided work for 8 million people. Among its more than 250,000 projects were hospitals, bridges, municipal power plants, post offices, school buildings, slum clearance, and the rehabilitation of army posts and naval stations.

The WPA also took into account the plight of the humanities and the arts, whose practitioners, like other workers, were left stranded by the Depression. Its projects in the fine arts, music, and the theater gave employment to painters, writers, actors, singers, and musicians. Still other projects resulted in the recovering of American folklore, interviews with more than two thousand surviving ex-slaves, and the recording of white and black spirituals, Indian songs, and folk tunes. On post-office walls all over the country WPA artists painted regional scenes and memorable local episodes. Americans who had never gone to a theater or concert flocked to federal theater performances, which charged no admission for those unable to pay.

No part of the New Deal drew more criticism than its relief program. The cost was truly enormous for the times, and the tax burden had to be shouldered by the depressed private sector of the economy. Many critics charged, usually inaccurately, that relief was inefficiently handled. Others, often justly, accused the administration of using

relief for political purposes. No part of the relief program drew more criticism than its support of cultural activities. Many Americans had no sympathy with the idea that musicians, writers, and artists had as much claim on the community as workers in other fields.

Even at its peak, however, the WPA had reached fewer than half of the unemployed. Despite the New Deal experiments in economic legislation, only once, in 1937, did the number of unemployed fall below 8 million. In 1940 it was back above that figure—a level five times as high as in 1929. This failure, some critics suggested, revealed a flaw in New Deal ideas about the essential soundness of the economic system it was trying to revive.

CHALLENGE AND RESPONSE

Most of the New Deal's famous "alphabet agencies"—NRA, TVA, AAA, SEC, CCC, PWA—were begun in the first hundred days of the Roosevelt administration. The opposition was for the moment shamed, shocked, or stunned into silence. Supported by the president's optimism, relief and reform measures were adopted almost unanimously. That same enthusiasm carried over to the polls. In the congressional elections of 1934 the Democrats scored overwhelming victories, swelling their majorities in the House and Senate.

But if the election of 1934 buried the conservative critics who thought Roosevelt was going too far too fast, it might have reminded him, if he needed reminding, of several things: the spirit of protest was still rising; recovery had not yet been achieved; and those who believed the New Deal moved too little and too slowly would be heard from. The most troublesome critics in the next several years would be those who took advantage of the growing despair of the lower middle class, many of whom had been badly shaken by the collapse of a system they had never thought to question. The despair was genuine and widespread enough to move the New Deal into some new areas.

Critics and Crusaders

Most formidable among the new breed of critics was Senator Huey Long of Louisiana. A skilled politician, he built up a national following on the strength of his Share Our Wealth plan. This called for confiscatory taxes on the wealthy, which would provide every family with an income of $2500, a homestead, and an automobile. The fear that Long might split the party by challenging Roosevelt's bid for reelection was ended by his assassination in September 1935.

A second popular challenge was mounted in California by Frances E. Townsend, an elderly physician. In January 1935 he announced the Townsend Plan, by which the government would give $200 a month to every citizen sixty years old or older. The cost would be paid by a sales tax. Each pensioner would be required to spend his or her allowance within the month. This would start such a wave of consumer buying that business would boom and make it easy for the rest of the country to bear the cost. Responsible economists dismissed the plan as a crackpot scheme. But Townsend Clubs, organized throughout the country, attracted desperate older men and women. Their combined membership was said to be about 3 million in 1935, and there were perhaps as many as 7 million additional supporters.

More forceful and yet more vague than Dr. Townsend was the "radio priest," Charles E. Coughlin, who broadcast weekly from Royal Oak, Michigan. Coughlin won an enormous audience with assaults on Wall Street and the international bankers, phrased in such a way that no one could doubt the role of these groups in the Depression. Originally one of Roosevelt's supporters, Coughlin broke with the New Deal in 1935, drifted toward fascism and anti-Semitism, and lost most of his popular appeal.

The popularity of Long, Townsend, and Coughlin, coming as it did with organized labor's growing discontent, suggested in the spring of 1935 that Roosevelt's mass appeal, so strong in the early months of the New Deal, might soon dissolve. The president well understood the genuine grievances underlying the broad appeal of these critics; privately he even spoke of doing something "to steal Long's thunder." The Revenue Tax Act, the Social Security Act, the National Labor Relations Act, and other actions were all responses to this pressure. "I am fighting Communism, Huey Longism, Coughlinism, Townsendism," Roosevelt told one of his critics. "I want to save our system, the capitalistic system; to save it is to give some heed to world thought of today. I want to equalize the distribution of wealth." The result was more reform.

New Directions: The 1935 Reforms

Responding to the challenge of his critics, President Roosevelt initiated a new wave of reform legislation. The Revenue Tax Act of 1935, sometimes called the wealth tax or the soak-the-rich law, was inspired by the administration's desire to stop the growth of gigantic personal fortunes. Some also suspected it was Roosevelt's way of responding to Long's Share Our Wealth scheme. Tax rates, which had already been raised by earlier New Deal measures, were now pushed much higher, reaching 75 percent on individual incomes over $5 million. Holding companies used for the management of private fortunes were also taxed heavily, and corporation taxes were raised.

The Social Security Act was another reform enacted in 1935. For the first time, the federal government would make payments, directly or through the states, for pensions to the aged and the infirm, for unemployment insurance, and for benefits to dependent mothers and children. Federal pensions of up to fifteen dollars a month to the poor over sixty-five years of age were expected to be matched by the states. Federal retirement funds, ranging from ten to eighty-five dollars a month, were to be paid to workers who retired at sixty-five and who had participated in the plan before their retirement. Agricultural workers, household servants, government employees, and those working for nonprofit religious or charitable organizations were among those excluded. The money for those included was to be raised by a payroll tax on employers and employees. Most states promptly set up old-age pension and unemployment-insurance systems conforming to the provisions of the act. A worker who lost his or her job could collect from five to fifteen dollars a week for a period of about fifteen weeks while looking for new work.

By 1940, about 50 million workers were protected by social security. From time to time since then, new classes of workers have been covered, money payments increased, and the period for receiving unemployment insurance extended.

Labor

When the Supreme Court found the NIRA unconstitutional and invalidated its labor guarantees, Congress responded in July 1935 by enacting the National Labor Relations Act, often called the Wagner Act after the New York senator who championed it. The act guaranteed collective bargaining and prohibited employer interference with organizing activities. It provided that the representative of the majority of the employees in any plant should be the exclusive bargaining representative of all the employees. It empowered a newly established National Labor Relations Board to investigate and certify the proper representatives and to hold supervised elections when there was a dispute over which union should represent employees. The long-run effects of this measure for the political future of the New Deal, for the Democratic party, and for the country were as profound and lasting as its economic consequences. Membership in trade unions continued to grow, particularly in the unorganized mass-production industries, until in 1941 it reached 10.5 million. By then, the NLRB had handled 33,000 cases affecting more than 7 million workers.

But the rise of organized labor was accompanied by conflict not only between workers and employers, but also within labor. The AFL was badly split. The leaders of the old craft unions that had first come together in the federation sought to retain their power and standing as the aristocracy of labor. Not wanting to bring in the unskilled and semiskilled workers of mass-production industries, they also refused to permit other leaders to organize such workers in new unions. The issue came to a head at the national AFL convention in October 1935, when a majority of the delegates stood fast for craft unionism. A month later, John L. Lewis of the United Mine Workers and seven other AFL leaders met separately and organized the Committee for Industrial Organization, intending to advise the AFL on how to organize the mass-production industries. Lewis became chairman of the committee. In January 1936 the AFL executive council ordered the CIO to disband. The CIO leaders refused. Expelled from the AFL in March 1937, they took with them unions representing 1.8 million workers. A massive organizing campaign followed, and there were a record 4740 strikes that year. Early in 1938, when the CIO had nearly 4 million members, the leaders formed a new, organization with the same initials, the Congress of Industrial Organizations.

One of the CIO's new weapons, outlawed by the Supreme Court in 1939, was the sit-down strike. Instead of walking off the job and picketing, workers went to their posts in the plants and stayed there, making it difficult for others to replace them. Sit-down strikes against two giant automobile companies, General Motors in January 1937 and Chrysler in April, won the CIO recognition as the bargaining agent for their workers. In March 1937 the United States Steel Corporation, once the terror of organized labor, also gave in. "Little Steel" proved harder to crack. On Memorial Day 1937, Chicago police killed ten pickets during a strike against the Republic Company, Little Steel's leader. Other strikes brought violence in the Ohio cities of Youngstown, Massillon, and Cleveland. Little Steel did not fall until 1941, when the companies signed contracts conforming to the NLRB order to reinstate workers fired during the 1937 struggle.

As labor grew more aggressive and important in politics as well as business, the split in its ranks caused many difficulties. A peace movement finally brought about a merger of the AFL and CIO in 1955.

The Roosevelt Coalition: White and Black

Although the New Deal failed to resolve the economic crisis, it did give the American people a sense of direction and hope.

Through his personal leadership and the legislation he had helped to bring about, Roosevelt had managed to build an extraordinary political coalition by the end of 1935. Underpinning this coalition was traditional Democratic strength in the Solid South, which was satisfied for the time being with the price improvements in such staples as cotton and tobacco, and Democratic loyalty in northern cities, where FDR chose to use rather than destroy the party machines.

The success of the New Deal's agricultural program among commercial farmers attracted many normally Republican midwesterners to the Roosevelt coalition. At the same time, labor's newly organized millions swelled the Democratic ranks, along with intellectuals who were heartened by the administration's receptivity to ideas and experts and by its readiness to assist unemployed artists, scholars, and writers. Nor, for that matter, were businessmen altogether hostile to Roosevelt. He counted many loyal personal friends among businessmen. Additional support came from consumer-goods manufacturers, chain- and department-store owners, and other retailers who benefited directly from gains in mass purchasing power brought about by New Deal reform and relief measures.

Blacks had good reason not to support the administration. Almost all NRA codes, for example, discriminated against black workers in the areas of employment, wages, and job-improvement opportunities. AAA crop-control payments went mostly to farmers with large acreage, which left black sharecroppers in a precarious economic position and forced many of them off the land altogether. The CCC began as a lily-white agency: fewer than 3 percent of the first quarter-million enrolled were blacks. Even when black participation grew, segregation remained the rule. This was also true in the model towns established by the TVA. And the New Deal housing program encouraged the development of racially segregated neighborhoods. Most important, the New Deal had not made a significant dent in black unemployment. And yet the president managed to convince American blacks that he cared about them. Black voters responded to the New Deal with enthusiasm and formed a strong part of the Roosevelt coalition. However little their share, they, like others, did get relief under the New Deal, where there had been little or none under Hoover. Despite almost universal second-class treatment, blacks, like others, did benefit from New Deal reforms. And they, like others, did share in economic recovery, perhaps most through the new labor movement the New Deal fostered. Roosevelt and many of his aides showed the same warmth to black leaders as they did to others, and the New Deal hired many black administrators. Finally, Eleanor Roosevelt's liberality of spirit and constant support of minorities helped to move urban black voters to the FDR bandwagon.

The Election of 1936

By the time of the 1936 elections, the New Deal had made most of the progress it was going to make. It had fostered business recovery and furthered labor organization. It had relieved distress on the farms and helped the unemployed. Economic statistics suggested that a good deal of recovery had been achieved in certain sectors of the economy. Farm income had gone up dramatically. Average weekly earnings of workers in manufacturing had risen since 1932 from $17 to almost $22. Although some 7 million remained unemployed, this figure had dropped by 4 or 5 million since Roosevelt took office, and the unemployed were receiving enough to live. The rise in national income from $40.2 billion in 1933 to $64.7 billion in 1936 reflected the general advance.

The Republicans attacked every aspect of the New Deal. "America is in peril," their 1936 platform began. "We invite all Americans, irrespective of party, to join us in defense of American institutions." For president, the convention nominated Governor Alfred M. Landon of Kansas; for vice-president, Frank Knox, a Chicago publisher. The Democrats renominated Roosevelt by acclamation. "These economic royalists," Roosevelt told the convention, "complain that we seek to overthrow the institutions of America. What they really complain of is that we seek to overthrow their power."

The critics came together in Cleveland to form a third party, the Union party. They nominated William Lemke, a Republican congressman from North Dakota. But the critics were far fewer now. The Social Security Act of 1935 had stolen much of Dr. Townsend's thunder, and Huey Long had been assassinated. Coughlin had received unmistakable evidence that the Roman Catholic church hierarchy found his political behavior embarrassing. Lemke polled fewer than a million votes and did not carry a single state.

In the balloting, Roosevelt carried all but two states, Maine and Vermont. His 27.75 million popular votes represented 60 percent of the total cast. In the cities his margins reached record levels. By winning even more overwhelmingly than in 1932, he made the Democratic party the accepted majority party of the country.

THE CLIMAX OF THE NEW DEAL

In his second inaugural address, FDR expressed no complacency over his victory or his achievement. The problems of depression and deprivation, as he frankly confessed, persisted: "I see one-third of a nation ill-housed, ill-clad, ill-nourished." Before attacking these problems, however, Roosevelt set out to neutralize a major obstacle to the realization of his reform vision—the Supreme Court.

The Court Fight

On February 5, 1937, Roosevelt proposed to Congress what was then called his court-packing bill: whenever a federal judge failed to retire within six months after reaching the age of seventy, an additional federal judge should be appointed. Although the proposal applied to the entire federal judiciary, it was obviously aimed at the Supreme Court, where six of the judges were already over seventy. Thus, as many as six judges could be added, bringing the full Court to fifteen.

Although the announcement came as a shock, the need for the bill seemed clear enough. The people had approved of the New Deal, but the Supreme Court had opposed its early legislation. In 1935 and 1936, the Court had struck down the NRA and the AAA. It had rejected a railroad retirement plan and the Bituminous Coal Act, which was intended to reorganize a sick industry. It had invalidated congressional legislation designed to protect farm mortgages, and it had thrown out a municipal-bankruptcy act. To those who sympathized with the New Deal social program, the Court seemed to be creating an area where neither state nor federal power could be used to solve critical problems.

The number of Supreme Court justices had, in fact, been changed several times in the past, but the present total of nine had become fixed for so long it almost had the sanction of constitutional authority. To attempt to reduce the Court's power by a con-

stitutional amendment would take years, and probably could not be done at all. Roosevelt's plan was a short cut. But his assertion that it was intended simply to help federal courts catch up with their business seemed not altogether true. Even for a large number of New Dealers, it gave weight to the charge that he was indeed seeking the dictatorial powers his opponents had said all along he wanted. On July 22 the Senate voted overwhelmingly, seventy to twenty, to recommit the bill to the Judiciary Committee, where it died.

And yet Roosevelt had a sort of triumph after all. Within a few weeks of his bombshell, certain justices appeared to rethink their position, and the Supreme Court quickly reflected the alteration of their views. On March 29, 1937, the Court sustained a state minimum-wage law by a vote of five to four, overruling a recent decision by the same majority. Even more important for the New Deal, the Court upheld the National Labor Relations Act on April 12. Six weeks later, in two five-to-four rulings, the Court sustained the social-security legislation. Moreover, some of the aging Court conservatives announced their intention to retire, and within a few years Roosevelt was able to place seven new men on the Court and thereby recast it. New Dealers had lost the battle but won the war, even though the whole procedure opened a lasting rift in the party and cost voter support.

Toward the Welfare State

Many reforms were gained or extended during FDR's second term. As in the Court fight, however, the political costs were high. The reform potential of the Democratic coalition was becoming exhausted.

New reforms attempted to strike harder at poor housing and low wages. The Federal Housing Administration had been established in 1934 to lend money mainly to middle-income families for the purpose of repairing old homes or building new ones. But positive action on low-income housing came only with the Wagner-Steagall Housing Act of September 1937. This measure created the United States Housing Authority and authorized it to make long-term, low-interest loans to state or city public-housing agencies, which would use the money to clear slums and build new houses that met federal standards. Occupancy of these homes was to be limited to those who could not pay rents high enough to induce private builders to construct dwellings for them. By 1941 the USHA had torn down more than 78,000 substandard buildings and built new homes for 200,000 families. This accomplishment met only a tiny portion of the need, but private building interests succeeded in stopping the program at this point.

The last major New Deal reform measure was the Fair Labor Standards Act of June 1938. The outcome of liberal agitation, this measure had failed to pass Congress on its first try. Finally, after Roosevelt gave it his open endorsement, it became law over the opposition of southern Democrats. The law included most industrial workers but, at the insistence of rural congressmen, omitted farm labor. It aimed for a minimum wage of forty cents an hour and a maximum work week of forty hours for those covered. Even these modest goals were to be reached only gradually. Beginning at forty-four hours, the work week was to be lowered to forty hours in three years. Beginning at twenty-five cents an hour, the minimum wage was to be raised to forty cents after eight years. The law also called for time-and-a-half for overtime. Many Americans were shocked to discover that over 750,000 workers were so poorly paid that they received immediate wage increases when the law first went into effect, in August 1938.

Farewell to Reform

Much of FDR's political difficulty came from the so-called Roosevelt recession of 1937, when no less than 4 million workers returned to the rolls of the unemployed. The reversal appears to have happened partly because the administration, encouraged by the business advance, had called for reducing spending by WPA and other New Deal agencies. The high taxes enacted in 1935 and 1936 seem to have cut private investment, and the accumulation of funds in the Treasury under the social-security laws cut purchasing power.

The speed with which lowering government expenditures started the downward trend suggested that neither the administration nor private industry could maintain economic growth without large-scale public spending. Early in 1938, the president and Congress put the spending program back into high gear. The business revival was resumed, but at a slower pace. In the meantime, FDR attacked the "economic royalists," who, he said, were choking American opportunity. He now launched the broadest trust-busting campaign since Taft. At his urging, Congress created the Temporary National Economic Committee and charged it with restudying the whole structure of American private enterprise.

These drastic steps seemed only to strengthen growing dissatisfaction with the New Deal. Roosevelt's actions just before the congressional elections of 1938 were similar to his efforts to pack the Supreme Court. He attempted to purge the Democratic party of conservative southerners and others who were alienated by the growing prestige of labor in the New Deal. Again, he succeeded only in adding numbers to the discontented while purging almost no one. In the elections, the Democrats—northern and southern—kept their majorities in both houses. But Republicans made large gains, raising their number in the House from 89 to 164 and in the Senate from 16 to 23.

The president was prepared to acknowledge that the reform urge in the New Deal was dead. In his annual message to Congress in January 1939, he talked about the need "to invigorate the processes of recovery in order to *preserve* our reforms." Two years earlier, Harry Hopkins had reached the conclusion that America had become "bored with the poor, the unemployed and the insecure." Recovery had not been achieved. It was not as though the ill-housed, ill-clad, and ill-nourished were any less visible. But the need to do something about them seemed less urgent, and the chances of getting more reform legislation were much poorer. By 1939, moreover, the war crisis in Europe and Asia was occupying the president's time and energy and tended to overshadow domestic problems.

The New Deal: An Assessment

Although the New Deal commanded the loyalty of the great majority of Americans, as shown by election results, it was fought at every turn. Conservative critics pointed out invasions of individual liberty, the failure to balance the budget, the enormous increase in the national debt (from $22.5 billion in 1933 to almost $43 billion in 1940), and the growing bureaucracy in the federal government (from 600,000 civilian employees in 1932 to more than a million in 1940). At the same time, critics noted that the New Deal had failed to restore the confidence of the business community, which held the real key to recovery. Critics on the Left raised questions about the soundness of the economic system that was being restored and the refusal of the New Deal to do the massive national and social planning to redistribute income. In 1939, when all the experiments were over, more than 8.7 million workers remained unemployed; millions more were poverty-ridden.

New Dealers preferred to emphasize the rise in national income from $40.2 billion in 1933 to $72.8 billion in 1939. Furthermore, if unemployment were measured in terms of real human suffering and social waste, it appeared to be less burdensome than a few years earlier. Whatever the methods by which reforms were achieved, farm prices did rise, enabling farmers to recover some of their lost purchasing power. Workers did gain from wage and hours legislation, and even more from protection of unionization and collective bargaining. The benefits of the New Deal may have gone mostly to the middle class, who gained the means to preserve their savings and their homes.

The New Deal placed on the statute books a number of measures intended to make life more comfortable and secure, measures that would benefit millions yet to be born. To achieve such results, the federal government assumed a new and greater role in the lives of Americans—social security, minimum wages and hours, collective bargaining, improved housing for low-income families, and the insuring of bank deposits. By the end of the New Deal, only a few, even among the Republicans, quarreled with this role.

When Roosevelt came into office in 1933, many Americans were flirting with thoughts of violence and doubts of democracy—political solutions of the extreme Right and the extreme Left. The New Deal restored their confidence in the ability of government to assume responsibility and to act. What the New Deal failed to restore was prosperity. Only with rearmament and World War II did the American people finally achieve economic recovery. Thus, the question of whether the New Deal alone would have been able to solve the economic crisis was left unanswered. To win the war, the government embarked on ambitious spending programs and national mobilization, including a commitment to full employment. The eagerness with which all Americans accepted national planning for the purpose of waging war raised some troublesome questions that would persist long after the war had ended.

SUGGESTED READINGS

J.K. Galbraith, *The Great Crash* (1955). S. Terkel, *Hard Times* (1970). W.E. Leuchtenburg, *Franklin D. Roosevelt and the New Deal* (1963). A.M. Schlesinger, Jr., *The Age of Roosevelt*, 3 vols. (1957-1960). E.W. Hawley, *The New Deal and the Problem of Monopoly* (1966). A. Brinkley, *Voices of Protest: Huey Long, Father Coughlin, and the Great Depression* (1982). D.E. Conrad, *The Forgotten Farmers: The Story of Sharecroppers in the New Deal* (1965). J. Agee and W. Evans, *Let Us Now Praise Famous Men* (1941). I. Bernstein, *Turbulent Years* (1969).

SUMMARY

The Great Depression, which began with the stock market crash of Black Thursday, October 29, 1929, had a profound and lasting effect not only on the United States, but on the entire world. Americans were devastated. For the first time in their history, there were bread lines; people were homeless and starving; there seemed to be no hope for the future. The election of Franklin Delano Roosevelt and the Democratic landslide in 1932 brought the first attempt at a turnaround, but even the New Deal did not solve the problems.

The stock-market crash pointed up the flaws in the economy. The Hoover administration did not see these flaws until much too late, and used only inadequate measures to try to fix them. The Republicans still held that federal intervention in the economy was to be avoided. FDR and his New Dealers thought the opposite: only massive federal programs could solve some of the most urgent problems.

Beginning almost on the day of his inauguration in March 1933, FDR moved to rescue the banks, stabilize business and agriculture, reduce unemployment, and provide assistance for the victims of the crash. Most banks were closed when Roosevelt took office. Using the Emergency Banking Act, passed by a special session of Congress, the government got the sound banks back in business and the bad ones closed permanently within a month. More bank reform followed, along with laws providing for closer supervision of the stock market.

Business recovery was attacked through the National Industrial Recovery Act, which set up the NRA, the first of the "alphabet" agencies of the New Deal. Agriculture was put under the AAA, the Agricultural Adjustment Administration. Laborers, sharecroppers, and farm tenants were helped by the RA, the Resettlement Administration. The federal government's first large-scale attempt at rural redevelopment was the TVA, the Tennessee Valley Authority. Unemployment was under the supervision of several agencies: the CCC (Civilian Conservation Corps), the PWA (Public Works Administration), and the WPA (Works Progress Administration). Thousands of roads, hospitals, bridges, schools, post offices, and other public facilities were built under their direction.

But all these efforts still did not break the back of the Depression. A new burst of reform was attempted in 1935, after the congressional elections of 1934. By this time, the administration had to contend with a variety of dissent movements—Huey Long in Louisiana, Dr. Townsend in California, and the "radio priest," Father Coughlin, in Chicago. Three reform laws were passed in August 1935: the Revenue Tax Act, to stop the growth of great personal fortunes; the Public Utility Holding Company Act, to stop manipulation and control of companies through the device of the holding company; and the Social Security Act, which for the first time set up the federal government as guarantor for Americans in economic trouble.

The National Labor Relations Act addressed the problems of the labor movement. It guaranteed collective bargaining and prohibited employer interference with organizing activities. The effects were deep and lasting. Company unions were broken up, and nationwide membership in trade unions grew until it had reached 10.5 million by 1941. During this decade organized labor split into two large organizations, the AFL and the CIO. The two remained separate until 1955, when they were joined in the AFL–CIO.

The New Deal gave Americans a sense of direction and hope, though it did not solve the economic crisis. Under FDR's leadership, the Democrats built a huge new coalition that joined Americans of all classes and colors: the solidly Democratic South, the Democratic machines in northern cities, the new immigrant groups and blacks, organized labor, intellectuals, and many farmers and businessmen. Even though the New Deal did nothing about black voting or lynching in the South, FDR convinced American blacks that he cared about them, and they responded.

In the election of 1936, FDR carried every state except two. This landslide made the Democrats the majority party of the country. In Roosevelt's second term many new reforms were gained and old ones extended, particularly housing for the poor and a minimum wage. But the reform drive was slowing, and by 1939, with many still unemployed, it was dead. By that time too, the crisis in Europe overshadowed all else.

24
World War II

Already shaken by the experience of the Great Depression, most Americans in the 1930s refused to believe that the United States might become involved in another war. But the news from abroad was ominous. The enthusiasm with which the embittered and depressed German people rallied around Adolf Hitler's pledge to redeem their pride, race, and economy was but one example. So was Mussolini's war on the Ethiopians, Stalin's purges of Communist officials, Japan's aggression in Manchuria and China, and the civil war in Spain. All these events fed and reinforced the insecurity that the deepening worldwide depression had helped set in motion.

The desire of most Americans to avoid any involvement in another war was not the same thing as indifference. Nazi Germany's aggressiveness and inhumanity troubled Americans. Although as late as 1939 popular polls showed 90 percent of Americans still opposed to involvement in the European war, 80 percent expressed sympathy for the Allies, Great Britain and France. Sensing this divided mood, FDR tried to balance the nation's desire to stay out of the war against the growing fear of Nazi Germany and the wish to help the Allies triumph.

Hitler's invasion of Poland in September 1939 set off a new general war. The distress of America's old allies, as well as the continuing struggle for supremacy in the Pacific, encouraged Japan to strike at the United States. What confronted Americans after the attack on Pearl Harbor, December 7, 1941, was quite simply the preservation of a way of life. The United States fought because it had been attacked, not to make the world safe for democracy. Recognizing such feelings, Roosevelt called World War II the War for Survival and indulged in less speculation about the postwar world than had Wilson.

In that war some 45 million people did not survive at all: among them were 17.5 million Russians, 6 million Jews, 4.2 million Germans, 2.2 million Chinese, 1.4 million Japanese, and 291,000 Americans. It was a time of extraordinary violence and brutality. While the casualties soared, the technology of extermination became even more sophisticated. The Germans employed assembly-line efficiency in carrying out the executions of some 6 million Jews, and the *men and women—the technicians—who acted as executioners looked upon themselves as perfectly normal and healthy human beings helping to build a new social order.*

BETWEEN THE WARS: 1920–37

The sources of international conflict after World War I increased as the worldwide depression deepened. The economic crisis became so severe that many peoples supported totalitarian movements and justified repression that promised a solution to their insecurities. Benito Mussolini in Italy and Adolf Hitler in Germany came to power at the head of movements that replaced democratic forms with police states and adopted militant and expansionist foreign policies. In Asia, Japan emerged as the dominant power after World War I. The Japanese took formerly German islands in the Pacific, kept some troops in Siberia, cast an eye on the the raw materials of Southeast Asia, and moved to shut the Open Door in China.

In the thirties, the United States often tried to interest European nations in collective action that would restrain Japan's ambitions. At the same time, the United States remained outside Europe's system of collective security. Both policies failed. Weakened by American isolation, European collective security collapsed in the face of Nazi aggression. With the Europeans in trouble at home, American efforts to involve them in the Far East were doomed.

Disarmament and Stability: The Washington Conference, 1921–22

To show that it had not abandoned its role as a great power, the United States took the lead after World War I to stop the naval race and to impose some kind of stability on the

With the dropping of the atomic bombs on Hiroshima and Nagasaki, World War II came to a close and the Atomic Age dawned. A world in upheaval found itself gripped by new tensions and anxieties.

Far East. President Harding invited Britain, Japan, France, Italy, and China to meet with the United States in Washington on Armistice Day, November 11, 1921.

Secretary of State Charles Evans Hughes electrified the delegates with a proposal for a ten-year suspension of construction of capital ships—battleships and cruisers. He also proposed that the capital-ship tonnage of the United States and Britain be limited to 500,000 and that of Japan to 300,000. This was in keeping with their then current power ratio of 5:5:3. But it also meant that Britain and Japan would have to get rid of no less than sixty-six ships, and the United States thirty ships. The conference ended in February 1922 with a five-power naval treaty that endorsed the 5:5:3 ratio almost at Hughes's tonnage figures. France and Italy were permitted capital-ship tonnage of 175,000. Although smaller ships were not covered by the agreement, the naval race was at least partially stopped.

Two other important agreements made at the Washington meeting were the so-called Four-Power Pact and the Nine-Power Pact. The first replaced an Anglo-Japanese alliance with a new agreement including the United States and France as well as England and Japan. The four powers pledged to keep the peace in the Pacific. In the second agreement, China, Italy, Belgium, the Netherlands, and Portugal joined the other four. They reaffirmed the Open Door in China and guaranteed that nation's sovereignty, independence, and territorial integrity. The treaties contained no real enforcement mechanism, and nothing was said about land and air forces or economic barriers to trade.

The Washington Conference was welcomed in most of the world as a triumph of diplomacy. When it was followed in 1928 by the Kellogg-Briand Pact, which renounced war as an instrument of national policy (sixty-two nations signed), a fragile international world seemed safer. Japan, however, was simply marking time.

Japan in China

Having already shattered the myth of the invincible white man by its triumph over Russia in 1904–5, Japan came out of World War I with renewed strength, determined to compete with the Western powers for economic advantages in Asia. If Japan came to believe that its destiny was a unified Asia under Japanese control, it was only asserting imperial ambitions that Great Britain, France, Germany, and the United States, among others, had asserted more than once in Africa, Asia, and Latin America. Japan's ambitions reflected its need for access to sources of raw materials to sustain its rapid industrialization and modernization. The Great Depression would make quite clear its economic vulnerability.

Since 1905, Japan had enjoyed special privileges in southern Manchuria, in the northeastern section of China. In the 1920s Chinese Nationalists under Chiang Kai-shek, intent on uniting the country and ridding it of foreign powers, threatened the Japanese in Manchuria; Japan chose to strike back. In September 1931, using as an excuse an incident on the Japanese-controlled Manchurian Railway, Japanese forces moved into Manchuria. The United States and the League of Nations promptly reminded Japan of its treaty responsibilities. But by January 1932 the Japanese army had crushed all re-

sistance in Manchuria and turned it into a puppet state.

When it was clear that reminders would have no effect, Western diplomats raised the question of economic sanctions. Secretary of State Henry L. Stimson suggested this possibility to President Hoover. But feeling that sanctions might lead the United States into war, the president opposed them. His decision, and the reluctance of the league powers to go beyond it, limited Western action to moral pressure. This Japan felt free to ignore. On January 7, 1932, Secretary Stimson stated in a note to Japan and China that the United States could not recognize any treaty or agreement in Asia that infringed its rights or violated Chinese territorial integrity. This policy of refusing to recognize territorial changes achieved by force of arms became known as the Stimson Doctrine.

The situation deteriorated after January 28, 1932. Japan invaded Shanghai, wiped out the Chinese force there, and killed civilians. When the League of Nations condemned Japanese aggression and refused to recognize the puppet regime in Manchuria, Japan's response was to withdraw from the league in March 1933. Less than two years later, Japan also renounced the Washington Conference naval agreement. When the United States and Britain refused in 1936 to grant Japan naval equality with themselves, it began an expansion program the other two felt they had to match. And the more Japan viewed its interests as being endangered by the refusal of the United States to recognize its conquests and ambitions, the closer it came to taking the chance of war.

The Soviet Union

Fear of Japan on the Asian mainland and of Hitler in Germany made the Soviet Union anxious to establish relations with the United States. All the other major powers, including Japan, had long since recognized the Soviet government. The United States had equally strong reasons to extend recognition. Mutual concern over Japanese intentions in Asia might have been sufficient justification. With the Great Depression, the pressure mounted. The prospect of trade with the Soviet Union attracted American businessmen, especially those in the machine-tool and agricultural-implement industries. At the same time, there was a growing interest among American intellectuals and writers in the Communist experiment.

Formal relations between the United States and the Soviet Union were set up by an exchange of notes in Washington on November 16, 1933. Mutual suspicion persisted, however. It was aggravated in the Soviet Union by memories of the postwar intervention and in the United States by fears of communism.

Latin America

Despite the pretense of isolationism in American foreign affairs after World War I, the United States pursued an active policy in Latin America. Strategic, diplomatic, and economic considerations led the United States to interfere in the governments of no less than ten countries.

Often American armed forces became involved—in Panama in 1921, in the Dominican Republic from 1921 to 1924, and in Honduras in 1923. Since 1912, United States marines had been in Nicaragua. When they were withdrawn in 1925, Nicaragua again became so unstable that Coolidge sent them back almost immediately. The establishment of a "democratic" government brought some order. But rebel leader Augusto César Sandino refused to be pacified. He retired to the hills and harassed

American marines until 1933, when the last of them were called home.

In Mexico, protection of private economic interests influenced United States policy. The Mexican Constitution of 1917 had reaffirmed the old Mexican principle, violated during the long Diaz regime (1877–1911), that the government retained ownership of all Mexican mineral and oil resources. American businessmen, encouraged by Diaz, had invested heavily in Mexican development. Now they feared confiscation of their properties. When President Plutarco Calles took office in 1924, he announced his desire to make just such a change. The Mexican Congress then provided that petroleum rights acquired in 1917 would be limited to fifty years.

The pressure of American oil interests and the influence of American Catholics, who resented Calles's anticlerical policy, together with the interventionist policy, soon brought talk of a new war with Mexico. But in 1927 the United States and Mexico reached a compromise by which American investors could retain permanently the oil properties they had held before the Constitution of 1917. Later confiscation under the Cárdenas regime in 1938 infuriated American oil companies, brought charges of Communist influence, and revived talk of intervention. Under a settlement reached in 1941, the Mexican government bought out American oil properties and other claims.

In his first inaugural address in March 1933, Franklin Delano Roosevelt said he hoped "to dedicate this nation to the policy of the good neighbor." His intentions were soon tested in Cuba, where in August 1933 the regime of Gerardo Machado was overthrown, perhaps with a push from Roosevelt's ambassador, Sumner Welles. The new government of Ramón Grau San Martín, however, was far too reformist to please Cuban business interests, including the substantial American business community. On the advice of Ambassador Welles, the president withheld recognition. With the encouragement of the United States, Martín's military backers, led by Sergeant Fulgencio Batista, conducted an election in January 1934. It brought the United States–backed candidate, the first in a string of Batista puppets, to the presidency. Roosevelt quickly recognized the new government. As a gesture of good will, the United States in May 1934 negotiated a treaty with Cuba giving up its right of intervention under the Platt Amendment. But it seemed clear that the United States reserved the right to impose order on the island if American economic interests or citizens were in any danger.

To improve the image of the United States in Latin America, Secretary of State Cordell Hull attended the Montevideo Conference of American States in 1933 and agreed to a proposal that "no state has the right to intervene in the internal or external affairs of another." Hull also announced a new plan to reduce tariffs through reciprocal trade agreements, further pleasing the delegates. By the time of the attack on Pearl Harbor, relations with Latin America had improved enough for the United States to be assured of cooperation in the hemisphere. But American economic domination persisted, setting the stage for more conflict after World War II.

Neutrality and Aggression

With the situation in Europe deteriorating rapidly, the desire of Americans to avoid involvement in military conflict became stronger in the mid thirties. The best way to stay out of war was to make it unprofitable under the law for citizens to trade with belligerents. The first test of this policy came in mid 1935 when the fascist dictator Benito Mussolini made it clear that Italy intended to annex Ethiopia. The Italians launched a full-scale attack in October 1935. By then Congress had passed the first of a series of Neutrality Acts authorizing the president, after proclaiming that a state of war existed between foreign nations, to forbid Americans to sell or ship munitions to them. (In February 1936, Congress extended this first Neutrality Act to May 1, 1937, and added loans and credits to belligerents to the ban.)

When Spanish Fascists under General Francisco Franco rebelled in July 1936 against their country's republican government, Mussolini and Hitler promptly sent assistance. Opinion in the United States was deeply divided over the Spanish war. Many Americans sided with the government, which the United States had long recognized. Some even went to Spain to fight for it. Soviet support of the government, however, lent weight to the Fascist charge that it was Communists they were opposing. It also made it easier for American Fascist sympathizers and Catholic supporters of Franco's uprising to get a joint resolution from Congress forbidding the export of munitions to either side (January 6, 1937). Naturally this action hurt the government more than the Fascists, who were receiving much foreign assistance. In May Congress adopted a new measure authorizing the president to decide not only when wars between nations existed, but also when civil wars like that in Spain endangered world peace. In such situations, an embargo was to begin at once on the export of munitions and on credits for them. A cash-and-carry plan, limited to two years, empowered the president to require belligerents buying nonmilitary goods in this country to take them away in their own ships. The act also made it unlawful for Americans to travel on vessels of belligerents.

In March 1939, after an exhausting

war, Franco's forces won. General Franco was under heavy obligation to Mussolini and Hitler. He managed to outlive both of them, and his anticommunism would win him new friends in the post–World War II era.

THE ROAD TO WAR

After Japanese and Chinese forces met at Peking in July 1937, the Japanese overran North China. Roosevelt attacked this aggres-

sion in his famous "quarantine speech" of October 5, 1937. Ninety percent of the people of the world wanted peace, he said, but their security was threatened by the other 10 percent. Peace-loving nations must act together to quarantine aggressors; otherwise the disease would spread uncontrolled.

The Crisis in Europe

Although no action was taken against Japan, Roosevelt got a billion dollars from Congress in May 1938 to enlarge the navy. Within

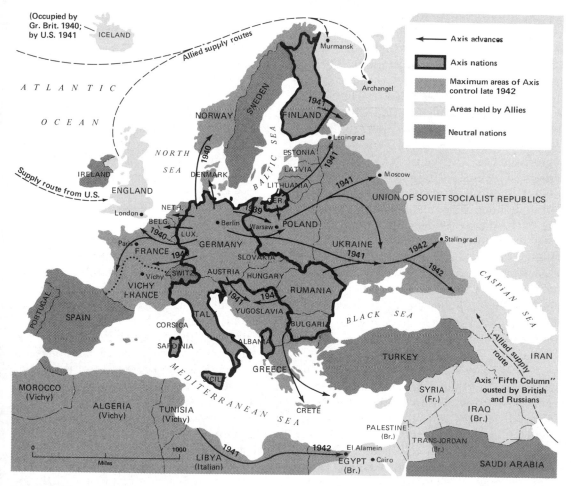

European Theater, 1939–1942

the year, aggression in Europe brought on a crisis there. Hitler had come to power in Germany in January 1933. Fifteen months later he renounced the Versailles Treaty's terms on German disarmament. In March 1936, while Mussolini's invasion of Ethiopia held the attention of western Europe, German forces occupied the Rhineland. Hitler had long been campaigning for the return of German territory lost in World War I. Now, in September 1938, he was poised to grab the Sudetenland of Czechoslovakia. France, along with Great Britain, remained unprepared to confront a rearmed Germany. At the disastrous meeting in Munich on September 29, they let Hitler have what he wanted.

Having gained the Sudetenland, Hitler promised to leave the rest of Czechoslovakia alone. In March 1939, however, he swallowed up the remainder of the small republic. Apparently safe on his western front, Hitler shocked the world by making a non-aggression pact in August with the Soviet Union on his eastern front. This double protection left him free to attack Poland. He had demanded that Poland return territory lost by Germany at Versailles, but Poland resisted, encouraged by France and Britain. The new pact left the Soviet Union free to strengthen its western frontier. On September 1, 1939, Hitler's troops invaded Poland while his air force bombed Polish cities. Two days later, Britain and France honored their commitments to Poland by declaring war on Germany.

As the law still required, Roosevelt invoked the Neutrality Act. But he did not repeat Woodrow Wilson's appeal for neutrality in thought as well as in deed. "Even a neutral," said Roosevelt, "cannot be asked to close his mind or his conscience." On his urging, Congress agreed in November 1939 to revise the neutrality laws to permit munitions to be sold to the old Allies. At the same time, Congress stipulated that the belligerents must carry their own cargoes. Lifting the arms embargo pleased the interventionists; restoration of cash-and-carry pleased the isolationists.

Aid Short of War

When Hitler delayed moving on the Western Front, many even in Europe were lulled by the "phony war." But when he did move, in April 1940, he did so with terrifying speed and force. Neutral Denmark, Norway, and the Low Countries—Belgium, Holland, and Luxembourg—and France itself were all defeated in seven weeks. During the summer and fall, in a tremendous effort to bring Britain to its knees, Hitler sent clouds of planes to bomb English cities. Tens of thousands of civilians were killed and wounded. But the Royal Air Force fought back with extraordinary courage, and by autumn it was clear that Hitler's attempt would fail. If Britain was to be conquered it would have to be by invasion.

Even as Roosevelt pledged to keep the nation out of war, he strengthened American defenses and took steps to assist Britain. Aid was rushed overseas throughout the summer of 1940. On September 3, Roosevelt took his most daring step. By executive agreement he transferred fifty old but still useful destroyers that Britain needed to keep off German submarines. In exchange, Britain gave the United States sites for naval bases in Newfoundland and Bermuda and rent-free leases on other sites in the Caribbean and South Atlantic. At the same time, Congress passed the first peacetime draft in American history and appropriated about $16 billion for airplanes, warships, and other defense needs.

In 1940 the Democrats broke the two-term tradition and renominated FDR for president, naming Secretary of Agriculture

Henry A. Wallace as his running mate. Republicans rallied behind a newcomer to politics, Wendell L. Willkie of Indiana, a public-utilities executive who had been a leader in the fight of private power interests against the TVA. His charm grew with his liberalism. By 1940 his stand on the war in Europe was close to Roosevelt's. This probably hurt more than it helped him in the campaign. It left him with a popular position but without an issue on which to set himself off from his opponent. Willkie lost by a popular vote of 22,305,000 to 27,244,000 and an electoral vote of 82 to 449. But he restored the Republican party to a strong position without accepting the views of its isolationist wing.

Roosevelt renewed the debate over foreign policy in a fireside chat to the people on December 29, 1940. Vowing to assist Britain, he called the United States "the great arsenal of democracy." One week later, the president proposed *lend-lease* as the most practical means by which the United States, remaining at peace itself, could help arm Britain and its allies. The lend-lease bill, which would supply Britain and its allies with arms, to be carried in their own ships and returned or replaced when the war ended, was fiercely opposed in Congress. But public opinion favored lend-lease, and Congress approved it.

To ensure that lend-lease ended up at its destination and not at the bottom of the sea, Roosevelt took steps to help Britain fight the packs of German submarines in the Atlantic. He soon extended American "defense" lines all the way to Greenland and Iceland. On May 15, 1941, a German torpedo sank the American merchant ship *Robin Moor* in the South Atlantic. Roosevelt responded by proclaiming an unlimited national emergency. Later in the year, after still another sinking, Congress authorized American merchant ships to sail well armed and to carry lend-lease supplies directly to Britain.

By the fall of 1941, the United States had become an open ally of Britain without formally declaring war. In August Roosevelt met with Winston Churchill, the British prime minister, on a British battleship at sea. The two leaders drew up a declaration named the Atlantic Charter, in which they proclaimed "certain common principles" that would ensure "a better future for the world": (1) no territorial aggrandizement; (2) self-government for all peoples; (3) free access to trade and raw materials; and (4) the abandonment of war as an instrument in international relations. The Atlantic Charter goals were very much like Wilson's Fourteen Points. Churchill accepted the self-government principle only with strong reservations regarding the British Empire.

While the war at sea continued, Hitler altered the entire course of the war in Europe by his decision on June 22, 1941, to invade the Soviet Union. Most likely he hoped to capture the wheat of the Ukraine, the oil of the Caucasus, and the greater part of the Soviet Union's industrial resources. Such conquests might make Britain and its friends across the sea more likely to negotiate rather than fight. Success might also inspire Germans with new hopes of total victory. Whatever his calculations, Hitler, like many Western leaders, underestimated the Soviet potential for resistance. When winter came, the Nazi armies were still outside Moscow and Leningrad and the Soviet Union was still mustering its strength. To reverse a generation of hostility and aid the Soviet Union against Germany created a predictable controversy within the United States. But Roosevelt thought this was no time to permit ideological differences to interfere with the urgent need to defeat Hitler. In November 1941, the United States extended lend-lease to the Soviet Union.

Toward Pearl Harbor

Since his quarantine speech, Roosevelt had been cautious in dealing with the Japanese. He refused to invoke the Neutrality Act because it might stop the movement of supplies to Chinese forces opposing Japan. Yet Americans continued to sell large quantities of scrap metal, steel, copper, oil, lead, and machinery to the Japanese. The president hesitated to impose an embargo, because he thought it would only cause Japan to look for these commodities by further conquest in Asia. In May 1940, as a deterrent to Japan, Roosevelt ordered the transfer of the United States Pacific fleet's base from San Diego, California, to Pearl Harbor, Hawaii.

As a further deterrent, after the fall of France in June 1940, Roosevelt ordered aviation gasoline withheld from Japan, a step that drew a strong Japanese protest. The next month Japan forced the helpless Vichy government in France (made up of French leaders tolerant of the Nazis) to surrender bases in northern Indochina. This move prompted Roosevelt, on September 25, to extend the embargo to iron and steel scrap and to grant a large new loan to Chiang Kai-shek in China. Two days later, Japan joined the German-Italian coalition.

The formation of the Berlin-Rome-Tokyo Axis to promote Hitler's "New Order" in Europe and a "Greater East Asia" under Japan was intended to warn the United States to keep hands off both. If America attacked any of the three, the other two agreed to come to the aid of the victim. In July 1941, Tokyo compelled the Vichy government to yield bases in southern Indochina. Roosevelt responded by freezing all Japanese assets in the United States. On August 17, he warned the Japanese that if they made any further moves to impose military domination on neighboring countries, the United States would take "all steps

which it may deem necessary toward safeguarding [its] legitimate right and interest."

In Japan the government of Prime Minister Fumimaro Konoye was forced to resign in favor of General Hideki Tojo in mid October 1941. Tojo feared that the army's morale would suffer if after years of sacrifice it had to yield China under American pressure. His cabinet agreed to speed up military preparations, and by November 3 the Tojo government had decided to attack Pearl Harbor if negotiations did not permit Japan to have its way. In those negotiations, Japan seemed to demand that the United States approve its conquests in Asia. The United States offered favorable trade relations in exchange for Japan's withdrawal of forces from China and Indochina and its signature on a nonaggression pact with other nations that had interests in the Far East.

Unknown to the American negotiators, a Japanese carrier force had just set out. On December 1, the special Japanese envoy in Washington dismissed the American demands as "fantastic." Roosevelt already knew of Japanese troop movements, which he thought meant only an attack in the Southwest Pacific on Thailand, Malaya, and the Dutch East Indies—which were, in fact, the main Japanese objectives. On December 6 the president sent the Japanese emperor a hasty peace appeal. The next day Japan made its move.

Early in the morning of Sunday, December 7, 1941, a strong carrier-borne force of Japanese planes swooped down on the American naval base at Pearl Harbor. Most American aircraft were destroyed on the ground, and the unprotected naval vessels suffered terrible damage. In this one assault, 2,355 American servicemen and 68 civilians died; 1178 were wounded. The next day a shocked Congress voted to declare war on Japan.

Roosevelt's critics later accused him of

having provoked Japan to attack in order to bring the United States into the war in Europe, and of having deliberately exposed the navy at Pearl Harbor in order to create a situation that would unite Americans behind his war. That Roosevelt wanted to enter the war by November and that he knew a firm stand against Japan might bring drastic action seem beyond doubt. However, had the United States stood quietly by while Japan conquered an immensely rich empire in China and Asia, Roosevelt would have been criticized for inaction. The notion that Roosevelt conspired to defeat and destroy a substantial part of the navy he had served and built up and that his administration and high military authorities were involved in the plot does not seem likely. No doubt there was fault both in Washington and Pearl Harbor. But to the very end it was thought the Japanese would strike elsewhere.

On December 11, four days after Pearl Harbor, Japan's Axis partners, Germany and Italy, declared war on the United States. Congress responded immediately with declarations of war against them. The United States was now engaged in global warfare.

THE HOME FRONT

To mobilize a people for war, to generate the kind of enthusiasm that will lead them to make sacrifices, it is almost always necessary to portray the enemy as an inhuman force. World War II was no exception. The Germans were the very incarnation of evil, prepared to invade the homes of American families. The Japanese were subhuman and treacherous. *Time* magazine caught the proper tone when it entitled the article on the Battle of Iwo Jima "Rodent Exterminators." "The ordinary unreasoning Jap is ignorant," *Time* observed. "Perhaps he is human. Nothing . . . indicates it."

Japanese-Americans

To unleash such hatred against a foreign enemy could be expected of any nation engaged in war. Less understandable was the decision in early 1942 to single out 110,000 Japanese-Americans, two-thirds of them citizens of the United States, remove them from their homes on the West Coast, and confine them in inland camps. The decision reflected racial rather than military considerations. It was the result of more than forty years of anti-Japanese sentiment and racial tension on the West Coast. No removal was ordered in Hawaii, where 32 percent of the population was of Japanese descent. Nor did anyone ever seriously consider doing the same to German-Americans or Italian-Americans. Earl Warren, attorney general of California, explained "that we can, in dealing with the Germans and the Italians, arrive at some fairly sound conclusions because of our knowledge of the way they live in the community and have lived for many years. But when we deal with the Japanese we are in an entirely different field and we cannot form any opinion that we believe to be sound." Although there was no evidence of Japanese sabotage on the West Coast after Pearl Harbor, that only confirmed the suspicions of those who advocated removal. The head of the Western Defense Command, in recommending removal to the secretary of war, concluded, "The very fact that no sabotage has taken place to date is a disturbing and confirming indication that such action will be taken."

Despite such hysterical racial repression, many units of Nisei (Americans of Japanese descent) performed heroically in the United States armed forces. Their work, along with the realization of how unfairly Japanese-American families had been treated, finally induced the federal government to pay more than $35 million to the

Japanese-Americans awaiting evacuation from the Pacific Coast. (National Archives, War Relocation Authority)

evacuees for property losses. But this was very little compensation for the immense damage that had been done. In a series of decisions near the end of the war, the Supreme Court upheld the essential features of the removal program.

Black Americans

Unlike World War I, when W.E.B. DuBois had urged his people to set aside their grievances and rally to the war effort, the black press and leadership vowed that World War II would be fought on two fronts: "victory over our enemies at home and victory over our enemies on the battlefields abroad." But the outlook for winning the war at home was often very bleak. Although more than one million blacks entered the armed forces, over half of whom served overseas, discrim- ination and segregation continued in the army, navy, and marines, in USO and service clubs, and even in Red Cross blood banks and entertainment centers. Nor did the war change traditional racial restrictions and segregation practices. Between 1940 and 1943, seventeen blacks were lynched. In 1943, race riots broke out in Los Angeles (directed at Mexican-Americans as well as blacks); Beaumont, Texas; Mobile, Alabama; New York; and, worst of all, Detroit, where twenty-five blacks and nine whites died.

Still, World War II marked a significant turning point in race relations. Even before Pearl Harbor, in early 1941, a threatened march of 100,000 blacks on Washington, D.C., forced Roosevelt to prohibit racial discrimination in defense industries and to establish a Fair Employment Practices Commission to protect minorities from job discrimination. During the war, blacks shared in employment opportunities. Migration of southern blacks to northern and western cities continued to change the nation's racial map. Overseas experience made black servicemen less willing to accept racial restrictions at home. Nor was the lesson of what had happened to 6 million Jews in Europe lost on black Americans. Finally, World War II generated revolutionary ferment in Africa and Asia that would eventually force the United States to reassess its racial policies.

Mobilization and Politics

At the time of Pearl Habor, an American army of 1.6 million men already existed, most of them recruited through the first peacetime draft. Eventually, all men between eighteen and forty-five were subject to military service, and for the first time women were permitted to volunteer for the armed forces. By war's end, 15 million men and more than 200,000 women had served in the army, navy, marines, and coast guard.

Almost complete conversion to war production was achieved. But private industry's fear of excess plant capacity forced the government, through the Defense Plant Corporation, to build about 85 percent of the new facilities needed. Most of the government-built plants were run during the war by private corporations under liberal contracts with the armed services and purchased afterward on generous terms. Corporate profits after taxes rose from $5 billion in 1939 to almost $10 billion in 1944, and many new fortunes were made. Depression unemployment also ended.

With the drafting of men into the armed forces, large numbers of women found wartime employment, particularly in the defense industries. By the fall of 1943,

with war production reaching peak levels, an estimated 17 million women made up a third of the total work force. Of these, some 5 million worked in war factories. Posters of Rosie the Riveter, along with popular songs, persuaded women to leave the home for war work as a patriotic duty and reassured them they could do factory work as easily as household work. Those who had already been working, usually in service and menial jobs, eagerly applied for the better-paying positions in war industries. Although war work increased the independence, income, and pride of women, men continued to dominate the supervisory positions. And the wage scales, despite government promises to the contrary, discriminated against women.

Although the farm population fell dur-

During the war millions of women found employment in the defense industries. (Gordon Parks)

ing the war (despite draft exemptions for many agricultural workers), farm production soared. In 1945 the output per farm worker, responding to favorable weather and scientific aids, was almost double that from 1910 to 1914, agriculture's golden years. Farm income also doubled. The war showed that a small farm labor force, working with improved agricultural techniques, could meet the normal needs of the domestic market. This demonstration soon began to influence farm and financial policies.

Even before Hitler's seizure of Czechoslovakia, Nazi scientists had become the first in the world to release energy by splitting the uranium atom. They worked feverishly to find a way to use this incredible energy in a deliverable weapon. Late in 1939 Albert Einstein, who had fled Germany when Hitler took power, and two other refugee scientists had managed to make FDR understand what atomic science could do. Roosevelt promptly established an advisory committee on uranium. But the crash program to produce an atomic bomb was not decided upon until the spring of 1941. At that point the British, whose atomic research was considerably ahead of that in the United States, agreed to share their knowledge. From the very first, the scientists knew they could keep their findings from political leaders who would want to use atomic energy in warfare. Almost to a man, however, they had suffered under Axis regimes. Their hatred and fear of Hitlerism had grown as strong as the new physical force itself. In 1943 responsibility for building a practical bomb was given to Robert J. Oppenheimer and the brilliant team of British, American, and European scientists he gathered at Los Alamos, New Mexico. On July 12, 1945, final assembly of the first atomic bomb began. Four days later, at the Alamogordo air base in New Mexico, the weapon was detonated.

By mid 1943 American war costs, including those for atom-bomb development, were running at $8 billion a month, as high as the *yearly* budgets of the peacetime New Deal. In 1945, for the first time in history, the federal government spent over $100 billion. The total cost of the war to the United States was about $350 billion—ten times the cost of World War I. After July 1, 1943, employers began to collect income taxes for the government by withholding them from employee payrolls. Income and other taxes paid for two-fifths of the war's huge cost. Yet between 1941 and 1945, the national debt rose from about $48 billion to $247 billion.

Politics was not suspended in the war years. In the congressional elections of 1942, Republicans gained by capitalizing on public discontent with military defeats. But by 1944 the military situation had changed, and the Republicans had to contend once again with Roosevelt's popularity. Thomas E. Dewey, governor of New York, became their candidate. The Democrats, with the third-term tradition shattered, again nominated Roosevelt. But Vice-President Wallace, unpopular with city bosses and southern conservatives, was dropped in favor of Senator Harry S. Truman of Missouri. Roosevelt won by a vote of 25,602,000 to 22,006,000 and by 432 to 99 in the electoral college.

THE WAR FRONTS

In the spring of 1942, the United States and the Allied powers did not expect to win the war quickly, if they could win at all. The Axis powers had enormous labor resources in central Europe, the occupied part of the Soviet Union, and the Southwest Pacific. Occupied France and friendly Spain could contribute by helping to make the Atlantic and the Western Mediterranean dangerous for Allied shipping. Axis forces occupied North Africa from Tunis to the Egyptian border, and Germany's formidable Afrika Korps, under Field Marshal Rommel, seemed about to smash eastward into Egypt, close the Suez Canal, and force Turkey to join the Axis. In southern Russia, the Germans were hammering at the Caucasus, threatening to drive through to Iraq and Iran and complete the conquest of the routes to the East.

The situation was no better in the Pacific. Japan followed up Pearl Harbor with successful attacks on the Philippines, Wake Island, Guam, Hong Kong, British Malaya, and Thailand. American troops in the Philippines under General Douglas MacArthur made several brave stands, but after MacArthur managed to escape to Australia, the last American stronghold surrendered in May 1942. In the Southwest Pacific, the Japanese paralyzed the British navy and then captured Singapore and crushed resistance in the Netherlands Indies. By March 1942 they had conquered Burma and closed the Burma Road, the supply route to China.

Early in the war, military planners in the United States and Britain made an important decision. They would conduct a holding operation in the Pacific until the United States could mobilize enough aid for Britain and the Soviet Union to take the offensive in Europe. After the Axis had been defeated in Europe, Japan's turn would come.

The War in Europe and Africa

To win the war in Europe, it was vital for the Western powers to gain control of the sea and the air. For months after the United States entered the war, German submarines roamed the Caribbean and the waters off the Atlantic and Gulf coasts. Ship sinkings were extremely high. Few submarines were sunk, however, until a new system of convoys was worked out and coastal waters were patrolled. Still, the cost in tonnage and lives continued, and it was only the tremendous rate of American merchant-ship production that offset the submarine damage.

In the air, supremacy had passed to Britain's Royal Air Force during the clashes over England in 1940. By 1941, when British aircraft production surpassed Germany's, the RAF went on the offensive. It returned the terrible attacks Germany had inflicted on British cities. In August 1942 American airmen joined the British in raids over the Continent, supplementing RAF nighttime saturation bombings with precision daylight bombing. Between them, the two air forces dropped more than 2.6 million bombs. When the time came for the Allies to invade the Continent, Germany found its defenses gravely weakened by the damage inflicted on railways, roads, and bridges at home and in France, and by shortages of fuel for planes, tanks, and other vehicles.

With an all-out assault on France still too risky, Churchill and Roosevelt decided to attack in Egypt, where the Afrika Korps was pressing toward the Suez Canal. On October 23, 1942, the first great Allied land offensive of the war confronted Rommel at El Alamein, on the Mediterranean, and sent his forces streaming back toward Libya. Broadening the assault on November 8, 1942, three Allied armies under General Dwight D. Eisenhower (who had been named supreme Allied commander in the Mediterranean theater), began landing at various points in North Africa. These forces were expected to join up with the Allied troops that had been defending Egypt and the Suez from Rommel's attacks.

The momentum of the offensive in North Africa, strengthened by the Soviet stand at Stalingrad in November, gave hope

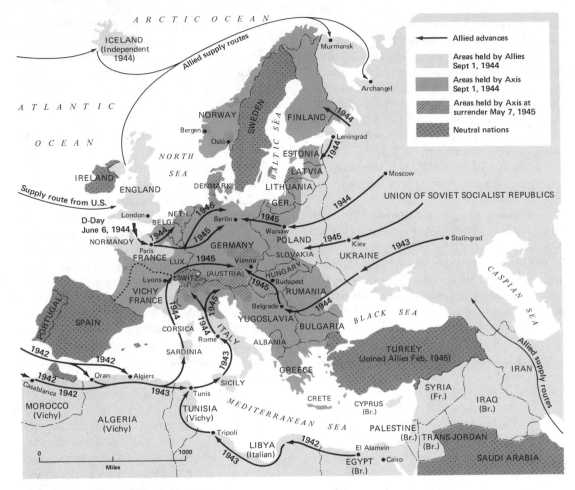

Legend:

← Allied advances

Areas held by Allies Sept 1, 1944

Areas held by Axis Sept 1, 1944

Areas held by Axis at surrender May 7, 1945

Neutral nations

European Theater, 1942–1945

to Allied planning. When Churchill and Roosevelt met at Casablanca in January 1943, they made plans for victory on all fronts. The Allied leaders decided to invade Sicily and Italy after victory in North Africa. They agreed to send enough forces to the Pacific to take the offensive there, and promised to ease the pressure on the Soviets by setting up another front in Europe. They also announced that they would accept only the unconditional surrender of the Axis. Following the conference, the Allies took full possession of North Africa. Although

Rommel evaded capture, his army of 350,000 men surrendered in Tunisia. The southern Mediterranean again became available to the Allies at normal wartime risk, and pressure on the Middle East was eased.

The attack on Italy began on July 10, 1943. By September, Sicily had been cleared and Mussolini had been deposed. The new Italian government signed an unconditional surrender. But Italy itself was still occupied by strong German forces, which Hitler strengthened. The Italian campaign turned into an agonizingly slow and costly war. The

Allies captured Naples on September 28, 1943. Rome, only 100 miles north, did not fall until June 4, 1944, only two days before the cross-channel invasion of France was to begin. On April 28, 1945, Italian partisans captured Mussolini, murdered him, and mutilated his body. But the Nazis in Italy fought on until May 2, five days before the Reich itself collapsed.

Roosevelt and Churchill met several times after the Casablanca Conference. The need to include Stalin in these meetings became more and more important. This occasion was finally set for Teheran, the capital of Iran, late in November 1943. On the way to Teheran, FDR met with Chiang Kai-shek and Churchill at Cairo. To keep Chiang willing to fight to the finish, the three leaders promised to continue the struggle until Japan surrendered unconditionally. Occu-

pied territories, including Manchuria and Formosa, would then be returned to China. They also foresaw a "free and independent Korea." All of this was in the Cairo Declaration, announced December 1, after the Russians had endorsed it at Teheran. At Cairo, Roosevelt and Churchill also agreed that Eisenhower would become the supreme commander of the forces that would invade Europe.

The Big Three conference at Teheran set the Normandy invasion, under the code name Overlord, for May or June 1944. It was to be linked with a Russian offensive against Hitler from the east. Stalin also confirmed an earlier promise to enter the war against Japan after Germany was defeated. The Grand Alliance agreed to aid Marshal Tito and the Yugoslav partisans in ridding their country of German forces. Poland

Stalin, Roosevelt, and Churchill at the Teheran Conference, 1943. (Library of Congress)

would again be sliced, the USSR taking some of its eastern land. But the Poles would be compensated on the west at Germany's expense. Germany was to be destroyed as a military power.

For four years Hitler had concentrated on making northern France the strongest wall of his fortress. For six weeks Allied air attacks pulverized this wall and the communication lines leading to it. By June 1944 a force of nearly 2.9 million men, supported by 2.5 million tons of supplies, 11,000 airplanes, and a vast armada of ships, had been assembled in England for the invasion. On D-Day, June 6, the first assault troops established beachheads along the coast of Normandy. Although caught by surprise because they had expected the attack elsewhere, the Nazis were able to mobilize quickly. But by July 24, more than a million Allied troops had taken 1500 square miles of Normandy and Brittany. The next day, General George S. Patton, Jr.'s Third Army swept after the Germans and turned their retreat into a rout. On August 25, Patton, assisted by a Free French division, liberated Paris. Two days later General Charles de Gaulle, exiled leader of the Free French, installed himself as president of a provisional government.

If Hitler had any thoughts about reinforcing his troops in the west, the Red Army made that impossible. By D-Day in Normandy, the Red Army had completed the recapture of the Crimea and was advancing along the entire front. Elimination of Nazi forces in the Balkans started in the summer of 1944. In Greece, Churchill sent troops to turn the civil war there to the conservative side. Elsewhere in the Balkans, the Soviets were able to establish Communist regimes. By February 1945 Finland was in Soviet hands and Poland had been organized as a Communist state. Hungary had fallen,

Czechoslovakia had been penetrated. Vienna was about to collapse. At the time of the Yalta Conference (February 4–11, 1945) Soviet armies were only fifty miles from Berlin. No people besides the Jews had suffered more from Nazi atrocities than the Russians. None of the Western Allies had sacrificed as much in the fighting itself. Understandably, the Soviet Union was concerned about its future security. Stalin now pressed that concern in all discussions over how the postwar world would be reorganized.

Although Stalin agreed at Yalta to hold "free and unfettered elections as soon as possible" in Poland, he was determined to have no unfriendly governments on his borders. To negotiate Soviet dominance in eastern Europe was now like asking the United States to negotiate the Monroe Doctrine. Later critics would charge that Roosevelt had given up too much at Yalta. But the fact remains that in the final phase of the war, the Red Army had overrun Eastern Europe. Stalin gave no indication of withdrawing his troops, and the United States was not about to drive them out. Neither Roosevelt nor Churchill gave Stalin anything that was in their possession.

Anxious to get Soviet participation in the Asian war, Roosevelt made some territorial concessions to Stalin at the expense of Japan. Stalin, in turn, promised to join the war "two or three months" after the surrender of Germany. Tentative decisions at Yalta provided for the multiple administration of Berlin, the partitioning of Germany, and trials of "war criminals." (These decisions would be confirmed at the Potsdam Conference in July and August 1945.) Finally, Stalin agreed to a United Nations Conference to be held in San Francisco in April 1945, at which a permanent international organization would be established. In Roosevelt's eyes, Stalin's agreement to participate in a United Nations was an important achievement. And with the atomic bomb still untested, American leaders welcomed Soviet action in Manchuria to help bring about the surrender of Japan.

The European war ended after still tough and costly fighting. On March 7, 1945, the Allies at last went across the Rhine over the railroad bridge at Remagen, the only bridge still standing. On April 25, American and Soviet troops made contact at the Elbe River. On or about May 1, Hitler committed suicide in Berlin, and the next day the capital surrendered. On May 7 General Jodl, chief of staff of the German army, signed the unconditional surrender at Eisenhower's headquarters. Within a week, half the American air force in Europe was bound for the Pacific and the demobilization of the massive American army had begun.

On April 12, 1945, in Warm Springs, Georgia, Roosevelt died suddenly of a cerebral hemorrhage. Not since the assassination of Lincoln had the death of a president so moved the American people. Many could not even recall living under any other president. Most appalled of all, perhaps, was FDR's successor, Harry S. Truman, who even as vice-president had not known the war's best-kept secret—that an atomic bomb was being developed.

The War in the Pacific

The Japanese mounted a new offensive even before they had time to absorb the great area conquered in their initial thrusts after Pearl Harbor. This offensive was aimed at nailing down a naval and air line of defense from Attu, the westernmost of the Arctic Aleutians, to Port Moresby, the best harbor in New Guinea. Anchor points were to be at Japanese-held Wake and American-held Midway. Inside this line Japan expected to chew up China and perhaps India. But these plans were changed in the spring of 1942 in two important naval engagements. One was the Battle of the Coral Sea, in which a Japanese assault on Port Moresby was turned back. The second Allied victory came in the Battle of Midway Island, June 3 to 6. Japanese capture of Midway would have made Pearl Harbor unusable. To save the island, Admiral Chester Nimitz mobilized what was left of the American fleet in Pearl Harbor and sent it out to meet the much larger Japanese force. Despite heavy losses, the Americans gave the enemy its first major naval defeat.

After their failure at Midway, the Japanese made an immense effort to retake Guadalcanal in the Solomon Islands. (American and Australian forces had gained a foothold there in August and intended to use the island as a starting point for an offensive on Japan's more exposed positions.) Huge naval actions covering reinforcement attempts by both sides raged in the surrounding waters until a turning point in the Allies' favor came in mid November. Finally, on February 9, 1943, the Japanese evacuated the island.

After Guadalcanal, the Japanese became occupied with defending the Pacific and mainland positions they still held as a screen for their home islands. To roll back this defense, island by island, atoll by atoll, man by man, would occupy a generation and still not guarantee success. MacArthur's command devised the bold alternative of island hopping, a strategy designed to open a path to the heart of Japan. Air power would neutralize the uncleared rear. Even so, armies as large as those that once conquered nations fought hundreds of battles on tiny unknown atolls. Every assault involved co-

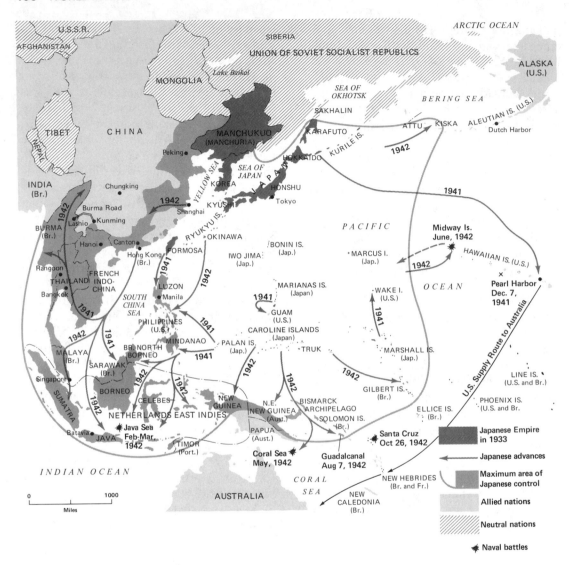

The War in the Pacific

ordination of sea, land, and air forces. None was easy. By August 1, 1944, Tokyo was within range of land-based bombers. The capital and other home-island cities were systematically assaulted with fire bombs that consumed their wooden buildings and devastated the civilian population.

The island-hopping strategy opened a path from New Guinea to the Philippines. On October 9, 1944, a grand armada carrying MacArthur and 250,000 men set out for the Philippine island of Leyte. Four days later, virtually the entire Japanese navy converged on Allied transports in Leyte Gulf, and from October 23 to 25 the greatest sea battle in history was fought. At its end the United States emerged in complete command of the Pacific. Manila fell to MacArthur's forces on February 23, 1945. But not until July 5 were the last of the Japanese rooted out. By then, Iwo Jima and Okinawa had been taken at a cost of 70,000 men. *Kamikaze* attacks—the plunging of bomb-laden planes into American ships by Japanese suicide fliers—accounted for many of the American casualties at Okinawa.

The island-hopping campaigns finished all but the remnants of the Japanese navy and air force. American submarines had sunk more than half of Japan's merchant marine, which had kept it supplied with the oil, rubber, tin, and grain of their mainland conquests. These conquests had been under strong attack by British and American forces since the winter of 1943. The Allies struggled to get Chiang Kai-shek to fight harder in China. But Chiang was preparing for a showdown with the Communists, who were gathering forces in the Chinese north.

The Atomic Victory

On July 16, 1945, at precisely 5:30 A.M., an atomic bomb was successfully detonated in the New Mexican desert. Ten days later, Allied leaders assembled at Potsdam sent an ultimatum to the enemy: "The alternative to surrender is prompt and utter destruction." No surrender came, because Japanese military leaders overruled the government. On August 6 the first atomic bomb to be used in warfare was dropped on Hiroshima, killing instantly nearly 75,000 persons and injuring 100,000 more in a city of 344,000;

many more would die from the effects of radiation. Still no word from the government. Two days later, as it had promised at Yalta, the Soviet Union entered the war and overran Japanese forces in Manchuria. On August 9, a second bomb was dropped, this time on Nagasaki. At last, on August 10, Tokyo sued for peace, but on one condition: that Emperor Hirohito be permitted to retain his throne. This condition was accepted by the Allies. On September 2, 1945, formal surrender ceremonies were conducted in Tokyo Bay on the battleship *Missouri*, with General MacArthur accepting for the victors.

The most terrible war in history had ended in the most terrible display of force. The decision to use the bomb on a country already on the brink of collapse aroused much controversy in the world community. Those who defended the decision argued that it actually saved the lives of hundreds of thousands of Americans and Japanese by bringing the war to a quick end and making unnecessary an invasion of the Japanese mainland. But critics contendend that it was unnecessary, that Japan would have surrendered soon even if there had been no bomb, invasion, or Soviet entry into the war. Still another factor was suggested by Secretary of State James F. Byrnes, who thought the new weapon would "put us in a position to dictate our own terms at the end of the war" and "make Russia more manageable in Europe." But to President Truman, use of the bomb was a foregone conclusion: "I regarded the bomb as a military weapon and never had any doubt that it should be used. The atomic bomb was no great decision, not any decision you had to worry about." Most likely, the bomb was dropped to force Japanese leaders to agree to a quick surrender. That its use would also dramatize to the

Soviet Union the supremacy of the United States reinforced more immediate military objectives. In any event, the United States assumed an awesome image in the world by becoming the only nation to have used the bomb.

The war against the Axis had been won more convincingly than the war on the Great Depression. Yet we may question how well American political institutions, already profoundly altered to meet the domestic crisis, survived the international one. The massive national mobilization significantly enlarged the role of the military in the economy, in education, and in other areas of American life. The unleashing of atomic energy at the moment of final victory, and then the international rivalry for atomic power, gave militarism new life. It also invited new worldwide responsibilities and irresponsibility—and speeded up change at home. The war brought the end of empire: colonial domains established by Europe in

Asia and Africa over some three centuries, sources of immense manpower and natural wealth, were dissolved almost entirely in the fifteen years that followed the war. And contending for the loyalty and resources of the new nations would be the two superpowers—the United States and the Soviet Union. Both were intent on remaking the postwar world in their own image.

SUGGESTED READINGS

R. Dallek, *Franklin D. Roosevelt and American Foreign Policy, 1932-1945* (1979). R.A. Divine, *The Illusion of Neutrality* (1962). H. Feis, *The Road to Pearl Harbor* (1962). J.M. Blum, *V Was for Victory* (1976). R. Daniels, *The Politics of Prejudice* (1962) and *Concentration Camps USA* (1971). J. Hersey, *Hiroshima* (1946). M.J. Sherwin, *A World Destroyed: The Atomic Bomb and the Grand Alliance* (1975).

SUMMARY

From 1920 to about 1937, the United States went its own way in world affairs. It remained outside the European system of collective security, and got nowhere in trying to persuade other nations to help restrain Japan in the Far East. In 1931, in the face of Japanese moves into Manchuria, the United States proclaimed the Stimson Doctrine, a policy of refusing to recognize territorial changes achieved by force of arms. Japan continued its war in China, however, and resigned from the League of Nations in 1933.

In the meantime, Fascist governments had come to power in Italy and Germany. In

1936 Spanish Fascists under Franco began a civil war that lasted until 1939, when with the help of Germany and Italy Franco won. All these governments favored aggressive, expansionist foreign policies centered in military conquest. Mussolini took Ethiopia in Africa in 1935; German forces occupied the Rhineland in 1936. In September 1938, Hitler took the Sudetenland; at the Munich Conference, Britain and France, unprepared, let him get away with it. In March 1939, Hitler took the rest of Czechoslovakia; three weeks later, Mussolini took Albania. In August, Hitler made a nonaggression pact with the Soviet Union in order to protect his eastern flank.

Then, on September 1, Nazi troops and planes invaded Poland. Two days later, Britain and France, honoring their commitments to Poland, declared war on Germany.

The United States was officially neutral, and public opinion was sharply divided. But then in April 1940, Hitler's blitzkrieg (lightning war) rolled over Denmark, Norway, Belgium, Holland, Luxembourg, and even France in seven weeks. The British were left to stand alone. During the summer and fall of 1940, Hitler made a tremendous effort to bomb them into surrender. He did not succeed, and at the end the British had regained control of the air.

American policy was to strengthen its own defenses while giving aid to Britain to keep it from collapsing. Roosevelt, reelected in 1940 for a third term, began pressing the foreign-policy debate in public. The lend-lease program was passed by Congress in early 1941, and the United States moved steadily closer to war in the Atlantic. At an August meeting, Churchill and Roosevelt drew up the Atlantic Charter, which set forth their goals for the postwar World. By the fall of 1941 the United States had become an open ally of Britain without having formally declared war. In November, lend-lease was extended to the Soviet Union, now under attack as Hitler opened his eastern front.

In the Pacific, American response to Japanese pressure had been first to embargo aviation gasoline and then iron and steel-scrap shipments to Japan. Two days after the extension of the embargo in September, Japan joined the German-Italian coalition. Although negotiations with Japan continued in Washington through the autumn, the Japanese made plans to attack if the outcome was not satisfactory. These plans were carried out on Sunday, December 7, 1941, when a carrier-borne force of Japanese planes destroyed the Pacific fleet at Pearl Harbor in Hawaii. The next day Congress declared war on Japan, and four days later Germany and Italy declared war on the United States. America was again engaged in global war.

The home front was mobilized for war. It was also mobilized in a propaganda campaign of hatred for the enemy. One result was the internment of Japanese-Americans in camps far from their West Coast homes. At the time of Pearl Harbor, an American army of 1.6 million men had been recruited in the first peacetime draft. The draft was extended to all men between certain ages, and women were allowed to volunteer. Behind the 15 million men and more than 200,000 women in active service were American industry, agriculture, labor, and science. Depression unemployment ended. Many women went to work, especially in the defense industries. Men continued to dominate in supervisory positions, and wage scales discriminated against women. Blacks continued to be segregated, even in the armed forces.

The Allied powers did not expect to win quickly. Germany had conquered most of Europe, and Japan had taken a good bit of the Pacific islands and Southeast Asia. The Allied decision was to concentrate on Europe first and leave Japan for later. The next decision was to gain control of the sea and air before beginning land invasions.

The first land operation was conducted in North Africa, where the Germans were moving toward the Suez Canal. It was followed by the invasion of Italy in July 1943, and then by the invasion of Normandy by *a huge force on D-Day, June 6, 1944. Throughout the war, Allied leaders met constantly to plan strategy and conduct diplomacy. Conferences were held in 1943 at Casablanca in January, at Moscow in October, and at Cairo and Teheran in November. By the time of the Yalta Conference in February 1945, Soviet armies were only fifty miles from Berlin. The European war ended on May 7, 1945, with the unconditional surrender of Germany.*

President Roosevelt died on April 12, and Harry S. Truman became president. By this time the campaign in the Pacific, based on an island-hopping strategy, was close to Japan itself. It was Truman's decision to use the atomic bomb, the first ever used in war, to bring the conflict to a quick end and avoid a long and costly land campaign. The most terrible war in history thus ended in the most terrible display of force. And at the end there were two superpowers, the United States and the Soviet Union, both out to reshape the postwar world according to radically opposite ideologies.

25

The Search for Security

The United States emerged from World War II as the most successful and dominant nation in the world, possessing, as its president said, "the greatest strength and the greatest power which man has ever reached." If greatness was measured by national income, industrial productivity, a trained work force, natural resources, scientific expertise, or the average daily caloric intake of the population, the United States had no equal. In contrast, the Soviet Union had seen its industrial capacity reduced by more than 40 percent. Great Britain and France faced desperate problems of economic recovery, even as nationalist movements in Africa, Asia, and the Middle East dismantled their colonial empires. Germany and Japan were shattered and conquered territories. China was about to be engulfed by civil war. As if to underscore the position of the United States in the world community, it was also the only nation that had the atomic bomb.

But within two years after V–J Day, Americans discovered that despite all the power they commanded, their position in the world was by no means secure. Not only were nationalist movements shaking co-

lonial empires and threatening to upset the political balance of power, but the Soviet Union had some different ideas about how the postwar world ought to be reorganized. The United States and the Soviet Union were engaged in a Cold War, a new experience for Americans. It was a war of rhetoric, the subversion and countersubversion of other governments, direct intervention in the affairs of other nations, and an armaments race with no limits. Over the next two decades, this unresolved conflict would use up a large portion of the national wealth for the perfection and accumulation of weapons designed to defend the country from nuclear destruction. It would demand from the American people the kind of loyalty usually reserved for a hot war.

The search for security was unlike anything in the American past. A nation that had always avoided "entangling alliances," the United States now entered into mutual-defense pacts with forty countries. For a nation that had confined its intervention to the Caribbean and Central America, the United States found reasons to intervene, covertly or openly, in the Middle East (Iran and Lebanon) and in Asia (Korea, Vietnam, *and Lebanon) and in Asia (Korea, Vietnam, Cambodia, and Laos), as well as in its own "sphere of influence" (Cuba, the Dominican Republic, and Chile). But even with*

this commitment, and with American forces stationed at bases in some thirty countries, the security Americans sought eluded them.

THE NEW INTERNATIONAL ORDER

The old League of Nations had failed as badly as traditional balance-of-power arrangements in keeping world peace. Whatever stability the new United Nations would be able to impose on the world rested largely on cooperation between the two dominant powers, the United States and the Soviet Union. But mutual suspicions had been aroused before the UN even had a chance to take shape. Only eleven days before his death, Roosevelt sent Stalin a sharp message about "the lack of progress" in implementing the political decisions reached at Yalta, particularly those regarding free elections in Poland. Stalin had also grown skeptical of Western actions and intentions. No less disturbing to Stalin was the Western challenge to Soviet domination of Eastern Europe after the war. Stalin held off until the last moment before sending a delegation to San Francisco, where work on the United Nations charter began April 25, 1945.

The United Nations

The charter of the United Nations Organization provided for two major agencies, the General Assembly and the Security Council. Each member nation had a seat in the General Assembly, which was primarily an arena for discussion and debate of international questions falling within the scope of the charter. The Security Council, which was to remain continually in session in or-

der to settle international disputes as they arose, consisted of five permanent members—the United States, the Soviet Union, Great Britain, France, and China—and six others elected for two-year terms. The council had the power to apply diplomatic, economic, or military sanctions against any nation threatening the peace. Any of the permanent members, however, could block action by exercising its veto power. This decision virtually ensured that the council would be unable to oppose aggression by the major powers.

Founded with 51 charter nations, the UN had by 1982 tripled in membership to 157 nations, more than two-thirds of them in the Third World. In the early years, the United States exercised considerable influence over the organization. In 1950, for example, it obtained General Assembly sanction for military intervention in Korea. And until 1961 it saw to it that the question of seating the People's Republic of China was not placed on the agenda. By the early 1970s, however, that dominance had clearly passed. China had been seated, and the United States ambassador to the UN was openly expressing his concern over a new "tyranny of the majority."

The existence of the United Nations ensured that some questions affecting world peace would be debated with words rather than with weapons. Some of its subsidiary units, such as the World Health Organization (WHO) and the United Nations Educational, Scientific, and Cultural Organization (UNESCO), made important strides toward international cooperation in vital areas. But the UN failed to exert the kind of power or influence that could successfully control an armaments race, deal with the dissolution of the overseas empires of Western powers, or resolve the question of what to do with the conquered Axis powers. As the Cold War developed, those issues became more and more important.

Atomic Energy

The UN was forced to confront atomic warfare and a potential atomic-arms race as its first major problem. Scientists in all industrial countries knew of the work on the atom in the 1930s, although only those in the United States could mobilize the funds, labor, and technical equipment required for A-bomb development and manufacture during the war. Once the bomb was dropped, many of the scientists involved wanted to harness the monster they had created. At the same time, the evidence of its power spurred others to develop the bomb in self-defense.

In 1946, Bernard M. Baruch, the American delegate to the recently created UN Atomic Energy Commission, submitted a plan for control of atomic weapons. It called for the creation of an international agency to which the United States would turn over its atomic secrets. The agency would be able to inspect atomic installations in any country and see that weapons were not being manufactured. It could punish violators, and its decisions would not be subject to veto. As soon as the inspection system was working, the United States would destroy its stock of weapons and manufacture no more.

But the USSR was suspicious of any international agency likely to be dominated by the United States, and was unwilling to tolerate inspection. It proposed instead an international agreement to abandon atomic warfare and prohibit the making of weapons. The Soviet plan had no provision for inspection, and this was unacceptable to the United States. When the USSR detonated its own first atomic bomb, in September 1949, security by balance of terror became part of the new world order.

The Conquered Nations

The problem of settling the fate of the conquered nations also revealed the tension between the Soviet Union and the West. On July 17, 1945, Truman, Churchill, and Stalin met at Potsdam, Germany, to deal with the future of the old Axis members. (Following the startling defeat of his party in the British elections on July 26, Churchill gave way to the new prime minister, Labor-party leader Clement Attlee.) At Potsdam the new Big Three reaffirmed a four-power occupation of Germany, worked out details of German reparations payments, and tentatively settled the Polish-German frontier.

During 1945 and 1946, the leading Nazis were tried at Nuremberg before an international military court on charges of starting the war and conducting it in ways that violated fundamental human decency. The trial revealed the full story of Nazi barbarity: the systematic torture and murder of millions of Jews and Slavs, along with other defenseless civilians. Never before had such brutality been so fully documented. Ten leading war criminals were executed. Similar trials in Japan led to the execution of former premier Tojo and six other war leaders. A generation later, these trials were to be recalled to the discomfort of some of the accusers, including the United States. For in the fighting against formerly colonial peoples, Europeans and Americans themselves broke many of the rules of war.

In 1948 the Soviets, irked by the friction arising from the administration of Germany, ordered a blockade of Berlin. That city, though situated deep in their zone, was jointly administered by the USSR and the Western powers. By threatening the Germans in the Western zone of Berlin with starvation, the Soviets hoped to force the Allies to leave Berlin altogether. The challenge was met with an airlift. Food and supplies were delivered to the city by continuously shuttling cargo planes. In the end, it was the USSR that gave in and lifted the blockade in May 1949. Frustrated by the failure to reach agreement on Germany, the Western powers met in June 1948 and consented to the creation of an unarmed German Federal Republic, embracing the three Western zones. The new state was launched in September 1949. One month later, the Soviets established the German Democratic Republic in the east.

No such divisions occurred in conquered Japan, where the United States assumed full command under General Douglas MacArthur. A new constitution, which went into effect in May 1947, turned the fundamental powers of government over to representatives elected by the people. The emperor renounced his claim to divinity, and the constitution renounced war as a right of the nation. In September 1951, following the Communist triumph in China (1949) and the outbreak of the Korean conflict (1950), forty-nine nations signed a general peace treaty with Japan restoring its "full sovereignty," including the right to redevelop an armaments industry and armed services. The treaty was negotiated at the urging of the United States (the USSR did not sign), which wished to rebuild Japan in order to offset communism in Asia—as Germany was soon to be strengthened so that it could help offset communism in Europe. At this time, mutual-security agreements were also made with the Philippines, Australia, and New Zealand.

THE TRUMAN ADMINISTRATION AT HOME

The death of Roosevelt in April 1945 had brought to the presidency Harry S. Truman, a relatively obscure New Deal Democrat whose bland folksiness contrasted sharply with FDR's urbanity. During World War I, Truman, a farm boy from Independence, Missouri, became an artillery captain. Soon after the demobilization in 1919, he opened a men's-clothing store in Kansas City. When this business died in the postwar depression, the Pendergast political machine, which controlled Kansas City politics, invited Truman to run for county judge. When the same machine needed a "clean" candidate for the United States Senate in 1934, it chose Truman. After his reelection in 1940, he became chairman of a Senate committee that investigated defense contracts. His zeal in working over wartime big business brought him notice and won him the Democratic vice-presidential nomination four years later. Neither in political wisdom nor in the ability to command confidence was he a match for FDR. But it was left to Truman to lead the nation out of one war while alerting it to the threat of still another. The problems he faced at home were enough to worry the most experienced of statesmen: a people eager to return to a peacetime footing but wanting to give up none of the economic benefits the war had brought them. The memories of the Great Depression were still much too vivid.

Demobilization and Reconversion

Once the war ended, in August 1945, Americans' profound war weariness manifested itself in the rapid demobilization of military personnel. The Servicemen's Readjustment Act of 1944, commonly known as the GI Bill of Rights, and later measures provided veterans with government loans for building homes and enabled them to begin or continue a college education. The act also entitled discharged servicemen and -women to medical treatment at veterans' hospitals and one year's unemployment insurance.

Not long after the demobilization of military personnel, the Truman administration moved to reorganize the military establishment. A Department of Defense was established at the cabinet level. The uniformed chiefs of the three services (army, navy, air force), along with the president's chief of staff, were to make up the Joint Chiefs of Staff and be the principal military advisors to the president. The act also created the National Security Council, to be presided over by the commander in chief. The act placed under this council a Central Intelligence Agency (CIA) to coordinate all government intelligence activities.

With the end of the war, Americans longed for the material comforts that had been denied them when industry converted to wartime production. Backing up this longing was the massive $140 billion in savings in bank accounts and government war bonds that Americans had come out of the war anxious to spend. The many new luxuries available to consumers, such as television sets and automatic dishwashers and clothes dryers, were quickly made into necessities by a revitalized advertising industry. The business community went on a spree of private expenditure for new plant construction. At the same time, Americans were able to make certain decisions the war had postponed, such as marriage and having children. The average age of marriage declined, and birth rates increased rapidly. To accommodate more and larger families, the

construction industry created a kind of society new to most Americans—suburbia.

The liberal heritage of the New Deal survived the war, but the sense of urgency about social and economic reform was no longer present and the mood of the country was more conservative. To stimulate postwar business, Congress cut taxes an estimated $6 billion in November 1945. In November 1946 Congress swept away all wartime price controls except those on rents, sugar, and rice, despite Truman's earlier veto of such a measure as "a sure formula for inflation." With these incentives, industrial production soared, as did the inflationary spiral. Between 1945 and 1947 food prices increased more than 25 percent.

Inflation broadened the wave of strikes that swept the country after the removal of wartime restraints. Labor found that wages were simply not keeping pace with the cost of living. One of the most far-reaching strikes was that of the United Mine Workers in April 1946. Although Truman ordered government seizure of the coal pits, the mine workers eventually made important wage gains. A nationwide railroad strike, followed by fruitless labor-management negotiations, prompted Truman to seize the railroads in May 1946. Only a last-minute settlement halted the passage of stern antiunion legislation. The president's actions no doubt reflected the lingering spirit of wartime discipline. Yet the atmosphere had changed: militant unionism received no encouragement in the postwar decades. That was in step with the prevailing conservative mood that suddenly brought life and hope back to the Republican party.

The Eightieth Congress

The postwar inflation and labor conflicts hurt the Democratic party, especially in the cities. Despite Truman's tough anti-Soviet stand in foreign relations, the Republicans harped on the New Deal's "softness" on communism and the possibility that highly placed Americans had participated in spy rings. Using these issues, the Republicans won majorities in both houses of the Eightieth Congress in the elections of 1946. In March 1947 Congress passed the Twenty-second Amendment to the Constitution, limiting the president to two terms, a back-handed slap at FDR. This amendment was declared ratified in February 1951. With his own eye on the 1948 presidential campaign, Truman pressed on the Republican-dominated Congress the liberal measures with which he hoped to rebuild Democratic urban strength. Among his proposals were comprehensive medicare and civil-rights bills. As anticipated, this program died in Congress, the victim of a Republican-Southern Democrat coalition. Seeking to save something of the civil-rights program, and perhaps to maximize the effectiveness of the armed forces, Truman used his authority as commander in chief to issue an executive order in July 1948 for racial equality (desegregation) in the armed services.

The Eightieth Congress's most controversial domestic measure, adopted over Truman's veto in June 1947, was the Taft-Hartley Act. This measure, first, outlawed the closed shop (unions could not compel employers to hire only union members) but allowed the union shop (unions could negotiate contracts with employers by which newly hired workers would then have to join the union). Second, it legalized "right-to-work" laws, by which states could prohibit the requirement of union membership as a condition of employment. Third, it permitted the government to impose on unions a sixty-day "cooling-off period," before the end of which they could not strike. Last, it required union leaders to file affidavits that

they were not Communists. If they did not do so, their unions could not be certified as bargaining agents under the National Labor Relations Act. Labor leaders denounced Taft-Hartley. Although the act made organizing new kinds of workers more difficult, it did weld unions together and speed the move toward unification of the AFL and the CIO. It also assured Truman of solid union support in the 1948 election.

The Election of 1948 and the Fair Deal

As the presidential election neared, Truman's prospects appeared poor. The Eightieth Congress had blocked most of his social legislation. Southern Democrats were angry over the growing concern of party liberals with civil rights. As early as 1946, moreover, Henry A. Wallace, Truman's secretary of commerce, had broken with the president over his Cold War policies and been dropped from the cabinet. In December 1947, Wallace announced he would run for president on a third-party ticket. Some analysts believed he might win 5 to 8 million votes, enough to sink any Democratic candidate. The Republicans renominated Governor Thomas E. Dewey of New York for president and named Governor Earl Warren of California for vice-president. They adopted a platform that was internationalist on foreign policy and moderate on domestic issues.

The Democrats nominated Truman and adopted a liberal platform defending the New Deal tradition, denouncing Taft-Hartley, and promising civil-rights legislation. That prompted some white southerners to bolt the party. Meeting in Birmingham, Alabama, these so-called Dixiecrats formed the States' Rights Democratic party and nominated Governor J. Strom Thurmond of South Carolina for president. Five days later, the Wallace liberals formed the Progressive party and named their favorite as standard-bearer. Wallace had hoped to offer an alternative to Truman's bipartisan Cold War foreign policy and the growing repression of civil liberties in the name of that policy. The fact that the Communist Party endorsed Wallace and played an active role in his campaign only alienated prospective supporters and tarnished his candidacy. Although Wallace's views deserved a wider hearing, he found himself harassed during the campaign and driven out of public life.

The failure of the efforts at unity made Truman's cause seem hopeless. But the Dixiecrat defection enhanced his appeal to the strategically important black voters of the North, and Wallace's campaign clearly illustrated that Truman was no friend of the radical Left. Dewey never caught the imagination of the voters. Truman, aware of the fight he had to make, stormed up and down the country denouncing "the do-nothing, good-for-nothing Eightieth Congress." When the ballots were counted, Truman had pulled off the greatest upset in American political history, winning 24,105,000 popular and 303 electoral votes to Dewey's 21,969,000 and 189. Thurmond carried only four Deep South States; Wallace carried not a single one. In the Eighty-first Congress, moreover, the Democrats had a Senate majority of twelve and a House majority of ninety-three.

Convinced that he had received a popular mandate to carry on what he now called the Fair Deal, Truman drew up a program designed to go the New Deal one better. At vital points the newly influential coalition of conservative Democrats and Republicans blocked him, but he made headway. In 1949 he secured an amendment to the New Deal's Fair Labor Standards Act raising the minimum wage from forty to seventy-five cents an hour. A new Social Security Act, in August 1950, added almost 10 million people to those eligible for benefits. A National Housing Act, passed in July 1949, provided large sums to cities for aid in slum clearance and the construction of over 800,000 units for low-income families. Congress, however, defeated the Brannan Plan (an ambitious program for stabilizing farm

After winning the 1948 election in a surprise upset, Harry Truman waved a copy of the strongly Republican *Chicago Daily Tribune*, which had gone to press confident of a Dewey landslide. (UPI/Bettman Archive)

income), turned down a strong civil-rights program for blacks, and refused to repeal or significantly amend the Taft-Hartley Act.

THE TRUMAN ADMINISTRATION AND THE COLD WAR

While Americans attempted to resume politics as usual at home, the United States and the Soviet Union clashed over the reorganization of the postwar world. To the United States, the USSR was a revolutionary monolith dedicated to the triumph of world communism, whether by subversion or force of arms. The foreign policy of the United States was based on the inevitable danger of Soviet military aggression and the need to find ways to contain it. With equal conviction, the USSR perceived the United States as a power anxious to preserve and extend American institutions and capitalism, whether by atomic diplomacy, subversion, or force of arms. With the horrors of World War II and Nazi occupation still paramount in the minds of the Russian people, the foreign policy of the Soviet Union rested in part on the conviction that its security demanded a weak Germany and friendly governments on its borders—the kind of security the United States enjoyed in the Western Hemisphere.

The United States and the Soviet Union viewed each other's moves in the world arena as a confirmation of these perceptions and fears. And decision makers in each nation capitalized on those perceptions and fears to justify greater expenditures for military arms and military alliances with friendly nations. It was imperative as well for each nation to keep intact its own nearby sphere of influence (Eastern Europe and Latin America) and to win friends among the noncommitted nations of the world.

Containment Through Foreign Aid

With the Communists in firm control of Eastern Europe, the first skirmishes of the Cold War were fought in the Middle East, Turkey, and Greece. Seeking to establish Soviet influence in oil-rich Iran, Stalin backed a Communist movement in Azerbaijan, Iran's northernmost province on the Soviet border, and tried to secure oil concessions similar to those enjoyed by Anglo-American companies. To maintain the pressure, he chose to ignore the Big Three agreement at Teheran in 1943, which called for the removal of all Allied troops from Iran by March 2, 1946. On March 5, after Iran had complained to the UN of Soviet interference, Truman sent Stalin a stiff note. By May 1946 the troops had been withdrawn.

For centuries Russia had sought access to the Mediterranean by way of the Turkish straits leading out from the Black Sea. When in 1945 the Soviet Union renewed its demands for joint control of the straits, the United States sent a naval task force. This action, in addition to stern American and British notes, deterred the Russians but also led them to shift the pressure westward onto Greece. Until February 1947, British forces had assisted the Greek government against Communist guerrillas who sought the overthrow of the right-wing monarchist regime. But the British were in financial trouble. On February 24 they notified the United States that they could no longer afford the burden of resisting communism in the Mediterranean. They planned to withdraw troops from Greece and to terminate aid to Turkey.

This step was an acknowledgment of the end of British supremacy in the Mediterranean. In March 1946 Britain had acknowledged the independence of Trans-Jordan (renamed Jordan in 1949). In April 1947, it turned over the future of Palestine to the UN. This led in May 1948 to the creation, with mixed United States reactions, of the independent state of Israel. France, meanwhile, had completed its promised withdrawal from Syria and Lebanon by August 1946. If only by default, leadership for the non-Communist world, with all the obligations it entailed, fell to the United States.

Determined to bolster the pro-Western governments in Greece and Turkey, Truman went before Congress on March 12, 1947, to enunciate what has been known since as the Truman Doctrine. He asked Congress for $400 million to assist Greece and Turkey. In addition, he wanted authority to send American civilian and military advisers to those countries, at their request, to oversee the use of American grants and to train Greek and Turkish soldiers. To sell this program to the American people and a budget-minded Congress, Truman set down the classic justification for Cold War policies. The images and language he used would be repeated by every succeeding president, from Dwight D. Eisenhower to Ronald Reagan.

> At the present moment in world history nearly every nation must choose between alternative ways of life. The choice is too often not a free one.
> One way of life is based upon the will of the majority, and is distinguished by free institutions, representative government, free elections, guaranties of individual liberty, freedom of speech and religion, and freedom from political oppression.
> The second way of life is based upon the will of a minority forcibly imposed upon the majority. It relies upon terror and oppression, a controlled press and radio, fixed elections, and the suppression of personal freedom.
> I believe that it must be the policy of the United States to support free peoples who are resisting attempted subjugation by armed minorities or by outside pressures.

> . . . If we falter in our leadership, we may endanger the peace of the world—and we shall surely endanger the welfare of our own Nation.

If some American critics felt Truman had oversold the Communist menace, still others questioned aid to regimes whose only virtue was their opposition to communism. But Congress responded favorably. Between 1947 and 1950, the United States spent about $660 million on aid to Greece and Turkey, and their political stability was preserved.

Through the development of the Marshall Plan in 1947, the United States again took the initiative in the Cold War. The economic predicament of Western Europe underscored this region's political vulnerability as well. To restore "the confidence of the European people in the economic future of their own countries," the United States proposed to help reconstruct the entire European economy. General George C. Marshall, the first military man to become secretary of state, announced the new program in his commencement address at Harvard on June 5:

> Our policy is directed not against any country or doctrine, but against hunger, poverty, desperation, and chaos. Its purpose should be the revival of a working economy in the world so as to permit the emergence of political and social conditions in which free institutions can exist.

The Soviet Union, although invited to participate in the Marshall Plan, saw it as a project to revive and preserve Western capitalism. Most likely, the United States neither expected nor wanted Soviet participation, particularly with a Republican Congress controlling appropriations. Western European leaders welcomed the program and immediately drew up plans for using it.

After considerable debate, Congress provided $5.3 billion in April 1948 for the first twelve months of Marshall Plan aid. Between 1948 and 1952 about $12 billion was distributed, more than half of the total going to Britain, France, and West Germany. By 1952, economic recovery in these countries was complete. Western Europe was launched on a long business boom, and the advance of communism within the West had been checked.

Containment Through Military Alliances

The idea behind the Truman Doctrine and the Marshall Plan was *containment*, which after 1947 became the cornerstone of American foreign policy. If the Soviet Union and her allies could be contained within their existing boundaries, internal divisions and failures might in time so weaken them that they would no longer threaten the security of the Western world. But in the meantime, the Cold War persisted. With every new diplomatic move, the United States and the Soviet Union made assumptions about the other's motives that resulted in even more rigid and inflexible policies. What had begun as economic and military aid to nations threatened by communism soon evolved into a policy of military alliances.

The Marshall Plan and an earlier treaty of economic cooperation and military alliance laid the ground for the North Atlantic Treaty, signed April 4, 1949, by twelve Western nations and ratified overwhelmingly (eighty-two to thirteen) by the United States Senate. An armed attack upon any member would be considered an attack upon all; each member promised to assist the one attacked by whatever action was thought necessary, "including the use of armed force." (In 1954 West Germany was granted full sovereignty, admitted to NATO with full equality, and permitted to raise an army of twelve divisions so that it could become part of the NATO force.)

On September 22, 1949, President Truman made the momentous announcement that the Soviet Union had successfully exploded an atomic bomb. Congress that same month passed the Mutual Defense Assistance Act, aimed at building up the military strength of the members of the North Atlantic Treaty Organization (NATO). During the next four years, the United States would supply almost $6 billion worth of arms and other military material to European allies and another $1.7 billion to other countries. But NATO soon came to depend on air power as the principal deterrent to the Soviet Union, particularly on the American Strategic Air Command (SAC), organized in 1951. SAC, in turn, imposed on the United States the need for air bases in many parts of the world. And this need sometimes awkwardly but decisively influenced diplomatic decisions.

The urgency of the Cold War stirred the Truman administration to solidify hemispheric defenses. At the Inter-American Conference near Rio de Janeiro in August and September 1947, the United States helped draw up a hemispheric mutual-defense pact. A second step was the creation at Bogotá, Columbia, in March 1948 of the Organization of American States (OAS) to oversee the Rio Pact and other inter-American contacts. New requests were made for aid—like that of the Marshall Plan—through the OAS. When the United States rejected them, whatever small gains had been made were undone. The Rio Pact and the OAS underscored the United States' concern for political stability. But the depth of poverty in Latin America, combined with a growing revolutionary ferment, made the status of some United States–backed regimes increasingly uncertain.

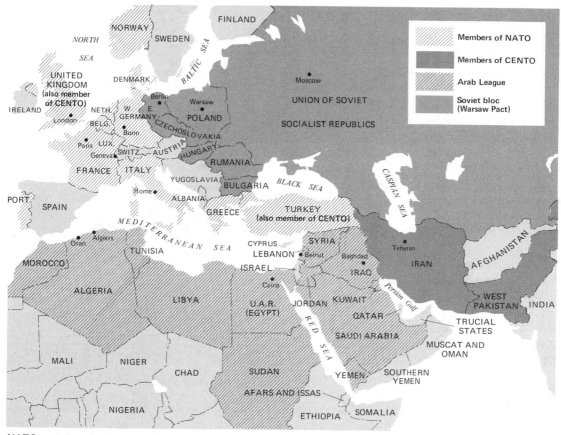

NATO and Eastern Europe

The People's Republic of China

Containment worked well enough in Europe, but in the Far East an entirely different situation developed with the triumph of the Communist forces in China in October 1949. These forces, under the leadership of Mao Tse-tung, had come into existence long before World War II. Throughout the war the United States and Britain, each for its own purposes, had tried to get them and the Nationalists under Chiang Kai-shek to work together to defeat Japan. The policy failed dismally. At the war's end, the Chinese Communists, encouraged by the Russians, received the surrender of Japanese armies independently, amassed their own arms,

and even engaged in skirmishes with the Nationalists. By late 1945, they controlled 225,000 square miles and more than 105 million Chinese.

Even as Truman sent several emissaries to the divided country, Chiang's regime continued to falter in the civil war that swept through China. Having rested his power on military strength, continued American assistance, and an oppressive landlord class, Chiang was unable to withstand the well-disciplined Communist forces, who had the support of millions of poverty-stricken peasants. Large numbers of Nationalist troops defected, and nearly 80 percent of the American supplies sent to Chiang fell into Communist hands. By December 1949, Nationalist forces had withdrawn to the island of Taiwan (formerly Formosa). In the meantime, on October 1, scarcely a week after the Soviet Union had exploded its first atomic bomb, the People's Republic of China was proclaimed. In February 1950, a treaty of alliance and mutual assistance was concluded with the USSR.

With the collapse of Chiang, the State Department issued a lengthy white paper in August 1949 on the Chinese question. It revealed, among other items, that from 1945 to 1949 the Nationalists had received $3 billion in American aid, most of which had been squandered or permitted to fall into Communist hands. In his introduction to the white paper, Secretary of State Acheson claimed that "the ominous result" of the civil war in China had been beyond the control of the United States. Nevertheless, Acheson still anticipated a time when the Chinese people would overthrow the "foreign yoke" of communism. Perhaps to speed that day, until the 1970s the United States, unlike Britain and other major nations, viewed Chiang's government in Taiwan as the legitimate government of China and refused to recognize the People's Republic of China or consent to its admission to the UN. In October 1971 the UN admitted the People's Republic and expelled Nationalist China; in February 1972 President Nixon's trip to China opened the way for United States recognition of the People's Republic.

The Korean Conflict

The hot war between Chiang and the Communists in China had an almost instant sequel in nearby Korea. During World War II, the Allied powers had agreed that Korea, occupied by Japan, should be made independent. In August 1945, the Soviet Union agreed to accept the surrender of the Japanese in Korea north of the thirty-eighth par-

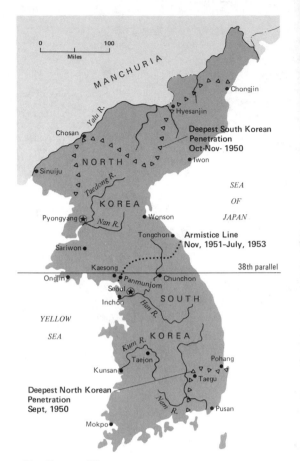

The Korean War

allel. It left the United States, on the arrival of its forces in September, to accept the surrender below that line. Although both the United States and the Soviet Union favored a united Korea, mutual suspicion and the unwillingness to accept unification under Communist or anti-Communist control led to the establishment of separate regimes.

Elections were held in May 1948 for a national assembly in the United States zone. The new assembly then adopted a constitution, elected Syngman Rhee (a devout anti-Communist who had spent many years in the United States) as the first president, and on August 15 proclaimed the Republic of Korea. The United States and thirty other nations promptly recognized the new nation. That very day, elections above the thirty-eighth parallel led to formation of the rival Democratic People's Republic of Korea, which the Soviet Union and its allies promptly recognized. North and South Korea thus faced each other across an artificial border, each backed by a rival great power and committed to unification on its own terms. Border skirmishes soon threatened to broaden into civil war. On June 25, 1950, North Korea sent its forces across the thirty-eighth parallel.

Truman, concluding that the attack endangered American interests, both in Asia and Europe, responded decisively. At his urgent request, the UN Security Council met on the afternoon of the invasion and by a vote of nine to zero held North Korea accountable for "a breach of the peace." (The Soviet Union was boycotting the council over its failure to seat Communist China in place of Chiang's government.) After the

Security Council urged positive action in support of South Korea, Truman broadened his earlier military instructions and with other nations sent ground troops. Although the operation was ostensibly under UN auspices, American troops made up about four-fifths of the UN forces in Korea, and General Douglas MacArthur was in firm command.

The Korean fighting was as savage as many World War II campaigns, and losses ran high. By the end of August 1950, the outnumbered UN forces had been pushed almost into the sea in the area around the port of Pusan. After being heavily reinforced, however, MacArthur opened a counterattack with an amphibious landing in September at the port of Inchon behind North Korean lines. A full-scale offensive drove the North Koreans back toward the thirty-eighth parallel and destroyed a considerable part of their army. Taking advantage of their momentary military su-

U.S. Marines move slowly down a muddy road on the Korean front. (UPI/Bettmann Archive)

periority, UN forces pushed across the thirty-eighth parallel on October 9, 1950, and pressed on toward the Yalu River—the boundary between North Korea and China. MacArthur called for the surrender of North Korea, and he chose to ignore Chinese threats of intervention if American troops approached their border. On November 26, Chinese forces moved into Korea, trapped and inflicted heavy casualties on American and South Korean troops, and pursued the fleeing armies below the thirty-eighth parallel. Although American troops finally regrouped and counterattacked, the war was now a military stalemate.

Restive over the restraints imposed on him by the strategy of conducting a limited war for the limited objective of restoring South Korea's frontier, General MacArthur publicly expressed his dissatisfaction with the UN and President Truman. Even at the risk of becoming involved in an open war with China, a development many observers believed might lead to war with the Soviet Union, MacArthur urged an all-out effort that included the bombing of Chinese troops and supplies in Manchuria, a naval blockade of mainland China, and the use of Nationalist Chinese troops. General Omar N. Bradley, chairman of the joint chiefs of staff, warned that a major war against China would be "the wrong war at the wrong place, in the wrong time and with the wrong enemy." MacArthur rejected this decision and finally caused President Truman, on April 11, 1951, to relieve him of his Korean command and of his control of the occupation forces in Japan. MacArthur returned to the United States, where he received a hero's welcome from the public.

Negotiations leading to an armistice began on July 10, 1951, and proceeded for two entire years, during which fighting often broke out. During the 1952 presidential campaign, General Eisenhower, the Republican candidate, dramatically announced that if elected he would fly to Korea to bring about a cease-fire. In December, a month after his victory at the polls, Eisenhower made the trip. But the cease-fire was delayed another seven months. It would have been delayed even longer, in his opinion, had he not threatened once more to extend the war beyond the Korean peninsula, unleash Chiang Kai-shek, and—despite the deep misgivings of the British and other Europeans—to employ "tactical" atomic weapons.

The touchy armistice was at last resolved on July 27, 1953. It was a return to the prewar division at the thirty-eighth parallel. By then the war had cost the United States over $15 billion, 54,000 dead, and 103,000 wounded. The outcome was a military and political draw; Korea was still divided but now war-ravaged as well.

McCARTHYISM: REPRESSION AT HOME

Within the United States, the strains of the Cold War manifested themselves in a desperate search for internal security. Nothing in their historical experience had equipped the American people to deal with a cold war. The same level of unity and bipartisanship asked of a people at war was now demanded in different circumstances. Never before had an individual's loyalty to country seemed more important. How to measure that loyalty was sufficiently clear—the intensity and consistency of a person's anticommunism.

In conducting foreign policy, Truman reinforced traditional American fears of the Soviet Union and of communism itself. At times, the threat seemed real enough. The spectacular revelations of spy rings, such as that uncovered in Canada in 1946, fed the growing suspicion that certain highly placed people were conspiring to overthrow or subvert American institutions.

Actually, the United States Communist party exerted little influence in the postwar period, even on the American Left. What had robbed it of power was not so much anti-Communist vigilance as disillusionment with the Stalin purges, the Hitler-Stalin pact, and the repressive character of Soviet communism. That helps to explain why the sensational exposures of the late forties and the fifties were so often exposures of past political sins, committed largely during the Great Depression, when the party was respectable in intellectual circles. But if the postwar Communist hunt did little for internal security, it did serve up numerous scapegoats. By 1950, substantial numbers of Americans were ready to believe Senator Joseph R. McCarthy of Wisconsin when he branded "the whole group of twisted-thinking New Dealers" as Communists who "have led America near to ruin at home and abroad."

Loyalty Tests

Before Senator McCarthy embarked on his crusade, the groundwork for what came to be called McCarthyism had been laid by Republicans and Democrats, by both the Truman administration and the Republican-controlled Eightieth Congress. Responding to fear of internal subversion, President Truman in March 1947 ordered a full-scale "loyalty investigation" of all present and prospective federal employees. No source of information, however questionable, was to be ignored. Among the "standards for refusal of employment or removal from em-

ployment" was "sympathetic association" with any foreign or domestic organization designated by the attorney general as subversive.

In compliance with the president's order, Attorney General Tom C. Clark in December 1947 issued a list of ninety organizations considered disloyal to the United States. None of these organizations had the right to defend itself. Since the list had been prepared by the federal government, with the assistance of the FBI under the direction of J. Edgar Hoover, it quickly became the principal reference for the detection of disloyalty. Not only federal agencies but private organizations, business establishments, trade unions, newspapers, entertainment agencies, and schools consulted it to discover "subversives."

When the federal investigation of loyalty was completed in April 1951, the records of no less than 3,225,000 civil servants had been examined. Under the pressure of the inquiry, 2900 had resigned; only 300 had been dismissed. Because of the broad criteria for what constituted subversion, it is possible that none of these individuals was a Communist, although some might have been at one time. Little that Joseph McCarthy ever managed to do in the United States Senate could compare with the steady, although less spectacular, subversion of constitutional liberties under Truman's loyalty program. In the name of internal security, Americans had been encouraged to spy on each other. Almost any "derogatory information" uncovered could deprive a person of job and livelihood. Rather than soften any abuses of the system, the Loyalty Review Board, which was empowered to oversee the federal program, conducted proceedings that denied the accused the right to confront the witnesses who testified against them.

HUAC

Even as President Truman established his own anti-Communist credentials, Republicans in the Eightieth Congress revived the House Un-American Activities Committee. What HUAC did was to manipulate various channels of publicity to reveal the political associations of individuals who had unorthodox ideas. By holding over each witness a threat to his or her career, the committee exerted tremendous power. Refusal to answer the committee's questions or cooperate with its investigation was like an admission of guilt. The committee's most audacious adventure was a two-week foray in Hollywood in October 1947, "to expose those elements that are insidiously trying to . . . poison the minds of your children, distort the history of our country, and discredit Christianity." The attempt to prove extensive Communist influence in the film industry was a dismal failure. Nevertheless, it did frighten movie executives into an indiscriminate house cleaning. It soon spread to radio and television, and to the blacklisting of actors, writers, directors, and others, some of whom could not get work twenty years later.

The Hiss case, HUAC's most far-reaching triumph, began on August 3. Whittaker Chambers, an admitted former Communist who said he quit the party in 1937, was brought before the committee to support earlier testimony about the Communist "apparatus" in Washington. Chambers, an editor of *Time* magazine, told a sensational story. He named members of the Washington Communist apparatus of the 1930s, including Alger Hiss, a former State Department official and since 1947 president of the Carnegie Endowment for International Peace. On learning of Chambers's accusation, Hiss telegraphed a full denial to the committee and asked for a hearing, which

was granted on August 5. This and subsequent hearings, interspersed with reexaminations of Chambers, brought additional details of Hiss's activities in the thirties, including membership (with Chambers) in a Soviet spy ring in Washington and the passing of classified government documents to the Russians. Hiss persisted in his denials. Neither could be prosecuted for espionage, since the acts had taken place more than seven years before and thus, under the statute of limitations, were beyond legal reach. But Hiss was indicted for perjury. After two trials, the first one ending in a hung jury, Hiss was found guilty and sentenced to five years in prison and fined $10,000. In March 1951, after appeals to higher courts had upheld the verdict, Hiss went to prison. The controversy about Hiss's guilt or innocence continued for several decades without being satisfactorily resolved. Despite the Hiss coup, HUAC failed to turn up any significant number of "subversives" in government, at least none that could safely be brought to trial. Meanwhile, J. Parnell Thomas, chairman of HUAC during the Eightieth Congress, was convicted of fraud on December 3, 1949, and sent to prison.

The Supreme Court yielded to the demands of "internal security" when it ruled in the *Dennis* case. In July 1948, the Justice Department got the indictment of eleven high-ranking Communist leaders (including Eugene Dennis) under the Smith Act of 1940. This act made it illegal for a person to advocate "overthrowing . . . any government in the United States by force," or to "affiliate" with groups teaching this doctrine. Their conviction by the federal district court in New York in October 1949 and their heavy fines and prison terms were upheld by the Supreme Court, six to two, in June 1951. "Certain kinds of speech are so undesirable," Chief Justice Fred M. Vinson said for the Court, "as to warrant criminal prosecution." The Dennis ruling also encouraged states and municipalities, under local acts and ordinances similar to the Smith Act, to pursue thousands of alleged subversives, sometimes on the basis of hearsay or even lies.

The news of the first Soviet atomic-bomb explosion late in September 1949, followed in October by the Communist triumph in China and in February 1950 by the mutual-security pact between the People's Republic of China and the USSR, deepened the fears of Communist expansion and subversion and provoked charges that the State Department itself was filled with Communists. Senator McCarthy, having learned his lessons well from Democrats and Republicans who had successfully used the Communist issue, now pounced on this theme.

McCarthy and McCarthyism

In a speech in Wheeling, West Virginia, on February 9, 1950, Senator McCarthy declared that the United States, the strongest nation on earth on V–J Day, had been shorn of its strength "because of the traitorous actions of those who have been treated so well by this nation." None were worse than "the bright young men" in the State Department "born with silver spoons in their mouths." To add substance to his charges, McCarthy added, "I have here in my hand [the names of] two hundred and five men that were known to the Secretary of State as being members of the Communist party and who nevertheless are still working and shaping the policy of the State Department."

McCarthy could never make good on his startling revelation. He gradually backed away from the figure of 205, keeping in the limelight with new numbers until, in the end, he was unable to substantiate a single name. But nothing was done to restrain the accuser, and events soon played into McCarthy's hands. While he was playing "the numbers game" with Communists in the State Department, British authorities arrested Klaus Fuchs, a German-born nuclear physicist and naturalized British subject who had worked on the American bomb at Los Alamos in 1944, for atomic espionage. Fuchs admitted the charges and was sentenced to fourteen years in prison. He also implicated certain American Communists in his activities. Acting on Fuchs's information, the FBI in the summer of 1950 arrested Ethel and Julius Rosenberg and their friend Morton Sobell. They were charged with passing atomic secrets to the Soviets and speeding up Russian success with the bomb.

For a crime "worse than murder," in the words of the trial judge, the Rosenbergs, in March 1951, were sentenced to death. Sobell was sentenced to thirty years. After many appeals failed, the Rosenbergs were executed on July 19, 1953. The punishment in this case suggested the kind of fear and hysteria that had overtaken the American people.

Meanwhile McCarthy's charges grew in reach and recklessness as the "limited" Korean conflict eroded American morale. A low point was touched on June 14, 1951, when McCarthy implicated General Marshall and General Eisenhower in a conspiracy to serve the world policy of the Kremlin. *McCarthyism* had by then passed into the language as an expression for wild and unfounded charges of disloyalty. But many Americans came to believe, as the senator himself told his home following in Wisconsin, that "McCarthyism is Americanism with its sleeves rolled." His most spectacular feats still lay ahead of him. So did his downfall.

The search for national security was a bipartisan effort, involving senators of such diverse politics as (left to right) Sam Ervin, Jr., Henry Jackson, John McClellan, and Joseph McCarthy. Standing behind them is their Chief Counsel, Robert Kennedy. (UPI/Bettmann Archive)

The McCarran Acts

Congress also responded to the national obsession with anticommunism. On September 23, 1950, over Truman's veto, it passed the McCarran Internal Security Act, making it unlawful to conspire "to perform any act which would substantially contribute to the establishment within the United States of a totalitarian dictatorship." All "communist-action" and "communist front" organizations were assumed to be such conspiracies and required to register with the attorney general. The act authorized the president, in case of an "internal security emergency," to arrest and detain any individuals for whom there was "reasonable ground" to suspect that they would "probably" engage in acts of espionage or sabotage. Any alien, moreover, with the slightest "subversive" taint was to be excluded from admission to the United States. In his veto message, Truman characterized parts of the Internal Security Act as "the greatest danger to freedom of speech, press, and assembly since the alien and sedition laws of 1798."

On June 30, 1952, Congress supplemented the Internal Security Act with the McCarran-Walter Immigration Act, passed again over Truman's veto. This act updated but hardly liberalized the widely attacked quota system, which imposed exceptional hardship on displaced persons and refugees from Communist countries. More to the point, it required the attorney general to screen out "subversives" within the permitted quotas and empowered him to deport such persons even after they had become naturalized American citizens.

The McCarran Acts, like Truman's loyalty program and the actions of the FBI, intensified the preoccupation with internal security. McCarthy had effectively used the issue in the congressional elections of 1950 to defeat a Maryland senator, Millard F. Tydings, who had been bold enough to oppose his reckless charges. With equal effectiveness, McCarthy capitalized on fears of communism to win reelection in 1952, and the Republican party employed such fears that same year to return to the White House.

The Election of 1952: Eisenhower

The platform adopted by the Republican party in 1952 promised to repudiate any commitments, such as Yalta, that made possible "Communist enslavement" and attacked the containment policy that "abandoned" so many millions to it. Yet many Republicans remained committed to bipartisanship in principle and to the Truman version of it in practice. Passing over the twice-defeated Thomas E. Dewey and the deeply conservative Senator Robert A. Taft, Republicans nominated the immensely popular wartime hero, Dwight David Eisenhower. The Taft people took what solace they could from the nomination for vice-president of Richard Nixon, the former HUAC member who had won a seat in the United States Senate after effectively using the communist issue against his opponent.

During the 1952 campaign, Nixon's successful use of innuendo to smear opponents came back to haunt him. Even as he charged that a Stevenson triumph would ensure "more Alger Hisses, more atomic spies, more crises," newspapers revealed the existence of a "secret" contingency fund that had been raised by friends to keep Nixon in "financial comfort." With Eisenhower now on the verge of dropping him from the ticket unless he placed "all the facts before the people, fairly and squarely," Nixon took to nationwide television to explain that the fund had been used for campaign expenses, not for himself or his family. The public responded favorably to what came to be known as the "Checkers speech" (referring to the family dog he refused to give up), and Eisenhower reaffirmed his confidence in Nixon's integrity.

After Truman announced that he would not run for reelection, the Democrats drafted his choice, Adlai E. Stevenson, governor of Illinois. Stevenson conducted a vigorous and unusually eloquent campaign that won him many supporters among intellectuals. To no one's surprise, however, Eisenhower's vast appeal, enhanced by his campaign pledge to fly to Korea and end the stalemate there, carried him to a striking triumph. He received 33,824,000 popular votes to Stevenson's 27,314,000. In the electoral college, his margin was 422 to 89, and for the first time since 1928 the Solid South contributed to the Republican total. Yet the Republicans had grounds for worry. Even Eisenhower's great popularity brought the party a mere majority of eight in the House and a standoff in the Senate. With a Republican–southern Democratic coalition able to control Congress, however, the conservative mood still prevailed.

The election of Eisenhower ended twenty years of Democratic rule in the White House. But few Americans anticipated any startling changes. By this time, much of the New Deal social legislation, like social security, had become so much a part of American life that no Republican leader thought of tampering with it. The foreign policy of the United States, despite Republican charges, was still bipartisan. Democrats and Republicans alike operated from the premise that the Soviet Union represented a constant and inevitable threat to the "free world" and needed to be contained. Even the search for internal security had been largely a bipartisan effort. Finally, no political figure so exemplified the spirit of bipartisanship to the American people as did Eisenhower, a candidate both parties had eagerly sought.

SUGGESTED READINGS

W. LaFeber, *America, Russia, and the Cold War*, rev. ed. (1976). S.E. Ambrose, *Rise to Globalism: American Foreign Policy since 1938*, rev. ed. (1983). T.G. Paterson, *On Every Front: The Making of the Cold War* (1979). G. Kennan, *American Diplomacy, 1900–1950* (1951). J.L. Gaddis, *Strategies of Containment* (1982). R.J. Donovan, *Conflict and Crisis* (1977) and *Tumultuous Years* (1984). B. J. Bernstein, *Politics and Policies of the Truman Administration* (1970). D. Caute, *The Great Fear* (1978). V. Navasky, *Naming Names* (1980). T.C. Reeves, *The Life and Times of Joe McCarthy* (1982).

SUMMARY

The United States after World War II was a superpower engaged in a rivalry with the other superpower, the Soviet Union, for world domination. Wartime cooperation soon returned to mutual suspicion and distrust.

The United Nations was created as the war ended. Envisioned as an international organization that would be more effective than the old League of Nations, it had fifty-one charter members. Its charter set up two major agencies, the General Assembly, to which all members belonged, and the Security Council, made up of the Great Powers as permanent members plus a few rotating members. The council was given authority to apply sanctions to maintain peace, but each of the permanent members had a veto that could block action.

By 1982 the UN had 157 members. Over the years, it influenced some world issues. But the arms race, the dissolution of overseas empires, and the Cold War were be-

yond its power to solve. So was atomic energy and the development of more and more sophisticated nuclear weapons. For once the Soviet Union had detonated its own atomic bomb in September 1949, security by balance of terror became part of the new world order.

In Europe, the map was far different from what it had been before the war. Germany had been divided into two states, and the leading Nazis had been tried for war crimes by an international tribunal. In Asia, Japan was occupied by the United States until 1950, when a general peace treaty was signed. At home Truman, taking office after Roosevelt's death, had to face the problems of demobilization, reconversion of the economy to a peacetime footing, reorganization of the military establishment, and satisfaction of the pent-up demands for consumer goods.

The 1948 election is remembered as the greatest upset in American history. Tru-

man won the presidency against Thomas E. Dewey, whom everyone had expected to win. Truman's domestic program was called the Fair Deal, and it was designed to expand the New Deal's social programs. In foreign affairs, Truman had to deal with the Cold War and the new postwar world.

The Soviets had moved to secure their borders in Europe by creating a sphere of influence in Eastern Europe like American control in the Western Hemisphere. The rest of the world became a battleground for an ideological war between the United States and the Soviets. And the American policy set during this period—containment of Russia and the spread of communism through foreign aid and military alliances—was to last unchanged for more than a generation.

The Truman Doctrine provided aid to bolster pro-Western governments in Greece and Turkey. The Marshall Plan, developed in 1947, helped restore the shattered European economy and stop the advance of communism in Western Europe. Collective defense in Europe was set up through NATO, the North Atlantic Treaty Organization. Its counterpart in Latin America was the Rio Pact of 1947 and the Organization of American States (OAS), set up in 1948. In the Far East, the victory of the Communists in China in 1949, despite all the aid America had given Chiang Kai-shek and the Nationalists, led the United States to extend its defense perimeter to include Japan, Okinawa, and the Philippines.

The first open conflict came in Korea, which had been divided in two after the war. When North Korea, backed by the Soviet Union, invaded the South on June 25, 1950, Truman went to the UN and then ordered American forces into the conflict. The fighting went on for two more years, and at the end no one had won: Korea remained divided, and the armistice of July 1953 was a return to the prewar boundary of the thirty-eighth parallel. The futile conflict had cost the United States more than 140,000 casualties and more than $15 billion.

At home, Cold War tensions erupted in an obsessive concern with internal security and subversion. HUAC, the House Un-American Activities Committee, looked for Communists everywhere. Senator Joseph McCarthy, who came to symbolize the mania for loyalty, took as his special target the State Department. McCarthyism became a new word in the American vocabulary, and it came to mean wild and unfounded charges of disloyalty. He never managed to prove a single one of the many accusations he hurled in public. The McCarran Acts of 1950 and 1952 were the congressional response to the national obsession with communism at home.

All these tensions and fears, plus the popularity of General Dwight D. Eisenhower, brought a Republican president in 1952 after twenty years of Democrats in the White House. But there were to be no startling changes: the New Deal was not dismantled, and bipartisanship and the Cold War continued.

26
Superpowers in the Missile Age

With the presidency of Dwight D. Eisenhower, the United States embarked on a unique period of peace and relative good times. Since the end of World War II, the American people had been involved in economic reconversion, an obsessive concern with internal security, and a Cold War that defied resolution. And there was no assurance that the Eisenhower presidency would bring relief. His victory came at a moment in the Cold War when the American way of life seemed threatened by events around the world and at home as well. The nuclear arms race had assumed terrifying proportions. The Soviet Union had exploded its first atomic weapon in 1949. The United States three years later produced the even more destructive hydrogen bomb, and the Soviet Union in turn developed its hydrogen bomb and in 1957 reported the first successful tests of an intercontinental ballistic missile (ICBM).

Confronted with this balance of terror and with international developments they could neither control nor at times understand, the American people found in President Eisenhower the security and self-assurance they needed so badly. Although his "dynamic conservatism" envisioned a more limited role for the federal government, he did little to undo the Fair Deal or the New Deal. Although his foreign policy took on a "new look" and used the language of "massive retaliation" and "brinksmanship," the substance and goals remained the same: containment by alliance and superior military power. His middle-of-the-road approach satisfied most Americans, as did his refusal to commit American youths to combat situations. Through two terms, he remained for most Americans the symbol of order, stability, and military might in the White House—precisely what the time seemed to demand.

John F. Kennedy succeeded Eisenhower to the presidency. The youngest person elected to that office and the first president born in the twentieth century, he brought to the White House a certain flair that it had not known since the days of FDR. Perhaps it was simply his youth that made the difference, that seemed to inspire hope in the youthful population of the entire world. He conveyed the impression of new *and imaginative approaches to old problems, even if his actual policies were not so different.*

Two events of 1960, seemingly unrelated, heralded the decade of turbulence that lay ahead. On February 1, four black students in Greensboro, North Carolina, violated segregation laws and customs by taking seats at the lunch counter of the local F. W. Woolworth store. On May 13, the House Un-American Activities Committee tried to hold hearings in San Francisco and ran into a massive demonstration, made up in part of students from the nearby Berkeley campus of the University of California. If these rumblings represented an undercurrent of dissatisfaction, they were barely understood in 1960. But comprehension came soon enough. The optimism with which the sixties began and with which many young Americans responded to Kennedy's vision of a New Frontier would be shattered by assassination, racial strife, and a deepening involvement in a country previously unknown to most Americans—Vietnam.

CONSERVATIVES IN POWER

In campaigning for the presidency, Eisenhower had promised to clean up the "mess in Washington," purge the disloyal, spend less money, and stem the tide of "creeping socialism." But Eisenhower discovered, like any new president, that it was not so easy to put campaign rhetoric into action. Successful businessmen and corporation lawyers dominated the cabinet. But the president was less successful in his efforts to cut government expenses. Although few New Deal and Fair Deal programs were enlarged, few were canceled, and in September 1954, on the eve of the congressional elections,

President Dwight David Eisenhower and Vice-President Richard Nixon. (UPI/Bettmann Archive)

Eisenhower signed an act adding more than 7 million persons to those eligible for social-security benefits.

The America Eisenhower venerated was best exemplified by his own boyhood home of Abilene, Kansas, which lay almost at the exact geographic center of the United States. No one stressed more than the president his dedication to the middle way. But even while Eisenhower was taking, as he believed, "that straight road down the middle," events were polarizing the nation and world in profound and disconcerting ways.

The Decline of McCarthy

Determined to expand the dragnet for Communists, the president issued his own "loyalty order" on April 27, 1953. The categories for "security risks" in government employment were made broader and vaguer. If charges were brought against a federal employee, he or she could now be suspended. Although the administration boasted it had fired 1456 federal employees under this program, not one Communist could be found. Truman's program had yielded even more "risks." The net result of the Democratic-Republican loyalty purges was the demoralization of federal employees.

The search for internal security knew few limits. In December 1953, Eisenhower dismayed the scientific community by ordering a "blank wall" to be placed between J. Robert Oppenheimer, the distinguished nuclear physicist who had directed the making of the first atomic bomb, and all secret atomic data. Oppenheimer, at this time head of the Institute for Advanced Study at Princeton, also served as chairman of the general advisory committee of the Atomic Energy Commission. The administration learned that McCarthy was on Oppenheimer's trail, and it wanted to get him first. After a humiliating hearing, a special review board cleared Oppenheimer of disloyalty. But in the eyes of the AEC he remained a "misfit," unemployable because of "fundamental defects in his character."

Although Congress and the presidency had often knuckled under to McCarthy, his star began to wane in the summer of 1954. The senator's reckless attack on the "coddling" of Communists in the United States Army led to the spectacular Army-McCarthy hearings. Before a nationwide television audience, McCarthy failed to sustain his charges. He conducted himself in a manner that embarrassed many of his associates. In December 1954, by a vote of sixty-seven to twenty-two, the Senate censured him for "conduct unbecoming a member." Less than three years later, he died virtually unsung. Although *McCarthyism* entered the American vocabulary as a word for indiscriminate allegations and unsubstantiated charges, such fame actually distorted the senator's importance. He had exploited the art, yet the origins lay in the Cold War itself. The earliest practitioners had been Democrats and Republicans, conservatives and liberals, including many who thought McCarthy had simply carried it too far.

Black Rights and White Laws

Even as the United States posed abroad as a defender of oppressed peoples, it found its credentials seriously undermined and challenged at home by its own black citizens. The revolution of rising expectations in the newly liberated colonial empires in Africa and Asia also stirred the black community in the United States. Despite the persistence of traditional racial practices, a new mood emerged in black America. The presidency, moreover, could no longer feel immune to the possible consequences of racism in the United States. During the Truman administration, a Committee on Civil Rights, composed of leaders of both races, made clear the extent to which the American image abroad and the Cold War demanded a new and more realistic view of race relations: "The United States is not so strong, the final triumph of the democratic ideal is not so inevitable that we can ignore what the world thinks of us or our record."

Since the 1930s, the National Association for the Advancement of Colored People (NAACP) had attacked the inequality of black educational facilities. Encouraged by a series of favorable court decisions that began to erode the separate-but-equal principle, blacks challenged segregation itself in *Oliver Brown et al.* v. *Board of Education of Topeka, Kansas.* Speaking for a unanimous Supreme Court in May 1954, Chief Justice Earl Warren, an Eisenhower appointee and former governor of California, ordered the end of public school segregation:

> To separate [black children] from others of similar age and qualifications solely because of their race generates a feeling of inferiority as to their status in the community that may affect their hearts and

minds in a way never to be undone. . . . We conclude that in the field of public education the doctrine of "separate but equal" has no place. Separate educational facilities are inherently unequal.

Much has been made of the sudden and shocking character of the Warren Court's ruling. No doubt it shocked millions who had never given a thought to the issue. It probably stunned the president. Yet the particular cases had been before the courts for years. And great care was taken in its implementation, which was placed in the hands of local courts. They were permitted to use guidelines reflecting local situations.

In the border states, considerable progress was made toward compliance within two years. In the Deep South it became clear that compliance would take time and might involve violence. In September 1957 Little Rock, Arkansas, became the focal point of southern resistance. Governor Orval E. Faubus used the National Guard to prevent nine black children from entering that city's Central High School. President Eisenhower countered by providing the children with federal military protection, and they were

Elizabeth Eckford, a black student attempting to integrate a white school in Little Rock, Arkansas, tries to ignore the abuse of white protesters. (Wide World Photos)

subsequently enrolled. The handful of black students in Little Rock were subjected to such harassment, however, that the local school board soon asked for a suspension of the integration program. Attorneys for the school board argued that it could not at present put integration into effect because of "the total opposition of the people and of the State Governor of Arkansas." Over a reasonable length of time, perhaps, the situation would change. Attorneys for the NAACP, led by their chief counsel, Thurgood Marshall, replied, "There can be no equality of justice for our people if the law steps aside, even for a moment, at the command of force and violence." The Supreme Court agreed and on September 12, 1958, unanimously denied the request. Seventeen days later it delivered an unprecedented written opinion on the case in which, to underscore their unanimity, all nine justices were listed as coauthors. This opinion declared that

> The constitutional rights of respondents [Negro children] are not to be sacrificed or yielded to . . . violence and disorder. . . . The constitutional rights of children not to be discriminated against in school admissions on grounds of race or color declared by this court can neither be nullified openly and directly by state legislators or state executives or judicial officers, nor nullified by them through any evasive scheme for segregation.

The outlook, however, remained bleak. By 1959, of the 2985 biracial southern school districts, only 792 had been integrated. None were in the Deep South or Virginia, which had taken the lead in adopting the official policy of "massive resistance." The governor could close any school ordered integrated by the courts.

While concentrating first on the school issue, blacks soon broadened their campaign for equality to every phase of life.

What was at issue was not only school integration, but the entire range of southern laws and customs that confined black people to separate and almost always inferior facilities. On December 1, 1955, Rosa Parks, a middle-aged black woman, refused an order to give up her seat to a white person on a bus in Montgomery, Alabama. After her arrest, local blacks under the leadership of a young Baptist clergyman from Atlanta, Martin Luther King, Jr., organized a movement to boycott the city buses. The boycott lasted for an entire year, until the Supreme Court ruled in favor of blacks and forced the city to desegregate its public transportation system. That proved to be only the beginning of a massive nonviolent campaign to disrupt and undermine the racial caste system in the South.

Responding to blacks' rising militancy, Congress passed the first federal civil-rights acts in almost a century in 1957 and 1960. Broad at the outset, these acts, as adopted, were confined largely to the right to vote. They made the procedure for federal intervention in this critical field so difficult that any gains were nullified. Nevertheless, these two measures revived dormant federal commitments. "I don't believe you can change the hearts of men with laws or decisions," Eisenhower had said, urging caution in implementing the *Brown* ruling. A few years later King observed, "The law may not change the heart—but it can restrain the heartless." That much and more, sometimes with far-reaching consequences, the law and continued black agitation were to undertake.

THE "NEW LOOK" IN FOREIGN POLICY

The Republicans took office promising a "new look" in foreign policy. Rather than pursue what they perceived to be the negative Democratic policy of containment, they proposed to "liberate" the nations in communism's grip, "roll back" Soviet power in Eastern Europe, and "unleash" Chiang Kai-shek in Asia. The architect of this ambitious program, John Foster Dulles, was an intractable and evangelical anti-Communist. But despite the considerable influence Dulles exerted on foreign policy, the Eisenhower years marked no significant break with the containment policies of the previous administration. Eisenhower moved more cautiously than Dulles's rhetoric dictated. His military experience had taught him to hate war, and his search for conciliation and compromise appeared to be genuine. Dulles actively pursued a diplomacy of rhetoric and alliance. He sought to bolster anti-Communist regimes and to undermine Communist regimes. But even if Eisenhower placed few restraints on this policy, he kept American troops out of combat.

Diplomacy by Rhetoric

For the president, "fiscal morality" meant balancing the budget, a goal attainable only by reducing military spending. Conforming to the president's guidelines, the National Security Council announced a new military strategy as early as October 1953. Dulles soon called it massive retaliation. Under the new "basic decision," dependence on the army's costly ground forces would be reduced or eliminated. As a bonus, the United States would no longer be lured into police actions like that in Korea. Instead, security would be attained by emphasis on air power, in which the United States still led the world. The administration would simply let the Communists in Moscow and Peking know that any new menace to American security would be met by nuclear and thermonuclear assaults on their cities and civilians.

By the end of 1954, massive retaliation had become synonymous with massive annihilation. The USSR had detonated its own thermonuclear bombs and had developed delivery systems like SAC's. America was confronted with a balance of terror. Dulles responded with still another empty verbal triumph: brinksmanship, the art of going "to the brink of war without being scared." But when it came to new nationalist movements that threatened American interests, the United States would not rely on rhetoric alone.

The New Nationalism: Iran, Guatemala, and Vietnam

With the collapse of colonial rule in Asia, Africa, and the Mideast, the United States faced the task of converting nationalist movements into anti-Communist allies. There were times when that objective could be realized only by helping to destroy or immobilize the movements themselves.

In Iran, Mohammed Mossadegh headed a movement that seized power in 1951 and proceeded to nationalize the Anglo-Iranian Oil Company—a combine that exploited Iran's oil reserves largely for the profit of non-Iranians. When American officials concluded that the new government was coming under Communist influence, the United States provided the military support that enabled the shah of Iran to regain control in August 1953. The payoff came in the form of a pro-Western ally, much greater Iranian oil production, and a legacy of American intervention in the internal affairs of Iran that came back to haunt the United States twenty-six years later when the shah's repressive regime was finally toppled.

Encouraged by its success in Iran, the United States prepared to deal with a challenge in its own hemisphere. In Guatemala, a Communist-backed reformist, Colonel Jacobo Arbenz Guzmán, headed up a new government and confiscated lands belonging to the monopolistic United Fruit Company. Although Arbenz had come to power in a democratic election, the Central Intelligence Agency engineered a coup that toppled his government in 1954.

With considerably less success, the United States sought to bolster its defenses in Asia, where a nationalist movement was threatening to undermine one of the last bastions of colonialism: Indochina, a mid-nineteenth-century creation consisting of the three old kingdoms of Laos, Cambodia, and Vietnam. With Britain and Holland on their way out as Asian powers, the United States wished to help the French retain these valuable possessions, especially after China's intervention in Korea.

The principal nationalist group in Indochina was the Vietminh in Vietnam, whose standing by the end of World War II was enhanced by its success in liberating portions of the north from the Japanese. In September 1945, its leaders had proclaimed the Democratic Republic of Vietnam, with Hanoi its capital and Ho Chi Minh (who had begun to work against French rule long before World War II) its president. While colonialism crumbled elsewhere, the French sought to maintain full control over Indochina. In September 1946, Ho Chi Minh returned from consultations in Paris disenchanted with the French attitude toward independence. By December, clashes in the north had grown into a general war. The rivalry grew more intense after June 1949. The French, having successfully set up former native rulers as puppets in Cambodia and Laos, now tried the same tactic in Vietnam. Their puppet here was Bao Dai, a member of an old ruling family, who had no popular following and preferred Paris or the French Riviera to Saigon.

This challenge led the Vietminh to intensify and extend its military activity. The emergence of the People's Republic of China in October 1949 gave a tremendous boost to Vietminh morale and soon to Vietminh strength as well. Early in 1950 China formally recognized the Hanoi regime. The United States and Britain, concerned at this time about French support for NATO in Europe, responded by recognizing the Saigon regime of Bao Dai. More than that, the Truman administration began to offset Chinese aid to Ho with American aid to Bao. When the Korean conflict ended, the United States greatly enlarged its assistance to the French. By the end of 1953, American taxpayers were paying two-thirds of the cost of the French military effort, or about $1 billion per year. But it could not save the French after their main army allowed itself to be trapped at Dienbienphu early in 1954.

The siege of Dienbienphu intensified the debate in Washington. Eisenhower had already stated that Southeast Asia was of "transcendent importance" to American security: "You have a row of dominoes set up, and you knock over the first one, and what will happen to the last one is the certainty that it will go over very quickly." But even while taking this stance, Eisenhower resisted the advice to commit American troops.

By the time Dienbienphu surrendered to Ho Chi Minh on May 7, 1954, the representatives of nine powers—France, the People's Republic of China, the USSR, Britain, the United States, the two Vietnams, Cambodia, and Laos—had already convened at Geneva to work out some arrangements in the light of the inevitable collapse. The armistice agreement, secured on July 20, provided for a military truce between the Vietminh and the French military command, the latter openly acting for its Saigon puppet regime. The truce divided Vietnam along the seventeenth parallel. North of the line, Vietminh armies were to "regroup"; south of it, the armies of the French. Although Ho Chi Minh controlled two-thirds of the country, he withdrew his forces to the north, convinced that he would easily win the countrywide elections in July 1956.

Not until January 1955 did the French turn back the Saigon regime to Bao Dai and his strong man, Prime Minister Ngo Dinh Diem. Fearful of a Communist victory, Diem found reasons for putting off the 1956 elections. Meanwhile, the United States gradually replaced the French in South Vietnam and increased its aid to Diem's regime, despite a campaign of suppression and political and religious murders that offended even his American friends.

Within South Vietnam, the Vietcong—pro-Communist guerrillas—stepped up their attacks on the Diem regime. By 1959 the North was openly aiding these attacks, and in September 1960 Ho formally recognized the Vietcong as the National Front for the Liberation of South Vietnam. Within the first year of the Kennedy administration, the Vietcong force grew to nearly 10,000. The South Vietnamese Army was unable to restrain them, and the new president felt it necessary to send his vice-president, Lyndon B. Johnson, on a fact-finding mission. Obviously, the debate over the United States role in Vietnam had by no means been settled.

Diplomacy by Alliance

Frustrated in his efforts to "liberate" Eastern Europe, Dulles envisioned encircling the Communist world with a series of military alliances by which the United States promised to defend member nations against aggression. Diplomacy by alliance would become, in fact, a hallmark of the Dulles "new look" in foreign affairs. The policy met with

varied success. In Asia, repeated failures to check communism led Dulles to seek a collective organization that would serve as a counterpart to NATO in Europe. But he was turned down by significant new countries such as India, Burma, Indonesia, and Ceylon. They resented American intrusion and feared that efforts to isolate China might just provoke that country.

Two mainland countries, Pakistan and Thailand, along with the Philippines, Australia, and New Zealand, proved more responsive. At Manila in September 1954 they met with the United States, Britain, and France and created the Southeast Asia Treaty Organization. The signers agreed to meet any "common danger" from "Communist aggression" in accordance with their own "constitutional processes." No SEATO armed force similar to NATO's was contemplated or created; thermonuclear weapons were to provide security.

Between SEATO countries in the Far East and NATO countries in the West lay the oil-rich Middle East. Arab nationalism, already inflamed by the creation of Israel in 1948, was reinforced after 1952 by the overthrow of King Farouk in Egypt. A new Egyptian republic emerged, with Colonel Gamal Abdel Nasser as its strong man. He had ambitions to unite the neighboring Arab lands under Egyptian leadership. An obvious first step was eliminating the remains of colonialism.

To close the gap between SEATO and NATO and thereby "create a solid band of resistance against the Soviet Union," Dulles had been promising a Middle East defense organization. In February 1955, Turkey and its neighbor Iraq, meeting at Baghdad, signed a mutual-defense treaty. Britain, Pakistan, and Iran also subscribed. These arrangements became known as the Baghdad Pact, under which the Middle East Treaty Organization was formed. The United

UNION OF SOVIET SOCIALIST REPUBLICS

BERING SEA

SEA OF OKHOTSK

Irkutsk •   *Lake Baikul*

(U.S.S.R.) (U.S.)   ATTU

KISKA

• Ulan Bator

SAKHALIN I. (U.S.S.R.)

MONGOLIA   MANCHURIA   Vladivostok •

KURILE IS. (U.S.S.R.)

Beijing •   NORTH KOREA   *SEA OF JAPAN*

Pyongyang •

• SOUTH KOREA

Seoul •

C H I N A

JAPAN

TIBET

• Tokyo

• Shanghai   TACHEN IS.

• BONIN IS.

PACIFIC

NEPAL   MATSU I.

QUEMOY I.

RYUKYU IS. (Jap.)

OKINAWA

• IWO JIMA

E. PAKISTAN   Hanoi •

TAIWAN (FORMOSA)

• MARCUS I.

Calcutta •   BURMA   LAOS   Hong Kong (Br.)   PESCADORES IS.

OCEAN

INDIA   NORTH VIETNAM

WAKE I. (U.S.)

Rangoon •   Vientiane •   *SOUTH*

THAILAND

PHILIPPINE

• MARIANAS IS.

BAY OF BENGAL   Bangkok •   SOUTH VIETNAM   *CHINA*

• Manila

SEA

GUAM (U.S.)

CAMBODIA   • Saigon   *SEA*   PHILIPPINES (also member of SEATO)

M I C R O N E S I A

CEYLON   BRUNEI (Br.)

MARSHALL IS. (U.S. trust)

MALAYSIA

Kuala Lumpur •   SARAWAK

CAROLINE ISLANDS (U.S. trust)

• Singapore

GILBERT IS. (Br.)

SUMATRA   KALIMANTAN

M E L A N E S I A

I N D O N E S I A   SULAWESI   IRIAN (To U.S. 1962, Indonesia 1963)   NEW GUINEA (Aust.)

Djakarta •   JAVA

SOLOMON IS. (Br.)

ELLICE IS. (Br.)

PAPUA (Aust.)

TIMOR (Port.)

INDIAN

CORAL SEA

NEW HEBRIDES IS. (Br. and Fr.)

FIJI IS. (Br.)

OCEAN

NEW CALEDONIA (Fr.)

A U S T R A L I A

Brisbane •

• Perth

TASMAN

Sidney •

Canberra •

SEA

NEW ZEALAND

Melbourne •

TASMANIA

Wellington •

//// Members of SEATO

▨ Nations having bilateral treaties with the U.S.

▒ Communist bloc

Postwar Alliances

States agreed to "cooperate with" but not join the organization. Widespread sympathy for Israel, especially among American Jews, who contributed heavily to the urban vote, made the administration wish to avoid appearing to be too close to the Arab powers, who had sworn to destroy the Jewish state.

To Dulles's great discomfort, Egypt also stayed out. Nasser wished freedom of action in playing off the USSR and the West against each other. His policy paid dividends in September 1955, when Egypt and the Soviet Union made an arms deal. Dulles, along with Britain and the United Nations, soon offered to help Egypt build the Aswan Dam. The project was to make much more of the Nile's water available for irrigation. Nasser accepted the American offer in July 1956. But within a week, certain anti-Western gestures prompted Dulles to withdraw it. On July 26, Egypt responded by announcing the nationalization of the Suez Canal. Egypt would use the canal tolls to construct the dam itself.

Rising tensions led Israel to launch an invasion of Egypt in October 1956. Its declared objective was to destroy the bases from which raids had been made on its territory. Israel's action was followed by the remarkable Anglo-French invasion of the Suez region. Even more remarkable was the collaboration of the United States and the Soviet Union in the United Nations General Assembly, where they jointly condemned this resort to arms by NATO nations. The General Assembly then voted to organize a force to supervise a cease-fire. American threats combined with those of the USSR brought the Israeli invasion to a stop. The first detachments of the United Nations Emergency Force began to arrive on November 15 to help keep the peace. But this was only a stopgap measure that solved nothing in the Middle East.

When the Soviets continued to arm Arab nations, the President asked Congress in January 1957 for endorsement of the Eisenhower Doctrine, a unilateral warning to the USSR that the United States would defend the entire Middle East against Soviet attack. In March, a joint resolution of Congress gave the president the power to use American forces to help any Middle East nation, at its request, to resist "armed attack from any country controlled by international communism." In July 1958, following an anti-Western revolution in Iraq that led eventually to its withdrawal from the Baghdad Pact, the United States and Britain sent troops to Lebanon and Jordan to prevent similar uprising in those countries.

CONCILIATION AND CONFRONTATION

After Stalin's death in 1953, the Soviet Union made a series of conciliatory moves. It recognized the Federal Republic of West Germany, signed a peace treaty with Japan, and ended the four-power occupation of Austria and recognized its independence. In June 1955, Nikolai Bulganin, the new premier, and Nikita Khrushchev, the Communist party head, paid a visit to Marshal Tito's Yugoslavia. In defiance of Stalin in 1948, Tito had set up his own version of a Communist state. Now, Tito, Bulganin, and Khrushchev declared openly that "differences in the concrete forms of socialist development are exclusively the concern of the peoples of the respective countries." This acknowledgment of the first break in the Soviet structure was to have far-reaching consequences in Europe and Asia.

Although the United States and the USSR remained militarily the world's superpowers, each capable of annihilating the other, both were to find themselves increasingly frustrated in their attempts to control other nations. Preoccupied with each other, the two superpowers seemed incapable or unwilling to grasp the implications of the revolutions that were transforming large segments of the world. All too often, they failed to understand the need of colonial and oppressed peoples to determine their own destinies. That failure would have profound consequences for the future of peaceful coexistence in a rapidly changing world.

The Second Eisenhower Administration

Significant gaps in economic performance appeared during the first Eisenhower administration. But the business boom, given a strong boost by government spending, was genuine enough for the Republicans to campaign in 1956 on the slogan "Peace, Progress, and Prosperity." Dependent on the general's personal appeal, Republican leaders urged him to run again, despite his health. He was renominated by acclamation, along with Vice-President Nixon. The Democrats made what they could of the threat of a Nixon succession, economic discontent in the farm belt, and the failure of the "new look" in foreign affairs. But Eisenhower's personal attractiveness carried him to victory even more decisively than in 1952. With 34,751,000 votes to Stevenson's 25,427,000, he won 58 percent of the ballots. In the electoral college his margin was 457 to 73. At the same time, the Democrats maintained the majorities in the House and Senate that they had won in the congressional elections of 1954.

In his second inaugural address, on January 21, 1957, Eisenhower expressed his continuing hopes for coexistence: "We honor, no less in this divided world than in a less tormented time, the people of Russia. We do not dread, rather do we welcome, their progress in education and industry." A few months later the president and the American people suffered a shock that suggested they would not welcome Soviet progress quite so heartily after all.

On October 4, 1957, within six weeks of reporting the first successful tests of an intercontinental ballistic missile, the Soviet Union electrified the world by using the missile's rocket engine to launch the first unmanned space satellite, Sputnik I. The successful launching of four American satellites the following year brought some comfort, but this was dissipated on January 2, 1959, when the Soviets launched Lunik I, the first space vehicle to traverse the full 250,000 miles or so to the moon. Lunik did not hit the moon but soared into space to become the first artificial planet in orbit around the sun. On March 10, the United States successfully put a planet of its own in orbit.

During Eisenhower's second administration, the United States suddenly found itself shuffling along with a slowdown in business expansion, a disturbingly high level of unemployment, inflation, and serious racial strife. In mid 1958, moreover, the administration was hit by revelations of scandals so far-reaching that Sherman Adams, the confidential assistant to the president, was forced to resign. The depth of the party's trouble on all fronts was disclosed in the 1958 congressional elections, when it suffered a defeat like those of the early New Deal years.

Coexistence and New Tensions

At the Twentieth Party Congress in February 1956, Nikita Khrushchev startled the world by revealing the crimes of Stalin, supporting the idea of different paths to socialism and suggesting the need for less rigid restrictions than those sanctioned by Stalin. This bold move, along with Khrushchev's endorsement of peaceful coexistence, his trip to the United States, and his refusal to support Mao Tse-tung's call for wars of national liberation, would soon drive a wedge between the USSR and China. The Soviet Union found itself charged with appeasement of capitalism and with betrayal of Marxist-Leninist principles. When de-Stalinization led Poland and Hungary to seek those different paths to socialism, the Chinese used the occasion to exploit the weaknesses in Soviet leadership and to assert their own leadership in the Communist world.

Both the Polish and Hungarian "counterrevolutions" reached their turning points in October 1956, when the world and the UN were absorbed in the Mideast crisis. Convinced that the uprisings had been "provoked by enemy agents" rather than Stalinist oppression, Khrushchev sent troops to crush the Hungarian revolt and tightened controls elsewhere. At the same time, he secured his position at home. In March 1958 he became premier as well as party chief.

Bolstered by space triumphs and missile gains, Khrushchev took some steps to ease the Cold War tensions. During Nixon's visit to Moscow in July 1959, Khrushchev engaged in such a high-spirited TV debate with the vice-president that he came to believe the premier should get to know more about the United States at first hand. This led to a prompt invitation from the president, and on September 14 Khrushchev arrived. After a peaceable address at the UN and a lively cross-country speaking tour, he met with Eisenhower with such success that a summit conference to continue "the spirit of Camp David," the site of their talks, was informally agreed upon.

But the thaw proved to be short-lived. On May 5, 1960, less than two weeks before the scheduled summit conference in Paris, an American U-2 reconnaissance plane was shot down over Soviet territory. Before acknowledging the truth of Soviet protests that the plane was on a regular spying mission, the administration trapped itself in a web of denials and halftruths. Although Eisenhower announced that further surveillance flights over the Soviet Union had been suspended, the damage had been done. The spirit of Camp David instantly dissolved in Paris, Khrushchev demanding American apologies for "aggression" and punishment of those responsible. The summit conference ended within three hours.

Closer to home, Latin America had begun to erupt. The most important challenge to United States dominance came in Cuba. On January 1, 1959, Fidel Castro successfully completed a five-year struggle to overthrow the Batista regime. Adopting a hostile attitude toward the United States, Castro found a receptive audience in a people that had known only dependence on America.

Determined to effect a radical social revolution, Castro moved to end the colonial relationship that had bound the Cuban government and economy to the United States. The massive confiscation of foreign holdings he ordered simply reflected the extent of outside control. His economic program and repression of civil liberties angered the United States, and it led many middle-class Cubans to flee there. With *Fidelismo* threatening to spread elsewhere, the United States chose to rely on traditional ways of dealing with hemispheric trouble. Before Eisenhower left office, he agreed to a CIA plan by which an anti-Castro army of Cubans would be landed in Cuba in early 1961. The implementation of the plan was left to the next president.

Eisenhower's Farewell

Eight years in office proved a great strain on the Republican party, especially since it had failed to balance the budget, reduce the national debt, end the upward wage-price spiral, restore farm income, and significantly cut taxes. It had also failed to roll back the Communists and restore the good old days of continental security. When Republican delegates convened in the summer of 1960 to choose a candidate, the conservatives were in command of the party machinery. On the first ballot the convention named Richard M. Nixon for president. As a sop to the party liberals, it chose Henry Cabot Lodge, United States delegate to the UN, as his running mate.

After his extraordinary performance in a series of primaries, Senator John F. Kennedy of Massachusetts clearly overshadowed the other presidential aspirants at the Democratic convention in Los Angeles. He won on the first ballot. Fearful of the effects of the strong civil-rights plank and of Kennedy's Catholicism, the Democrats, in an attempt to hold the South, nominated Senator Lyndon B. Johnson of Texas for vice-president. In Kennedy's acceptance speech, he talked about "a New Frontier—the frontier of the 1960s—a frontier of unfulfilled hopes and threats."

The campaign was highlighted by the first television debates between presidential candidates, from which Kennedy seemed to have gained more than his opponent. Nixon, moreover, had aroused considerable controversy in his political past, much of it revolving around the tactics he had used to advance his career.

When the results were in, Kennedy had become the first Catholic president, and at forty-three the youngest ever to be elected. But his winning margin was a mere 113,000 out of a record 68.8 million votes cast. He won by less than two-thirds of 1 percent of the popular vote. What probably saved him from defeat was the solid support he received from Catholics and blacks.

Before leaving the White House, the still popular Ike wanted to give the American people the "most challenging message" possible, and he did so admirably in his famous farewell speech of January 17, 1961:

> This conjunction of an immense military establishment and a . . . permanent armaments industry of vast proportions . . . is new in the American experience. The total influence—economic, political, even spiritual—is felt in every city, every state house, every office of the federal government. We recognize the imperative need for this development. Yet we must not fail to comprehend its grave implications. . . .
>
> In the councils of government we must guard against the acquisition of unwarranted influence, whether sought or unsought, by the military-industrial complex. The potential for the disastrous rise of misplaced power exists and will persist. We must never let the weight of this combination endanger our liberties or democratic processes.

The warning came too late. By 1961, the military-industrial complex had virtually overrun the traditional instruments of American government. With confrontation in Asia and the Caribbean, the military ascendancy, like the Cold War itself, seemed destined to remain a part of the American way of life. The newly elected president must have sensed that, and he paid little heed to Eisenhower's warning. During the first year of the Kennedy administration, the military budget increased 15 percent.

JFK AND THE NEW FRONTIER

Young as he was when he delivered his first State of the Union message in January 1961,

John F. Kennedy had already served fourteen years in Congress, the last eight in the Senate. He had been exposed to politics even earlier, in the home of his father, millionaire Joseph P. Kennedy, ambassador to Britain under FDR. It took time for the politically conservative environment to wear off. In Congress, he had associated with the severest critics of his party's China policy, helped carry the McCarran Internal Security Act over Truman's veto, and refrained from criticizing McCarthy. Elected to the Senate in 1952, Kennedy made an unsuccessful bid four years later for the Democratic vice-presidential nomination. In winning the presi-

dential nomination in 1960, he demonstrated some important assets. His candor was credible, his humor fresh, his modesty unfeigned. And he possessed, besides, an excellent war record and an efficient campaign organization.

No sooner had Kennedy taken office than he surrounded himself with youthful advisers pledged, like himself, to get the country moving again. The Kennedy team, David Halberstam would later write, "carried with them an exciting sense of American elitism, a sense that the best men had been summoned forth from the country." The dynastic heir apparent, his younger brother Robert, became attorney general and exercised perhaps broader powers than any previous holder of that office. Robert S. McNamara, one of the statistical geniuses of the Ford Motor Company, was named secretary of defense. His assignment was, with the aid of computers, to bring Pentagon feuding under civilian control. McGeorge Bundy, a Harvard intellectual, became Kennedy's special assistant for national-security affairs. In that position he may have exerted more influence than the official secretary of state, Dean Rusk.

During the campaign, Kennedy had compared himself with his also youthful rival. Nixon, said Kennedy, "has the courage of our old convictions." But "the New Frontier is here, whether we seek it or not." The New Frontier promised to pioneer in new approaches to old problems and to get the country moving again. The directions in which the country moved—toward confrontation at home and abroad—suggested how dependent Kennedy's approaches remained on the policies of his predecessors.

Civil Rights and Civil Conflict

In his first State of the Union message, Kennedy enumerated the "unfinished and ne-

Before an audience of some 70 million TV viewers, candidate John F. Kennedy demonstrated coolness and good humor in his debate with Nixon. (National Archives)

glected tasks'' that faced his administration. Because of financial need, ''one-third of our most promising high school graduates'' prematurely ended their education. Persistent recession resulted in the ''highest peak in our history'' of ''insured unemployment.'' Long-term ''distressed areas'' continued to decay. The drain of American gold abroad, largely for military assistance, menaced the stability of the dollar. Growing numbers of poor old people, the ill, and others in need were being neglected. Natural resources as basic as the water supply were being wasted.

But all these issues paled before that of racial equality, which Kennedy failed to mention in 1961. By the summer of 1963, the hundredth anniversary of the Emancipation Proclamation, it dominated the headlines. Nearly a decade since the Supreme Court had ruled school segregation illegal, the pace of integration made a mockery of the court-ordered ''all deliberate speed.'' When blacks sought admission to state universities, moreover, the resulting showdowns required the application of federal force. At the University of Mississippi, Governor Ross Barnett tried to block the ad-mission of James Meredith. At the University of Alabama, Governor George Wallace stood in the doorway, as he had promised, to stop two black students from entering.

Meanwhile, the attack on segregation had broadened. The sit-in at the Woolworth lunch counter in Greensboro, North Carolina, on February 1, 1960, mushroomed into hundreds of similar demonstrations, all designed to desegregate public facilities and transportation. By deliberately violating Jim Crow laws, black youths defied traditions and customs that had maintained generations of white supremacy in the South. By 1963, an estimated 70,000 blacks and white sympathizers had participated in these demonstrations, and more were to come.

To the embarrassment of American foreign policy, the headlines of 1963 made known around the world the brutality with which civil-rights demonstrations were suppressed. Several weeks after Kennedy proposed his first civil-rights legislation to Congress, mass demonstrations began in Birmingham, Alabama. Before the summer was over, more than 800 cities and towns had had peaceful protests, often in the face

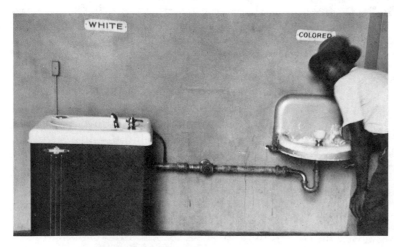

Segregated drinking fountains were symbolic of the separate worlds of the South until the 1960s. (Elliott Erwitt, Magnum Photos)

of dogs and fire hoses employed by the police. Leadership in the black nonviolent movement rested with Martin Luther King, Jr., barely in his thirties. If black people directed their appeal to the Christian conscience of white America, King argued, the walls of segregation and race hatred would inevitably crumble. What he asked of his followers was nonviolence, Christian love, and a belief in the essential decency of people. It would not be easy. The climax of the nonviolent campaign came on August 3, 1963, when over 200,000 blacks and sympathetic whites marched on Washington, D.C., demanding "freedom now." The march is best remembered for King's eloquent speech ("I have a dream") and the assembled multitude singing the anthem of the civil-rights movement, "We Shall Overcome."

On June 10, two months before the March on Washington, Medgar Evers, field secretary of the Mississippi chapter of the NAACP, was murdered by a sniper. Less than a month after the march, a bomb exploded in the Sixteenth Street Baptist Church in Birmingham, killing four black children. Perhaps, some argued, Martin Luther King had demanded too much of his people. His movement had yielded some positive results, but at a cost in human lives and frustration that many blacks found difficult to bear. The black movements, increasingly independent of white liberal sympathizers, began to take on different dimensions.

Although much of the activity was confined to the South, there were no grounds for optimism or smugness in the North. If anything, the frustration and betrayal of expectations were even deeper and potentially more explosive. Even as northern whites reacted with anger to the televised brutalities inflicted on southern

Martin Luther King. "We will not hate you, but we cannot obey your unjust laws. Do to us what you will and we will still love you. . . . But we will soon wear you down by our capacity to suffer. And in winning our freedom, we will so appeal to your heart and conscience, that we will win you in the process." (Bruce Davidson, Magnum)

blacks, they paid little attention to the discrimination in housing, employment, and education in their own region. Although northern blacks had the vote and civil rights, these were not of much value to a person facing unemployment and hunger. That was the message Malcolm X, a brilliant Black Muslim leader and separatist, was hammering home in the urban North, and he found an audience. "Well, I am one who doesn't believe in deluding myself," he said of white America. "I'm not going to sit at your table and watch you eat, with nothing on my plate, and call myself a diner. Sitting at the table doesn't make you a diner, unless you eat some of what's on that plate."

Space, Militarism, and Prosperity

To get the country moving again in the economic sphere, the new economists of the Kennedy administration explored every avenue for using the energies of the entire population. Early in 1962, the president proposed a broad tax cut for consumers as one way to stimulate demand for goods. But this measure, like so many of his proposals, made little headway in Congress. The president enjoyed far more success when he asked for appropriations for defense and space. During Kennedy's administration, annual space appropriations soared to over $5 billion.

The business upswing in 1962 and 1963 followed new expenditures and appropriations not only for the space program, but for the related missile program and other "national-security" items. While the strength of the country in foreign affairs depended on the strength of the domestic economy, it seemed that the strength of the domestic economy depended on the volume of military spending.

THE DIPLOMACY OF FLEXIBLE RESPONSE

Although Kennedy hoped to identify the country's power with its political ideals, its strength with its social values, he warned that "we must never be lulled into believing that either [the Soviet Union or China] has yielded its ambitions for world domination." Having accepted this basic premise of the Cold War, there were tragic ironies in Kennedy's attempts to find new approaches to foreign policy. While he tried to apply political solutions to "limited" international incidents, he felt obliged to build up

the armed services. In 1962, military expenditures went over the $50-billion mark for the first time since the Korean conflict.

By then, Kennedy had taken certain steps in pursuit of a more flexible response in foreign policy. The Peace Corps, in which young men and women would volunteer their technical skills to help underdeveloped nations, was a different and more creative approach to diplomacy. Far less imaginative was the president's response to continuing trouble in Latin America.

Cuba: The Bay of Pigs and the Missile Crisis

In one of his last acts as president, Eisenhower had broken off diplomatic relations with Cuba in protest against "a long series of harassments, baseless accusations, and vilifications." At least one of those accusations, however, soon proved far from baseless. For nine months, as Castro had charged, about 1500 anti-Castro Cuban exiles had been secretly training in Guatemala under United States CIA men for an invasion of their island.

After repeated assurances by a unanimous Joint Chiefs of Staff, some of his own "new frontiersmen," and an enthusiastic Allan Dulles (who reminded Kennedy of how his CIA had overthrown Guatemala's Marxist government), the new president permitted the invasion to start. At the same time, he assured the press that "there will not be, under any conditions, any intervention in Cuba by United States forces." Five days later, on April 17, 1961, the exile forces attempted to land at the Bay of Pigs, ninety miles from Havana. The anticipated popular uprising failed to happen, and the assault instantly collapsed.

Castro then tried to strengthen his defenses against any further United States aggression. But when the Soviet Union took this opportunity to install missile sites in Cuba, manned by Soviet technicians and capable of obliterating targets within a range of 2000 miles, that was more than the United States was willing to tolerate. On October 22, 1962, on nationwide television, Kennedy took a calculated risk that brought the world to the brink of nuclear war. He ordered Khrushchev to remove the missiles and instructed the navy to intercept and turn back Soviet ships headed for Cuba. (The Joint Chiefs of Staff and former secretary of state Acheson had argued instead for a direct air strike on the missile sites.) Recognizing the gravity of Kennedy's stand, the Soviet Union agreed to recall the ships and to remove the missile bases. Kennedy, on his part, assured the Soviet leader—but only in the form of a tacit understanding— that the United States would refrain from offensive action to overthrow the Castro regime. Both leaders had made their point, though it was Kennedy who emerged with the enhanced prestige.

Despite the Cuban confrontation and the ongoing Berlin crisis, new hopes for a détente between the Soviets and the West came out of the deepening split between the USSR and China. These hopes were strengthened in July 1963 when the three nuclear powers (the United States, Britain, and the USSR) signed a treaty pledging themselves to end nuclear testing that "causes radioactive debris" outside their own borders. The three powers invited others to sign the treaty. In the West, Germany had misgivings. France, eager for nuclear arms of its own, was openly hostile. In the East, China denounced the Soviets and the Western powers. In the United States, and no doubt in the USSR, armament had gained the irreversible momentum of which Eisenhower had spoken in his farewell.

Kennedy and Southeast Asia

Despite Kennedy's emphasis on developing political options, the most obvious product of flexible response became the elaboration and application of the concept of limited war. The fatal test of this policy came in Vietnam. Although Diem had refused to hold all-Vietnam elections in 1956 (correctly fearing he would lose) and had vio-

The Vietnam War

lated his pledge to Eisenhower to make needed reforms, the United States remained committed to his regime. In October 1961, General Maxwell Taylor went to South Vietnam as Kennedy's special representative to appraise the situation. The result of that mission was a speed-up in the flow of American instructors, pilots, and other military personnel. By the end of 1962, after Taylor had become chairman of the Joint Chiefs, the number of Americans in South Vietnam had reached 10,000.

Although Kennedy at first resisted both the overmilitarization and over-Americanization of the war in Vietnam, he soon found himself approving the growing military intervention. Embracing Eisenhower's domino theory, he declared in July 1963 that a United States withdrawal would "mean a collapse not only of South Vietnam but Southeast Asia. So we are going to stay there." American military assistance to the Diem regime soared, and the number of American military personnel edged toward 17,000. Bolstered by this demonstration of American support and confidence, Diem stepped up his attacks not on the Vietcong but on the Buddhists, who made up most of the opposition to the French-oriented Catholic ruling class.

In September 1963 Kennedy declared of the South Vietnamese, "In the final analysis, it's their war. They're the ones who have to win it or lose it. We can help them as advisers but they have to win it." To improve the prospects of winning, South Vietnamese general Duong Van Minh, with American encouragement, overthrew the Diem regime on November 1, 1963, and shortly thereafter executed Diem and his brother. The new government (the first of nine in the next five years) was given prompt American recognition. By the time of Kennedy's assassination, however, it had won few military laurels.

Death of the President

On reviewing his first two years in office, Kennedy acknowledged a large degree of frustration. "The responsibilities placed on the United States are greater than I imagined them to be and there are greater limitations upon our ability to bring about a favorable result than I had imagined them to be. . . . It is much easier to make speeches than it is finally to make the judgments."

The German problem remained unsolved. The Communists made it even more vivid by building a wall, early in August 1961, separating East from West Berlin. Periodic crises raised the threat of armed confrontation. In Africa, emerging nations were throwing off the last vestiges of colonialism and moving toward a neutral position in the East-West conflict. In Asia, the United States deepened its involvement in Vietnam. In space, Soviet scientists continued to set the pace.

Congress generously appropriated funds for defense and space, but proved more reluctant when it came to social legislation and the protection of civil rights. As the black movement spread, white resistance hardened. Black frustrations made Martin Luther King's hold on black leadership more precarious, and the prospect of violent confrontation grew. Meanwhile, Kennedy's civil-rights program went nowhere in Congress, along with his proposals to enlarge federal aid to education and extend medicare to the aged.

On November 22, 1963, Kennedy was in Dallas, Texas, to bolster his political position in that state. While riding in an open car, to the cheers of crowds lining the streets, the president was shot in the neck and head by an assassin. He died almost instantly. The tragic death of the young president threw the nation and the world into shock, mourning, and disbelief. The disbelief was compounded by the bizarre series of events that followed. Two days later, while a nationwide television audience looked on, Lee Harvey Oswald, the suspected assassin, was shot to death by Jack Ruby, the proprietor of a small Dallas nightclub, as he was being escorted to the county jail. Although a special committee headed by Chief Justice Earl Warren could find no conspiracy in Kennedy's assassination, doubts and rumors persisted. In 1979, a congressional inquiry raised serious questions about whether Oswald had acted alone.

SUGGESTED READING

D.T. Miller and M. Nowak, *The Fifties* (1977). D. Riesman, *The Lonely Crowd* (1950). W.H. Whyte, Jr., *The Organization Man* (1956). J.K. Galbraith, *The Affluent Society* (1958). S.E. Ambrose, *Eisenhower* (1983). H.S. Parmet, *JFK: The Presidency of John F. Kennedy* (1983). R. Kluger, *Simple Justice: The History of Brown v. Board of Education and Black America's Struggle for Equality* (1976). M.L. King, Jr., *Stride Toward Freedom* (1958). James Baldwin, *The Fire Next Time* (1963). *On Vietnam, see books suggested in Chapter 27.*

SUMMARY

The eight years of the Eisenhower presidency were a time of relative peace and prosperity, although both domestic and international forces were building beneath the surface. The Eisenhower administration, dedicated to the "middle way," was led by businessmen and lawyers. But even they were unable to cut government spending or stabilize agriculture. And the search for internal security continued, although Senator McCarthy's star began to wane in 1954, when he was censured by the Senate.

The most important domestic event of Eisenhower's first term was the Brown v. Board of Education *decision by the Supreme Court, which ordered the desegregation of the public schools. Under Chief Justice Earl Warren, the Court began to actively protect the civil rights of racial and political minorities. The mood of black America now was far different: there was a new militancy and a new determination. The events at Little Rock, Arkansas, in 1957, when the president sent federal troops to enforce the desegregation of the high school, symbolized both the depth of the*

resistance and the national commitment to change. The bus boycott in Montgomery, Alabama, in 1955–56, marked the beginning of a massive nonviolent campaign to end the racial caste system in the South.

The "new look" in foreign policy, carried out by Secretary of State John Foster Dulles, was based on the idea of rolling back communism all over the world. It was a diplomacy of rhetoric, threat, and alliance in which the United States sought to bolster anti-Communist regimes and undermine Communist regimes. It relied on massive retaliation and brinksmanship to meet threats to world peace.

As a result of this policy, the United States intervened actively in Iran, Guatemala, and Vietnam to convert nationalist movements into anti-Communist allies. In Vietnam, the French were losing the war against the Vietminh, the Nationalist regime based in the North. Eisenhower had resisted the pressure to commit American troops, although the United States did extend aid to the French and did join in the truce negotiations at Geneva after the disaster of Dienbienphu in May 1954. Gradually, the United States replaced the French in South Vietnam in supporting a repressive anti-Communist regime. Pro-Communist guerrillas, supported by the North Vietnamese, continued the war—but now against the South Vietnamese Army instead of the French. These events and others in Southeast Asia led Dulles to set up a new collective-security alliance, SEATO, the counterpart of NATO in Europe, in 1954. But no military force was created; thermonuclear weapons were to provide security.

In the Middle East, conflict between the oil-rich Arabs and the new state of Israel was a source of constant tension. In July 1956, Egypt nationalized the Suez Canal. In October, Israel invaded Egypt; this act was followed by an Anglo-French invasion of the Suez. It took American-Soviet cooperation through the United Nations to force a cease-fire and avoid a new world war. But the peace was shaky, and the Middle East continued to be a powder keg. Soviet-American hostility and tension soon returned to pre-Suez levels. The arms race and the rivalry continued.

Eisenhower's second administration was marked by spectacular Soviet advances in rocketry, a business slowdown, inflation, and racial strife. It was also marked by dissent within the Communist camp between China and Russia, by harshly suppressed uprisings in Poland and Hungary in 1956, and by the U-2 crisis in 1960, when an American reconnaissance plane was shot down over Soviet territory. Nearer home, on January 1, 1959, Fidel Castro successfully completed a five-year struggle to overthrow the American-supported Batista regime. His hatred of the United States, fueled by American business's exploitation of Cuba, changed the whole situation in the Caribbean.

The election of 1960 brought John F. Kennedy to the White House—a Democrat, a Catholic, and the youngest president in American history. The Kennedy administration was staffed by youthful advisers and pledged to getting the country moving again, to the New Frontier. But many of its approaches to foreign and domestic problems were no different from those of preceding administrations.

Conflict over civil rights escalated, and the attack on segregation broadened. Before the summer of 1963 was over, peaceful protests had occurred in more than 800 towns and cities, and 200,000 blacks and whites had marched on Washington. But by this time there was division within the black leadership between the more moderate Martin Luther King, Jr., and separatist militants such as Malcom X.

Cuba continued to be a problem. Its leader had turned not only to the Soviet Union, but to the task of spreading Fidelismo throughout Latin America. American responses were conventional: an American-supported invasion, at the Bay of Pigs, which ended in a fiasco in April 1961, and the threat of nuclear war in October 1962 over Soviet missile bases installed on the island, only ninety miles from the United States.

In Southeast Asia, Vietnam continued to be plagued by guerrilla war, and the United States continued to be involved. By the end of 1962, there were 10,000 Americans in South Vietnam. By late 1963, the number was 17,000 and the predictions were still for an early and easy victory.

On November 22, 1963, John F. Kennedy was assassinated in Dallas while riding through the city in an open car. The New Frontier was over.

27

Crumbling Consensus

On Air Force One, which was bringing the body of John F. Kennedy back to Washington, the most dramatic presidential succession in American history took place. Jacqueline Kennedy, her clothing still stained with the blood of her husband, looked on as the oath of office was administered on November 22, 1963, to the new president, Lyndon B. Johnson. Even as Americans recovered from the shock of presidential assassination, they would learn to live in the next decade with new violence, turbulence, and uncertainty. The deepening war abroad and civil strife at home shattered whatever remained of the consensus and complacency of the fifties. There were moments when the very survival of American society seemed threatened—not, as in the previous decade, by nuclear holocaust or Communists, but by America's own disenchanted.

The kinds of investigatory commissions established in the sixties said a great deal about what absorbed the American people. The concerns and revelations were far different from those of the fifties. The Warren Commission examined the circumstances surrounding Kennedy's assassination. The

Kerner Commission, appointed by President Johnson on July 27, 1967, investigated widespread racial violence. It concluded that the basic cause was the white racism that pervaded American society. The Cox Commission examined the violent student outbreak at Columbia University in 1968 and charged that campus administrators, by their "attitude of authoritarianism," had "invited mistrust." Major investigations of drugs and pornography were also undertaken. And America's sudden awakening to the contamination of the environment would produce a huge investigatory literature that warned of cosmic disaster.

The American experience in the sixties has been compared to weird pieces of science fiction or comic-book fantasy. The scenario features assassinations, cities burned out by their own people, street warfare, masked soldiers in fogs of tear gas, massed youth sprawling over the countryside at rock festivals, campus buildings under siege, cult murders, terrorist bomb factories, and courtroom shoot-outs. The crises of the decade were made to order for the mass media. Television brought all of life into focused image, turning all kinds of people into media performers. Combat teams and tormented villagers in Vietnam, starving children in Biafra, astronauts bound for the moon, protest marchers, hippies, yippies, and revolutionaries, celebrities from the world of sport and entertainment—all entered the living rooms of America.

Throughout the upheavals of the sixties, the war in Vietnam persisted and widened. Except for the Civil War, no previous conflict had so divided and alienated American society. With each passing month, with each new casualty list, with every promise of success, the divisiveness and disenchant-ment grew. To some critics, it was Lyndon Johnson's war. But that would be a gross distortion of the historical record. The war was not the exclusive responsibility of any one president. Although Congress had not declared war, it had given the president— by overwhelming majorities—the power and the "hardware" required to wage it. The deepening involvement in Vietnam proved to be a tragic inheritance for LBJ, who had envisioned a Great Society that would unify the nation and inspire the world. By 1968, President Johnson himself had concluded that the only way to unify the nation was to end the war and his own political career.

THE GREAT SOCIETY

Few American presidents entered the White House with a longer career in politics than Lyndon Johnson. The contrast between the personalities and political styles of Johnson and Kennedy could hardly have been more striking. Johnson's wealth had been self-made, not inherited. He had none of Kennedy's charisma or urbaneness and few of his cultural pretensions. He was as skeptical of intellectuals as they were of him. But LBJ knew how to get things done. He was a shrewd manipulator, and he had already demonstrated in his long years as Senate minority and then majority leader an uncanny mastery of political techniques. He invited and praised "consensus," while making certain his position always prevailed.

LBJ's vision of the Great Society, although absorbing much of Kennedy's New Frontier, was influenced more heavily by his admiration of the New Deal. The ambitious domestic program he proposed was aimed at improving the quality of American life, maximizing opportunities for those who had been denied access to the "affluent society." Like FDR, he felt the need to secure Americans from the fear of hunger, unemployment, and old age. Unlike FDR, he felt the need to attack the special problems plaguing black Americans. Although Johnson's civil-rights record in the Senate had been spotty, he seemed ready to extend his commitment to social justice to black people. The racial strife and agitation Johnson inherited as president also provided a stimulus for action exceeding that of any previous occupant of the White House.

Not all the Great Society measures proved workable. Some were too hastily drawn, and others suffered from lack of funding. But the commitment of the federal government to the concept of the welfare state seemed unquestioned. And it was this aspect of the Great Society that would arouse the most controversy and backlash in the seventies and eighties. For Johnson, the more immediate problem was how to wage a war on poverty while expanding the war in Vietnam. The cost of pursuing both wars at once proved too much. In the clash of priorities, the Great Society and the people of Vietnam were the principal victims.

The Transition Years

No sooner had Johnson become president than he proposed to Congress, as an appropriate memorial to Kennedy, that it act on a long-delayed prosperity tax cut and a civil-rights bill. The tax-reform bill helped a sagging economy. The Civil Rights Act of 1964, the most sweeping such legislation in American history, enlarged federal power to protect voting rights, to provide open access for all races to public facilities, to speed up school desegregation, and to ensure equal job opportunities in business and unions.

At the same time, Johnson set the stage for his Great Society program. In his first State of the Union message, in January 1964, he told Congress, "Unfortunately, many Americans live on the outskirts of hope, some because of their poverty and some because of their color, and all too many because of both." To raise the hopes of such people, he proposed a "war on poverty in America." This war Congress also endorsed, in August 1964, when it appropriated almost $950 million for ten separate antipoverty programs to be supervised by a newly established Office of Economic Opportunity. Key features included (1) a Job Corps, which would train underprivileged youth for the labor market; (2) work-training programs that would employ them; (3) a domestic peace corps (officially, Volunteers in Service to America, VISTA), which would enlist the privileged on behalf of the poor; and (4) a Community Action program, which would involve the poor themselves in the adminstration and planning of the war.

Encouraged by his legislative triumphs, Johnson eagerly anticipated the presidential election of 1964. What he wanted was a massive triumph at the polls that would make him president in his own right. The Republicans nominated Senator Barry Goldwater of Arizona, star of the strong conservative wing of the party. Although segregationist Governor George C. Wallace of Alabama also entered the race by running in a number of Democratic primaries, Goldwater's nomination had deprived him of conservative support. At the Democratic convention, Johnson easily won the nomination; after a spirited contest for LBJ's nod, Senator Hubert H. Humphrey of Minnesota, identified with the liberal wing of the party, won the vice-presidential spot.

Goldwater stood for dismantling the welfare state, and many Americans suspected that the social-security system would be among the victims. Nor did he help his candidacy when he suggested that NATO commanders be permitted to employ tactical nuclear weapons in a crisis. During the campaign, new uncertainties in world affairs made such statements seem particularly irresponsible. Nikita Khrushchev was out of power in the USSR, and China exploded an atomic bomb. While Goldwater evoked visions of atomic confrontation, Johnson appeared to be a man of peace and moderation.

Gaining 61 percent of the popular vote, Johnson surpassed even FDR's record in 1936. It was the sweeping mandate he had sought, and he intended to make the most of it. Even while preparing to escalate the Vietnam war, Johnson assured the American people that "this nation is mighty enough—its society is healthy enough—its people are strong enough—to pursue our goals in the rest of the world while still building a great society here at home."

Great Society Legislation

The Great Society was the central theme of LBJ's first message to the Eighty-ninth Congress, in January 1965. When that Congress finished its business in the fall of 1966, it had compiled one of the most constructive records in history. It had approved nearly every one of the Great Society measures the president had proposed.

The first, adopted in April 1965, was the Elementary and Secondary Education Act, which made available for the first time massive amounts of federal aid ($1.3 billion) to all pupils in school districts. If further incentive was needed for desegregation, this act provided it. As a condition for federal aid, the United States Office of Education now demanded proof that beginning with the school term of 1966–67, desegregation both for students and for teachers had been undertaken in good faith. Despite vigorous opposition to these new "guidelines," significant increases were reported in the number of blacks going to school with whites.

A second far-reaching measure was the adoption of the medicare amendments to the Social Security Act, which the president approved on July 30, 1965. The aged had won a significant victory over the relentless lobbying of the American Medical Association. Medicare provided hospital insurance and certain posthospital care for virtually all Americans upon their reaching the age of sixty-five. It also made available inexpensive medical insurance covering doctor bills, diagnostic procedures, and other medical services and supplies.

In addition, the Eighty-ninth Congress ended the discriminatory national-origins quota system in immigration; provided special assistance for improvement of conditions in the depressed states of the Appa-

lachia region; enacted programs that promoted the purification of smog-laden air and the restoration of polluted waterways; created the National Foundation of the Arts and Humanities in order to encourage cultural and artistic development; and passed a Truth in Lending Act in order to give consumers greater protection in credit transactions. Recognizing the critical problems of urban Americans, Congress agreed to a rent-supplement program for low-income families and established the Department of Housing and Urban Development (HUD). Massive new appropriations were made for earlier Great Society programs, including the War on Poverty, the regeneration of cities, and the space program.

When the Eighty-ninth Congress adjourned in October 1966, the American economy had enjoyed six solid years of extraordinary economic expansion. But the Great Society, like the New Frontier, raised the expectations of many Americans without necessarily fulfilling them. Despite the prosperity, social dissatisfaction deepened. Life on many family farms remained dreary; city dwellers were exposed to unprecedented violence and fears. Black Americans still found it hard to get jobs or to share in the affluence that was so visible around them. They were constantly exposed to success, and yet denied it. So frustration mounted, especially among the young.

The Black Revolution

While the "We Shall Overcome" spirit generated by the March on Washington still prevailed, the struggle to achieve racial justice in the South continued to attract national attention. During the Freedom Summer of 1964, thousands of young blacks and white students converged on Mississippi to register its nearly one million black residents. By the end of the summer, three youths—two whites and one black—had been murdered by terrorists in Neshoba County. Numerous civil-rights workers had been beaten, more than a thousand had been arrested, and scores of churches and homes had been burned or bombed.

The civil-rights coalition achieved its most dramatic hour in early 1965. The failure of certain southern states to enforce the voting provisions of the Civil Rights Act of 1964 had brought a new wave of black demonstrations, particularly in the town of Selma, Alabama. On February 1, 1965, Martin Luther King, Jr., and 770 other blacks were arrested. Early in March, Alabama state troopers and auxiliaries, using tear gas and whips, frustrated an attempted civil-rights march from Selma to Montgomery, the state capital. After President Johnson federalized the Alabama National Guard and ordered it to protect the marchers (Governor Wallace had earlier refused to do so), the procession of some 25,000 blacks and sympathetic whites from all over the country began. The night the march ended, one participant—a white woman from Detroit—was killed by Ku Klux Klan gunfire. Earlier, a Boston minister was slain. Their deaths enlarged the decade's toll of political activists.

With President Johnson himself now declaring that "we shall overcome," Congress responded by passing the Voting Rights Act of 1965. This measure suspended literacy tests and other devices still used to confine voting to whites. It empowered federal examiners to register qualified voters. The act also directed the attorney general to start suits against the surviving poll taxes in state elections. (The Twenty-fourth Amendment to the Constitution, ratified January 1964, had abolished the poll tax in federal elections.) On March 17, 1966, the last of the poll taxes was killed by the Su-

preme Court. By then a new drive to register the 2 million eligible blacks in eleven southern states was under way, and many black candidates soon appeared on the ballots.

Although many whites had sympathized with black efforts to register voters and desegregate public facilities in the South, they had far less feeling for the grievances that were mounting in the urban North. Discrimination in employment, housing, and schooling persisted, even as more blacks poured into the cities and more whites poured into the suburbs. When Martin Luther King, Jr., prepared to attack the problems of urban blacks and staged massive demonstrations in Chicago in 1967 to mobilize support for a national open-housing bill, he met resistance similar to that in the South. When his strategy failed and challenges to his leadership grew, King found himself addressing a hostile black audience in Chicago. He thought he knew why.

> For twelve years I, and others like me, had held out radiant promises of progress. I had preached to them about my dream. I had lectured to them about the not too distant day when they would have freedom, "all, here and now." I had urged them to have faith in America and in white society. Their hopes had soared. . . . They were now hostile because they were watching the dream that they had so readily accepted turn into a nightmare.

The frustrations finally exploded. Between 1964 and 1967, more than 100 riots shattered the peace of urban America. Few were planned. Indeed, it was the spontaneous quality of the uprisings that revealed the very depths of black disillusionment and despair—the felt need to expose the deprivation and desperation of the black ghettos and ghetto dwellers and the complicity of white businessmen, shop owners, and police in maintaining those conditions.

Even as King reaffirmed his faith in nonviolence and integration, others suggested that they be abandoned as the movement's primary tactic and goal. The persistence of white hostility and disillusion with the betrayal of expectations encouraged the organization of new movements, the development of new strategies, and the enunciation of new ideologies. The most pervasive of these was the concept of *black power*, by which black people would assume control of their own communities, lives, and destinies, establish their own economic institutions, and end the "colonialism" that had tied them to white institutions.

The assumptions underlying the concept of black power had been forcefully explained by Malcolm X, the Black Muslim

Malcolm X. "The day of nonviolent resistance is over. If they have the Ku Klux Klan nonviolent, then I'll be nonviolent. . . . But as long as somebody else is not being nonviolent, I don't want anybody coming to me talking any nonviolent talk." (UPI/Bettmann Archive)

leader. His father, the Reverend Earl Little, a Baptist minister in Omaha, Nebraska, was a devout follower of Marcus Garvey, whose campaign for racial dignity, community control, and the liberation of Africa from colonial rule had had the allegiance of many blacks in the twenties. The violence and humiliation Reverend Little's family suffered from "the good Christian white people" in the urban North deepened his son's alienation. By the age of twenty-one, when Malcolm X was convicted of theft and sentenced to prison, he found himself in a subculture of prostitutes, pimps, hustlers, numbers runners, and narcotics dealers.

In the religion of Islam, and in Elijah Muhammad's Black Muslim movement, Malcolm X found a path from the ghetto experience he recounts so vividly in his autobiography. "Yes, I'm an extremist," he conceded. "The black race here in North America is in extremely bad condition. You show me a black man who isn't an extremist and I'll show you one who needs psychiatric attention." Strife that arose within the black-nationalist movement after Malcolm X formed his own Organization of Afro-American Unity appears to have brought about his assassination, February 21, 1965, while he was on stage at the Audubon Ballroom in upper Manhattan. The violent death of Malcolm X only compounded the frustration and alienation that had overtaken so many blacks.

In still another violent setback, the civil rights movement lost its apostle of nonviolence. On April 4, 1968, Martin Luther King, Jr., was assassinated in Memphis, Tennessee. King had come to Memphis to support a strike of the city's garbage men, most of them black. He was shot while standing outside his motel room, speaking to some of his co-workers. The assassin, James Earl Ray, an escapee from the Missouri state penitentiary, was later caught and convicted.

Although King had been the apostle of non-violence, his assassination set off a new wave of rioting across the country, once again requiring the intervention of federal troops. This time the explosion centered in Washington, D.C. What Americans saw on their TV screens was the spectacle of the Capitol lit up by the nearby fires while federal troops and troop carriers patrolled the streets.

The persistence of racial violence dramatized continued frustration in the ghettos and the limited significance of civil-rights legislation in the day-to-day lives of most black people. Economic differences between black and white Americans loomed larger than ever. Yet the picture was not entirely bleak, and there were some significant breakthroughs. Middle-class blacks got substantial benefits from the black revolution. Certain kinds of employment, formerly closed to them, were opened. Blacks were more conspicuous now in business, the professions, on the TV screen, in sports and entertainment, and on college campuses. The 1970 census revealed that the proportion of black families whose annual incomes exceeded $10,000 had increased from 11 percent to 28 percent during the sixties. This decade, then, was significant for black people in a number of ways, perhaps most spectacularly in enhanced racial consciousness and self-pride. Recognizing the immense problems that still persisted, Martin Luther King, Jr., had sounded a note of optimism: "Lord, we ain't what we oughta be. We ain't what we wanna be. We ain't what we gonna be. But thank God, we ain't what we was."

La Raza

Since the mid nineteenth century, Mexican-Americans had found themselves dispossessed of their lands, stereotyped, segregated, harassed, and deported at the whim of law officers. By World War II their numbers had sharply increased, usually to meet demands for cheap labor. An unorganized labor reserve, politically powerless, they lived in *barrios* or *Mex-towns* in the cities.

In the 1960s and 1970s, however, the nearly 5 million "Spanish-surnamed" Americans (as the Census Bureau defined them) manifested a new sense of cultural identity. Although *Chicano* (a form of *Mexicano*) had once designated Mexican refugees in the United States, it now included all Mexican-Americans, particularly those committed to the cause of *La Raza* (the Mexican "race"). Few events dramatized their quest for economic justice more than Cesar Chavez's battle in California to organize a farm laborers' union. The seasonal nature of agricultural labor, the movement from one crop to the next, and vigorous opposition from well-organized growers and corporate farmers had foiled previous efforts. But in 1965, grape pickers in California struck for higher wages, improved working conditions, and union recognition. Soon the grape strike (*la huelga*) and a national consumer boycott of nonunion grapes became a rallying point of Chicano protest.

Like those he sought to organize, Chavez spent his youth in farm labor camps, left school at the seventh grade, and was a devout Roman Catholic. Like Martin Luther King, Jr., he made his religion a weapon for social justice and pledged his movement to nonviolent resistance. Through his National Farm Workers Association, Chavez hoped not only to raise the living standards of Mexican-Americans, but to establish a precedent that would affect more than 4 million farm workers—brown, black, and white—who lacked job security and economic power. By the end of the 1970s, his efforts had aroused considerable support and controversy. Most important, the union

Cesar Chavez marching in support of the boycott of nonunion growers. (UPI/Bettmann Archive)

had improved wages and working conditions for thousands of farm laborers. At the same time, and inseparable from the struggles of the farm workers, Mexican-Americans organized around a new ethnic consciousness, broadened their efforts to improve the quality of life of *barrio* dwellers, and made some significant political gains.

Native Americans

Improvements in public health and New Deal relief policies had helped to turn the "vanishing Americans" into one of the fastest-growing groups in the United States. Their number, including Eskimos, had risen to over 800,000 by 1970—an increase of more than half a million in eighty years. But Indian troubles were far from over. During World War II, about 25,000 Indians served in the armed forces. The experience increased their awareness and resentment of the discrimination they suffered. Wartime employment outside the reservations led many Indians to remain in the cities, and some of these moved into the white culture. To speed that assimilation among all Indians, westerners in Congress took the lead in trying to get "the government out of the Indian business." At their urging, Congress adopted two unfortunate measures in 1953 that set back Indian-white relations. One, a joint resolution, set forth the intent, once and for all, to end federal responsibility for the surviving tribes. The second, a step in this direction, gave the states authority over criminal and civil issues on the reservations. The sudden ending of certain reservations threw the Indians on them into turmoil and caused them immense losses in jointly held property and business enterprises. Individual Indians lost homes, public services, and security; many were thrown on welfare. Finally, in September 1958, Secretary of the Interior Fred A. Seaton ordered that no tribe be terminated without its consent.

The Great Society programs of the 1960s tried to restore purpose and incentive to Indian lives by redirecting federal policy toward such matters as health, education, housing, and vocational training. More important, the Indians themselves showed a growing ethnic consciousness. Indian groups and individual leaders in the 1970s sought to awaken their people to a new sense of dignity, self-respect, and cultural pride. Even the television and motion-picture screens began to reflect a reconsideration of Indian-white relations. "The whites told only one side," Yellow Wolf of the Nez Percé Indians once complained. "Told it to please themselves. Told much that is not true. Only his own best deeds, only the worst deeds of the Indians has the white man told." But the 1970s gave clear indication that this complaint was finally being listened to.

Even so, years of repression and neglect could not be wiped away simply by the correction of historical accounts. Prob-

lems persisted. In the 1970s, Indians still had one of the highest infant-mortality rates in the country; their life expectancy of forty-four years was far below the national average; and disease continued to take a great toll. Their average family income was well below that of other groups, and the unemployment rate on some reservations was as high as 50 percent.

To draw attention to these problems and to what they considered a paternalistic government policy, Indian militants in 1973 occupied the Bureau of Indian Affairs office in Washington, D.C., and seized Wounded Knee, South Dakota. Some years earlier, in 1969, Indians had invaded Alcatraz Island, near San Francisco, and asked that it be converted to an Indian cultural center. None of these actions proved to be anything more than symbolic reminders that native Americans, like their black and Chicano contemporaries, were no longer content to remain

To call attention to their cause, American Indians briefly occupied Alcatraz Island in 1969 and took over Wounded Knee, South Dakota, in 1973. (UPI/Bettmann Archive)

passive spectators; they demanded a voice in the decisions affecting their lives.

LBJ AND THE WORLD

The trouble with foreigners, Lyndon Johnson once said, "is that they're not like folks you were reared with." One trouble with Lyndon Johnson's foreign policy was his urge to make the world more congenial to Americans by making all people similar to ourselves. It was the familiar assumption, made most explicit by Woodrow Wilson, that American society could serve as a model and inspiration for all humankind. Wilson envisioned that day when the Stars and Stripes "shall be the flag not only of America but of humanity." Johnson told the American people, as if they needed reassurance, that "our cause has been the cause of all mankind." He repeated with approval Wilson's pronouncement that the United States was determined to make the world safe for democracy. Like his predecessors, LBJ formulated his policies from the same set of assumptions about the worldwide Communist conspiracy. "If we don't stop the Reds in South Vietnam," he instructed one senator, "tomorrow they will be in Hawaii, and next week they will be in San Francisco." Publication of the secret Pentagon Papers by the *New York Times* in mid 1971, an "objective and encyclopedic" study of the Vietnam war ordered by Secretary of Defense McNamara, documented how successive American presidents had acted on that same premise in extending the American commitment in Vietnam. The policies of American decision makers were based as well on the unchanging nature of world communism and on the assumption that any nationalist revolution influenced by communism posed a threat to American security. That Vietnam was no departure in

American foreign policy was revealed much closer to home—in Latin America.

Latin America and the Middle East: Seeds of Future Conflict

Whatever the professions of support for self-determination, neither Kennedy nor Johnson thought it inconsistent to differentiate between Communist take-overs and right-wing military coups. The United States seemed determined to crush the former, as in Cuba (1961), while tolerating if not encouraging the latter, as in Guatemala (1954) and Brazil (1964). The first major test of LBJ's Latin American policy came in the Dominican Republic in April 1965, when the president intervened in the civil war there by dispatching 400 marines to protect American lives. By May 5 American forces had exceeded 20,000 men, a number many thought incredible. The president went on nationwide TV to justify his action as a necessary step for preventing the Dominican Republic from falling into the hands of Communist conspirators. Evidence of such a conspiracy was far from convincing, and the entire episode enlarged the credibility gap already evident in White House reporting on the Vietnam war.

The United States position appeared to be stronger in the Middle East. But the American moral commitment to Israel and the simultaneous dependence on Arab oil suggested how difficult that position could suddenly become. In May 1967, complying with the demand of Nasser of Egypt, United Nations troops were withdrawn from the Suez region; they had kept Egypt and Israel apart for ten years. The Egyptian leader immediately called for a "holy war" of Arabs against the Jewish state. Israel, however, beat him to the punch with an overpowering assault in the Six-Day War, June 5 to 10. The extent of the defeat humiliated Egypt and the USSR as well, for it was Soviet aid that had encouraged Nasser's militancy.

But Israel's victory only intensified the already volatile tensions and fostered a bigger arms buildup. After the war, moreover, Israel cited its own security as justification for keeping some of the territory it had occupied: the Sinai Peninsula, the Golan Heights, the Gaza Strip, and the West Bank of the Jordan River. In November 1967 the UN Security Council called upon Israel to withdraw its forces from the occupied territories, while urging all states in the region to acknowledge each other's sovereignty and independence. The result was a stalemate that defied solution.

Israel continued to ignore the plight of the thousands of Palestinian refugees who had been made homeless by previous conflicts and whose mounting discontent would soon manifest itself in organized resistance movements. The Arab states cynically exploited the Palestinians as part of their overall plan to destroy Israel. With the vast oil resources at their disposal, the Arabs appeared to have time on their side. By the mid 1970s, when that oil became a potent political and economic weapon, the United States, like much of the world, would be forced to reassess its Middle East policies.

The Lengthening Shadow of Vietnam

Few wars in history have been marked by such an array of inconsistent, contradictory official pronouncements as to its purpose and progress as the American war in Vietnam. Nothing contributed more to public discontent over the war, except for the growing casualty lists, than the mistrust created by confusion, secrecy, and deceit. Even Congress was deliberately misled or kept ignorant by the executive department, largely for self-serving rather than security reasons.

No incidents in the war were more clouded by contradictory pronouncements and the classification of essential documents than the events in the Gulf of Tonkin, off North Vietnam, in August 1964. Neither side later denied that on August 2, North Vietnamese PT boats attacked the U.S. destroyer *Maddox* in the gulf, and were driven off with the help of carrier-based fighter planes. The *Maddox* suffered neither damage nor casualties. The United States asserted that the attack was "unprovoked"; *Maddox* was "on routine patrol in international waters." But Hanoi declared that Saigon vessels had raided North Vietnamese fishing boats and that, under the cover of an American destroyer, had bombarded two North Vietnamese islands. The attack on *Maddox*, Hanoi held, was made to stop such activities. Secretary McNamara denied American complicity. Four years later, McNamara admitted before a congressional hearing what the Pentagon Papers also confirmed—that North Vietnamese islands had been bombarded and that the United States and South Vietnam had made joint raids against North Vietnam. It was also made clear that the bombardment was part of a secret United States policy adopted in early 1964 to exert "new and significant pressures on North Vietnam." The point was to force North Vietnam to commit acts that would gain congressional authorization for whatever else "is necessary with respect to Vietnam."

On August 4, the Defense Department announced that North Vietnam had attacked both *Maddox* and a companion destroyer. North Vietnam denied that any such attack had taken place. (Congress did not learn until several years later that evidence of such an attack was, at best, inconclusive.) That very night, allowing no time for detailed investigation and without consulting Congress, the president went on television to announce that in response to "repeated acts of violence against the armed forces of the United States," American planes were now engaged in action "against gunboats and certain facilities in Vietnam." Just prior to his telecast the president informed legislative leaders that the next day, he would send Congress a retroactive joint resolution to be adopted before dark and without amendment. This resolution the administration viewed as a functional equivalent of a formal declaration of war in Southeast Asia. Restating the United States version of the events of August 2 and 4, the Tonkin Gulf Resolution of August 7, 1964, declared, "The Congress approves and supports the determination of the President, as Commander in Chief, to take all necessary measures to repel any armed attack against the forces of the United States and to prevent further aggression." Rushed into session in a crisis mood, the House and Senate adopted the resolution with virtually no dissenting voices.

Armed with the resolution, President Johnson escalated the war. During the spring of 1965, the administration developed a program for the systematic bombing of North Vietnam. With every new Vietcong provocation, Johnson stepped up the raids. And Congress, by huge majorities, voted the necessary "hardware." The more intensive bombing, however, only reinforced North Vietnam's determination to resist. In what were described as search-and-destroy missions, American ground troops engaged the Vietcong in direct fighting for the first time in June 1965. By the end of the year, American forces in Vietnam numbered above 200,000. The South Vietnamese also promised to step up their efforts after Air Vice-Marshal Nguyen Cao Ky took over as premier of the eighth South Vietnamese government since the end of Diem.

By the end of 1966, American forces in Vietnam had reached 380,000. In April, their casualties exceeded those of the South Vietnamese for the first time; 4800 American soldiers were killed in action that year. Meanwhile, American hardware commitments now probably exceeded those of any other war in history. But victory seemed no closer. Part of the frustration lay in the estimate that search-and-destroy missions destroyed six civilians for every Vietcong. Widespread chemical warfare and the use of other new weaponry, largely concealed from Americans at home, also contributed heavily to the devastation of South Vietnam while contributing little to "pacification" of the Vietcong. By May 1967, Secretary McNamara himself recoiled from what was happening. He noted that the bomb tonnage dropped every week on North Vietnam exceeded that of all the bombings of Germany in World War II.

By the end of 1967, United States troop strength in Vietnam was approaching 475,000 men, and casualties rose proportionately. In May, total American casualties exceeded 10,000. The futility of bombing North Vietnam and its immense political cost at home and abroad were now being acknowledged openly. McNamara admitted it publicly in August 1967, three months before his departure from the cabinet.

North Vietnam's Tet (New Year's) offensive against Saigon and other South Vietnamese cities in February 1968 suggested that despite the bombing, Ho could launch massive assaults that would catch hardened United States field commanders by surprise. It also revealed that the USSR would not leave North Vietnam to confront American military technology only with captured or stolen American weapons. In the Tet offensive, Hanoi used Soviet jet planes and tanks for the first time. Although American and South Vietnamese troops recaptured several of the population centers lost in the Tet offensive, the cost was immense, and confidence in ultimate victory was seriously undermined. United States forces soared to 549,000 in April 1968, while combat deaths reached 22,951.

Worldwide pressure for peace had grown very heavy by this time. Television filled America's living rooms with firsthand reports from Vietnam that were all too realistic. The sight of American troops on search-and-destroy missions setting fire to peasant huts raised doubts that were deepened by the weekly announcements of soldiers killed in action. Riots and demonstrations on college campuses attested to the antiwar sentiment there, even among usually conservative and nonpolitical students. The flow of draft resisters to Canada had reached 10,000.

The strength of the peace movement became evident in the showing of one of its leading congressional advocates, Senator Eugene J. McCarthy of Minnesota, in the Democratic presidential primary in New Hampshire on March 12, 1968. Although given little chance against LBJ, McCarthy shocked the administration by taking 42 percent of the votes to the president's 49 percent. On March 31, Johnson said on nationwide TV: "We are prepared to move immediately toward peace through negotiations. So tonight, in the hope that this action will lead to early talks, I am taking the first step to deescalate the conflict." This step was his order to halt all air and naval bombardment of North Vietnam, except in the area just north of the demilitarized zone where the enemy arms build-up was strongest. Even more dramatic was the president's gesture toward unifying the country: he announced that he would not seek reelection.

The North Vietnamese response came quickly. On April 3, Ho Chi Minh's government declared its readiness to talk about peace, and one month later preliminary

American soldiers in Vietnam. (Donald McCullin, Magnum Photos)

talks began in Paris. But even as Johnson restricted the bombings, he increased the troop level in Vietnam to 535,000. On June 4 the United States command in Vietnam announced that American battle deaths in the first six months of 1968 exceeded those of all 1967. On June 23, reckoning from December 22, 1961, the date of the first death of an American serviceman in Vietnam, the war there became the longest in American history. The direct cost of the war had soared to an acknowledged $25 billion a year. There were also unacknowledged costs for weapons development and other programs associated with the conflict.

Conflicts over the roles of South Vietnam and the Vietcong at the Paris peace talks ended Johnson's hopes of a quick end to the war through negotiation. LBJ left the White House with the war still unresolved. Not only his political career but his vision of the Great Society had become a casualty of the war and of the mounting dissension and strife at home.

The Silent Majority on Trial: The Election of 1968

The presidential election of 1968 may be said to have begun with the decision to bomb North Vietnam in February 1965. The ranks of doves swelled not only among McCarthy's colleagues in the Senate, but among the youth of the nation as well. McCarthy's performance in the New Hampshire primary in March 1968 showed that he had grown strong enough to split the party. When Senator Robert F. Kennedy of New York decided a few days later to enter the campaign, it seemed that the opposition to the administration would also be split. Johnson's withdrawal two weeks later deepened the conflict among his would-be Democratic successors.

The Kennedy mantle and mystique drew millions of American young people, black and white, to the Kennedy camp. On June 5, however, the very night of his victory in the California primary, Robert Kennedy was shot by Sirhan Sirhan, a young Arab nationalist resentful of Kennedy's support for Israel. Coming only two months after King's murder, the Kennedy assassination shocked the nation and changed the political scene.

The Democratic nomination was now a virtual certainty for Hubert H. Humphrey, Johnson's vice-president and a firm supporter of the war. He did not enter any primaries, but his quest for delegates did not end until the first ballot at the Democratic convention in Chicago, August 26–29. Although he easily won the nomination, the narrow victory of the plank on Vietnam revealed deep rifts in the party. What happened outside the convention center exposed even sharper divisions in the nation.

The International Amphitheater, where official sessions of the Democratic convention were held, took on the appearance of a fortress under siege. It was ringed with barbed wire, broken only by checkpoints for entering delegates, reporters, and guests. Several blocks around the amphitheater and around major downtown hotels swarmed with police, federal agents, and finally with more than 5000 National Guardsmen called in to keep away antiwar demonstrators. In the almost inevitable confrontation between the security forces and the demonstrators, the result, an investigative report subsequently charged, "was unrestrained and indiscriminate police violence"—that is, a police riot. With pandemonium inside and outside the convention hall—and all visible to millions on TV— Humphrey accepted the Democratic nomination. The next day he announced, and the convention confirmed, his choice for vice-president, Senator Edmund S. Muskie of Maine.

The Republican convention, comparatively peaceful, featured the remarkable political comeback of Richard M. Nixon. Despite his defeat in the California gubernatorial election of 1962, he had remained active in Republican politics and was now given a second chance at the presidency. The platform warned that "lawlessness is crumbling the foundations of American society," and the campaign itself stressed the need for law and order. In his acceptance speech, Nixon welcomed as the core of his constituency the "silent majority" of "forgotten Americans"—"the non-shouters, the non-demonstrators, that are not racist or sick, that are not guilty of the crime that plagues the land." He selected as his running mate Governor Spiro T. Agnew of Maryland.

In opposing school busing and vowing to appoint "strict Constitutionalists" to the Supreme Court, Nixon may have taken some of the wind out of the sails of a third candidate for president, George C. Wallace, the Alabama segregationist thought by many to be strong enough to deprive both regular-party candidates of the electoral majority needed to win. Wallace delighted audiences with his assaults on "scummy anarchists," "pseudo-intellectuals," federal meddlers, and those who coddled criminals. But he found it difficult to outdo the determination of Nixon and Agnew to bring law and order to the country.

With exceptional support from the old Democratic coalition of urban liberals, organized labor, and minority groups, Humphrey made a remarkably strong finish in the big industrial states. Nixon carried the critical states of Ohio, Illinois, New Jersey, and California by small majorities. Humphrey won in Michigan and Texas, as well as New York and Pennsylvania. Wallace's poor southern showing outside the few Deep South states he was certain to carry also helped Nixon gain a clear electoral majority. Like Eisenhower in 1956, however, he failed to carry enough legislative candidates with him to change the Democratic majorities in the House and Senate. Nixon also failed to gain a popular majority. His margin over Humphrey, a mere 510,000 out of 73.2 million votes cast, gave him only 43.4 percent of the popular vote, the lowest for a successful candidate since Wilson in 1912. Humphrey gained 42.7 percent of the popular vote, and Wallace 13.5 percent.

The new president clearly embodied the sentiments of tens of millions of Americans, angry over the threats to their personal safety, frightened by the racial violence, and frustrated by a costly and futile war. In Richard Nixon and Spiro Agnew, they found forceful spokesmen to articulate their grievances, fears, and hopes. Few could have envisioned the fate that awaited these two apostles of law and order. For the tens of thousands of young political activists who had enlisted in McCarthy's crusade to bring the war to an end, the disillusion was bound to be severe. The violence at the Chicago convention, the nomination of Humphrey, and the election of Nixon and Agnew reinforced for many of them the conviction that they had become strangers in their own land.

THE DISSENTING GENERATION

F. Scott Fitzgerald once said of his generation, which came of age in the 1920s, that it had found all gods dead, all wars fought in vain, and all faiths shaken. The generation of the 1960s, often described in similar terms, was thus not as unique as it preferred to believe. Even the relatively apathetic and silent generation of the 1950s had managed to produce the "rebel without a cause." When asked in the film *The Wild One* (1954) what he was rebelling against, the character portrayed by Marlon Brando replied, "Whadda ya got?" In the sixties, there was no end to the causes around which young people rallied. They ranged from the war in Vietnam, which they wanted to stop, to an adult society they considered corrupt and hypocritical, and which they expected to remake in their own image. What most of these "rebels" had in common was the middle-class inheritance they longed to renounce. But in the end, their staying power proved brief; the dominant society succeeded in absorbing both the rebels and the rebellion.

Sources of Disillusionment

For the generation that had experienced the Great Depression and World War II, the relative stability of the fifties had been welcome, along with the affluence many of them managed to acquire. If they cherished their security and the comfortable homes they purchased in suburbia, if they took pride in what they were able to pass on to their children in the way of educational and economic opportunities, they had only to remind themselves of the thirties, the wartime sacrifices, and the struggles they had endured to make all this possible. If they chose not to be skeptical of their major institutions and of the Protestant ethic of hard work, it was because these had served them well.

The generation of white middle-class youth that came of age in the sixties—products of the postwar baby boom—had good reason, then, to feel secure and hopeful about the society they entered. Neither their families nor their teachers suggested anything else. This was the first generation to have been raised in the age of television. If they took their values and attitudes from the TV screen, they found little reason to question the dominant institutions of American society. If they responded to politics, it was to the youthful appeal of John F. Kennedy and his call for young Americans to make a commitment to the New Frontier. Some enlisted in the Peace Corps; others were drawn into the civil-rights struggle and helped to register black voters in the South.

But the idealism and hope with which many young Americans entered the sixties began to come apart after the assassination of President Kennedy and the Freedom Summer of 1964. The vision of a more humane society gave way to a nightmare of violence—not the manufactured variety they had become accustomed to on TV, but real

The Free Speech Movement at the University of California at Berkeley received massive support on campus and soon spread to other universities. (Joe Wakabayashi)

violence: the assassinations of Robert F. Kennedy, Martin Luther King, Jr., and Malcolm X; the murder and beatings of civil-rights demonstrators; police violence in the ghettos; and the massive and organized violence the United States was inflicting on the people of Vietnam.

What middle-class youth began to perceive was the enormous contradiction between the ideals and virtues they had been taught by family, school, and television set and the spectacle of racism and poverty, and of the brutality of the war in Vietnam. The universities many of them were attending were so impersonal and bureaucratized as to be unable to see their own deep complicity in the war abroad and racism at home. The awakening came to different people at different times. Many of them enlisted in The Movement (as it came to be called) only after observing at first hand the attempts to repress it. When the radical Students for a Democratic Society (SDS) drew up their manifesto (the Port Huron Statement), the signers agreed that the civil-rights struggle, more than any other cause, had brought most of them "from silence to activism."

The presidential election of 1964 had no sooner ended than the Free Speech Movement (FSM) on the Berkeley campus of the University of California revealed the degree to which many middle-class youths were prepared to reject the apathy and indifference of their predecessors. What began as a protest over restrictions on campus political expression—800 students staged a nonviolent sit-in at the university administration building—evolved into a movement that directly challenged the dominant values and assumptions of American society. The effects would soon be felt on campuses across the country—and with ever-greater intensity as American involvement in Vietnam deepened and as frustration and tension mounted at home.

The Counterculture

A youth culture (some called it a counterculture) characterized by distinct forms of expression and consciousness, including new styles of dress, social behavior, and music, emerged in the sixties. Few exerted any greater influence on these styles than the Beatles, an English rock group that first visited the United States in 1963. The contagion of the Beatles and innumerable other groups and individual artists proved impossible to contain. The music suggested far different attitudes toward life and society from what the adult generation had been accustomed to hear. There was an intensity to the music, moreover, that was inseparable from the message conveyed. In form, content, and volume, the new music heralded a liberation from traditional restraints and conventions.

For many young people, the way to self-expression lay not through politics but through the adoption of a radical lifestyle, a redefinition of sexual mores, and the use of hallucinatory drugs. They substituted the "be-in" and the "love-in" for the protest meeting and preached an ideology of anti-ideology. Few protest marches or political rallies attracted as many young people as the countless rock festivals. The most spectacular and exhilarating was at Woodstock, New York, in the summer of 1969, when some 400,000 came together.

The dominant society, however, demonstrated immense staying power. With its usual agility, it curbed and absorbed radical impulses, whether political or cultural. It appropriated the youth culture itself—the hair styles, the clothes, the dancing, the music, the language, even the pot parties. Meanwhile, the political side of The Movement succumbed to slogans, communication by invective, and sectarianism. Sporadic riots, street warfare, bombings, and mass marches did not make a revolution. The Movement failed to make any inroads into the working class—the people who had to send their sons into the war. Nor had liberating lifestyles and musical expression affected the inequalities in the urban ghettos and *barrios*. With Richard Nixon's decisive victory over George McGovern in the 1972 presidential election, the familiar feeling of powerlessness, apathy, and cynicism once again gripped the college campuses. "Everything we thought was wrong is still wrong," wrote Elinor Langer, who had once shared the optimism of her generation, "but we are without the institutions, the influence, or the understanding to change it."

SUGGESTED READINGS

G. Hodgson, *America in Our Time* (1976). F. Fitzgerald, *Fire in the Lake* (1972). M. Herr, *Dispatches* (1977). W. Shawcross, *Sideshow: Kissinger, Nixon, and the Destruction of Vietnam* (1979). S. Karnow, *Vietnam* (1983). Malcolm X, *The Autobiography of Malcolm X* (1964). H. Sitkoff, *The Struggle for Black Equality, 1954–1980* (1980). H. Raines, *My Soul is Rested: Movement Days in the Deep South Remembered* (1977). N. Mailer, *The Armies of the Night* (1968) and *Miami and the Siege of Chicago* (1968). G. Marcus, *Mystery Train: Images of America in Rock 'n Roll Music* (1976).

SUMMARY

The 1960s was a decade of crises and war. It was also a decade of widespread social changes.

Lyndon Johnson, who had become president in the midst of the national shock of Kennedy's assassination, set into motion new and major domestic programs: the Great Society and the war on poverty. The commitment of the federal government to the concept of the welfare state seemed unquestioned. But Johnson faced the problem of waging the War on Poverty at home while waging a full-scale war on communism in Vietnam. Among his Great Society measures were the Civil Rights Act of 1964, the most sweeping such legislation in American history; a tax-reform bill; and the establishment of the Office of Economic Opportunity to supervise ten separate antipoverty programs

In the election of 1964, Johnson won a sweeping victory over the conservative Republican Barry Goldwater. Beginning in January 1965, the Eighty-ninth Congress

approved nearly all the Great Society measures the president proposed: the Elementary and Secondary Education Act; the medicare amendments to the Social Security Act; special assistance for Appalachia; the end of the immigration quota system; antipollution legislation; the Truth in Lending Act; the National Foundation for the Arts and Humanities; and a new cabinet department, the Department of Housing and Urban Development.

But the Great Society, like the New Frontier, raised the expectations of many Americans without necessarily fulfilling them. For blacks, frustration mounted as they found it hard to share in the affluence so visible around them. The civil-rights movement reached a peak in early 1965 with the dramatic march in Alabama; Congress responded to the violence with the Voting Rights Act of 1965, a significant triumph for southern blacks.

In the North, however, discrimination in employment, housing, and schooling per-

sisted. Whites poured out into suburbs as blacks poured into the cities. The frustrations finally exploded in urban rioting that continued from 1964 through 1967. Watts in Los Angeles, Newark in New Jersey, and Detroit were the scenes of major violence. There were also new confrontations in the South. New black movements, more militant and separatist, developed. On April 4, 1968, the apostle of nonviolence, Martin Luther King, Jr., was assassinated.

Black activism spurred activism on the part of other minorities. Cesar Chavez battled in California to organize a farm laborers' union; others organized Mexican-Americans around the cause of La Raza, racial and ethnic pride. Native Americans brought their cause to the public consciousness with demonstrations at Alcatraz and Wounded Knee. During the decade, minority groups enhanced their racial consciousness and self-pride and made some genuine gains in education, jobs, and political power.

In international affairs, the United States found itself in more and more difficulty. It intervened in the Dominican Republic in 1965 to prevent the establishment of a Communist government. At the end there were 20,000 American troops in that small country, and the United States had again smashed a nationalist movement that seemed to have popular support.

In the Middle East, the situation remained explosive. In May 1967 Egypt and Israel went to war again. Israel humiliated Egypt with an overpowering assault in the Six-Day War in June. It then kept some of the territory it had occupied in the war—the Sinai Peninsula, the Golan Heights, the Gaza Strip, and the West Bank. The result was an angry stalemate that defied solution.

For the United States, Vietnam overshadowed everything else as deepening involvement and confusion, secrecy, and deceit created mistrust and discontent at home. Events in the Gulf of Tonkin in August 1964 led to the president's demand for, and congressional approval of, a resolution that gave him almost sole authority to act as he saw fit. The war escalated, and by February 1965 bombing of North Vietnam had become a systematic policy. On the ground, search-and-destroy missions brought American troops in direct contact with the Vietcong. Both activities only stiffened resistance in North Vietnam.

By the end of 1966, there were 380,000 troops in Vietnam; by the end of 1967 troop strength exceeded that at the peak of the Korean War. Casualties mounted accordingly. By the end of 1967, the futility of United States policies was being openly admitted. The Vietnamese success in the Tet offensive of early 1968 brought heavy pressure, both domestic and worldwide, to end the war. There were riots and demonstrations on American campuses, and more draft resisters fled to Canada.

In March 1968, LBJ announced an end to air and naval bombardment of North Vietnam. He also announced that he would not seek reelection. Peace talks began in Paris in April. But the number of American troops in Vietnam continued to rise, and by June the war had become the longest in American history.

LBJ left office with the war still unresolved. Both his career and the Great Society were additional casualties. The election of 1968 was itself a period of tragedy and violence. Robert Kennedy was assassinated in June in California, only two months after Martin Luther King, Jr., had been killed. The

Democratic convention in Chicago was the scene of a police riot with antiwar demonstrators. Hubert Humphrey, Johnson's vice-president and a firm supporter of the war, lost to Richard Nixon and Spiro Agnew, who campaigned for law and order and the rights of the silent majority.

All these events had been accompanied by a vast youth movement of dissent and protest, and by the growth of a counterculture whose values were far different from those of the Establishment. This political and cultural movement was characterized by distinct forms of expression and conscious-ness, including new styles of dress, social behavior, and music. It was a revolt by white middle-class youth disillusioned with the world of their parents, and it focused on the confusions and contradictions of the visible tragedy of Vietnam. But The Movement was quickly invaded by exploiters. The drug culture itself became a tragedy for many young Americans, and political activism turned into slogans, communication by invective, sectarianism, and terrorism. In the end, its staying power proved brief; the dominant society succeeded in absorbing both the rebels and the rebellion.

28

The Politics of Righteousness

Toward the end of his administration, President Jimmy Carter thought it necessary to convene a domestic summit conference to assess the state of the nation. For six days in July 1979, he conferred with cabinet members, political and civic leaders, bankers, clergymen, corporation executives, university professors and presidents, trade unionists, and economists. The concerns that prompted such an assessment were clear enough—an energy and environmental crisis, inflation and unemployment, economic stagnation and an eroding standard of living, a hostile and revolutionary world, and public-opinion polls that revealed a loss of confidence in the ability of the president to meet these challenges.

These concerns had dominated most of the decade. Some ten years earlier, Richard M. Nixon, in his inaugural address, acknowledged the deepening mood of desperation in the United States: "We are torn by division, wanting unity. We see around us empty lives, wanting fulfillment." He then invoked the familiar political promise to unite the nation and rally it around the proper goals. But Nixon's attempt to unite

the American people and regenerate them spiritually ended in abuses of public power unprecedented in the history of the nation. His successors—Jerry Ford and Jimmy Carter—restored honesty and integrity to the presidency. But Americans remained deeply troubled and frustrated about problems that seemed to defy solution. Raised on the gospel of progress, few wanted to be told that there were limits to the nation's capacities, powers, and natural resources. Nor did Americans accommodate easily to recession, inflation, and unemployment, polluted air and water, deteriorating neighborhood services and rising crime rates, new tax burdens, and the declining quality of public education.

Feeling helpless to control their destinies, Americans turned to various remedies, not all of them political. The 1970s came to be called the Me Decade, and best-seller lists were dominated by books on the pleasures of self-improvement and self-awareness, how to make oneself more powerful and wealthy, and how to refurbish one's body and psyche. Spectator sports reached new heights of popularity, as did individualized forms of recreation such as jogging. Many Americans satisfied their emotional hunger by becoming "born again" or by embracing one of the new religious cults.

In the same decade, women experienced a self-awareness that went beyond psychological self-fulfillment. The march of 50,000 women up New York's Fifth Avenue in 1970 heralded a decade in which women organized to improve the quality of their lives and their future prospects. Inspired by the civil-rights movement of the previous decade, they sought to liberate themselves from demeaning cultural stereotypes, job and wage discrimination, and sexual harassment. Although the movement embraced a number of goals, it came to focus on a proposed Equal Rights Amendment to the Constitution: "Equality of rights under law shall not be denied or abridged by any state on account of sex." Passed by Congress early in the decade and submitted to the states for approval, it failed to win the number of states necessary for ratification. In the meantime, women made progress in the work force, particularly in the professions and in business, and achieved reforms in abortion laws. But they faced strong resistance as well, reflecting divisions among women as well as the hostility of many men to changes in traditional female roles.

Watergate and Vietnam cast their shadow over much of the seventies. Lacking any real parallel in the past, they proved to be bitter and emotionally draining experiences. Even as Americans sought for ways to improve themselves individually, they needed reassurance about the nation's moral fiber, power, virility, and destiny. Presidents Nixon, Ford, and Carter failed to provide those reassurances. That failure would be effectively exploited in 1980 by Ronald Reagan. In electing him to the presidency, the American people, according to pollsters, had chosen the individual they deemed most likely to "make America feel good about itself again."

RICHARD NIXON IN POWER

Nixon had always prided himself on his ability to know what people wanted. He claimed to understand the sources of their fears and frustrations. He felt in touch with the prevailing mood. The America that had elected him, as Nixon viewed that "silent majority," had grown weary of mounting welfare rolls crammed with chiselers, federal intervention in state and community affairs, soft and overindulgent judges, and moral permissiveness. Upon entering the White House, Nixon moved on several fronts to act on a new set of priorities.

Retreat from Liberalism

The reluctance of the Nixon administration to press school desegregation in the face of local resistance reflected the president's sense of the national mood. In October 1970, the U.S. Commission on Civil Rights reported that "a major breakdown" in enforcement of civil-rights legislation had occurred, for which the federal government bore principal responsibility. The president was undisturbed by this finding. He knew his constituents well, and he no doubt knew of the public-opinion polls that showed some 78 percent of the people opposed to the idea of busing school children in order to effect racial integration. Most of these people, including many Democrats who had not voted for him, applauded the president's recommendation that school-busing orders by federal courts be set aside until an alternative solution could be found. This was an issue by no means confined to the South; it aroused strong emotions and resistance elsewhere in the nation.

Vacancies on the Supreme Court gave the president the opportunity to redeem his campaign promise to appoint strict-constructionist justices and to satisfy the southern constituency that had made his election possible. Nixon's selection of Warren E. Burger of Minnesota to replace Earl Warren as Chief Justice was confirmed by the Senate in June 1969. But the president's move to name a southerner to the Court led to confrontation with the Senate. The dispute had less to do with the regional background of the nominees than with Nixon's selection of mediocrities with highly questionable records.

Economic Game Plans

Depending on which economist or government expert made the assessment, recession or depression had overtaken the American economy by mid 1970. To check the inflationary spiral, President Nixon sought tighter money policies and a reduction in federal spending. But prices continued to rise. At the same time, unemployment, especially among the underprivileged and the young, added significantly to the cost of welfare. The overexpanded war industries were hard hit by the winding down of American involvement in Vietnam. Educated, middle-income technicians and engineers suddenly found themselves out of work and competing for jobs in a glutted market. Structural unemployment, once limited to pockets of declining industries such as coal mining in Appalachia and textile manufacture in New England, spread to most central cities. Its predominantly racial character made it a social as well as an economic issue.

The president's proposal for *revenue sharing* between federal and state governments became the avowed keystone of his domestic program; labeled the New Federalism, it proposed to return federal funds to the states and thereby encourage state and local management of federal programs. With some 10 million Americans on welfare rolls in 1969, Nixon hoped to clean up the "welfare mess" by shifting the burden of payments from the states to the federal government. At the same time, to check the inflationary surge, Nixon ordered a ninety-day wage-price freeze in 1972. Once the freeze ended, a pay board and a price commission would have the authority to rule on wage and price increases. To regain American markets abroad, the president also declared virtual economic warfare on other industrial nations.

Even as hard times settled on the nation, the American people enjoyed the dividends of a long-term government investment in space conquest. Only six months after entering the White House, President Nixon could boast of a masterful achievement by the United States. The first successful manned space mission to the moon, Apollo 11, was launched on July 16, 1969. Four days later, the lunar module came down on a rock-strewn plain on the Moon's Sea of Tranquility. When Neil Armstrong set foot on the moon's "very, very fine grained surface," he declared, "That's one small step for man, one giant leap for mankind." But whatever Apollo 11 did for

United States prestige in the world community, the persistent war in Vietnam continued to undermine it.

THE PRESIDENT AT WAR

The management of foreign affairs became the principal concern of Nixon's first administration. During the 1968 campaign, he ventured the opinion that the nation "could run itself domestically without a President. All you want is a competent Cabinet to run the country at home. You need a President for foreign policy; no Secretary of State is really important. The President makes foreign policy." In foreign affairs, Henry A. Kissinger and his White House staff of 110 overshadowed not only Secretary of State William P. Rogers and the 11,000 State Department employees, but the Department of Defense and the National Security Council as well. Both as special assistant for national-security affairs and later as secretary of state, Kissinger preferred secret diplomacy.

The foreign policy constructed by Nixon and Kissinger recognized that the Communist world was no longer unified. The growing tension between the Soviet Union and China underscored that recognition. Even as the United States pressed the war in Vietnam, it sought to improve relations with both major Communist powers based on mutual acceptance of the prevailing balance of power. At the same time, Nixon made clear the willingness of the United States to "participate in the defense and development of allies and friends." But he preferred, he said, to leave the basic responsibility to those allies and friends, particularly when it came to military action. In Southeast Asia, however, that policy proved unworkable. Success eluded the United States—with tragic consequences.

Initiatives for Peace

Although Nixon entered the White House with the reputation of a hardened cold warrior, he took the initiative to thaw the Cold War and establish a stable world order based on détente with the Soviet Union and the People's Republic of China. In August 1971 he announced that he had accepted an invitation from Premier Chou En-lai to visit China. None of his initiatives revealed the president's turnabout more dramatically and elicited such excitement and anticipation. The peace mission, as Nixon called it, came in February 1972 and resulted in mutual expressions of good will and an agreement to settle differences peacefully and to expand trade and cultural relations. What few Democratic presidents might have been willing to risk, Nixon had achieved.

Committed to a strong defense establishment, Nixon moved cautiously in the sensitive area of disarmament. With the United States and the Soviet Union spending $130 billion annually for defense, the need for some kind of mutual limitation on the balance of terror had long seemed desirable. Nixon agreed to enter strategic-arms-limitation (SALT) talks. To ensure the strongest possible bargaining position, however, he urged upon Congress a missile program designed to enlarge the already great strategic capacity of the United States. Several months after his successful China mission, Nixon capped his détente diplomacy with a trip to Moscow. On May 26, 1972, the president and Leonid Brezhnev agreed to limit the number of defensive missile sites and strategic offensive missiles.

The Middle East remained a source of international tension. Lacking adequate guarantees of its security, Israel defied the United Nations resolution of 1967, which called upon it to withdraw from territories it had occupied in the Six-Day War. The United States backed Israel with military aid and political support, while the Soviet Union helped arm Egypt and Syria. The continuing plight of Palestinian refugees and the demand for an independent Palestinian state complicated Kissinger's efforts to arrange a peace settlement among Egypt, Syria, and Israel.

In October 1973, hostilities again broke out as Egypt and Syria attacked Israel on the holy day of Yom Kippur. Both sides suffered heavy casualties, but Israel soon demonstrated its military superiority. The United Nations Security Council adopted a resolution that called for a cease-fire and peace negotiations based on its 1967 resolution. At the same time, the oil embargo imposed by the Arab nations impressed the entire world with the new reality of a unified bloc of oil-exporting nations. It raised havoc with available domestic supplies, sent gasoline prices skyrocketing, and made suddenly urgent the long-debated energy question.

But even as the Nixon administration tried to stabilize the situation in the Middle East and effect a détente with the Soviets and China, it needed to confront the continuing war in Southeast Asia.

Toward Vietnamization

Despite the Paris peace talks, the Vietnam war showed no signs of subsiding. At the time Nixon became president, United States troop strength in Vietnam had reached a peak of 542,500. The number of Americans killed in action was about to exceed the 33,639 killed in the Korean War. More bomb tonnage had been dropped on Vietnam than had been expended by the Allies on all of Europe during World War II. Moreover, the United States was spending more than $25 billion a year on what had become the most unpopular war in the nation's history.

In June 1969, Nixon announced his program for Vietnamization of the war. The idea was simple: the United States would maintain military pressure in the air while the South Vietnamese assumed the bulk of the casualties and fighting on the ground. There was nothing particularly new about Vietnamization; both Kennedy and Johnson had talked about the Vietnamese doing their own fighting. But it had not worked. How could a hopelessly corrupt and inefficient South Vietnamese government function without large-scale American assistance?

The War at Home

Although Nixon stepped up his Vietnamization program, neither the pace of American withdrawal nor the progress of the war satisfied anyone. On October 15, 1969, in the largest public protest since the war began, hundreds of thousands across the country, most of them students and other young people, observed Vietnam Moratorium Day. The most impressive of the demonstrations took place one month later in Washington, D.C., where more than 250,000 gathered.

The demonstration had no apparent effect on the president. Convinced that the great silent majority stood behind him, the president lashed back at his critics: "North Vietnam cannot defeat or humiliate the United States. Only Americans can do that." He explained that the alternatives in Vietnam were to admit defeat and order an immediate and humiliating withdrawal, or to press the Vietnamization program and secure an honorable peace. When the choice was put that way, most Americans—some 77 percent, according to a Gallup poll—backed the president.

But support of the war rapidly eroded. The television and press coverage reminded people daily of the brutality and futility of the conflict. Early in 1970, for example, the full details were revealed of an American attack in March 1968 on My Lai, a Vietnamese hamlet. Led by Lieutenant William L. Calley, Jr., a company of United States soldiers had massacred at least 175 and perhaps more than 500 Vietnamese, mostly old men, women, youths, and infants. The Army's official inquiry found the troops guilty of "individual and group acts of murder, rape, sodomy, maiming and assault on noncombatants and the mistreatment and killing of detainees." The operation appeared to have been based on false intelligence reports.

Although wartime atrocities were hardly unique, the degree of American complicity disturbed a nation accustomed to seeing itself as civilized and decent. The conviction of Calley by a military court raised equally disturbing questions about who bore ultimate responsibility and whether My Lai had been an exceptional and isolated incident. At his own trial, Calley's commander declared, "Every unit of brigade size had its My Lai hidden some place." Moreover, the United States had long followed a policy of destroying hamlets suspected of harboring Vietcong guerrillas. Lieutenant Calley's platoon had simply performed the task with the thoroughness characteristic of the more impersonal aerial bombardment.

From War by Tantrum to Peace with Honor

On April 20, 1970, President Nixon announced that Vietnamization and the phased withdrawal of American troops were proceeding successfully. Within ten days, however, he ordered United States troops into neighboring Cambodia to clear out "enemy sanctuaries." Unknown to Congress or the American people, United States planes had already been engaged for over a year in bombarding Cambodia. The administration denied that the invasion was an undeclared war on an independent nation. It was not even an invasion, said the White House, but an "incursion" (a brief raid). By June 29 all American forces had been withdrawn, their objective presumably gained.

The casualties of the expanded war reached into the very heartland of America. College students responded to Nixon's latest move with massive protests that exceeded anything yet seen. Some schools were forced to close altogether, and disruptions hit colleges barely affected by previous protests. At Kent State University in Ohio, National Guardsmen called out during campus demonstrations fired into a crowd of students, killing four and wounding nine. Although Nixon deplored the incident, he reminded Americans "that when dissent turns to violence, it invites tragedy."

To speed up Vietnamization, President Nixon resumed full-scale bombing of North Vietnam in November 1970. Although the attacks were called protective retaliation strikes, they amounted to the most massive aerial bombardment in history. Meanwhile, South Vietnamese troops did little to advance the cause of Vietnamization, and in March 1972 North Vietnamese and Vietcong were able to launch a major offensive in the South. When the Paris negotiations again broke down, the president ordered B-52 bombers over Hanoi and other major northern cities in mid December 1972. The assaults were massive, thorough, and round-the-clock. Hospitals, schools, and residential areas were not spared. It had come to be, as one columnist put it, war by tantrum. Vietnamese casualties mounted, as did the number of American planes shot down and prisoners taken.

With both sides pressing for a settlement, intensive negotiations between Kissinger and Le Duc Tho of North Vietnam finally produced a cease-fire in late January 1973. United States troops would be withdrawn while North Vietnam was releasing American prisoners of war. Peace with honor, the jubilant and relieved president announced, had finally been achieved. What remained questionable was the enormous price the United States had paid in waging the war and how long the peace could last.

Reflecting the recent Vietnam experience, Congress moved to limit the power of the president to wage war without congressional approval. The War Powers Act provided that if the president should send troops to a foreign country, he must fully explain the action to Congress within forty-eight hours. Moreover, he was obliged to halt the operation within sixty days unless Congress thought otherwise. President Nixon angrily vetoed the measure, but the House and the Senate overrode the veto on November 7, 1973.

The Election of 1972

While the war in Vietnam was still raging, the Democratic convention of 1972 had nominated Senator George McGovern of South Dakota, an avowed antiwar candidate. That convention was unique in the history of the party. Changes in delegate selection had resulted in far greater representation of minority groups, women, and young people than in any previous party convention. The party's old guard, many deprived of their traditional seats as delegates, could only look on in dismay. The expanded role of young people reflected not only their stake in the Vietnam war, but also the Twenty-sixth Amendment to the Constitution (ratified June 30, 1971), which lowered the voting age to eighteen.

If McGovern lacked the political savvy of the professional politician, he possessed an antiwar record and a commitment to social reform that attracted the party's new constituency. But his nomination badly split the party, and the Republicans exploited domestic fears of radicalism. The incumbent president rested on his record: the China mission, détente with the Soviet Union, and a Vietnamization program that had reduced the number of American casualties. McGovern campaigned on the peace issue. Just before the election, however, Kissinger said "Peace is at hand," and the president assured the people it would be an honorable peace. McGovern called the Nixon administration "the most corrupt in history," but most Americans did not believe him. With 61 percent of the popular vote, Nixon won the victory he had coveted.

Shortly after Nixon's second inaugural, the Vietnam war ended in an uncertain truce. The president turned to persistent and mounting domestic problems. After his decision in early 1973 to substitute voluntary restraints for price and wage controls, the cost of living soared to new heights. In keeping with his political philosophy, Nixon tried to reduce federal spending, and the cuts came, predictably, at the expense of social programs. Even when Congress appropriated funds for such programs, the president often refused to spend the money, thereby redefining the constitutional relationship of Congress and the presidency.

Although Nixon had won a resounding electoral mandate, he secluded himself from Congress and the public. Press conferences were infrequent. Despite his pledge to return power to the people, the White House bureaucracy seemed more formidable and unapproachable than ever. The "palace guard" was headed by two men: John D. Ehrlichman (domestic-affairs adviser) and H. R. (Bob) Haldeman (White House chief of staff). They operated as the president's shield, controlled access to him, and placed loyalty to him above the law itself. With so much power in the hands of so few, abuses were inevitable. Few people suspected their extent, and fewer still thought them possible.

ABUSE OF POWER

From the beginning of the Nixon administration, the war in Vietnam and its escalation had sharply divided the American people. On college campuses and in the streets, antiwar demonstrations had grown more militant, as had the efforts to control them. Confronted with massive protests and disruptions, the Nixon administration came to view the opposition as if they were conspirators, made up of the president's traditional foes: liberals, intellectuals, and reporters. To combat these foes, the Nixon White House encouraged and justified, in the name of national security, clandestine activities infringing on the fundamental liberties of American citizens. Through a series of events known as Watergate, the American people would come to learn of the full extent of these activities. That was more than enough to destroy President Nixon's credibility, strip his administration of any moral authority, and pave the way for his downfall.

Break-in and Cover-up

On June 17, 1972, a security guard at the elegant Watergate hotel-apartment-office complex in Washington, D.C., reported to police that a burglary was under way in the headquarters of the Democratic party. Among the suspects arrested were two officials employed by the Committee to Re-Elect the President and a former CIA agent and White House aide. Attorney General Mitchell expressed his dismay over the burglary, and President Nixon affirmed on August 29 "that no one in the White House staff, no one in this administration presently employed, was involved in this very bizarre incident."

The president knew better. He decided, as the nation would learn only later, to tell a calculated lie. New revelations would force him to repeat that lie on numerous occasions. The Watergate break-in proved to be part of a massive, deliberate, and illegally financed operation to sabotage the opposition's campaign and ensure the reelection of Richard Nixon. Only a few persons in the White House knew all the details of the operation. The arrest of the Watergate Seven moved these individuals to immediately cover their tracks by destroying relevant evidence, paying hush money to maintain the silence of the defendants, and lying to the grand jury of the District of Columbia. The president realized that a full probe of this affair might reveal too much about White House intelligence operations, including those directed at Democratic opponents and at critics of the Vietnam war. Less than a week after the break-in, Nixon agreed to the first stage of a cover-up. Using the pretext of national security, he instructed the CIA to intercede with the FBI to stop any further investigation of Watergate. By June 23, 1972, President Nixon had become a co-conspirator in the criminal obstruction of justice.

Revelations and Purges

The trial of the Watergate defendants opened in early 1973. Five of the defendants pleaded guilty to wiretapping, burglary, and attempted bugging; two others were convicted by a jury. Before imposing sentences, the presiding judge read the court a letter from one of the convicted burglars charging that highly placed White House advisers had known in advance of the break-in and that perjury had been committed during the trial. He soon revealed everything he knew to a grand jury, implicating others who would be called to testify. On April 30, 1973, as the cover-up began to unravel, the president went on nationwide television, the first of several such appearances relating to Watergate, to affirm his innocence and his determination to bring the guilty to justice and "maintain the integrity of the White House." More dramatically, he announced the resignations of his key advisers and legal counsel—Haldeman, Ehrlichman, and John Dean. He would, at the same time, authorize a new attorney general, Elliot Richardson, to appoint a special prosecutor to investigate Watergate.

The summer of 1973 proved to be a turning point. On May 17, 1973, the Senate Watergate Committee (as it came to be called), headed by Senator Sam J. Ervin, Jr., of North Carolina, began public hearings. Millions of television viewers across the country watched the mountain of testimony add up to an ugly record of deception and political sabotage carried out by the highest echelons of the White House: top-level discussions of executive clemency, destruction

of evidence, complicity of top aides in the cover-up, and how the break-in fitted into a pattern of political subversion. Nixon aides, moreover, had tried unsuccessfully to use the Internal Revenue Service and the threat of tax audits to harass individuals thought to be hostile to the president. With each new revelation, the credibility crisis escalated and the president's support eroded. On August 15, the president reaffirmed his innocence to a nationwide television audience. "Not only was I unaware of any cover-up, I was unaware there was anything to cover up."

The Watergate scandal had in no way implicated Vice-President Agnew, who had been second only to Nixon in his moral preachments on law and order and his attacks on "permissiveness" in the courts and the "coddling" of criminals. But even as Agnew expressed "total confidence in the President's integrity," serious questions were raised about his own. He found himself under investigation for bribery, extortion, conspiracy, and tax evasion—charged with extorting bribes from contractors while he was a Maryland county official and governor in exchange for influencing the awarding of government contracts.

Agnew protested his innocence. But with evidence of criminal conspiracy and graft mounting, the vice-president opted on October 10, 1973, to secure immunity from further criminal prosecution and thereby escape a prison term. After bargaining with the Justice Department, he pleaded no contest to lesser charges of tax fraud and resigned as vice-president. The court fined him $10,000 and placed him on three years' probation. At the same time, the Justice Department released an exhaustive summary of his illegal activities. It marked the first time a vice-president had been forced from office as a convicted criminal. As a successor to Agnew, Nixon selected Gerald R. Ford, a veteran Michigan congressman and the House minority leader.

During the Senate Watergate inquiry, a former White House operations aide revealed that the president had installed secret recording devices in his office that automatically taped telephone calls and office conversations. Obviously, the Senate committee was anxious to hear those tapes, as was Archibald Cox, whom Attorney General Richardson had appointed as the special prosecutor in charge of the Watergate case. The president, however, refused to turn them over, claiming the tapes were confidential and protected by executive privilege. When Cox persisted, Nixon ordered Richardson to fire him. Richardson refused, as did the deputy attorney general, and both men resigned their positions. The public reacted with outrage, and for the first time in more than a century the House Judiciary Committee launched an inquiry to determine if there were adequate grounds for impeachment. If only to weather this fire storm, Nixon agreed to appoint a new special prosecutor and provide him with whatever materials he needed.

Toward Impeachment

Despite Nixon's attempts to mobilize public support, the scandal gained momentum and reached closer to the president. In March 1974, a grand jury indicted three of Nixon's most intimate associates—Haldeman, Ehrlichman, and Mitchell—and four other White House aides on charges of conspiracy, obstruction of justice, and perjury. Meanwhile, new charges were brought against the president, including illegal income-tax deductions and the expenditure of public funds to improve his Florida and California estates. Nixon appeared to be under siege. At one point, the American people were presented with the sad spectacle of their president assuring them in a televised press conference, "I am not a crook."

On April 30, 1974, Nixon took his case to the people in still another television address. With pressure mounting on him to provide additional tapes, he declared his intention to make public 1254 pages of transcribed tape recordings containing "all the relevant" White House conversations about Watergate. Rather than calm the storm, however, the edited transcripts of White House conversations eroded still further the president's support. No matter in what context they were read, the transcripts did nothing to instill confidence in the president's leadership or truthfulness. The edited transcripts, moreover, contained sufficient ambiguities and contradictions to raise more questions than they answered. The president had not, as he had assured the public, revealed all the relevant information. In refusing to turn over additional tapes to the House Judiciary Committee and Special Prosecutor Leon Jaworski, Nixon argued that to do so would only "prolong the impeachment inquiry without yielding significant additional evidence." The president knew that was not true.

While the Supreme Court readied its judgment on Nixon's refusal to provide additional materials, the House Judiciary Committee proceeded with its impeachment investigation. On July 30, 1974, after months of private and public hearings, the committee, with the support of several of its Republican members, adopted three articles of impeachment. The president was accused of obstructing justice, violating his oath of office, abusing his presidential powers, subverting the constitutional rights of citizens, and willfully disobeying lawful subpoenas for White House records and tapes. It appeared almost certain that the House would sustain the committee's recommendations, impeach the president, and thereby set the stage for a trial in the Senate.

The Downfall

The climax came suddenly and spectacularly. By August 1, 1974, Nixon's credibility was nil, his state of mind suspect. He had virtually sealed himself off from the outside world. Adding to his troubles, the Supreme Court on July 24 had unanimously ruled that executive privilege could not be invoked to withhold evidence needed for a criminal trial and had ordered Nixon to turn over the additional subpoenaed tapes to the special prosecutor. On August 5, the president agreed to release the new material, which revealed beyond any question his direct involvement in the cover-up in a criminal obstruction of justice. Nixon conceded that he had withheld relevant evidence from the House Judiciary Committee as well as from his own lawyers and that the newly released tapes were "at variance with certain of my previous statements."

With these final revelations of criminal wrongdoing, the Nixon presidency lay in shambles. Even Nixon's supporters on the House Judiciary Committee, confronted now with evidence of statutory crime, reversed their positions and made the vote recommending impeachment unanimous. Republican leaders in the House and Senate advised the president that he would be impeached and convicted. Rather than face this prospect, Richard Nixon went on television on August 8 to announce his resignation. He was the first president in American history to do so.

Less than two years after he won reelection by as huge a margin as any in the nation's history, he departed from the White House in defeat and humiliation. He left to avoid impeachment and conviction, and he still faced the prospect of criminal prosecution. In his final message to the people, Nixon admitted to no serious wrongdoing, only to exercising poor judgment, and he showed no remorse. He had acted, he insisted, "in what I believed at the time to be in the best interests of the nation." While Nixon was still en route to his California home, Gerald Ford took the oath of office. "Our long, national nightmare is over," he declared. Nearly one month later, President Ford made a move to heal the nation's wounds and avoid the spectacle of a former president under criminal indictment. On September 8, he granted Nixon "full, free, and absolute pardon . . . for all offenses against the United States which he . . . has committed or may have committed or taken part in" during his presidency. Rather than end the nightmare, the pardon raised questions about a double standard of justice; the president had been permitted to stand above the law while those who carried out his orders were punished.

By early 1975, nearly forty officials of the Nixon administration, including the vice-president, four cabinet officials, and top White House aides, had been named in criminal indictments. The range of the criminal charges against Nixon's men in the White House presented a sorry record: obstruction of justice, fraud, extortion, burglary, perjury, illegal campaign activities, violation of campaign-funding laws, illegal wiretapping, eavesdropping, destruction of evidence, and conspiracy to commit illegal acts. Along with the ending of the Vietnam war and détente with Red China and the Soviet Union, they would constitute the mixed legacy of the Nixon presidency.

Throughout his long political career,

Richard Nixon had found it difficult to tolerate criticism or to admit defeat. His hatred of the media was matched only by the contempt he felt for many of his political enemies. Eventually, these obsessions consumed him and encouraged him to stand above the law and to violate his public trust. With the pardon and the convictions, the Watergate case came to an end. The lessons of Watergate, however, would persist, if only to remind the nation of the dangers of unbridled executive power and the possibilities for political abuses in the name of national security.

THE FORD PRESIDENCY

The new president was personable, hardworking, and honest. To most Americans, these were attractive qualities after their recent political experience. On no issue—domestic or foreign—were there discernible differences between Ford and Nixon. Since 1949, when Ford was elected to the House, he had reflected the views of his conservative Michigan constituency. As House minority leader he had won the respect of Democrats and Republicans, largely because of his amiability and even temper. He also possessed an openness that reflected the confidence with which he voiced the views of Middle America: "It's the quality of the ordinary, the straight, the square that accounts for the great stability and success of our nation. It's a quality to be proud of."

Middle America in Power

After the exhausting Watergate ordeal, the good feelings that characterized the opening weeks of the Ford administration came as a relief. His regular consultations with Congress provided a welcome contrast with the infrequent appearances of his predecessor.

His leniency program for Vietnam draft evaders and deserters reflected the national mood of reconciliation. But the Nixon pardon abruptly ended the political honeymoon, and the growing economic crisis provoked confrontations between Ford and a Democrat-controlled Congress.

Upon assuming office, Ford had declared war on inflation, calling it public enemy number one. The administration relied largely on fiscal restraint and tight monetary policies. By early 1975, however, the United States faced the grim prospect of the worst economic slump since the Great Depression and the highest percentage of jobless in the work force since 1941. Although the inflation rate was reduced the following year, unemployment and the high cost of living remained acute problems that neither the Democratic Congress nor the Republican president did much about.

Vietnam: End of an Era

The withdrawal of United States troops in early 1973 did not bring peace to war-torn Vietnam. The fighting continued, both sides violating the truce. South Vietnam remained dependent on United States support—$3.8 billion in 1973 alone, almost all of it for military aid. The end came quickly and unexpectedly. In March 1975, President Nguyen Van Thieu of South Vietnam ordered his forces to abandon several outlying northern provinces (nearly one-fourth of the country) that had come under Communist attack. This "strategic withdrawal" turned into a headlong retreat. Within weeks, Communist troops were in the outskirts of Saigon, Thieu had fled the country along with thousands of refugees, the South Vietnamese army had lost its will to resist, and Congress was refusing to invest any additional funds. In late April, Saigon and the government fell. After thirty years of war and more than a decade of American involvement, peace had finally come to Vietnam. At the same time, Cambodia fell under Communist control and Laos came under predominantly Communist influence.

With the fall of Indochina, an era in American history ended. Four American presidents had presided over United States intervention, some 56,000 Americans had died, more than 300,000 had been wounded, and $150 billion had been spent. To Eisenhower, the future of Vietnam had assumed "a most terrible significance"; to Kennedy, Vietnam represented "the cornerstone of the Free World in Southeast Asia"; to Johnson, it was a question of confronting the Communists in Vietnam or having to face them in Hawaii or San Francisco; and to Nixon, Vietnam would be recorded in history as "one of America's finest hours." But in the end, the war's greatest significance had been in teaching the United States a difficult lesson about the limits of its power.

The Bicentennial Election: 1976

On the occasion of America's two hundredth birthday, the nation's voters would be given the opportunity to decide who should lead them into the third century. Memories of Vietnam, Watergate, and the Nixon pardon reinforced popular suspicions of those in power. As the incumbent, Gerald Ford should have had no difficulty in securing the Republican nomination. But he had to mobilize all his political resources to defeat challenger Ronald Reagan, a former Hollywood actor and governor of California who had emerged as the spokesman of the Republican right wing. Even as Ford nosed out Reagan for the nomination, with the support of the party's professional politicians, Reagan tightened his hold at the party's grass-roots level.

Among the many Democratic contenders, James (Jimmy) E. Carter, Jr., former governor of Georgia, was the least known. In the primaries, this Annapolis graduate, nuclear engineer, successful agrarian businessman, and born-again southern Baptist deacon exploited the public's discontent with professional politicians and bureaucrats and their same old programs. The American people, Carter insisted, were searching for "new voices, new ideas, new leaders," and he managed to turn into a virtue his position as an outsider.

The strategy worked. Bolstered by his primary victories, Carter won the nomination at the Democratic convention and named as his running mate Walter F. Mondale, an able and liberal senator from Minnesota and a protégé of Hubert Humphrey. In the campaign, Ford defended his record of restoring honesty, integrity, and stability to government, and he promised more of the same. Carter appealed to liberal Democrats with pledges of full employment and social legislation. At the same time, he appeased moderates and conservatives by promising to eliminate bureaucratic waste in government and to balance the budget. To the American people, he promised moral leadership—decency, truthfulness, fairness, and compassion.

Despite Carter's sizable lead in the early polls, the election itself was close: 40.8 million votes for Carter to 39.1 million votes for Ford (a plurality that exceeded the winning margins of Kennedy in 1960 and Nixon in 1968), and an edge in the electoral college of 297 to 241. For the first time in forty-four years, an incumbent president had been defeated. And for the first time since before the Civil War, the nation had turned to the Deep South for a president. To win, Carter had needed to revive the New Deal coalition of urban blacks, Catholics, Jews, and blue-collar workers, along with the South. He did so, but the old coalition had been very weak: only blacks rallied around Carter in substantial numbers (about 87 percent). Without them he would have lost the election. Only 53 percent of the people of voting age had chosen to vote. What remained uncertain was whether the results were a personal triumph and mandate for Carter the outsider, or a rejection of Ford as the candidate of a political party still under the shadow of Watergate.

THE CRISIS OF THE AMERICAN SPIRIT: THE CARTER PRESIDENCY

In his election campaign, Carter had successfully exploited the outsider theme. But once elected, he needed to surmount persistent doubts about his capacity to govern. The issues he confronted were as formidable as any recent president had faced, and the American people looked to Carter to make good on his promise to be a "strong, independent and aggressive President." Four years later, with those issues still largely unresolved, many Americans had come to view him as weak, indecisive, and ineffectual. "The insiders have had their chances," Carter had declared in 1976, "and they have not delivered. Their time has run out." His Republican opponent in 1980 would campaign on essentially the same theme.

The Outsider in Power

President Carter inaugurated his administration with a dramatic move. Ford had hoped to end the Watergate era with his pardon of Nixon. Carter wanted to end the Vietnam era by offering full pardons to those who had resisted the draft during the Vietnam war. By issuing pardons, he insisted, he was not justifying their actions but merely granting forgiveness. It was less than the antiwar activists had demanded, and more than some Americans thought they deserved.

In the conduct of foreign policy, an area in which Carter seemed least experienced, the president had a mixed record of impressive successes and unexpected failures. He strengthened relations with the People's Republic of China. Over strong opposition, he managed to win the Senate's ratification in 1977 of a treaty that would gradually (by the year 2000) yield to Panama control of the Panama Canal. In Africa, the United States improved its standing by supporting black majority rule in Rhodesia (Zimbabwe) and Southwest Africa (Namibia). Even more spectacular, Carter initiated a flexible American response to the ongoing Mideast crises and, in a personal triumph, brought together in 1978 the leaders of Egypt and Israel at Camp David and helped them work out the framework for a peace agreement. Any permanent settlement, however, depended on resolution of the still critical issue of the Palestinian refugees and their claims to nationhood.

Early in his presidency, Carter moved to make respect for human rights a cornerstone of American foreign policy. In this endeavor he encountered difficulties, some of them of his own making. He singled out for condemnation Soviet treatment of dissidents and apartheid in South Africa, and he chastised several Latin American nations and South Korea for their repressive policies. But the president found it necessary to reconcile his strong convictions about human rights with pledges of support for repressive anti-Communist regimes that were thought essential to national security. He praised the shah of Iran, for example, and approved a multibillion-dollar arms sale to this "island of stability." That support soon plunged Carter into a crisis that defied any quick resolution and rapidly eroded popular support for his presidency.

Since the shah's return to power in 1953 (with the assistance of the United States), Iran had been a valuable ally against communism in the Middle East. While providing a steady flow of arms to back up the regime, successive American administrations had tended to ignore the domestic discontent with the shah's policies. In 1979, a revolution deposed the shah and sent him into exile. Seeking to eliminate all traces of the shah's westernizing influence, Iranians embraced a religious depotism under a Muslim spiritual leader, the Ayatollah Ruhollah Khomeini. At the same time, Iranians vented their anger on the United States for its long support of the shah.

When Carter agreed to permit the exiled shah to enter the United States for med-

ical treatment, mobs in Teheran attacked the American embassy and held the Americans there as hostages. Iran demanded as the terms for their release that the shah be returned for trial. Meanwhile, the Muslim nationalism unleashed by the revolution in Iran was being felt elsewhere in the Middle East, and threatened to bring chaos to a region that supplied more than half the world's imported oil. After the shah died in exile in Egypt, Iran continued to hold the American hostages, now demanding the return of the shah's wealth and the release of Iranian funds Carter had frozen in retaliation for that nation's actions. The president sent a military force to rescue the hostages, but the mission failed. By the time the hostages were finally released in January 1981, after more than a year in captivity, they had come to symbolize to Americans the im-

On the first day of the occupation of the U.S. Embassy in Teheran, the blindfolded American hostages were paraded before the mob by their captors. (UPI/Bettmann Archive)

potence of the United States abroad—an issue the Republican candidate in 1980 successfully exploited.

Even as President Carter grappled with the Iranian issue, he was plunged into a new crisis in Soviet-American relations. From the outset of his presidency, his criticism of the Soviet Union for its persecution of dissidents had cooled relations between the two countries. Nevertheless, after lengthy negotiations that had begun during the Ford presidency, Carter concluded the SALT II treaty, which imposed restrictions on strategic nuclear weapons. But the treaty foundered in the Senate, where critics charged that America's military defenses had been compromised. Then in December 1979 Soviet troops moved into Afghanistan to bolster the Communist regime there. Carter reacted with outrage. He withdrew SALT II from the Senate (where its chances for passage were slim anyway), imposed a partial grain embargo on the Soviet Union, called for a boycott of the 1980 Olympic Games in Moscow, reduced cultural and technological exchanges with the Soviets, and asked Congress to authorize the registration of young Americans for a military draft. Moreover, vowing to prevent "any outside force" from gaining control of the Persian Gulf region, Carter declared the region vital to American interests and sent in a naval force.

The Misery Index

The most conspicuous failure of the Carter presidency was its inability to stop the inflationary spiral that threatened the American people. His efforts to stimulate the economy and reduce unemployment were no more successful than his attempts to balance the budget and combat inflation. In the 1976 campaign, Carter had compiled a "misery index" by adding the levels of unemployment and inflation, and he had used it effectively against his opponent. Four years later the misery index stood even higher—a point his Republican opponent repeatedly stressed. To increase employment, the president proposed various programs, including job training, public-service jobs, and tax incentives to private employers. But these proposals either ran aground in Congress or proved too feeble for the president to make good on his promise to reduce an unemployment level he had found unacceptable.

Nor did Carter persuade Congress to accept his watered-down program for national health insurance or his proposed reform of a tax system he had called "a disgrace to the human race." Although he made some progress in reorganizing the civil service, he was only partly successful in reducing the "bureaucratic mess" in Washington. Carter had vowed to make the conservation of energy a top priority, calling it "the moral equivalent of war." But his energy program was less ambitious than such rhetoric suggested. Special-interest groups lobbied against various provisions, and Congress dismantled much of it. The United States was able to reduce its oil imports, but Americans paid higher prices for gasoline.

The achievements of the administration—in foreign policy, in energy conservation, in environmental protection, and in the unprecedented numbers of qualified minorities and women appointed to judgeships and government positions—were not enough to make up for the most conspicuous domestic and foreign failures. What ultimately undid Carter's presidency was his failure to inspire confidence. Whether any president could have dealt successfully with the domestic and foreign crises of the time was less important than the public's perception that Carter could not.

The Election of 1980

Encouraged by the rapid decline in Carter's popularity, the Republicans entered the 1980 election brimming with confidence. This time there was no mistaking the clear choice of the party's rank and file—Ronald Reagan. The Republican convention was dominated by the party's right wing, which pushed through a platform promising tax cuts, a balanced budget, increased defense spending, constitutional amendments banning nontherapeutic abortions and reinstating school prayer, the appointment of judges who opposed abortion, and opposition to the Equal Rights Amendment. For vice-president, Reagan chose George Bush of Texas, a former congressman and CIA director who had made an impressive run in the primaries.

The Democrats, rejecting a bid by Senator Edward Kennedy of Massachusetts, renominated Carter and Mondale. But a mood of fatalism dominated the convention, and Kennedy's challenge in the primaries had already split the party. In the campaign, Reagan successfully exploited domestic economic distress and international instability; he proclaimed his belief in reducing government interference in the lives of Americans while increasing the nation's military arsenal. To broaden his appeal, he moderated his previous hostility to social programs, and he tried to assure voters that he would not lead the country into needless foreign conflicts. In speaking to unemployed workers and to union audiences, he capitalized on dissatisfaction with inflation and promised to put people back to work. To a middle class weary of government programs and the taxes needed to pay for them, he promised a sharp reduction in federal spending (except for defense) and tax relief. To Americans concerned with the humiliating events in Iran and with the declining position of the United States in the world community, he promised to shed the guilt over Vietnam and restore the nation's power and credibility.

Reagan won over the nation's increasingly white and middle-class voting population, and he effectively buried the old New Deal coalition, even in the South. Only black voters remained loyal to the Democratic party. The election results, while an overwhelming triumph for Reagan, revealed a new low in voter turnout: only 52 percent of the eligible voters had chosen to participate. The new president entered the White House having received a "landslide" of only 26 percent of the electorate. Although Reagan's election had been expected, the success of the Republicans in securing control of the Senate for the first time in twenty-six years had not been. And the ideological makeup of the new senators confirmed the election of 1980 as an impressive triumph for conservative principles.

REAGANISM TRIUMPHANT

The Reagan presidency sought to redirect the nation's priorities. It advocated a strong military establishment, the reduction of federal regulations, the dismantling of the welfare state, and a balanced budget. To achieve these objectives was presumably to restore America's military superiority and economic prosperity. The new president had come to power on a wave of disillusionment with the government's ability to resolve fundamental problems. In proclaiming that the federal government itself was the root of the problem and in promising to "get the government off the backs of the people," he signaled a new departure for the American people—a sharp retreat from the New Deal tradition that both Democratic and Republican presidents had helped to sustain. In

Promising a sharp break with past policies, Ronald Reagan embarked on his presidency with the support of a broad spectrum of crisis-weary Americans. (UPI/Bettmann Archive)

proclaiming the Soviet Union to be "the focus of evil in the modern world," he signaled a return to a Cold War rhetoric that divided the world, irreconcilably, into camps of good and evil.

The Domestic Program: Reaganomics

Reagan chose a cabinet and White House staff dominated by businessmen who shared his political philosophy and priorities. His most controversial appointment, James Watt as secretary of the interior, had previously represented private interests anxious to exploit the public domain; the policies he supported in regard to natural resources and public lands shocked environmental groups and kept him embroiled in controversy. But Watt's views meshed with those of Reagan, and the new president moved quickly to act on his conservative

principles. Although Reagan often professed an admiration for Franklin Delano Roosevelt ("I was an enthusiastic New Deal Democrat," he wrote in his autobiography), he took his cues as president from the example of Calvin Coolidge, whom he admired for his success in reducing taxes and government expenditures. Those same ends would constitute the cornerstone of Reagan's domestic program.

In confronting "the worst economic mess since the Great Depression," President Reagan placed his confidence in orthodox conservative ideology and in supply-side economics. He proposed to cut income taxes across the board; the principal benefits would go to wealthy individuals and corporations who would use their windfalls to improve industrial productivity and revive the stagnant economy. At the same time, sharp reductions in government spending would compensate for the lost tax revenue.

By 1984, Reagan promised, the federal budget would balance government revenues and expenditures. The budget he sent to Congress in 1981 called for cutbacks in social programs. Public pressure forced the president to retreat on his plans for reductions in social-security benefits, but he did achieve significant reductions in government spending on welfare, food stamps, child nutrition, and employment and training programs. Congress went along with the president's program, mostly along party lines. In the Democratic-controlled House, a sufficient number of conservative southern Democrats voted with the Republicans to give Reagan most of what he had demanded. The president had similar success in 1981 in obtaining a three-year rate reduction on both individual and corporate taxes. The prospect of a balanced budget by 1984, however, seemed dim, largely because Reagan's increases in military spending outweighed the reductions in domestic spending.

Through most of Reagan's first term, the economic revival remained an unfulfilled promise. The policy of reviving the economy through substantial tax cuts could not be easily reconciled with the Federal Reserve Board's attempt to check inflation through credit restraints. By early 1982, the United States was experiencing the longest recession and the highest levels of unemployment since the Great Depression. The basic industries, such as steel and automobiles, were especially hard hit, and this accelerated their decline, which had begun much earlier. Many businesses went bankrupt, unemployment exceeded 10 percent of the work force (some 12 million workers were without jobs by the end of 1982), and interest rates for borrowed money remained discouragingly high. By late 1983, however, the economic had improved sufficiently for Reagan to claim a victory for his supply-side

economic theories. Inflation had been checked, interest rates came down, and factory production and employment increased. Whether the revival would be permanent, however, was as debatable as the means used to achieve it. Huge increases in military spending and the consequent growth of the federal deficit to unprecedented levels raised serious questions about the health of the economy. Reagan's response in the budget he submitted to Congress in 1984 was to propose still larger reductions in social programs, necessary again to offset increases in military spending. He defended his priorities in the name of national security, the still urgent need to contain international communism.

Foreign Policy: Peace Through Strength

Like the heroes he admired in Hollywood films, Ronald Reagan wanted to make Uncle Sam respected and feared once again in the world community. The recent humiliations in Vietnam and Iran, he thought, had been debilitating experiences for the American people. But respect would come only from military strength and preparedness, and his determination to raise the level of defense spending rested firmly in that belief. His choice for secretary of state, Alexander Haig, a former Nixon aide and NATO commander, shared the commitment to a tougher foreign policy. "There are things worse than war," Haig told a Senate committee, and he vowed that the United States would not enter any war it was not prepared to win. The inauguration had hardly ended before Reagan himself unleashed a verbal attack on the Soviet Union that had not been heard since the days of the Cold War. "They don't subscribe to our sense of morality," he said of the Soviets; "they don't believe in an afterlife; they don't believe in a God or a religion. And the only morality they recognize, therefore, is what will advance the cause of socialism."

Midway through Reagan's administration, Haig's ongoing feud with White House staff members resulted in his resignation under pressure. To replace him, Reagan turned to George Shultz, a former Nixon cabinet member who was regarded as more of a team player than Haig. But the change in secretaries brought no lessening of the growing tension in Soviet-American relations. The assumption persisted that the Soviet Union was at the head of a monstrous international conspiracy bent on world conquest and the destruction of the American way of life. To confront and contain Soviet power and international communism became once again the guiding principle of American foreign policy. Persuaded that the Soviets understood only force, Reagan proceeded with his massive military build-up. He did agree to resume arms-control talks with the Soviets, focusing on mutual and balanced reductions in nuclear arsenals. But no agreement could be reached by the end of 1983, the date on which the United States had promised to deploy in Western Europe intermediate-range Pershing 2 and cruise missiles aimed at the Soviet Union. The United States and NATO contended that the deployment was in response to the Soviet modernization of its missiles aimed at Western Europe. The Soviet Union claimed that a balance of destructive weapons already existed and that deployment of the new missiles destabilized the nuclear power balance. Refusing to believe the Reagan administration was interested in reaching an agreement, the Soviets broke off the arms-control talks in December 1983.

The Reagan administration "linked" any reduction of Cold War tensions to a demonstrated improvement in Soviet behavior. The Soviet Union, on the other hand, argued that its behavior in international affairs reflected a concern over threats to its own national security. Such a concern kept Soviet armed forces in Afghanistan in a frustrating, costly, and only partially successful effort to bolster the communist government there. Even more momentous in its implications was the emergence in Poland of an independent-trade-union movement (Solidarity). That Polish authorities were forced to recognize Solidarity as a legitimate trade union was in itself an impressive triumph in a communist nation. But when Solidarity then insisted on still more fundamental reforms—an implied challenge to Communist hegemony in Poland and Eastern Europe—officials in both Warsaw and Moscow knew that a confrontation was unavoidable. In the winter of 1981, the Polish government imposed martial law and dissolved Solidarity. The United States denounced the action as Soviet-inspired and imposed some sanctions on both Poland and the Soviet Union. Two years later, martial law was lifted but not the ban on Solidarity.

Mounting tensions and distrust between the United States and the Soviet Union had a tragic consequence on September 1, 1983, when a Soviet fighter plane shot down a South Korean airliner that had strayed off course into militarily sensitive Soviet territory. The 269 passengers aboard were all killed, including a number of Americans, and the world expressed profound shock over the incident. The United States condemned it as outright murder. The Soviet Union defended the action, claiming the Korean airliner was on a spying mission. Subsequent investigations suggested that Soviet air-defense personnel had not known it was a commercial plane before ordering the attack. Ultimate responsibility, however, lay in the tensions that had provoked such a paranoiac response.

In the Middle East, the Reagan administration, much like its predecessors, sought a strong Israel aligned with "moderate" Arab states that would serve to discourage Soviet intrusion into the region and keep Western oil supplies flowing from the Persian Gulf. But the United States never seemed to grasp the dimensions and complexity of the various religious, ethnic, and revolutionary movements that made up this volatile area. The position of Palestinians, including the 1.2 million in Israeli-occupied Gaza and the West Bank, continued to deteriorate. In June 1982 Israel invaded Lebanon, ostensibly to secure its northern border. But the major objectives appeared to be the destruction of the military strength of the Palestine Liberation Organization (PLO) and the restructuring of Lebanon. Israeli troops reached Beirut, inflicting heavy losses on the PLO. The United States, England, Italy, and France agreed to dispatch "peace-keeping" troops to Lebanon to replace the Israelis and to bolster the new Christian-led Lebanese government. But these troops soon became embroiled in a long-standing civil war among Muslims and Christians, and the loss of American lives, including some 240 marines and sailors in a suicide attack on the barracks-headquarters, shocked the American people. In Congress, questions were raised about the wisdom of an operation designed to prop up a Christian-led government in a predominantly Muslim country. But President Reagan, using language that evoked memories of Vietnam, defended the American presence in Lebanon as "central to our credibility on a global scale" and necessary "to stop the cancerous spread of Soviet influence." In February 1984, however, he bowed to heavy pressure and reluctantly withdrew the marines from Beirut.

Consistent with the administration's view of the Soviet Union as an expansionist power, the United States insisted on the need to combat Communist influence wherever it appeared and no matter what form it assumed. In a shift from the position of the Carter administration, Reagan's policy makers made it clear that the United States would in the future be more flexible in applying human-rights standards to friendly (anti-Communist) governments. The most conspicuous example was in Central America, where El Salvador had become a battleground between leftist guerrillas and a repressive military regime. The danger of a guerrilla victory took precedence over invasions of human rights and right-wing terrorism, and the Reagan administration gave its full support to the beleagured anti-Communist regime. The United States was no less concerned with a Marxist government that had come to power in Nicaragua. That was reason enough to grant covert military support to rebels (*contras*) seeking the overthrow of the government. To underscore its new determination in Central America and the Caribbean, the United States also resorted to some old remedies. On October 25, 1983, Reagan ordered the invasion of the small island of Grenada in the eastern Caribbean in order to replace the Marxist regime with "governmental institutions responsive to the will" of the people—and presumably friendlier to the United States. "Years of frustration were vented by the Grenada invasion," one Congressman explained. "I hardly get a call in my office about Grenada where people don't mention the Iranian hostage situation. So people feel their frustration relieved, and members of Congress sense that."

As he announced his determination to seek a second term, Ronald Reagan enjoyed an impressive amount of popularity, at least among white Americans. His skills as a communicator no doubt helped, as did the improvement in economic conditions and the reduced rate of inflation and unemployment. But many of the same sources of concern persisted. The soundness of the economy remained debatable. Unemployment (particularly among black Americans) continued to exact a heavy personal toll. The quality of public education continued to deteriorate. And with the president asking for still further reductions in government spending on programs for poor people, the issue of the proper role of government was certain to remain a potent political issue. Nor did Americans agree about the results of President Reagan's massive increase in military spending. Some viewed the cost as necessary for successful bargaining with the Soviet Union; others feared the consequences of additional rounds of nuclear escalation. Despite enormous military expenditures by both the Soviet Union and the United States, neither felt any more secure. That was a development not even a George Orwell had envisioned for his nightmarish world of 1984.

The American Dream in the 1980s

The Reagan presidency's inaugural celebration, costing nearly $11 million (much of it donated), heralded an era of opulence and splendor. The new president talked of boundless opportunities, of an "energy-rich nation," and of "an era of renewal." He vowed to restore to Americans a pride in their country and a confidence in its destiny. He evoked memories of an America that had conquered many new frontiers.

> I'm talking about the very essence of what it is to be an American. We are different. We have always been different. If we all feel that way the world will once again look on in awe at us, astonished by the miracles of education and freedom, amazed by our rebirth of confidence and hope and progress, and when they are amazed and when it happens we'll be able to say to the

world, "Well, what did you expect? After all, we're Americans."

But the number of Americans who could share in the American Dream reaffirmed by Reagan remained questionable. Many found themselves in deep economic distress, unable to pay their bills and exhausting their savings. The nation was experiencing difficulties absorbing the vast numbers of new refugees flocking to its shores, mainly Cubans, Haitians, and Vietnamese seeking better lives. For black Americans, the gains of the civil-rights movement were eroding, along with their standard of living. The number of black poor far exceeded the number of blacks who had managed to attain middle-class standing.

In the American myth of success, any person could make it to the top on the basis of hard work and ambition. But for many Americans in the 1980s, the principal concern was not so much with lifting themselves up the economic ladder as with trying to keep from falling lower. If they worked, they often worked at joyless jobs that permitted them no opportunity for self-expression and little chance for advancement. Few people expressed these feelings of frustration more eloquently than Mike Lefevre, a steel worker interviewed by Studs Terkel in 1974:

> I'm a dying breed. A laborer. Strictly muscle work . . . pick it up, put it down, pick it up, put it down. We handle between forty and fifty thousand pounds of steel a day. . . . It's hard to take pride in a bridge you're never gonna cross, in a door you're never gonna open. You're mass producing things and you never see the end result of it. . . . It isn't that the average working guy is dumb. He's tired, that's all. . . . At seven it starts. My arms get tired about the first half-hour. After that, they don't get tired any more until maybe the last half-hour at the end of the day. I work from seven to three thirty. My arms are tired at seven thirty and they're tired at three o'clock. I

hope to God I never get broke in, because I always want my arms to be tired at seven thirty and three o'clock. 'Cause that's when I know that there's a beginning and there's an end. That I'm not brainwashed. In between, I don't even try to think. It's not just the work. Somebody built the pyramids. Somebody's going to build something. Pyramids, Empire State Building—these things just don't happen. There's hard work behind it. I would like to see a building, say, the Empire State, I would like to see on one side of it a foot-wide strip from top to bottom with the name of every bricklayer, the name of every electrician, with all the names. So when a guy walked by, he could take his son and say, "See, that's me over there on the forty-fifth floor. I put the steel beam in." Picasso can point to a painting. What can I point to? A writer can point to a book. Everybody should have something to point to. . . .

Yes. I want my signature on 'em, too. Sometimes, out of pure meanness, when I make something, I put a little dent in it. I like to do something to make it really unique . . . just so I can say I did it. . . . I'd like to make my imprint. . . .

This is gonna sound square, but my kid is my imprint. He's my freedom. . . . You know what I mean? This is why I work. Every time I see a young guy walk by with a shirt and tie and dressed up real sharp, I'm lookin' at my kid, you know? That's it.*

*Pantheon Books, a Division of Random House, Inc., for Studs Terkel, *Working: People Talk About What They Do All Day and How They Feel About What They Do.* Copyright 1974.

Two hundred years after the birth of the nation, the American Dream, though flawed and losing its luster, persisted. Ronald Reagan vowed to make that dream a reality in the lives of all Americans. But so had every American president in the twentieth century. Reconciling technological advances with persistent economic failures and a decline in the quality of life would be a formidable challenge for any president of the 1980's. Nor was the challenge unique to the United States. The betrayed aspirations of masses of people were making for an increasingly turbulent and revolutionary world.

SUGGESTED READINGS

G. Hodgson, *All Things to All Men: The False Promise of the Modern Presidency* (1980). W.E. Leuchtenburg, *In the Shadow of FDR: From Harry Truman to Ronald Reagan* (1984). A.M. Schlesinger, Jr., *The Imperial Presidency* (1973). G. Wills, *Nixon Agonistes: The Crisis of the Self-Made Man* (1970). J. Schell, *The Time of Illusion* (1976).C. Lasch, *The Culture of Narcissism: American Life in an Age of Diminishing Expectations* (1979).B. Friedan, *The Feminine Mystique* (1963).

SUMMARY

Richard Nixon began his presidency in 1968 with a clear program and a clear mandate from a silent majority of Americans to retreat from the liberalism of the New Deal, the Fair Deal, the New Frontier, and the Great Society. For Nixon, this meant slowing down desegregation and appointing conservatives to Supreme Court vacancies. His economic game plan offered revenue sharing, tight money policies, and a reduction in federal spending. But prices and unemployment continued to rise. And although the triumph of the moon landing raised America's prestige, Vietnam continued to undermine it.

Foreign affairs became the major concern

of the first Nixon administration, and a balance of power a major goal; military action would be left to the discretion of allies and friends. The administration did succeed in effecting détente with the Soviet Union and China, and made an effort to stabilize the Middle East. But Vietnam was different: nothing seemed to work—not more troops, more bombs, or Vietnamization.

At home, protest against the war mounted on and off the campuses, fueled by revelations of American atrocities in Vietnam. Nixon secretly ordered the bombing of Cambodia in 1969, and a resumption of full-scale bombing of North Vietnam in 1970. But neither the bombings nor "incursions" into Laos helped. A cease-fire was negotiated in January 1973—but still the war continued, in Vietnam and in Cambodia.

The election of 1972 brought Nixon back to office with an overwhelming victory. But illegal campaign activities, along with Nixon's campaign to undermine his critics and the antiwar movement, soon erupted into what became known as the Watergate scandal. Before it was over, more than forty highly placed Nixon-administration officials, including the president's closest aides and the attorney general, had been indicted, and the president himself had been implicated in lies, crimes, and systematic deception. Faced finally in the summer of 1974 with impeachment proceedings, Nixon resigned in disgrace. His presidency was a shambles, and the American people's faith in government had been profoundly shaken. To make matters worse, Nixon's vice-president, Spiro Agnew, had been forced to resign in 1973 to escape a prison term for tax fraud, bribery, extortion, and conspiracy.

Gerald Ford took office on August 9, 1974,

and served out the remaining two years of Nixon's second term. He brought refreshing personal qualities to the office and tried to restore good feelings by such acts as leniency programs for Vietnam draft evaders and deserters. But his pardon of Nixon, along with the growing economic crisis and confrontation with the Democrat-controlled Congress, ended the political honeymoon.

In Vietnam, where the fighting had continued after the American troop withdrawal of early 1973, the South Vietnamese were close to collapse by early 1975. Saigon fell in April. At the same time, Cambodia and Laos came under Communist influence and control. The policy of four American presidents had failed, and the United States had learned a difficult lesson about the limits of its power.

In the bicentennial election of 1976, Americans turned to a political outsider, Jimmy Carter, and rejected Ford. But Carter's promises to "clean up the mess in Washington" and to balance the budget were not kept. Neither was his promise to provide moral leadership.

Economic and social problems worsened. Carter's success in the Middle East in 1978 was more than offset by what Americans saw as his failure in Iran in 1979, and the humiliation of having American citizens kept hostage there for more than a year. In 1980 Americans saw him as indecisive and ineffectual; they rejected his bid for re-election by turning to the Republican party and to Ronald Reagan, spokesman of its right wing.

In reordering the nation's priorities, Reagan placed particular emphasis on strengthening its military capability. He expected supply-side economics to cure the nation's economic ills. Through tax cuts and an easing of federal regulations, individuals and corporations would be induced to invest and stimulate economic growth. Reduced spending on social programs would help pay for the increased military budget and soften the impact of the tax cut. The economy did revive by late 1983, though not before unemployment had reached the highest levels since the Great Depression. The nation still faced unprecedented federal-budget deficits, which reflected the imbalance between cuts in domestic spending and massive increases in military spending.

Reagan's foreign policy was directed at containing Soviet influence and revolutionary communism. Soviet-American relations plummeted to a new low, exacerbated by Reagan's rhetoric, the deployment of new missiles in Western Europe, Soviet actions in Afghanistan and Poland, and the Soviet downing of a South Korean airliner. To check Communist influence, the United States also became involved in civil wars in the Middle East and Central America.

Appendix

The Declaration of Independence

When in the course of human events it becomes necessary for one people to dissolve the political bands which have connected them with another and to assume, among the powers of the earth, the separate and equal station to which the laws of nature and of nature's God entitle them, a decent respect to the opinions of mankind requires that they should declare the causes which impel them to the separation.

We hold these truths to be self-evident, that all men are created equal; that they are endowed by their Creator with certain unalienable rights; that among these are life, liberty, and the pursuit of happiness. That, to secure these rights, governments are instituted among men, deriving their just powers from the consent of the governed; that, whenever any form of government becomes destructive of these ends, it is the right of the people to alter or to abolish it, and to institute a new government, laying its foundation on such principles, and organizing its powers in such form, as to them shall seem most likely to effect their safety and happiness. Prudence, indeed, will dictate that governments long established should not be changed for light and transient causes; and, accordingly, all experience hath shown that mankind are more disposed to suffer, while evils are sufferable, than to right themselves by abolishing the forms to which they are accustomed. But when a long train of abuses and usurpations, pursuing invariably the same object, evinces a design to reduce them un-

der absolute despotism, it is their right, it is their duty, to throw off such government and to provide new guards for their future security. Such has been the patient sufferance of these colonies, and such is now the necessity which constrains them to alter their former systems of government. The history of the present King of Great Britain is a history of repeated injuries and usurpations, all having, in direct object, the establishment of an absolute tyranny over these States. To prove this, let facts be submitted to a candid world:

He has refused his assent to laws the most wholesome and necessary for the public good.

He has forbidden his governors to pass laws of immediate and pressing importance, unless suspended in their operation till his assent should be obtained; and, when so suspended, he has utterly neglected to attend to them.

He has refused to pass other laws for the accommodation of large districts of people, unless those people would relinquish the right of representation in the legislature; a right inestimable to them and formidable to tyrants only.

He has called together legislative bodies at places unusual, uncomfortable, and distant from the depository of their public records, for the sole purpose of fatiguing them into compliance with his measures.

He has dissolved representative houses, repeatedly for opposing, with manly firmness, his invasions on the rights of the people.

He has refused, for a long time after such dissolutions, to cause others to be elected; whereby the legislative powers, incapable of annihilation, have returned to the people at large for their exercise; the state remaining, in the meantime, exposed to all the danger of invasion from without and convulsions within.

He has endeavored to prevent the population of these States; for that purpose, obstructing the laws for naturalization of foreigners, refusing to pass others to encourage their migration hither, and raising the conditions of new appropriations of lands.

He has obstructed the administration of justice by refusing his assent to laws for establishing judiciary powers.

He has made judges dependent on his will alone for the tenure of their offices and the amount and payment of their salaries.

He has erected a multitude of new offices and sent hither swarms of officers to harass our people and eat out their substance.

He has kept among us, in time of peace, standing armies, without the consent of our legislatures.

He has affected to render the military independent of, and superior to, the civil power.

He has combined with others to subject us to a jurisdiction foreign to our Constitution and unacknowledged by our laws, giving his assent to their acts of pretended legislation—

For quartering large bodies of armed troops among us;

For protecting them by a mock trial from punishment for any murders which they should commit on the inhabitants of these States;

For cutting off our trade with all parts of the world;

For imposing taxes on us without our consent;

For depriving us, in many cases, of the benefit of trial by jury;

For transporting us beyond seas to be tried for pretended offences;

For abolishing the free system of English laws in a neighboring province, establishing therein an arbitrary government, and enlarging its boundaries, so as to render it at once an example and fit instrument for introducing the same absolute rule into these colonies;

For taking away our charters, abolishing our most valuable laws, and altering, fundamentally, the powers of our governments;

For suspending our own legislatures and declaring themselves invested with power to legislate for us in all cases whatsoever.

He has abdicated government here by declaring us out of his protection and waging war against us.

He has plundered our seas, ravaged our coasts, burnt our towns, and destroyed the lives of our people.

He is, at this time, transporting large armies of foreign mercenaries to complete the works of death, desolation, and tyranny already begun with circumstances of cruelty and perfidy scarcely parallel in the most barbarous ages, and totally unworthy the head of a civilized nation.

He has constrained our fellow citizens, taken captive on the high seas, to bear arms against their country, to become the executioners of their friends and brethren, or to fall themselves by their hands.

He has excited domestic insurrections amongst us and has endeavored to bring on the inhabitants of our frontiers, the merciless Indian savages, whose known rule of warfare is an undistinguished destruction of all ages, sexes, and conditions.

In every stage of these oppressions, we have petitioned for redress in the most humble terms; our repeated petitions have been answered only by repeated injury. A prince whose character is thus marked by every act which may define a tyrant is unfit to be the ruler of a free people.

Nor have we been wanting in attention to our British brethren. We have warned them, from time to time, of attempts made by their legislature to extend an unwarrantable jurisdiction over us. We have reminded them of the circumstances of our emigration and settlement here. We have appealed to their native justice and magnanimity, and we have conjured them, by the ties of our common kindred, to disavow these usurpations, which would inevitably interrupt our connections and correspondence. They, too, have been deaf to the voice of justice and consanguinity. We must, therefore, acquiesce in the necessity which denounces our separation, and hold them, as we hold the rest of mankind, enemies in war, in peace, friends.

We, therefore, the representatives of the United States of America, in general Congress assembled, appealing to the Supreme Judge of the world for the rectitude of our intentions, do, in the name and by the authority of the good people of these colonies, solemnly publish and declare, that these united colonies are, and of right ought to be, free and independent states; that they are absolved from all allegiance to the British Crown, and that all political connection between them and the state of Great Britain is, and ought to be, totally dissolved; and that, as free and independent states, they have full power to levy war, conclude peace, contract alliances, establish commerce, and to do all other acts and things which independent states may of right do. And, for the support of this declaration, with a firm reliance on the protection of Divine Providence, we mutually pledge to each other our lives, our fortunes, and our sacred honor.

The Constitution of the United States of America

We the people of the United States, in order to form a more perfect union, establish justice, insure domestic tranquility, provide for the common defense, promote the general welfare, and secure the blessings of liberty to ourselves and our posterity, do ordain and establish this Constitution for the United States of America.

Article I

SECTION 1. All legislative powers herein granted shall be vested in a Congress of the United States, which shall consist of a Senate and House of Representatives.

SECTION 2. 1. The House of Representatives shall be composed of members chosen every second year by the people of the several States, and the electors in each State shall have the qualifications requisite for electors of the most numerous branch of the State legislature.

2. No person shall be a representative who shall not have attained to the age of twenty-five years, and been seven years a citizen of the United States, and who shall not, when elected, be an inhabitant of that State in which he shall be chosen.

3. Representatives and direct taxes[1] shall be apportioned among the several States which may be included within this Union, according to their respective numbers, which shall be determined by adding to the whole number of free persons, including those bound to service for a term of years, and excluding Indians not taxed, three fifths of all other persons.[2] The actual enumeration shall be made within three years after the first meeting of the Congress of the United States, and within every subsequent term of ten years, in such manner as they shall by law direct.

The number of representatives shall not exceed one for every thirty thousand, but each State shall have at least one representative; and until such enumeration shall be made, the State of New Hampshire shall be entitled to choose three, Massachusetts eight, Rhode Island and Providence Plantations one, Connecticut five, New York six, New Jersey four, Pennsylvania eight, Delaware one, Maryland six, Virginia ten, North Carolina five, South Carolina five, and Georgia three.

4. When vacancies happen in the representation from any State, the executive authority thereof shall issue writs of election to fill such vacancies.

5. The House of Representatives shall choose their speaker and other officers; and shall have the sole power of impeachment.

SECTION 3. 1. The Senate of the United States shall be composed of two senators from each State, chosen by the legislature thereof,[3] for six years; and each senator shall have one vote.

2. Immediately after they shall be assembled in consequence of the first election, they shall be divided as equally as may be into three classes. The seats of the senators of the first class shall be vacated at the expiration of the second year, of the second class at the expiration of the fourth year, and of the third class at the expiration of the sixth year, so that one third may be chosen every second year; and if vacancies happen by resignation, or otherwise, during the recess of the legislature of any State, the executive thereof may make temporary appointments until the next meeting of the legislature, which shall then fill such vacancies.[4]

3. No person shall be a senator who shall not have attained to the age of thirty years, and

---

[1] See the Sixteenth Amendment.
[2] See the Fourteenth Amendment.

[3] See the Seventeenth Amendment.
[4] See the Seventeenth Amendment.

been nine years a citizen of the United States, and who shall not, when elected, be an inhabitant of that State for which he shall be chosen.

4. The Vice President of the United States shall be President of the Senate, but shall have no vote, unless they be equally divided.

5. The Senate shall choose their other officers, and also a president pro tempore, in the absence of the Vice President, or when he shall exercise the office of the President of the United States.

6. The Senate shall have the sole power to try all impeachments. When sitting for that purpose, they shall be on oath or affirmation. When the President of the United States is tried, the chief justice shall preside: and no person shall be convicted without the concurrence of two thirds of the members present.

7. Judgment in cases of impeachment shall not extend further than to removal from office, and disqualification to hold and enjoy any office of honor, trust, or profit under the United States: but the party convicted shall nevertheless be liable and subject to indictment, trial, judgment and punishment, according to law.

SECTION 4. 1. The times, places, and manner of holding elections for senators and representatives, shall be prescribed in each State by the legislature thereof; but the Congress may at any time by law make or alter such regulations, except as to the places of choosing senators.

2. The Congress shall assemble at least once in every year, and such meeting shall be on the first Monday in December, unless they shall by law appoint a different day.

SECTION 5. 1. Each House shall be the judge of the elections, returns and qualifications of its own members, and a majority of each shall constitute a quorum to do business; but a smaller number may adjourn from day to day, and may be authorized to compel the attendance of absent members, in such manner, and under such penalties as each House may provide.

2. Each House may determine the rules of its proceedings, punish its members for disorderly behavior, and, with the concurrence of two thirds, expel a member.

3. Each House shall keep a journal of its proceedings, and from time to time publish the same, excepting such parts as may in their judgment require secrecy; and the yeas and nays of the members of either House on any question shall, at the desire of one fifth of those present, be entered on the journal.

4. Neither House, during the session of Congress, shall, without the consent of the other, adjourn for more than three days, nor to any other place than that in which the two Houses shall be sitting.

SECTION 6. 1. The senators and representatives shall receive a compensation for their services, to be ascertained by law, and paid out of the Treasury of the United States. They shall in all cases, except treason, felony, and breach of the peace, be privileged from arrest during their attendance at the session of their respective Houses, and in going to and returning from the same; and for any speech or debate in either House, they shall not be questioned in any other place.

2. No senator or representative shall, during the time for which he was elected, be appointed to any civil office under the authority of the United States, which shall have been created, or the emoluments whereof shall have been increased, during such time; and no persons holding any office under the United States shall be a member of either House during his continuance in office.

SECTION 7. 1. All bills for raising revenue shall originate in the House of Representatives; but the Senate may propose or concur with amendments as on other bills.

2. Every bill which shall have passed the House of Representatives and the Senate, shall, before it become a law, be represented to the President of the United States; If he approves he shall sign it, but if not he shall return it, with his objections, to that House in which it shall have originated, who shall enter the objections at large on their journal, and proceed to reconsider it. If after such reconsideration two thirds of that House shall agree to pass the bill, it shall be sent, together with the objections, to the other House, by which it shall likewise be reconsidered, and if approved by two thirds of that House, it shall become a law. But in all such cases the votes of both Houses shall be determined by yeas and nays, and the names of the persons voting for and against the bill shall be entered on the journal of each House respectively. If any bill shall not be returned by the President within ten days (Sundays excepted) after it shall have been presented to him, the same shall be a law, in like manner as if he had signed it, unless the Congress by their adjournment prevent its return, in which case it shall not be a law.

3. Every order, resolution, or vote to which the concurrence of the Senate and the House of Representatives may be necessary (except on a question of adjournment) shall be presented to the President of the United States; and before the same shall take effect, shall be approved by him, or being disapproved by him, shall be re-passed by two thirds of the Senate and House of Representatives, according to the rules and limitations prescribed in the case of a bill.

SECTION 8. The Congress shall have the power

1. To lay and collect taxes, duties, imposts, and excises, to pay the debts and provide for the common defense and general welfare of the United States; but all duties, imposts, and excises shall be uniform throughout the United States;

2. To borrow money on the credit of the United States;

3. To regulate commerce with foreign nations, and among the several States, and with the Indian tribes;

4. To establish a uniform rule of naturalization, and uniform laws on the subject of bankruptcies throughout the United States;

5. To coin money, regulate the value thereof, and of foreign coin, and fix the standard of weights and measures;

6. To provide for the punishment of counterfeiting the securities and current coin of the United States;

7. To establish post offices and post roads;

8. To promote the progress of science and useful arts, by securing for limited times to authors and inventors the exclusive right to their respective writings and discoveries;

9. To constitute tribunals inferior to the Supreme Court;

10. To define and punish piracies and felonies committed on the high seas, and offenses against the law of nations;

11. To declare war, grant letters of marque and reprisal, and make rules concerning captures on land and water;

12. To raise and support armies, but no appropriation of money to that use shall be for a longer term than two years;

13. To provide and maintain a navy;

14. To make rules for the government and regulation of the land and naval forces;

15. To provide for calling forth the militia to execute the laws of the Union, suppress insurrection and repel invasions;

16. To provide for organizing, arming, and disciplining the militia, and for governing such part of them as may be employed in the service of the United States, reserving to the States respectively, the appointment of the officers, and the authority of training the militia according to the discipline prescribed by Congress;

17. To exercise exclusive legislation in all cases whatsoever, over such district (not exceeding ten miles square) as may, by cession of particular States, and the acceptance of Congress, become the seat of the government of the United States, and to exercise like authority over all places purchased by the consent of the legislature of the State in which the same shall be, for the erection of forts, magazines, arsenals, dockyards, and other needful buildings; and

18. To make all laws which shall be necessary and proper for carrying into execution the foregoing powers, and all other powers vested by this Constitution in the government of the United States, or any department or officer thereof.

SECTION 9. 1. The migration or importation of such persons as any of the States now existing shall think proper to admit, shall not be prohibited by the Congress prior to the year one thousand eight hundred and eight, but a tax or duty may be imposed on such importation, not exceeding ten dollars for each person.

2. The privilege of the writ of habeas corpus shall not be suspended, unless when in cases of rebellion or invasion the public safety may require it.

3. No bill of attainder or ex post facto law shall be passed.

4. No capitation, or other direct, tax shall be laid, unless in proportion to the census or enumeration hereinbefore directed to be taken.[5]

5. No tax or duty shall be laid on articles exported from any State.

6. No preference shall be given by any regulation of commerce or revenue to the ports of one State over those of another: nor shall vessels bound to, or from, one State be obliged to enter, clear, or pay duties in another.

7. No money shall be drawn from the treasury, but in consequence of appropriations made by law; and a regular statement and account of the receipts and expenditures of all public money shall be published from time to time.

8. No title of nobility shall be granted by the United States: and no person holding any

---

[5] See the Sixteenth Amendment.

office of profit or trust under them, shall, without the consent of the Congress, accept of any present, emolument, office, or title, of any kind whatever, from any king, prince, or foreign State.

SECTION 10. 1. No State shall enter into any treaty, alliance, or confederation; grant letters of marque and reprisal; coin money; emit bills of credit; make any thing but gold and silver coin a tender in payment of debts; pass any bill of attainder, ex post facto law, or law impairing the obligation of contracts, or grant any title of nobility.

2. No State shall, without the consent of the Congress, lay any imposts or duties on imports or exports, except what may be absolutely necessary for executing its inspection laws: and the net produce of all duties and imposts laid by any State on imports or exports, shall be for the use of the treasury of the United States; and all such laws shall be subject to the revision and control of the Congress.

3. No State shall, without the consent of the Congress, lay any duty of tonnage, keep troops, or ships of war in time of peace, enter into any agreement or compact with another State, or with a foreign power, or engage in war, unless actually invaded, or in such imminent danger as will not admit of delay.

Article II

SECTION 1. 1. The executive power shall be vested in a President of the United States of America. He shall hold his office during the term of four years, and, together with the Vice President, chosen for the same term, be elected, as follows:

2. Each State shall appoint, in such manner as the legislature thereof may direct, a number of electors, equal to the whole number of senators and representatives to which the State may be entitled in the Congress: but no senator or representative, or person holding any office of trust or profit under the United States, shall be appointed an elector.

The electors shall meet in their respective States, and vote by ballot for two persons, of whom one at least shall not be an inhabitant of the same State with themselves. And they shall make a list of all the persons voted for, and of the number of votes for each; which list they shall sign and certify, and transmit sealed to the seat of the government of the United States, directed to the president of the Senate. The president of the Senate shall, in the presence of the Senate and House of Representatives, open all the certificates, and the votes shall then be counted. The person having the greatest number of votes shall be the President, if such number be a majority of the whole number of electors appointed; and if there be more than one who have such majority, and have an equal number of votes, then the House of Representatives shall immediately choose by ballot one of them for President; and if no person have a majority, then from the five highest on the list the said House shall in like manner choose the President. But in choosing the President, the votes shall be taken by States, the representation from each State having one vote; a quorum for this purpose shall consist of a member or members from two thirds of the States, and a majority of all the States shall be necessary to a choice. In every case after the choice of the President, the person having the greatest number of votes of the electors shall be the Vice President. But if there should remain two or more who have equal votes, the Senate shall choose from them by ballot the Vice President.[6]

3. The Congress may determine the time of choosing the electors, and the day on which they shall give their votes; which day shall be the same throughout the United States.

4. No person except a natural born citizen, or a citizen of the United States, at the time of the adoption of this Constitution, shall be eligible to the office of President; neither shall any person be eligible to the office who shall not have attained to the age of thirty-five years, and been fourteen years a resident within the United States.

5. In case of the removal of the President from office, or of his death, resignation, or inability to discharge the powers and duties of the said office, the same shall devolve on the Vice President, and the Congress may by law provide for the case of removal, death, resignation or inability, both of the President and Vice President, declaring what officer shall then act as President, and such officer shall act accordingly until the disability be removed, or a President shall be elected.

6. The President shall, at stated times, receive for his services a compensation which shall neither be increased nor diminished during the period for which he shall have been elected, and he shall not receive within that period any other

[6] Superseded by the Twelfth Amendment.

emolument from the United States, or any of them.

7. Before he enter on the execution of his office, he shall take the following oath or affirmation:—"I do solemnly swear (or affirm) that I will faithfully execute the office of President of the United States, and will to the best of my ability, preserve, protect and defend the Constitution of the United States."

SECTION 2. 1. The President shall be commander in chief of the army and navy of the United States, and of the militia of the several States, when called into the actual service of the United States; he may require the opinion in writing, of the principal officer in each of the executive departments, upon any subject relating to the duties of their respective offices, and he shall have power to grant reprieves and pardons for offenses against the United States, except in cases of impeachment.

2. He shall have power, by and with the advice and consent of the Senate, to make treaties, provided two thirds of the senators present concur; and he shall nominate, and by and with the advice and consent of the Senate, shall appoint ambassadors, other public ministers and consuls, judges of the Supreme Court, and all other officers of the United States, whose appointments are not herein otherwise provided for, and which shall be established by law: but the Congress may by law vest the appointment of such inferior officers, as they think proper, in the President alone, in the courts of laws, or in the heads of departments.

3. The President shall have power to fill up all vacancies that may happen during the recess of the Senate, by granting commissions which shall expire at the end of their next session.

SECTION 3. He shall from time to time give to the Congress information of the state of the Union, and recommend to their consideration such measures as he shall judge necessary and expedient; he may, on extraordinary occasions, convene both Houses, or either of them, and in case of disagreement between them with respect to the time of adjournment, he may adjourn them to such time as he shall think proper; he shall receive ambassadors and other public ministers; he shall take care that the laws be faithfully executed, and shall commission all the officers of the United States.

SECTION 4. The President, Vice President, and all civil officers of the United States, shall be removed from office on impeachment for, and conviction of, treason, bribery, or other high crimes and misdemeanors.

Article III

SECTION 1. The judicial power of the United States shall be vested in one Supreme Court, and in such inferior courts as the Congress may from time to time ordain and establish. The judges, both of the Supreme and inferior courts, shall hold their offices during good behavior, and shall, at stated times, receive for their services, a compensation, which shall not be diminished during their continuance in office.

SECTION 2. 1. The judicial power shall extend to all cases, in law and equity, arising under this Constitution, the laws of the United States, and treaties made, or which shall be made, under their authority;—to all cases affecting ambassadors, other public ministers and consuls;—to all cases of admiralty and maritime jurisdiction;—to controversies to which the United States shall be a party;[7]—to controversies between two or more States;—between a State and citizens of another State;—between citizens of different States;—between citizens of the same State claiming lands under grants of different States, and between a State, or the citizens thereof, and foreign States, citizens or subjects.

2. In all cases affecting ambassadors, other public ministers and consuls, and those in which a State shall be party, the Supreme Court shall have original jurisdiction. In all the other cases before mentioned, the Supreme Court shall have appellate jurisdiction, both as to law and fact, with such exceptions, and under such regulations as the Congress shall make.

3. The trial of all crimes, except in cases of impeachment, shall be by jury; and such trial shall be held in the State where the said crimes shall have been committed; but when not committed within any State, the trial shall be at such place or places as the Congress may by law have directed.

SECTION 3. 1. Treason against the United States shall consist only in levying war against them, or in adhering to their enemies, giving them aid and comfort. No person shall be convicted of treason unless on the testimony of two witnesses to the same overt act, or on confession in open court.

---

[7] See the Eleventh Amendment.

APPENDIX **499**

2. The Congress shall have power to declare the punishment of treason, but no attainder of treason shall work corruption of blood, or forfeiture except during the life of the person attainted.

Article IV

SECTION 1. Full faith and credit shall be given in each State to the public acts, records, and judicial proceedings of every other State. And the Congress may by general laws prescribe the manner in which such acts, records and proceedings shall be proved, and the effect thereof.

SECTION 2. The citizens of each State shall be entitled to all privileges and immunities of citizens in the several States.[8]

2. A person charged in any State with treason, felony, or other crime, who shall flee from justice, and be found in another State, shall on demand of the executive authority of the State from which he fled, be delivered up to be removed to the State having jurisdiction of the crime.

3. No person held to service or labor in one State under the laws thereof, escaping into another, shall, in consequence of any law or regulation therein, be discharged from such service or labor, but shall be delivered up on claim of the party to whom such service or labor may be due.[9]

SECTION 3. 1. New States may be admitted by the Congress into this Union; but no new State shall be formed or erected within the jurisdiction of any other State; nor any State be formed by the junction of two or more States, or parts of States, without the consent of the legislatures of the States concerned as well as of the Congress.

2. The Congress shall have power to dispose of and make all needful rules and regulations respecting the territory or other property belonging to the United States; and nothing in this Constitution shall be so construed as to prejudice any claims of the United States, or of any particular State.

SECTION 4. The United States shall guarantee to every State in this Union a republican form of government, and shall protect each of them against invasion; and on application of the legislature, or of the executive (when the legislature cannot be convened) against domestic violence.

Article V

The Congress, whenever two thirds of both Houses shall deem it necessary, shall propose amendments to this Constitution, or, on the application of the legislatures of two thirds of the several States, shall call a convention for proposing amendments, which in either case, shall be valid to all intents and purposes, as part of this Constitution, when ratified by the legislatures of three fourths of the several States, or by conventions in three fourths thereof, as the one or the other mode of ratification may be proposed by the Congress; Provided that no amendment which may be made prior to the year one thousand eight hundred and eight shall in any manner affect the first and fourth clauses in the ninth section of the first article; and that no State, without its consent, shall be deprived of its equal suffrage in the Senate.

Article VI

1. All debts contracted and engagements entered into, before the adoption of this Constitution, shall be as valid against the United States under this Constitution, as under the Confederation.[10]

2. This Constitution, and the laws of the United States which shall be made in pursuance thereof; and all treaties made, or which shall be made, under the authority of the United States, shall be the supreme law of the land; and the judges in every State shall be bound thereby, any thing in the Constitution or laws of any State to the contrary notwithstanding.

3. The senators and representatives before mentioned, and the members of the several State legislatures, and all executive and judicial officers, both of the United States and of the several States, shall be bound by oath or affirmation to support this Constitution; but no religious test shall ever be required as a qualification to any office or public trust under the United States.

Article VII

The ratification of the conventions of nine States shall be sufficient for the establishment

[8] See the Fourteenth Amendment, Sec. 1.
[9] See the Thirteenth Amendment.

[10] See the Fourteenth Amendment, Sec. 4

of this Constitution between the States so ratifying the same.

Done in Convention by the unanimous consent of the States present the seventeenth day of September in the year of our Lord one thousand seven hundred and eighty-seven, and of the independence of the United States of America the twelfth. In witness whereof we have hereunto subscribed our names.

[Names omitted]

* * *

Articles in addition to, and amendment of, the Constitution of the United States of America, proposed by Congress, and ratified by the legislatures of the several States, pursuant to the fifth article of the original Constitution.

Amendment I [First ten amendments ratified December 15, 1791]
Congress shall make no law respecting an establishment of religion, or prohibiting the free exercise thereof; or abridging the freedom of speech, or of the press; or the right of the people peaceably to assemble, and to petition the government for a redress of grievances.

Amendment II

A well regulated militia, being necessary to the security of a free State, the right of the people to keep and bear arms, shall not be infringed.

Amendment III

No soldier shall, in time of peace be quartered in any house, without the consent of the owner, nor in time of war, but in a manner to be prescribed by law.

Amendment IV

The right of the people to be secure in their persons, houses, papers, and effects, against unreasonable searches and seizures, shall not be violated, and no warrants shall issue, but upon probable cause, supported by oath or affirmation, and particularly describing the place to be searched, and the persons or things to be seized.

Amendment V

No person shall be held to answer for a capital or otherwise infamous crime, unless on a presentment or indictment of a grand jury, except in cases arising in the land or naval forces, or in the militia, when in actual service in time of war or public danger; nor shall any person be subject for the same offense to be twice put in jeopardy of life or limb; nor shall be compelled in any criminal case to be a witness against himself, nor be deprived of life, liberty, or property, without due process of law; nor shall private property be taken for public use, without just compensation.

Amendment VI

In all criminal prosecutions, the accused shall enjoy the right to a speedy and public trial, by an impartial jury of the State and district wherein the crime shall have been committed, which district shall have been previously ascertained by law, and to be informed of the nature and cause of the accusation; to be confronted with the witnesses against him; to have compulsory process for obtaining witnesses in his favor, and to have the assistance of counsel for his defense.

Amendment VII

In suits at common law, where the value in controversy shall exceed twenty dollars, the right of trial by jury shall be preserved, and no fact tried by a jury shall be otherwise reexamined in any court of the United States, than according to the rules of the common law.

Amendment VIII

Excessive bail shall not be required, nor excessive fines imposed, nor cruel and unusual punishments inflicted.

Amendment IX

The enumeration in the constitution of certain rights shall not be construed to deny or disparage others retained by the people.

Amendment X

The powers not delegated to the United States by the Constitution, nor prohibited by it to the States, are reserved to the States respectively, or to the people.

Amendment XI [January 8, 1798]

The judicial power of the United States shall not be construed to extend to any suit in law or equity, commenced or prosecuted against one of the United States by citizens of another State, or by citizens or subjects of any foreign State.

Amendment XII [September 25, 1804]

The electors shall meet in their respective States, and vote by ballot for President and Vice President, one of whom, at least, shall not be an inhabitant of the same State with themselves, they shall name in their ballots the person voted for as President, and in distinct ballots, the person voted for as Vice President, and they shall make distinct lists of all persons voted for as President and of all persons voted for as Vice President, and of the number of votes for each, which lists they shall sign and certify, and transmit sealed to the seat of the government of the United States, directed to the President of the Senate;—The President of the Senate shall, in the presence of the Senate and House of Representatives, open all the certificates and the votes shall then be counted;—The person having the greatest number of votes for President, shall be the President, if such number be a majority of the whole number of electors appointed; and if no person have such majority, then from the persons having the highest numbers not exceeding three on the list of those voted for as President, the House of Representatives shall choose immediately, by ballot, the President. But in choosing the President, the votes shall be taken by States, the representation from each State having one vote; a quorum of this purpose shall consist of a member or members from two thirds of the States, and a majority of all the States shall be necessary to a choice. And if the House of Representatives shall not choose a President whenever the right of choice shall devolve upon them, before the fourth day of March next following, then the Vice President shall act as President, as in the case of the death or other constitutional disability of the President. The person having the greatest number of votes as Vice President shall be the Vice President, if such number be a majority of the whole number of electors appointed, and if no person have a majority, then from the two highest numbers on the list, the Senate shall choose the Vice President; a quorum for the purpose shall consist of two thirds of the whole number of Senators, and a majority of the whole number shall be necessary to a choice. But no person constitutionally ineligible to the office of President shall be eligible to that of Vice President of the United States.

Amendment XIII [December 18, 1865]

SECTION 1. Neither slavery nor involuntary servitude, except as a punishment for crime whereof the party shall have been duly convicted, shall exist within the United States, or any place subject to their jurisdiction.

SECTION 2. Congress shall have power to enforce this article by appropriate legislation.

Amendment XIV [July 28, 1868]

SECTION 1. All persons born or naturalized in the United States, and subject to the jurisdiction thereof, are citizens of the United States and of the State wherein they reside. No State shall make or enforce any law which shall abridge the privileges or immunities of citizens of the United States; nor shall any State deprive any person of life, liberty, or property, without due process of law; nor deny to any person within its jurisdiction the equal protection of the laws.

SECTION 2. Representatives shall be apportioned among the several States according to their respective numbers, counting the whole number of persons in each State, excluding Indians not taxed. But when the right to vote at any election for the choice of electors for President and Vice President of the United States, representatives in Congress, the executive and judicial officers of a State, or the members of the legislature thereof, is denied to any of the male inhabitants of such State, being twenty-one years of age, and citizens of the United States, or in any way abridged, except for participating in rebellion, or other crime, the basis of representation therein shall be reduced in the proportion which the number of such male citizens shall bear to the whole number of male citizens twenty-one years of age in such State.

SECTION 3. No person shall be a senator or representative in Congress, or elector of President and Vice President, or hold any office, civil or military, under the United States, or under any

State, who having previously taken an oath, as a member of Congress, or as an officer of the United States, or as a member of any State legislature, or as an executive or judicial officer of any State, to support the Constitution of the United States, shall have engaged in insurrection or rebellion against the same, or given aid or comfort to the enemies thereof. But Congress may by a vote of two thirds of each House, remove such disability.

SECTION 4. The validity of the public debt of the United States, authorized by law, including debts incurred for payment of pensions and bounties for services in suppressing insurrection or rebellion, shall not be questioned. But neither the United States nor any State shall assume or pay any debt or obligation incurred in aid of insurrection or rebellion against the United States, or any claim for the loss or emancipation of any slave; but all such debts, obligations, and claims shall be held illegal and void.

SECTION 5. The Congress shall have the power to enforce, by appropriate legislation, the provisions of this article.

Amendment XV [March 30, 1870]

SECTION 1. The right of citizens of the United States to vote shall not be denied or abridged by the United States or by any State on account of race, color, or previous condition of servitude.

SECTION 2. The Congress shall have power to enforce this article by appropriate legislation.

Amendment XVI [February 25, 1913]

The Congress shall have power to lay and collect taxes on incomes, from whatever source derived, without apportionment among the several States, and without regard to any census or enumeration.

Amendment XVII [May 31, 1913]

The Senate of the United States shall be composed of two senators from each State, elected by the people thereof, for six years; and each senator shall have one vote. The electors in each State shall have the qualifications requisite for electors of the most numerous branch of the State legislature.

When vacancies happen in the representation of any State in the Senate, the executive

authority of such State shall issue writs of election to fill such vacancies: *Provided,* That the legislature of any State may empower the executive thereof to make temporary appointments until the people fill the vacancies by election as the legislature may direct.

This amendment shall not be so construed as to affect the election or term of any senator chosen before it becomes valid as part of the Constitution.

Amendment XVIII[11] [January 29, 1919]

After one year from the ratification of this article, the manufacture, sale, or transportation of intoxicating liquors within, the importation thereof into, or the exportation thereof from the United States and all territory subject to the jurisdiction thereof for beverage purposes is thereby prohibited.

The Congress and the several States shall have concurrent power to enforce this article by appropriate legislation.

This article shall be inoperative unless it shall have been ratified as an amendment to the Constitution by the legislatures of the several States, as provided in the Constitution, within seven years from the date of the submission hereof to the States by Congress.

Amendment XIX [August 26, 1920]

The right of citizens of the United States to vote shall not be denied or abridged by the United States or by any State on account of sex.

Congress shall have the power to enforce this article by appropriate legislation.

Amendment XX [January 23, 1933]

SECTION 1. The terms of the President and Vice resident shall end at noon on the 20th day of January and the terms of Senators and Representatives at noon on the 3d day of January, of the years in which such terms would have ended if this article had not been ratified; and the terms of their successors shall then begin.

SECTION 2. The Congress shall assemble at least once in every year, and such meeting shall begin at noon on the 3d day of January, unless they shall by law appoint a different day.

SECTION 3. If, at the time fixed for the be-

[11] Repealed by the Twenty-first Amendment.

ginning of the term of President, the President-elect shall have died, the Vice President-elect shall become President. If a President shall not have been chosen before the time fixed for the beginning of his term, or if the President-elect shall have failed to qualify, then the Vice President-elect shall act as President until a President shall have qualified; and the Congress may by law provide for the case wherein neither a President-elect nor a Vice President-elect shall have qualified, declaring who shall then act as President, or the manner in which one who is to act shall be selected, and such person shall act accordingly until a President or Vice President shall have qualified.

SECTION 4. The Congress may by law provide for the case of the death of any of the persons from whom the House of Representatives may choose a President whenever the right of choice shall have devolved upon them, and for the case of the death of any of the persons from whom the Senate may choose a Vice President whenever the right of choice shall have devolved upon them.

SECTION 5. Sections 1 and 2 shall take ef fect on the 15th day of October following the ratification of this article.

SECTION 6. This article shall be inoperative unless it shall have been ratified as an amendment to the Constitution by the legislatures of three-fourths of the several States within seven years from the date of its submission.

Amendment XXI [December 5, 1933]

SECTION 1. The Eighteenth Article of amendment to the Constitution of the United States is hereby repealed.

SECTION 2. The transportation or importation into any State, Territory, or possession of the United States for delivery or use therein of intoxicating liquors in violation of the laws thereof, is hereby prohibited.

SECTION 3. This article shall be inoperative unless it shall have been ratified as an amendment to the Constitution by conventions in the several States, as provided in the Constitution, within seven years from the date of the submission thereof to the States by the Congress.

Amendment XXII [March 1, 1951]

No person shall be elected to the office of the President more than twice, and no person who has held the office of President, or acted as President, for more than two years of a term to which some other person was elected President shall be elected to the office of the President more than once.

But this article shall not apply to any person holding the office of President when this article was proposed by the Congress, and shall not prevent any person who may be holding the office of President, or acting as President, during the term within which this article becomes operative from holding the office of President or acting as President during the remainder of such term.

This article shall be inoperative unless it shall have been ratified as an amendment to the Constitution by the legislatures of three-fourths of the several States within seven years from the date of its submission to the States by the Congress.

Amendment XXIII [March 29, 1961]

SECTION 1. The District constituting the seat of Government of the United States shall appoint in such manner as the Congress may direct:

A number of electors of President and Vice President equal to the whole number of Senators and Representatives in Congress to which the District would be entitled if it were a State, but in no event more than the least populous State; they shall be in addition to those appointed by the States, but they shall be considered, for the purposes of the election of President and Vice President, to be electors appointed by a State; and they shall meet in the District and perform such duties as provided by the twelfth article of amendment.

SECTION 2. The Congress shall have power to enforce this article by appropriate legislation.

Amendment XXIV [January 23, 1964]

SECTION 1. The right of citizens of the United States to vote in any primary or other election for President or Vice President, for electors for President or Vice President, or for Senator or Representative in Congress, shall not be denied or abridged by the United States or any State by reason of failure to pay any poll tax or other tax.

SECTION 2. The Congress shall have power to enforce this article by appropriate legislation.

Amendment XXV [February 10, 1967]

SECTION 1. In case of the removal of the President from office or of his death or resignation, the Vice President shall become President.

SECTION 2. Whenever there is a vacancy in the office of the Vice President, the President shall nominate a Vice President who shall take office upon confirmation by a majority of both Houses of Congress.

SECTION 3. Whenever the President transmits to the President pro tempore of the Senate and the Speaker of the House of Representatives his written declaration that he is unable to discharge the powers and duties of his office, and until he transmits to them a written declaration to the contrary, such powers and duties shall be discharged by the Vice President as Acting President.

SECTION 4. Whenever the Vice President and a majority of either the principal officers of the executive departments or of such other body as Congress may by law provide, transmit to the President pro tempore of the Senate and the Speaker of the House of Representatives their written declaration that the President is unable to discharge the powers and duties of his office, the Vice President shall immediately assume the powers and duties of the office as Acting President.

Thereafter, when the President transmits to the President pro tempore of the Senate and the Speaker of the House of Representatives his written declaration that no inability exists, he shall resume the powers and duties of his office unless the Vice President and a majority of either the principal officers of the executive departments or of such other body as Congress may by law provide, transmit within four days to the President pro tempore of the Senate and the Speaker of the House of Representatives their written declaration that the President is unable to discharge the powers and duties of his office. Thereupon Congress shall decide the issue, assembling within forty-eight hours for that purpose if not in session. If the Congress, within twenty-one days after receipt of the latter written declaration, or, if Congress is not in session, within twenty-one days after Congress is required to assemble, determines by two-thirds vote of both Houses that the President is unable to discharge the powers and duties of his office, the Vice President shall continue to discharge the same as Acting President; otherwise, the President shall resume the powers and duties of his office.

Amendment XXVI [June 30, 1971]

SECTION 1. The right of citizens of the United States who are eighteen years of age or older to vote shall not be denied or abridged by the United States or by any State on account of age.

Index